How To Create Successful CATALOGS

Maxwell Sroge Publishing
Colorado Springs, Colorado

ISBN Number: 0-942674-08-1
Library of Congress Catalog Card Number: 85-60190

First Printing 1985

Contents

Preface

This book is designed to be *used,* not merely "read." Browse through it, enjoy it, mull it over, learn from it, even argue about it. In these pages you'll find the step-by-step guidance of hands-on catalog experts . . . dissecting, explaining, illustrating every aspect of a catalog's creation. Whether you're a catalog "pro" or a "beginner," you'll find value in the techniques exposed here. This book can be used by *anyone* who wishes to create a catalog and to do so *successfully.*

Each chapter is self-sustaining. Use them as separate guidelines to a particular area of your interest, or use them together. Though there are many approaches to each step in creating a catalog, there also are some basics which must be followed by both experienced cataloger and novice. These are the methods which will produce a *good* catalog: one which attracts the target customer, has appropriate style, and compliments the product line (and the image of the catalog house) with its graphics and copy approach. A "good" catalog is one which *sells.*

The methods presented in this book are proven. The fresh ideas and approaches here are founded on these proven methods and will result in a professional catalog with plenty of selling punch.

To "begin at the beginning," Chapter 1 reflects on the origins of catalogs, and Chapter 2 deals with the all-important technicalities of planning and scheduling (a first step, after all). But those of you *creating* your first catalog should start with Chapter 3, Forming an Approach, and move to Chapter 5, Photography and Art, and Chapter 6, Copy. The excitement and detailing of catalog creation are found in these later chapters and prepare you to tackle the more tedious, but basic and vital elements found in Chapter 2, such as scheduling.

Chapter 3 defines the purpose of the three major catalog sections: front cover, back cover and inside pages. Design approaches are discussed and basic methods are explained. Execution techniques are provided with blueprints (grids) for various styles of page layouts. Chapter 4 leads you through methods of deciding upon the art and copy approaches which are most appropriate for your product line and your target customer. Here is where you discover "product work sessions," the "scientific" basis for your "creative" decisions. Chapter 5 tackles the exciting and awesome task of how to present your visuals. You are guided through the four basic photographic techniques, as well as when to use artwork instead of photography. In Chapter 6, copywriting skills are described. Here you'll find a formula to produce good product copy, clinching the sale and building credibility for your products and your company. Chapter 7 addresses the guarantee — that element which either can provide credibility for your catalog, or create doubts in the mind of your prospective customers. Closing the sale in the easiest way is described in Chapter 8, The Order Form. Techniques used here practically place the pen in the hand of the customer, encouraging that final step, placing the order. The "how-tos" of print production, from choosing the right paper to communicating with your printer and lettershop, are addressed in Chapter 9. Chapter 10 alerts you to the fact that many of your actions when creating a catalog may have legal ramifications as well.

It is a pleasure to acknowledge the following individuals whose thoughts, work and ideas enhance this book. Their knowledge and experience have also contributed to articles printed in The Catalog Marketer and The Business-To-Business Catalog Marketer, newsletters published by Maxwell Sroge Publishing.

Richard L. Bencin, President
Richard L. Bencin & Associates
Brecksville, OH

Gordon F. Bieberle, President
Bieberle Associates
Des Plaines, IL

Robert W. Bly
Copywriter/Consultant
New Milford, NJ

Jim Coogan, Vice President
Woodworker's Supply
Albuquerque, NM

James M. Doyle, Mkt. Mgr.
Webcraft
North Brunswick, NJ

Dean Powell, President
Dean Powell Design
New York, NY

Arthur Pryor
Pryorities Advertising, Inc.
Tamarac, FL

Sally Richman Rogers
SR Enterprises
Los Angeles, CA

Ernest H. Schell, President
The Communications Center
Jenkintown, PA

John Schmid, President
J. Schmid & Associates
Shawnee Mission, KS

Mark Favus, Vice President Mktg.
Foote & Davies
Atlanta, GA

Frank Gesualdi, Prod. Consultant
Lincroft, NJ

Rene Gnam
Rene Gnam Consultation Corp.
Holiday, FL

Erwin J. Keup, Attorney at Law
Newport Beach, CA

Joyce Kole, Account Manager
Webcraft, Inc.
North Brunswick, NJ

James E. Lentz, Exec. VP
Lehigh Press
Pennsauken, NJ

James A. Semsar
The Studio
Baraboo, WI

Henry Spitz, Vice President
Brodie Advertising Service
Chicago, IL

Warren Swanson
Warren K. Swanson Studio, Inc.
Ringwood, IL

Zane Tankel, Pres./CEO
Collier Graphic Services
New York, NY

Arthur Winston
Winston & Sherman, P.C.
New York, NY

It is also with pride and gratitude that the very special comments and advice that you see in sidebar form throughout this book were given by the following:

Scott Ashley
Annie's Attic
Big Sandy, TX

James J. Casey, Pres.-Direct Mktg.
Eddie Bauer
Redmond, WA

Len Carlson
Los Angeles, CA

Judith Diehl, Dir. Advertising
Taffy's
Cleveland, OH

Richard Halpern
Data General Direct
Milford, MA

John Hawkins, Advtg. Mgr.
B.A. Pargh Co., Inc.
Nashville, TN

Estin Kiger, Corp. Creative Dir.
Inmac
Santa Clara, CA

Larry Lefavor, Catalog Dir.
DRI Industries
Bloomington, MN

A. Lee Maynard
Lee Maynard
Santa Fe, NM

Frank B. Merritt
The Colonial Williamsburg Fdn.
Williamsburg, VA

Walter K. Noel, Creative Art Dir.
New England Business Service
Groton, MA

Norm Sherwood, Dir. of Advtg.
Current, Inc.
Colorado Springs, CO

Patrick D. Smith, Jr., Prd. Mgr.
Calif. Polytechnic State Univ.
San Luis Obispo, CA

John C. Schenck
Avon Fashions
New York, NY

Grateful acknowledgement is made of all the catalogs used to illustrate examples of photography, art and copy for the critiques and commentary throughout How To Create Successful Catalogs.

As you use this book, please record your ideas and comments. We'd appreciate hearing suggestions for additions and improvements, as well as learning the results of your efforts and experiences in creating a catalog.

The Editors

Lou E. Smith
Cecile Wood Gort
Maxwell H. Sroge
Gary D. Hennerberg
Bradley D. Highum

Special thanks to the following people, without whose dedication this book would not have been possible:

Alice Kimsey	Production
Dallas Cline	Art
Sally Calton	Proofreading
Jeannie Smith	Proofreading

Chapter 1

The Mail Order Catalog

Where did the word ''catalog'' originate and what does it mean? It was derived from the Greek KATALOGOS . . . meaning ''to list.'' List may seem rudimentary, but even today the catalogs we produce are ''listings.'' They are most often both visual and verbal listings of products for sale. Page after page of products are pictured with informational copy designed and worded to entice the customer to buy. The sophistication of design, photographs, art, ink, paper has transformed the original unadorned ''list'' into one which is fully costumed, ready to entertain, educate and sell with the flip of a page.

The first catalog, a listing of books during the 15th century, was produced in Europe. Here in America, the first version of a mail order catalog was produced by Ben Franklin, the first postmaster of the United States, in 1744. It was a listing of several hundred books. The catalog was a natural outcome of Mr. Franklin's profession as a postmaster and publisher. In those days, postmasters could send any type of printed matter through the mail, at no charge, so Ben had a pretty good deal.

But the individual most publicly recognized for starting the first mail order *catalog* is Montgomery Ward. In 1872 he put out a small flier (catalog) *listing* such items as handkerchiefs, coats, and table cloths at below-retail prices. Low prices were achieved by quantity purchasing and the elimination of the middle-man. This first flier was only a single page -- a few years later it grew to eight pages. The 1985 Spring-Summer Montgomery Ward catalog is perfect bound and has 376 four-color pages, with professional photographs of each product complete with information and pricing.

The current day trend is to offer specialized merchandise such as shoes, jewelry, specific foods, computer supplies, butcher products, auto parts in catalogs by themselves. Then, refining the selection of the mailing list to those who are interested in purchasing that specific category of product so, when mailed, catalogs produce more orders and are more profitable.

Since the first mail order catalog, enormous strides have been made in the type of merchandise offered and the manner in which it is offered. Today the mail order catalog is most often a glossy, four-color jewel with page after page of enticing pictures and informative copy. Through catalogs, small towns like Big Sandy, Texas (the home of Annie's Attic), Millstone, West Virginia (the home of Alice in Wonderland Creations), and Freeport, Maine (the home of L.L. Bean), can all sparkle as brightly as New York City to the customer. Fifth Avenue, with its multitude of merchandise, is transported into the customer's home. The general consumer is educated, entertained and pampered with thousands of wonderful catalogs containing millions of products to be purchased at one's will. And what could be more convenient than shopping from your own home at the kitchen table, propped up in bed or in your favorite easy chair?

The business-to-business world is just awakening to what mail order catalogs can mean to their success. Costs for sales calls are skyrocketing. One sales call costs in excess of $200 for large corporations and a whopping $291 for companies with fewer than ten sales people (Laboratory of Advertising Performance, McGraw Hill Research). Because of these costs, many small customers would have to be ignored if it weren't for catalogs. A company can easily service accounts and inform their customers about the products carried or services offered. Time delay is kept to a minimum through toll-free numbers and warehouse fulfillment centers across the United States — even around the world. In fact, an individual can now select the product to be purchased from a catalog, call the order in, and receive the merchandise the next day. That's convenience shopping!

Convenience shopping . . . customers want it and look to mail order catalogs for it! Indeed convenience is only one percentage point below "merchandise not available elsewhere" as the most important factor for shopping by mail, according to the October, 1983 Consumer Report Magazine. Why? One of the most significant factors influencing how the consumer shops is the changing role of women in society. Fifty-one percent of the labor force is now women (over seventy percent of the twenty to twenty-nine-year-olds are working women). Over thirty-one percent of all household have two incomes, allowing for more discretionary income. More women have less time outside of their work and family obligations. Shopping in retail stores can be exhausting and time consuming, sapping energy and taking away time which could be used for job, family, and recreation. Shopping by mail order catalog has become a pleasurable, no hassle experience . . . an almost required method of life for *thirty percent of the general consumer* population to spend an estimated fifty billion dollars in 1985.

Catalogs have also become a relied-on source of accurate and detailed product information. How many times have you walked into a retail store and asked a clerk for some information about a product only to receive a blank stare, mumbled words, or a bland "I don't know." A catalog that presents products well, both visually and verbally, informs the customer thoroughly about each product listed. It should enthusiastically present products in such a way as to build confidence and encourage the customer to make a purchase. *This is why the way a catalog is created is so important.*

This book deals with the fundamentals of creating a successful catalog. It starts after your company concept has been formed, your products selected, and your business plan made. This book does not propose to include every approach or every aspect there is to creating a mail order catalog. It does, however, endeavor to give you successful, workable methods for creating a successful catalog. It will complement and guide your skills so you can create a new catalog or improve methods used before on other catalogs. Now, turn to Chapter 2 to read about how and why planning is such an important factor in creating a successful mail order catalog.

Chapter 2

Planning A Catalog

The catalog plan can be compared to the rudder of a ship. Without one there is no control or direction and therefore the desired end result is seldom met. Your basic concept may become diluted, your approach will be weak, deadlines may not be made, and a very carefully planned mailing date might be missed. How do you go about making a plan? What are the elements to include? Many subjects talked about in this chapter are gone into more fully in other chapters. You may find it advantageous to refer to this chapter later as you achieve a better understanding of the steps from other areas of the book.

Seven Major Tasks

Creating a catalog can be broken down into seven major tasks — dummying the catalog based on products selected, product review, design/layout, copy, photography, reproduction preparation, and printing/lettershop. Planning and scheduling must be built around these tasks.

Dummying a catalog is the placement of products within the catalog pages once the products (old and new) have been selected. Categories of products must be placed in groupings or in some kind of order in the catalog according to product popularity and season. Consideration must be given to retail prices and space justification. The bottom line is that all products must be placed where they will justify their being, *collectively*, with the most sales.

1. **Dummying the catalog** is primarily the job of the merchandiser. Why? Isn't the visual effect of the catalog important in attracting the customer and selling the products? Doesn't it matter what products are put side-by-side? Yes, to all questions, except that the merchandiser is aware

of product sales and seasonality, and it is the merchandiser who must be concerned with placement, creating additional sales with specific products, and taking advantage of catalog ''Hot Spots'' (discussed in Chapter 3) to boost selected product sales.

Merchandiser dummies catalog

The format you choose for your catalog (the way you group your products, such as by product category, theme-function category, mixed product) and the technique you choose (the physical design of the grouping, such as symmetrical or asymmetrical) dictate how soon and how deeply the graphic designer and product artist become involved with the dummying process. If you have chosen to have a symmetrical layout with a product or theme/function format, it is fairly easy for the merchandiser to proceed with the dummying. Art and copy sizes are balanced proportionately and may be predetermined by the merchandiser because of a limited number of common sizes. Keeping the products in categories such as stationery, kitchen, office forms, desks, and twine is pretty cut-and-dried. But when an asymmetrical layout is chosen, requiring different sizes per individual product, the knowledge, talent, and guidance of a graphic designer and artist become critical to the outcome. (Symmetrical and asymmetrical layouts are fully discussed in Chapter 3.) All of these factors must be considered when you're making up a schedule: a symmetrical layout will take less time and most likely involve fewer people; the asymmetrical layout will take longer to dummy and will involve a number of people and perhaps several meetings.

Don't miss product work sessions!

2. Product review by the copywriters and artists, along with the merchandiser and other product buyers, is how the selling message to the customer begins. In Product Work Sessions, new products are introduced to the creative staff and the catalog art and copy are planned. Chapter 4 is devoted to these sessions — who should attend, the material to have on hand, and what should be discussed. These sessions are vitally important and productive. A minimum of fifteen minutes should be devoted to each new product, to bring out why it was selected, why the customer will purchase it, which competitors have run it, how the art might be approached, and what needs to be included in the copy. If you have only a few new products (nine or ten) you might be able to get by with one long review session. But if you have 100 new products, you may have to schedule many sessions. *Do not expect the artist to work on layout or design or the copywriter to produce copy without the benefit of these meetings — your bottom line will suffer if they are skipped.*

3. Design layout will take considerable time. Even though the products have been assigned to their pages and the basic idea as to how they should be presented has been formed, ample time should be allowed for the artists to wave their creative wand . . . the visual presentation must catch the customer's eye. Chapters 3, 4 and 5 all deal with presentation.

4. Copy. The copywriters must assemble the facts, emphasize the benefits, and sell the customer. If legal releases from the manufacturer are needed for copy claim protection — this takes extra time. Rewrite time must be considered, too. And the duty of revising copy on old products or for seasonal changes usually falls on the shoulders of the copywriter. Don't shortchange this time. Chapters 4 and 6 deal with copy approach and writing.

5. Photography can be either extremely involved (if done on location in Greece) or less complicated (if done in the studio). But do not think that photographing catalog products is easy just because the photograher is provided with detailed, to-size layout sketches of how the shot should look. The right props have to be found, the models arranged for, the background readied, and lighting planned. The layout provided for the photographer may not work well once the real products are positioned and viewed through the photographic lens. Time for reshooting needs to be allowed. Chapters 4 and 5 deal with photography and visual presentation.

6. Press preparation. Much is included in this task. Typesetting, mechanical paste-ups, transparency assembly, and color separation all take a good share of time. The better prepared the work is, the fewer problems will occur at press. If the camera-ready art is expertly done — no smudges, photography/art edges smooth, no headlines, type, inserts or photos missing, everything in line — the printer won't have to piece things together and there will be minimal error. So the time spent at this stage will save time and trouble at press. Chapter 9 deals with production planning.

7. Printing/lettershop. The time it takes at this stage is pretty standard. Four-color printing generally takes six weeks from the time the job is received by the printer to the time the first catalog drops in the mail. (If your camera-ready art is slick-as-a-whistle and the color separations have been provided — maybe five weeks, but don't count on it.) Chapter 9 on production planning goes into this step more thoroughly.

Work Communication

It is crucial that all elements be able to communicate on a significant level and to maintain totally professional attitudes during sometimes long and tedious days. Conflicts of aesthetics are terribly stressful and can ruin a job as well as everyone's day!

Judith Diehl
Director, Advtg.– Mail Mktg.
Taffy's
Cleveland, OH

Allow enough time for tasks

You need to plan each step, which means you must assign a deadline for each step and keep each deadline. If yours is an established catalog company with an established mailing pattern — and you know exactly how many different catalogs will be published during your fiscal year and when they need to be mailed — a schedule for each publication date should be made. This can and should be done once the mail dates have been set. Why? This will allow you to see the demands for all areas (buyers, copy, art, pricing, computer entry, printing, and lettershop) and how these demands overlap for each catalog. All people involved will be able to adjust their time to make the deadlines. Catalogers just starting up will want to carefully structure their schedule, working back from the mail date (chosen with extra time built-in if possible). A successful catalog is one with a well-thought-out plan that is carried through.

How To Set Up A Catalog Creative Schedule

Once you have decided to produce a catalog, a mail date must be set. The mail date is the most important date in structuring a creative catalog schedule. It is the one deadline that cannot be missed. So you have the mail date — what happens now? You start working backwards from the mail date to establish other deadline dates. There are certain elements of production which have fairly set time frames for completion from the time camera-ready artwork is provided. These time frames establish other important dates. For example, catalog printers generally take five to six weeks to prepare and print your catalog (this includes lettershop functions). Envelope printers need only two weeks if one or two colors are involved, or four weeks if your envelope is four-color. But the envelopes should be on the catalog printer's floor two weeks prior to the catalog press date. These are a few of the more defined periods of time you will work with. But remember, if Christmas, New Year's, or Thanksgiving falls in the scheduling period, build an extra week for each holiday into the schedule.

A Catalog Production Schedule

Thirty-eight steps to publication. This schedule covers a twenty-one-week countdown and could be considered a fairly tight catalog production schedule. However, some catalogers, especially business-to-business, might consider it generous. In the fast-moving field of electronics, for example, product developers and buyers may scream at a three-month-out closing date for new products. While merchandisers and creative people must be lenient and understanding of such a fast-moving product development world, they must also be realistic. Mail dates need to be met in order to take advantage of ideal selling periods, and the creative process demands a fair amount of time to produce the vehicle which will sell the products. This twenty-one week countdown is a fair schedule for an average size catalog (up to 100 pages), though only if enough staff people are involved and if all intermediate deadlines are met.

38 Steps to Catalog Production

1. Preliminary review of products, old and new.
2. Special promotion products selected.
3. New products finalized.
4. Catalog dummy complete.
5. Art and copy review meeting.
6. Photography and art started.
7. Art and copy review meeting.
8. Old products finalized.
9. Product releases sent.
10. Envelope/order form design started.
11. Late product closing.
12. All art and copy reviewed.
13. Layout finalized.
14. Cover design/art finalized.
15. All products to photographer.
16. Cover complete and to printer.
17. Envelope/order form art to printer.
18. Product changes, final review.
19. Copy to typesetter.
20. Begin paste-ups.
21. Selling prices reviewed and finalized.
22. Copy releases accounted for.
23. All prices and copy changes to typesetter.
24. Copy repros pulled.
25. Envelope proof received, returned to printer.
26. Cover press proof received.
27. Color printer spreads viewed.
28. Color spreads to separator.
29. Paste-ups corrected.
30. Proofing complete, camera-ready art to the printer.
31. Envelopes received by printer.
32. Catalog proof received.
33. Catalog proof returned to printer.
34. Catalog on press.
35. Catalog published.
36. Transparencies returned.
37. Files broken down.
38. Gather bound catalogs.

Week Countdown	Task
Week 21	**1. Preliminary review of products, old and new.** The total product needs of the catalog are reviewed. Sales figures for all previously-run products and product categories should be analyzed to determine the final merchandise needs. Decisions on old (carryover) product inclusion and sizing are determined according to performance and season. The number of new products needed is finalized, and their space allotment is indicated. Completing this step will take several weeks.
Week 19	**2. Special promotion products selected.** "Special promotion" includes any free gift or incentive-priced merchandise. Also included are products placed on sales-boosting pages (explained in Chapter 3): front cover, back cover, order form. These products will not only influence the design, layout and copy in the catalog, but they will also need special attention in the purchasing department because of the above-average sales volume which their placement produces.
Week 17	**3. New products finalized.** All new products should now be selected. Information on material, availability, and cost should be on file for art and copy use. Production samples should be in-house. Products needing special attention such as copy releases, official test document claims, and warranties should be marked for needed action.
Week 16	**4. Catalog dummy complete.** Each product being cataloged should now have an assigned catalog page number. If the catalog is symmetrical in design, sizes may be assigned at this time by the merchandiser. If the catalog is asymmetrical, meetings with the art and copy department will help in assigning final space allotment.
Week 16	**5. Art and copy review meeting.** This is the first of the product work sessions (Chapter 4) in which you will be thoroughly going over each new product. A minimum of fifteen minutes should be allowed for each product, since competitors' listings must be reviewed, test results combed, and manufacturer's information looked at. A full understanding of the product (why it was selected, its main benefit, and why the customer will purchase it) influences how the art is presented and the copy approached. The product shots requiring models or extensive proofing should have precedence over the straight shots because their photo prep and shooting take longer. These meetings are intense and therefore should not last over three hours. Several may need to be scheduled.
Week 16	**6. Photography and art started.** If you're working with symmetrical layout, some individual product layouts may be ready to send to the photographer — the sooner

Week Countdown	Task

the better. Even if your photographer doesn't start shooting until all products for one catalog have been sent, sending some of the products early will allow the photographer to look for props and to have plenty of time for setup.

Week 13 **7. Art and copy review meeting.**

Just the same as step number five. More meetings will need to be scheduled if there are over twenty or so new products.

Week 13 **8. Old products finalized.**

All repeat products should by now have been verified for availability and possible changes from the manufacturers. Shaky products (slow sellers or those with availability problems) will have been dropped, and product specifications that have changed should be reviewed for art and copy changes.

Week 12 **9. Product releases sent.**

Some catalog companies get a signed release form from the manufacturer for every product they carry. Essentially, the catalog copy is sent for specification review and an accuracy check. Some companies ask for releases only on critical items where copy claims may be subject to doubt, because of the nature of the product. Exercise equipment, ointments, diet pills, bunion pads, ingested items, and electronics products are a few areas considered critical. Getting a signed release stating all claims are true, relieves catalog companies from any doubts, as well as any legal problems. Plenty of time must be allowed to ensure that the signed release (or correct copy) is on file when camera-ready art is sent to the printer.

Week 12 **10. Envelope/order form design started.**

Any products appearing on the order form should be verified by now. Design and finished art must be completed so the envelopes can be sent to the printer in plenty of time. Also, actual printed samples must be double-checked for accuracy in gluing, perfing, and folding.

Week 12 **11. Late product closing.**

This is it — the last chance for the buyers and product developers to get products in this catalog. If there are some new products at this date, review them and get the art and copy going.

Week 11 **12. All art and copy reviewed.**

All of the product work sessions should be over and the catalog layout nearly complete. If more than the two scheduled art and copy review sessions are needed — they should have been done before now.

Week Countdown	Task
Week 11	**13. Layout finalized.** The catalog layout and all product layouts must be okayed. Any problems with visual presentation must be worked out *now;* no more time is left.
Week 11	**14. Cover design/art finalized.** Photographs must be finalized (both front and back cover), original art and design okayed.
Week 11	**15. All products to photographer.** The last of the product layouts and products must go to the photographer. Sending anything later will not allow for reshots if they are needed. Many catalogers attend the photo sessions themselves to offer guidance and on-the-spot approval for props and changes.
Week 10	**16. Cover and photography/design complete and to printer.** The cover needs to go early so a press proof can be pulled, if desired. Many catalog companies request a press proof of the cover because of the cover's critically important function — attracting the customer's attention. Getting the right color tones and combinations becomes vitally important — errors can be caught and corrected now.
Week 10	**17. Envelope/order form art to printer.** Camera-ready art needs to be sent off. Be sure to review postal charts, special messages, and products.
Week 9	**18. Product changes, final review.** This is the last go at old or new product changes to be included in copy or art. Double-check your "Change Memo System" (discussed directly after this catalog production schedule) and manufacturer product confirmations.
Week 9	**19. Copy to typesetter.** Send all of the copy (old with changes and new) to the typesetter. Be sure that clear instructions are sent regarding width, line length, style, size, and weight of type — include the catalog layout if it's an asymmetrical design where copy may "wrap around" the design or products.
Week 8	**20. Begin paste-ups.** Now the process of preparing camera-ready artwork begins. Each individual page is laid out on boards with the design and photo designations exactly to-size and in position as they will appear in the catalog. Copy headlines and blocks are placed in their exact positions, too. Most symmetrical mechanicals have "windows" placed where the photographs will appear. The windows are generally made with rubylith (a screening material which, when photographed, produces a clear or dropped out area for photographs or drawings). For an asymmetrical layout, a pencil sketch or black and white velox

Week Countdown	Task

or color transparency is put in place, indicating the exact position and form of the illustration. The finished (camera-ready) boards are photographed and incorporated as an element of the black plates.

Week 8 **21. Selling prices reviewed and finalized.**

All costs and retails need final approval for inclusion in the typesetting process. Old products should be cost checked and any new prices established. New products should have all cost workups done and prices set.

Week 8 **22. Copy releases accounted for.**

Don't forget to follow up on the requested copy releases. If any changes resulted from them, now is the time to make them.

Week 8 **23. All prices and copy changes to typesetter.**

These changes are easily made on the copy proofing galleys which are pulled as part of the final copy procedure. Be sure to double-check changes on old items through your "change memo system."

Week 8 **24. Copy repros pulled.**

All corrections are made by the typesetter and checked by you — then a camera-ready reproduction of all product copy and headlines is printed to be used in paste-up.

Week 8 **25. Envelope proof received, proofed, returned to printer.**

Your final chance to view envelope and order form art and copy before it's printed and shipped to the catalog printer. Be sure to keep a copy — double-check glue coverage and position, perf-positioning, and type of perf. Ask that printed samples be air expressed to you as they come off the press.

Week 7 **26. Cover press proof received.**

Check for color, blotches, position — how the art and photographs blend. Is the paper the proof was pulled on the same as what it will be printed on — it makes a difference. (See Chapter 9.)

Week 7 **27. Color printer spreads viewed.**

All new product photographs — in fact, *all* catalog product photographs — should have been reviewed for correctness and acceptance, with changes made and transparencies assembled in page form. Generally the photographs are to-size and butted end-to-end in position with an acetate overlay indicating side borders. Pages are separated in groupings (gang separating) for position accuracy and cost savings. When photographs are individually separated, cost is considerably more. (See Chapter 9.)

Week 7 **28. Color spreads to separator.**

If you deal directly and select your own color separator, you know whether the mechanicals need to be shot and the type stripped in at this time. Some separators strip headlines and type into place; others just separate the color transparencies and leave it to the printer

Week Countdown	Task
	to assemble. If you have a printer who does the color separating or handles it for you, you will not have to worry about sending material to another party before it goes to the printer. Just send them to your printer.
Week 5	**29. Paste-ups corrected**. All changes that have come in due to manufacturer changes in the product, price increases, or the pulling of doubtful products should now be complete. The art boards should be in perfect shape, ready to be photographed for platemaking.
Week 5	**30. Proofing complete, camera-ready art to the printer**. A full-blown proofing session should be done on the paste-up boards. This is the last chance to make reasonably inexpensive changes. From here on, changes will involve film and plates — major costs when compared to changes made on paste-ups.
Week 5	**31. Envelopes received by printer**. Always keep checking on how all production is doing. You should have been in contact with your envelope printer to make sure that the envelope went on press, when the printing was complete, and when the envelopes were shipped to your catalog printer. Your checking samples should have been air freighted to you and approved before the main shipment to the catalog printer was made.If the envelopes have not been received on time (two weeks prior to catalog press date), find out where they are and get them to your printer.
Week 4	**32. Catalog proof received**. There are a number of names for a proof — blueline, silverline, brownline — it depends on the process used when making them. You should have two proofs — one to send back to the printer with the corrections marked, and one to be kept by you. This way, you'll both understand what to talk about if questions arise about the changes because at this point you are not at the printshop. (If extensive changes are requested, you may want a second proof copy pulled to check before the presses roll.) At this point, a really hot product can still be included if the art and copy are ready and another product taken out to make room. It is not preferable, but it can be done.
Week 4	**33. Catalog proof returned to printer**. Make sure all corrections are clearly marked and any material needed to make the corrections has been sent. The best approach is to make a separate list of the corrections wanted, in page order — this acts as a check list for the printer and better assures that corrections will be made.

Week Countdown	Task
Week 3	**34. Catalog on press.** Be there! Check the press sheets as they come off the press against any last-minute changes you may have made. See how the color is running once the press is up to speed and the pressmen have had a chance to balance colors. If colors need adjustment, work with your representative and pressman for the best result. When everything looks good, that sheet will become the control to follow for the rest of the job. Get a handful of press sheets to take back for others to see and use.
Week 1	**35. Catalog published.** It's in the mail — at least the first segment. Many high-volume companies have mail patterns that extend over a one- to two-month period before one catalog version mailing is complete. This allows stable order inflow and smoother work handling for fulfillment and operations. It also allows a regional timing factor, boosting sales with more timely delivery in different sections of the country.
Week 1	**36. Transparencies returned.** Be sure to get the transparencies back so they can be disassembled and filed for use in the next catalog. (This simple step is very easily forgotten. Then when transparencies are needed, they must be hunted down, if possible, and prepared for use, wasting valuable time and causing unneeded frustrations.)
Week 1	**37. Files broken down.** This does not sound very creative, but it too is a chore which — if not done — causes chaos in all departments. Break the files down right away, getting the needed information to the appropriate departments such as bookkeeping, data processing, and warehouse control.
Week 1	**38. Gather bound catalogs.** Don't forget to have a few hundred catalogs shipped from the printer to the marketing department for future creative use. Too often *no* catalogs are set aside, and the catalog company ends up not having a copy for its own records or use.

This 38-step countdown is just a skeleton to help guide you along. Additional steps will need to be added for each individual demand. Just be sure to take your schedule seriously, be reasonable in setting the deadline dates, and adhere to the deadlines set!

How To Prevent Errors In Your Catalog When Products Undergo Changes

A **"Change Memo System"** will help keep track of changes in your catalog production. Details can be uninteresting and no fun — especially when no immediate action is required or when the impact of these details is unknown or not understood. But the importance of a Change Memo System should not be minimized. The detail of recording possible product changes and following through when the changes are needed may seem to have few rewards. Not true! *A Change Memo System collects facts and institutes actions that allow the cataloger to have a "clean" catalog,* a catalog that is *error free*. This must be made clear so the people involved realize the importance of their actions.

Here's the flow of a Change Memo System: the five steps to take, plus the why . . . and the reward.

First — **Choose a vehicle to record changes** . . . such as a wire-bound memo book with two-up or three-up memos, and the ability to make at least one copy from a built-in carbon. A bound upright version can be referred to easily and stored on a shelf or in a desk drawer.

Second — **Identify catalog areas of change** . . . four major areas are affected most seriously:

1. Supply. Product supply may be cut off or it may be too small. Sometimes factories really do burn down or other complications arise which temporarily make the product unavailable. The merchandiser may have to omit a product from the catalog until it's available again.

Changes in more than one area

2. Art. If product style, color, size, function, or raw material changes, the visual of the product also changes . . . and catalog art must reflect the difference.

3. Copy. If the product style, color, size, or function changes, or the number of components differs, the copy must reflect this. Your customer relies on good, thorough, correct information provided by copy explanation. Reflecting any change is vital.

4. Selling Prices. A cost increase from a supplier generally means a price increase to maintain an acceptable profit margin when the product is run again. Your catalog must reflect the most current and desirable prices.

Third — **Identify in-house and out-of-house departments which must know of the change.** Two major areas of concern exist within the cataloging department: active and inactive products. Active are those products running in the current catalog or slated for the catalog being prepared for press. Inactive are those products not presently running, but still viable for future catalogs. Three other departments exist outside the cataloging department: Data Processing, Plant (order entry, warehouse, customer service), and Ad Agency. These departments will need to know any changes affecting them.

Fourth **Record the change**. All changes must be recorded in such a fashion that they are easily implemented. Here are three important facts to be sure to record:

1. Product identifying number and name.

2. Nature of change.

3. Date change needs to be implemented.

And here's an example of a typical Change Memo:

H 50555 Weather Stripping.
Cost increase from J.W. Jones Manufacturing, to $24.00/dz., effective 10-83. Price change, effective for Jan. '84 catalog, to $8.95.

Attach the original copy of the memo to the copy used for catalog paste-up (wherever it is stored). Then, when the item is again run, the change will be seen. Also, the cost of making the change will not be incurred if the product is not run again. Keep a duplicate memo in a special file (according to product number) and send other duplicates to departments also affected (such as your ad agency).

Fifth **Make the change**. When a catalog is being assembled, the Change Memo File becomes paramount in importance. All the changes needed for all old products are in one place and therefore easily made. The Art Department needs only to refer to the file to make sure the right art is used. The Copy Department needs only to make the changes these memos record to have accurate, updated copy. The merchandiser can rest easy that products are represented properly and retails meet profit structure requirements.

Memo all departments

Reward: A catalog that is outstanding and complete in product representation for the customer, and with profitable products for the company. Details can be rewarding, but only if we all understand their importance.

Don't shortchange yourself or your catalog by sidestepping or putting little effort into the planning stages. Allow plenty of time for each step in your plan, and then stay on schedule. You'll be rewarded with happy employees, happy suppliers, a terrific looking catalog, and buying customers.

Chapter 3

Forming An Approach

The Front Cover . . . What Is Its Role? *To Attract Attention!*

Attracting attention is certainly the catalog cover's primary job. Many factors influence accomplishing this feat. The type of merchandise you carry needs to be identified in some way so the customer will pick up the catalog with anticipation of what is inside. But just presenting a pretty cover does not insure customer interest; there is too much competition from other catalogs, magazines, and direct mail packages. Your cover must attract attention in such a manner that it captures the type of customer who will buy your products. We may all dream that customers are waiting to pounce on our catalog as soon as it arrives, peruse its every detail, and tally up a massive order. This seldom happens — and it never happens by accident!

Orders are achieved by generating the desire to purchase and then motivating that desire. Once a product line is established, it is the cover's job to create desire and *motivate the customer inside;* to get your cover to do this, *you must attract the right kind of attention in the right way*. In creating a cover, you need to ask: Should it create just an image which will attract attention, or should it also sell your services and products? Do you gain enough by using your cover design merely as a "hook" to get the customer inside your catalog? Is promoting an image enough? Or could you gain more, including extra sales?

In creating a cover, remember: it represents your company image, your products — even the customer himself. It communicates to your customers and prospects the overall position of your company. The cover projects your appeal, and gives the viewer a myriad of hints about what you offer and what the customer can expect regarding:

Cost of merchandise (high-end, middle range, inexpensive, discounted)

Type of merchandise (clothes, gifts, general merchandise, food, computer accessories, nuts and bolts, stationery, sports gear)

Attitude and image of catalog house (serving-the-customer-since-1900 reliability, brand-new-company excitement, urbane sociability, down-home neighborliness, sweepstake seduction, banker's reliability)

Seasonality of merchandise (Christmas gifts, summer fun, spring fix-up)

Type of customer to whom you are appealing (affluent/middle-class; country/city; intellectual/physical; refined/simple tastes; business/homebodies).

And there is the constant argument that rages among many prominent and experienced catalogers: (a) always put products on the front cover, or (b) never put products on the front cover. Many feel that the catalog image is lost or cheapened when products are put on the front cover. Others feel that it is poor judgment not to make this space available for sales or service promotions because it is the most powerful sales space in the whole catalog. The majority of catalogers compromise between image and product by attempting to project image and sell items concurrently. But no matter what the decision is, one must always remember what the primary job of the cover is: *The number-one job* of a catalog cover is to *attract the customer's attention*!

Three ways to get Front Cover attention!

Both the general and the business-to-business customer receive a lot of advertising mail, a lot of catalogs. Mailboxes are full of catalogs, direct mail, and sample offerings. Incoming office mail has traditionally been heavy with direct mail packages and advertising fliers. Now catalogs are becoming a necessarily popular business-selling device because of economics and convenience. This all adds up to heavy competition for even a first glance, let alone the opportunity to make a sale. How can your catalog cover command the viewer's attention? There are three basic approaches:

1. Dramatic Impact
2. Product Line Identification
3. Sales/Benefits

1. Dramatic Impact

The **Dramatic Impact** approach is aesthetically the most preferable. It grabs the customer's attention with a startling design, commanding photo, or unusual presentation. Most often this approach does not picture products; it is more artistic in effect. Catalog companies often become known for a specific type of dramatic effect which then becomes a trademark for the company.

General Consumer Figure 3-1 is from the Patagonia catalog, which offers casual outdoor apparel. The total cover is a reproduction of a rugged snowcapped mountain in the country of Argentina. It is an arresting cover photo — one which will grab the attention of anyone viewing it. Only the catalog name and season are added to maintain simplicity and effect. (''One Dollar,'' a catalog value

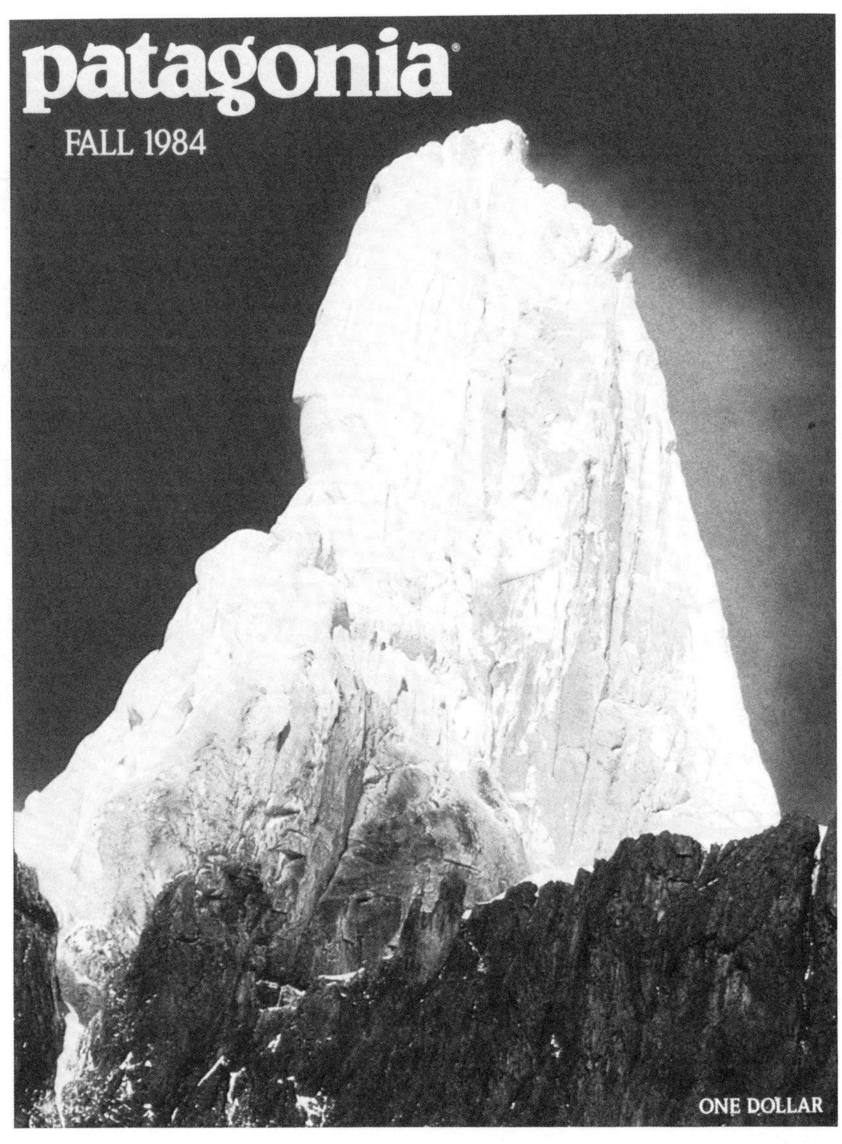

3-1

attempt, serves only to distract and defeats the desired effect of high-end outdoor apparel.) For the Patagonia customer, breathtaking outdoor scenes have become a trademark of the catalog, which is instantly recognizable and immediately picked for viewing and ordering, while other catalogs are cast aside.

The prospective customer receiving the catalog for the first time is attracted because of the dramatically effective visual representing the outdoors, and Patagonia is counting on the cover to qualify the viewer's interest, strongly suggesting the catalog be opened for additional appreciation of the outdoors.

Business-to-Business Figure 3-2 illustrates how a business-to-business company, OK Industries Inc. (a tools, equipment, electronic accessories and telecommunications firm) creates an interestingly dramatic effect with angular blocks wrapped with photos of

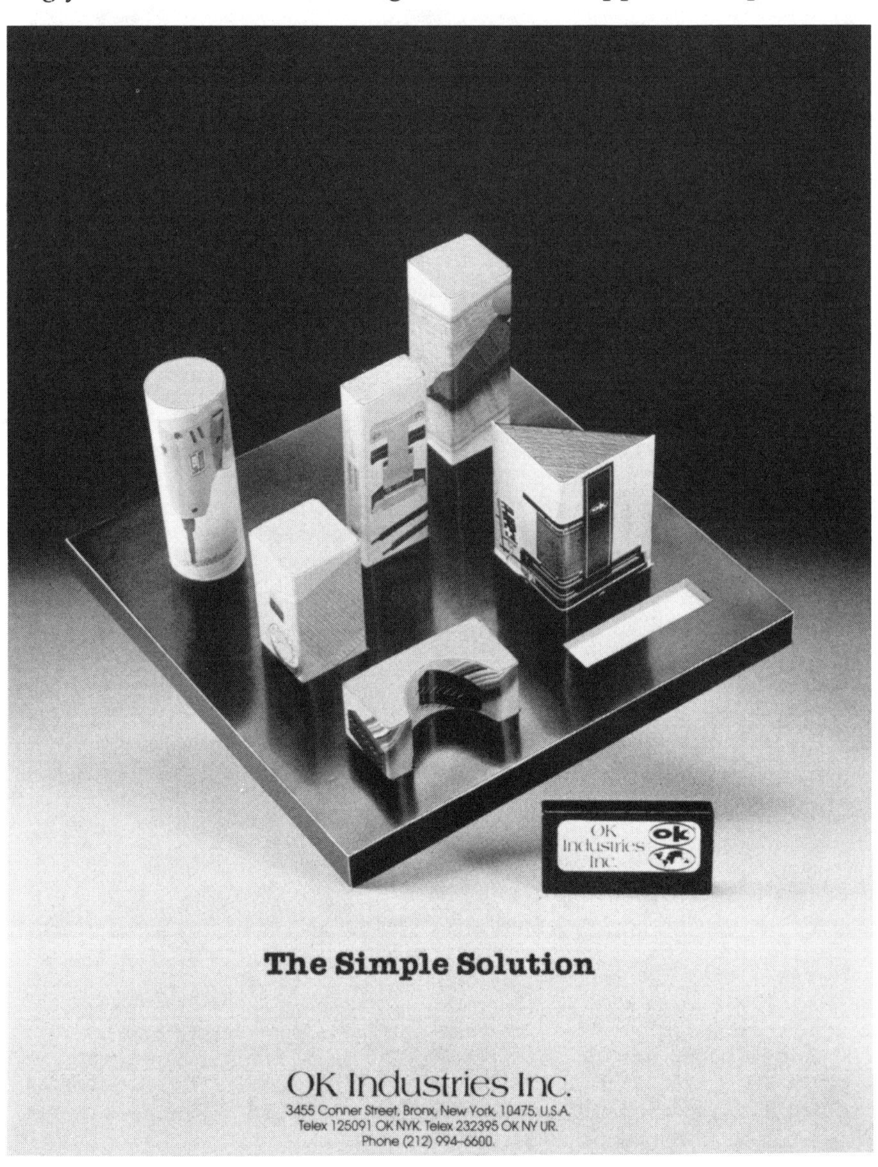

OK Industries Inc.
The Simple Solution
OK Industries Inc.
3455 Conner Street, Bronx, New York, 10475, U.S.A.
Telex 125091 OK NYK. Telex 232395 OK NY UR.
Phone (212) 994-6600.

3-2

products which the customer will find inside. The design is visually commanding and interesting, suggesting an office building complex or an internal office plan. The picturing of the products is secondary and was used as only a minor part of the design.

Neither of these examples directed the customer inside with an invitational phrase, nor did either announce any special offers or use any other motivational methods of getting the customer to look inside. Most catalogs choosing the dramatic impact approach miss these prime opportunities because of the misconception that the dramatic effect would be lost. (Patagonia could easily have used something like, ''See Page 22 for popular classic Pile Jacket - new and improved,'' without destroying anything; in fact, the company might add to its image and increase sales by eliminating the $1.00 price tag.)

Rather than rely on distinct product line identification, OK Industries has chosen to artfully suggest a businesslike atmosphere via clean-cut shapes, lines, and colors. Only the company's name, address, phone number, and logo are added, along with the statement ''The Simple Solution,'' maintaining the efficiency and dramatic effect of the cover. This approach in the business-to-business customer area is often chosen in hopes that the catalog, because of its attractiveness, will be kept around the office for a greater length of time than a competitor's.

Advantages	**Disadvantages**
Total aesthetic appeal; possibility of catalog being kept around longer or kept in view, because of attractiveness; possibility of getting customer's attention due to visual impact.	Catalog being overlooked because of magazine appearance; non-identification of product type; missed opportunity to sell products or verbally direct the customer inside.

2. Product Line Identification

Put top selling products on the cover

Selected merchandise is pictured either alone with plain background or shown in use. Often just one product is presented; however, several can be pictured. The product or products chosen should be proven top sellers or new products which are very similar to the cataloger's top sellers. Seasonal aspects should be brought in and most likely will be if top sellers are chosen. This approach is by far the most often used. Generally it can be aesthetic in feel while simultaneously identifying the product line.

General Consumer The cover of the Hills' Court Fall 1983 catalog (Figure 3-3) leaves no doubt as to the product type carried. An attractive, wholesome-looking model leans up against the fencing around a tennis court, smartly clad in tennis shoes and a warm-up

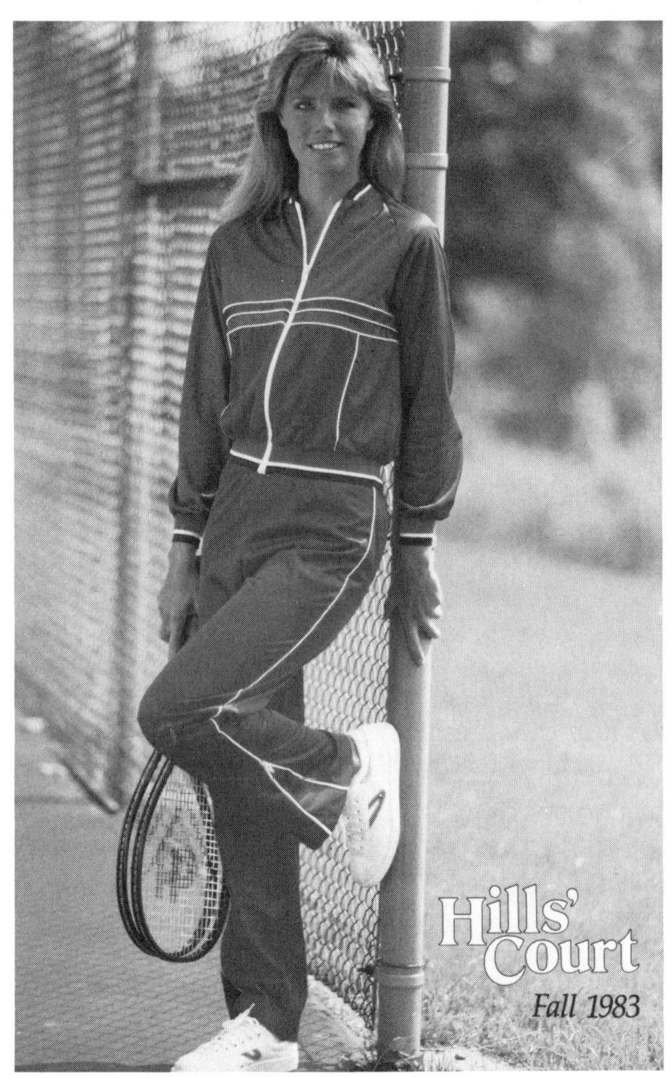

3-3

suit, with her rackets in hand. Not only does the clothing announce the product line, but the background setting complements the appeal while helping to identify the product line, too. The total impact neatly does the job of identifying and defining the appeal. Customers choosing to pick up and open this catalog will not be disappointed when they look inside and find tennis apparel and related products. The company will not be disappointed either; orders will come in because of the cover's ability to identify product line, on the cover as well as to appeal aesthetically to the customer. One opportunity which is missed, and one which would not detract from the visual appeal, is a reference to the inside page on which the product appears.

Business-to-Business DECdirect (Figure 3-4) sets up an office situation which displays many of the personal computer accessories and support products carried inside. These products surround an evidently happy and successful executive. The scene framed in the window suggests a busy and important setting: the

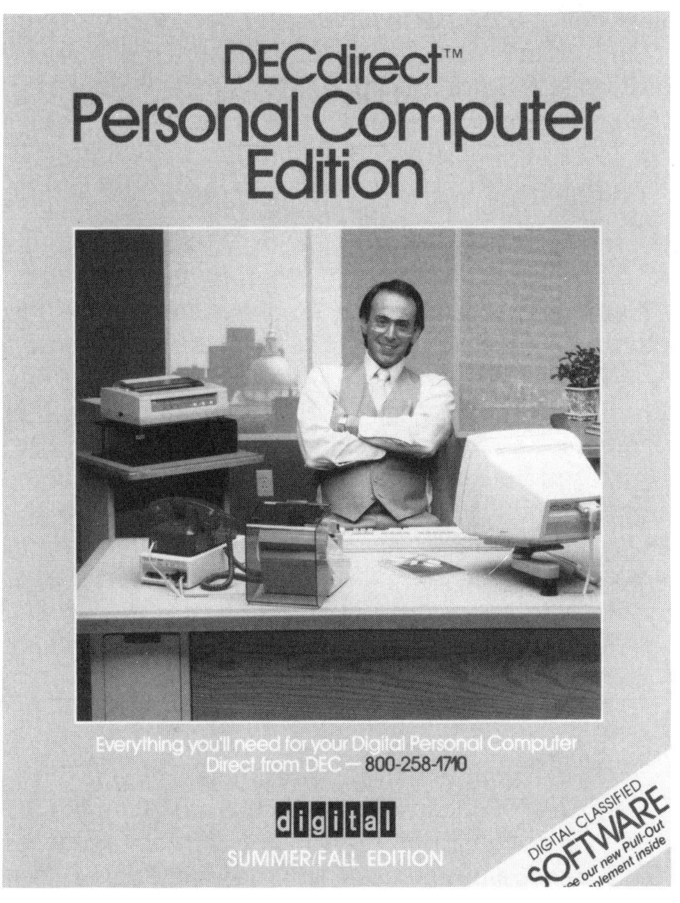

DECdirect™
Personal Computer
Edition
Everything you'll need for your Digital Personal Computer
Direct from DEC — 800-258-1710
digital
SUMMER/FALL EDITION
DIGITAL CLASSIFIED
SOFTWARE

3-4

male executive looks intellectual, physically fit, and happy with his job and with his *surroundings* — which are the products offered by the catalog company. The total cover image is appealing as well as clear in product identification. Ease of ordering is announced by the toll-free number. An attempt is made at directing the customer inside with reference to the software supplement. However, more sales would be realized if page numbers had been referenced for the six products appearing in the cover picture and other products within, or if, perhaps, a mini-index of categories had been presented.

Advantages
Product type immediately identified; getting the customer's attention via area of interest and attractive presentation; visual motivation to look inside; verbal reference motivating inside interest; additional sales.

Disadvantages
Possibility of unattractive cover due to poor product selection and awkward and unclear presentation.

3. Sales/Benefits

In the sales/benefits approach, a product or products are pictured with copy and pricing directly on the cover. Benefits or incentives are directly stated. Since this approach directly or indirectly sells a product, it is perhaps the most logical use of the most valuable sales space available in the catalog. Need aesthetic appeal be lost and image destroyed, resulting in a hard, unappealing look? We think not.

General Consumer The Hanover House cover (Figure 3-5) accomplishes both visual appeal and direct sales, plus the announcement of a 50th Anniversary giveaway. This low-ticket catalog (mostly $1.99 to $10.00 range) has managed to select a product which is appealing (spiral sippers), picture it in an attractive manner (in use, filled with a beverage, and propped with tantalizing fruit), and give it dramatic lighting. In addition a full product description allows the customer to order directly from the cover! Value is boldly announced, along with the inside reference to the $550,000 Giveaway Sweepstakes. All of this is accomplished on a small (5⅜″ ×8¼″), digest-size cover format. For a direct sales/benefits cover, it does everything well.

Price $1.00
Better Buys By Mail Since 1934
HANOVER, PA 17333
Hanover House
SUMMER 1984
Spiral Sippers
Sale $1.88
3 for Only $4.99
Win one of 50 2-carat diamond rings in our 50th ANNIVERSARY $550,000 GIVEAWAY!
See insert
BOTTOMS UP the easy way with our unique spiral sipper glasses. A glass with a new "twist"—the colorful straw wraps around the outside of the glass and enters at the bottom, so you are actually drinking from the bottom up. You get every drop, minus drip or clog! They're fun to look at and are the life of the party or summer picnic.
They're designed to last . . . and good news: when the party's over and it comes to clean-up time, these ingenious tumblers are top-rack dishwasher safe. Be sure to order plenty for all your summer festivities. Assorted colors. Very specially priced!
C556042–Spiral Sippers . . . $1.88; 3/$4.99

3-5

Business-to-Business The Bencone cover (Figure 3-6) clearly identifies the product, gets the customer inside with a page reference, and announces a bunch of benefits. Two models attractively attired in Bencone uniforms cheerfully greet the customer and announce what the catalog is all about. At the base of the photo is a page reference for these cover products. Bencone also verbally tells the customer what its product line is (''Professional Uniforms and Accessories'') and that it has been a ''Value Leader in Fashion Uniforms for Half a Century!'' Four benefits are listed: 1. ''The latest fashions for . . .,'' 2. ''Inflation-fighting '2-for' Values,'' 3. ''Special! Free pair of Knee-Hi Hose,,'' and 4. ''SPECIAL OFFER. . .with the purchase of $35 or more!'' All are fine incentives designed to attract the customer and make a sale. Ease of ordering is shown with the toll-free phone number plus days and hours available. All is accomplished with clean, sharp design and no confusion — overall, a convincing sales/benefits cover.

Sell directly from the Front Cover

3-6

Advantages
Product line identification; visual motivation to look inside; verbal reference motivating inside interest; credibility building via benefits; direct or additional sales.

Disadvantages
Possibility of unattractive cover due to product selection and presentation; cluttered effect due to too much information; customer confusion due to too much information or cluttered design.

One Product Category — Three Approaches

Most interesting at this point might be a comparison of three different general consumer covers offering the same type of merchandise: clothing. The differences in image created by the chosen approach of each catalog are immediately apparent, and so are the differences suggested by each cover regarding the cost and appeal of the products inside.

Dramatic Impact Brooks Brothers' Summer cover (Figure 3-7) is a beautiful watercolor of a craggy New England shoreline, stormy skies, sailboat, and a turn-of-the-century couple gazing out at the choppy waters and seagoing activities. This creates a dramatically attractive visual while defining a classic American feel for the upscale merchandise inside.

Product Line Identification Lane Bryant's cover (Figure 3-8) shows actual photos of a product offered. Picturing five color choices plus headline benefits and product references makes a busier cover. This immediately takes the catalog out of the expensive category, and this fact is underlined with cover copy: ''Your dollar buys more at Lane Bryant.''

Sales/Benefits Lana Lobell (Figure 3-9) uses a specific item which is sold directly from the cover. The price is very low and, even though the garment is on the dressy side, it definitely is not haute

3-7

3-8

3-9

couture. The pricing, informational copy, and visual impact obviously set the tone for the low-end clothing line found within.

Though the merchandise category is exactly the same, each of these three covers immediately implies the taste, lifestyle, and budget of a different kind of target customer, and how the products inside will suit that individual. In each case the customer has a good idea, before opening the book, exactly what to expect inside.

The style and mood which have been set by each catalog are maintained with every new catalog that company creates. The customer immediately recognizes the source, and each new catalog mailing reinforces the company's image. Existing customers develop loyalty and confidence through familiarity, and prospects in the same target group become customers because they see a format with which they are comfortable.

Remember, the basic rule for your cover is to *Attract Attention*. Also remember, when you are determining the approach needed, that you are establishing your *image*, which will set the tone for the entire catalog. This is an image you will want to keep and which becomes representative of your catalog company, an image which will build customer loyalty and bring in new customers.

What Else Can a Catalog Cover Do?

After the general approach of the cover is decided, there are various promotional elements which can be included on the cover:

1. Payment Methods (charge card logos, in-house credit) tell the customer he has immediate credit with which to make a purchase. It also suggests how easy it is to order from the company.

2. Toll-Free Service immediately tells the customer it is easy to order. It also suggests fast service because it will take less time to place the order and, therefore, fill the order. If for some reason your company does not have a toll-free number, use your regular number; the effect is similar.

3. Ordering Incentives — whether a free gift, sweepstakes, discount, or sale — encourage customers by letting them know they will be rewarded for ordering.

4. Credibility Builders such as number of years in business, customer testimonials, and a strong guarantee can relieve the customer's mind about the reliability of the company and build confidence in placing an order.

Each of these elements is applicable to any product area and any target group, from gifts for consumers to forms for business. In effect, everything you put on your cover is a device for getting customers' attention and then getting them into your catalog. Remember: every square inch of your catalog costs you money to produce and, consequently, must produce dollars for you. Logic suggests that using cover space for product presentation may bring in more dollars in the long run.

But first, you must **Get the Customer's Attention.**

Front Cover Checklist:

- ☐ Establish Theme.
- ☐ Determine Approach.
- ☐ Select Merchandise.
- ☐ Select Special Messages.
- ☐ Design Cover.

Always:

1. Put company name on cover.
2. Show continuity of theme.
3. Indicate seasonality.
4. Motivate the customer to look inside, both visually and verbally.

Strongly Consider:

1. Charge card availability.
2. Toll-free number.
3. Credibility factors like company longevity, customer testimonials, guarantees.
4. Ordering incentives such as free gift, sale, discount, sweepstakes.

The Back Cover . . .
What Is Its Role?
To Identify the Recipient — Plus!

The back cover is the second most visible part of your catalog. In fact, it is most likely the first part viewed as the customer pulls the catalog out of the mailbox. Why? When postal employees sort the mail and match it to the delivery address, the name/address side must be viewed and, therefore, is the side which is ''up'' when the catalog is placed in the mailbox or business in-box. The importance of the back cover becomes very evident. The role it plays is *major*.

The primary job of the back cover is to act as an *identifier* of the receiver and the sender. The back cover carries the customer's name and address so the catalog can be delivered, plus the catalog company's name and address for company identification. After performing its purpose of identifying, there are three basic services the back cover can perform:

1. Image Carryover
2. Direct Sales Promotion
3. Referral Sales Promotion

1. Image Carryover.

Back Cover identifies theme too

The theme or look established on the front cover is carried over onto the back cover via artwork, design, or color. A minimal amount of product or service reference is used. This approach is aesthetically appealing and can allow easy general information reference such as service, phone number, a quick index. In the general consumer area, this category includes coffee table catalogs which are aesthetically appealing enough to compete with attractive magazines. Some business-to-business catalogs strive to achieve an attractive, uncluttered cover which will be kept around the office and, hopefully, inspire continued use. Generally with all such books, the thematic look of the front cover is also desired on the back.

General Consumer Earlier, in this chapter, we saw how the Patagonia catalog created a showstopper cover with an arresting mountain scene in Argentina. Now let's take a look at how that image and impact are carried over onto the back cover (Figure 3-10). An evening campsite scene in Cedar Mesa, Utah, carries the stark and challenging feel of the outdoor struggle for survival. No reference is made to product or product type. Creative credits are acknowledged and store locations given. Nothing competes with establishing

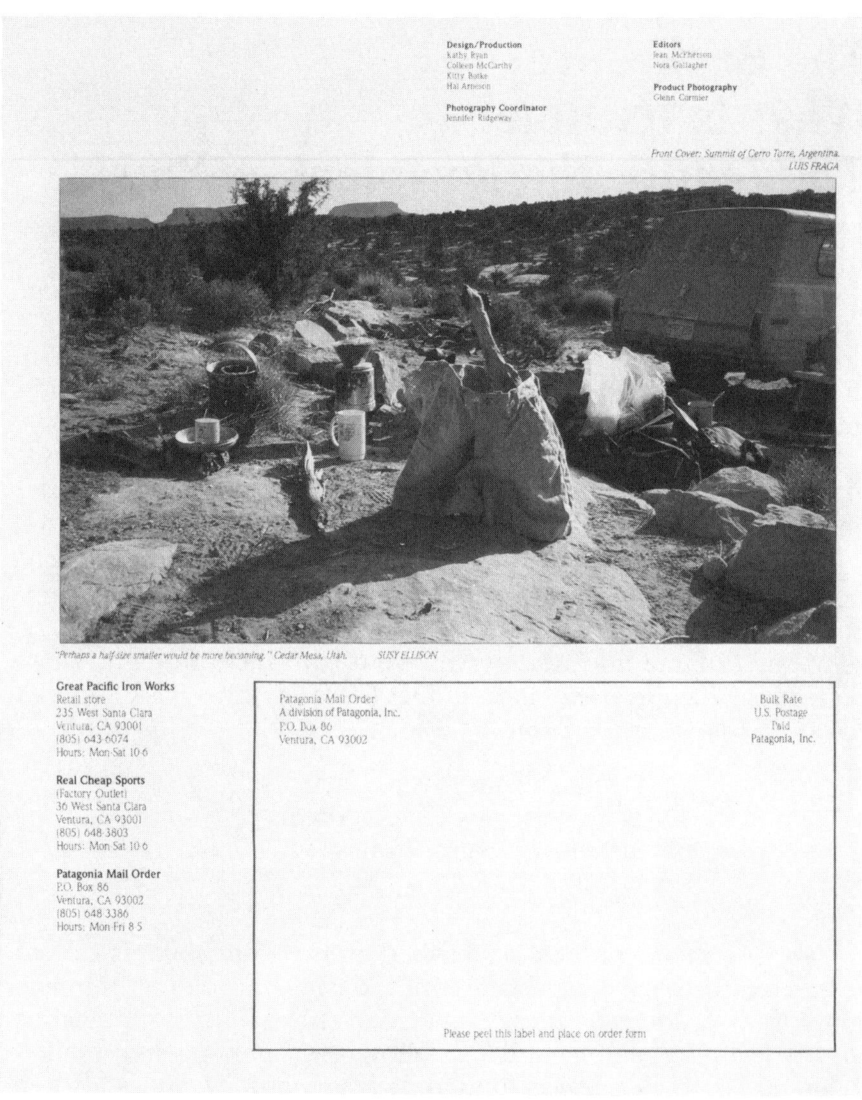

Design/Production
Kathy Ryan
Colleen McCarthy
Kitty Batke
Hal Arneson
Photography Coordinator
Jennifer Ridgeway
Editors
Jean McPherson
Nora Gallagher
Product Photography
Glenn Carmier
Front Cover: Summit of Cerro Torre, Argentina.
LUIS FRAGA
"Perhaps a half size smaller would be more becoming." Cedar Mesa, Utah. SUSY ELLISON
Great Pacific Iron Works
Retail store
235 West Santa Clara
Ventura, CA 93001
(805) 643-6074
Hours: Mon-Sat 10-6
Real Cheap Sports
(Factory Outlet)
36 West Santa Clara
Ventura, CA 93001
(805) 648-3803
Hours: Mon-Sat 10-6
Patagonia Mail Order
P.O. Box 86
Ventura, CA 93002
(805) 648-3386
Hours: Mon-Fri 8-5
Patagonia Mail Order
A division of Patagonia, Inc.
P.O. Box 86
Ventura, CA 93002
Bulk Rate
U.S. Postage
Paid
Patagonia, Inc.
Please peel this label and place on order form

3-10

an image and mood for the catalog. A visual dramatic effect has been given the sole responsibility for enticing the customer inside to look at the array of outdoor apparel.

Business-to-Business Also we earlier saw how OK Industries achieved a dramatic impact with the use of blocks and angles to form an unusual design to attract the customer's attention. The back cover (Figure 3-11) carries the theme of eye-catching design with a line drawing on a stark black background. The only additions are the catalog identification number, logo, business address and phone. No allowance is made for the name-address panel, as the catalog is sent in an outer envelope.

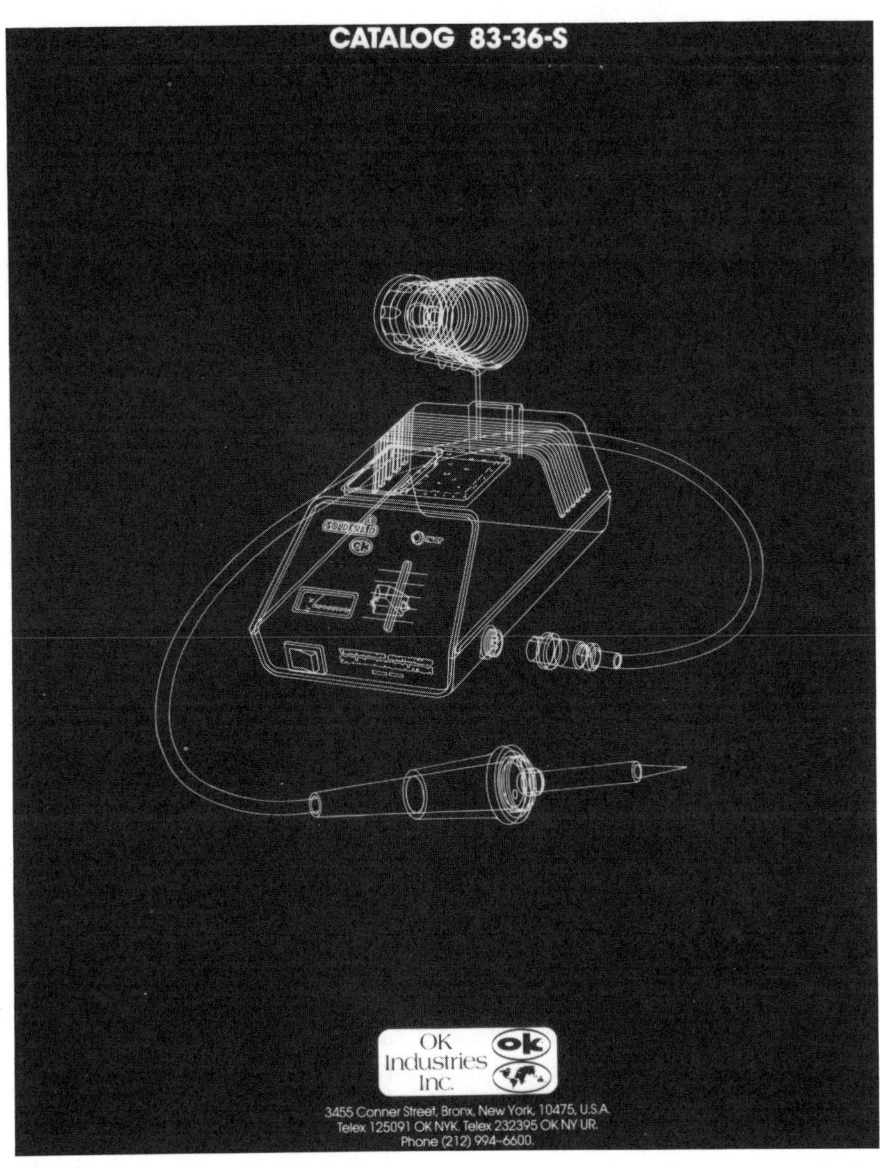

3-11

Advantages
Aesthetic appeal maintained; little problem created for address panel space; clutter and confusion eliminated.

Disadvantages
Loss of valuable sales and reference space; lost additional dollar sales; minimal product line identitification.

2. Direct Sales Promotion

The back cover may picture a product or products not shown elsewhere in the catalog, with all information necessary for placing an order, including the retail price. The products presented on the back cover will enjoy a healthy sales increase (two to three times more than the same listing inside the catalog) and, therefore, should be chosen wisely. Products must meet two criteria before they are put in this important position:

(a) Products should be strong sellers. Consider not only the staple items in your line, but also items with seasonal pull (toys for Christmas, industrial-strength bug killers in the summer).

(b) Products should have excellent profit margins. Extra sales should bring in maximum profits.

This direct sales promotion is the approach most commonly used for back covers, and it is perhaps the most profitable because of its powerful sales pull. For example, Sears Roebuck regularly runs bedspreads on the back cover because of their popularity and consistent profit margin.

General Consumer David Kay Inc., a garden and gift catalog (Figure 3-12), sells as many products on the back cover as it does on a typical inside page. Here, artful planning has allowed the top product (a set of Christmas tree ornaments) to become a lovely decoration adding to seasonal holiday appeal. Each of these products should sell well above its average pull, while serving as an attraction to the customer. A tidy address panel area gives the company name and address and bulk rate permit. Unfortunately, the phone number and an opportunity for an inside page reference are lost.

Business-to-Business Inmac, a computer supplies, accessories, furniture, cables and data communications devices catalog (Figure 3-13), chooses an exclusive product to sell directly: an adjustable keyboard shelf. The product is illustrated both solo and in use, and a photo silhouette illustrates its versatility. Not a chance is lost to attract the customer for a sale. Approximately one-third of the page is used for illustrating one inside page and referring the customer to four others. This is very smart and should produce some nice additional sales for those referenced products. However, the page numbers are so hard to find and to read that some of the advantage is lost. A startling move is the omission of a phone number, as up to 90 percent of business-to-business orders are placed over the phone.

Advantages
Identification of product line; additional direct sales; customer interest qualified; visual motivation for customer to look inside catalog.

Disadvantages
Possible clutter in design; chance of confusion.

3-12

Sell directly from the Back Cover

3-13

3. Referral Sales Promotion

Attracting the customer with back-cover visuals and then referencing the inside page numbers is an approach which will move the customer inside your catalog. There are several variations on this approach. Descriptive copy can accompany the picture of the product, the product alone can be pictured, or there can be only verbal mention. The products referenced will enjoy a 25 to 35 percent increase in sales. The important step is to get the customer to open up your catalog via inside page references.

3-14

General Consumer DRI Industries (Figure 3-14) pictures ten products and references eleven pages on its back cover. No sales copy accompanies the picture, just the product name and the inside page it appears on. A little over a quarter of the page is devoted to purchasing incentives: Complete Selection, Complete Comfort, Save Money, Charge it, 100% Guarantee of Satisfaction, Save Time and Gas. Every point made is another good reason to deal with DRI. These are six customer convenience points that will help persuade the customer to purchase and will also build confidence. Only minimal space for the customer's name and address is allowed.

Business-to-Business Blanchard Training and Development, Inc. (Figure 3-15), the company which produced the best-selling book, *The One Minute Manager*, does a wonderful job of picturing six basic products and referencing ten of the eighteen inside pages (56 percent of the catalog!). The crisp, modern graphic design implies efficiency, just as the products offered are designed to be efficient. A small descriptive copy block accompanies each photo, thumbnailing the product. Prominently displayed is the toll-free number, smartly announcing convenience and prompting order placement.

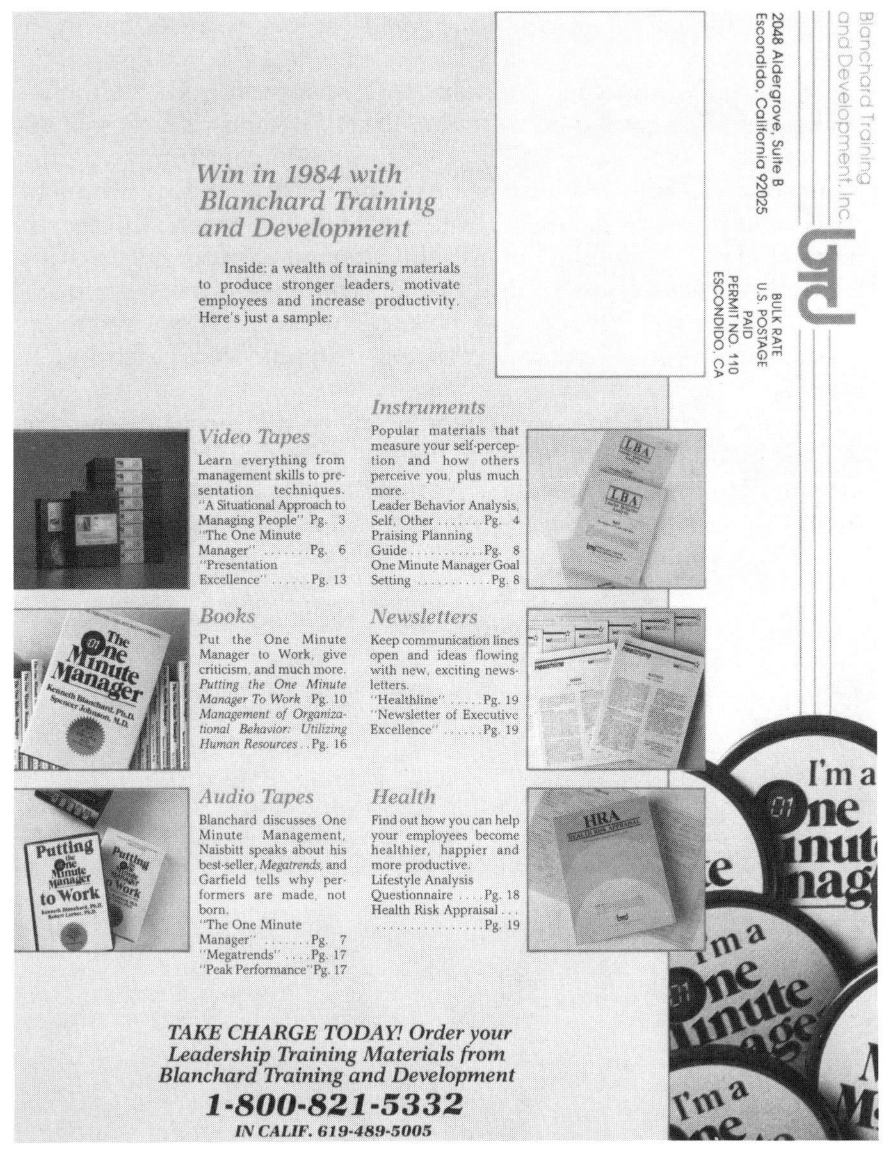

3-15

Advantages
Product line identification; direct motivation to get the customer inside the catalog; opportunity to increase sales of products directly referenced and other products on pages referred to.

Disadvantages
Possibility of cluttered design; possibility of customer confusion.

Both the direct sale and referral sale approaches direct customers to the order form by referencing popular products, thereby motivating them to place an order. This act of ordering automatically references the two additional catalog pages which surround the order form and increases viewing time for those pages, resulting in increased sales.

A good approach, perhaps the most preferred one for the back cover, is a combination of the direct sale and referral sale approach. Increased sales will be realized when a picture and complete ordering information are provided for one or two products. Also, when inside pages are referenced, not only are customers motivated to look inside, but also the referred-to products enjoy increased sales, as do the surrounding products on the same page. When referring to inside pages, be sure the products referred to are on different pages. That way more products are viewed and more sales are made.

Combine approaches

Remember: the back cover is one of the most visible areas of your catalog. It is important to maintain your *image*, but it is more important to make *product sales*. Work with your designer so the back cover *attracts the attention of the customer,* just as the front cover should.

Back Cover Checklist:

- ☐ Determine Method of Front Cover Theme Carryover.
- ☐ Select Direct-sale Merchandise.
- ☐ Select Referral-sale Merchandise.
- ☐ Determine Size of Address Panel.
- ☐ Determine Address Correction Message.
- ☐ Design Back Cover.

Always:

1. Put company name and address on back cover.
2. Put toll-free or regular telephone number.
3. Show charge card acceptance visually.
4. Refer customer inside the catalog in some way.

Strongly Consider:

1. Credibility factors such as company longevity, customer testimonials, guarantees.
2. Special offer announcements: sale, free gift, contests.
3. Mini-index.
4. Retail store location.
5. Phone specials.
6. Guarantee statement.
7. Customer testimonials.

Inside Pages . . .
How Should You Handle Them?

Once the customer has been intrigued into viewing the inside pages of the catalog, one would think the hard part was over. All that remains is for customers to choose which products they wish to purchase. The truth is, the hard work has just begun. The customer's interest must be carried over eagerly from the cover and held on every page throughout the catalog. Each product must call for attention independently without overpowering other products being offered. The catalog designer must exercise great skill in creating eye flow while calling attention to special offers and product benefits. One must always be governed by customer convenience, while making sure to motivate the customer towards placing the order. To do all this, one must first decide:

How the Catalog Is To Be Organized. Even before the format of your catalog or the graphic design and layout can begin to take shape, you must understand what factors dominate the organization of a catalog. Then apply these factors to your own situation so you can move forward.

Sales Boosting Pages The Natural Hot Spots

There are a few pages within a catalog which will produce greater sales than other pages. They are often called the catalog ''Hot Spots,'' and are the *natural* sales boosters in all catalogs. Remember, the most powerful sales pages in the entire catalog are the front and back cover. Here are the inside hot spots in order of effectiveness:

1. **Inside Front Cover (page 2)** is certainly the most natural because most customers ''naturally'' turn to the next page once their attention has been captured by the front cover presentation.
2. **Page 3**, opposite the inside front cover, benefits in much the same manner as page 2 and for the same reason.
3. **Middle Pages** (center spread) of the catalog produce greater sales because of the natural tendency of the catalog to fall open due to the method of binding. Most catalogs have ''stitch'' binding which employs a metal staple or glue method of binding to hold together the pages. Trimming or burring down for perfect binding, used for larger publications such as books, eliminates this area as a sales booster. A majority of catalogs bind-in the order form/envelope here.

4. **Inside Back Cover** enjoys a moderate increase in sales because some people look at a catalog from the back to the front. Many extra sales opportunities that normally would be gained by this position are actually realized by pages 1 and 2. Once customers are attracted by the back cover, it is their natural inclination to turn the catalog over to see the front cover and start viewing from that point.
5. **The Page Opposite the Inside Back Cover** is ''hot'' for the same reasons as the inside back cover.

Contrived Hot Spots

There are *contrived* hot spots, too. These are areas where greater sales are enjoyed because the cataloger has made a special effort to produce them. The three most common contrived spots are:

1. **Front Cover Referenced Pages**. Products pictured on the front cover are then page referenced inside for complete information needed to make the sale. Or, there may be verbal references to individual products, product groupings, or special offers. Products and pages referred to will enjoy greater sales.
2. **Back Cover Referenced Pages**. Products both pictured and referenced from the back cover will enjoy more sales than products simply referenced. Specific categories of products such as home exercisers or computer accessories, whose inside page numbers are referenced, will enjoy a moderate sales boost.
3. **Bind-In Areas**. The opportunity to bind-in an order form is present in between every signature printed to comprise a catalog. Signatures are generally printed in multiples of 8, 16 or 32 pages — depending on the type of printing and type of printing press being used. For example, in a 96-page catalog printed in 32-page signatures, there would be three opportunities to bind-in material: between pages 16-17 and 80-81, pages 32-33 and 64-65, and between 48-49 (the middle of the catalog). Again, most catalogers bind-in an order form in the middle of the book. However, as that is a natural hot spot, why not take the opportunity of binding into the other available spots and creating additional sales which might otherwise not be realized?

Guide customers through your catalog

Being aware of these special areas will allow you to dummy the catalog more intelligently and more profitably. One should always make sure these contrived reference areas and natural hot spots do not carry the same products. More sales will be realized by avoiding duplication and moving the customer on to new and different products.

Now that you know a few of the ground rules, you are ready to select:

The Format In Which To Present Products

How do you determine the makeup of a catalog? Many things influence you, but the price range and type of merchandise will be the governing factors. So once your merchandise is selected, you have already made a big step in determining which type of format to use. The other major determining factor is whether you are appealing to the general consumer or the business-to-business customer. The general consumer has, traditionally, approached purchasing by mail in a fairly relaxed manner. Because the general consumer is able to choose the time and place for shopping and tends to have a broad interest in products, this type of customer makes catalog shopping time a leisurely browsing time. Business-to-business customer's time is limited to fit within working hours. Their interests tend to be more narrow because they are job-oriented; therefore, they need a more orderly and expeditious way of selecting their merchandise.

Here are the three major formats, or ways a catalog can be made up:

1. Product Category (Products are grouped according to category.) For a more general line, put all kitchen products together, all garden products, all toys. The business-to-business cataloger would put all roof repair supplies together, all paint, all screen doors. If you have a specialized line, this method is still functional. For an audio electronics catalog, organize all stereos, then all tape recorders, then all car radios.

General Consumer The Spiegel Christmas catalog beautifully categorizes product type into groups throughout the catalog. Figure 3-16 is an example of one of the twenty jewelry pages within the front section devoted to this category. The catalog was not only formatted according to category, but also classified into subgroupings within a category — in this case, pearls. Interestingly enough, Spiegel's indexing is broken down into only two categories, Fashion World and Home World, with product categories sublisted, while the catalog itself is broken into many category sections.

Business-to-Business The Vocational Education Productions 1984 catalog, put out by Cal Poly State University Foundation, is targeted to the field of education. It lists all sorts of instructional materials for the agricultural area. A mini-index on page three lists eleven different product categories. Figure 3-17 shows the first page of the ''Field Crop Production'' section. At the top, a silhouetted cluster of grapes and grape leaves identifies the section, too.

2. Theme/Function Category (Products are presented with mini-subject themes or product function is broken into groups.) A food specialty catalog, for example, could put all steaks together, fowl, sauces, desserts. A business-to-business software catalog would put all word processing together, then accounting, then organizers. A more general line could be organized within broad categories, such as all rings together, all bracelets.

3-16

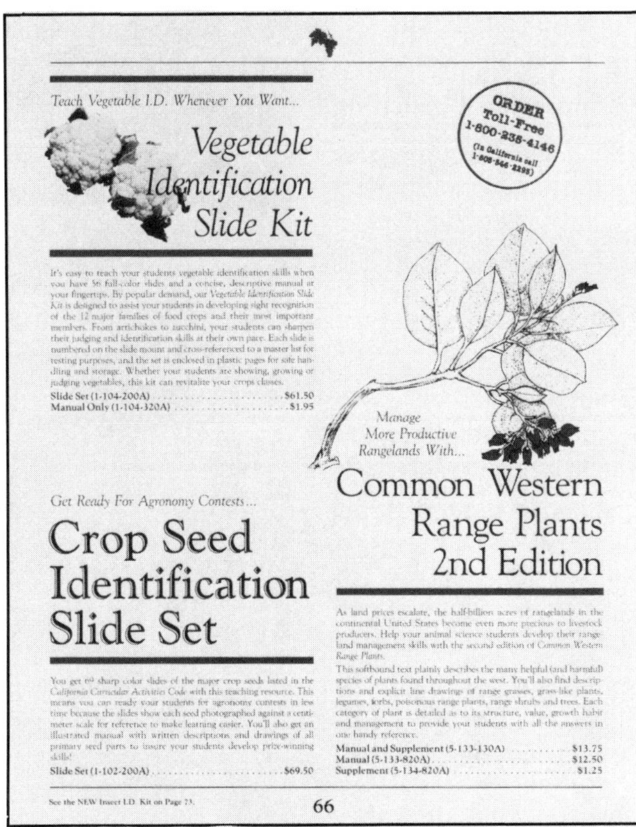

3-17

Advantages	**Disadvantages**
Easy customer reference; easy graphic design; copy (a page theme can be developed, a general category comment or educational blurb can be added, or background colors are more easily dealt with); easy like-product comparison; allows product line selection to appear large; easier specific product selection.	Greater possibility of the same look to all products within a category, plus boring layouts and then boring subject matter; missed chances for additive selling (lost opportunities for sales of coordinated or allied products).

General Consumer The Early Winters 1983 Winter Catalog (an outdoor equipment and apparel catalog) puts products together by function. If you want to look after your feet, you can do so by looking at five consecutive pages in this catalog, where the company offers heel pads, insoles, silk socks, anti-blister socks, foot-warming powder, Afghan socks with or without soles, and so on. The same goes for hand care products, bed and lounging products, packs. Figure 3-18 is one of two facing pages carrying silk products — a category. Customers see how they can keep warm with two products (scarf and balaclava), and be a little stylish with yet another (Wallace Beery shirt).

Business-to-Business The Data General DIRECT catalog is neatly portioned out into nine sections, each dealing with specific computer functions and accessories. Going with the theory that the

3-18

Pure silk with a taste of the thirties.

Rough-and-ready Wallace Beery popularized this shirt in the 30's. Now it's yours, for rough-and-ready outdoor action, in luxurious and hard-working silk.

You'll love the way silk feels against your skin. So warm, so strong, yet so supple—it's the ideal natural insulator.

Discover the sheer pleasure of silk.

Colors: Red, Blue   Warm wash, lay flat to dry.

Sizes (= men's / women's):
XS (30-32 / 6-8), S (34-36 / 10-12), M (38-40 / 14-16), L (42-44 / 18-20), XL (46-48 / —)

Wallace Beery Shirt, No. 14-0995 ...... $24.50

Warm & nearly weightless!

Try the face-saving protection of a silk balaclava. At just ¾ oz., it packs tiny, provides a luxurious shield from chapping and chilling winds.   One size fits all.

Colors: Red, Blue, Silver

Silk Balaclava
No.14-1021—$8.95
Save $2.00—
2 for $15.90

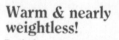

Wrap up in warmth.

Dazzle the eye. Check the wind. Swathe your neck in a wrap of pure Chinese silk.

Whether you wear it with a flight jacket, windbreaker, or dressy coat, it makes effective and elegant warmth.

12X60 inches, double layer

Silk Scarf
No. 14-0997 ...... $14.95

up-front pages are the biggest sales motivators and customer interest-catchers, the company has devoted ten pages to an attractive assortment of new products. Within that section, printers and print stands are laid out together, formatted and unformatted diskettes, and so on. Figure 3-19 shows how product function is tied together within Data General's basic product category. A Terminal Survival Stand, which needs to be mounted to a table, is offered on the same page as a table workstation. In Figure 3-20, one page in a ten-page hardware section, the main product offered is a printer. Four other products are attachments which can be used with the printer. This kind of presentation is smart because it makes it easier for customers to assess what they want and, in turn, boosts sales. Also note the small dark area on the bottom right of the page. It is color-coded (red), identifying the hardware category. Other categories have different colors. This is another customer convenience offered by Data General.

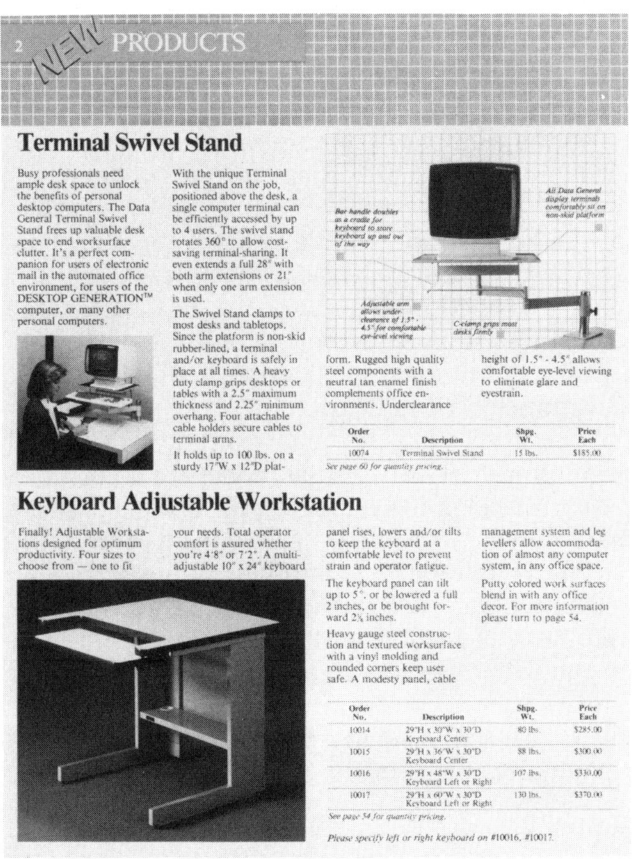

2 NEW PRODUCTS

Terminal Swivel Stand

Busy professionals need ample desk space to unlock the benefits of personal desktop computers. The Data General Terminal Swivel Stand frees up valuable desk space to end worksurface clutter. It's a perfect companion for users of electronic mail in the automated office environment, for users of the DESKTOP GENERATION™ computer, or many other personal computers.

With the unique Terminal Swivel Stand on the job, positioned above the desk, a single computer terminal can be efficiently accessed by up to 4 users. The swivel stand rotates 360° to allow cost-saving terminal-sharing. It even extends a full 28" with both arm extensions or 21" when only one arm extension is used.

The Swivel Stand clamps to most desks and tabletops. Since the platform is non-skid rubber-lined, a terminal and/or keyboard is safely in place at all times. A heavy duty clamp grips desktops or tables with a 2.5" maximum thickness and 2.25" minimum overhang. Four attachable cable holders secure cables to terminal arms.

It holds up to 100 lbs. on a sturdy 17"W x 12"D platform. Rugged high quality steel components with a neutral tan enamel finish complements office environments. Underclearance height of 1.5" - 4.5" allows comfortable eye-level viewing to eliminate glare and eyestrain.

Bar handle doubles as a cradle for keyboard to store keyboard up and out of the way

All Data General display terminals comfortably sit on non-skid platform

Adjustable arm allows underclearance of 1.5" - 4.5" for comfortable eye-level viewing

C-clamp grips most desks firmly

Order No.	Description	Shpg. Wt.	Price Each
10074	Terminal Swivel Stand	15 lbs.	$185.00

See page 60 for quantity pricing.

Keyboard Adjustable Workstation

Finally! Adjustable Workstations designed for optimum productivity. Four sizes to choose from — one to fit your needs. Total operator comfort is assured whether you're 4'8" or 7'2". A multi-adjustable 10" x 24" keyboard panel rises, lowers and/or tilts to keep the keyboard at a comfortable level to prevent strain and operator fatigue.

The keyboard panel can tilt up to 5°, or be lowered a full 2 inches, or be brought forward 2⅜ inches.

Heavy gauge steel construction and textured worksurface with a vinyl molding and rounded corners keep user safe. A modesty panel, cable management system and leg levellers allow accommodation of almost any computer system, in any office space.

Putty colored work surfaces blend in with any office decor. For more information please turn to page 54.

Order No.	Description	Shpg. Wt.	Price Each
10014	29"H x 30"W x 30"D Keyboard Center	80 lbs.	$285.00
10015	29"H x 36"W x 30"D Keyboard Center	88 lbs.	$300.00
10016	29"H x 48"W x 30"D Keyboard Left or Right	107 lbs.	$330.00
10017	29"H x 60"W x 30"D Keyboard Left or Right	130 lbs.	$370.00

See page 54 for quantity pricing.

Please specify left or right keyboard on #10016, #10017.

3-19

Hardware 45

Letter-quality printer — 4518

This printer is a tabletop unit that produces high quality hardcopy at up to 35 CPS, with 12 characters per inch spacing. Exceptional print quality as found in word processing applications make this a very attractive printer.

A choice of four forms handling options transforms this printer into an exceptionally versatile printer. A Bi-Directional Forms Tractor simplifies forms handling. The Single Sheet Feeder allows single cut sheet paper use. The Dual Sheet Feeder Adaptor allows simultaneous use of different types of paper. The Cut Sheet Guide simplifies loading and prevents misalignment.

An ASCII 96-character upper and lower case print element is supplied. Many other character thimbles including international sets are available for diverse fonts tailored to various print requirements.

This receive only unit has a serial interface that operates at 300, 600 and 1200 BPS. It can be interfaced to any Data General computer including the DESKTOP GENERATION computer system. It can run on CEO software. It is an exceptionally versatile printer that can even print on computer fanfold paper having up to 7 parts plus an original.

Order No.	If printer connected to:	Shpg. Wt.	Price
4518-J	Modem via 25' cable	46 lbs.	$2,800.00
4518-N	CPU via 25' RS-232 cable	46 lbs.	$2,800.00

The above Printers require one I/O port.

Bi-Directional Forms Tractor

The Data General Bi-Directional Forms Tractor enables precise forward and reverse paper motion necessary to print subscripts, superscripts, complex graphics and tables. Designed for feeding of side-sprocket-hole paper, this versatile, popular option is ideal for printing presentation quality text and business graphics, as well as engineering and scientific reports.

The tractor is fully adjustable to handle up to six-part continuous forms with ease. It features automatic paper-out sensing.

Paper Width: 3" to 16"
Paper Weight: 13# to 22#

Order No. 4522
Shpg. Wt. 5 lbs.
Price Each $300.00

Single Sheet Feeder

The Single (Cut) Sheet Feeder stores, and feeds single cut sheet paper to eliminate the need for fanfold paper or forms. It automatically feeds and stacks standard paper or letterhead and is ideal for moderate to heavy volume printing applications. A bin feeds the paper into the printer and a stacker receives the printed forms.

A removable, easy loading, paper out, and paper jam detectors and simple controls provide fast dependable operations.

Paper Width: 5" to 11.7"
Paper Weight: 17# to 28#
Paper Length: 4.3" to 14"
Tray Capacity: 180 sheets of 18# stock

Order No. 4523
Shpg. Wt. 15 lbs.
Price Each $1400.00

Dual Sheet Feeder Adaptor

The Dual Sheet Feeder Adaptor converts the single sheet feeder Order No. 4523 to a 2 bin paper inserter. This enables the use of different weight papers at the same time. Order No. 4524 is attached to Order No. 4523. The 2 paper types may be fed in under program control to produce presentation multi-page letters, reports and other important documents. An adjustable paper tray can be easily attached in minutes.

Paper widths: 5" to 11.7"

Order No. 4524
Shpg. Wt. 15 lbs.
Price Each $350.00

Cut Sheet Guide with Automatic Load

Now there's a simple low-cost option available to speed the printing of single sheet paper by eliminating slow, manual paper insertion and positioning. A ruled scale and adjustable alignment guide ensures fast and accurate paper positioning. A built-in paper detect/paper out sensor controls printer operation.

Paper Width: 5" to 16"
Paper Length: 3.5" to 16.5"
Paper Weight: 13# to 25#

Order No. 4526
Shpg. Wt. 5 lbs.
Price Each $165.00

3-20

Advantages

Requires only the function to be known, not the specific product — makes for fast, easy referencing; easy comparison of products performing the same functions; easy presentation of customer education and specific promotional copy areas.

Disadvantages

Possible sales decline for less popular product styles; boring page layouts; lost product coordinating opportunities; undesirable carryover when there is not enough area for all products in one section.

3. Mixed Product (Any product type can be dummied on any page with any other product.) At first this may appear to be the ideal way to go because of seemingly easier product placement. However, this layout is very difficult to execute well. Products should not be offensive when mixed, such as a cake pan and a kitty litter box. Certain products demand greater area because of high sales (a shelving storage unit sells better in January than in the fall gift season and so should be given larger space in January), because of price (a product bearing a high retail such as JS&A's radio/telephone unit at $179.95 can justify a larger space than a Walter Drake $1.99 smile sticker), because of size (a full-size kit model body which fits over an existing chassis needs more space than an ashtray for adequate visual presentation), or because of the nature of the product (a product with a number of features such as Day-Timer's pocket planner needs much more area for presentation because of its many functions than does a brass button set for a blazer). Mixed product is the most popular format in the general consumer area because of the ease of mixing and because sales are less dependent on product grouping by function or category. It is almost totally undesirable in the business-to-business world because of the need to categorize by function or brand, so an example has been omitted.

General Consumer Trifles (Figure 3-21), a general gift catalog, is one of the masters at utilizing the mixed product approach. This wonderful page offers personalized stationery, an enormous handblown vase, clear marbles for arranging flowers, a porcelain ashtray, and a Japanese robe which is on sale! These products are carefully illustrated to compliment one another. Tones of blue are in every picture. The stationery is trimmed in blue, the vase has a blue tint in the water and reflection on the table, the ashtray has a blue design, and the robe is blue. The mixed product approach seems orderly because of the color coordination. It has also allowed product coordination with the vase and the marbles. This type of format occurs on page after page in the Trifles catalog.

Advantages
Lively, appealing visual format; product coordination; color coordination; individual product appeal; size flexibility of product presentation; encourages browsing.

Disadvantages
Possible increase in preparation and production costs due to different layout and different product presentation in each issue; scattered customer attention; inability to index easily; no reference ability for product category or product function.

E

E. Improve your personal correspondence. Blue and green bordered personalized cards and letter sheets to call your own, with personalized companion blue and green stripe lined envelopes. For thank-yous, invitations or notes to friends. Makes a thoughtful gift, too. 5⅜" x 4¼" cards and 5⅜" x 8½" letter sheets. Specify full name, and two-line address. Please allow six weeks for delivery.
50 cards and 50 lined envelopes. #XY796 20.00 (3.00)
50 sheets and 50 envelopes.; #XY797 20.00 (3.00);
50 cards, 50 letter sheets and 100 envelopes. #XY798 36.00 (3.00)

H/I

F. TRIFLES SPECIAL!
Traditional Japanese robe called a "yukata". Wrap styled kimono with deep sleeves in a blue and white cotton printed just for Trifles. One size fits anyone. Washable. #XV897 36.00 value
NOW JUST 25.00 (2.95)

F

G

G. Blue and white Oriental dragon hand decorated on a brass backed porcelain ashtray. Makes the perfect decorative touch to any room. 7½" diameter. #XM527 14.00 value **SPECIAL 10.00 (2.90)**

H. An enormous hand blown glass bubble is the perfect vase for a long stemmed bouquet. 14" diameter. (Sorry, gift box is not available.) #XL759 34.00 (6.30)

I. Clear glass marbles are the perfect arranger for a clear vase. Three pounds in a net bag. #XI614 9.00 (3.00)

Page Layout

Now that the type of format has been determined, you can reasonably select the style of layout which is best for your products, price level, and image. The term layout simply means the physical arrangement of the design (in the case of catalogs, the products) throughout the catalog. Layouts are affected by how you decide to group your product line (formatting choices), and your product grouping, in turn, is affected by how your customer will respond. Perhaps you have chosen the theme/function category because you are business-to-business and your customers like the easy reference afforded by this method of category classification. If you appeal to the general consumer, chances are you have chosen the mixed product method because your customer likes to browse while shopping and enjoys the stimulation of "impulse buying." You must now decide which of the two basic layout types will best serve your customer effectively: which will most enhance your merchandise line; which will produce the greatest amount of sales.

a layout selection guide

By answering the following questions, you will have guidelines for selecting the best layout approach for your catalog — one which compliments your product line and one of which you can make continual use.

1. What products are you putting in the catalog?
2. What method of organization do you wish to use?
3. Who is the customer to whom you are trying to appeal, and what is the "tone" with which these customers will feel most comfortable?

Then consider these questions when selecting your catalog's layout style:

4. Which style do you feel you can handle most efficiently, not just for one catalog, but on a regular schedule?
5. Will the style you're inclining toward create budgetary problems or problems with your ability to execute it?

This helps you along the road to deciding which layout is best for you.

Layout techniques fall into two basic approaches: *symmetrical*, a measured grid format, and *asymmetrical*, a nonproportional grid format.

There are three other layout technique approaches, one of which may work better for you: • art separated from copy, • product grouping and • one-item-to-a-page. First, let's look at the two basic approaches, symmetrical and asymmetrical.

1. Symmetrical

In a symmetrical layout, art and copy are generally in balanced proportions, or there is a measured ratio of art to copy (for example, art taking one-third of the allotted area and copy taking two-thirds). Again, low-end merchandise generally works well in this type of layout. The major factor is that a greater number of products can be put on a page with the least effort and expense. Because of sales requirements per page to make a profitable catalog and because of individual products' low retail price, a low-end cataloger must put more products on a page in order to make a profit. The mechanics of layout for each catalog are easy because of measured space, and economical because the size of the art and copy areas almost never changes.

General Consumer Walter Drake and Sons is a low-end general merchandise catalog that is a perfect example of one of the most traditional symmetrical catalog layouts in the industry. As you can see in Figure 3-22, the copy and art share an almost identical amount of space. The layout has a very measured effect. The copy area is always identical in width (flush left and right), and the number of lines is always within a line or two of the same length. The typeface is traditional (Century Schoolbook), readable, and printed in black against a white background for greater clarity. The pages are equally balanced, and the art and copy on every page of the catalog have the same characteristics. And yet all pages are not identical. (Some pages use this layout vertically; some are changed to horizontal across the top and vertical across the bottom.)

Look now at a similar layout from another low-end general merchandise catalog, Spencer Gifts (Figure 3-23), with photographs that are bled off the page. The elimination of the border of air to frame the page, along with the narrower spaces between each art and copy block, makes the page seem constrained and tight. This seemingly minor alteration in spacing causes the items to "run into" each other, and the layout is not as crisp. The sacrifice of air around the photographs allows them to be somewhat larger in size than those in the Walter Drake catalog, but it also prevents each individual photo from having any "snap." Though this layout strives for a more interesting look than the previous one, it actually seems more cluttered and the eye does not want to relax and stay a while on each item. When this occurs, customers have not viewed the item long enough to learn what they need to know in order to make a purchasing decision.

The next example, Hanover House (Figure 3-24), again a low-end merchandise product line, begins to loosen up the symmetrical theme. The balance between artwork and copy is no longer equal. The photos are no longer identical in size, nor are all copy blocks. The copy now is flush left, ragged right, allowing a freer look. The right-hand photos bleed off the page, but there is enough air separating all art and copy so that this technique now works well. The order found in all symmetrical-

PERKY POLKA DOT RAIN CAPE AND HOOD give you instant, pretty protection! Always ready for sudden showers, this see-thru cape slips comfortably over bulky clothes . . . keeps you snug and dry with heat-sealed seams, sewn hem, and button closures for lasting wear. Folds into handy case to tuck in purse or glove compartment. Heavy-duty vinyl; one size fits all.
N3098 Rain Cape $4.99

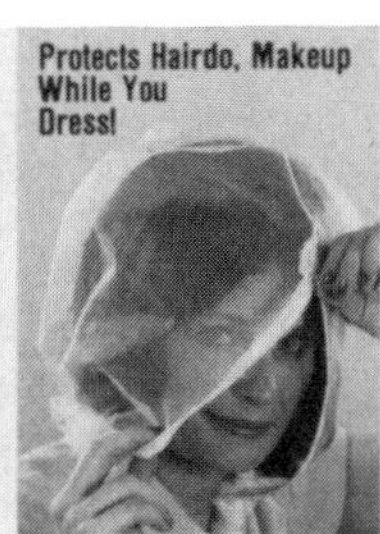

NEW PROTECTIVE HOOD keeps hairdo in place and makeup fresh while you dress! Zippered hood protects hairdo when slipping clothes on over your head . . . protects expensive clothing from messy make-up stains—helps end costly cleaning bills! Handy while dressing for work or evenings out. Great when trying on clothes while shopping! Nylon netting; one size fits all.
N2146 Hood $4.99

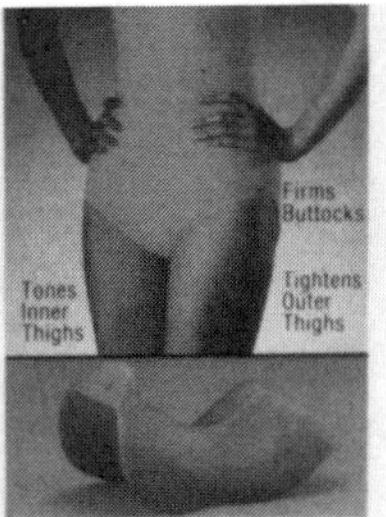

MELT AWAY FAT in just minutes a day! Easy new Squeeze Me® helps trim flabby thighs and sagging buttocks—without strenuous exercises! Special design uses isometric pressure to get rid of excess inches — all you do is squeeze! You'll look slimmer, trimmer in no time! About 8x7", specially contoured plastic; easy instructions incl. Guaranteed results in just 10 days!
F4194 Squeeze Me® $8.99

Satisfaction Guaranteed!

SECRET BRA POCKET lets you tote extra cash and valuables safely, out of sight! Helps end worry of loss or purse-snatching. Just tuck Secret Pocket into bra or slip . . . snap around straps to secure in place. Jewelry or cash slips into flapped pocket for perfect safe keeping. 3x4" lace-patterned washable nylon with plastic lining. So comfy you'll forget you're wearing it; won't show under clothes. Great peace of mind!
N2079 Secret Bra Pocket $1.19

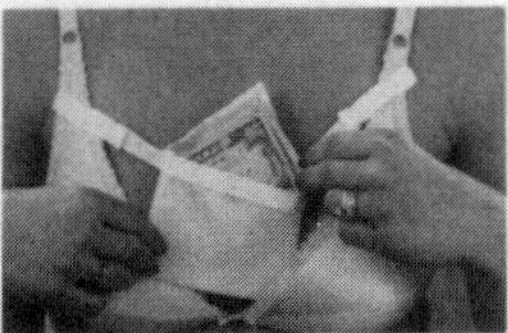

NEW PIERCED EAR PROTECTORS AND EXTRA BACKS. Special protectors end red, swollen, irritated ears . . . let you wear all types of pierced earrings, even with sensitive skin! Just slip poly shields over metal posts or wires; invisible when worn. Set of 4 pairs. Also available . . . extra backs to replace lost ones! End maddening searches, switching backs. Set of 24; surgical grade, non-allergic polyethylene.
N6161 Pierced Ear Protectors, 4 Pairs $2.98
N3129 Extra Backs, Set of 24 99¢

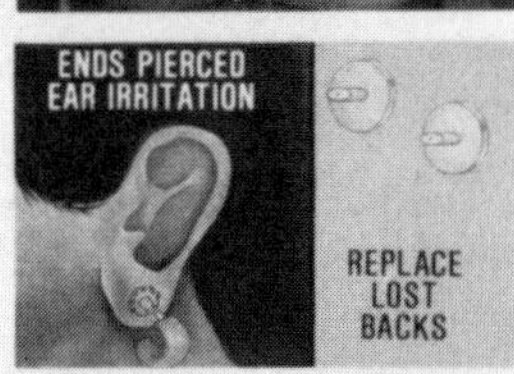

EXTRA LARGE HOOD FOR YOUR DRYER! Throw away that old, tight-fitting bonnet—this hood is made extra large . . . wear it comfortably over your jumbo rollers! And drying time is cut in half, since air circulates more freely! Plastic hood fits all makes of hair dryers, thanks to special patented socket. Add new flexible plastic hose with coupling; 40" long. Fits all dryer models.
N1002 Super-Size Hair Dryer Bonnet $3.98
N1082 Hair Dryer Hose $3.98

33

3-22

style layouts is retained because of the "columnar" format, both horizontally and vertically.

Sometimes a symmetrical grid layout is almost the only way to retain clarity and ease for the customer. This need occurs frequently in business-to-business catalogs, but is also found in

3-23

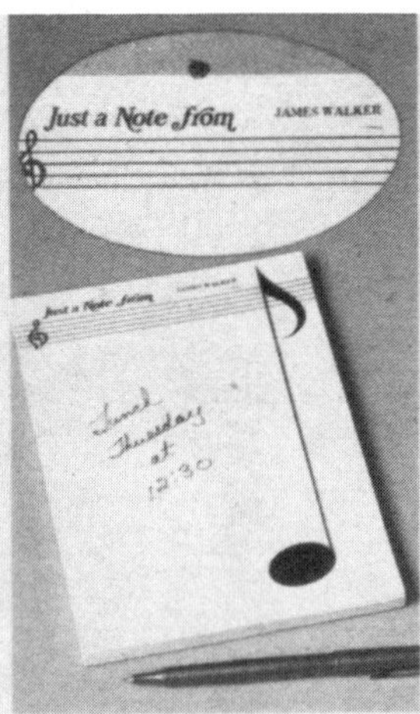

NOTEWORTHY MEMO PAD . . . CUSTOM-PRINTED WITH YOUR NAME! Striking quarter note design adds a distinctive flair to your messages. Whimsical heading "Just A Note From" & your name are cleverly underlined by a musical staff. Unique way to identify your memos. Pad of 100 sheets, ea 8¼" x 5½". **Specify full name.**
☐ **"Note" Memo Pad** (DT-63008) **$2.99**
SAVE! 2 Pads for only $4.99

HISTORIC FLIGHT DECK CAP is personally yours! Designed exclusively for the U.S. Apollo astronauts—it's customized just for you—with your name (or message)! Smart military styling with golden embroidered "scrambled eggs" on the visor; braid trim. Adjustable back tab. Crisp poly-knit for lightweight comfort. One size fits all. **State name or message (2 lines, 9 letters per line).**
☐ **Personal Flight Cap** . . **$5.99**
Red (PT-79491) **Navy** (PT-79509)

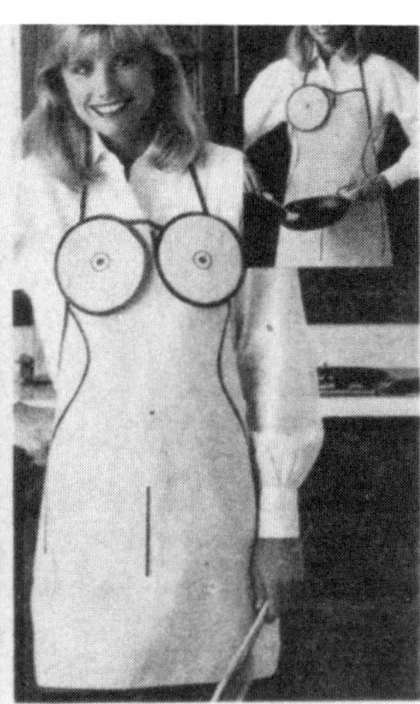

"SEXY LADY" APRON HAS 2 STRATEGICALLY PLACED PADDED POTHOLDERS! Secured with Velcro* tabs, they pop off & on with ease. Shapely lines complete the au naturel look that turns any cook into a curvaceous eye-catcher—in the kitchen or at a barbeque! Washable natural canvas; brown trim & detailing. Full bib; waist tie. 28" lg.
☐ **Sexy Lady Apron** (T-50880) **$6.99**

SHAMPOO WAVES & CURLS! Our protein Waving Shampoo curls while it cleans! Washes in long-lasting natural waves . . . all you do between shampoos is dampen your comb & brush curls in place. Eliminates streaking before bleaching; gives uniform shade before dyeing! 6 oz.
☐ **Curl Shampoo** (T-25775) ~~$1.99~~

THE PERFECTLY ORGANIZED

WALLET HANDBAG

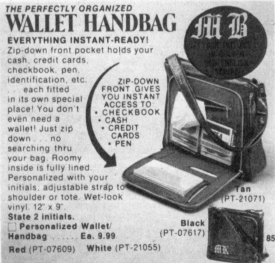

EVERYTHING INSTANT-READY! Zip-down front pocket holds your cash, credit cards, checkbook, pen, identification, etc. . . . each fitted in its own special place! You don't even need a wallet! Just zip down . . . no searching thru your bag. Roomy inside is fully lined. Personalized with your initials; adjustable strap to shoulder or tote. Wet-look vinyl, 12" x 9". **State 2 initials.**

ZIP-DOWN FRONT GIVES YOU INSTANT ACCESS TO
• CHECKBOOK
• CASH
• CREDIT CARDS
• PEN

☐ **Personalized Wallet/Handbag** . . . . . **Ea. 9.99**
Red (PT-07609) **White** (PT-21055) **Black** (PT-07617) **Tan** (PT-21071)

85

consumer-oriented books which must present long lists of merchandise in many subcategories, with many styles or product numbers and many individual products on a page.

Business-to-Business DLM, Developmental Learning Materials, produces an instructional materials catalog for educational

3-24

MORNING AFTER MUG
Last night's pink elephants respectfully tiptoe across this 10-oz. "shakes"-resistant ceramic mug!
G555334—Hangover Mug $2.99

PRETTY NURSE DINNER BELL
Very, very special gift for a favorite nurse, sweet young girl in old fashioned nurse's uniform and cap rings daintily to tell you she's brought in dinner on a tray. Handpainted bisque porcelain collectible measures 4¾" tall. Gift boxed.
G556183—Nurse Bell $3.99

3 CAST IRON SKILLETS FOR EVEN HEATING, NO NONSENSE
When all's been said, done and experimented with, the best cooks come back to cast iron for unsurpassed excellence in heat distribution and wear. Heavy duty frying pans with pouring edges measure 10½", 8", and 6½" diameter. You can hang them up for a nostalgic touch in your kitchen, and their good looks are only enhanced with age.
If this is your first cast iron cooking experience, you're in for a pleasant surprise . . . no wonder generations of cooks have depended on it!
G555797—Cast Iron Skillet Set . . . . 3/~~$15.99,~~ SALE 3-Pc. Set $12.88

METALLIC GIFT TAPE SET
Adds a sparkle, a touch of class to any holiday wrapping job. Sticks on all surfaces—mix 'n match, create designs. Assortment of 4 merry colors. 7/16" wide.
G556423—Tape 4-Roll $1.99

COMPLETE TRAVEL KIT KEEPS YOU ORGANIZED
A necessity for the smart traveler, keeps bathroom needs in one convenient see-through plastic snap-shut tote. Includes: soap box/lid; screw-top bottle; toothbrush and holder; emergency sewing kit with thread, needle, threader, pins, buttons, snaps, scissors; clever collapsible drinking glass with lid! 10½x6" tote.
G556258—Travel Kit $4.99

Appealing layouts must have clarity

institutions. The company's product line ranges from language arts, filmstrips, and assessment tests to computer education software. Retails range from $3.50 to $300 plus. Figure 3-25 is a typical illustration of how a measured symmetrical approach compliments DLM's products. Equal area (one-fourth page) for both art and copy is allowed each of the four products presented. A headline banner at the top of the page announces the section, Language Arts, and the subject, grammar. Bold headlines and price lines identify each product and its cost, while the body copy utilizes a no-nonsense sans serif type. Each page in the catalog employs the banner technique to identify the section/subject and a measured (one-third, one-fourth, two-thirds) approach to layout.

Many business-to-business catalogs must contend with hundreds, sometimes even thousands, of listings in one single catalog. Figure 3-26, a page from the Rio Grande jeweler's supply catalog, is a perfect example of how clarity need not be boring when a cataloger is faced with such a problem. Though the page is covered with lists of various wires and must show dimensions and weights, interest has been added with the silhouettes of the various wires. Space has been used judiciously so that the list is not overwhelming, and balance has allowed the page to remain appealing. Keeping appeal in a layout like this is not easy, yet it is vital to encouraging the customer's desire to read the material. Whenever an attitude of "I have to plow through this" is created, instead of "This is clear and it will be easy for me to locate what I need," sales will be lost.

Advantages

Easy matching of copy with artwork; facilitates all products sharing equal prominence; easy interchange of product listings throughout the book because of equality of space allotment; economies from this ability to interchange art and copy; rapid layout because so many of the items use exactly the same amount of copy and art space; minimal creative and production costs, as once the photograph is taken and the copy is written and typeset, it can be used over and over again; customer appreciation of measured neatness and orderliness in a book like this.

Disadvantages

Static and boring style without careful variation of other page layouts throughout the book, from vertical to horizontal; same look for all pages; the inability to easily vary the size of copy and art, hurting adequate treatment of items needing more space for optimum presentation or products needing dramatic presentations; tendency of customers to think they have seen this page before.

LM LANGUAGE ARTS Grammar

NTRACTION BOARDS

-correcting! Students work independently as they learn simple and complex contractions. Convenient answer make it easy to correct work as students match the outs to corresponding sentences. All contractions are ht in context in easy-to-read sentences. Contraction rds measure 8½" x 11" and are made of heavy stock.

4Z Contraction Boards (Set of 3) $8.95

ACTION VERB BOARDS

Students learn to identify 32 common action verbs! The friendly, engaging format of these three beautifully rendered Action Verb Boards encourages children to have fun as they match verbs to corresponding illustrations. Convenient answer keys make it easy to correct work. The versatile boards measure 8½" x 11" and are made of heavy stock.

533Z Action Verb Boards $11.50

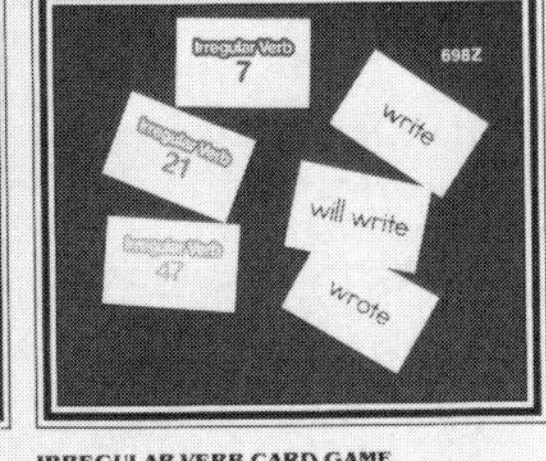

RB-TENSE BOARDS

ctice in present-past, past-future, and future-perfect verb ses! This versatile classroom set of three durable Verb-se Boards is perfect for all curriculums involving gram- and oral language development. Each 8½" x 11" board is -correcting and includes cut-outs that students will have matching to simple sentences.

2Z Verb-Tense Boards $8.50

IRREGULAR VERB CARD GAME

The past, present, and future tenses of 60 irregular verbs are included in this lively card game. Designed to be enjoyed individually or by a small group of players, the Irregular Verb Card Game easily supplements your instructional sequence in grammar and oral language. There are 180 cards to the set.

698Z Irregular Verb Card Game $6.50

3-25

3-26

SHEET SILVER

Gauge	1/1000"	Approx. Size, oz.	Actual Weight
14	.064	6"×½"	1.053
16	.051	6"×⅝"	1.046
18	.040	6"×¾"	.9945
20	.032	6"×1"	1.050
22	.025	6"×1¼"	1.017
24	.020	6"×1⅝"	.990
26	.016	6"×2"	1.048
28	.013	6"×2⅝"	1.038
30	.010	6"×3⅜"	1.071
32	.008	6"×4"	1.044

ROUND WIRE

Gauge	1/1000"	Length per oz.	Oz. per foot
4	.204	5½"	2.12
6	.162	9"	1.35
8	.128	14½"	.852
10	.102	22"	.536
12	.081	3'	.337
14	.064	4'8"	.212
16	.051	7½'	.133
18	.040	12'	.084
20	.032	19'	.053
22	.025	31'	.033
24	.020	48'	.021

HALF ROUND

Gauge	1/1000"	Length per oz.	Oz. per foot
2	.257	7"	1.650
4	.204	11"	.940
6	.162	1'6"	.680
8	.128	2'4"	.424
9	.114	3'	.335
10	.102	45"	.280
12	.081	6'	.168
14	.064	9'6"	.106
16	.051	15'	.061

TRIANGLE WIRE

No.	Base × Ht. 1/1000"		Approx. Length per oz.	Oz. per foot
1	.380	.225	3¾"	3.30
1½	.325	.200	5"	2.45
2	.258	.160	7¾"	1.80
2½	.193	.140	9¾"	1.10
3	.215	.097	14½"	.90
4	.175	.090	19½"	.60
5	.156	.111	17½"	.70
6	.122	.095	2'	.50
7	.103	.081	2'6"	.40
8	.080	.064	51"	.21

SQUARE WIRE

Gauge	1/1000"	Approx. Length per oz.	Oz. per foot
6	.162	7½"	1.75
8	.128	11"	1.09
10	.102	1'6"	.682
12	.081	2'4"	.429
14	.064	3'9"	.269
16	.051	6'	.169
18	.040	9'6"	.107

LOW-DOME

No.	Base × Ht. 1/1000"		Approx. Length per oz.	Oz. per foot
1	.608	.077	5½"	2.45
2	.515	.072	7¼"	1.75
3	.412	.062	9⅝"	1.15
4	.232	.072	13¾"	.90
5	.170	.040	33"	.39

1·800·545·6566
ORDERS ONLY PLEASE!

BEAD WIRE

Gauge	1/1000"	Approx. Length per oz.	Oz. per foot
8	.128	20"	.60
10	.102	32"	.38
12	.081	4'	.29
14	.064	6'6"	.15
16	.051	10'6"	.10

HALF-BEAD

Gauge	1/1000"	Approx. Length per oz.	Oz. per foot
8	.128	3'	.33
10	.102	4'	.19
12	.081	8'	.125
14	.064	9'	.11

TWIST-WIRE

Gauge	Base × Ht. 1/1000"	Approx. Length per oz.	Oz. per foot
8	.128	1'7"	.63
12	.084	3'8"	.27
14	.067	5'7"	.18
16	.054	8'9"	.11

NOTE: ALL SHEET SILVER COMES 6" WIDE. WE WILL CUT ANY LENGTH YOU WISH FROM ½" UP TO 36". PLEASE STATE DIMENSIONS (6" × 12¼", FOR INSTANCE). AND BE SURE TO SPECIFY GAUGE DESIRED.

PRICES SUBJECT TO CHANGE WITHOUT NOTICE.

2. Asymmetrical

Asymmetrical layouts utilize a nonproportional approach for individual art and copy sizes, seemingly in every page of the catalog. Most mid-to-high retail catalogers employ this type of layout. The majority of general consumer catalogs use some form of asymmetrical layout, and many business-to-business catalogs do, too. The mechanics of this technique are more difficult and more costly because of needed art and copy changes for each new catalog produced. Generally, this type of layout also requires more experienced creative talent.

General Consumer The Lillian Vernon catalog (Figure 3-27) uses silhouette photographs (where the backgrounds have been dropped out — a technique more typical in an asymmetrical layout), as well as photographs placed in windows. One side of the copy block is always flush to the relevant item, making it easy for the customer to match the item's copy to its photograph. The other side of the copy is ragged, allowing the page to retain a graceful, freer look. Air is balanced against occupied space in a way that encourages the eye to flow rhythmically from item to item, never having to jump gaps that are too large, or struggle with crammed areas. This style

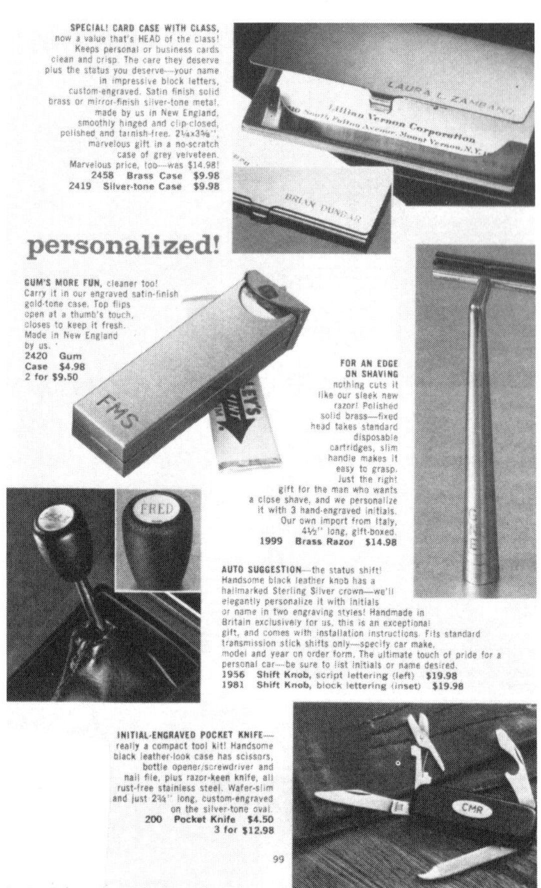

3-27

of layout is a fine balance between discipline and freedom. It inspires the customer to give equal attention to every item, yet continue to move through the book, viewing each page in turn. In its many variations, asymmetrical is probably the most frequently seen style of layout in cataloging.

Business-to-Business Taffy's Showstoppers is a dance costume catalog. The company takes advantage of its product category in producing a lovely asymmetrical layout throughout that flows on every page of the catalog. Figure 3-28 shows Taffy's application of a nonproportional approach. This two-page spread utilizes a continuous common background, devoting the major portion of one page to illustrating one dance skirt, Cascade. Skillful insetting allows ten additional products to be featured. Different photo sizes, overlapping and angled, carry the eye easily over the pages. Clever billboarding of copy on solid color backgrounds allows easy reading. Identifying numbers below the photos appear in the order of product presentation for easy referencing. Plain italic sans serif type is easily read and does not compete with the visual presentation. Confusion is avoided; clarity is achieved.

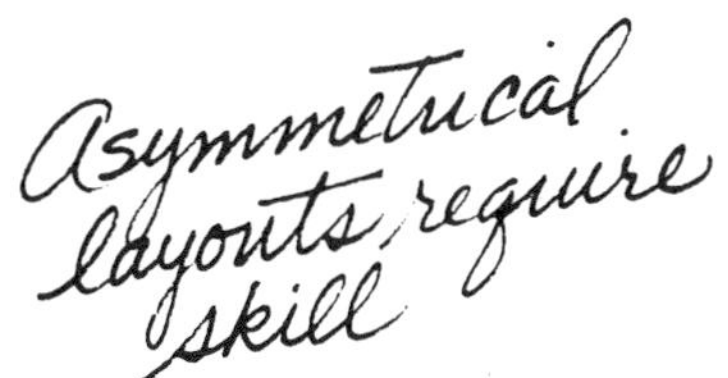
Asymmetrical layouts require skill

To see how art and copy in a basic asymmetrical layout can

SHOWSTOPPERS '83
CONCERT DANCEWEAR
FAB 405 CASCADE SKIRT
Ballet Pink, Black, Kelly, Light Blue, Lilac, Orange, Peacock, Purple, Red, Royal Blue, White, Yellow. LC, SA, MA, LA $11
FAB 402 CLASSIQUE SKIRT
Ballet Pink, Black, Kelly, Light Blue, Lilac, Orange, Peacock, Purple, Red, Royal Blue, White, Yellow. LC, SA, MA, LA $14
FAB 403 JOANIE SKIRT
Ballet Pink, Black, Kelly, Light Blue, Lilac, Orange, Peacock, Purple, Red, Royal Blue, White, Yellow. SC, MC, LC $9.50 SA, MA, LA $10.50
FAB 401 SHE'S A LADY
Ballet Pink, Black, Kelly, Light Blue, Lilac, Orange, Peacock, Purple, Red, Royal Blue, White, Yellow. LC, SA, MA, LA $11.50
FAB 407 SHORT HANKY SKIRT
Ballet Pink, Black, Kelly, Light Blue, Lilac, Orange, Peacock, Purple, Red, Royal Blue, White, Yellow. LC, SA, MA, LA $10
FAB 400 WHISPER SKIRT
Ballet Pink, Black, Kelly, Light Blue, Lilac, Orange, Peacock, Purple, Red, Royal Blue, White, Yellow. SC, MC, LC $7 SA, MA, LA $8

SHOWSTOPPERS '83
FAB 350R Not available
FAB 406 LONG HANKY SKIRT
Ballet Pink, Black, Kelly, Light Blue, Lilac, Orange, Peacock, Purple, Red, Royal Blue, White, Yellow. LC, SA, MA, LA $13
FAB 413 DEMI-HANKIE SKIRT
Triple layered demi-skirt in pretty pastel combinations. Yellow/Lilac/Kelly, Peacock/Lilac/Yellow. LC, SA, MA, LA $11.75
FAB 518 NYLON CAMISOLE LEOTARD
Ballet Pink, Black, Copen, Cranberry, Gold, Kelly, Light Blue, Mint, Navy, Orange, Peach, Peacock, Purple, Red, Royal Blue, Rust, Slate Grey, Toast, White, Yellow. SC, MC, LC $9 SA, MA, LA $10

3-28

SATIN GLASS BATH SET gleams with a subtle luster, its softness echoed in sensuous curves and seashell shapes. Generous soap dish is $5\frac{3}{8}$'' across, scalloped like the shell that inspired it—stands on three feet, seems to float with a fluid grace. Oval tumbler is sculpted with two scallop shells in relief, $3\frac{5}{8}$'' tall, holds 6 oz. Remembrance of an Art Deco past in blush pink, the set is our exclusive import from Italy.
7726 Pink Shell Bath Set.
1 Set $10.98

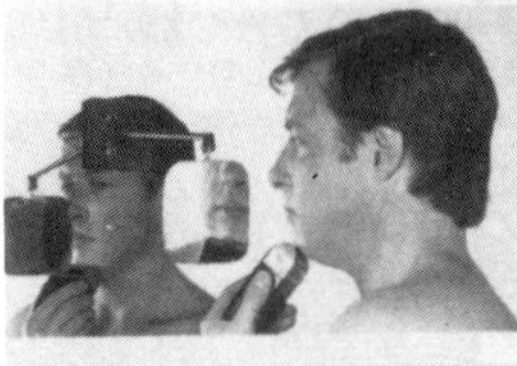

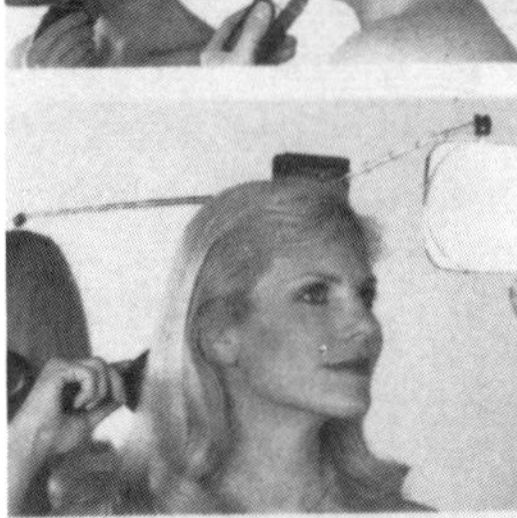

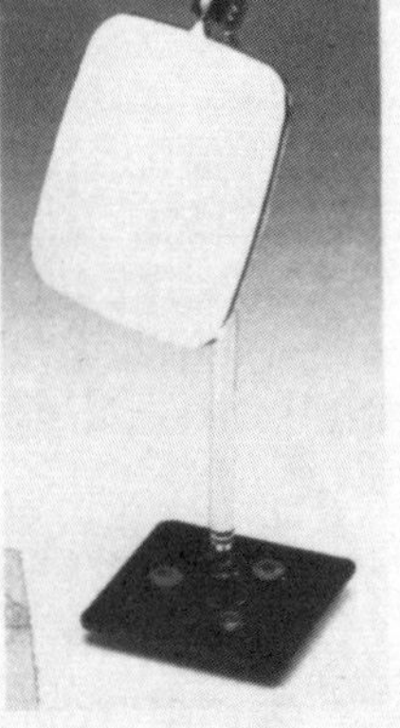

TERRIFIC FOR TRAVEL—won't break, folds flat, weighs less than 5 oz. Imagine a two-way extension mirror that goes everywhere, does everything: clings to any smooth surface, extends from $6\frac{1}{2}$'' to 28'', swivels to any angle for side and back views, flips from plain to double magnifier. A must for hair styling, makeup or shaving—square shape of the $4\frac{1}{4}$'' mirror adds extra viewing area. Precision-made throughout—smooth telescoping arm of chrome-plated brass, sturdy ball joints, tough plastic base with three sure-grip suction cups. Handy at home, great at the office—comes in its own travel case; tucks into drawer or attaché. AND great value—it's $15 elsewhere.
6567 Travel Mirror $11.98

OVER-DOOR HANGER, handsome anywhere, handy everywhere for towels, ties, pants, many things. Sculptured elegance, ingenious design that assembles in a wink without tools. No installation—hang it over any door, move it any time. American-made of tough ivory styrene with brass-plated steel rods, blends with any decor. 18'' wide, 25'' long.
4720 Door Hanger $10.98
2 for $19.98

HANDMADE BATH BRUSHES for a super glow, top to toe—fine natural bristle set in solid pine. A back-scrub first, then slip off the handle for a $5\frac{1}{4}$x$2\frac{7}{8}$'' brush with fabric hand-strap. Now the $3\frac{3}{4}$'' nail brush on fingers and toes—all done, fit 'n' fresh! From West Germany, $17\frac{5}{8}$'' long handle has hole for hanging.
4771 Back and Nail Brushes. 1 Set $7.98
8945 Back Brush only $5.98
4770 Nail Brush only $2.50

CHARGE IT on MasterCard or Visa—see order form for details, or charge by phone! Call 914-699-1420.

97

3-29

be used for another catalog without changing size or reshooting, and yet be different, let's look at the Lillian Vernon catalog again. Generally this catalog features four products to a page; however, some versions do have five products and occasionally even more. In the two examples, Figures 3-29 and 3-30, you can see that the lower portion of each page is identical, but one item in the upper

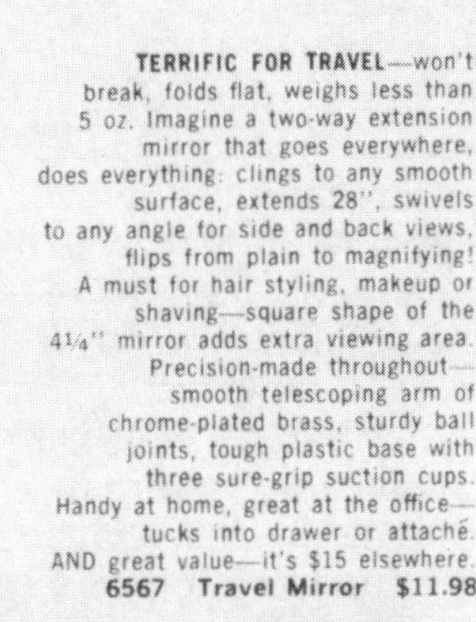

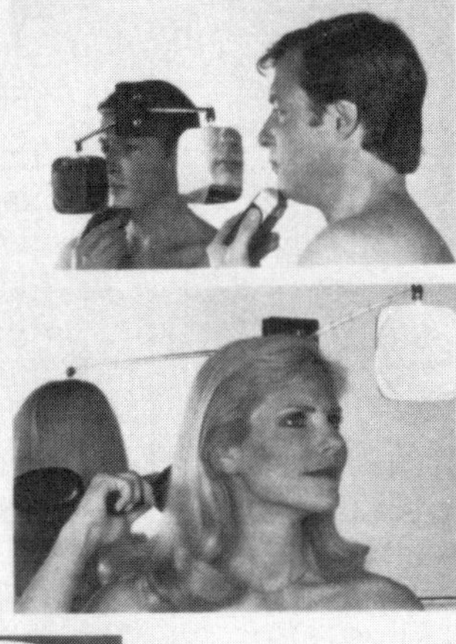

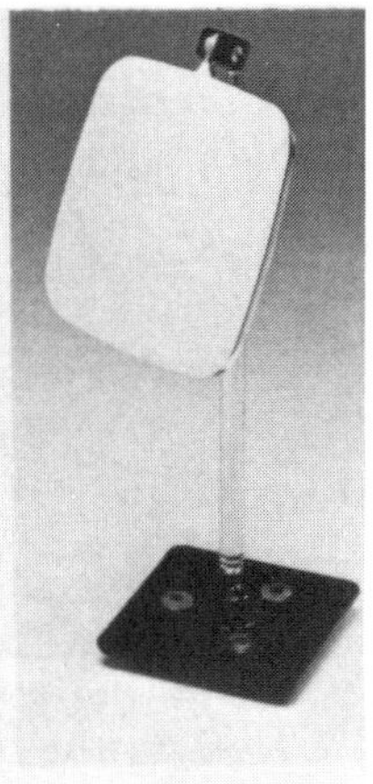

TERRIFIC FOR TRAVEL—won't break, folds flat, weighs less than 5 oz. Imagine a two-way extension mirror that goes everywhere, does everything: clings to any smooth surface, extends 28", swivels to any angle for side and back views, flips from plain to magnifying! A must for hair styling, makeup or shaving—square shape of the 4¼" mirror adds extra viewing area. Precision-made throughout—smooth telescoping arm of chrome-plated brass, sturdy ball joints, tough plastic base with three sure-grip suction cups. Handy at home, great at the office—tucks into drawer or attaché. AND great value—it's $15 elsewhere.
6567 Travel Mirror $11.98

TRADITIONAL JAPANESE DESIGN leads the way in the new Oriental look for the bath. Clear, bold strokes of color on purest white porcelain—orange day lilies, slender blue and green leaves, rims of genuine 24K Gold. 4⅜x2⅜x3" tall toothbrush caddy holds 4, has oval for toothpaste tube in center, bud at the back. Soap dish is gracefully shaped, 5⅝x3⅝" to hold large bars. Tumbler is 3¾" tall, holds 5 oz. Our own imports from Japan—save when you buy all three!
6650 Complete Set. 1 Set $12.98
6649 Toothbrush Holder. $5.98
6648 Soap Dish and Tumbler. 1 Set $8.98

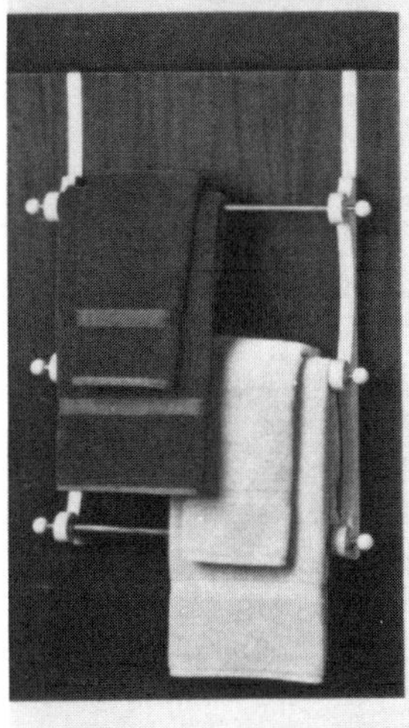

OVER-DOOR HANGER, handsome anywhere, handy everywhere for towels, ties, pants, many things. Sculptured elegance, ingenious design that assembles in a wink without tools. No installation—hang it over any door, move it any time. American-made of tough ivory styrene with brass-plated steel rods, blends with any decor. 18" wide, 25" long.
4720 Door Hanger $10.98
2 for $19.98

HANDMADE BATH BRUSHES for a super glow, top to toe—fine natural bristle set in solid pine. A back-scrub first, then slip off the handle for a 5¼x2⅞" brush with fabric hand-strap. Now the 3¾" nail brush on fingers and toes—all done, fit 'n' fresh! From West Germany, 17⅝" long handle has hole for hanging.
4771 Back and Nail Brushes. 1 Set $7.98
8945 Back Brush only $5.98
4770 Nail Brush only $2.50

CHARGE IT on MasterCard or Visa—see order form for details, or charge by phone! Call (914) 699-1420.

97

3-30

half of the page (the Japanese design bath set in Figure 3-30), has been replaced with another item (see Figure 3-29). Perhaps for aesthetics, the travel mirror at the top of the page was repositioned when the new item was added. This caused the copy to be reset. In the new layout, the copy is flush left; in the old layout it was flush right.

Advantages
Easy adjustment of space allotted to individual copy and art areas permits the cataloger to show each item to its best advantage, because every item does not have to fit into the dimensions of a specifically defined ''block''. The same is true for the copy, which allows the copywriter to write to the demands of the item (longer or shorter); easy interchange of items occur because certain sizes are standard throughout the book, even including the silhouette; permits possible rewriting of copy, or at least re-typesetting, if it is necessary to change the margin from flush left to flush right; rhythmical feel to pages retains the customer's interest, allows the eye's travel from item to item and page to page because of the controlled free-form positioning of the items.

Disadvantages
Greater care needed to size the art and copy so that the air between items is appropriately balanced to retain eye flow (this means that judgments have to be made continually, which requires extra time and money, as well as allowing the possibility of errors in that judgment. This format also requires more attention — again, time and money — to the line-for-line positioning of copy, at least for the graphics accompanying the initial listing, plus additional expense in the resetting of copy when adjustments to an item's positioning are made); longer lead time to put together the catalog, which also adds to cost; possible problems in the copy-to-artwork match-up, creating a risk that the customer cannot easily find the proper product description; possibility that errors in creative judgment will cause layout to appear chaotic, disrupting eye flow and, consequently, sales.

Before showing three other commonly practiced page layout approaches, let's look at what grids are and how they are used.

An Exercise in Grid Design: How Layouts Grow From Grids

A grid is any combination of overlapping horizontal and vertical lines which will ultimately aid in the page design of a catalog. A catalog may utilize one grid design or several. Grids may be symmetrical or asymmetrical. Their main function is to act as guides to the designer in identifying margins, space, and columns. The grid design approach is the backbone of the electronic design used in computer graphics and the wave of the future. It can be a catalog designer's best friend.

1. Symmetrical Grid Layout

In the symmetrical grid layout, the art and copy are perfectly balanced and proportioned; art and copy blocks are placed in exact or logical relation to one another.

General Consumer Let's look at an example of how a perfectly balanced symmetrical layout was achieved from a four-column grid. Figure 3-31 is a four-column, 8½″ × 11″ page grid. Note how each column is divided into five equal squares, allowing room for ten products to be displayed on the page in a balanced, systematic way. Figure 3-32 from The Sharper Image shows how the designer easily utilized the grid. The two middle column squares are each used for same-size product photos, just combining the top two middle squares into one photo and dropping in a silhouetted side view of the diamond pendant at the top left of the second photo down. The two outside columns are used for product description copy. Note how the balance of individual copy length and the air around these copy blocks is proportioned (i.e., long, short, short, long, long) so when the copy is positioned with the photos the whole becomes a perfectly balanced visual. Another version of the four-

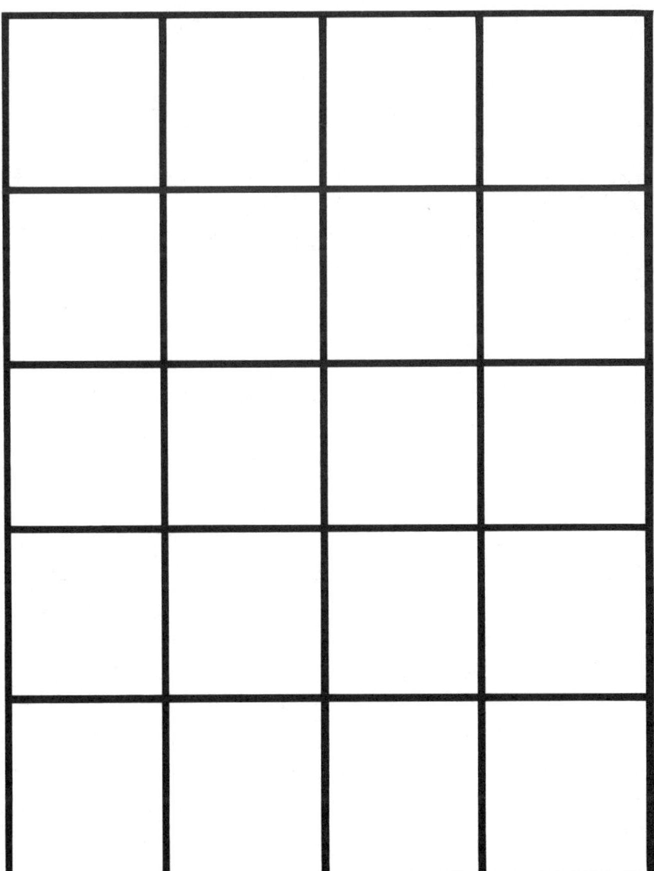

3-31

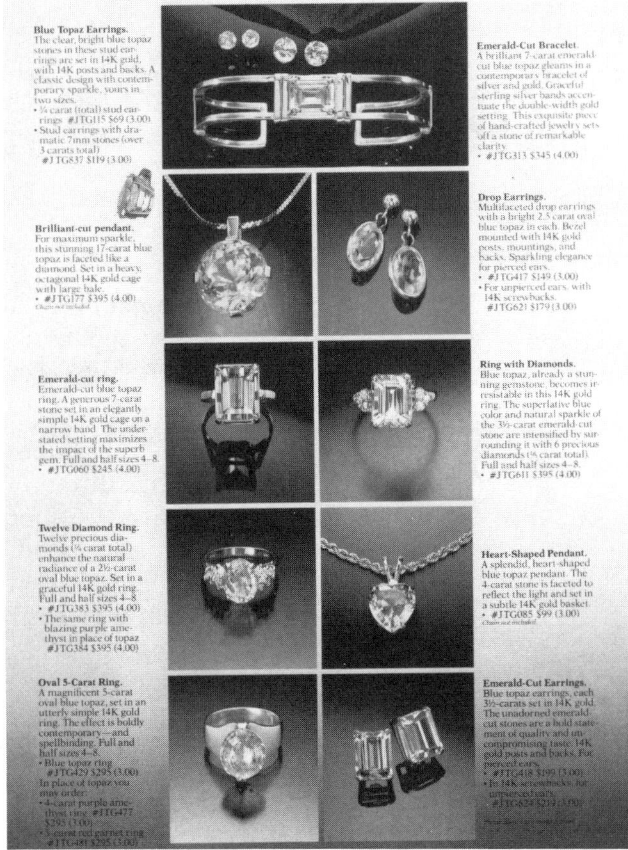

3-32

column grid is seen in the same Sharper Image catalog. Figure 3-33 shows how the symmetrical grid is used to produce a horizontal product presentation which is perfectly balanced in the top 60 per-

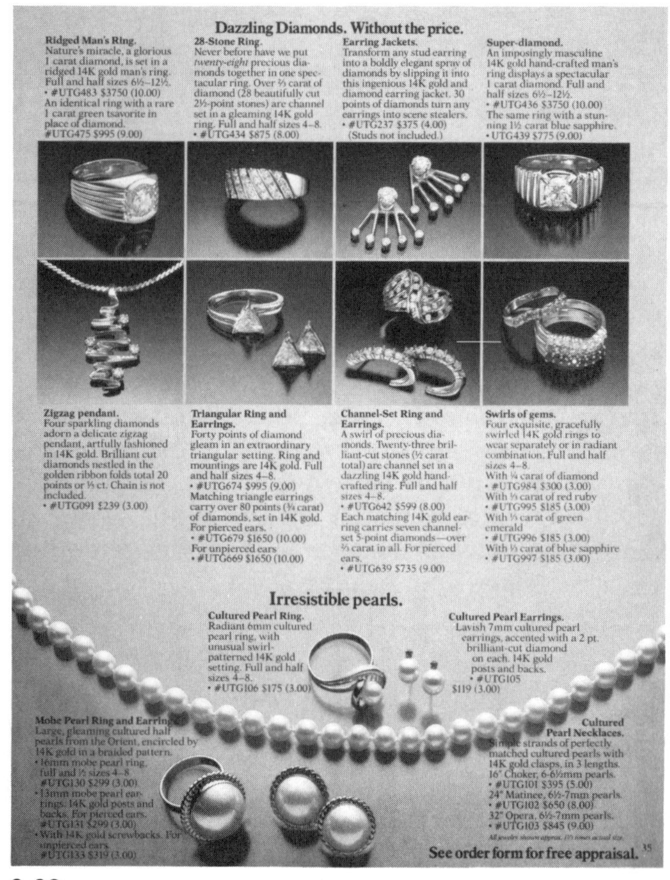

Dazzling Diamonds. Without the price.

Ridged Man's Ring.
Nature's miracle, a glorious 1 carat diamond, is set in a ridged 14K gold man's ring. Full and half sizes 6½–12½.
• #UTG483 $3750 (10.00)
An identical ring with a rare 1 carat green tsavorite in place of diamond.
#UTG475 $995 (9.00)

28-Stone Ring.
Never before have we put *twenty-eight* precious diamonds together in one spectacular ring. Over ⅔ carat of diamond (28 beautifully cut 2½-point stones) are channel set in a gleaming 14K gold ring. Full and half sizes 4–8.
• #UTG434 $875 (8.00)

Earring Jackets.
Transform any stud earring into a boldly elegant spray of diamonds by slipping it into this ingenious 14K gold and diamond earring jacket. 30 points of diamonds turn any earrings into scene stealers.
• #UTG237 $375 (4.00)
(Studs not included.)

Super-diamond.
An imposingly masculine 14K gold hand-crafted man's ring displays a spectacular 1 carat diamond. Full and half sizes 6½–12½.
• #UTG436 $3750 (10.00)
The same ring with a stunning 1½ carat blue sapphire.
• UTG439 $775 (9.00)

Zigzag pendant.
Four sparkling diamonds adorn a delicate zigzag pendant, artfully fashioned in 14K gold. Brilliant cut diamonds nestled in the golden ribbon folds total 20 points or ⅕ ct. Chain is not included.
• #UTG091 $239 (3.00)

Triangular Ring and Earrings.
Forty points of diamond gleam in an extraordinary triangular setting. Ring and mountings are 14K gold. Full and half sizes 4–8.
• #UTG674 $995 (9.00)
Matching triangle earrings carry over 80 points (¾ carat) of diamonds, set in 14K gold. For pierced ears.
• #UTG679 $1650 (10.00)
For unpierced ears
• #UTG669 $1650 (10.00)

Channel-Set Ring and Earrings.
A swirl of precious diamonds. Twenty-three brilliant-cut stones (½ carat total) are channel set in a dazzling 14K gold hand-crafted ring. Full and half sizes 4–8.
• #UTG642 $599 (8.00)
Each matching 14K gold earring carries seven channel-set 5-point diamonds—over ⅔ carat in all. For pierced ears.
• #UTG639 $735 (9.00)

Swirls of gems.
Four exquisite, gracefully swirled 14K gold rings to wear separately or in radiant combination. Full and half sizes 4–8.
With ¼ carat of diamond
• #UTG984 $300 (3.00)
With ⅓ carat of red ruby
• #UTG995 $185 (3.00)
With ⅓ carat of green emerald
• #UTG996 $185 (3.00)
With ⅓ carat of blue sapphire
• #UTG997 $185 (3.00)

Irresistible pearls.

Cultured Pearl Ring.
Radiant 6mm cultured pearl ring, with unusual swirl-patterned 14K gold setting. Full and half sizes 4–8.
• #UTG106 $175 (3.00)

Cultured Pearl Earrings.
Lavish 7mm cultured pearl earrings, accented with a 2 pt. brilliant-cut diamond on each. 14K gold posts and backs.
• #UTG105 $119 (3.00)

Mobe Pearl Ring and Earrings.
Large, gleaming cultured half pearls from the Orient, encircled by 14K gold in a braided pattern.
• 16mm mobe pearl ring, full and ½ sizes 4–8
#UTG130 $299 (3.00)
• 13mm mobe pearl earrings. 14K gold posts and backs. For pierced ears.
#UTG131 $299 (3.00)
• With 14K gold screwbacks. For unpierced ears.
#UTG133 $319 (3.00)

Cultured Pearl Necklaces.
Simple strands of perfectly matched cultured pearls with 14K gold clasps, in 3 lengths.
16" Choker, 6-6½mm pearls.
• #UTG101 $395 (5.00)
24" Matinee, 6½-7mm pearls.
• #UTG102 $650 (8.00)
32" Opera, 6½-7mm pearls.
• #UTG103 $845 (9.00)

See order form for free appraisal. 35

3-33

cent of the page. The remaining 40 percent of the layout is still guided by the four columns but becomes asymmetrical in design. The orderliness of the symmetrical design is maintained with the balanced placement of the copy blocks.

Business-to-Business DRI Industries employs a two-column grid throughout its 96-page catalog with variations which allow the layout to become asymmetrical. Figure 3-34 shows the basic two-column grid dividing an 8½″ × 11″ page into eight equal parts. Figure 3-35 shows how DRI presents four different tool shops. Each copy block is dropped slightly below each picture division, allowing a small and interesting visual element to add variety to the page and encouraging the eye to travel down the page. Figure 3-36 shows how enlarging the grid areas for one product and utilizing the silhouette technique of dropping out part of the product picture onto the second column area gives the impression of an asymmetrical design. Also, note that part of the copy description is formed around the silhouetted product, further adding to the more relaxed presentation. Figure 3-37 is yet another page in the same DRI catalog which deals very successfully with multi-item listing. Twenty-two products are picture-listed, all falling nicely into the two-column grid guide. Interest is added to the page with category headers containing a crisp

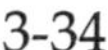

3-34

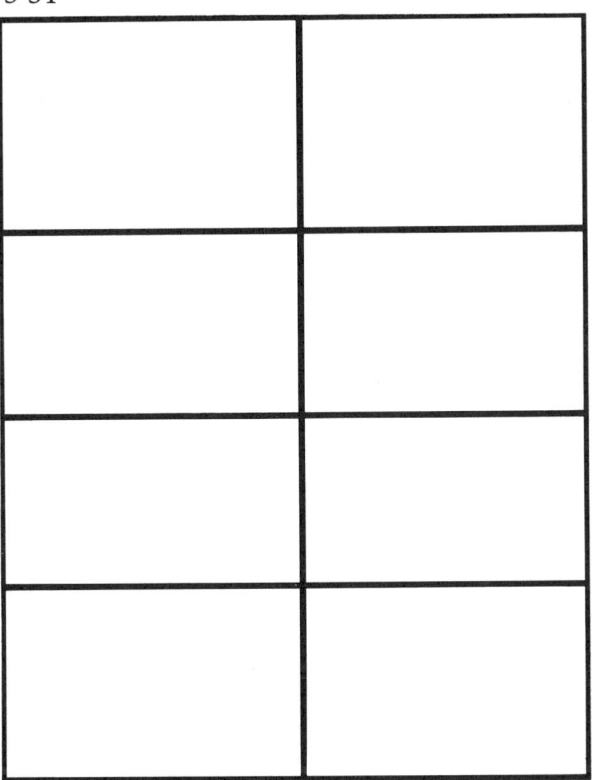

3-35

THREAD REPAIR INSERT SHOP

No professional mechanic would be without these inserts. They provide a perfect-match repair for damaged machined threads in metal. You'll be able to use a bolt of the same diameter and thread pitch. No more drilling out oversize and using a larger bolt where it just isn't practical. No need for a Tap & Die Set. They can be used for exhaust manifold bolts, carburetor hold down bolts . . . also can be used in cast iron and even in wood. You'll be able to install machine threads in all types of materials. Inserts are self-tapping and once installed, they're permanent. No special tools are needed for installation.

You get a total of 34 thread repair inserts — 102 pieces total

102-Piece, Self-Tapping $44.50 Value
Thread Repair Shop, Catalog Number 80000100
Your Price Only $24.99

For bulk Thread Repair Inserts, see Page 44.

THREADED INSERT SHOP

Made of brass alloy for superior corrosion resistance, threaded inserts provide permanent machine threads in porous material, wood, plastic or soft metals . . . anywhere frequent removal of a normal wood screw or sheet metal screw tends to wear out the self-tapped threads in the material. They provide a machine screw thread for unlimited assembly or disassembly and go in permanently, flush with the surface. Slotted end is for driving in with a screwdriver or they can be installed with a hex bolt or machine screw with a lock nut. (The same as Thread Repair Inserts.) The coarse external threads are engineered for maximum resistance to backout and loosening. They can be used instead of large, bulky wood screws and eliminate the worry of wood splitting.

The Shop includes . . . 185 threaded inserts

***High-impact, divided plastic case**

185-Piece, Brass, $70.95 Value
Threaded Insert Shop, Catalog Number 80000046
Your Price Only $38.99

For bulk Threaded Inserts, see Page 45.

TINNERMAN "J" NUT SHOP

"J", Multi-Thread Tinnerman Nuts are made to be used with machine screws and cap screws in areas of sheet metal assembly where it is difficult to hold a nut on the other side. They slip easily over the edge of sheet metal, plastic or chassis material. They also can be slipped through a slotted hole in sheet metal. Most often found on autos and appliances, you can use them to replace original equipment parts or on new projects.

The Shop contains a variety of sizes for use with machine screws or bolts. All contained in a divided carry case.

The Shop includes . . .

***High-impact, divided plastic case**

46-Piece, Multi-Thread, Spring Steel, $36.00 Value
Tinnerman "J" Nut Shop,
Catalog Number 80000016
Your Price Only $19.99

TINNERMAN NUT SHOP

Tinnerman Nuts with single thread are used to hold light to medium loads and eliminate the need for lock washers or flat washers. They assemble faster than traditional hex nuts and usually require no more than finger pressure to hold while tightening. They're used as original equipment on many cars, trucks, appliances and tools.

You get a total of 500 pieces . . . a complete size range of Tinnerman Nuts for use with sheet metal screws, machine screws and studs.

Here's what you get . . .

***High-impact, divided plastic case**

500-Piece Single Thread, Spring Steel, $40.00 Value
Tinnerman Nut Shop,
Catalog Number 80000015
Your Price Only $24.99

19

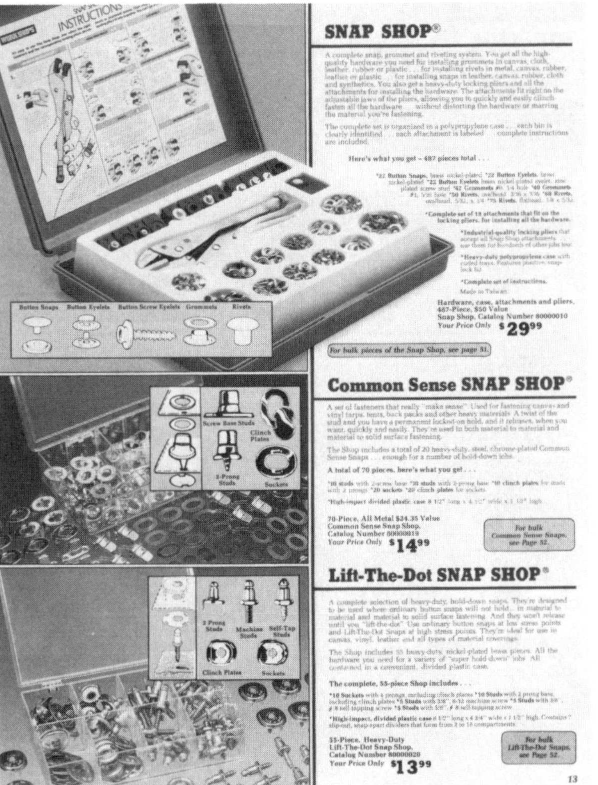

SNAP SHOP®

A complete snap, grommet and riveting system. You get all the high-quality hardware you need for installing grommets in canvas, cloth, leather, rubber or plastic . . . for installing rivets in metal, canvas, rubber, leather or plastic . . . for installing snaps in leather, canvas, rubber, cloth and synthetics. You also get a heavy-duty locking pliers and all the attachments for installing the hardware. The attachments fit right on the adjustable jaws of the pliers, allowing you to quickly and easily clinch-fasten all the hardware . . . without distorting the hardware or marring the material you're fastening.

The complete set is organized in a polypropylene case . . . each bin is clearly identified . . . each attachment is labeled . . . complete instructions are included.

Here's what you get – 487 pieces total . . .

***Complete set of 18 attachments that fit on the locking pliers, for installing all the hardware.**

***Industrial-quality locking pliers**

***Heavy-duty polypropylene case**

***Complete set of instructions.**

Made in Taiwan

Hardware, case, attachments and pliers,
487-Piece, $50 Value
Snap Shop, Catalog Number 80000010
Your Price Only $29.99

For bulk pieces of the Snap Shop, see page 51.

Common Sense SNAP SHOP®

A set of fasteners that really "make sense". Used for fastening canvas and vinyl tarps, tents, back packs and other heavy materials. A twist of the stud and you have a permanent locked-on hold, and it releases, when you want, quickly and easily. They're used in both material to material and material to solid surface fastening.

The Shop includes a total of 20 heavy-duty, steel, chrome-plated Common Sense Snaps . . . enough for a number of hold-down jobs.

A total of 70 pieces, here's what you get . . .

70-Piece, All Metal $24.35 Value
Common Sense Snap Shop,
Catalog Number 80000013
Your Price Only $14.99

For bulk Common Sense Snaps, see Page 52.

Lift-The-Dot SNAP SHOP®

A complete selection of heavy-duty, hold-down snaps. They're designed to be used where ordinary button snaps will not hold . . . in material to material and material to solid surface fastening. And they won't release until you "lift-the-dot". Use ordinary button snaps at low stress points and Lift-The-Dot Snaps at high stress points. They're ideal for use in canvas, vinyl, leather and all types of material coverings.

The Shop includes 55 heavy-duty, nickel-plated brass pieces. All the hardware you need for a variety of "super hold-down" jobs. All contained in a convenient, divided plastic case.

The complete, 55-piece Shop includes . . .

55-Piece, Heavy-Duty
Lift-The-Dot Snap Shop,
Catalog Number 80000020
Your Price Only $13.99

For bulk Lift-The-Dot Snaps, see Page 52.

13

3-36

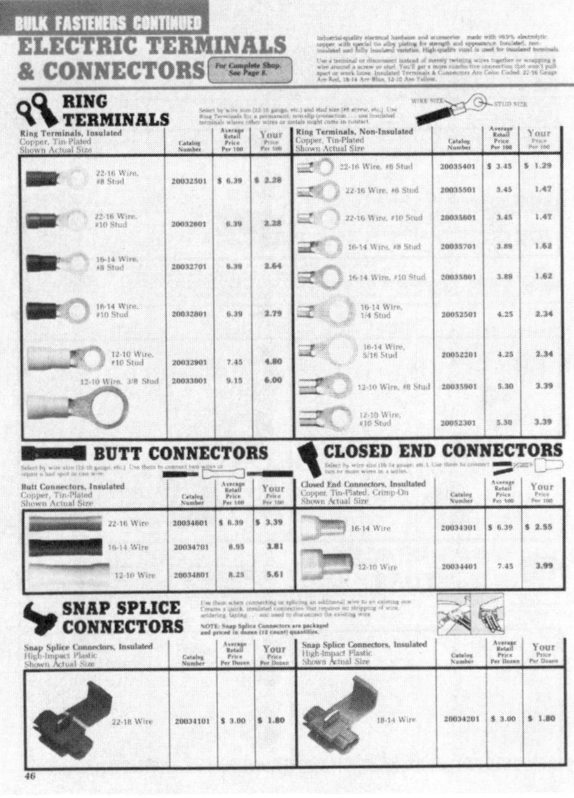

BULK FASTENERS CONTINUED

ELECTRIC TERMINALS & CONNECTORS

For Complete Shop, See Page 8.

RING TERMINALS

Ring Terminals, Insulated Copper, Tin-Plated Shown Actual Size	Catalog Number	Average Retail Price Per 100	Your Price Per 100
22-16 Wire, #8 Stud	20032501	$ 6.39	$ 2.28
22-16 Wire, #10 Stud	20032601	6.39	2.28
16-14 Wire, #8 Stud	20032701	6.39	2.64
16-14 Wire, #10 Stud	20032801	6.39	2.79
12-10 Wire, #10 Stud	20032901	7.45	4.80
12-10 Wire, 3/8 Stud	20033001	9.15	6.00

Ring Terminals, Non-Insulated Copper, Tin-Plated Shown Actual Size	Catalog Number	Average Retail Price Per 100	Your Price Per 100
22-16 Wire, #6 Stud	20035401	$ 3.45	$ 1.29
22-16 Wire, #8 Stud	20035501	3.45	1.47
22-16 Wire, #10 Stud	20035601	3.45	1.47
16-14 Wire, #8 Stud	20035701	3.89	1.62
16-14 Wire, #10 Stud	20035801	3.89	1.62
16-14 Wire, 1/4 Stud	20052501	4.25	2.34
16-14 Wire, 5/16 Stud	20052201	4.25	2.34
12-10 Wire, #8 Stud	20035901	5.30	3.39
12-10 Wire, #10 Stud	20052301	5.30	3.39

BUTT CONNECTORS

Butt Connectors, Insulated Copper, Tin-Plated Shown Actual Size	Catalog Number	Average Retail Price Per 100	Your Price Per 100
22-16 Wire	20034601	$ 6.39	$ 3.39
16-14 Wire	20034701	6.95	3.81
12-10 Wire	20034801	8.25	5.61

CLOSED END CONNECTORS

Closed End Connectors, Insultated Copper, Tin-Plated, Crimp-On Shown Actual Size	Catalog Number	Average Retail Price Per 100	Your Price Per 100
16-14 Wire	20034301	$ 6.39	$ 2.55
12-10 Wire	20034401	7.45	3.99

SNAP SPLICE CONNECTORS

NOTE: Snap Splice Connectors are packaged and priced in dozen (12 count) quantities.

Snap Splice Connectors, Insulated High-Impact Plastic Shown Actual Size	Catalog Number	Average Retail Price Per Dozen	Your Price Per Dozen
22-18 Wire	20034101	$ 3.00	$ 1.80
18-14 Wire	20034201	$ 3.00	$ 1.80

46

3-37

silhouette of general product shape and bold identifying headline classifications.

The symmetrical grid method is an easy and fairly expeditious way of doing proportional page layouts. It offers both the easy art and copy coordination and the orderliness which are often appreciated by the customer.

2. Asymmetrical Grid Layout

The horizontal and vertical lines forming the asymmetrical grid act mostly as a guide to identification of certain perameters such as column measures, margins, and space possibilities within a page. It is a less stringent format than the symmetrical grid. Designers need to be able to apply the principles of proportion in such a manner that their creative abilities dominate the final design. The layout will result in a seemingly looser, more relaxed page.

General Consumer Brookstone's Homewares catalog is a joy to view, mainly because of the way the designer laid out the 98-page catalog with a three-column, nine-item grid as a guide. Figure 3-38 is the basic grid with three 2½″ columns acting as the layout guide for an 8¼″ × 9″ page. Figures 3-39, 3-40, and 3-41 illustrate the expert page layout throughout the catalog. In Figure 3-39 the designer has chosen to highlight an expensive ($300) product with a nice one-half point border, taking up approximately one-fourth of the page. Note how the boxed area overlaps the right margin edge and the left column. The designer has completed the page with silhouette drop-outs (top left and middle left) and fully bordered photos with accompanying copy blocks. Secondary vertical lines become promi-

3-38

3-39

nent layout guides (see our added dotted lines in Figure 3-39 indicating secondary guides). Figure 3-40, another seven-product page, highlights of the page's most expensive product by silhouetting the set of bowls (upper right) and overlapping the outer margin and, this time, the right columnar line. In Figure 3-41, Brookstone presents a collection of lower-priced kitchen merchandise (ten products in all). Rhythm and eye flow are achieved even on this product-packed page by bordered photos, product silhouetting, and a combination of both. The designer has chosen to use the vertical line columnar grids as part of the design. These lines have created interest and eye flow where, without them white space might have let the photos and copy "float" without purpose or direction. The designer has pulled together all the products on each page have been pulled together to present a total viewing occasion, retaining individual product interest.

Easy eyeflow

Business-to-Business A good business-to-business catalog with a layout which follows the same three-column grid approach is Inmac, a computer accessories catalog. Here are three 8½″ × 11″ pages, each illustrating the different look and feel which can be created, depending on the demands of the product being presented. Figure 3-42 shows how the descriptive copy falls into the three-column format, resulting in what is very near to a magazine page. The main illustration uses two-thirds of two columns to show the product, a Mobile Micromaster organizer system, and to highlight the company's guarantee, which is smartly bordered to maintain

3-40

3-41

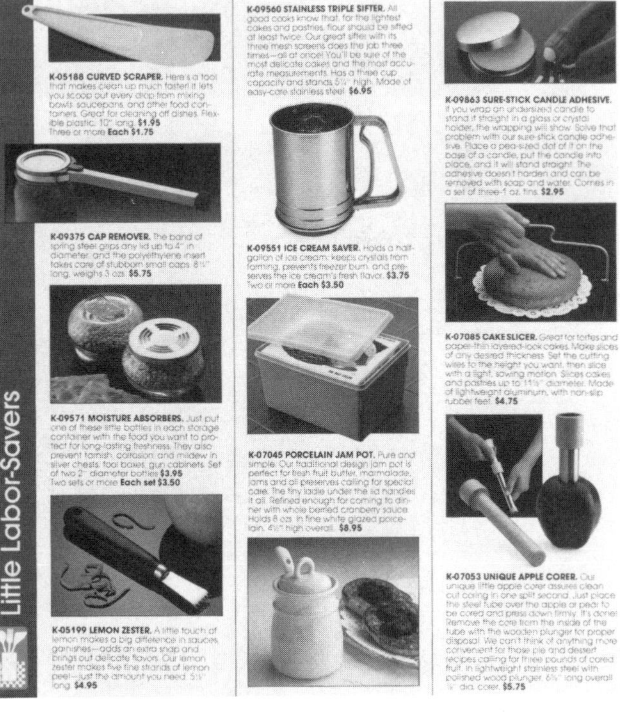

3-42

58
Furniture and Storage

Announcing the end of PC clutter. MicroMaster™… The workstation that mobilizes your entire system!

MicroMaster is the first truly complete PC support system available anywhere!

Its revolutionary design integrates orderly paper and cable management like no other office furniture we know of. And, for maximum PC usage and functionality, mobile MicroMaster can be moved from one location to another easily and safely. Best of all, MicroMaster is so well-made, we guarantee it for life.

Designed with your comfort in mind.

On its heavy-duty 4" wheels, mobile MicroMaster is the perfect height for keying—26½" from the floor. An optional monitor shelf mounts on either the left or right hand side of the station. This handy shelf quickly adjusts to whatever height is most comfortable for the user, and it tilts your CRT up or down to the angle that best reduces monitor glare. There's even room for your most frequently used documentation!

For additional "creature comforts"—like extra workspace, or modems, hard disk drives and T-switches—you can add an optional 15-inch-wide by 30-inch-deep side extension to an already generous 10 square feet of worksurface.

Keeps your cables out of sight, out of mind.

MicroMaster puts an end to unsightly and potentially dangerous cables and electrical cords. Instead of just "hanging around," they're carried through slots in the worksurface where they're tucked out of sight in special troughs. Power cords are then routed invisibly down a channel built into the leg.

For even greater convenience and safety, you may plug your components into either of our 2 optional power strips … standard or specially surge-protected. Mounted under the worksurface (conveniently out-of-sight), these power strips give you one-switch control over six outlets right where you need them. And it enables you to have only one cord to plug/unplug when moving your MicroMaster. (The surge-protection model protects your sensitive equipment from AC-line spikes that occur daily in most electrical environments. These dangerous spikes can cause critical computer malfunctions or loss of data.)

Simplifies paper handling.

If you've ever had printout snaking all over your desk or crawling back into your printer, you'll really appreciate how MicroMaster handles paper for you!

Two slots let paper pass from below to your rear- or bottom-feed printer.

A third slot carries output to the optional paper-catch basket mounted beneath or behind the worksurface. Neat and easy!

And a special advantage of MicroMaster's paper-catch basket is that it mounts either behind or beneath the worksurface. That saves valuable office space, while still giving you easy access to your printout.

Truly mobile.

When someone else needs to use your PC, it's a snap to move it to their area. (With the power strip, you'll only have to unplug one cord.)

MicroMaster is specially designed so that its keying height on wheels is the standard 26½". To make mobility even easier, an optional paper dolly attaches to the stand and rolls on its own casters. With the dolly, you'll never have to disconnect your paper supply when you move your computer system.

Use the chart on the next page to order your Mobile MicroMaster today.

Inmac's Lifetime Guarantee Plus a 45-day Trial.

Our MicroMaster is guaranteed for life against defects in material and workmanship. If the product fails we'll replace the defective item free.

You also have a 45-day no-nonsense trial period. If you're not completely satisfied with your MicroMaster, you may return it within 45 days. Just send it back with proof of purchase to the nearest Inmac branch, freight prepaid, for prompt exchange, refund or credit.

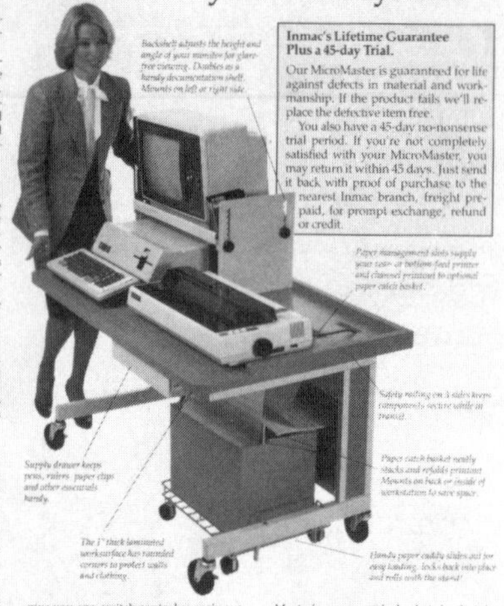

Puts you in control of your completely organized system.

3-43

98
Cables & Connectors

At last! A snap-together way to reconfigure cable assemblies!

Our EIA Line-Link is the fastest way we know to reconfigure mismatched EIA RS232 connectors.

It's compact, yet rugged enough to be used as a permanent "fix."

No special tools needed.

Plug your cable into one of the connector shells. Using the jumpers, match the pin and socket functions to the other connector shell and plug your other cable into that connector. The signal matrix between the cables is now compatible. Snap the plastic cover on and you're in business.

Each Line-Link includes a 2-pc. cover, a 25-position connector shell, mounting hardware and 1 insertion/extraction tool.

Male-Female EIA Line-Link. Includes 10 M-F jumpers, 2 F-M/F "Y" jumpers, and 2 M-M/F "Y" jumpers.
No. 308 .... $20 each

Extra Jumpers. 10 M-F jumpers, 2 F-M/F "Y" jumpers and 2 M-M/F "Y" jumpers.
No. 307 .... $9 each

Male-Male EIA Line-Link. Includes 10 M-M jumpers and 4 M-M "Y" jumpers.
No. 305-1 .... $20 each

Extra Jumpers. Includes 10 M-M jumpers and 4 M-M/M "Y" jumpers.
No. 307-1 .... $9 each

Female-Female EIA Line-Link. Includes 10 F-F jumpers and 4 F-F/F "Y" jumpers.
No. 305-2 .... $20 each

Extra Jumpers. Includes 10 F-F jumpers and 4 F-F/F "Y" jumpers.
No. 307-2 .... $9 each

Line-Link reconfigures cable assemblies quickly.

The jumpers match the wiring schemes of the connectors.

Your cables plug into the EIA RS232 connectors.

The 2-piece cover snaps together tightly to seal out dust and dirt.

Adding terminals? Use our self-contained null modems for quick hook-up!

Our new self-contained null modems (or cross-over cables) can get two DTE devices or two DCE devices talking in minutes.

Just plug one into the EIA cable between the devices you want to communicate. Unlike some null modems, there's no extra cable to hook-up.

Internal pin configuration: 1-1, 2-3, 3-2, 5 & 6 & 8-20, 20-5 & 6 & 8, 7-7.

These null modems are completely self-contained for easier connection.

Price each	Qty. 1	2-4	5-9
Molded Null Modem. (M-M). No. 314-1	$25	$23.50	$22
Molded Null Modem. (F-F). No. 314-2	$25	$23.50	$22
Molded Null Modem. (M-F). No. 314-3	$25	$23.50	$22

How to make moving peripherals easier!

Moving peripherals from station to station is easy when you wire your building with our dataports.

Each two-part box lets you conveniently wall-mount an EIA cable without removing the connectors. Order several.

Dataport box for 25-pin connectors. Includes mounting hardware (excluding connector). Cover dimensions: 2¾"w. x 2⅓"h. x 1¼"d. Wt. 1 lb. White.
No. 393 .... $10 ea.

Dataports are easy to install. They contain everything you need to wall-mount a cable.

Gender-changer fixes non-mating cables!

Here's the money-saving alternative to replacing or modifying EIA RS232 cables that won't mate because they've got connectors of the same gender.

Just plug your cables into our self-contained gender-changer.

All 25 pins are live so it'll work with any EIA cables you already have.

Modifying or replacing non-mating EIA RS232 cables is a snap with our compact gender-changer.

Keep several on-hand. They're indispensable when reconfiguring terminals or modems. Call us with your order and we'll ship them to you the same day.

Compact gender-changer (F-F).
No. 328 .... $35 ea.

Compact gender-changer (M-M).
No. 329 .... $35 ea.

Our modem bypasses can quickly configure your terminal devices —without using modems!

Modem bypass allows direct connections.

Now you can connect two DTE (Data Terminal Equipment) devices or two DCE (Data Communications Equipment) devices without using modems. Each modem bypass has a pair of RS232 connectors wired together to form a 12-inch cable.

General Purpose Modem Bypass (F-F).
No. 276 (7 signals, plus ground) .... $30 ea.

General Purpose Modem Bypass (M-F).
No. 277 (7 signals, plus ground) .... $30 ea.

HP-Compatible Modem Bypass (F-F). Equivalent to HP part #13232U.
No. 275 (13 signals, plus ground) .... $34 ea.

DEC/DGC-Compatible Modem Bypass (F-F). Equivalent to DEC part #H312A.
No. 270 (9 signals, plus ground) .... $32 ea.

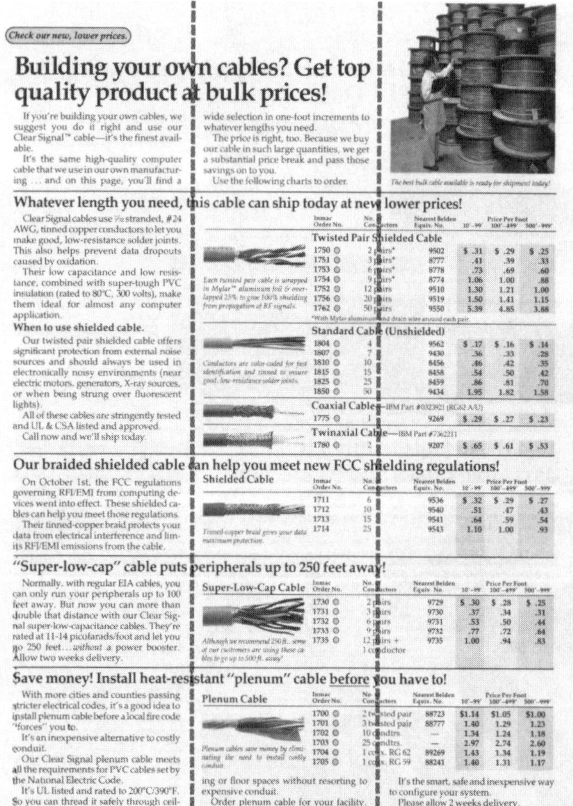
Check our new, lower prices.

Building your own cables? Get top quality product at bulk prices!

If you're building your own cables, we suggest you do it right and use our Clear Signal™ cable—it's the finest available.

It's the same high-quality computer cable that we use in our own manufacturing … and on this page, you'll find a wide selection in one-foot increments to whatever lengths you need.

The price is right, too. Because we buy our cable in such large quantities, we get a substantial price break and pass those savings on to you.

Use the following charts to order.

The best bulk cable available is ready for shipment today!

Whatever length you need, this cable can ship today at new lower prices!

Clear Signal cables use 7/32 stranded, #24 AWG, tinned copper conductors to let you make good, low-resistance solder joints. This also helps prevent data dropouts caused by oxidation.

Their low capacitance and low resistance, combined with super-tough PVC insulation (rated to 80°C, 300 volts), make them ideal for almost any computer application.

When to use shielded cable.

Our twisted pair shielded cable offers significant protection from external noise sources and should always be used in electronically noisy environments (near electric motors, generators, X-ray sources, or when being strung over fluorescent lights).

All of these cables are stringently tested and UL & CSA listed and approved.

Call now and we'll ship today.

Inmac Order No.	No. of Conductors	Nearest Belden Equiv. No.	Price Per Foot 10'-99'	100'-499'	500'-999'
Twisted Pair Shielded Cable					
1750	2 pairs*	9502	$ .31	$ .29	$ .25
1751	3 pairs*	8777	.41	.39	.33
1753	6 pairs*	8778	.73	.69	.60
1754	9 pairs*	8774	1.06	1.00	.88
1752	12 pairs	9510	1.30	1.21	1.00
1756	20 pairs	9519	1.50	1.41	1.15
1762	50 pairs	9550	5.39	4.85	3.88
Standard Cable (Unshielded)					
1804	4	9562	$ .17	$ .16	$ .14
1807	7	9430	.36	.33	.28
1810	10	8456	.46	.42	.35
1815	15	8458	.54	.50	.42
1825	25	8459	.86	.81	.70
1850	50	9434	1.95	1.82	1.58
Coaxial Cable—IBM Part #0323921 (RG62 A/U)					
1775	1	9269	$ .29	$ .27	$ .23
Twinaxial Cable—IBM Part #7362211					
1780	2	9207	$ .65	$ .61	$ .53

*With Mylar aluminum and drain wire around each pair.

Each twisted pair cable is wrapped in Mylar™ aluminum foil & overlapped 25% to give 100% shielding from propagation of RF signals.

Conductors are color-coded for fast identification and tinned to insure good, low-resistance solder joints.

Our braided shielded cable can help you meet new FCC shielding regulations!

On October 1st, the FCC regulations governing RFI/EMI from computing devices went into effect. These shielded cables can help you meet those regulations.

Their tinned-copper braid protects your data from electrical interference and limits RFI/EMI emissions from the cable.

Shielded Cable: Inmac Order No.	No. of Conductors	Nearest Belden Equiv. No.	Price Per Foot 10'-99'	100'-499'	500'-999'
1711	6	9536	$ .32	$ .29	$ .27
1712	10	9540	.51	.47	.43
1713	15	9541	.64	.59	.54
1714	25	9543	1.10	1.00	.93

Tinned-copper braid gives your data maximum protection.

"Super-low-cap" cable puts peripherals up to 250 feet away!

Normally, with regular EIA cables, you can only run your peripherals up to 100 feet away. But now you can more than double that distance with our Clear Signal super-low-capacitance cables. They're rated at 11-14 picofarads/foot and let you go 250 feet… *without* a power booster. Allow two weeks delivery.

Super-Low-Cap Cable: Inmac Order No.	No. of Conductors	Nearest Belden Equiv. No.	Price Per Foot 10'-99'	100'-499'	500'-999'
1730	2 pairs	9729	$ .30	$ .28	$ .25
1731	3 pairs	9730	.37	.34	.31
1732	6 pairs	9731	.53	.50	.44
1733	9 pairs	9732	.77	.72	.64
1735	12 pairs + 1 conductor	9735	1.00	.94	.83

Although we recommend 250 ft., some of our customers are using these cables to go up to 500 ft. away!

Save money! Install heat-resistant "plenum" cable before you have to!

With more cities and counties passing stricter electrical codes, it's a good idea to install plenum cable before a local fire code "forces" you to.

It's an inexpensive alternative to costly conduit.

Our Clear Signal plenum cable meets all the requirements for PVC cables set by the National Electric Code.

It's UL listed and rated to 200°C/390°F. So you can thread it safely through ceiling or floor spaces without resorting to expensive conduit.

Order plenum cable for your facility. It's the smart, safe and inexpensive way to configure your system.

Please allow 2 weeks delivery.

Plenum Cable: Inmac Order No.	No. of Conductors	Nearest Belden Equiv. No.	Price Per Foot 10'-99'	100'-499'	500'-999'
1700	2 twisted pair	88723	$1.14	$1.05	$1.00
1701	3 twisted pair	88777	1.40	1.29	1.23
1702	10 condtrs.	—	1.34	1.24	1.18
1703	25 condtrs.	—	2.97	2.74	2.60
1704	1 coax. RG 62	89269	1.43	1.34	1.19
1705	1 coax. RG 59	88241	1.40	1.31	1.17

Plenum cables save money by eliminating the need to install costly conduit.

3-44

the single-column approach. A small, one-column photo in the lower left shows how easy the product is to use. Figure 3-43 shows again how the three-column format is utilized for 16 different products. One-point line rules help divide the page, adding order and interest. The designer has used the upper left one-third of the page to sell Inmac's special Line-Links. Interest and asymmetry are achieved with "wandering" or columnar overlapping of silhouetted product photos. Figure 3-44 shows how the three-column grid can look like a horizontally dominated layout while really being based on a vertical three-column format. Note the top of the page showing the conformity to the three columns. Now follow our added gray dotted lines downward (lines not printed in the actual catalog) to see how the three columns are carried through.

Following is an example from the Neiman-Marcus catalog (Figure 3-45), which illustrates how a single page when viewed alone is asymmetrical.

However, this (Figure 3-46) same page, when paired with its opposite page, becomes perfectly balanced and symmetrical.

The flexibility of the asymmetrical approach is limited only by the imagination and ability of the designer. Many catalogers find the absence of uniformity more to their liking but the budget a little strained because of more costly photography. If the product is run in a later catalog, art and copy may have to be reshot or resized because of new layout demands, creating additional expense. Asymmetry does cost more and demands different graphic design talent.

Art visits art. The furs of Neiman-Marcus are photographed in the open-air Sculpture Garden of the new Dallas Museum of Art.

20A,B

Jerry Sorbara designs exclusively for N-M, opening our Christmas fur pages with typical innovation. **20A.** Her jacket is natural sable from the U.S.S.R. Luxuriantly full, and fashioned in the progressive technique of working the fur skin-on-skin. A full shape with extended shoulders, and a new eye to length. Sizes 6-14. 55,000.00. **20B.** Sorbara shapes a greatcoat in wedge silhouette for him. Natural Blue Iris mink is a step ahead in men's fashion. A steel-grey that hovers toward blue with the shift of light. Sizes 36-44. Fur: U.S.A. 12,500.00.

20C

The famed Italian couturier André Laug designs furs exclusively for Neiman-Marcus. Shown, a sculptural jacket of rare natural brown Russian broadtail with knife-edge inverted box pleats front and back. The sleeves are full, gathered at the shoulder and buttoned at the wrist. The collar is a detachable ring cowl of natural Russian sable. 6-16 sizes. Fur: U.S.S.R. 15,000.00.

THE Furs of N-M

3-45

Art visits art. The furs of Neiman-Marcus are photographed in the open-air Sculpture Garden of the new Dallas Museum of Art.

20A,B

Jerry Sorbara designs exclusively for N-M, opening our Christmas fur pages with typical innovation. **20A.** Her jacket is natural sable from the U.S.S.R. Luxuriantly full, and fashioned in the progressive technique of working the fur skin-on-skin. A full shape with extended shoulders, and a new eye to length. Sizes 6-14. 55,000.00. **20B.** Sorbara shapes a greatcoat in wedge silhouette for him. Natural Blue Iris mink is a step ahead in men's fashion. A steel-grey that hovers toward blue with the shift of light. Sizes 36-44. Fur: U.S.A. 12,500.00.

20C

The famed Italian couturier André Laug designs furs exclusively for Neiman-Marcus. Shown, a sculptural jacket of rare natural brown Russian broadtail with knife-edge inverted box pleats front and back. The sleeves are full, gathered at the shoulder and buttoned at the wrist. The collar is a detachable ring cowl of natural Russian sable. 6-16 sizes. Fur: U.S.S.R. 15,000.00.

James Galanos, eminent American designer. His exclusive fur collection for Neiman-Marcus evokes the past and the future with equal ease. So intricately detailed, they might have been cut from fabric.

21A

One of a kind, a floor-length regality in rare white ermine. Wrapped in clouds of white fox at neck and cuffs, and decorated with hand-attached rows of ermine tails. The natural white ermine is from the U.S.S.R. Fox (brightener added), is from Norway. Subject to prior sale. 50,000.00.

21B,C

A remarkable construction that combines two furs. Unsheared natural Lunaraine mink is formed into a full shawl collar to trim the cardigan jacket of sheared Blue Iris and Lunaraine mink, worked together in a lattice pattern. Sleeves gather at the shoulders for extension of line. **21B.** Sizes 6-14. Fur origin: U.S.A. 8,995.00. **21C.** The belt, a sash of soft, elephant-printed grey leather with decorative buckle. One size. 750.00 (9.10).

THE Furs of N-M

3-46

A Master Grid For A Digest-Size Catalog

The grid actually acts as a blueprint for a catalog page, meant to guide and aid the artist in laying out the catalog pages. Figure 3-47 is the master grid used to design the 16 grid combinations on the opposite page. The vertical lines on a grid are meant to act as column guides, to designate the space between columns, and to indicate the inner and outer margins. The horizontal lines aid in the depth of type and the placement of visual material and headlines, and they indicate the upper and lower page margins. This grid is designed for a 5½″ × 8½″ digest-size page.

3-47

Good layout requires skillful use of air

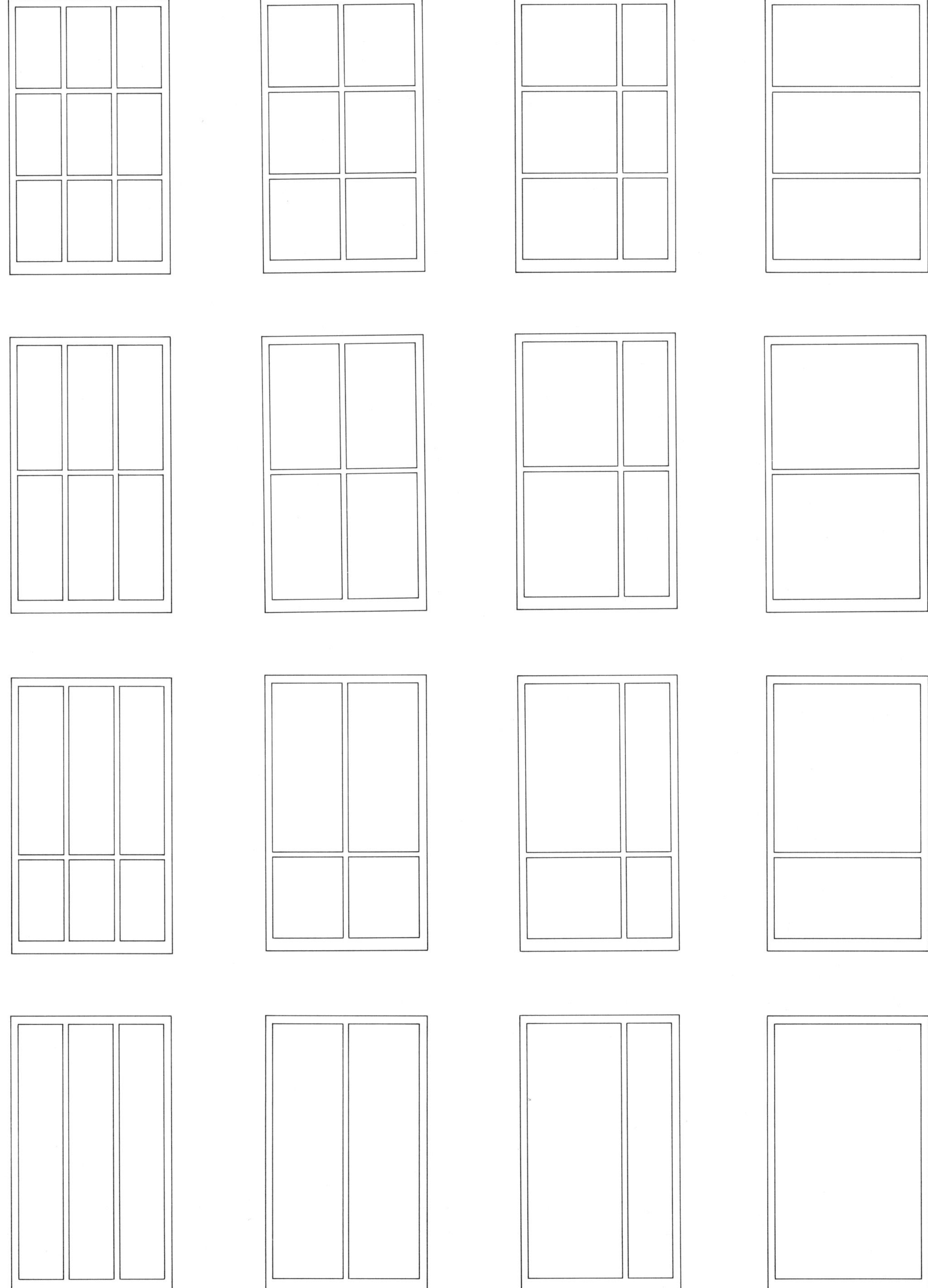

Two Different Layouts From One Grid Design

In Figure 3-48, we see a basic three-column, nine-unit grid designed to be used for a horizontal catalog page. Figure 3-49 illustrates how the artist has applied a symmetrical layout in presenting four basic products. An attractive, full column view of the pivotal and most expensive product, a dress, is seen at the left of the page. The top and bottom margins are indicated by the horizontal lines of the top and bottom grid units. The middle column guides the placement of the headlines and type. Even though the right margins of the type are ragged, they still stay within the perimeters of the middle column vertical guidelines. The three units in the right-hand column of the grid act as exacting guides for the photographs of the three accessory products. Figure 3-50 shows how the artist has maintained the full left column to present the main product and has still come up with an asymmetrical page design. The artist has created an easy flow starting with the logo and headline, directing the eye over to the photo of the scarves in the upper right. Because of the angle of the scarves, the eye is pointed back into the page and over to the wallet. The corner of the wallet is silhouetted outside of the bottom border to direct the eye down to the copy and over to the handbag. This is a wonderful job of directing the eye over the entire page. The copy is essentially still in the middle column, but it overlaps onto the right column in the upper part of the page and then falls into the middle column perimeters at the bottom. The art treatment of silhouetting the scarves and handbag loosens up the page and acts as an attractive visual aid to the asymmetrical design. By using the basic grid as a guide, the artist was able to come up with two very different and attractive page layouts.

3-48

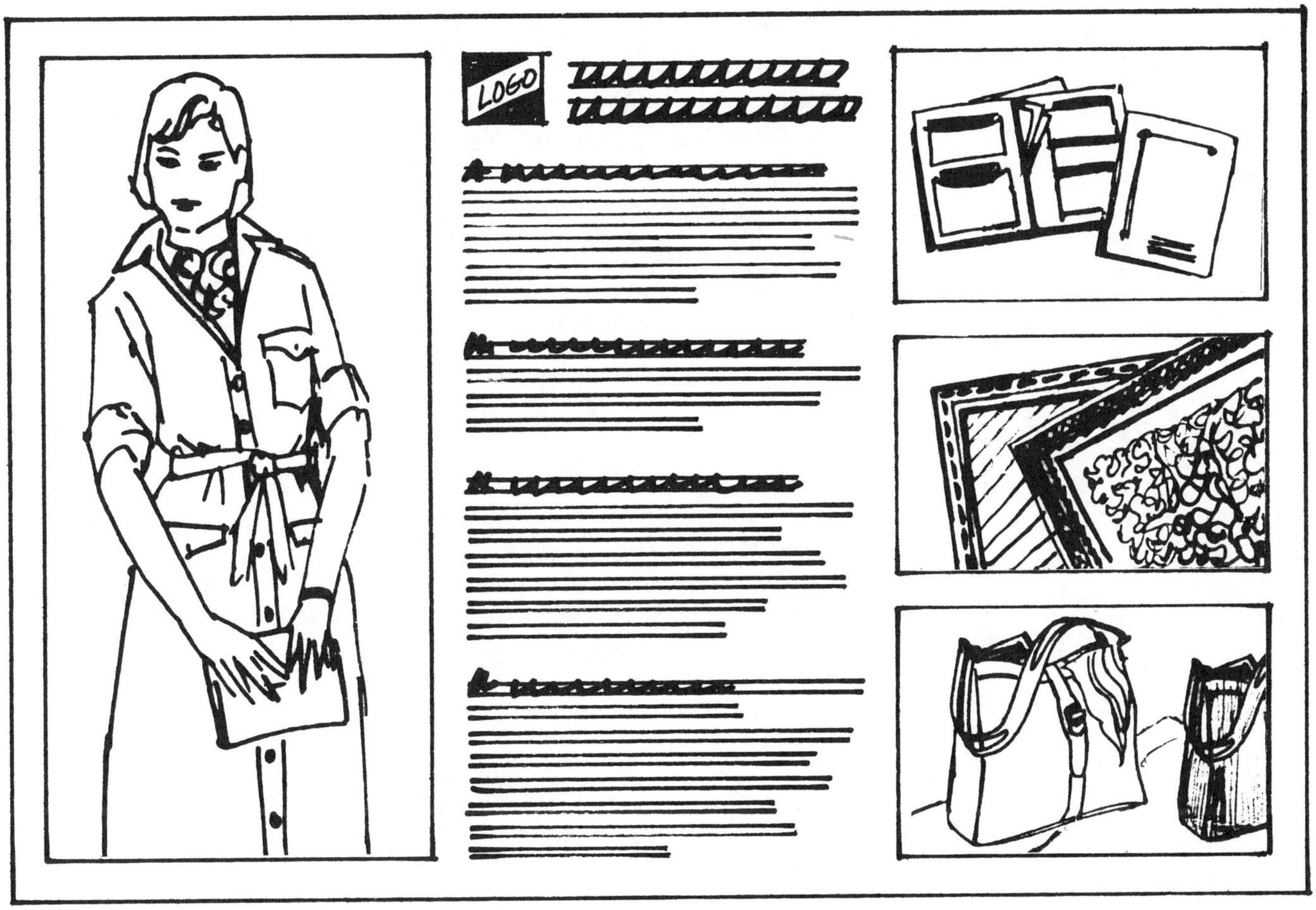

LOGO

3-49

LOGO

3-50

3. Art Separated From Copy

This format is especially interesting because it can retain the orderliness of the symmetrical layout along with the rhythm of the asymmetrical. Individual product shots are grouped on one section of the page or on a separate page entirely, while the accompanying copy is in a separate area or page. Such a format functions well for catalogs appealing to a variety of retail segments, high-ticket to low-ticket, although it must be handled differently for each one, particularly in the use of air.

General Consumer Examine this example (Figure 3-51) from Crate and Barrel. Varying the size of individual photos within a firm, geometrical area keeps the layout interesting. The copywriter is working within the discipline of making the copy for all items fit into the double-page spread, but retaining the advantage of being able to adjust the length of each item's description. If the copy on a right-hand page had been allowed to run to the next page, causing the customer to turn the page to read about an item pictured on the previous page, an inconvenience would have been introduced. Whenever a situation makes things less convenient for the customer, sales are affected negatively.

A low-end general merchandise catalog using this same technique is Bruce Bolind (Figure 3-52). Here you can see a very com-

26
THE CRATE AND BARREL CATALOGUE
SUMMER 1984

A Bird feeder. Certain to be a favorite port of call for chickadees, warblers and other small birds, this delightful new bird feeder from Bennington Potters is made of unglazed terra cotta, has a natural grape vine perch. #2775. $9.95 ($2.00).

B Folding rocker. Beautifully crafted of clear Canadian maple, this ingenious rocker folds to a compact 6". Remarkably comfortable, the ease with which it stores makes it an ideal choice for a summer home, a small nursery or anyone who occasionally enjoys the hypnotic security of a rocking chair. #2769. $64.95 ($5.00).

C "Verho" dress. This year's chemise is next year's cast-off. But a dress from Marimekko is destined to become a classic in any wardrobe. Simplicity and distinctive fabrics are two of the keys to the timeless appeal of Marimekko. The "Verho" dress, for example, is beautifully detailed with soft tucks at the yoke and full, gathered sleeves, but it never becomes fussy. The fabric is a delicately pin striped cotton batiste in a cool, flattering celadon green. For 1984, wear it blousy and belted low with its wide self belt. In the years to come, wear it with confidence any way it pleases you. It will look right, any way, anywhere. Sizes: XS (6-8), S (8-10), M (10-12), L (14-16). Please specify size when ordering. #8705. $175.00 ($2.00).

D Window basket. Enjoy the beauty of flowering plants all year with this handwoven Spanish willow window basket. Filled with a seasonally changing assortment, it is lovely on a sun porch or sheltered window sill or as a table centerpiece. 20"x6"x6," it comfortably holds three 6" pots. #2770. $19.95 ($2.00).

E Willow picnic hamper. This spectacular willow hamper is constructed of peeled whole willow that will mellow to a warm golden hue over the years. Its sturdy construction, fortified by a wooden brace woven into the base, promises years of use. Handwoven in Spain, it measures a spacious 24"x15½"x10". A Crate and Barrel exclusive design. #2771. $49.95 ($2.25).

F Willow basket. Handcrafted in Spain, this basket represents an extraordinary blend of function and beauty. Details such as the twisted handle, undulating border and slightly rounded sides require special

3-51

mon problem. In this layout, each piece of artwork can readily run into another, making it difficult for the customer to isolate the individual items. This collision occurs partly because the individual photographs in this layout have been formatted too tightly: the items are either too large within each individual frame, or they are cropped too closely, leaving no air inside the frame to relax the eye. When photographs are cropped in this manner, they require more air on the outside of the frame. The copy descriptions can also run together (though this did not happen here) if not properly gapped, or if each new copy block does not have something isolating it from the previous one, such as a boldface headline.

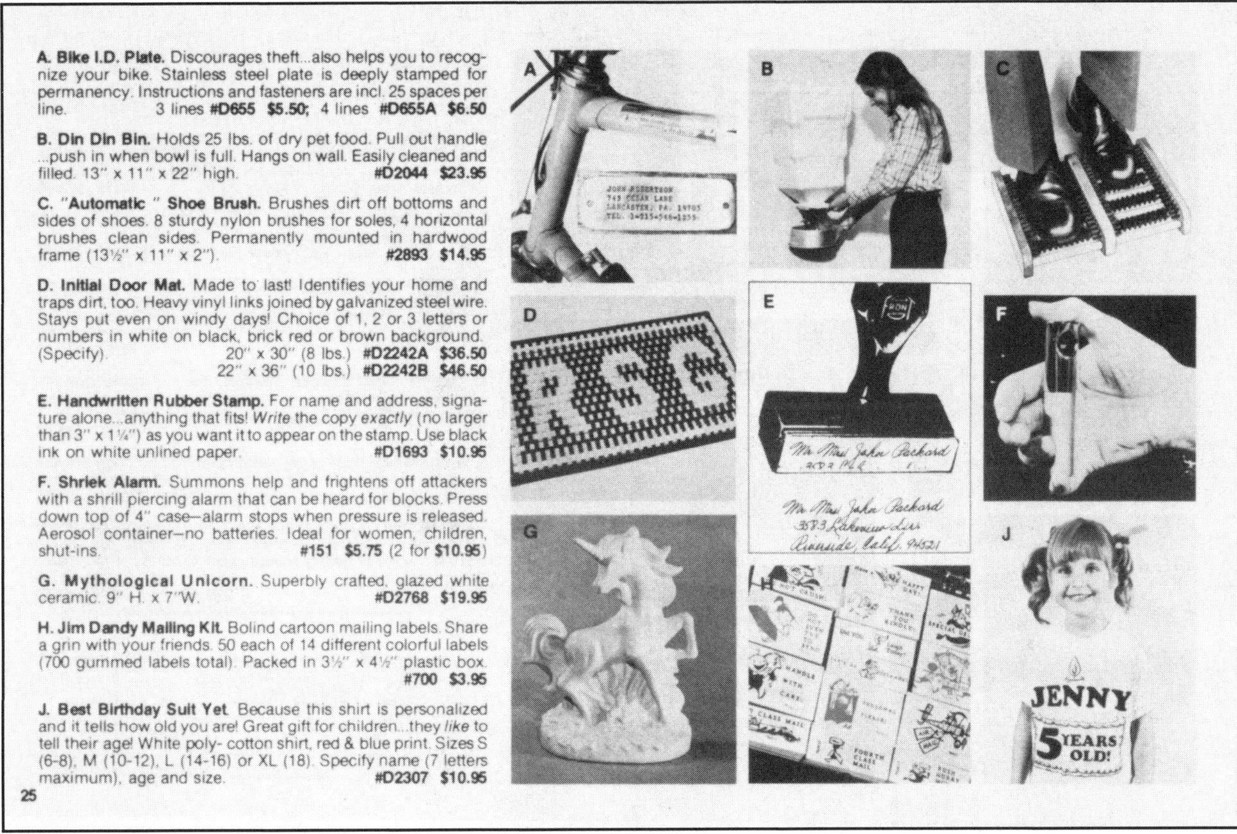

A. Bike I.D. Plate. Discourages theft...also helps you to recognize your bike. Stainless steel plate is deeply stamped for permanency. Instructions and fasteners are incl. 25 spaces per line. 3 lines **#D655 $5.50;** 4 lines **#D655A $6.50**

B. Din Din Bin. Holds 25 lbs. of dry pet food. Pull out handle ...push in when bowl is full. Hangs on wall. Easily cleaned and filled. 13" x 11" x 22" high. **#D2044 $23.95**

C. "Automatic " Shoe Brush. Brushes dirt off bottoms and sides of shoes. 8 sturdy nylon brushes for soles, 4 horizontal brushes clean sides. Permanently mounted in hardwood frame (13½" x 11" x 2"). **#2893 $14.95**

D. Initial Door Mat. Made to last! Identifies your home and traps dirt, too. Heavy vinyl links joined by galvanized steel wire. Stays put even on windy days! Choice of 1, 2 or 3 letters or numbers in white on black, brick red or brown background. (Specify). 20" x 30" (8 lbs.) **#D2242A $36.50**
22" x 36" (10 lbs.) **#D2242B $46.50**

E. Handwritten Rubber Stamp. For name and address, signature alone...anything that fits! *Write* the copy *exactly* (no larger than 3" x 1¼") as you want it to appear on the stamp. Use black ink on white unlined paper. **#D1693 $10.95**

F. Shriek Alarm. Summons help and frightens off attackers with a shrill piercing alarm that can be heard for blocks. Press down top of 4" case—alarm stops when pressure is released. Aerosol container—no batteries. Ideal for women, children, shut-ins. **#151 $5.75** (2 for **$10.95**)

G. Mythological Unicorn. Superbly crafted, glazed white ceramic. 9" H. x 7"W. **#D2768 $19.95**

H. Jim Dandy Mailing Kit. Bolind cartoon mailing labels. Share a grin with your friends. 50 each of 14 different colorful labels (700 gummed labels total). Packed in 3½" x 4½" plastic box. **#700 $3.95**

J. Best Birthday Suit Yet. Because this shirt is personalized and it tells how old you are! Great gift for children...they *like* to tell their age! White poly- cotton shirt, red & blue print. Sizes S (6-8), M (10-12), L (14-16) or XL (18). Specify name (7 letters maximum), age and size. **#D2307 $10.95**

25

3-52

Business-to-Business Eastman, Inc., an office products catalog (Figure 3-53), takes a symmetrical approach allowing for the art and copy to appear in a three-column format. The six pieces of artwork are nicely surrounded with air and clearly identified with alpha characters, which are matched with each individual copy block. The copy blocks appear in one column, stacked one on top of the other, allowing for a nice area of air at the bottom of the column. This small allowance relieves the eye, loosening up what is normally a fairly rigid approach. The outcome is a very easy and pleasing page for the customer to view.

A

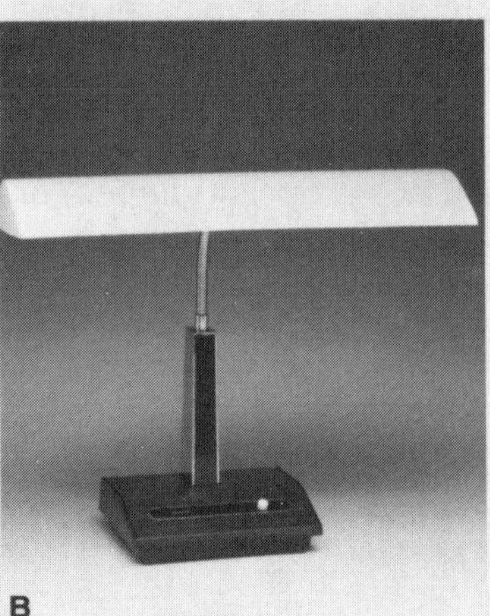

B

C

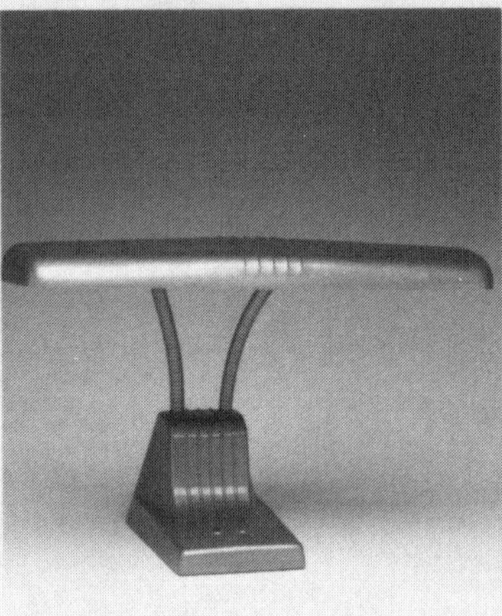

D

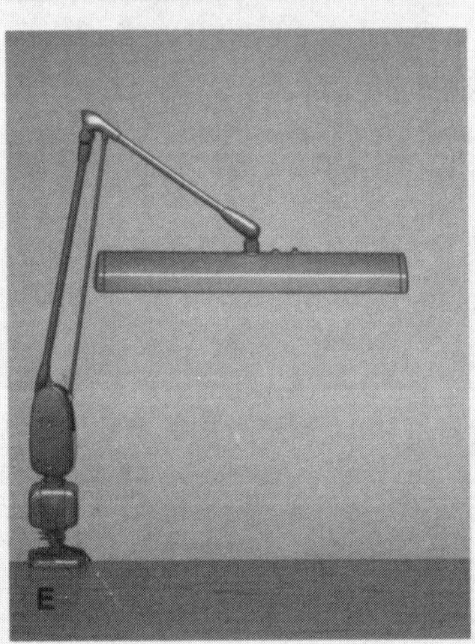

E

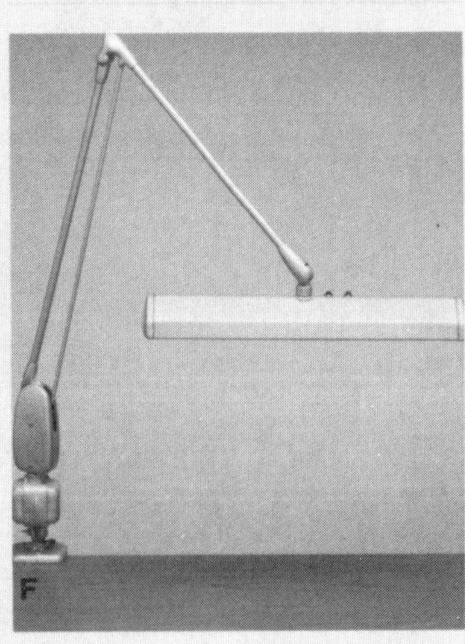

F

Panasonic

A Flexible arm single tube desk lamp with weighted wood base, equipped with power booster to increase wattage of 15 watt tube to 22 watts. Adjustable goose neck stem, transluscent reflector, 8⅞"x 6" base.

Order No.
FS-300E (Tube included)

B Flexible arm single tube desk lamp. Simulated walnut grain vinyl finish weighted base. Adjustable goose neck stem. Translucent reflector. 8-9/16"x 6¼" base. 13½" high.

Order No.
FS-287E (Tube included, 15 watts)

C Flexible arm single tube desk lamp with black weighted base, adjustable goose neck stem. Transluscent reflector. 7½"x 7-5/16" base. 16" high.

Order No.
FS-586E (Tube included, 15 watt).

Replacement Tubes:

F15T8CW	18" 15 watt, fluorescent tube cool white.
F15T8D	18" 15 watt, fluorescent tube daylight.

DAZOR

D Fluorescent desk lamp, twin flexible arms, reflector adjusts from 8 to 14 inches. Weighted base. Requires two tubes (not included).

Order No.

D100BLK	Black
D100BRN	Statuary Bronze

E Floating 24" arm fluorescent lamp, universal clamp can be clamped or screwed to any horizontal sloping or vertical surface. Requires two tubes (not included).

Order No.
2124BRZ Frost Tan

F Floating 34" arm fluorescent lamp, universal clamp can be clamped or screwed to any horizontal sloping or vertical surface. Requires two tubes (not included).

Lamp Order No.

2134GRY	Gray
2134BRN	Statuary Bronze

Tubes For Dazor Lamps:

F15T8CW	18" 15 watt, fluorescent tube cool white.
F15T8D	18" 15 watt, fluorescent tube daylight.

Advantages
Specific sizing of art in advance of the shot, to fit into an area the exact dimensions of which are known; eliminates the risk of forcing the eye to jump around the entire page, which sometimes occurs in asymmetrical layouts, since all copy can be found in one area; easy viewing of all products one after another, without interruption.

Disadvantages
Requires greater attention to juxtaposition of items and air within the photographs, and air surrounding them, so the customer's eye is not confused; greater attention to gapping of the photographs; possibility that the page will not retain both a visual blend and a separation if background colors for photographs are not carefully coordinated; possibility of visual "run-together," adding confusion when used in a black and white catalog (black and white creates a solid mass from border to border in the area where the photos are abutted, discouraging visual differentiation introduced by varied colors in a four-color layout); difficulty in readily matching the description to the photo (letters referencing the photo to the copy block must be easily picked out in each area); greater probability of a cluttered layout if copy is not properly gapped.

4. Product Grouping

Less often seen is the style of layout which uses a single photograph consisting of a group of separately sold products. The success of this format is often dependent on how readily the eye can separate the individual products within the grouping. Copy is positioned separately.

General Consumer The Lillian Vernon At Home catalog (Figure 3-54) illustrates that this kind of layout can be the most difficult to deal with. Though each item in the photograph blends aesthetically into a "perfect" room, and the entire photo is attractive, it is difficult for the customer to isolate the individual items which are for sale. For example, the rustic bucket sitting on the hearth is almost impossible to see. In addition, the "key" letters used to match art with copy are difficult to find. (In this type of layout, it is especially difficult to position the letters properly and noticeably within the photo.) The customer has to work hard to pull together the necessary information to come to a purchasing decision.

Product grouping in one photo dangerous

A. OUR ONE-OF-A-KIND ANTIQUE STOVE an authentic European coal stove—probably 19th century Dutch. To own it is to evoke warm memories of kitchens past. Antique iron with inlaid blue porcelain tiles. H459, $1800.00

B. SOLID PINE JELLY CUPBOARD, ours alone! From a rustic antique, authentic to its hand-carved front, black metal hinges, wood turn-latch. Each handmade, signed, dated. 22x15x60" high, 4 shelves. H139, $325.00 (CC)

C. HAND-FORGED, HAMMERED and handsome—the perfect pot rack. ¼" carbon steel, its warm natural gray protected by clear finish, 17x36". Instructions and bolts for secure 2-point attachment. 16 staunch hooks. H120, $135.00 (9.25)

D. CALPHALON COOKWARE, famed for 20 years of professional use. Thick heavy-duty aluminum heats evenly—fused surface won't stick, crack, peel, discolor or react to minerals and acids. Functional cast iron handles, tinned and riveted. All have aluminum lids except omelet and butter

warmer. Easy to clean, just whisk in suds. H074, 2½-qt. pan $46.00 (3.80); H075, 5-qt. pan $79.00 (5.20); H076, 8-qt. stockpot $62.00 (5.20); H077 10" omelet $31.00 (3.80); H078 ½-qt. butter warmer $15.00 (1.90)

E. LE SMOCK in country blue, prettily piped and pocketed. Easy grip-front, machine wash/dry polyester/cotton. H478 petite, H479 small, H480 medium, H481 large, $28.00 (2.75)

F. HEART-SHAPED STOOL of fine walnut and cherry woods. Lovingly carved, lacquered—the original was a valentine gift from the artisan to his wife. 13½" across, 20" high. H195, $140.00 (4.25)

G. STONEWARE ART TILES for a counter, a strip, a whole wall—lovely alternated plain-and-posy. Handmade, blue underglaze designs, high-fired, water- and heat-resistant. 4⅜" squares ¼" thick, all 3 designs with corner motifs. H117 plain, H119 tulip, H118 violet, $4.00 each (1.40)

3-54 8

SCIENCE,

NATURE & MAN

6 The Illustrated Encyclopedia of Space Technology. From the first steps into space to today's Shuttle Program — a beautifully illustrated photographic history of space exploration. Foreword by Arthur C. Clarke. **$24.95**

7 The Audubon Society Encyclopedia of North American Birds. The first one-volume encyclopedia to cover all the birds that nest in North America (including Greenland and Bermuda). 320 full-color photographs. **$60.00**

8 The Dinosaurs. An affectionate yet historically accurate look at the giant beasts that once roamed the earth. Extensively illustrated with full-color and black and white plates. Sure to be treasured by adults and children alike. **$12.95,** paper.

9 Life On Earth. In this unique book, David Attenborough undertakes nothing less than the history of nature — from the emergence of tiny one-celled organisms more than 3,000 million years ago to apelike primitive man. **$22.50**

10 The Making of Mankind. Richard Leakey, the celebrated authority on ancient man, offers a sequel to his bestselling *Origins*. "A brilliantly illustrated story of the evolution of man." — *Discover.* Full color. **$24.95**

11 Arthur C. Clarke's Mysterious World. Arthur C. Clarke, whose novels of prophecy and origin are read by millions, investigates our suprascientific world and its unexplained phenomena. With Simon Welfare and John Fairley. **$9.95,** paper.

2

3-55

Business-to-Business The layout from B. Dalton (Figure 3-55) is successful because there is no great variance between the sizes of items. (Large items tend to overwhelm the viewer's attention; very small items get lost.) Because every item is essentially the same size and same category, the photographer experiences only minor difficulties in laying out the photograph. The photographer merely has to place the books in a pleasing, balanced manner, with as much of each book cover showing as possible, without the problem of balancing items of vastly different shapes or sizes. This photograph makes everything easy for the customer: reference numbers are easily seen and matched between art and copy, and the book titles in the photograph act as copy headlines.

Advantages
Encourages coordinated purchasing; aesthetically pleasing, although aesthetics are of value only if they encourage the bottom line; more interesting to view when all one category subject; lower production costs, in some cases (only one picture to take, one color separation, one photo to strip up instead of six, for example, if set-up can be kept simple, such as in the B. Dalton layout — however, may be more expensive for the Vernon shot because of photographer's fees for a more complicated photograph, requiring more time and originality).

Disadvantages
More difficult for items to retain individual attention from the customer, who often has to search for each one; more difficult art/copy match-ups because it is hard to place reference letters in the main photograph without making them either too prominent, causing a distraction, or too recessive (all of which forces the customer to work, which is a liability in creating an easy sales climate); difficulty of achieving the hoped-for use of association to lend greater appeal to each item in order to create more sales; in practice, possibly disastrous results by not calling proper attention to all of the merchandise available, causing lost sales.

5. One Product To A Page

This style of layout has many variations and may even extend to two pages in some catalogs. Basically, a full page is devoted to both art and copy in presenting one product. Of all styles, this one is most often dictated by the type of product being presented. It is quite often used when a product line offers many versions of the same product type, such as a "good, better, best" situation, or when one product has many features which need to be pointed out.

General Consumer The JS&A catalog (Figure 3-56) illustrates how a high-ticket product being offered in two model types (stan-

"Will Avanti get away with it?"

IBM Has Ball

But Avanti steals it in the last quarter of the typewriter revolution.

The score is IBM twelve million and Avanti a measly 175,000. That's the typewriter score between America's giant IBM and Japan's Avanti—the company that has copied IBM's popular typewriter concept. Will Avanti catch up?

NOT ON YOUR LIFE

IBM has been making the Selectric typewriter for over 25 years, perfecting it as they became the world's undisputed number one typewriter manufacturer.

IBM has created the standard in the ball-element typing system while Avanti is simply cashing in. From the onset, it would seem totally unfair. But wait. Advancing technology and Japanese innovation have a strange way of changing the direction of the ball game.

Avanti examined the American market and clearly saw that Americans loved the IBM product. And IBM wasn't stupid. They owned dozens of protective patents on their unit which made it practically impossible for anyone to steal, copy or duplicate their wonderful design.

But Avanti didn't give up easily. The Japanese are known for their persistence. "What if," they said, "we developed a typewriter that felt like the IBM, typed like the IBM and even used ball typing elements like the IBM, but didn't violate any of IBM's patents?"

GOOD IDEA

So those clever little guys over at Avanti worked for nine solid years. That's right, nine solid years. And the typewriter they developed was so unique that the only similarity with IBM was the interchangeable ball element and the fact that both typewriters are full-fledged, heavy-duty office typewriters.

But oh, the differences. The IBM has approximately 3200 separate parts or components. The Avanti, using the latest in technology, has reduced the parts count to approximately 1200.

But oh, what parts. Avanti uses C-50 carbon steel in all moving or contact parts—tougher steel than IBM uses. With the IBM, there are 270 separate adjustments that have to be made either at the factory or in the user's place of business. Avanti only has 80, and they're all done at the factory.

AEROSPACE TECHNOLOGY

The housing on the Avanti is Cyolac V521—a product from aerospace technology. It's tough, non corrosive and lightweight. IBM uses die cast metal. The Avanti weighs 21 pounds compared to IBM's 46.

If we sound rather one-sided, you should have heard the independent laboratory that tests typewriters. They categorically praised the Avanti as one of the best units they've ever tested and by far the best value.

In one of their 500-hour marathon typing tests, Avanti typed without a flaw while the IBM suffered numerous breakdowns. But what about consumers?

THEY LOVE THEM TOO

The ribbons on the Avanti snap right in with no levers to pull and nothing to twist or turn. Your hands stay clean. With the IBM, ...well, let's just say it's no joy. And a black carbon ribbon on an IBM will type 80,000 characters versus 300,000 on the Avanti 1400 model.

For fast typists, the Avanti avoids what is called "flicking," or the chopping off of a character when a typewriter types too fast. Why? Because the Avanti can type at 62 characters per second compared to 45 characters on the IBM. This also means you get an immediate tactile response when you touch a key on the Avanti compared to the buffered feel on most electronic units.

And what about service? IBM is known for their highly-trained servicemen who dress in nice suits, wear highly-polished shoes and are very polite. They even do a nice job of fixing your typewriter.

Avanti instead uses a national network of 150 independent service centers with three factory support groups. True, you have to mail or bring your Avanti typewriter in for repair, but it should require less service and cost you a lot less too. And Avanti has a 90-day limited warranty compared to IBM's 30 days.

MOTHERHOOD AND APPLE PIE

Why should you get an Avanti and not an IBM? Why should you support those Japanese upstarts when IBM is like motherhood and apple pie? The answer is quite simple. First, as a consumer, if you can get a better product for less, it's to your advantage. That's quite logical.

Secondly, if IBM had no competition, do you think they would have any incentive to lower their prices or produce even more innovative products? That's what the free enterprise system is all about.

If you were considering an IBM but can appreciate the alternative offered by Avanti, buy an Avanti. They'll never beat IBM, but they'll sure keep them on the ball.

Order an Avanti at no obligation, today.

Model 1400 (6120V) **$369**
Model 1500 (6121V) (avail late May) **469**

Note: There are two Avanti models. The 1400 has a correcting cover-up tape and the 1500 uses a special lift-off tape. We offer both.

17

3-56

dard and auto dealer) and needing extra-long copy can benefit from a full 8½″ × 11″ catalog page for presentation. Ample room allows the product itself to visually stand out, with complimentary white space surrounding. The large headline and subhead help identify the product, as well as calling attention to it. Two-thirds of the page, including headlines, is devoted to descriptive copy and a small inset, which helps to further identify a product feature and total function. JS&A's long, conversational copy complements the type of product offered by detailing information while, at the same time, selling in a very personal way. Easy art and copy reference is achieved. The fact that the catalog looks a great deal like a magazine targeted to the serious electronics buff is no accident, *as this is exactly the kind of customer to whom this catalog appeals.*

Easy art and copy reference

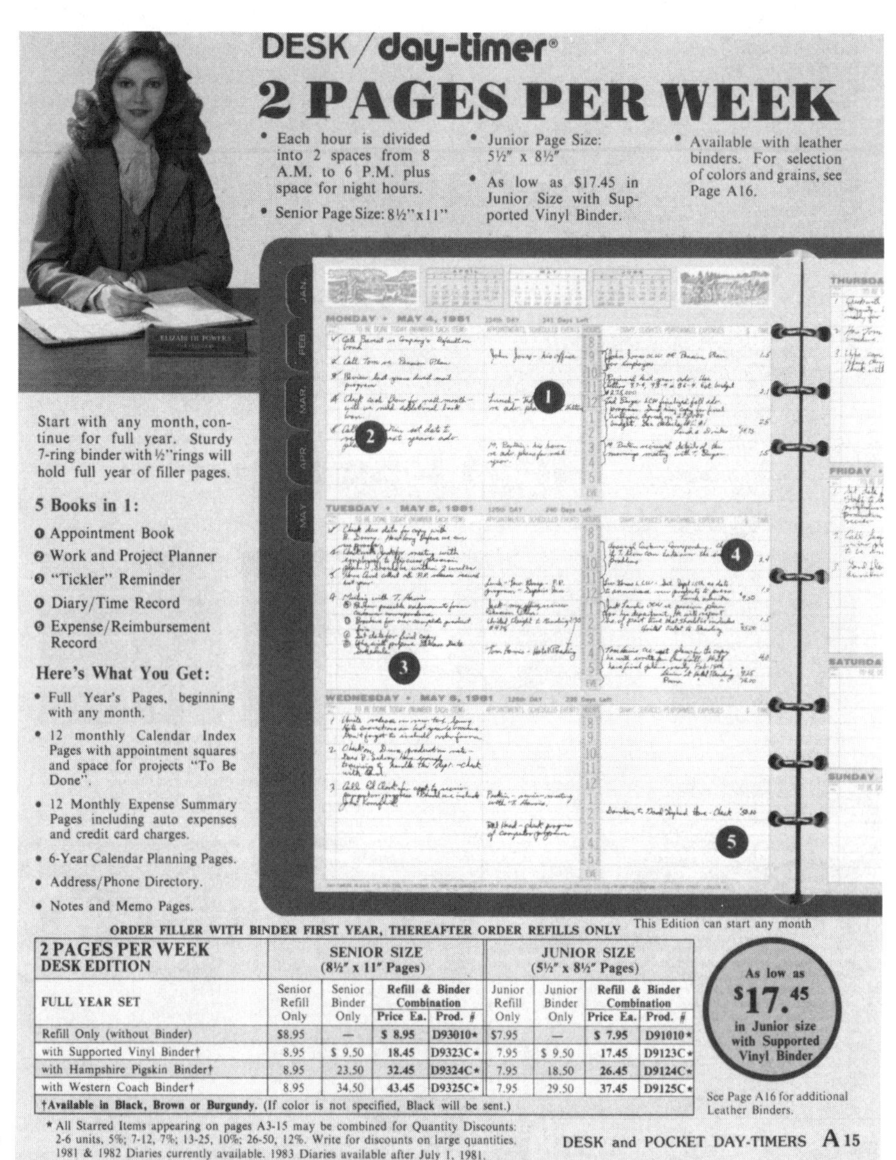

DESK / day-timer®

2 PAGES PER WEEK

- Each hour is divided into 2 spaces from 8 A.M. to 6 P.M. plus space for night hours.
- Senior Page Size: 8½"x11"
- Junior Page Size: 5½" x 8½"
- As low as $17.45 in Junior Size with Supported Vinyl Binder.
- Available with leather binders. For selection of colors and grains, see Page A16.

Start with any month, continue for full year. Sturdy 7-ring binder with ½"rings will hold full year of filler pages.

5 Books in 1:

1. Appointment Book
2. Work and Project Planner
3. "Tickler" Reminder
4. Diary/Time Record
5. Expense/Reimbursement Record

Here's What You Get:

- Full Year's Pages, beginning with any month.
- 12 monthly Calendar Index Pages with appointment squares and space for projects "To Be Done".
- 12 Monthly Expense Summary Pages including auto expenses and credit card charges.
- 6-Year Calendar Planning Pages.
- Address/Phone Directory.
- Notes and Memo Pages.

This Edition can start any month

ORDER FILLER WITH BINDER FIRST YEAR, THEREAFTER ORDER REFILLS ONLY

2 PAGES PER WEEK DESK EDITION	SENIOR SIZE (8½" x 11" Pages)				JUNIOR SIZE (5½" x 8½" Pages)			
FULL YEAR SET	Senior Refill Only	Senior Binder Only	Refill & Binder Combination Price Ea.	Refill & Binder Combination Prod. #	Junior Refill Only	Junior Binder Only	Refill & Binder Combination Price Ea.	Refill & Binder Combination Prod. #
Refill Only (without Binder)	$8.95	—	$ 8.95	D93010*	$7.95	—	$ 7.95	D91010*
with Supported Vinyl Binder†	8.95	$ 9.50	18.45	D9323C*	7.95	$ 9.50	17.45	D9123C*
with Hampshire Pigskin Binder†	8.95	23.50	32.45	D9324C*	7.95	18.50	26.45	D9124C*
with Western Coach Binder†	8.95	34.50	43.45	D9325C*	7.95	29.50	37.45	D9125C*

†**Available in Black, Brown or Burgundy.** (If color is not specified, Black will be sent.)

As low as $17.45 in Junior size with Supported Vinyl Binder

See Page A16 for additional Leather Binders.

* All Starred Items appearing on pages A3-15 may be combined for Quantity Discounts: 2-6 units, 5%; 7-12, 7%; 13-25, 10%; 26-50, 12%. Write for discounts on large quantities. 1981 & 1982 Diaries currently available. 1983 Diaries available after July 1, 1981.

DESK and POCKET DAY-TIMERS A15

3-57

Business-to-Business A look at this example from the Day-Timer catalog (Figure 3-57), shows that this one-item-to-a-page layout is particularly beneficial when a single item offers multiple benefits, or when a single product is made up of many components. The product shown in this particular layout, Desk/Day-Timer, is one of Day-Timer's basic products, the foundation of their line: a best-seller. The company is a major business supplier of calendar/planners and other desk accessories. It fills large multiple orders of this specific low-retail ($17.45) product and can therefore afford the exceptionally large space allotted.

Advantages	**Disadvantages**
Detail easily emphasized in both copy and art, affording the opportunity to relay to the customer all information for a buying decision; minimal "competition" between products; maximum space and attention allowed to each product in the catalog.	More difficult to achieve cost-effectiveness since one product must bring in enough sales to justify the cost of a full page; greater copy skill needed (long copy sometimes hard to keep lively and interesting).

An Exercise in the Use of Air

Figure 3-58 is an example of a double-page, art-separated-from-copy style layout from the Boston Proper that was created to position a maximum number of products in the space available. All of the product artwork falls within a grid which is almost square and occupies two-thirds of the double-page spread. Each photo is separated from the next by a thin white border which, because of its small size and light color, sometimes blends into the photos themselves, allowing the eye to become confused. The copy to the right is set fairly solidly, with very little space between each copy description block. A bright, attractive color (yellow) offers a nice background for the type and the connecting border encasing the product presentation. Overall, the art area has problems of confusion, clutter, and undefined product presentation. The copy also confuses the eye, because of type usage and poor use of air between copy blocks.

Now, let's see how subtle changes can help ease the appearance of this basically good double-page presentation. Without changing the grid design or deleting any items, we can make some improvements. Look at the altered example (Figure 3-59). Here the air between each frame has been slightly more than doubled (reducing the picture size somewhat), which helps the frames avoid running into each other. The air between each copy block has also been increased, relaxing the copy area and creating a greater desire to read it. (Seven copy lines have been deleted to achieve this, and the individual headlines for each copy block were set in all-caps.) The garlic bud jar and the grill have had their positions switched, so that the "busy" grill photo does not abut the "busy" orange juice squeezer. While these improvements are small, they would have a cumulative effect if accomplished on each of the 36 pages in this catalog. The viewer would have to work a little less hard on page after page, and the viewing eye would be more pleasantly satisfied.

Use air to avoid page clutter

These changes were all effected by the use of air. They are important not for aesthetics, but because a layout that looks cluttered can be harmful to sales volume. If the catalog readers experience confusion ending in boredom, they certainly are not going to give the merchandise the attention it might deserve. Sales

Smells Good! What's Cookin?

A. Sleek ivory toaster automatically adjusts from ⅜" to 1⅝" thick slices, including bagels. Cool wall construction prevents burning of fingers. Easy to clean.
Toast of the Town (3½"w x 6⅜"h x 15½"long), #B1091, **$39.95.**

B. For good measure, our five colorful porcelain measuring spoons. #B1029, **$11.00.**

C. The tickless timer. Our 2 hour quartz timer repeats an electronic beep for 2½ minutes. 2¼" sq. x ⅞"d. #B1135, **$20.00.**

D. A squeeze in the morning makes you feel great all day. Receive a bushel of juice laden Indian River oranges with the Mighty O.J., a manual juicer which uses a sturdy rack and pinion gear system to get virtually every drop of fresh juice from the orange with no seeds and just enough pulp. Polished chrome with baked enamel finish. 8" high with rubber feet to prevent slipping. To insure the tastiest oranges, orders will be shipped after Nov. 1. Please remember to order by Dec. 1 for a Christmas delivery. (Sorry, we cannot ship to Arizona, Alaska or Hawaii, or APO & FPO addresses.)
Mighty O.J. and Oranges, #BD1007, **$79.95.**

E. Knew you were comin' so I baked a cake. And displayed it in our 13" dia. cake stand of frosted and clear lucite.
Cake Stand, #B1099, **$50.00.**

F. Absorbent cotton dishtowels from India, 27" x 18".
Pasta Stripe, #B7591; **Happy Rainbow,** #B7592, **$11.25 each set of 3.**

G. Grill of my dreams. Our thermostatically controlled hot 'n toasty grills two golden-brown filled sandwiches in just minutes on a non-stick, non-stain surface. Features compact stand-up storage and over 70 recipes. 9" x 9" x 4½".
Hot 'n Toasty, #B1576, **$45.00.**

H. Your very own cookie jar of stoneware with a cork top and lead-free glaze. Be sure to order by Dec. 1 for a Christmas delivery. 7" dia. x 9" high.
Cookie Jar, #BD9536, **$35.00.**

J. Hold the garlic... in our glazed holder. Ventilated and dark to promote longer life to garlic and ginger root. 5"h x 5½"w.
Garlic Holder (from Design Imports), #B1095, **$16.50.**

K. Like you've never whisked before. Our rechargeable cordless electric whisk can do its job on 4 egg whites and 1 cup of heavy cream in 2 minutes flat. Dishwasher safe attachments store on a compact stand that also charges the whisk battery. The base charges for a full 35 minutes of rigorous whisking and has a comfortable, lightly-textured grip that won't slip off wet hands. 115 volt, 60 Hz motor. Measures 10½" x 5½" x 3½" and weighs 1¼ lbs. By Barbara Kafka.
Ready, Set, Whisk, #B1137, **$65.00.**

L. Grinds and brews while you snooze. Just put in the beans, pour in the water and set the timer to start when you wake in the morning. It programs easily for as much as 24 hours in advance, has dark and regular settings, and comes with a permanent stainless steel filter. The digital flourescent display shows the time of day, mill time and automatic start time. And the warming plate turns off automatically after 2 hours. 12½"h x 6½"d x 10½"w. 24 pg. recipe book included. From Toshiba.
My Café, #B1078, **$129.00.**

M. Pretty cotton quilt potholders, 8" square.
Rainbow Potholder (set of 3), #B1138, **$13.50.**

N. Best garlic press in the West. Just put peeled garlic cloves into the cylinder, insert the screw top and give it a little twist. It extrudes just enough fresh, rich garlic and stores the rest. Pop the whole thing into the refrigerator and don't worry about losing flavor and aroma. A tight-fitting cap seals it all up for the next zesty dish. Made of clear plastic and comes apart for easy cleaning. Approx. 6" high.
Garlic Machine, #B1136, **$15.00.**

12 13

3-58

cannot be made if the buyer's attention is lost. If you believe that your products or target audience demand the busy-layout philosophy, it is vital that you design this layout with care.

The major cause of page clutter is usually the dollar cost of catalog space. Seldom do art directors or grid designers say, "How little can I put on this page?" We all desire to use expensive catalog space efficiently, and most of the time this results in putting as many items on a page as possible, within the framework of the style of layout we choose.

Often the first thing that is considered dispensable is AIR: air around copy, air around artwork. But the *inclusion* of air accomplishes two things: (1) it *rests* the eye, and (2) it helps the eye to move. This means that the eye has a chance to relax between points of interest; therefore, the eye does not become exhausted and discouraged by its inability to instantly isolate elements. Conse-

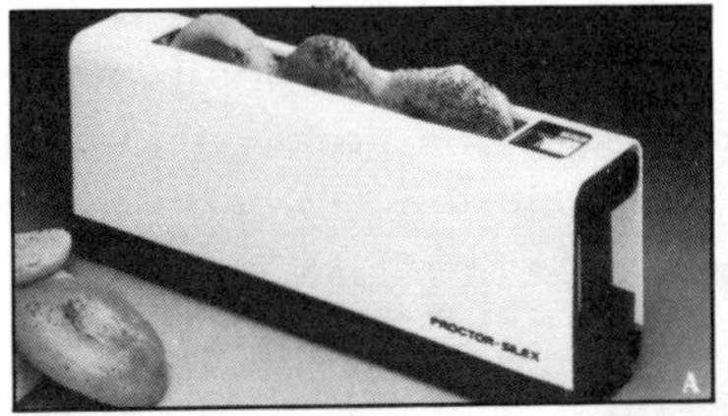

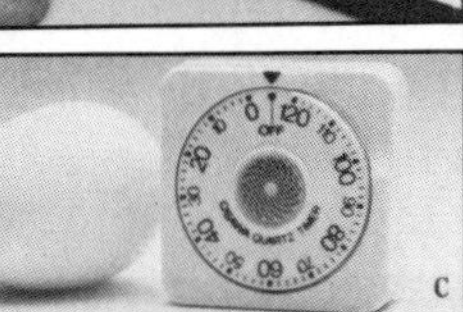

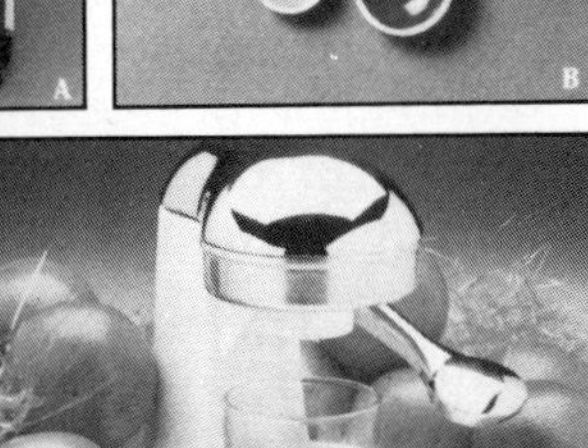

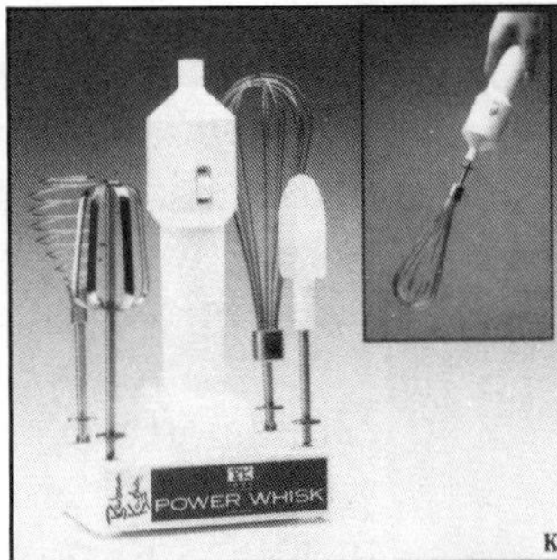

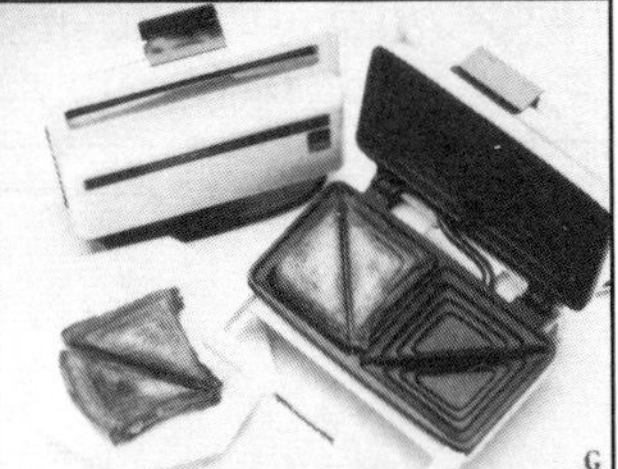

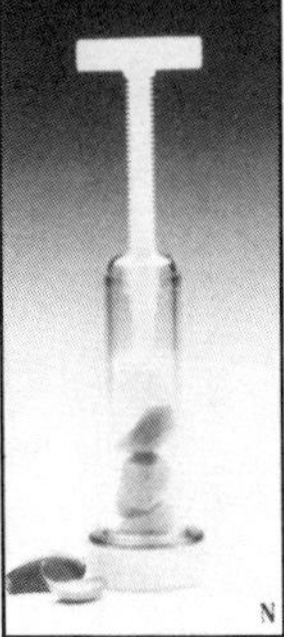

Smells Good! What's Cookin?

A. **SLEEK IVORY TOASTER** automatically adjusts from ⅜" to 1⅛" thick slices, including bagels. Cool wall construction prevents burning of fingers. Easy to clean. **Toast of the Town** (3½"w x 6⅜"h x 15½"long), #B1091, **$39.95.**

B. **FOR GOOD MEASURE,** our five colorful porcelain measuring spoons. #B1029, **$11.00.**

C. **THE TICKLESS TIMER.** Our 2 hour quartz timer repeats an electronic beep for 2½ minutes. 2¼" sq. x ⅞"d. #B1135, **$20.00.**

D. **A SQUEEZE IN THE MORNING** makes you feel great all day. Receive a bushel of Indian River oranges with the Mighty O.J., a manual juicer which uses a sturdy rack and pinion gear system to get virtually every drop of fresh juice from the orange with no seeds and just enough pulp. Polished chrome with baked enamel finish. 8" high with oranges, orders will be shipped after Nov. 1. Please remember to order by Dec. 1 for a Christmas delivery. Sorry, we cannot ship to Arizona, Alaska or Hawaii. **Mighty O.J. and Oranges,** #BD1007, **$79.95.**

E. **KNEW YOU WERE COMIN' SO I BAKED A CAKE.** And displayed it in our 13" dia. lucite cake stand. **Cake Stand,** #B1099, **$50.00.**

F. **ABSORBENT COTTON DISHTOWELS** from India, 27" x 18". **Pasta Stripe,** #B7591; **Happy Rainbow,** #B7592, **$11.25 each set of 3.**

G. **GRILL OF MY DREAMS.** thermostatically controlled hot 'n toasty grills two golden-brown filled sandwiches in compact stand-up storage and over 70 recipes. 9" x 9" x 4½". **Hot 'n Toasty,** #B1576, **$45.00.**

H. **YOUR VERY OWN COOKIE JAR** of stoneware with a cork. Christmas delivery. 7" dia. x 9" high. **Cookie Jar,** #BD9536, **$35.00.**

I. **HOLD THE GARLIC . . .** in our glazed holder. Ventilated and dark to promote longer life to garlic and ginger root. 5"h x 5½"w. **Garlic Holder** (from Design Imports), #B1095, **$16.50.**

K. **LIKE YOU'VE NEVER WHISKED BEFORE.** Our rechargeable cordless electric whisk can do its job on 4 egg whites and 1 cup of heavy cream in 2 minutes flat. Dishwasher safe attachments store on a compact stand that also charges the whisk battery. The base charges for a full 35 minutes textured grip that won't slip off wet hands. 115 volt, 60 Hz motor. Measures 10½" x 5½" x 3½" and weighs 1¼ lbs. By Barbara Kafka. **Ready, Set, Whisk,** #B1137, **$65.00.**

L. **GRINDS AND BREWS WHILE YOU SNOOZE.** Just put in the beans, pour in the water and set the timer to start when you wake in the morning. It programs easily for as much as 24 hours in advance, has dark and regular settings, and flourescent display shows the time of day, mill time and automatic start time. And the warming plate turns off automatically after 2 hours. 12½"h x 6½"d x 10½"w. 24 pg. recipe book included. From Toshiba. **My Café,** #B1078, **$129.00.**

M. **PRETTY COTTON QUILT POTHOLDERS,** 8" square. **Rainbow Potholder** (set of 3), #B1138, **$13.50.**

N. **BEST GARLIC PRESS IN THE WEST.** Just put peeled cloves into the cylinder, insert the screw top and give it a little twist. It extrudes just enough fresh, rich garlic and stores the rest. Pop the whole thing into the refrigerator and cap seals it all up for the next zesty dish. Made of clear plastic and comes apart for easy cleaning. Approx. 6" high. **Garlic Machine,** #B1136, **$15.00.**

3-59

quently, time is taken to view an item, and then desire to move along to the next item of interest occurs.

Too little air on a page discourages the eye's desire to travel, ending with the viewer saying: "This is too much for me; this clutter is boring." Conversely, too *much* air achieves the same end result via a different means: the viewer says, "This is too gappy; it's too much trouble to make my eye jump those gaps; what a boring thing to look at."

Though the foregoing illustration addresses a specific kind of layout, the philosophy of using air properly relates to every kind of layout that exists.

The style of layout you choose is an important decision for many reasons, but one of the most important is that it becomes an "identity" for your company. The recognition of *your* catalog's arrival is an important event for developing customer loyalty and shopping comfort. If customers are comfortable with your book, they're glad to shop there! For this reason, once you develop a style of layout, *stick with it*. If the style is truly successful for your customers, prospecting for new customers will cause similar kinds of people to respond to your book, and the growth of your customer list will fit a logical pattern.

In choosing your layout, give thought not just to the first catalog off the press, but also to your ability to continue to function within that format for subsequent books. Foresee the need to list products in more than one book. Do you want to make it easy to use the same photos and copy again? In many mail order catalogs, merchandise has a longer life than in retail establishments. This longevity, of course, depends on your product line. Do you want to have to redesign the layout of every catalog you produce (and would you have the time), or do you want the ability to work within a format that allows the repositioning of your particular ''standard-sized'' art and copy in each new catalog?

Inside Page Checklist:

- ☐ Determine Style of Format Best Suited.
- ☐ Review Key Sales Areas.
- ☐ Select Layout Approach.
- ☐ Determine Basic Page Design.

Always:

1. Consider customer convenience.
2. Consider individuality of product line.
3. Consider advantages of product comparison.
4. Choose the best approach for moving the customer through the catalog.
5. Understand your budget restrictions.

Strongly Consider:

1. Trying several of the basic approaches before making a final decision.
2. Choosing a layout approach you can live with always.

Chapter 4

Product Work Sessions

No matter how large or small your creative staff, you must gather them together for product work sessions. What are these and why bother? Product work sessions are meetings where your artists and copywriters meet with the merchandisers and buyers to review new products being placed in the catalog. This is likely to be the first time the artist and copywriter will have seen the product, and they will therefore need ample time for an in-depth introduction and to review each product. Why allow so much time when nobody ever has enough? The person who makes the selection decision knows why the product was chosen and why the product will appeal to a specific customer. This knowledge must be relayed to the art and copy people so they can present the product in its strongest light and so generate the greatest number of sales.

Remember, the most important factor for both art and copy is not the aesthetic self-satisfaction of design or poetry; it is the ability to attract and inform customers so they will purchase.

Prepare Ahead

There is a great deal to be done prior to any product work session if it is to be successful. Good merchandisers will have selected a product for a specific reason, not just because they liked it. Good buying decisions are based on some hard, proven guidelines. Therefore, it is the merchandiser's responsibility to bring these reasons and all backup material to the meeting. Here is a list of what to bring:

1. **Actual sample of the product** Preferably bring a production sample. If a prototype (a handmade product sample) is all you

have, watch out! Minor changes in style, function, or material may be made prior to actual manufacturing, and then art and copy will be incorrect and misleading. Following are just a few disasters that could result:

Don't use prototype sample

Art. The prototype sample may be. . .
(a) poorly put together and will not photograph well. *Consequence*: Art has little attraction. Sales suffer.
(b) or sometimes the prototype can be better or more functional. *Consequence*: Product misrepresented, quality and appearance may be disappointment when received.
(c) an incorrect color. *Consequence*: The product is misrepresented in photograph. Customers dissatisfied. Refund percentage will be higher than normal.
(d) not fully functional. *Consequence*: Art is unable to fully represent the product benefits. Sales lag.

Copy. The prototype sample may be. . .
(a) not representative of final color or colors. *Consequence*: Copy is unable to capitalize on color assets. Color choices are incorrectly given. Complaints run high.
(b) only visually correct, but performance is unclear. *Consequence:* Mechanics of product will not be fully described. Complete benefits are hazy. Copy is unable to "sell" customer.
(c) different in style or materials or size specifications from the final manufactured product. *Consequence*: Copy will be misrepresentative of the real product. Refunds will be high.

If you can't bring the product to the work session because of its size (computer, pool table, boat), try to schedule the creative people for a visit to the product.

2. **Art Clippings** Most products selected are already being run by someone else (your competitors). Gather competitors' presentations together for the creative people to view. You know the product is selling well by mail. Part of the reason for that is the clarity and purpose of your competitors' presentations. Your staff will want to learn and benefit from others' success. There may be many examples; bring them all. Mount them all on a piece of paper for easy comparison of selling points. Include any magazine or newspaper ads. If the manufacturer has furnished a photo, bring that, too, even though it will most likely not be used.

3. **Copy Clippings** These may or may not be included with the photos. Mounting copy separately will make it easier for everyone to study, and the mounted copy will ultimately be

given to the assigned copywriter. Much of the copy will be from competitors' catalogs but may also be from magazine and newspaper ads and from manufacturers.

4. **Testing Results** By the time a product has made it to the work session, it should have been fully tested. Merchandisers should have tested it themselves or assigned the testing to someone else to make sure the product is valid. Following are three areas of testing which help generate information your art and copy people need to know:

   (a) *Will the product do what the manufacturer claims? Example*: The manufacturer of a child's highchair makes specific safety claims. The chair should be tested to prove or disprove the claims. Catalogers can run their own tests or ask a consumer group or parents' organization to test for them. These groups are highly critical and will give the claims a thorough test.

   (b) *Is the product quality up to your company specifications? Example*: When listing quilted fabrics, test to see if they are washable. Will they bleed or shrink? Test to see if the fabrics are wrinkle-resistant. Your customer needs to know.

   (c) *Packaging . . . Will the item be delivered to your customer in good shape? Example*: You don't want your package to arrive broken open and badly dented with the item crushed. Ship a sample to a person in another state and ask this person to tell you the condition of the package when it arrives. If the item does not arrive intact, you have a quality problem with your packaging. *Note*: Be prepared to eliminate an item or two from your inventory line when you follow this procedure.

Test your own catalog products

5. **Manufacturer's Information** A product information form (see chapter 3 for a fuller explanation) should have been filled in by the manufacturer on each product being listed. It will tell what the product is made of, the colors, dimensions, etc. Additional information sheets may also be supplied by the manufacturer. Claims documentation should be provided. *Example*: The grower claims a dwarf fruit tree will bear full-size fruit. Obviously you cannot test in time for your next catalog. Ask the grower for documentation of the claim. All legitimate companies which have products such as plants, gas savers, nonallergenic items, and so on must have test documentation to back their claims. State or federal laws generally require this proof. (Ask your lawyer!)

6. **Merchandiser's Notes** The marriage of merchandise and market occurred the moment the buyer decided a specific product should be listed in your catalog. Why? Because products are selected for specific reasons having to do with customer wants, needs, and previous buying records. All buyers know what it is about any given product that will attract the customer, and therefore they know what must be described clearly. These are the types of facts and feelings which the artist and copywriter will benefit from — and so will sales.

(Merchandiser leads product work sessions)

The major individual responsible for this material is not the art director, not the copy chief, and not the creative coordinator. It is the merchandiser. The merchandiser (or buyer) is the one who knows *why the product was selected*. The art director and copy chief are the people who know how to channel the customer's attention in the direction you want *once they know what that direction is*. But do not let them choose the direction (though this does not mean they cannot contribute to it). The merchandiser has chosen the product and bears the ultimate responsibility for its sales.

How To Conduct a Product Work Session That Results in Sales!

Product work sessions are where you make the decisions on how to present products which will appear in your catalog. This is where you decide:

1. Why the customer will buy the item,
2. How to present it with photography (or artwork),
3. What to say about it in the copy description.

This is where the merchandiser orchestrates facts and presents the reasons the product was selected so the artist and copywriter can blend their interpretive and creative skills into a winning sales combination.

And since nobody knows the product and the reasons for its selection better than the merchandiser, this is the person who leads the product work session. The merchandiser comes armed with all of the material just discussed: samples, art clippings, copy clippings, test results, selection facts, and manufacturer's information.

The merchandiser should start the session by furnishing those attending with a list of products to be reviewed in that session. Then a sample of the first product to be discussed should be passed around so all can look at it, feel it, handle it.

The first area to discuss is "why the product was selected." Reasons for selecting an item frequently fall into the categories listed below. The merchandiser should be able to discuss the reasons fully from notes made when selecting the product. Use these as a check list of information which needs to be known by the creative staff in order for them to gear their presentations properly.

1. **Is the product UNIQUE?** Is the concept of this product new; does it have a feature never before offered; does it perform a new service? Unique qualities are powerful selling tools because they are not easy for customers to find.

2. **Is the product RARE?** Is the product not easily found in retail stores? This is a main benefit of shopping by mail, don't forget. If the product is a service, is it difficult to find or render? Will the offer be limited? Remember, it's human nature to want something that is hard to get.

3. **What BENEFITS does the product offer the customer?** Is it beauty, service, value, function, utility, or a combination? The more benefits, the better the sales. But generally one main benefit is promoted to focus the item in the customer's mind, with other benefits mentioned subsidiarily. If too many benefits are vying for attention, the presentation is usually diluted.

4. **Does the product SOLVE PROBLEMS?** Does it help stop a pipe from leaking, firm the muscles, make a job easier, tell how to do something? Customers need items that solve problems for them.

5. **Does the product have EGO APPEAL?** Will owning this product make customers the envy of their associates? Will it compliment masculinity or femininity? Ego is a strong sales element.

6. **Does the product make life more EFFICIENT?** Will it simplify the customer's life via organization? Can the product promise to make extra room in the kitchen? Will it make memos easier and faster to send for business customers? Will the purchase mean that the customer's budget, time, work day can be organized more efficiently? Will it save money?

7. **Does the product have a special PRICING? Does it have pocketbook VALUE?** Is this product priced more attractively than a competitor's item? Can it be offered at a bargain?

Discussing these reasons for selection will help focus on a main art and copy element: *where and how the product is used*. In the office, the home, a factory, a workshop? Customers will not purchase a product unless they can find a use relating to their own needs. (Don't forget that this use can even be "ego.") Some products may have a specifically defined area of use; others may have three or four areas where the product can be placed or several ways it can be used. Again, avoid confusing the customer. Present a main area and allow other areas to be secondary.

The second area to review is the merchandiser's art visualization and copy headline visualization.

1. **Art visualization**. How did the merchandiser visualize the product in the catalog when selecting it? A good merchandiser will have pictured the catalog presentation of the product as part of the selection process. Even if the image is hazy, discussion of the visualized impact will help trigger the artist's creativity and final composition.

2. **Copy Headline Visualization**. What were the words or the headline the merchandiser thought of when selecting the products? Headline visualization is often more prolific than art. The merchandiser's thoughts will be valuable to the copywriter, who will polish and add to that initial thought.

In-Use Photography

Remember: Your customers LOOK before they read. So, be sure to emphasize the visual.

Len Carlson
Los Angeles, CA

Next, the group should discuss the sales history (if any) of the product. The merchandiser might very well have selected the product for one of the following reasons:

1. **Proven sales by competitors**. The product may have run in one or more competitors' catalogs several times or may have appeared in space advertising. If run more than once, it is likely to be a good seller.

2. **Similarity to other good sellers**. The product may have been chosen because of another product which is very like it or whose function is very similar within your own product line.

3. **Revival of an old product**. A product which sold well several years ago but was dropped because of discontinuance, interrupted manufacturing, or slow sales may be worth listing again. Or a product may be cyclical in sales popularity and its time has come around again.

Know why product was selected

Art and copy clippings should now be reviewed. Peruse clippings of successful ads (your own or your competitors'). Discuss the main effect created by the artwork. What main element is emphasized? Is the product clearly shown? Which benefits are visually presented? From what angle was the shot taken? Be cautious if your creative staff wishes to take a different (especially a drastically different) approach. Remember, the product was chosen because of successful sales, and the art and copy you are viewing helped create that success. If your present product is slightly different, you must discuss whether or not the new product will benefit from the same approach.

In the area of copy, notice the kind of headline which was used previously. Notice the reasons and benefits the body copy gives for purchasing the product. Analyze the order in which those reasons are given to the customer. If you are viewing a competitor's copy, discuss how to apply your catalog image to the competitor's copy point. But again remember, the copy you are looking at has proven itself successful.

Check out the competition

Don't ever decide upon your art and copy presentation before viewing existing presentations. Competitor research is a powerful sales tool. Even the most innovative approach is built upon an accumulation of past knowledge. Thorough observation, inspection, and analysis of your catalog marketing competition gives you a basis upon which to make judgments. You may decide to ''imitate'' with a similar presentation, or your viewing may inspire an entirely new approach which may be even better. Though you cannot argue with someone else's success, there is still room for your own approach. If you're just beginning your first catalog, it's vital to watch others. And if you're an already successful cataloger, watching others will help guarantee continuing success. The need for careful observation never ends.

Competitor Analysis Exercise

Here is an example of the way you and your creative staff would use a product work session to analyze presentations created by others. Start with the premise that you want to see the results achieved by their efforts. (A competitor who has repeated a listing no doubt has a successful product, and his art and copy have aided that success.) Let's look at five different presentations of the same product and see what we can discern from them.

Example One This illustration from Taylor Gifts shows an embosser sitting on a book. (Figure 4-1)

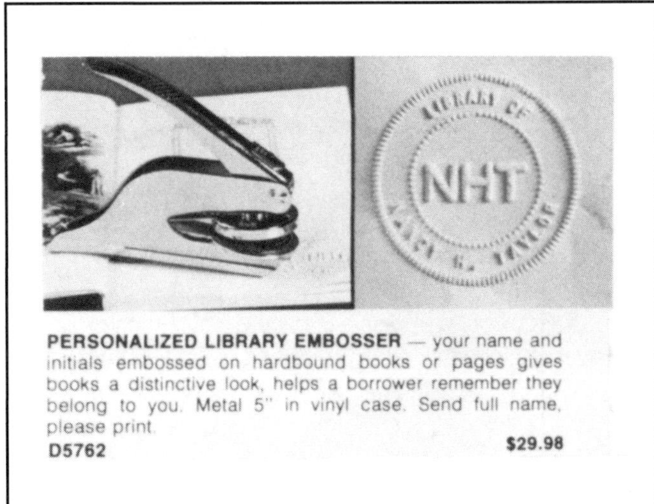

NHT
PERSONALIZED LIBRARY EMBOSSER — your name and initials embossed on hardbound books or pages gives books a distinctive look, helps a borrower remember they belong to you. Metal 5" in vinyl case. Send full name, please print.
D5762
$29.98

4-1

Art. The background is light, which does not accent the embosser. Was the book placement necessary, since the blow-up of the seal shows detail explicitly and it clearly says, ''Library of''? Or does the book act as an instant identifier of where the product is designed to be used?

Copy. The copy headline states, ''Personalized Library Embosser.'' The body copy states the location where the product can be used, but not the object it can be used on. Elsewhere in the copy, no details are given as to the actual size of the embossing, whether or not there are letter limitations on the length of name the customer can order, or how the embosser operates (by hand compression). Also, hardbound books are the only suggested use, unnecessarily excluding the possibility of paperbacks. The copy does provide a relatively unnecessary detail, ''Metal, 5 inches,'' and adds that the product comes in a vinyl case (not shown in the photo).

Example Two The next illustration is from the Bruce Bolind catalog. (Figure 4-2)

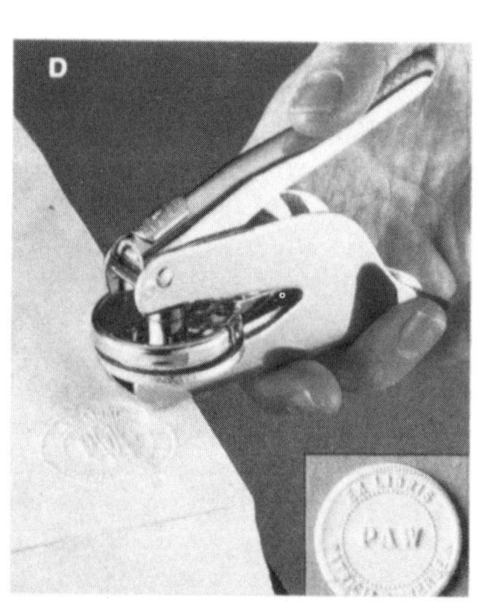

D. Book Embosser. Just like the libraries use. Personalizes books. 1½" diameter seal with "EX LIBRIS (name)" and 3 initials in center. 5" long.
Monogram (*underline* last initial) **#D2969A $29.95**
Block Initials (see insert) **#D2969B $19.95**

4-2

Art. The photo visually implies that the embosser has just completed the operation of embossing, because it shows the item in someone's hand with an embossed page immediately underneath. The dark background allows the light metal to stand out clearly. A small inset shows the actual embossing in detail.

Copy. The headline "Book Embosser" identifies where the product is to be used and what it does. The copy is minimal but states the diameter of the seal, and the price lines let the customer know that both a monogrammed style and a block initial style are available.

Example Three Joan Cook has chosen a different approach. (Figure 4-3)

Art. The angle of the photography is different, this time more from the position of the user. Is it better? The functional part of the embosser leads away from the viewer's eyes. The inset showing the seal is in the line of the embosser and therefore fairly prominent, but not large enough or clear enough to show the details well (thus diluting the main purpose of an inset). The highlights and shadows picked up allow the item to stand out from the light background. An art headline has been added, stating the main purpose of the product: "Personalize Your Books."

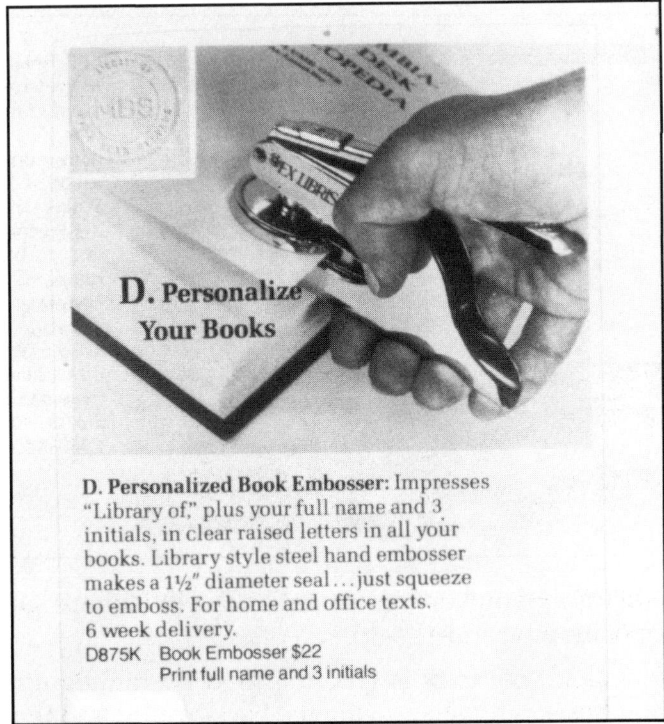

EX LIBRIS
D. Personalize
Your Books
D. Personalized Book Embosser: Impresses "Library of," plus your full name and 3 initials, in clear raised letters in all your books. Library style steel hand embosser makes a 1½" diameter seal...just squeeze to emboss. For home and office texts.
6 week delivery.
D875K Book Embosser $22
Print full name and 3 initials

4-3

Copy. The copy block headline clearly identifies the product: "Personalized Book Embosser." The copy goes on to explain the workings ("Impresses 'Library of'") and what personalization is furnished ("plus your full name and three initials") and mentions "raised" letters, to make the function very clear. It also mentions the size of the seal and that it is made of metal. It does not mention letter limitation but does mention delivery time.

Example Four Pennsylvania Station tries yet another approach. (Figure 4-4)

Art. The vinyl case has been added to the illustration. This catalog house has chosen a side-on view of a hand actually embossing. The seal has been brought up in size to a large inset for easy design identification. Was it necessary to show the product twice, or did doing so only add to presentation clutter?

Copy. The headline attempts to attract interest with uplifting wording ("Scholarly Seal"), but instead it achieved only vagueness. The size of the embossing is stated plus the reason for purchasing the product: "identifies your books." A full description of what is embossed is given and there is a clear request for information ("Send exact name and up to three initials"), but no letter limitation is given. Delivery delay notification is clear, too, although reversed copy makes it hard to read.

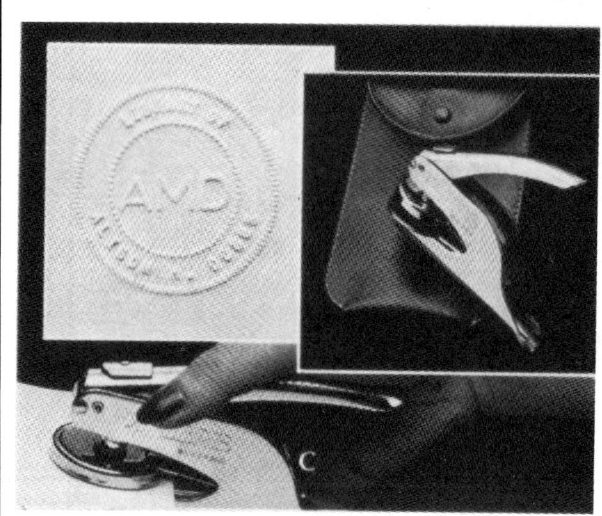

C. Scholarly Seal. Impressive 1½" personal embossing seal identifies your books with indisputable proof of ownership. Seal is stamped with the legend "Library of . . .". We add your full name around the perimeter and your initials in the center. Send exact name and up to 3 initials. Allow six weeks for delivery, please. C940890D, $20.00.

4-4

Example Five Henniker's presentation is a little more sophisticated in composition. (Figure 4-5)

Art. Good contrast is accomplished by highlighting the embosser and shadowing the background and the rest of the photo. The working part of the embosser is angled for easy viewing, but details are lost because of shadowing. Background props (book, stamps, glasses), which are wonderful aids in product identification, are also lost in shadowing. In an attempt to simplify the photo by eliminating an inset, the photographer has shown the embossing on stationery on which the embosser lies. Does the message get across? The art headline (''A Gift For The Person Who Has Everything!'') is hard to read because of thick-thin reversed type. The accompanying line drawing to the right of the photo is meant to identify the 15 design choices available but fails because of loss of detail.

Bring out details

Copy. Here there are different embossing choices and a two-step ordering method: ''The order card arrives with the embosser that we send you! Then simply designate the design(s) you want and send in the order.'' The copy becomes more complicated because the selling job is more

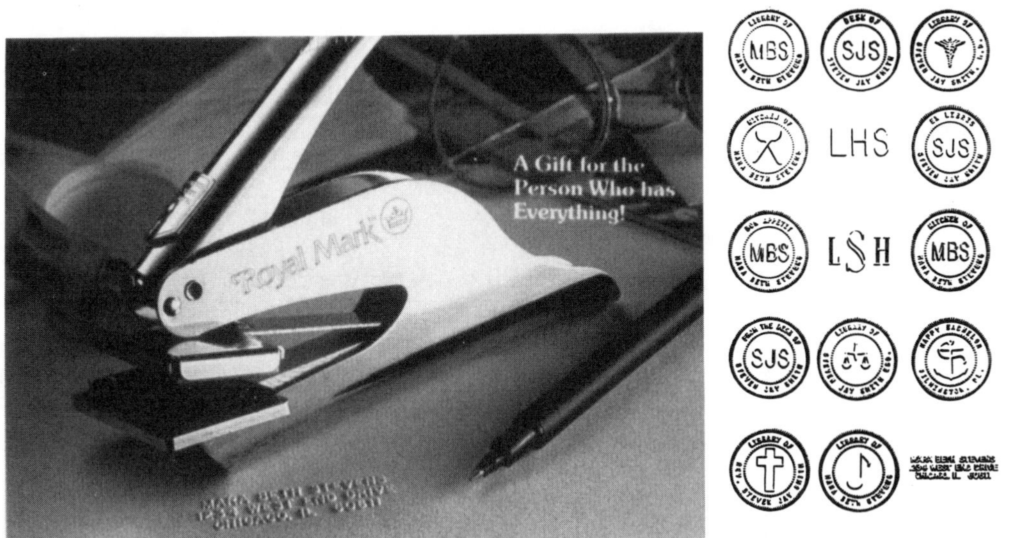

Choose Your Own Embossing! Pick One or Pick Them All!

We'll send you the basic embosser and then it's up to you to select from this wonderful variety of designs...everything from the "the library of"...to "Bon Apetit"...and with the center design of your choice: doctor, lawyer, sailor, religious, monogram, etc. A very creative item that will be multi-purpose. If you order different dies, you'll be able to emboss your books, your memos, your recipe cards, your stationery, etc. The order card arrives with the embosser that we send you! Then simply designate the design(s) you want and send in the order. Same embosser accommodates all dies...so it's a versatile and unique gift you won't want to be without! All steel construction, nothing to wear out or breakdown.
#23277 Embosser $21.95 (2.10)

4-5

complicated. A light approach is taken in the headline: ''Choose Your Own Embossing! Pick One or Pick Them All!'' The copy continues the lightness but comes off as indecisive with ''If you order'' instead of *when* you order; ''it's up to you to select'' instead of *just* or *simply* select; and so forth. The dimension of the die is not given. Nowhere is it mentioned that your name or initials are added for individual personalization!

After reviewing these five examples, what knowledge have we gained for our own presentation?

Art/Copy Checklist

Art. ■ Show contrast between product and background so product will stand out. (Bruce Bolind, Pennsylvania Station, Joan Cook).

■ Bring an example of the embossing up close for the customer to view. This is most easily accomplished by an inset. (Taylor Gifts, Pennsylvania Station).

■ Consider showing the product in use so the customer can easily relate. (Bruce Bolind, Joan Cook, Pennsylvania Station).

■ Consider having props which are easily identifiable and help explain the product function. (Taylor Gifts, Bruce Bolind, Joan Cook).

■ Consider an art headine which helps to identify product benefit. (Joan Cook).

Copy. ■ Make headline identify product or product benefit. (Bruce Bolind, Joan Cook).

■ Inform the customer of product benefit — personal book identification — in body copy. (Taylor Gifts, Bruce Bolind, Joan Cook, Pennsylvania Station).

■ Emphasize individual personalization appeal (ego) — ''your name'' for identification. (Taylor Gifts, Joan Cook, Pennsylvania Station).

■ Consider giving letter limitations for full name or initials. However, the actual limitation may be well over the number of letters in an average name, and refunding of the few exceptions may be better than using catalog space and possibly discouraging sales. (Bruce Bolind, Joan Cook, Pennsylvania Station).

■ Inform the customer of delayed delivery (for FTC compliance, see chapter 10) due to drop shipping and thus avoid informing after ordering if need arises. (Joan Cook, Pennsylvania Station).

■ Mention that a case is included, to enhance product, if space allows. (Taylor Gifts).

Pitfalls can be avoided if you look at other art/copy presentations. If you want a product photo background of book pages, you now know that the problem of making the light-colored item stand out from the light-colored background can be handled by photographic lighting. If you're using an inset, you'll realize that the lighting must be appropriate to make the embossing dominant, and the inset must be large enough to serve its purpose. Your copywriters are now alerted to the inclusion of all the facts. This is important. The omission of letter limitations could necessitate refunds, and this means loss of sales, internal processing expense, plus disheartened customers whose long names cannot be accommodated.

This embosser is not a complicated product to show. But many questions have been raised about the optimum presentation. Five catalogers have shown it differently. There's no doubt about it — your competition is one of your best "helpers" for doing a better job. Examined thoroughly, their art and copy will help you decide upon the best presentation for your book. Even if the product has never before been listed in mail order, it is still helpful to view presentations of similar items, both from competitors' books and your own.

There are two important facts always to remember:

1. The easier the product and its benefit are to identify, the greater product sales will be because of customer ease.
2. Competitors have repeated the product listing because of its success, based on proven art and copy presentation.

Now is the time to discuss testing results.

Granted, the product should not have gotten to this stage if it was faulty, below quality standards, or just no good. But during testing, you might have discovered exceptional ease of use, for example, and this might be a very important feature to emphasize. The mobility of an office table might be outstanding and provide expanded use the manufacturer neglected to emphasize. Product sizing may have to be clarified in copy or actually adjusted in referencing because of the manufacturer's nonconformity to normal or standard sizing. The copywriter should be extremely aggressive in questioning the testing phase so all the pluses and minuses are known.

Next, discuss the manufacturer's information.

You will need promotional sheets, wholesale catalog pages, photographs, clippings, claim documentation, warranties, field testing results, and a completed request for product information originated by your company. The completed product information form should answer questions for art and copy production and for retail pricing and also provide information for other areas in the company such as warehousing and purchasing. Complete answers should be provided for the following areas:

1. **THE SUPPLIER** (1) Company name, address, phone. (2) Person to contact, title. (3) Area marketing rep, phone. (4) Credit references.

   Tip: Large companies have regional, state, or local representatives with which to deal, but a greater discount may be realized if these are bypassed. However, a rep *can* help with delivery problems.

2. **THE PRODUCT** (1) Stock number, name of product. (2) Country of origin. (3) Dimensions, inches, ounces. (4) Materials: wood, metal. (5) Intrinsic details, such as UL listings, battery-operated, etc. (6) Sizes and colors available, percent of sales in each category.

   Tip: The stock number is the key for suppliers' processing; use it for speedier transactions. An import may need to be ordered early. Such things as materials or components are essential for catalog description. Knowing the mix of percent of sales helps you to project quantity needs and decide on which colors to list. (Drop the low sellers.)

Specify all information

3. **PRICING AND DROP SHIPPING** (1) Recommended price. (2) Cost each, quantity cost breaks. (3) Is product pre-priced; dollar amount. (4) How about a "guaranteed sales" deal? (5) Is drop shipping available? At what cost?

   Tip: The supplier may consider total quantity ordered during the life of your catalog for quantity discounts — ask! Pre-pricing can be a problem — ask if it can be deleted. You can avoid overstock with "guaranteed sales," but the product will cost more. When the supplier drop ships to your customer, you save costs of warehousing, freight, and overstock.

4. **PACKAGING** (1) Master shipping carton quantity. (2) Weight of master carton. (3) Individual packaging: display, bulk, poly bag, individual mailer.

   Tip: Suppliers prefer shipping full cartons; if shipping less, costs may be more. Display packaging crushes easily when mailed; a poly bag is less costly and may work as well.

5. **SHIPPING AND TERMS** (1) FOB point. (2) Shipping point. (3) Payment terms. (4) Freight allowance.

   Tip: Who pays the freight? Will terms or allowances help keep your costs down?

6. **AVAILABILITY** (1) Is item in stock; if not, when? (2) Is supply continuous, or are there seasonal lows? (3) What is normal on-hand supply? (4) How long will it take to ship after receipt of order?

Tip: Be sure the product is actually manufactured and in stock before cataloging. If you don't, you may find yourself refunding all orders.

7. **ADVERTISING AND PRODUCTION** (1) How many samples do you want? (2) How about a glossy photo or transparency? (3) Any supplier contributions toward cost of art and copy? (4) Any advertising allowances?
   Tip: Get enough samples for evaluation, testing, art, copy. If you're cataloging plants or food, the manufacturer often has a transparency you'll want to use. Many will contribute to photography costs. Some will pay an advertising allowance upon proof of publication — ask!

8. **PRODUCT SALES EXPERIENCE** (1) Any previous sales in mail order, and with whom? (Ask for a clipping.) (2) If product is sold in media, ask for a copy of advertisements. (3) Ask for company sales literature.
   Tip: Never miss a chance to see how the product has been previously presented. Get as much sales history as you can. Art and copy samples will help with your catalog presentation.

Miscellaneous Tips: (1) Ask about other items offered by the company; don't ever miss a chance to find new products. (2) State your mail order status on the form to indicate your need for jobber discounts and price protection once an item is catalogued. (3) Ask about product warranty protection on defective merchandise. Bona fide sources will tell you the amount of liability they carry. Use this protection if needed; it will keep your own insurance payments down. (4) Allow a space for the signature of an officer of the source company; it's more binding than a rep's.

Be sure to recap the main points which will make your customer purchase, so that the art and copy direction is clear. Because of the energy needed to profitably benefit from product work sessions, limit the number of products to be reviewed at one time. Overload and limited-time concentration are enemies of any long meeting, so break up the number of products to be reviewed into groups of 10 to 12 per meeting. You will be rewarded with quality art and copy presentation.

Product work sessions are vital to the success of your mail order catalog. This is where it all comes together: your merchandise, your market, and the creative approach that makes the sale!

Product Presentation

Your photos are critical. *A customer cannot touch your product, feel it, weigh it and hold it in his hands the way he can in a store. You have to show him all these things in your photos if he is going to buy from you.*

Scott Ashley
Annie's Attic
Big Sandy, TX

Don't overload product work sessions

Product Work Session Checklist:

Prepare Ahead

- ☐ Acquire Actual Product Sample.
- ☐ Gather Competitor Catalog/ Media Art Samples.
- ☐ Gather Competitor Catalog/ Media Copy Samples.
- ☐ Gather Similar Product Art and Copy Samples.
- ☐ Test Product.
- ☐ Acquire Manufacturer Information.
- ☐ Have List of Merchandiser/ Buyer Comments.

Actual Meeting

- ☐ Have Merchandiser Conduct Meeting.
- ☐ Have All Buyers Responsible for Product Selection Attend.
- ☐ Have Design and Layout Artists Responsible for Presentation Attend.
- ☐ Have Copywriter Responsible for Product Copy Attend.

Always:

1. Present actual production sample.
2. Review reasons for product selection.
3. Review competitor art presentations.
4. Review competitor copy descriptions.
5. Review merchandiser/buyer's art visualization.
6. Review merchandiser/buyer's copy headline visualization.
7. Review testing results.
8. Review manufacturer's information.

Strongly Consider:

1. Trying the product yourself or having your artist and copywriter do so to further understand the product.

Chapter 5

Photography and Art . . . What role do they play?

To Attract the Customer's Attention—*Again*

Ours is a visual world. We see before we can talk. We learn to depend on "looking" as a major factor in the process of making a decision. Color, forms, scenes, things in visual form attract our attention. The role of photography and art is to visually attract the customer's attention. The front and back cover both need to attract the customer's attention so your catalog will be singled out from all the rest. Each product must also attract the customer's attention so it may vie for its share of the almighty dollar and justify the space it occupies. How do you go about this visual feat? Whom do you turn to for help?

Where to Start?

Earlier, in Chapter 3, we talked about determining an approach. By now you should know what image you want to convey. If it is a value image, the front and back covers must signal this fact to the customer. Inside, your product photos will need to have this same flavor. This does not mean that quality should be sacrificed; it merely means that more elegant settings and presentations may not be needed or desired because the "value" message may not get across. On the other hand, an elegant and dramatic presentation may be just what you want if you are selling high-priced furs, jewels, or cruises. Almost always, photography is the means by which your image is conveyed. Therefore, *it's important to have the right photographer for your specific product line.*

How to Find the Photographer for You

You're looking for several important characteristics in one person: know-how, talent, and an ability to carry on a meaningful dialogue with you and your creative staff. If the photographers you're considering are missing any one of these three basics, you'll not get the kind of end result you want and need.

Use these guidelines when making your search for a photographer:

1. Look at portfolios. Viewing samples of photographers' work is a fast way to gain an impression of their talents, know-how, and specialties (for example, as photographers of high fashion, kitchen items, or industrial work). The best portfolios will present the original prints and transparencies, as well as the printed end results; and if all these are included, it will tell you much about the photographers' common sense and how much confidence you can place in each candidate's abilities. If the portfolios include sample catalogs, ask which specific photographs you should consider. Frequently, catalogs are shot by more than one photographer. Don't be swayed or dismayed by the total graphic impression of the printed piece you are viewing, since the quality of paper, graphic design, and other elements contribute to the total. Try to confine your analysis to each photographer's work itself.

2. Ask for and INVESTIGATE references. The portfolios will suggest things about the photographers' skills and talent, but references will help you assess on-the-job working relationships. Talk to people who've worked with the photographers. Ask about their speed and ability to meet deadlines. Inquire about their attitudes toward revisions or changes. Try to assess their communication skills and talent for working with others.

3. Question their workload. Will they really have the time to do your job? Ask how much volume each photographer can handle. Do they have a staff who will be helping, perhaps even taking some of your shots under their guidance? You must feel confident that the one you choose will not be too overloaded to accomplish your job in the time period important to you. You may also wish to anticipate their ability to grow with you as your business grows.

4. What support services can they furnish. Do the photographers have access to models, props, and sets? Do they process their own film, furnish retouching or stripping services? Areas such as these will affect the quality of work and your job's outcome.

If you are expecting them to furnish photo layout services (to-size sketches of the desired presentation), be specific. Though you may have a catalog layout, you may not be creating a layout for each item. Discuss how the photographers will expect you to convey the direction you want each shot to take. This will give you a good idea about how they work and will help ensure that the images produced will satisfy you.

5. Assess their ability to communicate with more than a camera. Telling your story on film is vital, but it usually cannot be accomplished if you and your creative staff cannot communicate with your photographer. Ask your candidates if you will be dealing directly with them when giving direction and instructions, or if you will be talking with someone on their staff. Try to look beyond photography into areas such as the style you're trying to achieve. Do the candidate photographers have a "feel" for what you're trying to sell and how you're trying to sell it?

Learn photographers' language

Because photography is a specialized field, it has its own special terminology, with which you may not be familiar. Learning to speak the photographers' language is important to you because it helps you communicate on common ground. Even if you think you know the meaning of some words your photographers are using, ask. A word as simple as "silhouette" can also be defined by the terms "outline," "C.O.B." (crop out background), and "dropout." They all mean an image to be printed without a background. So as you develop a relationship with your photographers, also be aware that it is important to define your terms (and theirs).

6. Are they willing to do a test or "spec" photograph? How far are they willing to go to get your business and show you how they work? Will they test photograph a sample product? Are they willing to photograph an item to the specifications you've furnished in a layout? Most photographers are willing to invest a little time and materials to prove they can produce what you want.

Depending on your needs, you may have to use more than one photographer. If you have a large product line or short schedules, you've got a good reason for more than one photographer. If your product line is extremely diverse in content, you may need one photographer who specializes in food shots and another who works with clothing and models. Photographers tend to be specialists, but a good catalog photographer must have the ability to do all things well. If you use several photographers, you must be sure that their styles are similar so that your catalog has a consistent, uniform look. Background materials and lighting techniques may have to be coordinated, in tonal qualities, among the different photographers shooting your book.

7. Establish charges. This isn't as obvious as it sounds. A simple $100 (or $1,000) per shot may seem straightforward, but can become a real bone of contention between photographer and cataloger. Misunderstandings don't usually arise over creative fees. But photographers charge for other services, and it's important to establish what those charges are.

For example, whose responsibility is it to pick up (or return) products to be photographed? Will review sessions between client and photographer be charged for? Who assembles products or touches them up in order to make them photograph properly? Suppose the photographer has to wait for products to be altered or delivered. Who pays for the reshot when it occurs because you, the cataloger, have changed your mind? (Photographers should absorb reshot costs when the error is theirs.)

If the photographer you are thinking of engaging is not specific about these areas, ask. If you don't, you risk receiving *less* than the job you expect, and paying *more* for it.

This kind of investigation into photographers' ability and style of working not only lets you assess whether or not they fit into your catalog image, but also defines the role and functions they will be performing in your particular organization. And remember, no matter how well your catalog is printed, nor how good the paper might be, the physical end result never will be better than the excellence of your art and photography.

Be an Effective Communicator

While you may have found the perfect photographer, the responsibility of direction still remains with you. And you will need material at your disposal to help you be effective in your direction. There are two main strategies which will help you know what you want and help you convey what you want to the photographer.

1. Competitor Clip Files. Back in Chapter 4, Product Work Sessions, we explained how to watch your competitors and the advantages of doing so. Now, all the art which you clipped and saved from your most interesting competitors is going to help you in the photography and art area. Even though product sketches "to-size" (the exact size which will appear in the catalog) should have resulted from the product work session, your competitors' art will be beneficial when you're talking to the photographer. Perhaps the lighting is especially good or maybe the background color compliments the product nicely. Or the product positioning or props could be undesirable. The photographer will want to know! By having something to show your photographer, you can be more certain the desired message will be understood.

2. General Clipping File. This file should consist of all catalogs, magazines, space ads from newspapers, trade journals, manufacturers' catalogs — anything that you like or dislike in product presentation. The products pictured need not be those in your product line. The importance of this file is to show effect, technique, and approach so you can easily convey your likes and dislikes to the photographer.

Look at successful catalog presentations

Now when you're reviewing each product with your photographer, you'll be able to indicate that you want "a background like this," or "an angle like that," or "lighting like this photo, not like that one." It's important, by the way, to have a sample of each product available for your photographer to see in advance of the shooting session. An item you may feel is "camera ready" may not fulfill the photographer's criteria. You may think that a prototype product sample with the logo pasted onto it is going to "blend in," but the photographer may know that this prototype status will be very apparent in the final photo. Be sure to listen to what the photographer has to say. This person's a professional and will have suggestions on how to present your merchandise or achieve the look you're after.

When we're putting together a catalog, our thoughts are naturally involved with the products that are going to be housed within the catalog. We are concerned about how to present them, finding the best photographer or artist to make them appear appealing to the customer. But we need to give careful consideration to what is going to happen on the front and back covers.

Chapter 3 should have given you information which helped you to decide what type of cover is best for your catalog. Now you have the job of creating a visually commanding cover that will *get the customer inside* where the action of buying occurs.

Front Cover Art and Photography

How can you get the most qualified attention with your cover? What approach will be best? Should you use products you sell? Would the customer be attracted more with an appealing country or city scene? Can stock photos be successfully used? Would a studio shot work better? All of these questions and more should be going through your mind when you plan your front cover. Some answers can be provided once the decision on approach has been made.

In Chapter 3 we discussed the three basic approaches to the front cover: (1) dramatic; (2) product line identification; and (3) sales/benefit. Once a direction is chosen, it will be easier for you to decide which method of presentation is the best. There are four basic options:

1. Studio shooting
2. Location shooting
3. Stock photos
4. Art illustration

Studio Shooting

Studio shooting is the most commonly used method. The reason is that the photographer can shoot a plain, unadorned shot of a product, a dramatically effective shot of products or objects, or simulate a setting which is indicative of the character of the products. In studio shots, the photographer has more control over lighting, wind, and rain, and studio shooting is generally less expensive than location and complicated art illustrations or renderings. A photographer or studio specializing in kitchen or other in-the-house room shots will have studio sets built for continual use: a built-in bathtub for shower products, a kitchen for kitchen products, a bedroom for bedroom products, and so on.

The Horchow catalog utilizes studio photography. Figure 5-1 is a dramatically commanding shot playing on the effect of objects and lighting. The objects, an antique Chinese plate and medicine bottle, are offered for sale inside but are not referenced. The artist's calligraphy brush is used for a dramatic accent. Figure 5-2 is another studio shot from a different Horchow catalog. This time, more products which are offered for sale inside are used to create an inviting setting. Both covers represent the upscale gift type of products carried inside and the upscale customer enjoyed by Horchow. The depth and feel of the photographs were achieved by a skilled photographer in a controlled studio environment.

Figure 5-3 is the cover of A Touch of Class, a catalog specializing in products for the bedroom. The photograph looks like a grand bedroom. It is, of course, a studio shot taken in a special room set built for multi-uses. (The same set is used for another bedroom setting inside the catalog.) This is an example of utilizing studio photography which appears to be photographed in its natural area of use.

Advantages	**Disadvantages**
Controlled atmosphere allows exacting lighting; weather not a bothersome factor; minimal costs.	Realism sometimes lost, thereby lessening credibility; aesthetic appeal sometimes minimized.

HORCHOW
THE HORCHOW COLLECTION
Early Fall 1984

5-1

Roger
Carolyn
Elizabeth
HORCHOW
THE HORCHOW COLLECTION
July-August 1984

5-2

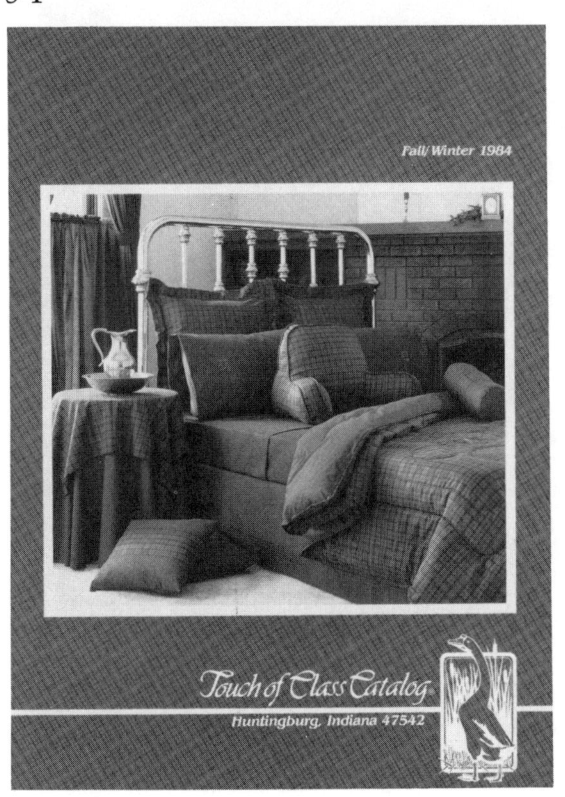
Fall/Winter 1984
Touch of Class Catalog
Huntingburg, Indiana 47542

5-3

Location Shooting

Location shooting is the most glamorous sounding. This is where the photographer, client, and entourage take off to some near or distant place to "shoot" the cover and maybe some inside product shots, too. Needless to say, it is also the most expensive. The cost of travel and accommodations on top of the time for the photographer and other needed personnel quickly becomes exorbitant and (usually) prohibitive to the budget. However, results can be very effective.

The Early Winters catalog specializes in outdoor gear. Their customers order tents, clothing, backpacks, cooking gear, and other products to help them meet and enjoy the challenge of the outdoors. In order to transmit the message of product durability, convenience,

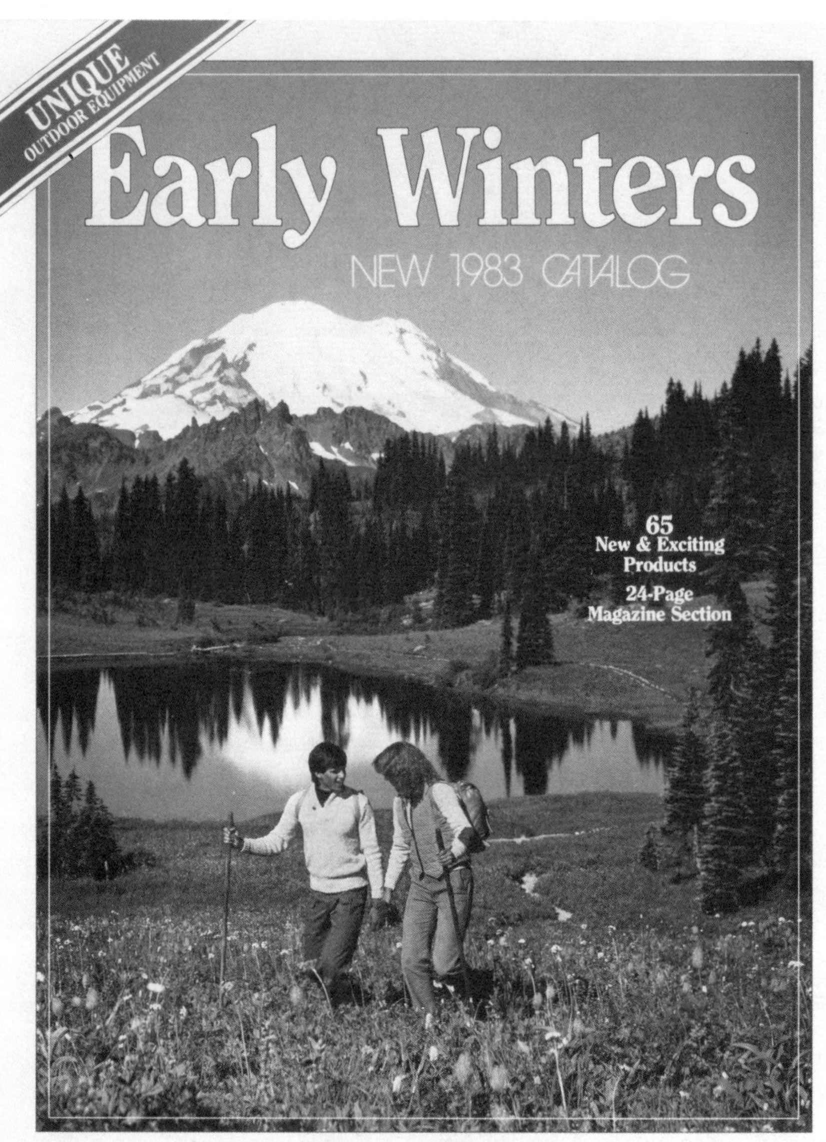

5-4

and enjoyment, Early Winters goes on location to shoot the front cover and various inside product shots. Figure 5-4 is a typical front cover. The location may be the North Selkirk Mountains of British Columbia, the islands of Barkley Sound, Carmel, Sierra, or Catalina Island.

Jean Grayson's Brownstone Studio specializes in women's vacation and career apparel. A recent issue takes the customer on a visit to Portugal. The cover (Figure 5-5) is at dockside in Obrigado, Portugal. The cover is not the only glimpse of this country seen in the catalog; inside are over 60 different product shots utilizing Portugal's beaches, ports, and countryside for background and theme carrythrough.

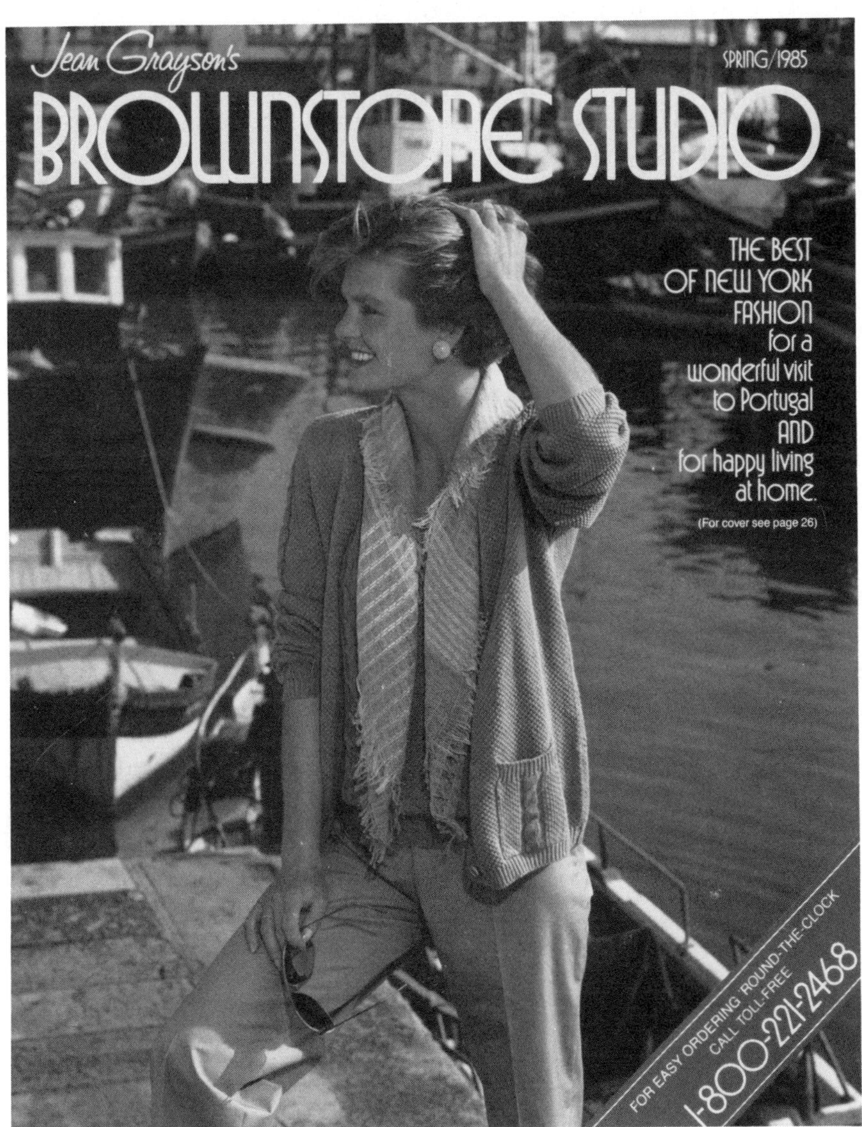

5-5

Twelve Hints For Location Shooting

1. Does a location's atmosphere *compliment the merchandise?* Will the product setting have an *important* effect on the customer's *perception of the merchandise quantity?*

2. *Does the setting suggest what the merchandise will look like when used by the customer? Does the setting enhance the believability* of the item or product?

3. *Stay as close to home as possible.* Plan the location to fit the seasons. Shoot summer shots in the south or southwest when it is winter in the north.

4. Consider cost and *plan every shot in as much detail as possible BEFORE you leave.*

5. *Shoot studio shots* concurrently with location shooting. Location photography is not an "add-on" to your schedule, but should "mesh" with it.

6. Know the ability of the photographer and *how many shots he can shoot in one day.* An expensive photographer who can shoot faster may be cheaper than one who appears less expensive but is slower.

7. Take along the support people (stylists, makeup artists and assistants) who are needed *so shots can be set up and broken down in a reasonable time frame.*

8. Hire local models. They go home at night and save on hotel bills and transportation costs.

9. Scout locations and finalize layouts before the day of shooting. Schedule in detail *so everything needed is possible in the time it takes to set up and shoot.* Nothing is worse than having to hunt for locations as models stand around, or send for items that are not on location when needed.

10. Work with travel agencies that can give you a *package deal.*

11. *Consider the weather* and anticipate problems which could arise from it.

12. *Negotiate cancel dates* with your photographers before you hire them. Allowances must be made for possible sickness, bad weather, or accidents; non-penalty cancel-dates must be understood.

Advantages	Disadvantages
Greater product appreciation because of natural setting; heightened product credibility; theme carry-through sometimes more realistic; heightened aesthetic effect.	Weather an interfering and troublesome factor (delays due to poor weather conditions); high costs due to travel, accommodations; difficulty in controlling photographic elements, such as lighting.

Stock Photos

Stock photos are many times the way to go if a certain feeling or effect is wanted when time, money, or skill will not allow otherwise. There are companies whose business is shooting pictures of different subjects for use by individuals and companies for a dollar fee. Many times the quality of the shot is very good, both in composition and reproduction aspects. When a certain subject is desired, such as a fall country scene showing the orange, gold, and red leaves depicting the season of the year, or an attractive, wholesome young woman meant to represent the typical catalog customer, the stock photo companies may offer the best choice. Let's say you want that fall scene. Get in touch with several stock photo companies so you will have a good range of pictures to choose from. They will send a selection to you. Some companies charge for this service, but the charge will be minimal. You will then be able to sit down with your artist and choose the photo which suits your needs best. And you will be able to judge the technical quality of the photograph for print reproduction — even consulting your printer if needed.

Work with more than one company

Figure 5-6 is a typical cover of a Walter Drake catalog. This catalog carries low-end gift merchandise and appeals to the middle-aged, middle-class woman of America. The wholesome attractiveness of the subject reflects this audience but eliminates the need for a photo of a particular product. The artist has taken the photo and designed a "cover-frame" around it.

Figure 5-7 is the cover of The Institute of Human Development. The products for sale are tapes and other products relating to self-development. The hot air balloons represent adventure and discovery, concepts difficult to convey with product photos.

If you become a regular customer of stock photo companies, they will tell you when they are going on shooting assignments pertaining to the subject you are interested in and will shoot some spec shots for you. If you don't have an on-staff photographer and if you don't use your own products on the cover, utilizing stock photos can be economical as well as satisfying.

5-6

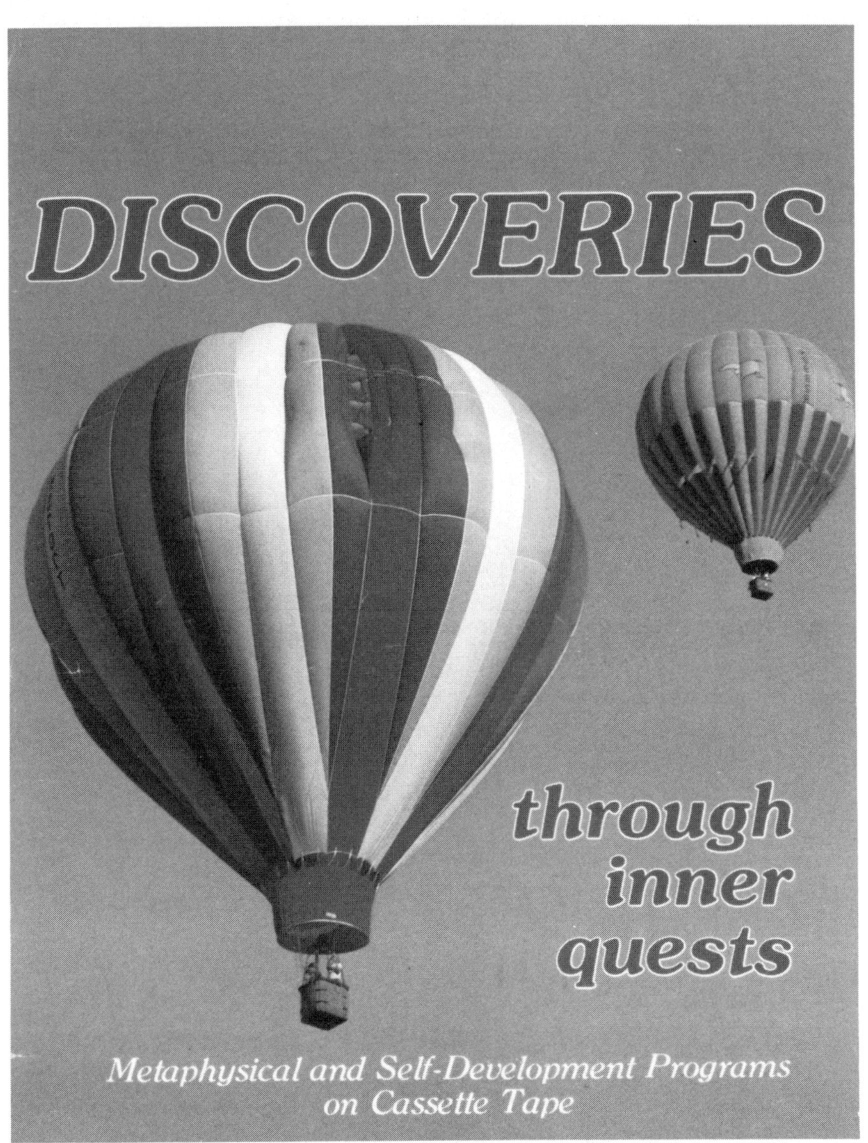

DISCOVERIES
through inner quests
Metaphysical and Self-Development Programs on Cassette Tape

5-7

Advantages
Large choice of subject matter; consistently good quality of photographs; low costs.

Disadvantages
Individual catalog personality sometimes lost; commercial and stilted appearance likely if selection process not carefully done.

Art Illustration

Product detail emphasized

Art illustration is the least utilized technique for catalog covers. Why? Most catalogers show products on the cover and they feel that photography displays them better and makes the visual message more believable. But illustration many times will make the catalog stand out from all the others received because it looks different. And an illustration can project the desired image, create the proper mood, and identify the category of product, as well as illustrate products realistically and in a desirable fashion.

The Brooks Brothers clothing catalog uses an old-fashioned scene (Figure 5-8) for a front cover illustration, thus giving the feeling of traditional stability and old-fashioned quality and service. Their cover focuses on clothing; they focus on a feeling — that of a privileged class in a romantic era.

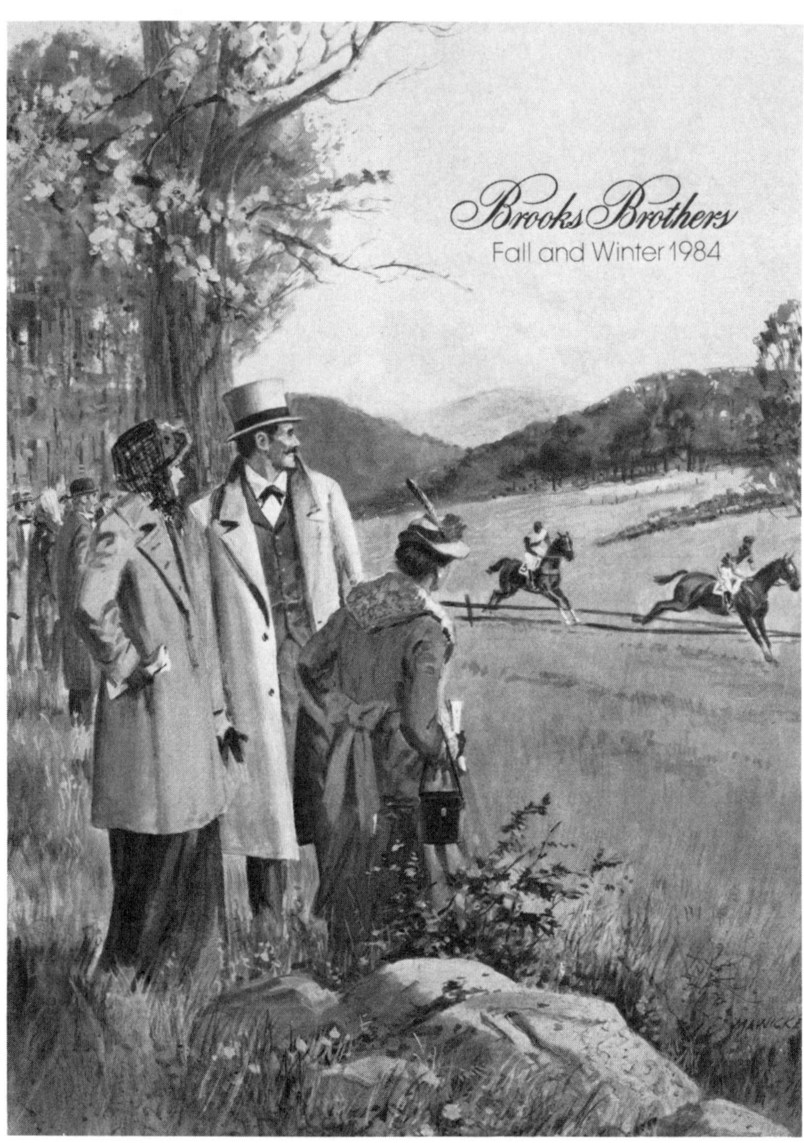

5-8

The Lands' End catalog (Figure 5-9) bears a watercolor wash which illustrates seven products carried inside. The lightness and freedom of the artist's technique and design create an appeal which carries you inside the catalog.

Figure 5-10 is the cover of the Banana Republic catalog. All of the paraphernalia (and more) piled on the boat dock can be found inside. The artist has created a feeling of anticipation, one of pending adventure. The customer wants to look inside to find out more.

5-9

5-10

All three of these general consumer catalog covers are appealing, individually calling attention to the catalog. The traditional appeal of a Brooks Brothers cover is representative of the clothing found inside — herringbone sports jackets, fur felt hats, oxford shirts. Lands' End's free and easy painting of casual clothes does, of course, tell what's to be seen inside, but it also creates the desire to ride along in a delightful, relaxing mood. The Banana Republic cover has not only created a traveling mood with the penciled dock and boat presentation, but has also qualified the customer's interest with clothing which appears inside — the overall golden hue of the drawing contributes to the prevailing feeling of a safari adventure.

Business-to-business catalogs make use of original art illustrations, too. The Business Book (Figure 5-11) uses an old-fashioned line drawing reproduced in brown to suggest tradition and dependability — just as Brooks Brothers created the same feeling with four-color watercolor. Dependability and service are important for a company to convey, especially when selling imprinted office forms, stationery, and office accessories.

The Developmental Learning Materials catalog (Figure 5-12) selling student instructional materials to teachers uses a beautiful watercolor painting of three young students on its cover. The customer receiving the catalog immediately relates to the students. The painting becomes an appreciated attention-getter.

The message of fast service, in-stock inventorying, plus a large selection of plant and warehouse furniture and equipment (as seen in Figure 5-13) is immediately transmitted with C&H Distributors' acrylic art rendering cover. An hourglass denoting time with a multitude of products carried and a prominent ''24 hour in-stock shipping'' message strategically placed in the middle of it gets all the information across better than a photograph could. By designing the illustration so it is off to the left side, the cover artist has left ample and proportionate room for printed information. Art illustra-

5-11

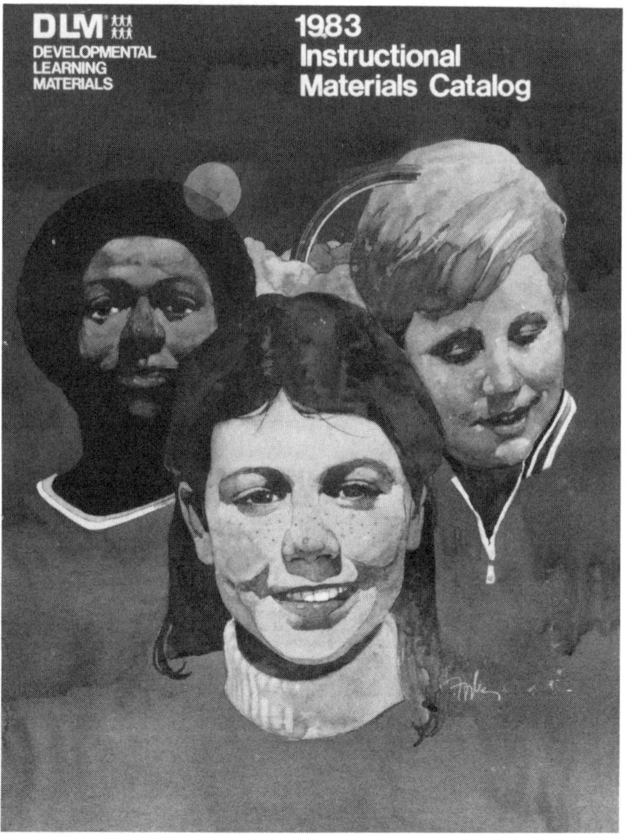

5-12

tion definitely has a different look and can many times convey just the image and message needed. And it will stand out from all the other catalog covers because it does indeed look different.

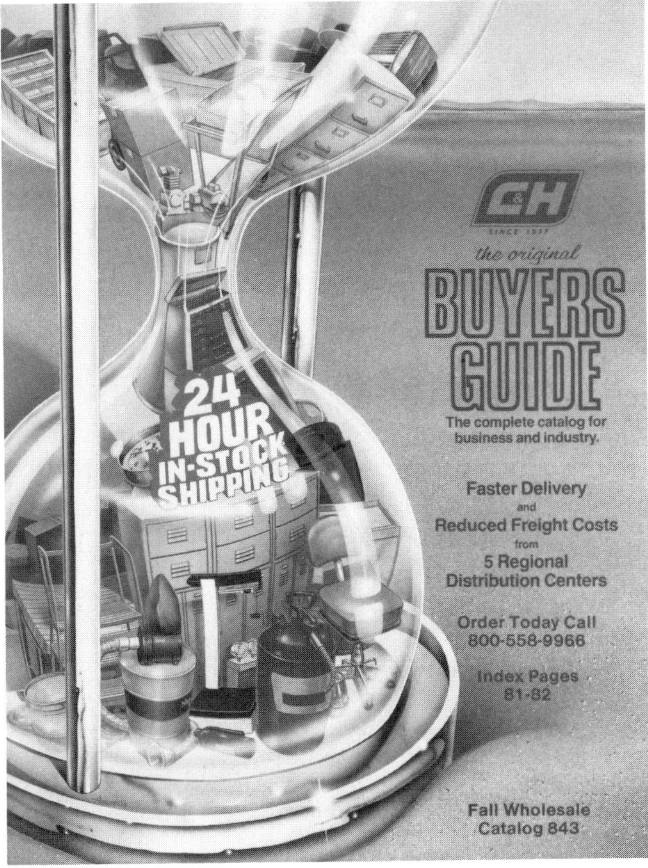

5-13

Advantages	**Disadvantages**
A different look for greater attention; easier emphasis on a desired area or mood; sometimes lower costs than photography; possibility of using cover design for product design, too.	Possible loss of realistic look; possible questioning of credibility if product or image carelessly distorted.

With these four options of approach available, there is no reason a good attention-getting cover can't be done. Meet with your artist — get the copy people in on the meeting too. It's important to have a good cover, so spend some time considering your options.

Front Cover Checklist:

- ☐ Define Approach To Take.
- ☐ Review Clip Files for Ideas.
- ☐ Decide Method of Creative Execution.
- ☐ Select Photographer.
- ☐ Select Artist.
- ☐ Consider Budget.

Always:

1. Consider your customers' tastes.
2. Consider using stock photos.
3. Consider going with an approach you can stay with and become recognized for.

Strongly Consider:

1. A separate and specialized photographer for cover shots.

Back Cover Photography

This always called-upon and often taken-for-granted space, the back cover, must be given every consideration in a photography and art planning session. As noted in Chapter 3, the back cover area must play many roles. From being an official carrier of the customer's name and address, the required postal indicia, and the catalog company's name and address to selling products, directing the customer inside, informing the customer of ease and convenience and playing the all-important role of attracting the customer's attention — that's a tall order! What can photography and art do to help fulfill this large and varied role?

theme carryover

Once the approach has been decided, the layout artist must give a lot of thought to how to deal with all of the elements to successfully execute an attention-getting plan which will meet address panel requirements, too.

If a dramatically inviting setting is chosen, the layout artist may wish to carry the feeling and visual image over onto the back cover. As an example of studio shooting, we looked at a Horchow cover that displayed products related to entertaining in one's home. Crystal, china, and place cards were invitingly positioned on a linen tablecloth and accented with fresh produce. Figure 5-14 shows how the setting was carried over on the back cover by simply extending the photograph. The required address panel elements, indicia and address label, are applied over the photograph. A panel to the left gives ordering, pricing, mailing list policy, and disclaimer information. A business-to-business catalog utilizing a similar approach is C&H Distributors, which we looked at earlier. The yellow-peach background color is carried over for the back cover background color, too. The front cover art approach is utilized in the upper lefthand corner (Figure 5-15). The artwork, a semi truck, bears the company logo and visually denotes the fast service guarantee stated alongside.

The approach most commonly used for a back cover is to treat it as a separate page whose job it is to bear the customer's name and address and to sell products and promote company services and policies. Typical back covers are seen in Figures 5-16, 5-17, 5-18, and 5-19.

Figure 5-16 is the back cover of L.L. Bean with photographs of two products sold only on the back cover of this specific catalog. The products are photographed the same as if they were for sale on an inside page.

Figure 5-17, Brooks Brothers' short sleeve pullover shirts were photographed especially for the back cover. Even though the general feeling and approach is the same as for inside product photos, this photograph is a horizontal shot, while all of the inside pages are

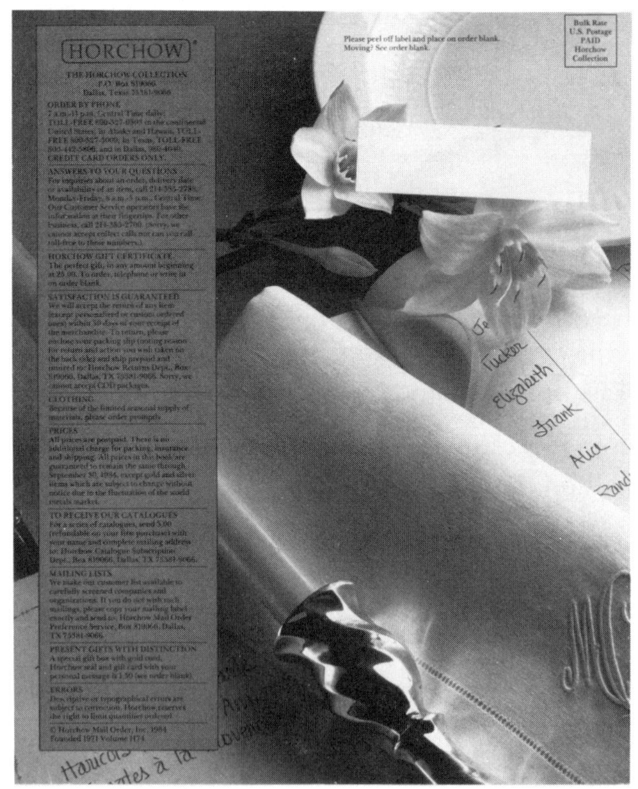

HORCHOW
THE HORCHOW COLLECTION
Please peel off label and place on order blank. Moving? See order blank.
Bulk Rate U.S. Postage PAID Horchow Collection

5-14

CH
Q.S.C. PROGRAM
Exclusive with C&H! When you place an order for any C&H compressor on our Q.S.C. Program, we guarantee that the compressor will be on its way to you within 24 hours or C&H will pay the freight!
EXTRA BONUS!
MAGNETIC MOTOR STARTER
BIG SAVINGS ON TOP QUALITY COMPRESSORS
25 HP UNIT
$4731.00 COMPLETE!*
SAVE 45%
Fully Accessorized, Ready to Go!
Outstanding Features for Long Service
$4731.00
5 FULL SERVICE DISTRIBUTION CENTERS
★ATLANTA (404) 524-6106
★DALLAS (214) 988-0830
★EDISON, NJ (201) 287-3888
★MILWAUKEE (414) 271-2250
★RENO (702) 356-0132
TELEX 26-687
CALL 800-558-9966
Thousands Of Items In Stock . . . Ready To Ship Within 24 Hours!
C&H DISTRIBUTORS, INC.
400 S. Fifth Street
P.O. Box 04499
Milwaukee, Wisconsin 53204
CATALOG 843

5-15

Bean Jean Jacket
Made of the same 14 oz. indigo-dyed cotton denim used in our jeans. Rugged and good looking, jacket gains character as it is worn. Lined with the same warm 100% cotton flannel as our Scotch Plaid Shirts. Collar is faced with soft 100% cotton corduroy to protect neck against chafing. Western styling with two button-flap chest pockets and two handwarmer pockets. Button cuffs and six-button front placket. Double-needle stitching throughout. Machine Wash (tumble dry medium).
Men's model has straight yoke, squared pockets and adjustable waist tab closures. Weight 2 lbs. 4 oz.
Men's even sizes: 36to46. Length about 23".
1462J Men's Bean Jean Jacket, $46.00 ppd.
Women's model has chevron yoke and rounded pockets. Weight 1 lb. 7 oz. Length about 23".
Women's even sizes: 6to16.
4566J Women's Bean Jean Jacket, $42.00 ppd.
To place an order call:
207-865-3111
We are here 24 hours each day, seven days a week.
Bean's® Blucher Moccasin
(For Men, Women and Boys)
Oil-tanned, smooth-grain uppers. True moccasin construction with hand sewed toe piece. Blucher style lacing for snug fit at heel and arch. Durable traction design rubber sole with molded arch support for walking comfort. Color: Brown.
Men's whole and half sizes: 6to13 Narrow, Medium and Wide (no size 12½). Weight about 2 lbs. a pair.
3421J Men's Blucher Moccasin, $46.25 postpaid.
Women's whole and half sizes: 5to10 Narrow and Medium. Weight about 1 lb. 8 oz. a pair.
4817J Women's Blucher Moccasin, $42.75 postpaid.
Boy's whole and half sizes: 1to6 Medium. Weight about 1 lb. 4 oz. a pair.
4818J Boy's Blucher Moccasin, $29.75 postpaid.
L. L. Bean, Inc.
Freeport, ME 04033
Order Telephone 207-865-3111
24 Hours — 7 Days
Please Deliver to Current Resident
BULK RATE U.S. POSTAGE PAID L. L. Bean, Inc.
72 L. L. Bean, Inc. Freeport, Me. 04033

5-16

Brooks Brothers
346 MADISON AVENUE, NEW YORK, N.Y. 10017
BULK RATE
U.S. POSTAGE
PAID
BROOKS BROTHERS
TELEPHONE
YOUR ORDER
CALL
TOLL FREE
1-800-
247-1000
000861
3DG
C7000
LOU SMITH
119 VIA VALLECITO
MANITOU SPRINGS
CO 80829
Men's Golden Fleece
A. A Brooks Brothers classic, this short sleeve mesh knit pullover of cotton-and-polyester embroidered with our famous Golden Fleece. Coral, royal blue, red, navy, white, bright green, wine or yellow. Small, medium, large or extra large. C333, $24 ($2.45).

5-17

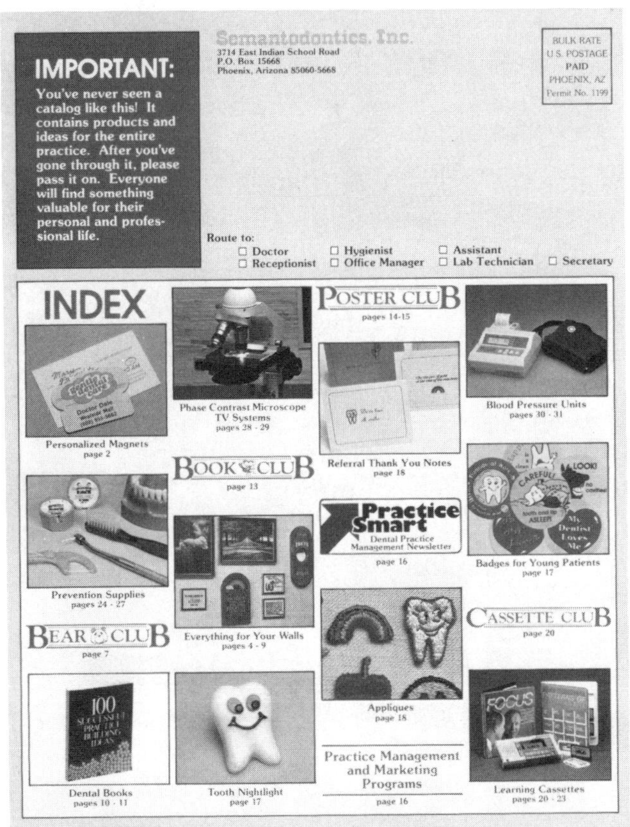
IMPORTANT:
You've never seen a catalog like this! It contains products and ideas for the entire practice. After you've gone through it, please pass it on. Everyone will find something valuable for their personal and professional life.
Semantodontics, Inc.
3714 East Indian School Road
P.O. Box 15668
Phoenix, Arizona 85060-5668
BULK RATE
U.S. POSTAGE
PAID
PHOENIX, AZ
Permit No. 1199
Route to:
☐ Doctor ☐ Hygienist ☐ Assistant
☐ Receptionist ☐ Office Manager ☐ Lab Technician ☐ Secretary
INDEX
Personalized Magnets
page 2
Phase Contrast Microscope TV Systems
pages 28 - 29
POSTER CLUB
pages 14-15
Blood Pressure Units
pages 30 - 31
BOOK CLUB
page 13
Referral Thank You Notes
page 18
Prevention Supplies
pages 24 - 27
Practice Smart
Dental Practice Management Newsletter
page 16
Badges for Young Patients
page 17
BEAR CLUB
page 7
Everything for Your Walls
pages 4 - 9
CASSETTE CLUB
page 20
Appliques
page 18
Dental Books
pages 10 - 11
Tooth Nightlight
page 17
Practice Management and Marketing Programs
page 16
Learning Cassettes
pages 20 - 23

5-18

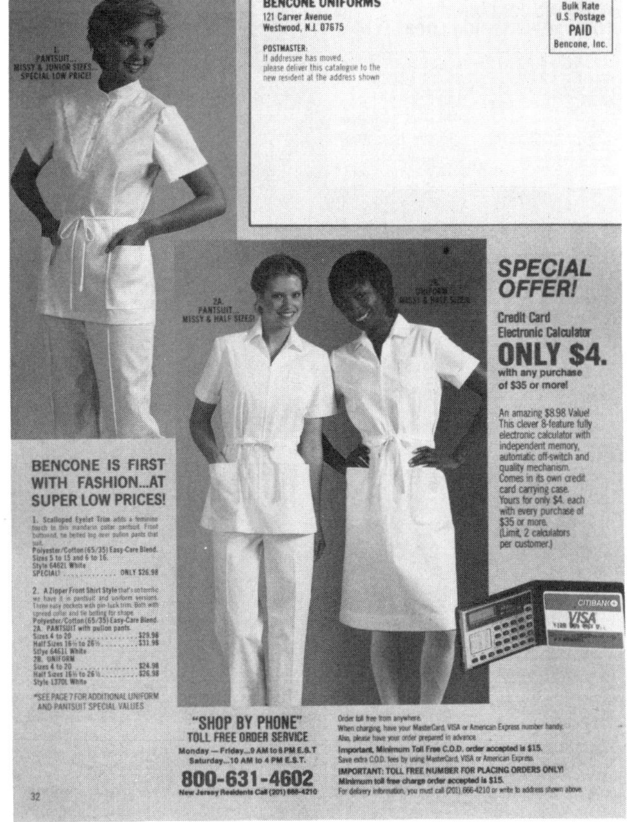
BENCONE UNIFORMS
121 Carver Avenue
Westwood, N.J. 07675
POSTMASTER:
If addressee has moved,
please deliver this catalogue to the
new resident at the address shown
Bulk Rate
U.S. Postage
PAID
Bencone, Inc.
1.
PANTSUIT...
MISSY & JUNIOR SIZES...
SPECIAL LOW PRICE!
2A.
PANTSUIT...
MISSY & HALF SIZES!
SPECIAL OFFER!
Credit Card
Electronic Calculator
ONLY $4.
with any purchase
of $35 or more!
An amazing $8.98 Value! This clever 8-feature fully electronic calculator with independent memory, automatic off-switch and quality mechanism. Comes in its own credit card carrying case. Yours for only $4. each with every purchase of $35 or more. (Limit, 2 calculators per customer.)
BENCONE IS FIRST WITH FASHION...AT SUPER LOW PRICES!
Polyester/Cotton (65/35) Easy-Care Blend.
Sizes 5 to 15 and 6 to 16.
Style 6462L White
SPECIAL! ONLY $26.98
Polyester/Cotton (65/35) Easy-Care Blend.
2A. PANTSUIT with pullon pants.
Sizes 4 to 20 $29.98
Half Sizes 16½ to 26½ $31.98
Style 6461L White
2B. UNIFORM
Sizes 4 to 20 $24.98
Half Sizes 16½ to 26½ $26.98
Style 1370L White
*SEE PAGE 7 FOR ADDITIONAL UNIFORM AND PANTSUIT SPECIAL VALUES
"SHOP BY PHONE"
TOLL FREE ORDER SERVICE
Monday — Friday...9 AM to 8 PM E.S.T
Saturday...10 AM to 4 PM E.S.T.
800-631-4602
New Jersey Residents Call (201) 666-4210
Order toll free from anywhere.
When charging, have your MasterCard, VISA or American Express number handy.
Also, please have your order prepared in advance.
Important, Minimum Toll Free C.O.D. order accepted is $15.
Save extra C.O.D. fees by using MasterCard, VISA or American Express.
IMPORTANT: TOLL FREE NUMBER FOR PLACING ORDERS ONLY!
Minimum toll free charge order accepted is $15.
For delivery information, you must call (201) 666-4210 or write to address shown above.
32

5-19

presented vertically. Notice how well planned the positioning of the shirts is in order to show the product well and provide the desired room for the company name and address and the customer name and address.

Semantodontics, a business-to-business catalog whose customers are dentists, uses a combination of product photos. (See Figure 5-18.) Some photos are the same as used inside, like the dental book and blood pressure unit. Others are croppings of a larger inside photograph ("Everything for your walls"), some are appliques, while still others are original photographs (learning cassettes and prevention supplies).

The back cover from Bencone Uniforms (Figure 5-19) uses photographs which are typical of inside product photos. Yet the products on the back cover are not sold inside this catalog issue.

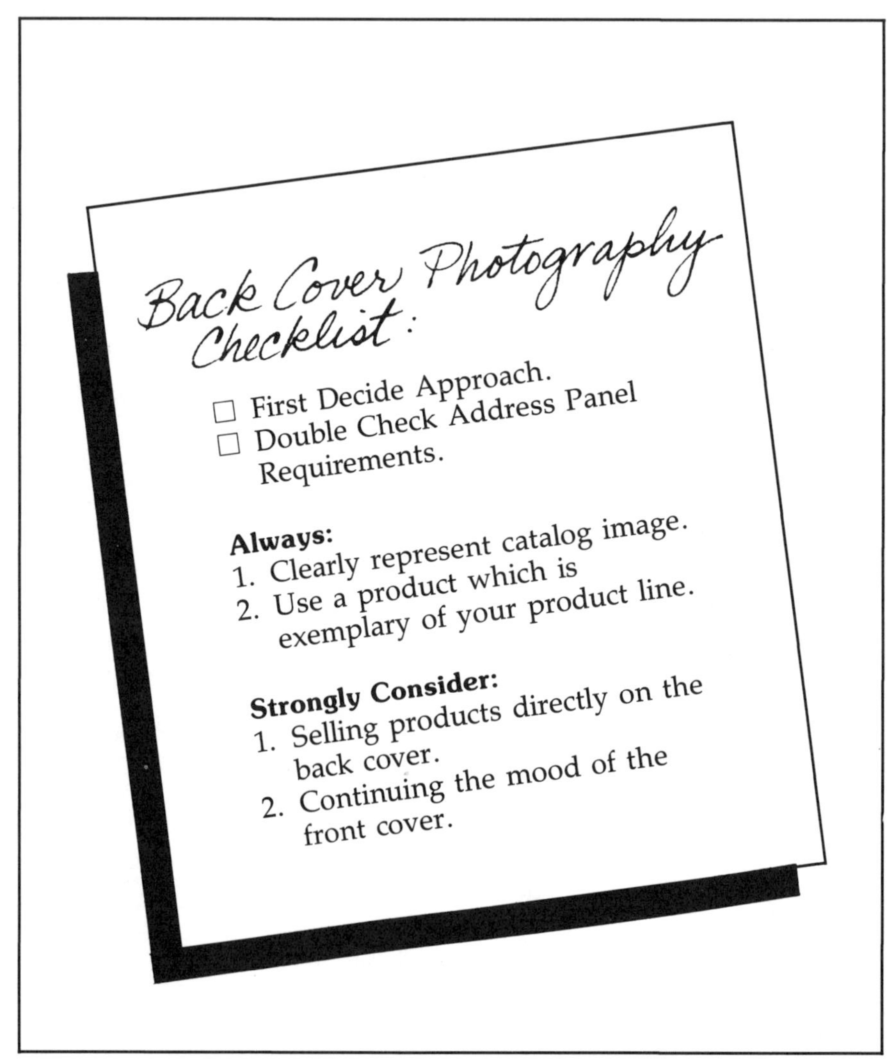

Back Cover Photography Checklist:
☐ First Decide Approach.
☐ Double Check Address Panel Requirements.
Always:
1. Clearly represent catalog image.
2. Use a product which is exemplary of your product line.
Strongly Consider:
1. Selling products directly on the back cover.
2. Continuing the mood of the front cover.

Inside Product Photography

You are now ready to tackle product presentation, so you should know that the first goal of any product illustration is — once again — *to attract the attention of your customer.* When you're thinking in terms of visual appeal, you generally must choose between a photograph of the product or an artist's rendering, such as a line drawing, a watercolor, or another form of mechanical illustration. The photograph is by far the more common choice, mainly because it performs one function a drawing cannot: a photograph encourages credibility. The customer trusts a photograph, and knows subliminally that an illustration can always "cheat." However, drawings and other art techniques have valuable uses, and sometimes can present an item even more truthfully than a photograph.

But before we discuss the actual presentation of products and the different methods used, let's prepare ourselves.

How To Direct Your Photographer

Earlier in this chapter we reviewed how to choose a good photographer. Now we need to know how to convey to your photographer the kind of shot you want. Though getting the best results with your catalog photography is directly related to your photographer's skill in communicating, don't forget that communication is not a one-way street. You've got an obligation, too. *You must be able to convey exactly what you're looking for.* A vague direction along the lines of "make this desk set look classy" is not enough.

If a verbal description isn't enough, what is? You have two basic approaches to choose from: a "clipping service" and a layout sketch.

1. Clipping service. If you have no art staff to furnish sketches of layouts, you're going to need to start a "clipping service." (In fact you need this even if you do have artists on your staff.) This point is fully discussed in Chapter 4. Professionals can look at a photo and know how to achieve the same results. They can tell you how the subject was lit, the kind of camera used for the shot, and how much time and expense was involved.

The clippings you have gathered for your Competitor Clip Files and General Clipping File (discussed in Product Work Sessions) will be of great help in communicating your wishes to the photographer. The background color you wish, the effect you desire, the total creative visual approach you desire can be easily communicated. You will be less frustrated in directing your photographer if you have the use of visual guides. Your photographer will be less frustrated when looking at a visual guide. And you will both be happy with the outcome because it is known — it is what you wanted to achieve.

2. Layout Sketch. More effective than furnishing clippings alone is to furnish them along with an artist's sketch of the layout you desire. This sketch is exactly the size the shot will run in your catalog. The layout will show exact placement of the item, the angle from which it is to be shot, the kind (and color) of background, the props to be used, and so on. Guidance for these layouts will have been given in your product work sessions (see Chapter 4) when competitor clippings were reviewed, discussion with your creative staff was held, and your merchandiser reviewed the reasons for selecting the product.

Product photography, in almost all cases, is shot to the size that the photos appear in the catalog. (This refers to those catalogs reproduced from transparencies which are stripped together in position in page form. A 35 mm or 2¼ x 2¼ camera is not used for this purpose, but rather a 4 x 5, 8 x 10 or even larger camera. The photographer must stage the photographs carefully, because they have to fit a given space and size. It's easy to see how vital the specifics of a layout can be: *the layout becomes the "frame" which the photographer uses as a guide.* When you develop your layouts, think of them as the frame for your ad. The photographer will appreciate the guidance . . . and you'll have a good idea of exactly what will appear in your book.

Here is an example of a to-size layout sketch and the final photograph resulting therefrom (Figure 5-20). Notice the artist's directions to the photographer:

> **Lighting instructions:** "Fade to a dark background at top," "Light from top — make it dramatic," and "Watch reflection here." These are detailed instructions which ensure the end result of a good photograph with the mood and effect wanted.

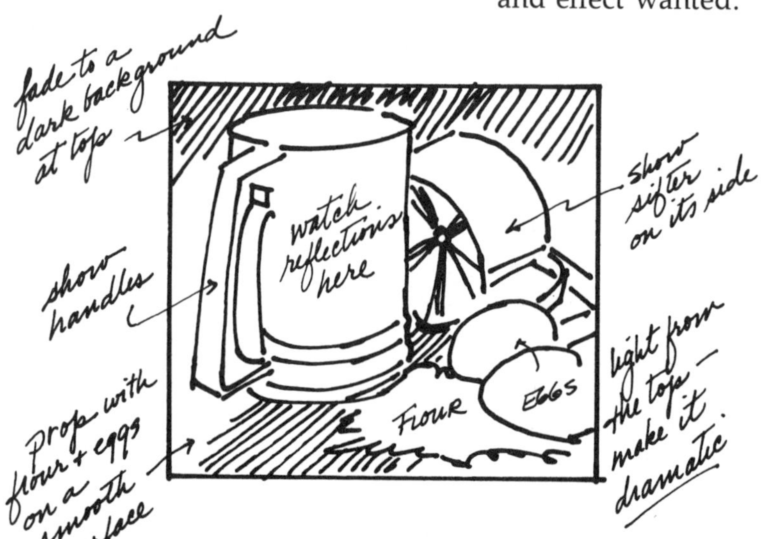

5-20

Product positioning: ''Show handles'' and ''Show sifter on its side.'' The important feature of the product is the ease-of-use which the handles allow. Therefore, the photo must visually show the customer the handles and the inner workings, thus telling the product's story and benefit.

Propping instructions: ''Prop with flour and eggs on a smooth surface'' further ensures the desired end result of a professional presentation by adding interest to the photo without detracting attention. This type of instruction is done by a talented and knowledgeable artist. The cataloger who does not have this kind of talent available must sit down with the photographer and carefully go over the product and the desired end result.

Once the customer's attention has been captured, the primary intent is to picture the product clearly and truthfully. In any discussion on product presentation, there is always a battle between reality and enhancement. Where you stand on this issue must be clearly understood by your photographer for each item you wish photographed. It's the photographer's job not to misrepresent the merchandise, but still to give it all the appeal it needs to attract the prospective buyer. Also, don't forget that the more truthfully you present the merchandise, the greater the customer's satisfaction. If ''what you see is what you get,'' a bond of loyalty and trust is established between cataloger and customer — a great incentive for future order placement. In the long run, your internal systems benefit from this approach as well, because there are fewer returns and fewer complaints.

Technical Effects Techniques

Being aware of photographic techniques helps you to convey your desires to the photographer, both verbally and in the layout form we've just seen. For instance, an art director who doesn't have some knowledge of what photographic lighting techniques can achieve (as well as the problems lighting could cause) will be hard pressed to issue the directions in the layout/photo example just given. There are technical aspects of photographic technique that you will want to be aware of. What techniques and elements help convey the product image you desire?

The style of photography you choose for your catalog contributes in two vital ways: (1) it suggests your ''image'' (who you are and to whom you wish to appeal), and (2) it presents your products effectively. From the cataloger's point of view, there are three photographic techniques and three elements of photography through which both image and products are interpreted:

The basic techniques: (a) background
(b) lighting
(c) camera type and focal length.

The basic elements: (a) shape and form
(b) detail and clarity
(c) texture.

Technical skill can be determined by how your photographer interplays between these two areas, because the photographer uses the techniques to effect the execution of the elements. In fact, these are the areas you would analyze in any photograph that you were putting to the test of whether or not it was "good."

Complimentary background vital to product sales

Background. Imagine a simple seamless sweep in a standard, straightforward background usually lighted for even, shadowless illumination across its width and depth to produce a "nonbackground." This is particularly suited to utilitarian images. But that same seamless sweep can become very dramatic when shadows and highlights are intentionally cast upon it, becoming quite appropriate for upscale images.

Backgrounds can be used to suggest mood and use of items, as well. High-tech images, for example, are often produced on "high-tech" backgrounds such as black slate-textured Formica, black Plexiglas, narrow-slatted metal window blinds, striped or checkered mirror, and black industrial floor matting with various textured surfaces. Wood-graining as a background can create many moods, from old-fashioned elegance to a business-office environment.

The important area of concern in the use of backgrounds is two-fold: don't let it overpower the item, but at the same time make sure it enhances the item. One of the major errors in the use of backgrounds is to choose a color or intensity that does not properly promote the item. A dark background with a dark item upon it attracts the eye less than a light background featuring a dark item. This is not a hard-and-fast rule, however, because many of these choices are affected by the style of the catalog.

In any catalog, backgrounds should be coordinated in range of color to give the catalog a coordinated, tied-together appeal. For example, the first choice you make in deciding upon your backgrounds is actually just like that of an artist who selects a specific color palette from which he will create a specific painting. No matter how many colors are chosen, they are all clear and bright (clear yellow, bright blue). Or perhaps they will be muted shades (grayish blue, pale lavender). If your catalog has various sections that are sharply defined in content, you can change this palette from section to section. But generally, each section retains the same mood/palette of background. Occasionally a surprise color can be interjected for effect, but this must be done with care so it does not look like a mistake.

Within the background palette, you can use several kinds and textures of backgrounds to avoid visual boredom, repeating the same backgrounds every few pages to add necessary continuity. *The background style must be planned in advance to visually pace the customer.*

Backgrounds are crucial because they help to move the viewer through the book by adding color flow without interjecting distraction.

The choice of a consistent palette assures you of having all of your new items match previously photographed products. The new products intermingle with the older ones, maintaining a coordinated look as you publish each catalog edition. If you create each one of your catalogs with an entirely new group of backgrounds, you can of course change your palette for each book. But this is the exceptional situation, rather than the rule. In a case such as this, or in a brand-new catalog, you would develop thumbnail layouts (at least) of the finished total catalog to be sure of continuity in the printed piece.

Catalogs can also achieve ''nonbackgrounds'' by utilizing silhouetted products instead of photographs in ''frames.'' This can open up the look of the catalog, especially a book with many dark backgrounds. The silhouetted products seem larger than they would when within a frame, and a light, airy look is achieved because a great deal of white space has been injected into the catalog.

Backgrounds are affected tremendously by the style and quality of light that is cast upon them, either directly or indirectly, which brings us to our next basic technique.

Lighting. The variables that can be achieved with lighting produced either in a studio or outdoors are almost infinite. The quality of light (hard or soft) and color temperature of light (warm, cool, neutral) affect the catalog's continuity as much as the backgrounds do. *For continuity and a look of planned cohesiveness, both quality and color temperature of lighting should remain the same on all products in the catalog.* Again, if a catalog is broken into obviously different sections, each section should be filled with images that reflect lighting continuity, but in this case, not necessarily the entire catalog. Exceptions to the continuity can be quite effective, but they must be carefully orchestrated by an art director. Each divergence must be planned to create a specific effect (and surprise alone is an acceptable reason) at a specific spot in the finished catalog.

Many effects are controlled by how your photographer lights the subjects for your catalog shots. The type of lights to use has always been debated, even among the best photographers. But the choices are natural daylight, strobe or electronic flash, and tungsten lights. Don't let anyone trap you into judging which is best, because each has its application and produces different results.

The most important decision you will have to make is not what kind of light your photographer uses, but what kind of RESULT you want. Light has a lot to do with how your customer reacts to the product. As an example, a soft light with open shadows or streaking sunlight can communicate a romantic feeling, great for fashion or nostalgic looks. Hard lighting with deep shadows can be very dramatic and create an impact or an attention-getting quality. This look might be appropriate for high-tech decorator items or for a business-to-business catalog selling computer hardware.

But the main concern should be how your *product* looks under the lighting used by your photographer, and whether or not the lighting helps delineate those important elements we mentioned earlier: shape, detail, and texture. Because your three-dimensional product is being translated to the two-dimensional printed page, these elements are vitally important.

Your product must be lighted so it has *shape, dimension, and form.* It should look real enough to lift off the page, with three distinct planes: top, side, and front. Flat lighting often fosters an unreal look, which subconsciously builds doubt in the viewer's eye. Often a photographer will use lighting to darken the background of a photograph to give the product more depth and dimension. This roundness, or form, is very important to the impact your product makes on the customer.

In addition, your product must be lighted so that it has detail. Don't let shadows hide important product details like switches or dials, engravings, or important lines of product design. Even on the dark, shadowed side of a subject, all the important details of the product still should be visible for scrutiny by your customer.

Light your product so its *texture* is properly represented. Chrome must look like chrome and gold like gold. You should be able to see — and have the illusion of feeling — the texture of leather, suede, plastic, wood, or corduroy. The lighting is the primary medium in showing texture. The *direction and intensity of light* usually are best determined on set to suit each product's unique demands. To a degree, this also is true of light quality. A broad, soft source is essential to make chrome or brass shine, while a hard, small source is a must to bring out texture in fur or high-pile fabrics. A cross light can bring out a rough texture, and the proper reflector can accent a smooth, shiny surface. The visual effect of these textures upon the viewer can make the difference between sale or no sale.

The underlying goal of all lighting is to make your product look as real and believable as possible by representing it as true-to-life as possible. Secondary lighting techniques can give the photo drama, excitement, or romance, but they must never steal the show from the product. Lighting, even dramatic lighting, should not be the obvious factor in the finished photo.

If through proper lighting of your product you can convey to the customer exactly what you are selling, you have eliminated one of the largest stumbling blocks of mail order resistance: disbelief in that product. Subconsciously your customer says: 'I know what I'm getting. I saw it clearly, realistically, honestly — as it is and will be when it arrives.''

Lighting ratio (the difference between brightness of highlights and shadows on a subject) *should remain the same, or nearly so, throughout a catalog for consistency.* If this is not done, a catalog can have a choppy effect, and the customer senses the jarring note and does not wish to continue moving through the book.

Camera type and focal length. Whether strict perspective control will be observed or abandoned throughout a catalog should be determined before the first image is recorded on film. Images with converging parallel lines are now showing up more and more often. This technique was once a definite no-no in professional photography, and it still is frowned upon by many conventional catalog marketers. But this break from the traditional can be effective, particularly for catalogs that feature high-tech merchandise or that appeal to the avant garde customer. Though perspective-controlled images and those with obvious distortion may be mixed in a catalog, the use of just one or two photos with mildly distorted perspective will look like a mistake or afterthought.

Telephoto lenses from normal to short are used for more traditional photos because they "see" products with minimal distortion, just as the eye normally sees them. In more upscale catalogs, wide-angle lenses frequently are used to purposely and dramatically distort perspective. This again reflects a contemporary acceptance on the part of catalog marketers and consumers alike. Not long ago, the product shape was sacred and could not be distorted either within itself or in relation to other subjects. Consumers just weren't sophisticated enough about visuals to realize that distortion was due to optics and not to a strangely-shaped product. Today, that is not so.

The two-drawer file in the center of this layout from The Sharper Image catalog (Figure 5-21) reveals how distorted perspective is being accepted in today's photography. The image was probably made with a medium-format camera that does not control converging vertical parallel lines. The distortion in the file cabinet is subtly but effectively offset by the outline halftone of the briefcase. The tilt of the left angle directly counters the tilt of the cabinet side closest to the briefcase.

Focus is another area which is often thought to make the difference between a good photo, and a bad one. Almost everyone thinks that all good photographs must be "sharp." But every rule is made to be broken, as each situation is unique and those rules cannot solve every problem. Creative focusing can be a strong force in the presentation of your offering.

Use of focus strengthens presentations

When everything is super sharp in your photograph, it gives a subliminal feeling of being technically correct. This is good to keep in mind if you are photographing a highly mechanical or technical product. In contrast, a soft-focus subject has the subliminal effect of being romantic, and this may be an excellent technique to use for lingerie. A deliberate soft-focus or misty technique can add immeasurably to the mood of the item.

Focus can usually be controlled within any photographic composition, and the areas where the photographer chooses to vary the focus become dramatic tools for effectively presenting your product. For example, when it is felt that the background will interfere with the presentation of a product, the composition can become stronger if the photographer puts the background out of focus (Figure 5-22

admired for your efficiency and taste.
• Kluge Portfolio #ZKT382 $79 (5.50)
h oak.
alternative
Drawers are 13½" deep, hold letter-size files and suspension folders. File measures 16 × 17½ × 28", weighs 45 lbs.

5-21

from Jones & Scully, Inc.). Note how the glass of the greenhouse becomes a complimentary light pattern helping to pop out the product, an orchid, when put out of focus. If the glass were in focus, it would compete with and distract from the product.

A soft focus or blur can also add the dimension of motion or speed to your product. This may be the very essence that helps describe and sell your product or service. See Figure 5-23 from the back cover of The Sharper Image catalog introducing a special "Rush Service." A slow shutter speed has allowed the movement of an item to be seen in a soft blur, indicating speed of delivery.

Even if you have a photograph you like, ask yourself if it could be improved if certain areas (foreground, background, subject) were to be refocused. Focus is an interesting tool, and one which truly can be exploited by "breaking the rules." All of these techniques we've discussed will be used in four basic layouts (or photographic styles of product presentation):

1. The straight shot
2. The propped shot
3. The in-use shot
4. The end-benefit shot.

The tone and image selected for your catalog can have a great deal of influence on which type of shot you choose to use. However, there are always two elements of concern: first, the item itself, and second, the prospective customer. The first question to ask is, "What benefit does this product provide the customer?" The second question is, "How can the benefit best be shown while maintaining the catalog image and customer appeal?"

5-22

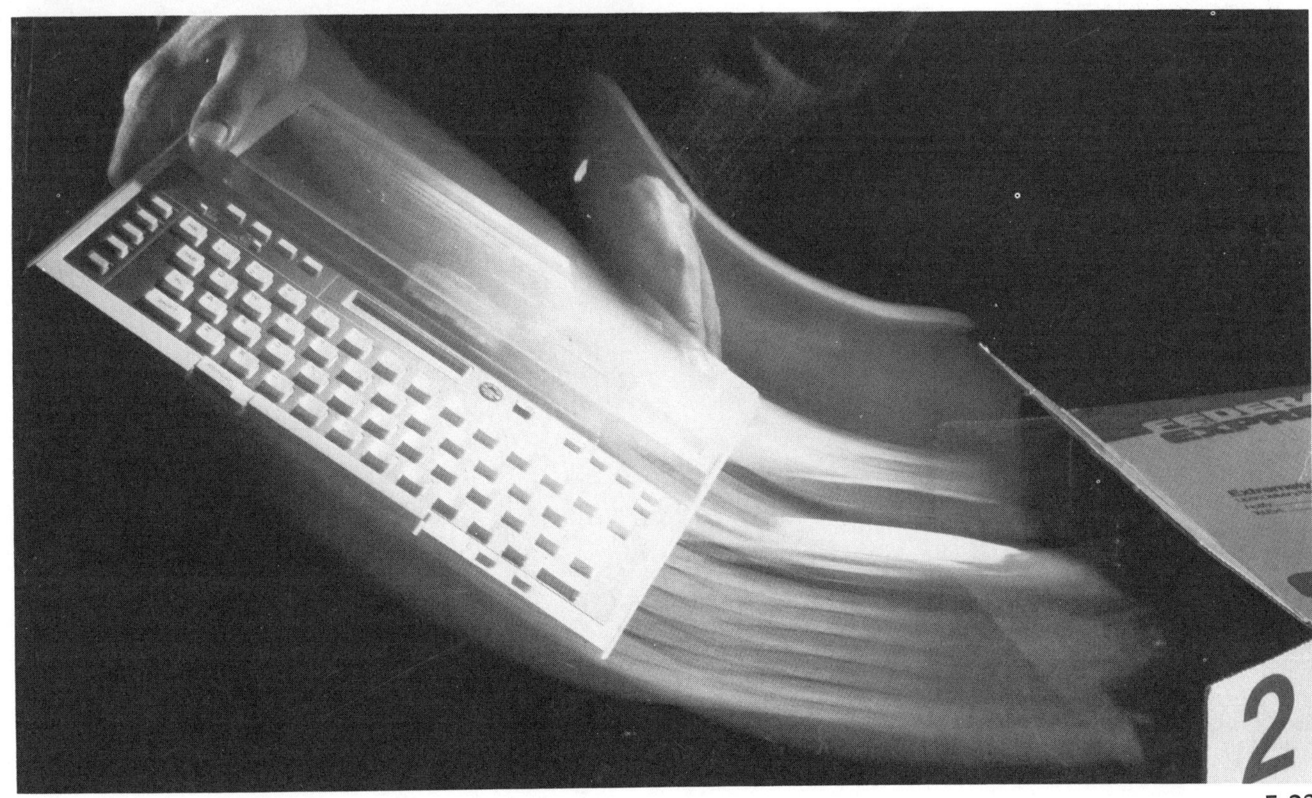

5-23

The Straight Shot. . . When should you use this approach?

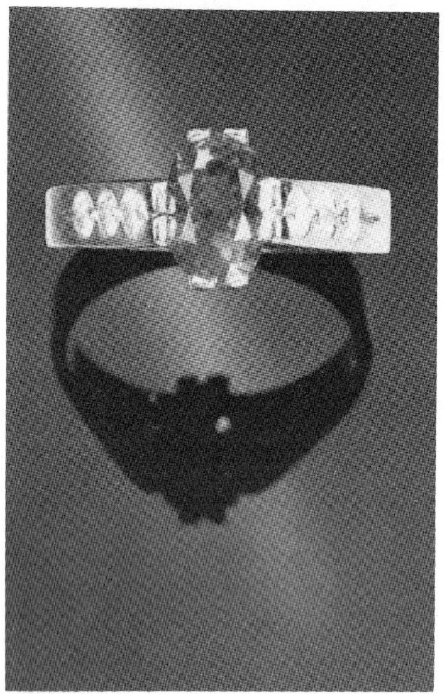

5-24

If an item does not need any "editorial comment" or enhancement to show what it is or what it does, then a straight shot can be used. Items which have no complications and are readily identifiable fall into this category. Higher-ticket items often utilize straight shots because the look of the catalog must be very clean to fulfill the aesthetics demanded by high price tags. Higher-ticket customers may feel patronized if, for example, in-use photos are utilized when not necessary. Items which require close-up views to maximize their details or importance also fall into this category. For instance, a necklace worn as an accessory to a dress being sold is difficult to sell from the same photo because the details which enhance the necklace cannot be seen. A straight shot does not have to be boring. Lighting techniques and backgrounds can enhance the product, further explaining it visually. A mood can even be created for its use.

Computer disks, car seat frames, or a professional butcher knife most often would suggest a straight shot when the products are common to the market where they are being sold: professional offices, auto repair companies, and meat packers. At the same time, a valued piece of art such as a collector's art print, paperweight, or pre-Columbian vase would generally benefit from a straight shot because of the intrinsic value of the product to the customer and the (most likely) high retail price. A straight shot would be placing

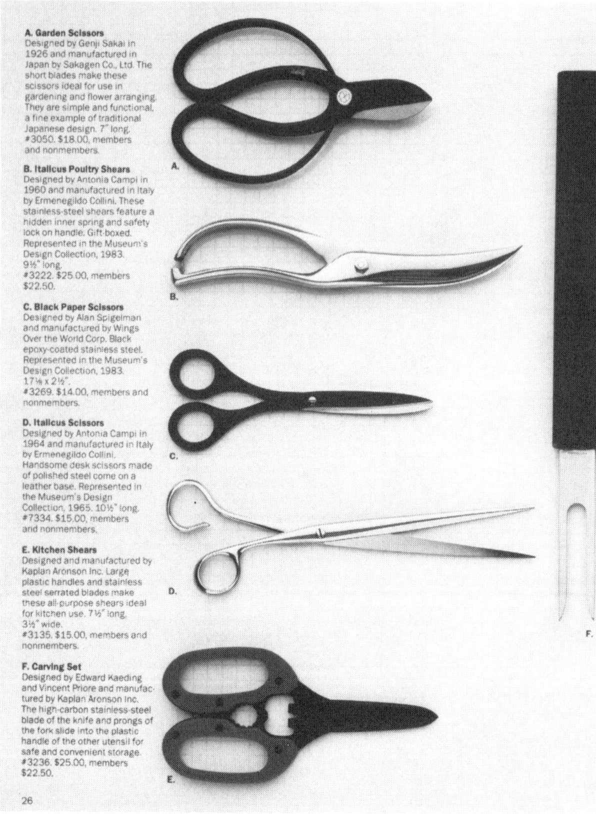

5-25

5-26

the product in a more natural "museum" setting to allow the customer to view the product without undue interference from props, people, and other competing factors.

General Consumer Figure 5-24, the Gemstones and Jewelry catalog by The Sharper Image, is a straight-on shot of a ladies' ring. A dramatic air has been achieved by careful lighting which casts a heavy shadow, giving the ring identity by presenting a dimensional side view while still allowing the front of the ring to be seen.

Figure 5-25 is a page from The Museum of Modern Art catalog. Six products are shot straight. All pertain to an act of cutting. The shapes, textures, and colors make them attractive designs, but would subtle props have helped identify their use and therefore attracted more potential buyers? Another typical straight shot subject matter seen in this catalog is greeting cards. Figure 5-26 is a page illustrating seven Christmas cards. Other common straight shots are seen in the home furnishings field. Figure 5-27 from the Scatters catalog shows four rugs spread out on the page, with three pillow designs inset in the lower right-hand corner. The products (rugs and pillows) could have been glamorized and put in an actual room setting, but the size of the product would have to be smaller and attention would have been diverted to objects other than the products themselves. This type of presentation is also less expensive.

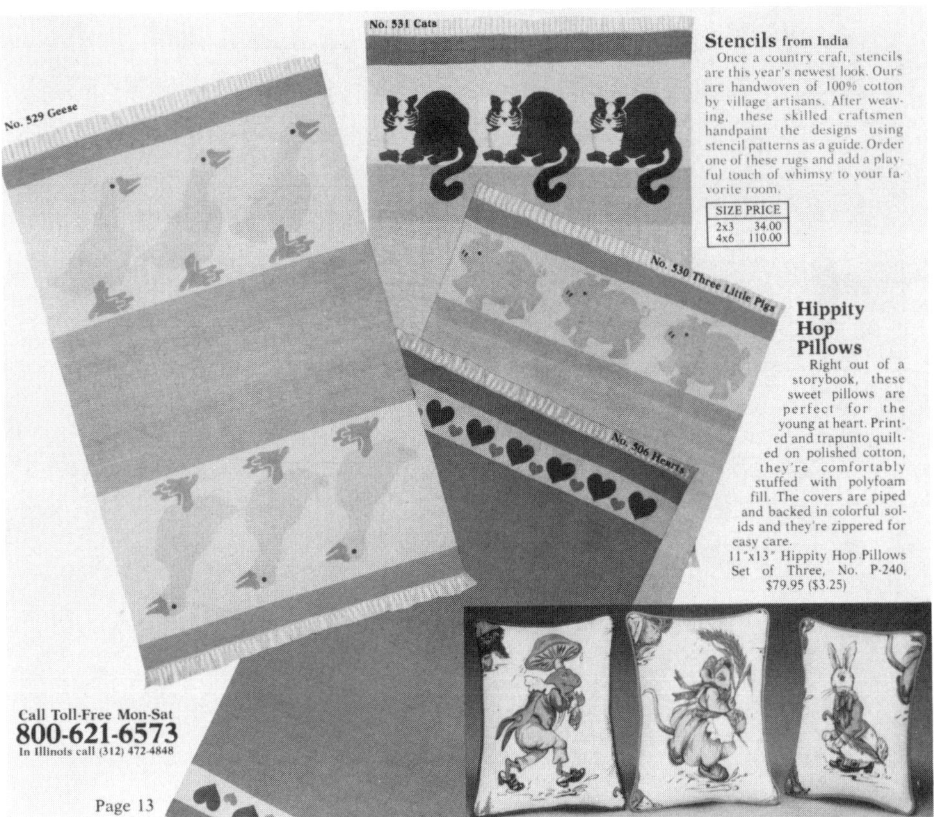

5-27

Business-to-Business Most business and industrial catalogs have, in the past, used the straight shot approach almost exclusively. It was felt that all that was needed was to show the box, bottle, or dental tool, and the salesman would do the informing and selling. Unfortunately, this attitude of presentation has been too often carried over to the business mail order catalog. Interestingly enough, there are still many instances where the straight approach is still the best approach in presenting business products. Data General illustrates most of its computer hardware with the straight shot approach. Figure 5-28 is a page from the Data General Direct catalog. A letter-quality printer is shot straight on while various attachments are presented singly and in straight solo shots. This is a clean approach showing the physical product. Figure 5-29 is from the Arrow Star catalog selling various plant equipment. All of the products on the

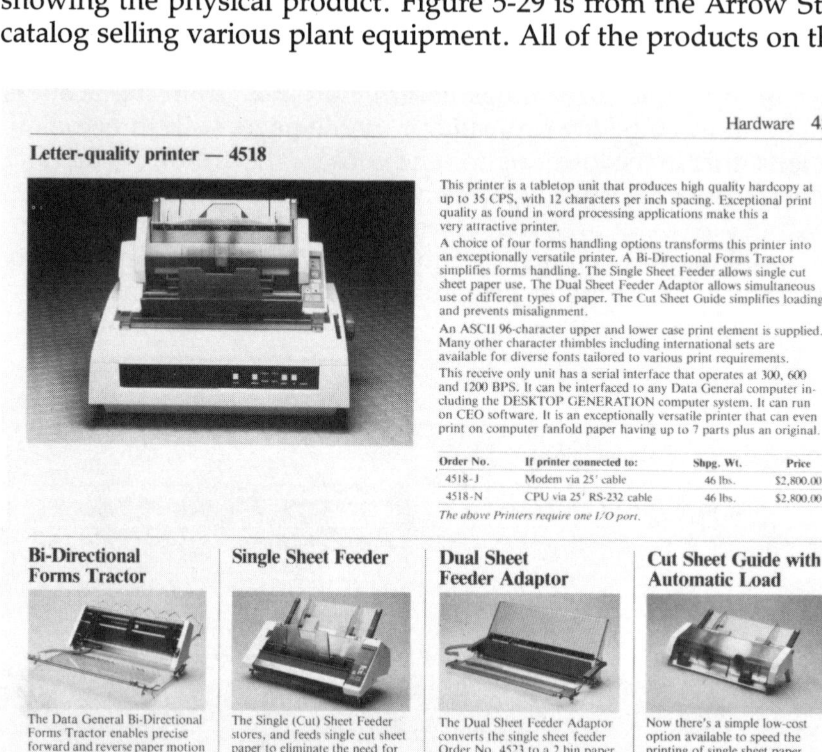
Hardware 45

Letter-quality printer — 4518

This printer is a tabletop unit that produces high quality hardcopy at up to 35 CPS, with 12 characters per inch spacing. Exceptional print quality as found in word processing applications make this a very attractive printer.

A choice of four forms handling options transforms this printer into an exceptionally versatile printer. A Bi-Directional Forms Tractor simplifies forms handling. The Single Sheet Feeder allows single cut sheet paper use. The Dual Sheet Feeder Adaptor allows simultaneous use of different types of paper. The Cut Sheet Guide simplifies loading and prevents misalignment.

An ASCII 96-character upper and lower case print element is supplied. Many other character thimbles including international sets are available for diverse fonts tailored to various print requirements.

This receive only unit has a serial interface that operates at 300, 600 and 1200 BPS. It can be interfaced to any Data General computer including the DESKTOP GENERATION computer system. It can run on CEO software. It is an exceptionally versatile printer that can even print on computer fanfold paper having up to 7 parts plus an original.

Order No.	If printer connected to:	Shpg. Wt.	Price
4518-J	Modem via 25' cable	46 lbs.	$2,800.00
4518-N	CPU via 25' RS-232 cable	46 lbs.	$2,800.00

The above Printers require one I/O port.

Bi-Directional Forms Tractor

The Data General Bi-Directional Forms Tractor enables precise forward and reverse paper motion necessary to print subscripts, superscripts, complex graphics and tables. Designed for feeding of side-sprocket-hole paper, this versatile, popular option is ideal for printing presentation quality text and business graphics, as well as engineering and scientific reports.

The tractor is fully adjustable to handle up to six-part continuous forms with ease. It features automatic paper-out sensing.

Paper Width: 3" to 16"
Paper Weight: 13# to 22#

Order No. 4522
Shpg. Wt. 5 lbs.
Price Each $300.00

Single Sheet Feeder

The Single (Cut) Sheet Feeder stores, and feeds single cut sheet paper to eliminate the need for fanfold paper or forms. It automatically feeds and stacks standard paper or letterhead and is ideal for moderate to heavy volume printing applications. A bin feeds the paper into the printer and a stacker receives the printed forms.

A removable, easy loading, paper out, and paper jam detectors and simple controls provide fast dependable operations.

Paper Width: 5" to 11.7"
Paper Weight: 17# to 28#
Paper Length: 4.3" to 14"
Tray Capacity: 180 sheets of 18# stock

Order No. 4523
Shpg. Wt. 15 lbs.
Price Each $1400.00

Dual Sheet Feeder Adaptor

The Dual Sheet Feeder Adaptor converts the single sheet feeder Order No. 4523 to a 2 bin paper inserter. This enables the use of different weight papers at the same time. Order No. 4524 is attached to Order No. 4523. The 2 paper types may be fed in under program control to produce presentation multi-page letters, reports and other important documents. An adjustable paper tray can be easily attached in minutes.

Paper widths: 5" to 11.7"

Order No. 4524
Shpg. Wt. 15 lbs.
Price Each $350.00

Cut Sheet Guide with Automatic Load

Now there's a simple low-cost option available to speed the printing of single sheet paper by eliminating slow, manual paper insertion and positioning. A ruled scale and adjustable alignment guide ensures fast and accurate paper positioning. A built-in paper detect/paper out sensor controls printer operation.

Paper Width: 5" to 16"
Paper Length: 3.5" to 16.5"
Paper Weight: 13# to 25#

Order No. 4526
Shpg. Wt. 5 lbs.
Price Each $165.00

5-28

page are straight shots, relying on the copy to inform or suggest use or obvious visual identification. Since this catalog goes to such a select audience (business and plant equipment purchasing agents), perhaps this is all that is needed. The Visible Computer Supply Corporation in many instances photographs the containers and packaging of the products. Figure 5-30 shows how typing paper and correction fluid appear in the catalog. This catalog carries over 2,000 products, with many variations in style or brand of products that all do the same thing. The background is flat and void of shadowing. This then becomes a less costly and more manageable method of presentation. On the other hand, Figure 5-31, from DECdirect, shows how background material with its high-tech look suggests the personality and interests of the end-user of the product through variation, texture, and depth. Though this is a straight shot, the way the

5-29

photographer has placed the item ("standing" and at an angle) gives it animation and vitality. The major difference between these two catalogs is that The Visible Computer Supply Corporation carries many different brands and a large variety of products for a varied audience, while DECdirect sells only Digital brand products and markets them to the customer who has previously purchased a Digital computer. DECdirect's market is narrower and more defined — and easier to profile into a selective audience.

Following are two catalogs, with similar customer profiles, which approach jewelry presentation very differently. Figure 5-32, La Shack, is selling eight different products on the page. The middle model is wearing a necklace color-coordinated with the outfit she has on. The necklace is for sale, but it is barely distinguishable in style or color. The detail needed to sell it simply is not there because of its small size in the catalog. Figure 5-33 is from the Esplande catalog. The model in the upper left of the page is wearing a necklace and earrings. But the catalog does not try to sell the jewelry

5-30

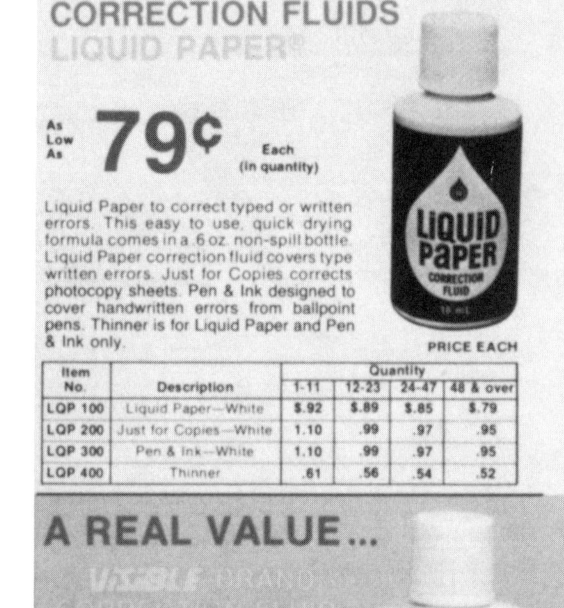

CORRECTION FLUIDS

LIQUID PAPER®

As Low As 79¢ Each (in quantity)

Liquid Paper to correct typed or written errors. This easy to use, quick drying formula comes in a .6 oz. non-spill bottle. Liquid Paper correction fluid covers type written errors. Just for Copies corrects photocopy sheets. Pen & Ink designed to cover handwritten errors from ballpoint pens. Thinner is for Liquid Paper and Pen & Ink only.

PRICE EACH

Item No.	Description	Quantity 1-11	12-23	24-47	48 & over
LQP 100	Liquid Paper—White	$.92	$.89	$.85	$.79
LQP 200	Just for Copies—White	1.10	.99	.97	.95
LQP 300	Pen & Ink—White	1.10	.99	.97	.95
LQP 400	Thinner	.61	.56	.54	.52

A REAL VALUE...

As Low As 54¢ Each (in quantity)

Visible brand correction fluid gives you top quality correction fluid at low Visible prices. White correction fluid covers typewritten errors. Pen and Ink for correcting handwritten errors of markers, ballpoint and fountain pens. Thinner for use with correction fluid. White correction fluid and Pen and Ink comes in 3/4 oz. non-spill bottles. Thinner comes in 1 oz. bottles.

PRICE EACH

Item No.	Description	Quantity 1-11	12-23	24-47	48 & over
VCF 100	Correction Fluid—White	$.65	$.62	$.58	$.54
VCF 200	Pen & Ink—White	.73	.70	.65	.60
VCF 300	Thinner	.57	.52	.49	.46

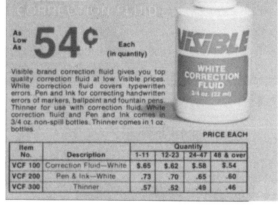

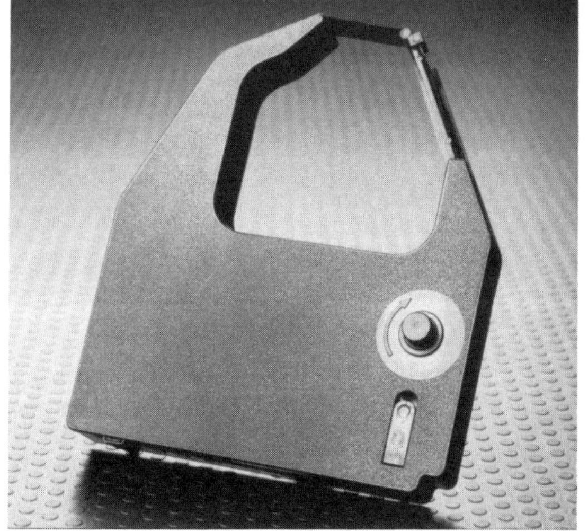

5-31

from this presentation. Straight shots of the jewelry are used as an inset (earrings) and the necklace is free formed on the background of the page. Product size has been brought up so the customer can see the detail and color of the items. The page is made visually interesting, too. Through this approach, all six products on the page command their share of interest and provide the customer with enough individual detail to show the product benefit.

Straight shots may work well for your catalog, but ask yourself these questions when deciding whether or not to use a straight shot:

1. Is the product perfectly identifiable on its own?
2. Can it be enhanced to evoke the purchasing emotion merely through use of lighting, background, and positioning of the item?
3. Are there any advantages which might result in greater sales by propping the item or showing it in use?

5-32

5-33

The Propped Shot . . . When is this approach the best?

The main reason to prop an item is that the item needs to be identified or clarified, or it has a characteristic which needs to be identified. Props can indicate the use of the product without an in-use shot. They are vital if a product's size needs to be scaled. But there are secondary reasons which are also important: complimenting the item to catch the customer's eye, or conversely, subliminally appealing to shoppers' hidden desires. Props are particularly useful when they explain the product at a single glance, or when they add ''sizzle'' to an item which might otherwise be commonplace. The majority of product types can benefit from this approach, if only to bring visual appeal which, in turn, calls attention to the product. Don't leave the choice of props to the photographer. Merchandisers can be most helpful and should work closely with the layout artist or the photographer to assure that props add appropriate definition of product benefit or purpose. There can be important, subtle differences in the intended use of a product: an enameled cash box intended as a ''stow-away'' spot for teenagers (and pitched that way in the copy) could easily be misunderstood by an unguided photographer and propped with a man's pocketknife and a hundred dollar bill.

General Consumer. Props can suggest the product use, imply a benefit, create a mood, or help call attention to the product; the majority of general consumer catalogs make use of them.

Choose your own props

Figure 5-34 from The Paragon catalog is an excellent example of declaring the product function. The salt and pepper shakers would look merely like ceramic decorations shaped like Scottish terrier dogs if it were not for the box of salt and can of pepper shown in the background. Using these as props shows the product function at a single glance. Following are two useful examples of props visually suggesting a benefit which may be derived.

Notice the subliminal suggestion created by the props in Figure 5-35 from the American Express catalog. The briefcase is propped with the Wall Street Journal and a pipe. The implication is that the briefcase is carried by a successful, upper-class individual. It is only a small jump in the mind of the viewer to the ''conclusion'' that by carrying this briefcase, the viewer, too, will appear (or be) successful. If this claim had been made in the copy description, the result would be ridiculous, even to the most unsophisticated customer. But the subtlety of this visual message can be accepted by anyone.

A macho, carefree message is related in Figure 5-36. The Sharper Image is selling a leather flight vest. To get the message across and to appeal to the most likely customer, the photographer has shown a silk scarf casually draped over the front side of the vest.

MORTON
SALT
BLACK
PEPPER
A. SALT AND PEPPER SCOTTIES. Perky little scotties shake-out the "black and white" to perform clever table service! Made of fine painted earthenware, each 3" x 3". The pair.
#2788 10.00 (1.55)
A

5-34

5-35

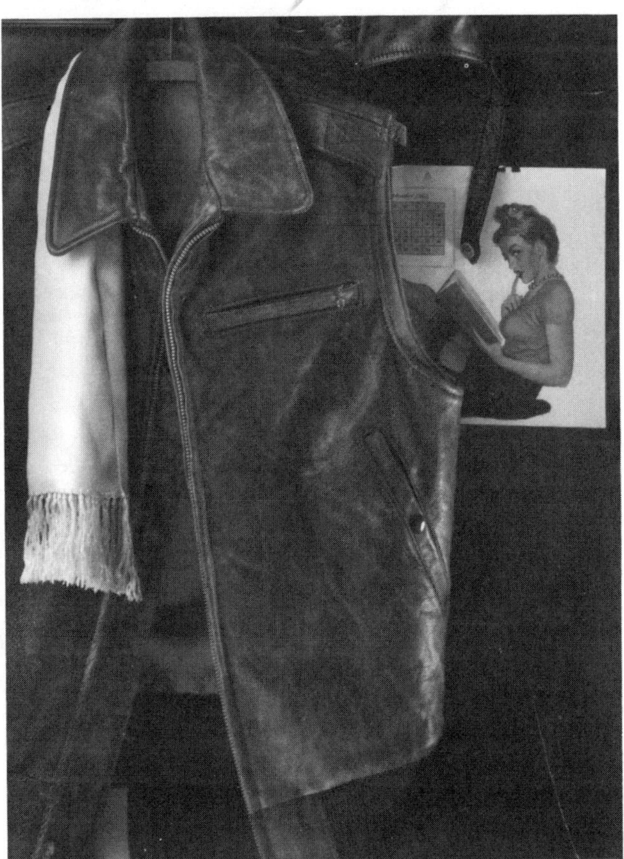

5-36

This not only suggests a carefree approach reminiscent of World War II, but also acts as an attractant because of its light color. An old black leather flight cap is barely seen in the upper right of the photo with a strap carefully hanging down on an old Varga pin-up-girl calendar. A romantic life of popularity is subtly suggested by this excellent use of props. The lighting adds to the effect, too, allowing highlights to play on the leather vest. The props have set a mood which implies a style of life which can be yours if you own the vest.

In Figure 5-37 we see how propping can make a presentation in the Horchow catalog more interesting in form or color, thereby helping call attention to the product as well as helping clarify the size of the product. Three oranges are placed around the two Chinese plates which are being sold. The plates are blue and white and would have been far less noticeable if it weren't for the lovely bright-orange oranges. Two cigarettes alongside suggest use. This small (approximately 2⅜″ × 1⅞″) presentation could have gone unnoticed on the large 9″ × 11″ page if it were not for the colorful orange props calling attention to it.

A small Analog Quartz alarm clock (Figure 5-38) from the Chris-Craft catalog is nicely scaled by the placement of a cloisonne pen alongside. Such scaling as this is especially effective when the product being photographed must be brought up in size to be noticed on the page. With propping to bring scale to the product, the customer will not be misled, and still the photograph of a small product is as large as those of other truly larger products on the page.

5-37

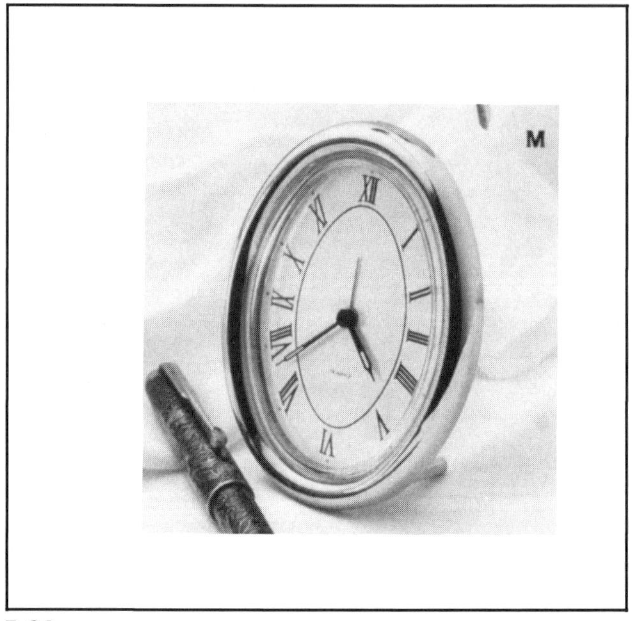

5-38

Business-to-business catalogs tend to use fewer props. In many cases photography is more or less treated like a visual listing. However, business-to-business catalog presentation could greatly benefit from more use of props. Business customers, remember, are people, too. They respond to mood and benefit, and they identify with a product and its setting as well as the general consumer.

Figure 5-39 is from the Inmac catalog. The photograph shows how the product Inmac is selling, Keyboard Keeper, neatly stores a computer keyboard when not in use. In the foreground of the photograph, a pen rests on the table surface, indicating the area ''freed'' because of the product being sold.

Sycom Forms and Supplies catalog (Figure 5-40) nicely props its appointment cards with a pen and letter holder, adding a professional air as well as indicating easy usage in the office. The wooden background surface helps indicate an office atmosphere, too. Figure 5-41, also from the Sycom catalog, is a four-stage illustration bringing out various product benefits. Each photograph is effectively propped with a pen, typewriter, tape dispenser, and stapler to create an office atmosphere and add visual interest to what would otherwise be a pretty dull product.

Data General (Figure 5-42) warms up a display terminal and keyboard presentation with a telephone and flowering plant placed alongside. These additions subliminally suggest that the products are approachable. They are not for some cold, futuristic utilization, but accessible and ready to use now. The placement (off to the side and in the background), the focus (the plant is slightly out of focus), and the lighting (shadowed while the products which are being sold are highlighted) are planned so they do not compete but compliment and help draw attention and set a mood of relaxed efficiency.

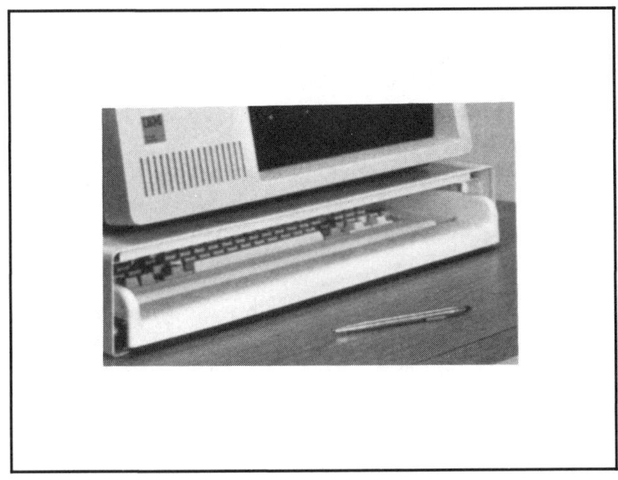

5-39

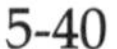

5-40

5-41

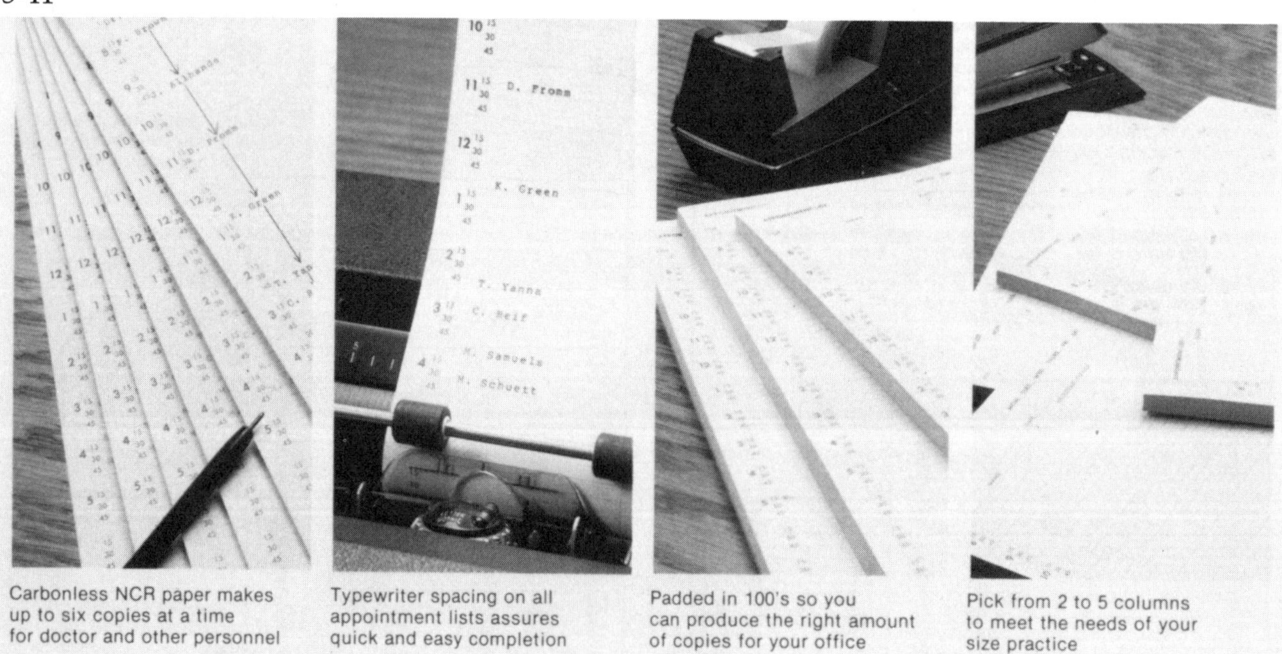

Carbonless NCR paper makes up to six copies at a time for doctor and other personnel

Typewriter spacing on all appointment lists assures quick and easy completion

Padded in 100's so you can produce the right amount of copies for your office

Pick from 2 to 5 columns to meet the needs of your size practice

5-42

There is some danger in the use of props, mainly that of overpowering the product, which should always be the main focus. Figure 5-43 from Leichtung's tool catalog shows a carved wooden duck as a prop for a kit with three woodburning tips. The product benefit (that of woodburning the feathers on the duck) is illustrated (though it may be a use that's a bit too vague for instant recognition). But the shot risks allowing the prop to be more prominent than the product. The technique that saves this from happening is the cropping of the prop. Including an entire prop in a photograph might confuse the customers — they don't know which item is being sold. Cutting into props concentrates customer attention on the product and creates "mystery," which induces customer interest.

Don't let props overpower products

5-43

Props, even ones that are highly related to the item, don't always add buyer motivation or interest to the catalog photograph. In this example from the Neiman-Marcus catalog (Figure 5-44), a plate, fruit, and coffee cup have been used to prop a set of folding tables. But the props do not illustrate a use that was otherwise indeterminate, nor do they add subliminal desire to make the purchase. Artistically they're too small to affect the composition of the photograph. Though this is not a bad photograph, it also is not an effective use of props.

Ask yourself these questions when trying to decide whether or not to prop the product:

1. Will the identity, function, or benefit of the product be clearer with a prop?
2. Is the item so visually dull that a prop will add appeal or draw the eye of the customer to the photograph?
3. Will it help the product sell by appealing to subliminal desires on the part of the customer?

5-44

The In-Use Shot. . . How can this approach benefit a presentation?

This technique can describe an otherwise unidentifiable product, show how to use the product or how the product functions, and indicate all the benefits of owning the product (easy or fun to use, elegant to wear). An in-use shot makes the benefits offered by the product seem readily within the customer's reach. Any type of product can be presented this way, but areas which particularly benefit are those featuring clothing, sporting goods or exercise equipment, office equipment, factory and plant equipment, and gardening items. An in-use shot often is called for if a product must move or be moved for the owner to derive its benefit. The use of colorful accessorizing in a propped shot, or dramatic lighting and backgrounds in a straight shot, have caused a gradual movement away from in-use catalog shots. But showing a product actually being used can make the illustration more interesting and compelling for the customer. And it is almost demanded when the product is complicated in function or when the resulting benefit is the major selling point.

General Consumer. This illustration (Figure 5-45) from the Chris-Craft catalog clearly shows how impossible it would have been for the viewer to know that the "binoculars" are actually a flask. Though the "eyepieces" are shot glasses, using them to catch the liquid would have added nothing to the photograph and might have been extremely confusing. This point is covered in copy, and rightfully so. Notice, too, that in the background of the top of this photo, a pennant has been used as a prop behind the binoculars. Perhaps this is supposed to suggest that the flask can be used at ball games, but one discovers the pennant only after examination. If a prop is not instantly recognizable, it does not achieve its main function. In this photograph, the pennant only adds clutter.

A standard in use shot for containers such as vases, dishes, or glasses is to show something in them. Figure 5-46 illustrates how effective a Chinese planter is when shown in-use. The tulips not only show visually how to use the product but also add color to the photo, thereby helping to attract attention. Another clever in-use example from the same catalog is seen in Figure 5-47. Designer rubber gloves are shown being worn and sudsing a dish. They would not have been nearly as attractive without this approach.

Some products need to be in-use in order to be identified visually. Following is the same product (a foot massager) as it is presented in two different catalogs. Figure 5-48 is from the American Express catalog. The use of the model's foot quickly tells the shopper that the item being sold is a foot product. Without the foot, viewers would have passed the photo by, but there is still doubt as to what the product is. The foot, although acting as an identifier, is really just a prop, so this is not an in-use shot. Frequently, new or high-tech items demand props in order to instantly tell customers what the item does. Figure 5-49 is from The Sharper Image catalog. They have literally shown the product in-use. The photographer has adjusted the camera to a slow shutter speed, thus picking up vibration

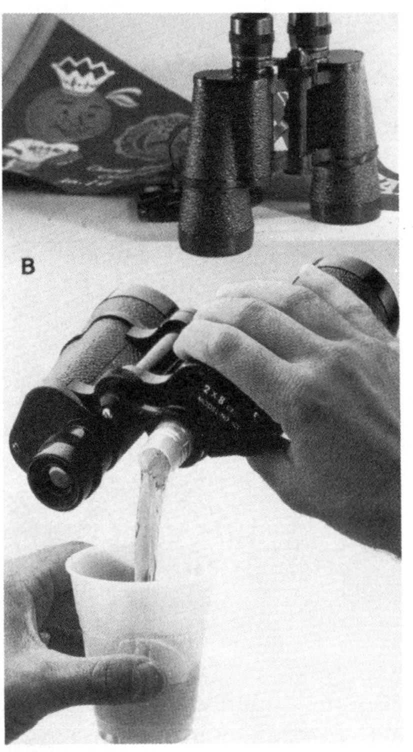

5-45

A contemporary Chinese porcelain planter, selected by Roger Horchow on his recent trip to Beijing (Peking). In a traditional hexagonal shape, handpainted in a blue and white design, the planter is a re-creation of an antique design. Ideal to use for spring bulbs or a year around plant. 12″ across, 7″ tall.
#F935G 150.00 value SPECIAL 99.90

5-46

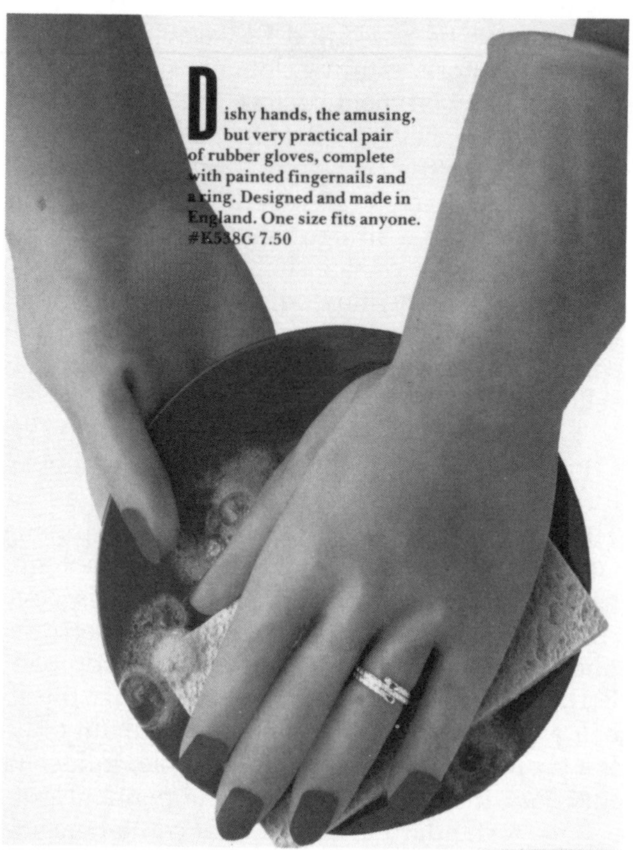

Dishy hands, the amusing, but very practical pair of rubber gloves, complete with painted fingernails and a ring. Designed and made in England. One size fits anyone.
#K538G 7.50

5-47

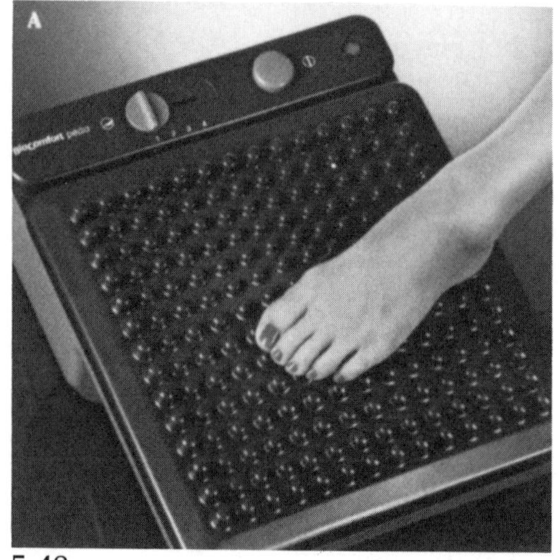

5-48

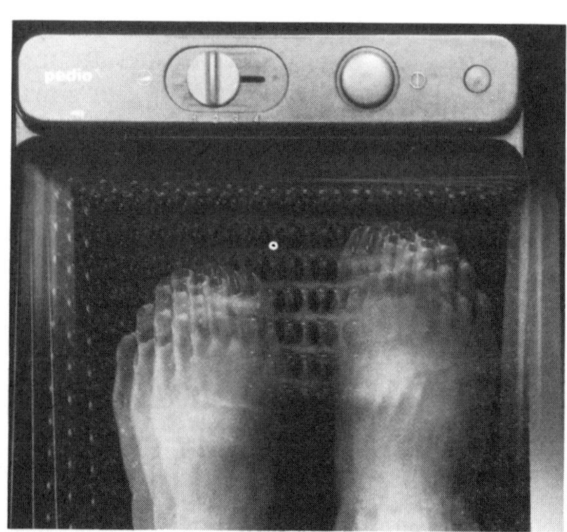

5-49

movement in the photograph, just as though the customer were actually using the product. A small straight shot of the product to one side allows the customer to see it in an unobstructed way. This approach identifies the product as well as the product use, so there is no doubt about what the product is.

Business-to-Business. There are many opportunites for in-use shots in business-to-business catalogs.

Figure 5-50 is a typical in-use application as seen in the Digital DECdirect catalog. A model representing an office worker is seated

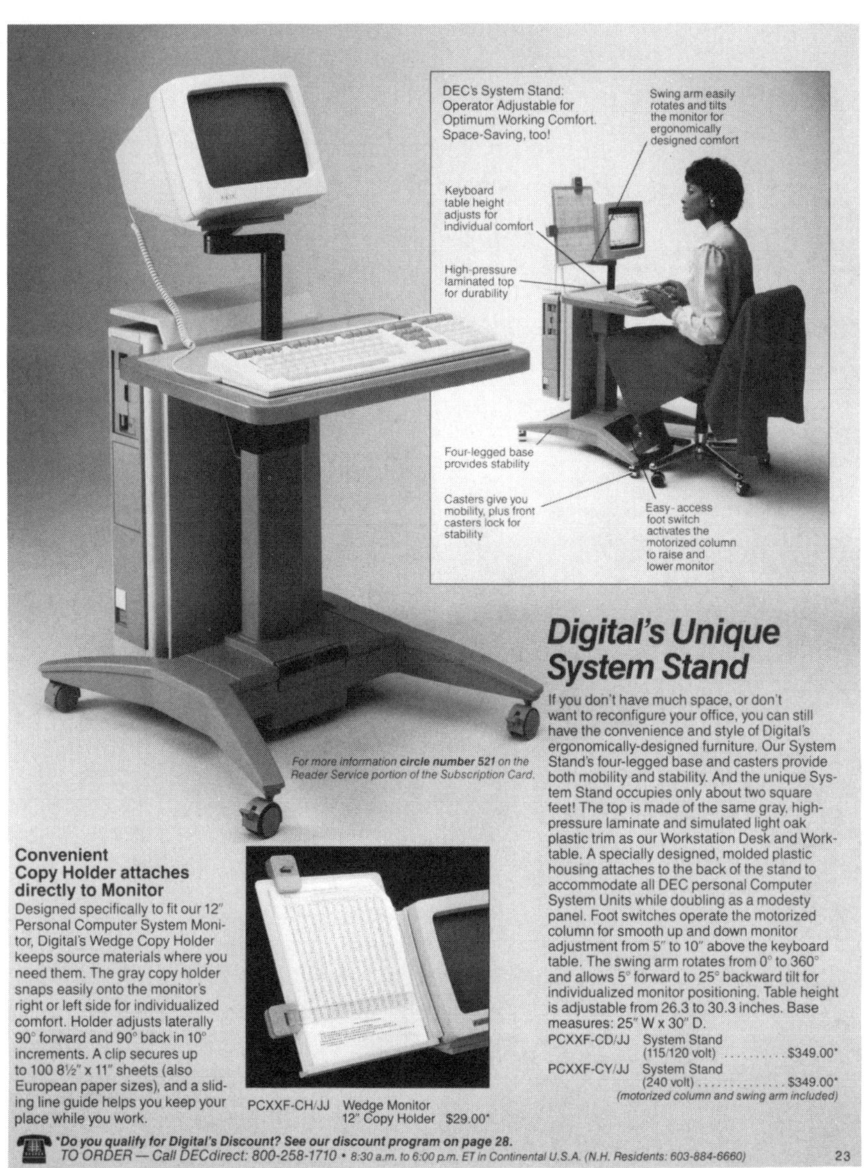

5-50

at the system stand and is using the copy holder — two products which are attached to a Digital computer (here, a prop). The model appears at ease and happy, exactly what is wanted in any office. Benefit call-outs are used to emphasize the various benefits of the two products being sold. A straight shot of each product dominates the space of the catalog page, but the in-use benefit shots command attention — partly because of the lighter background and the model in a red suit, but also partly because of the attitude of convenience produced by the technique.

Figure 5-51 is a simple in-use photograph silhouetted onto a lively color (yellow) background. Day-Timers has shown how easy it is to do an otherwise troublesome job of packaging with their sealing tape and dispenser. The one-hand action exemplifies the convenience and simplicity of use.

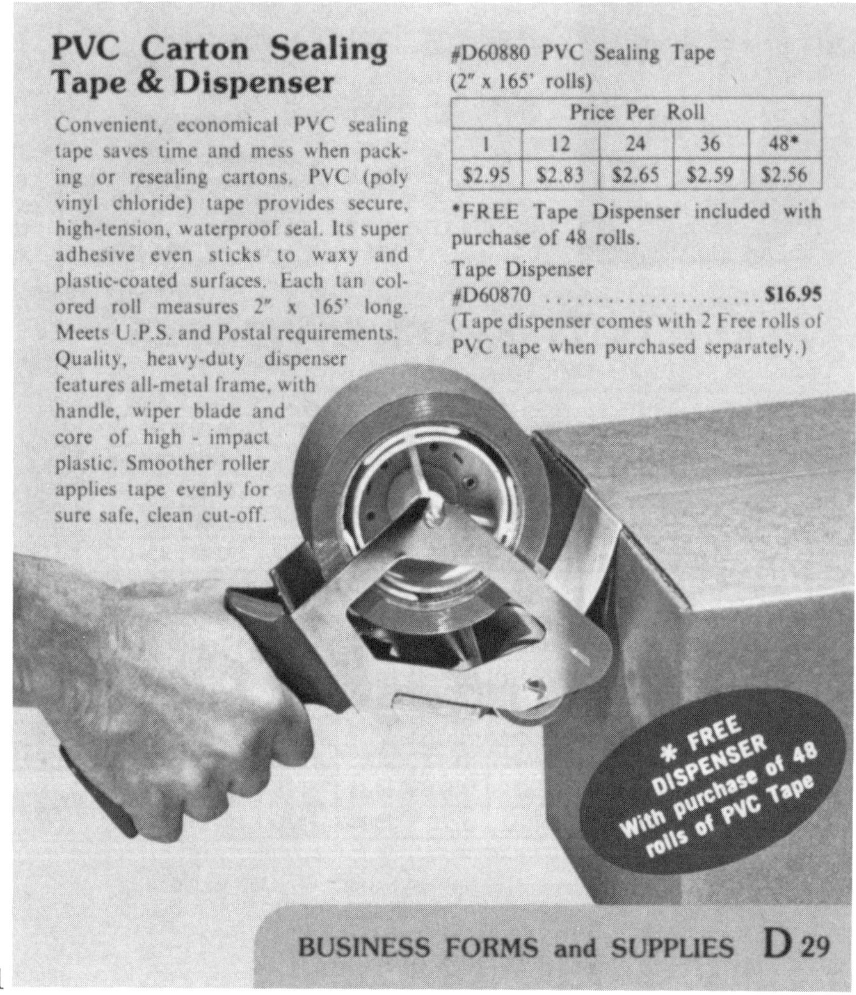

PVC Carton Sealing Tape & Dispenser
Convenient, economical PVC sealing tape saves time and mess when packing or resealing cartons. PVC (poly vinyl chloride) tape provides secure, high-tension, waterproof seal. Its super adhesive even sticks to waxy and plastic-coated surfaces. Each tan colored roll measures 2" x 165' long. Meets U.P.S. and Postal requirements. Quality, heavy-duty dispenser features all-metal frame, with handle, wiper blade and core of high - impact plastic. Smoother roller applies tape evenly for sure safe, clean cut-off.
#D60880 PVC Sealing Tape (2" x 165' rolls)
Price Per Roll
1 | 12 | 24 | 36 | 48*
$2.95 | $2.83 | $2.65 | $2.59 | $2.56
*FREE Tape Dispenser included with purchase of 48 rolls.
Tape Dispenser
#D60870 .... $16.95
(Tape dispenser comes with 2 Free rolls of PVC tape when purchased separately.)
* FREE DISPENSER With purchase of 48 rolls of PVC Tape
BUSINESS FORMS and SUPPLIES D 29

5-51

A three-step photo series shows how easy Garon's Instant Concrete is to use. (See Figure 5-52.) In just one hour's time (note the mock clock with time for each photo), the product being sold has solved with ease a common and irritating problem. This is an exceptionally fine example of how to present a difficult and uninteresting product in an attention-getting way. The visual presentation has told the story and sold the product too!

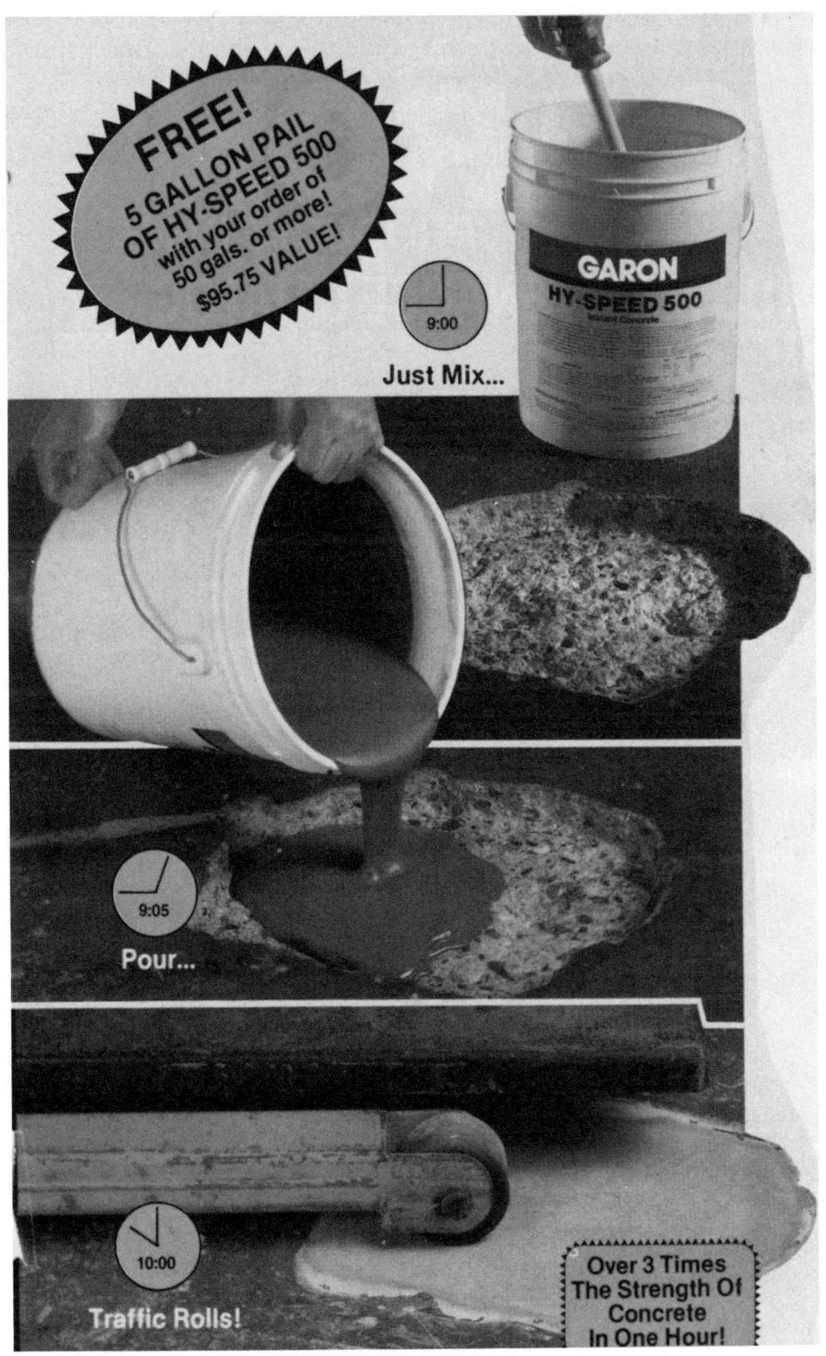

5-52

The product category emphasizing the in-use technique the most often and across the gamut of markets is apparel.

Neiman-Marcus (Figure 5-53) shows three likely partygoers walking down city streets in furs ranging in price from $8,000 to $30,000. The casualness of the scene reflects the mood only moneyed people create in such apparel. The very casualness of presentation will attract those who can afford the products.

Figure 5-54 from Spiegel's Wool catalog presents a chic coat appealing to currently popular style, but still with understated simplicity and a fairly high price ($405.00). The more stilted studio shot suits the appeal of the product and the target customer.

5-53

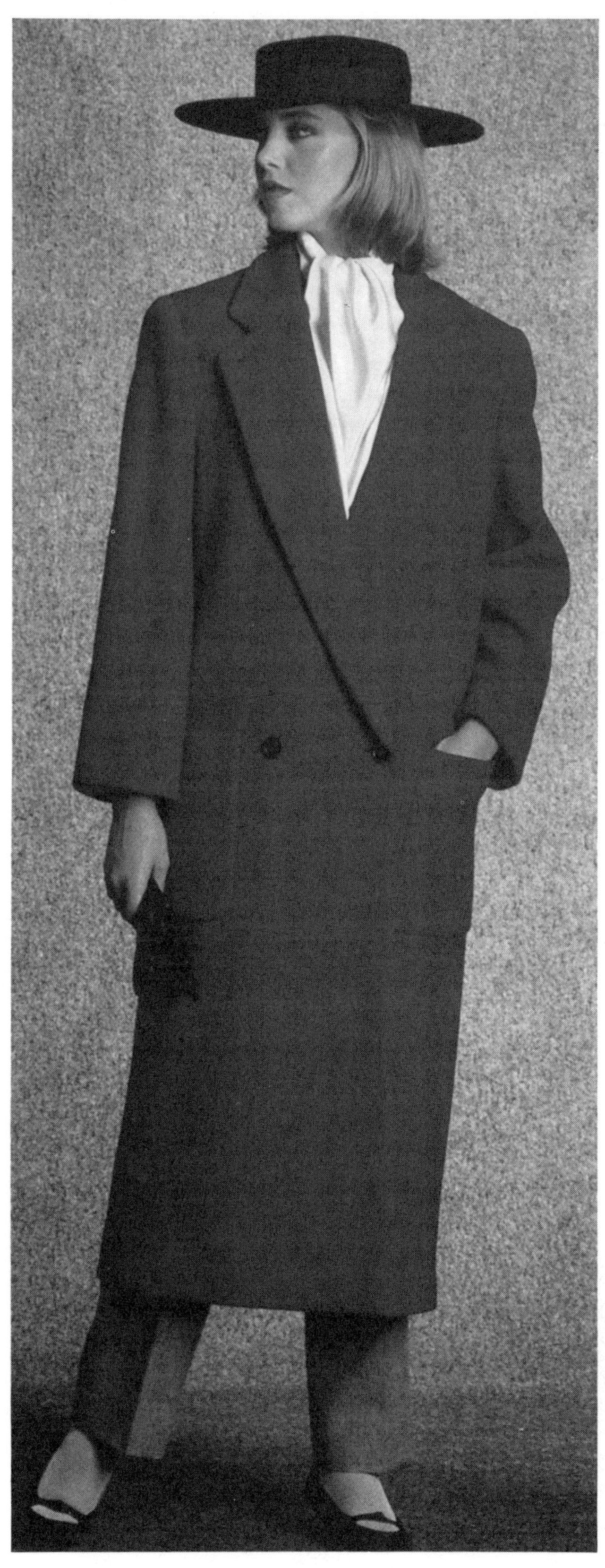
5-54

Jean Grayson's Brownstone Studio catalog appeals to a more middle-class market and is conservative in approach. The model is set in a more casual but modest outdoor pose (Figure 5-55). The style, mood, and price ($102.00) appeal to a more traditionally conservative customer.

5-55

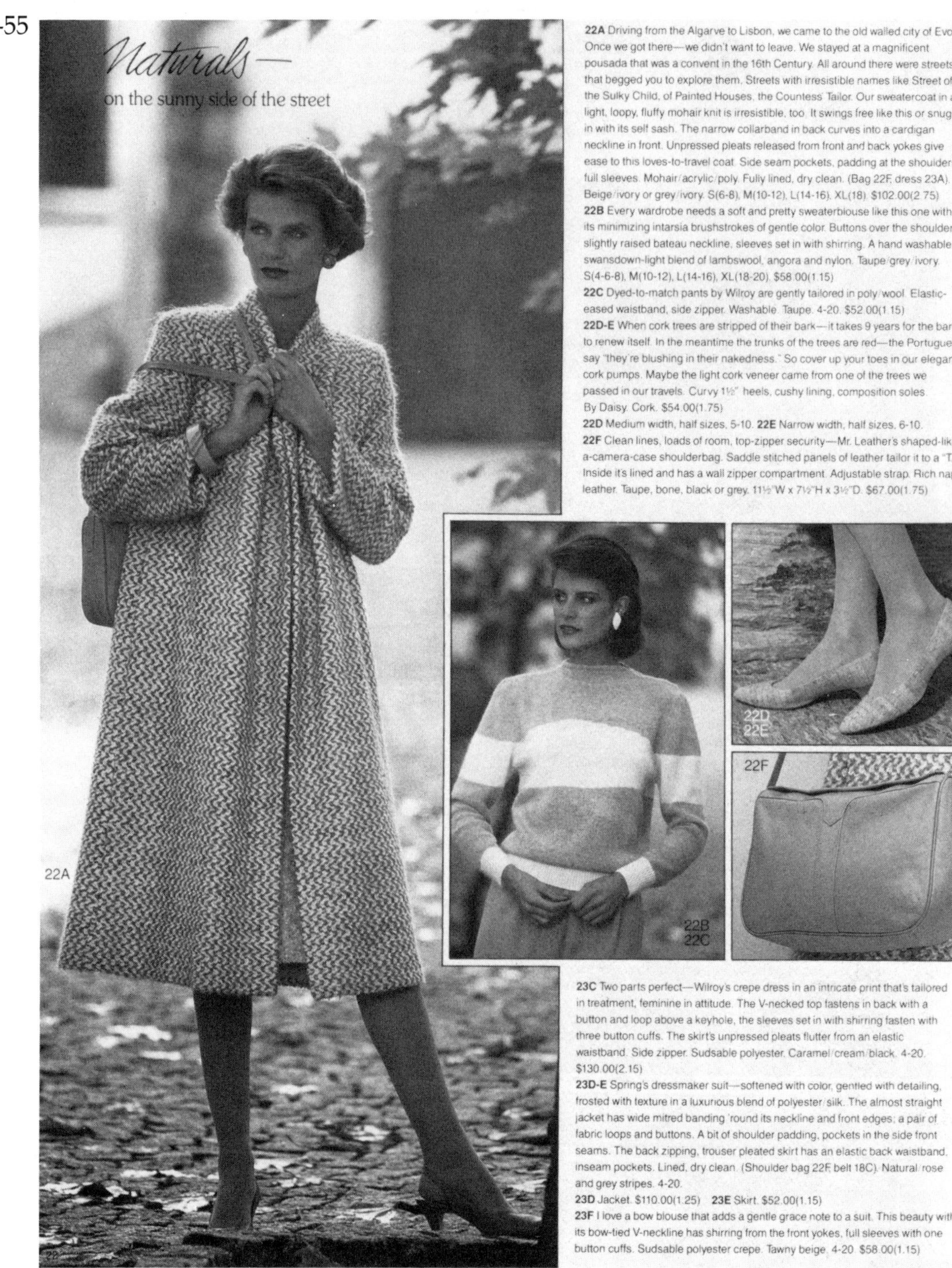

Naturals—
on the sunny side of the street

22A Driving from the Algarve to Lisbon, we came to the old walled city of Evora Once we got there—we didn't want to leave. We stayed at a magnificent pousada that was a convent in the 16th Century. All around there were streets that begged you to explore them. Streets with irresistible names like Street of the Sulky Child, of Painted Houses, the Countess' Tailor. Our sweatercoat in a light, loopy, fluffy mohair knit is irresistible, too. It swings free like this or snugs in with its self sash. The narrow collarband in back curves into a cardigan neckline in front. Unpressed pleats released from front and back yokes give ease to this loves-to-travel coat. Side seam pockets, padding at the shoulders, full sleeves. Mohair/acrylic/poly. Fully lined, dry clean. (Bag 22F, dress 23A). Beige/ivory or grey/ivory. S(6-8), M(10-12), L(14-16), XL(18). $102.00(2.75)

22B Every wardrobe needs a soft and pretty sweaterblouse like this one with its minimizing intarsia brushstrokes of gentle color. Buttons over the shoulder, slightly raised bateau neckline, sleeves set in with shirring. A hand washable swansdown-light blend of lambswool, angora and nylon. Taupe/grey/ivory. S(4-6-8), M(10-12), L(14-16), XL(18-20). $58.00(1.15)

22C Dyed-to-match pants by Wilroy are gently tailored in poly/wool. Elastic-eased waistband, side zipper. Washable. Taupe. 4-20. $52.00(1.15)

22D-E When cork trees are stripped of their bark—it takes 9 years for the bark to renew itself. In the meantime the trunks of the trees are red—the Portuguese say "they're blushing in their nakedness." So cover up your toes in our elegant cork pumps. Maybe the light cork veneer came from one of the trees we passed in our travels. Curvy 1½" heels, cushy lining, composition soles. By Daisy. Cork. $54.00(1.75)

22D Medium width, half sizes, 5-10. **22E** Narrow width, half sizes, 6-10.

22F Clean lines, loads of room, top-zipper security—Mr. Leather's shaped-like-a-camera-case shoulderbag. Saddle stitched panels of leather tailor it to a "T." Inside it's lined and has a wall zipper compartment. Adjustable strap. Rich napa leather. Taupe, bone, black or grey. 11½"W x 7½"H x 3½"D. $67.00(1.75)

22A

22B
22C

22D
22E

22F

23C Two parts perfect—Wilroy's crepe dress in an intricate print that's tailored in treatment, feminine in attitude. The V-necked top fastens in back with a button and loop above a keyhole, the sleeves set in with shirring fasten with three button cuffs. The skirt's unpressed pleats flutter from an elastic waistband. Side zipper. Sudsable polyester. Caramel/cream/black. 4-20. $130.00(2.15)

23D-E Spring's dressmaker suit—softened with color, gentled with detailing, frosted with texture in a luxurious blend of polyester/silk. The almost straight jacket has wide mitred banding 'round its neckline and front edges; a pair of fabric loops and buttons. A bit of shoulder padding, pockets in the side front seams. The back zipping, trouser pleated skirt has an elastic back waistband, inseam pockets. Lined, dry clean. (Shoulder bag 22F, belt 18C). Natural/rose and grey stripes. 4-20.

23D Jacket. $110.00(1.25) **23E** Skirt. $52.00(1.15)

23F I love a bow blouse that adds a gentle grace note to a suit. This beauty with its bow-tied V-neckline has shirring from the front yokes, full sleeves with one button cuffs. Sudsable polyester crepe. Tawny beige. 4-20. $58.00(1.15)

A lower-end catalog, First Editions (Figure 5-56), takes a conservative, posed approach in an outside setting. This approach shows the garment well and minimizes the photograph's cost because action shots, when done well, take more time to get just right and more skill from the model and the photographer.

PRICE BREAKER
63.00
A
SAVE 5.00
BUYS · BUYS
WAS $68.00
A. QUILTED VELOUR
pantsuit combines a sensational sensuous soft texture, with lavish contemporary detailing. New, bomber jacket looks fabulous with quilting all around and the newest neckline. Body is backed with acetate satin, the hem and wrists are elasticized. Paired beautifully with straight leg pants with elastic waist. Cotton/polyester velour. Washable. Salmon or Blue. S(8-10), M(12-14), L(16), J257238, $63.00
$66 VALUE
B. SWEATER-DRESSING
in three superb parts: an open front cardigan, a sleeveless shell and a pull-on skirt. Take note of the detailing, the gentle crochet-textured pattern of jacket and shell, the scalloping trim everywhere, the wide-ribbed A-line skirt. Knitted of rayon/acrylic. Hand wash. Natural. Sizes S(8-10), M(12-14), L(16-18), J225060, $59.95
PRICE BREAKER
59.95
B
SAVE 6.00
Only
88.00
D
larger sizes, too
PRICE BREAKER
47.00
C
WAS $49.00
12
C. SETTING THE PACE...
the classiest looking pump around. From Daisy in reptile look genuine leather with 2¼" heel and composition sole. Made in the USA. Full & half sizes 5-10 & 11. Medium. Wine, J300707B; Black, J300715B, $47.00
D. BEST COVERAGE...
the sweeping cape! Discover the elegance and pleasure of wearing one in exquisite suede that looks and feels like the real thing. It's washable... and resists rain and stains because it's Zepel-treated. Styled with button-front closing, a flattering collar, slit armholes and two shaped pockets. Breezy, warm and beautiful with top-stitching accents everywhere. In washable polyester fully lined with nylon taffeta. Beige or Mink Brown. J245829. S(8-10), M(12-14), L(16-18), $88.00 XL(38-40-42), $94.00

5-56

Not only does the in-use technique usually compliment the product but it also takes the place of "trying on" the clothing for the customer. Visualization becomes easier.

Ask yourself these three questions before deciding whether or not to choose an in-use shot:

1. Is the product function too complicated or indeterminate for a straight shot?
2. Is the product benefit or use the major selling point?
3. Will sales benefit from an in-use illustration?

The End-Benefit Shot. . . When It's The Best Way To Go

This kind of shot is most often dictated by the nature of the item itself. Products which have no visual attraction on their own, but have a splendid visual when utilized by the customer, should be presented in this manner. Use an end-benefit shot when you're selling the physical item not for its intrinsic look, but for the benefits received by the customer when using it. Catalogs which sell craft kits, seeds and bulbs, fruit and nut trees, diet and slimming aids, or training courses on tape or cassette can utilize this technique with effective results.

General Consumer. A perfect example of the end-benefit technique is seen in Figure 5-57 from the Park Seed Flower and Vegetable catalog. Over half a page is devoted to presenting Park's Pea, Sugar Snap, in three tantalizing photos. Not one photo shows the pack of seeds the customer receives or even the plants which will result. All three photos show the "picked" peas. The top photo even shows how the peas might be served when harvested and ready for the table. The two lower photos show peas being opened and cut away, thus revealing the superior quality of fully developed peas and their compact growth.

Williams-Sonoma's Catalog for Cooks (Figure 5-58) makes a full production in presenting a checkerboard cake pan set. Ingredients are shown in the background, and the product empty and in-use adds another step; but the most important element of the presentation is the end-benefit — the completely finished cake sitting on a cake stand. Without this part of the presentation, the purpose of the product could not visually be identified.

Craft catalogs whose products are kits, not a completed, ready-to-utilize product, show all the products in completed form. Figure 5-59 from the Herrschners needlecraft catalog photographs a finished quilt and dolls, not the thread, buttons, and material with marked stitches. Nowhere are these products seen in the form in which the customer will receive them. To do so would make a cluttered, unappealing, and uninteresting photograph that would act as a deterrence to purchase. Customers *want* to see benefit derived —

the attractive completed product — not the work to be done, even though they may derive enjoyment from performing it.

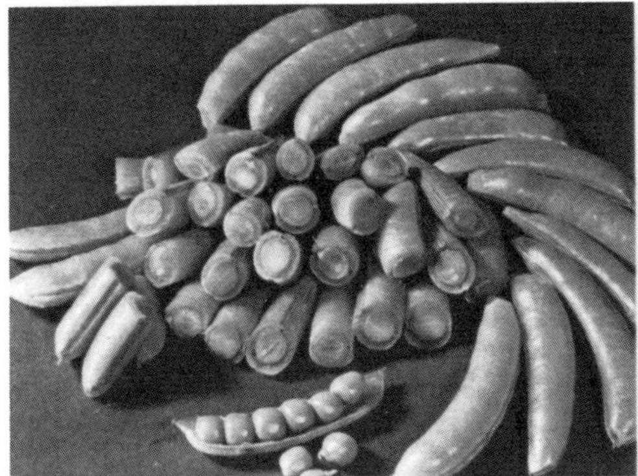
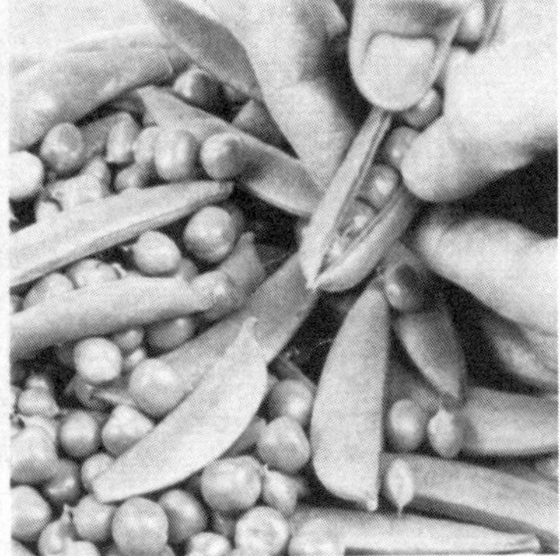

5-57

5-58

5-59

Business-to-Business. Many opportunities are available for business-to-business catalogers to take advantage of the end-benefit technique. How-to or self-help books and programs can picture the benefit derived from utilizing the product. A leadership program could picture a confident-looking person standing happily in front of a group of people, with the book or tapes overlayed in the foreground. Any problem-solving product could show the ''after'' treatment or application. Paper manufacturers could show specific completed products such as catalogs and books.

Garon Products (Figure 5-60) shows how their quick-set patching mortar and grout mix has patched difficult areas. Line drawings show other suggested areas it will repair. The actual product as it will be received occupies very little of the photo (note Garon bucket on top of loading dock).

Sycom Forms and Supplies catalog pictures three functions their product, Superbills, will perform (Figure 5-61), thus adding reality and interest to the presentation.

Inmac Computer Supplies catalog gracefully scatters different graph designs across the pages selling Inmac plotter pens to be used with various companies' computer printers (Figure 5-62). Also, at the top of the page is a true end-benefit shot picturing a successful and happy-looking gentleman presenting a brilliantly colored graphic chart before a group of people. This is visually saying, "You too can be successful because of the impact our pens will give to your presentations."

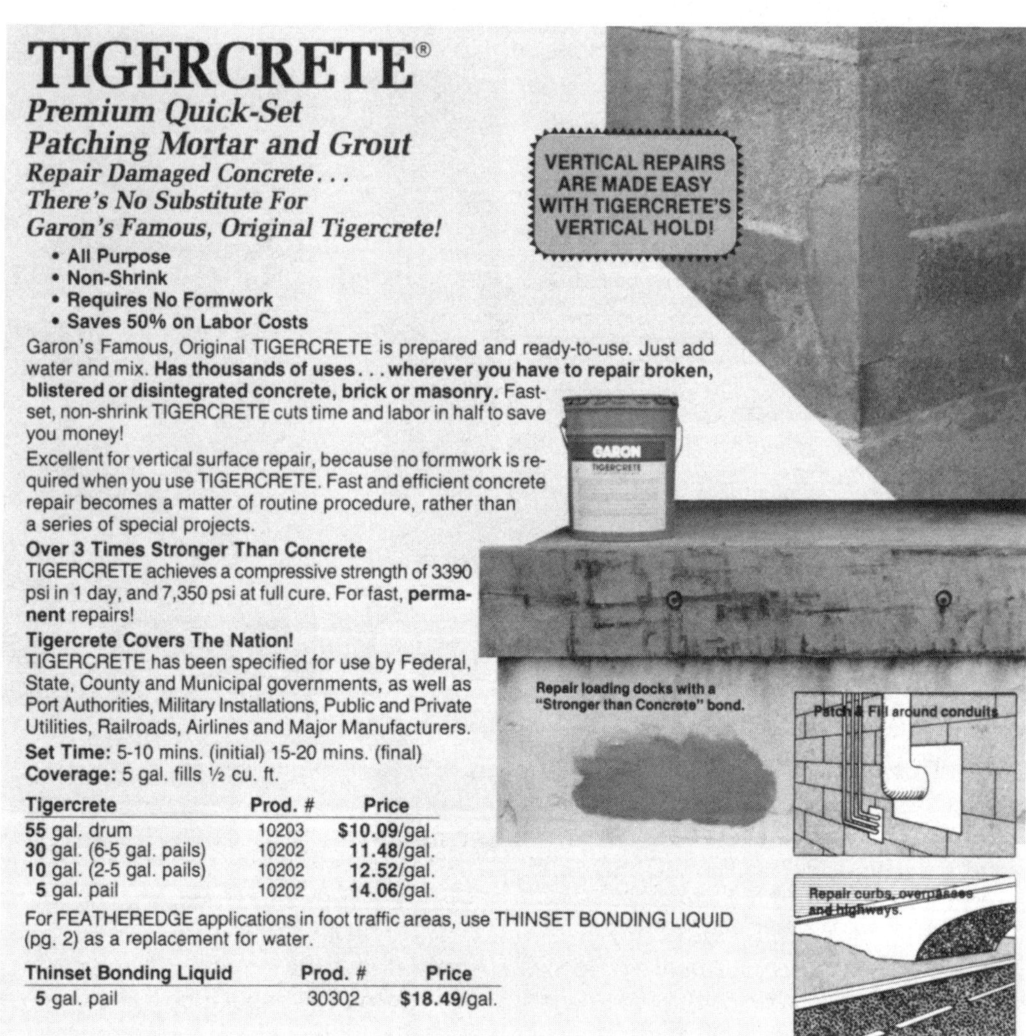

5-60

Speed up claims processing with our new superbills

[A] **Superbills.** Avoid messy carbons with 3-part NCR format. Accepted by most insurance carriers when attached to claim form's lower portion. Instructions for submitting claims printed on reverse side. Original is for doctor, canary for carrier, pink for patient. Includes space for benefits assignment, next appointment information. Exclusive format designed for quick, easy patient understanding. Select our standard optometric procedure codes (Item 875) or provide up to 36 codes suited to your special needs (Item 876). Please limit code descriptions to 23 characters/line (includes spaces). Provide doctor's name, address, telephone, social security, IRS and other identifying numbers for imprint at upper left. Printed in blue ink. For consecutive numbering see note below. Measures 5½" x 8½".

Item 875—standard codes	10,000 . . **$454.30**	5,000 . . **251.10**
Item 876—custom codes	2,000 . . **116.10**	1,000 . . **69.10**
	500 . . **40.20**	

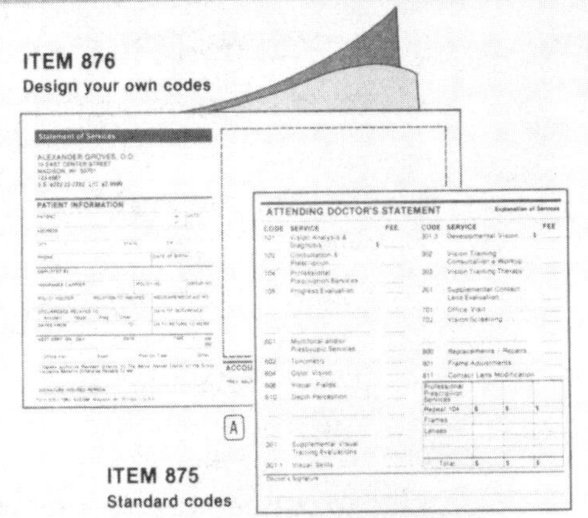

Superbills perform 3 important functions

Prompts immediate payment

Improves office communication

Speeds up claims processing

Note: Superbills can be consecutively numbered. Add $18.00 per 1000; minimum order of 1000.

5-61

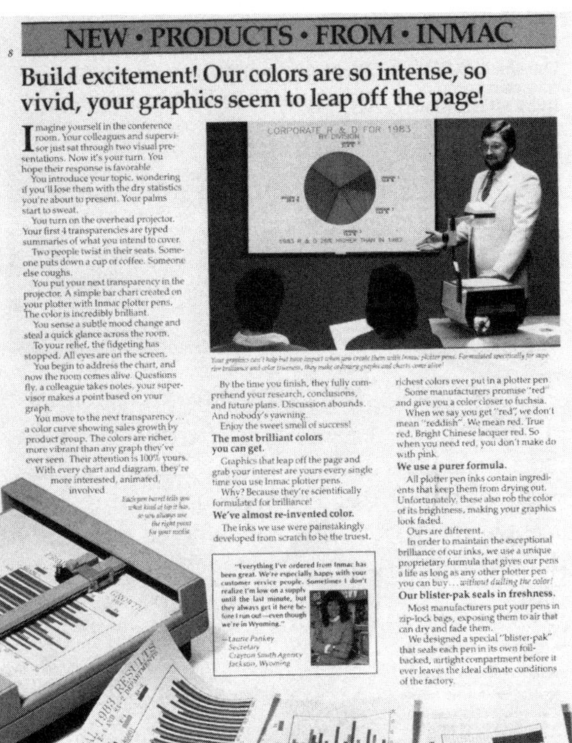

8

NEW • PRODUCTS • FROM • INMAC

Build excitement! Our colors are so intense, so vivid, your graphics seem to leap off the page!

Imagine yourself in the conference room. Your colleagues and supervisor just sat through two visual presentations. Now it's your turn. You hope their response is favorable.

You introduce your topic, wondering if you'll lose them with the dry statistics you're about to present. Your palms start to sweat.

You turn on the overhead projector. Your first 4 transparencies are typed summaries of what you intend to cover.

Two people twist in their seats. Someone puts down a cup of coffee. Someone else coughs.

You put your next transparency in the projector. A simple bar chart created on your plotter with Inmac plotter pens. The color is incredibly brilliant.

You sense a subtle mood change and steal a quick glance across the room.

To your relief, the fidgeting has stopped. All eyes are on the screen.

You begin to address the chart, and now the room comes alive. Questions fly, a colleague takes notes, your supervisor makes a point based on your graph.

You move to the next transparency . . . a color curve showing sales growth by product group. The colors are richer, more vibrant than any graph they've ever seen. Their attention is 100% yours.

With every chart and diagram, they're more interested, animated, involved.

By the time you finish, they fully comprehend your research, conclusions, and future plans. Discussion abounds. And nobody's yawning.

Enjoy the sweet smell of success!

The most brilliant colors you can get.

Graphics that leap off the page and grab your interest are yours every single time you use Inmac plotter pens.

Why? Because they're scientifically formulated for brilliance!

We've almost re-invented color.

The inks we use were painstakingly developed from scratch to be the truest, richest colors ever put in a plotter pen.

Some manufacturers promise "red" and give you a color closer to fuchsia.

When we say you get "red", we don't mean "reddish". We mean red. True red. Bright Chinese lacquer red. So when you need red, you don't make do with pink.

We use a purer formula.

All plotter pen inks contain ingredients that keep them from drying out. Unfortunately, these also rob the color of its brightness, making your graphics look faded.

Ours are different.

In order to maintain the exceptional brilliance of our inks, we use a unique proprietary formula that gives our pens a life as long as any other plotter pen you can buy . . . *without dulling the color!*

Our blister-pak seals in freshness.

Most manufacturers put your pens in zip-lock bags, exposing them to air that can dry and fade them.

We designed a special "blister-pak" that seals each pen in its own foil-backed, airtight compartment before it ever leaves the ideal climate conditions of the factory.

"Everything I've ordered from Inmac has been great. We're especially happy with your customer service people. Sometimes I don't realize I'm low on a supply until the last minute, but they always get it here before I run out—even though we're in Wyoming."

—Laurie Pankey, Secretary, Crayton Smith Agency, Jackson, Wyoming

5-62

Ask yourself these questions when deciding if you should use an end-benefit shot:

1. Is the product form merely a means to an end, with the end-result the reason for purchase?
2. Is the product dull or unidentifiable without showing it in its final form?
3. Will the end-benefit shot be a better road to sales?

Every one of these types of photographic presentation has the goal of clearly illustrating in an appealing way exactly what is being sold. The decision on which presentation to use occurs in thought and planning stages prior to the actual photography session. And the responsibility to execute each presentation effectively rests with the creative director and photographer. They must have the skills to convey the desired effect in each photograph and evoke the purchasing urge from the customer.

How Photography And Layouts Work Together To Sell Products

Every effective photograph needs a focal point . . . *and it must be your product*. While the techniques used by your photographer can help to focus the customer's attention on the product, the *placement* of the item within the frame of the photograph is vital. Prospects who view your catalog are not devoting themselves to intimate examination of every detail on every page. Most of the time the customer is browsing. Any impression you wish your product to make must be made *quickly*. And in a fast impression (which is probably all the time the customer will give you), *the product should be the first thing seen*. The first area of interest in the photograph should *not* be the color of the background, the location of the shot, or the props. It should *not* be the aesthetics of the photograph. It's the *product* you're selling.

Making sure the customer's eye focuses on the merchandise is easier said than done. Many subtle occurrences can cause the customer's eye flow to be disrupted or your viewer to focus on the wrong area. But a proper blend of the photographic techniques of background, lighting, and focus, along with the graphic technique of layout, can prevent these errors.

The major layout elements used to focus the customer's eye properly on the product are:

1. The *size* of the item in relationship to the photographic frame. Usually problems arise in this area because the product is shown either too large or too small within the photograph.
2. The *positioning* of the item within the photographic frame. Errors commonly occur here because the item is not placed in proper balance with other elements which might be present in the photo (such as models or props).
3. The *physical balance* between the item and its surroundings. This is a matter of how much ''air'' the item is surrounded by. Too much or too little will cause the viewer's eye to be bored.
4. The *color balance* (if a color photograph) or *tonal balance* (if a black and white photograph) between the item and background or other elements. The wrong balance between the item's color or tone and that of the background will cause either boredom or distraction.

You might think that layout would be a rather simple element. The camera is aimed right at the product, the photographic frame is filled with the product, and the shutter is clicked. Unfortunately, too much can go wrong, and following are a few illustrations of how this occurs.

For example, a simple product such as a coffee cup, shown against a simple background such as a sweep of color, seems as though it should be immediately apparent in a photograph. But even here, if the coffee cup is yellow and the background is gold, there may not be enough contrast between the two to make the cup ''snap'' out of its background. Lighting must then be used to make highlights play upon the cup to catch the viewer's eye. Would a navy background work instead? Yes, but maybe you don't want to have a high-contrast look to your catalog page. In that case, the way your photographer lights the item is the answer. And this must be indicated to your photographer by the layout. If that same cup is photographed quite tightly within the borders of the picture, there may not be enough air around the cup to help the viewer's eye rest upon it. Or if the cup is photographed with a great deal of background showing, there may be so much air that the item doesn't demand focus and the photograph is boring. Again, the viewer's eye skips right over the presentation.

Figure 5-63 shows (a) not enough air around the cup, (b) too much air around the cup, and then (c) the right amount of air around the cup to attract the viewer's eye.

There are other elements that can cause this simple cup in this simple photograph to end up as either an effective presentation, or a poor one. If the camera angle is too high, the cup will appear foreshortened and its proportions will not be represented realistically. If the angle is too "head on," the cup will not look interesting. So even with an item as straightforward as a coffee cup, shot without a complicated background or even a prop, *the elements of size, positioning, physical balance, and color balance all play an important role.*

5-63

How To Determine If your Layout Demands Focus For Your Product

When your customers are visually moving through your catalog, their eyes are moving fast and their minds are absorbing information rapidly. Anything that is not immediately apparent is either misunderstood or ignored. So while it seems obvious that photography is the tool for presenting the product clearly, there are two questions you should ask yourself *after* you create your product layout and *before* it is executed:

1. Does this layout *leave no doubt as to the indentity of the product* and its function?
2. Does this layout make sure that the *customer's eye is drawn to the product* — and not focused on a less important element?

If you can't answer yes to both of these questions, knowing that the product has been presented with the strongest possible focus, go back to the drawing board and start over. If there can be any confusion on the customer's part about these two issues, then your product sales will suffer.

Certain products which have many elements or functions can be even more difficult to deal with, simply because the multiple elements can cause confusion regarding the main product function. Also, products which resemble something which they are not, such as an item which looks like a pistol but really is a cigarette lighter, can fall into the difficult-to-present category. These kinds of products require extra thought in presentation, such as whether or not props will help make the product's function clear (using a cigarette and an ashtray with the pistol lighter, for example). And even those decisions are not as clear-cut as they initially seem. Are both the cigarette *and* the ashtray necessary — or would a pack of cigarettes or a single cigarette lying beside the lighter work even better? Which props provide the clearest enhancement and the least distraction to the main focus, the product itself? Again, all this must be indicated to the photographer by the layout you want followed.

The importance of lighting

Though you as the cataloger do not produce the actual photograph, you must direct the photographer toward the most effective presentation. This direction always begins with a decision about what the final photograph is expected to accomplish, and ends with conveying those demands to the photographer to carry out. More than one approach can be effective — there is no "right" or "wrong" style. But what may be effective for one catalog may not work for another. Some customers respond to bright colors, others to a soft or dramatic look. High-ticket items in high-ticket catalogs often demand a lot of image and status in backgrounds, lighting, and locale. You may want a "Horchow" look for your catalog, but in reality it may not be effective for your customer list. Knowing which approach to use is half the battle. Accomplishing it effectively is the other half.

Let's examine the elements of layout with some products and photographs that are more complicated than the coffee cup just illustrated.

Figure 5-64 from The Sharper Image shows a cordless telephone, which could have been photographed propless and with minimal background. But here is an excellent example of how the product remains the first thing seen, even in a situation with a complicated background, a model, and several props. The reason the focus remains on the product is that the product is *"sized" properly* in relationship to the other items; it is *positioned* forward and toward the center of the page it is on, which is the main focal area in almost any photograph; its immediate background (the car hood) does not "fight" with the item from either a "busy" standpoint or in terms of *balance;* and the *physical balance* of the house in the background and the hands in the foreground keep leading the eye to the prod-

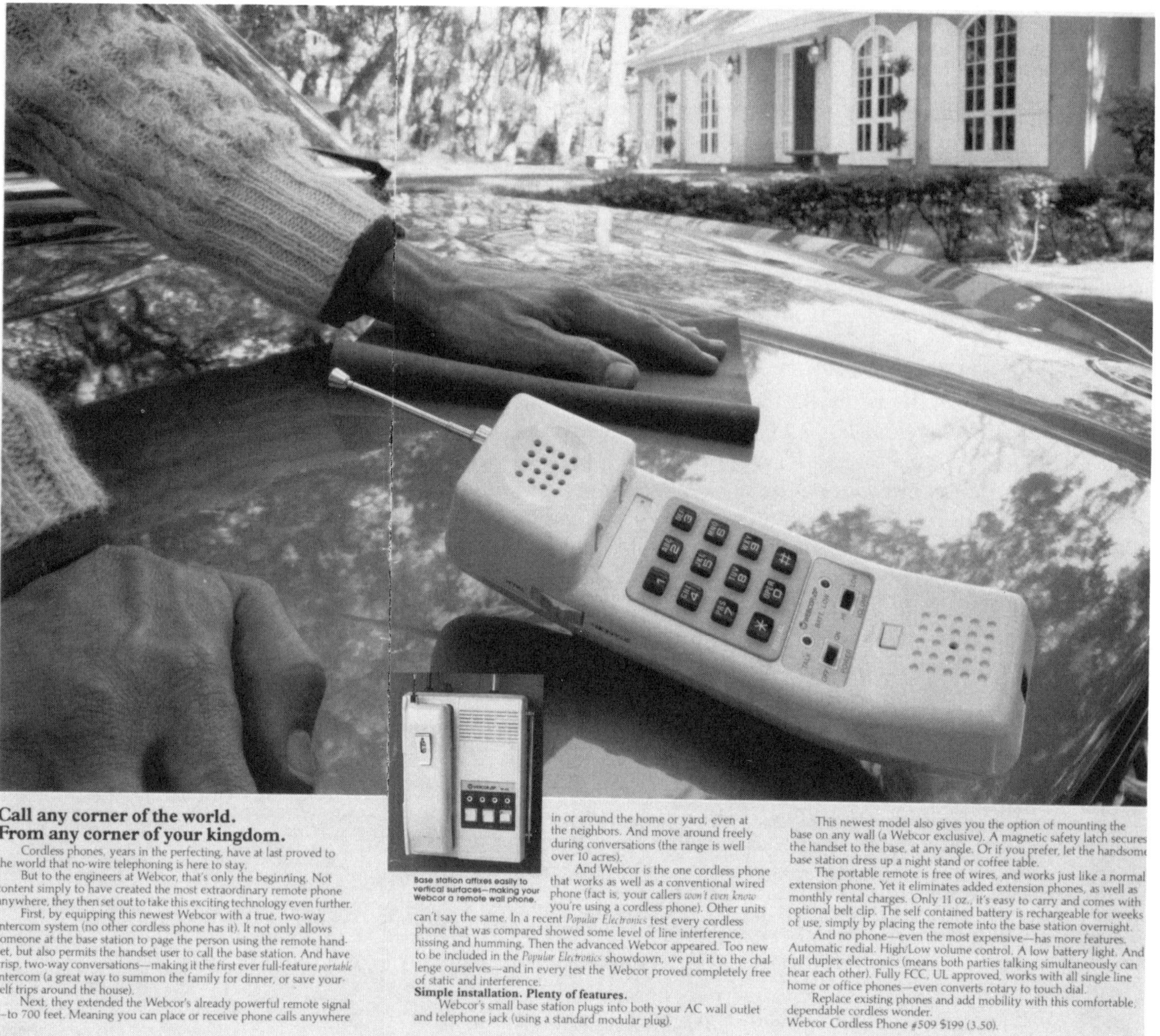

Call any corner of the world.
From any corner of your kingdom.
Cordless phones, years in the perfecting, have at last proved to the world that no-wire telephoning is here to stay.
But to the engineers at Webcor, that's only the beginning. Not content simply to have created the most extraordinary remote phone anywhere, they then set out to take this exciting technology even further.
First, by equipping this newest Webcor with a true, two-way intercom system (no other cordless phone has it). It not only allows someone at the base station to page the person using the remote handset, but also permits the handset user to call the base station. And have crisp, two-way conversations—making it the first ever full-feature portable intercom (a great way to summon the family for dinner, or save yourself trips around the house).
Next, they extended the Webcor's already powerful remote signal—to 700 feet. Meaning you can place or receive phone calls anywhere in or around the home or yard, even at the neighbors. And move around freely during conversations (the range is well over 10 acres).
And Webcor is the one cordless phone that works as well as a conventional wired phone (fact is, your callers won't even know you're using a cordless phone). Other units can't say the same. In a recent Popular Electronics test every cordless phone that was compared showed some level of line interference, hissing and humming. Then the advanced Webcor appeared. Too new to be included in the Popular Electronics showdown, we put it to the challenge ourselves—and in every test the Webcor proved completely free of static and interference.
Simple installation. Plenty of features.
Webcor's small base station plugs into both your AC wall outlet and telephone jack (using a standard modular plug).
This newest model also gives you the option of mounting the base on any wall (a Webcor exclusive). A magnetic safety latch secures the handset to the base, at any angle. Or if you prefer, let the handsome base station dress up a night stand or coffee table.
The portable remote is free of wires, and works just like a normal extension phone. Yet it eliminates added extension phones, as well as monthly rental charges. Only 11 oz., it's easy to carry and comes with optional belt clip. The self contained battery is rechargeable for weeks of use, simply by placing the remote into the base station overnight.
And no phone—even the most expensive—has more features. Automatic redial. High/Low volume control. A low battery light. And full duplex electronics (means both parties talking simultaneously can hear each other). Fully FCC, UL approved, works with all single line home or office phones—even converts rotary to touch dial.
Replace existing phones and add mobility with this comfortable, dependable cordless wonder.
Webcor Cordless Phone #509 $199 (3.50).
Base station affixes easily to vertical surfaces—making your Webcor a remote wall phone.

5-64

uct. Why was this item photographed in this manner, when a straight shot would have shown it just as well? Because the background and the props add subliminal feelings of distinction and elegance to the cordless phone. The benefit of owning this particular phone is not merely to use it as a communications vehicle, but to attain a certain status by the possession of this special phone. Features are not the only thing being sold. Benefits also are sold here. The small inset showing how the base station converts it to a wall phone is simply an added benefit.

The next illustration (Figure 5-65) from Bloomingdale's "The Taste of France" catalog also tries to sell benefits. Unfortunately, the immediate question occurring to the viewer is, "What is the prod-

5-65

uct?'' In this photograph, the product is *not* the first thing seen. The product is not the lace tablecloth; it is a group of products appearing on top of the table, including a bottle of mineral water, cherries in light syrup, and coffee. In this photograph, the *size* and *positioning* of products are dwarfed and subsidiary to background and props. The *physical balance* of the photo is disrupted by incorrect placement of all items. This negates orderly eye flow and positions a non-product, the block of lace, in the most prominent area. And the *color balance* is upset because the white lace draws the eye. Though this photograph attempts to sell benefits, it is not successful because the benefits do not relate clearly to the specific products being sold.

Basic product presentation rule: For any given product in any given catalog, take the *elements of layout* (size, positioning, physical balance, and color balance) *and combine them with the photographic techniques* of lighting and focus to control and illustrate your product's features and benefits. Do this after you consider how best to present these benefits to your specific audience.

An Exercise Comparing Two Product Presentations

Here, in practical terms, is the right (and wrong) way to approach product presentation. These two photographs of jewelry present a study in contrast. The first illustration (Figure 5-66) is from The Sharper Image Gemstones and Jewelry catalog. The subtleties used to focus the customer's eye on the merchandise abound. The photograph uses a model and prop (the fur) to sell benefits by adding glamour and "image" to possession of the jewelry. (These elements effectively "size" the product, as well.) But the addition of these elements does not prevent the jewelry from remaining the focal point — even though the amount of space occupied in the photo by the merchandise is small compared to the amount occupied by the model. How has this been achieved)? By *using the photographic techniques of lighting and focus in combination with elements of layout.*

Four important techniques

1. Lighting. The model's face does not demand the attention it would have if it had been lit with the same intensity as the rest of the photograph. Instead, it is "shadowed," which controls the balance of this area of the photograph. Because the jewelry is the most brightly lit area, it remains the focal point. This style of lighting also adds drama to the products.

2. Focus. The depth of field is shallow, making the jewelry the sharpest area of the photograph, giving a subdued feeling of soft-focus to the rest of the photo. Some photographs could exaggerate this technique even more strongly. They could use a filter to soft-focus the background, or conversely to make a "star" appear where a facet of the gemstone reflects the light.

3. Positioning. The merchandise is in the center of the photo with the arm angled toward the center and the fur framing the center point. Everything leads the eye to the grouping of neckpiece, rings and bracelet, which are in close juxtaposition. The eye does not jump across the photo trying to locate the items in different areas. No distractions occur because there are no jarring angles.

4. Color. Though you cannot see it in this black and white rendition, the blue topaz stones command attention within the neutrals of skin tone and white fur. Color balance has been effectively used to attract the viewer's eye to the product.

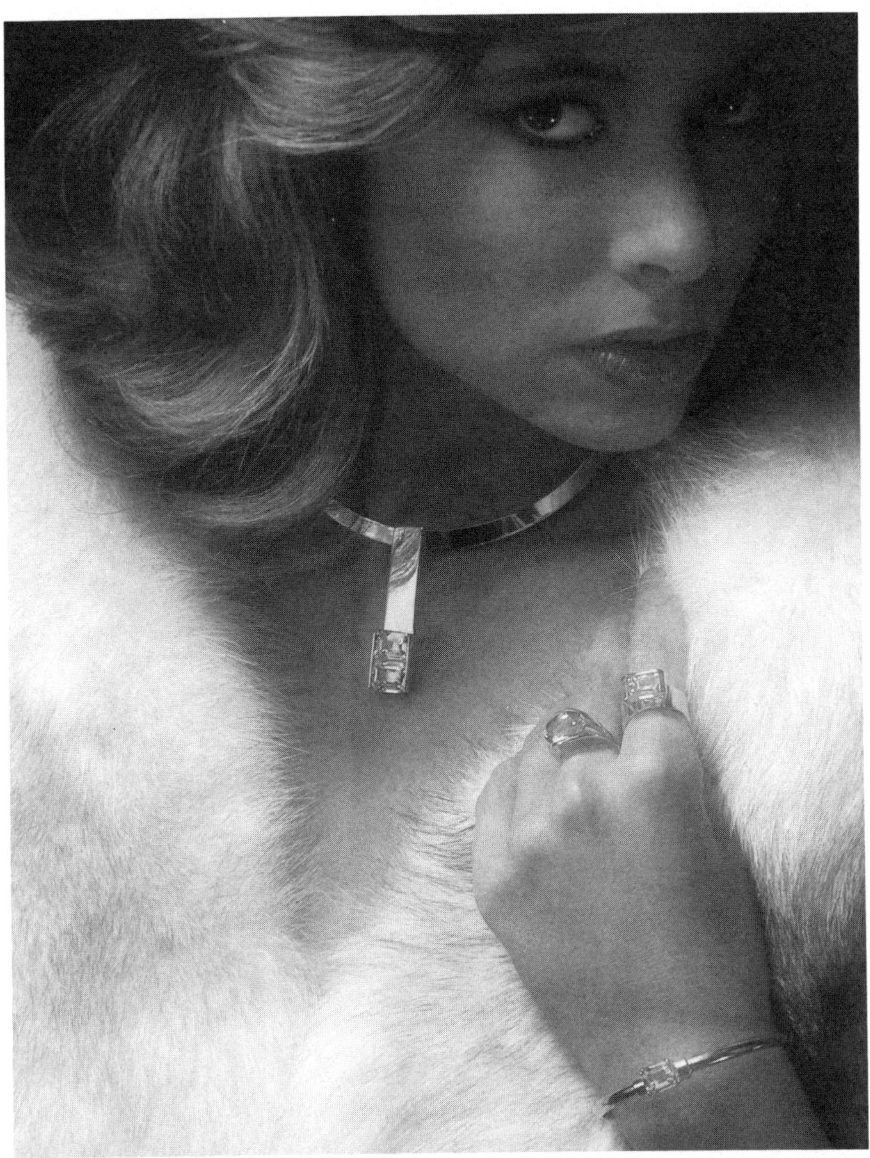

5-66

The next illustration (Figure 5-67) from an American Express catalog shows that bigger is not necessarily better. The original of this photo is a bit larger than the Gemstones example, but the merchandise featured here has been overwhelmed by the rest of the photograph. Its layout has destroyed the viewer's ability to focus on the products, and the photographic elements have not helped this situation. The photo could just as well be a skin cream ad. Let's take a look at the same elements used in the preceding photograph to see what happened.

1. Lighting. The lighting is soft, flat, even. No shadows, no highlights — nothing to force a glint or gleam from the diamonds, or to add drama, impact or mood — nothing to direct eye flow. Lighting does not help the eye focus on any area of the photograph.

2. Focus. Because the photo is a tight close-up, conflicting elements are in the identical plane (and identical focus), such as the model's eye and the ring. The technique is almost clinical — as though every inch of the photograph has to show subject matter with equal clarity.

3. Positioning. Here, the actual span between ring and pendant covers about the same area as on the model in the Gemstones

5-67

photograph, but this layout forces the eye to jump a much greater distance, with nothing guiding it along a "travel" route. The background dwarfs the items, making them appear insignificant in relationship to the expanse of skin and hand. The total diamond weight of the ring is one carat, but it appears unimpressive. Though the hand leads into the photograph, it points toward the eye — both pieces of merchandise remain on the fringes of interest.

4. Color. This photo is completely composed of neutrals, since diamonds are also colorless. But here is where the addition of "black" *via shadows* would have helped add contrast. The merchandise would have stood out with emphasis from a shadowy background, even if the items had remained on skin-toned hand and neck.

The customer must never be confused about where to focus (on the merchandise) and how the eye should travel (never at random, never jumping, always flowing). Good layout is not merely "position." It is control of the viewer's eye flow via all elements and techniques of photography. It is the forcing of the viewer's eye where you want it — on your product!

If The Main Focus Is The Item . . . Then What Is The Item's Main Focus?

Poor focus and layout often occur because techniques are badly used. But in addition, an ineffective presentation is frequently caused by confusion on the part of the catalog marketer about the main point of the product.

No matter what your product is — no matter how many features it offers the customer and no matter how complicated it is visually — any product has a certain area which offers a major advantage to the customer. Perhaps even a couple of areas. But never *all* the areas.

A frequent error in art and copy presentations is the *inability of the creative staff to choose (or decide upon) the main thrust of the product.* And every time a product is presented with all thrusts given equal weight (or almost equal weight), the presentation is diluted. This weakening usually occurs because the eye of the viewer is confused and has to work harder to draw conclusions about the item, and about whether or not to purchase it. There is no logical reason why you want to make your customers have any more difficulty making a purchasing decision than absolutely necessary. This problem of equally weighting all of the assets of a product is a concrete example of the old saw: 'More is less.' You'll often see this problem of presentation in catalogs geared to businesses, because the products offered for sale frequently have many features.

In layouts presenting products with many features, the copy often is as intrinsic to the visual presentation as the photograph. The copy not only tells about the item, but works in immediate juxtaposition to the artwork.

Complicated presentations must be made easy for the customer!

The example below from a Day-Timer catalog (Figure 5-68) indicates confusion between the main feature of the item and its subsidiary advantages. To determine what the item is and does, the customer must do a lot of scattered looking. The main feature, 5 Books in 1, is tucked into a small space to the right of the item photo. This main feature is printed in type which asks for the same attention as that asked by the auxiliary features below it (which occupy a great deal more space). The fact that a wallet is also involved (which can be personalized) is a confusing element sandwiched in between the main and the auxiliary features. If a customer is not familiar with the physical makeup of a Day-Timer, the logical question would be: 'What wallet?'' since none is apparent from the photograph.

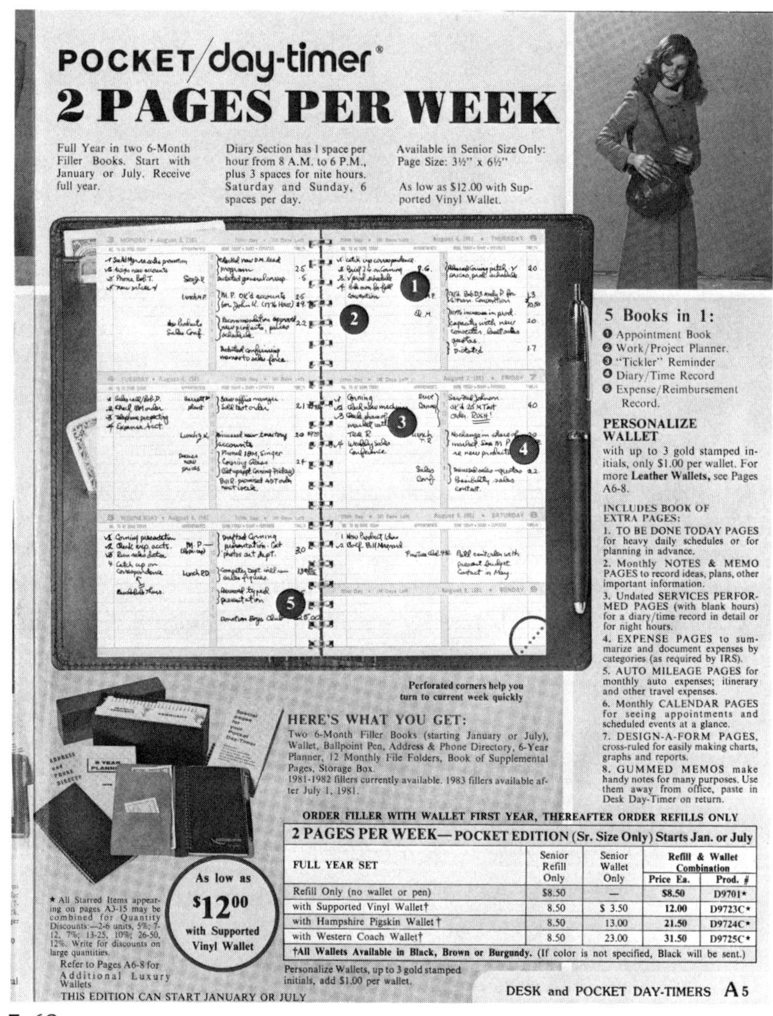

2 PAGES PER WEEK— POCKET EDITION (Sr. Size Only) Starts Jan. or July

FULL YEAR SET	Senior Refill Only	Senior Wallet Only	Refill & Wallet Combination	
			Price Ea.	Prod. #
Refill Only (no wallet or pen)	$8.50	—	$8.50	D9701*
with Supported Vinyl Wallet†	8.50	$ 3.50	12.00	D9723C*
with Hampshire Pigskin Wallet †	8.50	13.00	21.50	D9724C*
with Western Coach Wallet†	8.50	23.00	31.50	D9725C*
†All Wallets Available in Black, Brown or Burgundy. (If color is not specified, Black will be sent.)				

5-68

The copy below the main headline does not clarify any of the main features of the item. It begins, ''Full year in two 6-Month Filler Books,'' but it could have clarified the product by saying: 'Full year diary/planner in its own wallet.''

Random copy points are placed within the layout anywhere that space is available, rather than with forethought regarding size, position, and balance. The comment squeezed into the lower left of the ad is an example: 'This edition can start January or July.'' Another example is the copy block immediately above which talks about quantity discounts available for ''starred items'' in the ads. But it's hard to reference the starred items to this copy. (You'll find them in the right-hand column of the order information chart.)

And if a customer wanted to purchase a dozen of any of these products, the discount incentive isn't apparent in the chart (which is where it normally would appear and be noticed). This chart of ordering information is also confusing. There are product numbers in the right-hand column which seem to refer to the refill and wallet combination. But if the customer wants to order the refill or the wallet only, what product number should be specified? Yet at the top of the order chart, bold capitals instruct repeat customers to order refills, if they already own the wallet from a prior purchase.

This presentation is a plethora of confusion, not only in the lack of isolation of main product features, but also in the confusing placement of vital ordering incentives and information. And, incidentally, quite a bit of valuable space is used at the upper right to show a woman placing the item in her purse. Ostensibly this is shown to imply female usage, as well as male (because preceding ads for other Day-Timers picture men only).

Obviously the product is chock-full of features. Though it may not be too difficult to determine which are the main item points, it is certainly quite a project for the cataloger to decide how to emphasize and promote the features in a way which is orderly to the customer's eye . . . and which allows the eye to pick up and mentally absorb those points one by one. Compounding the problem are such things as quantity discount incentives. In the Day-Timer example, could this idea have been presented in a larger format in one main place in the catalog, instead of in the fine print used here (and in other individual ads)? Then the individual ads could have said: 'Quantity discounts — see order form.'' Some people argue the sensibility of making the customer flip elsewhere in the catalog. If this is a problem, then place the information in the chart, where it belongs.

As you can see, solving the problem of promoting the product's main point takes thorough analysis.

Product Photography Checklist:

- ☐ Obtain Actual Production Sample of Product If At All Possible.
- ☐ Determine Mood of Your Catalog To Be Transmitted in Photographs.
- ☐ Review Product Presentation with Artist, Merchandiser, Copywriter.

Always:

1. Focus on the product or resulting benefit.
2. Review background colors for visual coordination.
3. Review competitors' presentations.

Strongly Consider:

1. Utilizing insets for product detail or functional emphasis.
2. Using props to enhance visual attraction or to size product.
3. Using natural setting in which to photograph products.
4. Art presentation for greater definition of product or product function.

Presenting a Complicated Item

How To (Or How Not To) Present A Complicated Item In Your Catalog . . . The art and copy approach, and what makes it happen.

Certainly one catalog marketer with a hefty line of complicated products to show is Ambassador. This catalog house continually struggles to arrive at new ways to tell the same story because such a large part of its product lines is organizer-type handbags. Each one of Ambassador's handbags is hampered by the classic problem of "not being able to tell a book by its cover." That is, the hidden advantages of the compartments and accessories of each handbag cannot be seen by a casual glance at the exterior of the bag. What to do?

Let's assume that the product in the example from Ambassador which we are using in Figure 5-69 was chosen (or created) by merchandisers who have based their choice on previous customer response to other handbags. As mentioned earlier, the art and copy approaches to any presentation should always be based on this premise: what is there about the product which will make our customer list respond to it? These features must be instantly clear and observable when the customer views the photograph. But what do we see instantly in Figure 5-69? A woman's handbag with lots of "stuff." Is this observation as pointed as it could have been? Or are customers forced to isolate the features of the bag simply because they realize that the representation of so much "stuff" must mean something? Let's try to follow the thoughts which created this art and copy presentation by looking at the elements of the ad one by one.

1. This product is hoped to be one of the number-one sellers in the catalog. Why? It's shown on pages two and three of the catalog (a high visibility area) and it has been given a double-page spread. Other handbags with as many features and accessories, plus the same price points, are shown on single pages. Because of this, we must assume that a conscious decision was made to feature the purse, not that this amount of space was deemed necessary to show the bag. So, point number one: *How much space will the item occupy, and why?*

2. The product is getting a heavy "personal" touch. A scripted blurb is used in the upper left to encourage a personal touch between Joy H. and the customer. A logo accompanies the blurb featuring "An Ambassador Lifestyle™ Handbag," obviously used to suggest that this bag has an extra-special quality. Point number two: *"Personal touch" techniques are valuable — but if you use them, be sure they work hard for you.* The logo is crowded into the layout, hard to read, and, consequently, hardly worth the space it occupies. Couldn't less space have been taken to achieve the same result? Yes.

5-69

3. The main copy headline is positioned in the area immediately below the script and the logo, a weak area already because of its physical location, but even more so here because it fights the scripted headline and logo above it. Both the script/logo area and the main headline area occupy the same amount of space — a mistake because the reader's eye does not give precedence to one over the other. Though a paler blue print is used in the actual four-color ad, the "weight" of it is still too balanced with the bolder black print (a fact which does not appear in this black/grey rendition). Point number three: *When using headlines and subheads or banners, do not make them fight by giving them equality.*

4. Now comes the real problem, how to show the hidden essentials: an inner view of the handbag's compartments, a view

of the eight accessories, and an attempt to correlate the two. The inner view of the handbag is crowded by the large overlay of the handbag itself, so the more detailed view doesn't stand out as an entity. It is overprinted with eight circled numbers. Good — that seems to indicate there is something special here. Though the headline above this inner view photo tries to clarify the main features of the bag, the headline is too ''blocky'' to read at a glance, so it doesn't do its job. The reader cannot instantly figure out what the eight numbers refer to. Perusal shows that they indicate placement within the handbag of the eight accessories shown underneath. But the relationship requires study; it is not at-a-glance clear. The accessories are numbered (very indistinctly) to match the circled numbers. Point number four: *If you have to correlate two pieces of artwork, duplicate techniques in each to make the correlation logical.* For instance, if the accessories were numbered circles, with reversed colors from the numbers used for the inner view, the connection would be easier to make. This is just one suggestion for a solution to the problem. Or imagine a different headline above the inner view: ''6 special compartments keep you organized. . .'' continuing with a matching headline over the photo of eight accessories: '. . .with 8 accessories to tuck in the compartments!'' Each head would be printed in the same typestyle, with size and colors relating them to each other.

5. The large photo of the purse occupies the most prominent physical area of the layout — the upper right — and then some. An attempt was made to show that the handbag has zippered compartments because the model's hands are holding what appear to be the flaps of the zippers. But actually what has happened is that this conclusion cannot be drawn without study. Consequently, the hands occupy space within the ad to no purpose except that they clutter it and use up ''air'' which would have been better spent clarifying the photo. Point number five: *If you can't show a feature at a glance, better not try it.* Point number six: *Often bigger is not better, if it crowds space (or air).* Air is vital to help the reader's eye travel and absorb information.

6. Now to the copy block: the position is fine, but the point size of the type is somewhat small in comparison to the ad as a whole and the photographs specifically. This copy might have been clearer and had more punch if, instead of paragraphing, it were bulleted:

- Six compartments in all!
- 3 separate zippered compartments up top.

In summary, a slightly smaller main photo of the bag and the elimination of the hands (or at least the hand on the left) would give some air to the layout and would allow a main head to run across the top. A smaller personal message, combined with the extra air from the reduction of the main photo, would allow a better spatial placement of the headline under the script/logo area (which could use the rewrite mentioned earlier). An improvement in correlating the numbers in the accessory photo, plus a rebalancing of the accessory photo with the inner view photo, and presto! — the same ad would be clearer and more effective.

Artwork Versus Photos

Nothing is as believable to the viewer as a photograph of an item. Because of this, photographs are invariably the first choice when presenting a product visually. But there are times when photos simply will not work, or are too impractical to consider. It's vital for your artists, or art director, to be able to isolate these instances. The first would be:

> **1. Size of Item.** Usually the size becomes critical when items are so large or so long that fitting them in a photo causes the camera to back off so far that the item can no longer be clearly seen. This ineffectiveness occurs because photographs cannot control perspective in the same ways that artwork can. Figures 5-70, 5-71, 5-72, and 5-73 show the same item, a long-handled pulsating window washer, in three different catalog presentations, which achieve varying degrees of success.

Emphasis on detail

Figure 5-70 from Walter Drake and Sons is a full-color presentation. The creators of this ad have decided that two issues are the most important: (1) the length of the washer, and (2) the pulsating ability. The artwork warps the perspective of a two-story house to show the length, and uses an inset to show the head of the washer with a headline indicating the pulsating action. The copy headline, "Wash Second-Story Windows Easily," underlines the thrust of the artwork by clearly stating the main function. What has been ignored in this presentation? First, the showing of the various components of the washer, and secondly, the showing of the various functions of the washer. One would assume that these deletions were made in an effort to keep the main point of the washer prominently presented, not confusing the issue with secondary points. On the whole, this is an entirely satisfactory presentation, which a photograph could never have accomplished.

Figure 5-71 from Miles Kimball illustrates a similar approach — full-color artwork geared toward exaggerating the length of the washer. The long-handled feature is clear; the fact that the item is washing second-story windows is clear. But in this presentation, the inset has been used to feature an additional attachment, a gutter cleaner. This is not easy to show in the space allotted, mainly because the gutter cleaner has a mirror attached to it which confuses the artwork (though the copy explains it clearly). The mirror attachment is too unfamiliar a device to be instantly absorbed by the mind in such a small piece of art. Here is a situation where one wonders

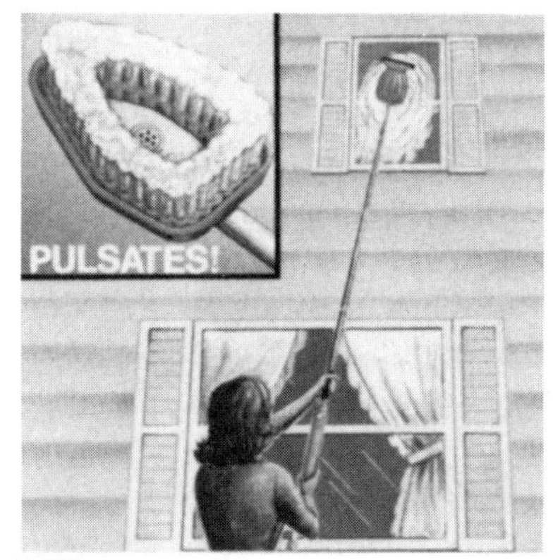

5-70

5-71

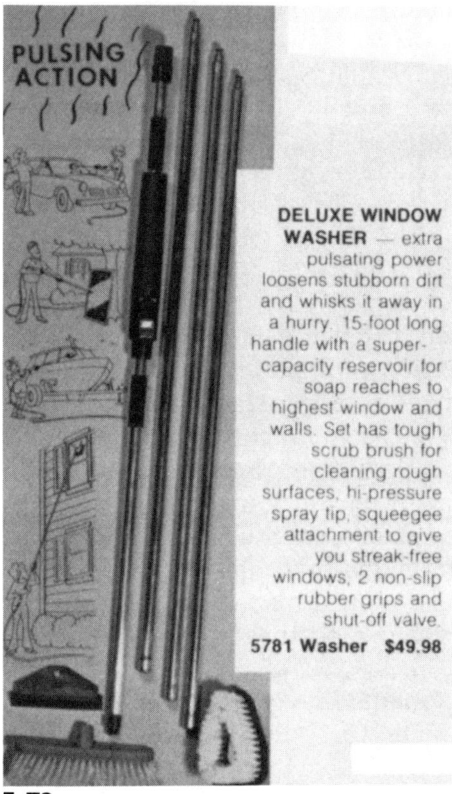

PULSING ACTION
DELUXE WINDOW WASHER — extra pulsating power loosens stubborn dirt and whisks it away in a hurry. 15-foot long handle with a super-capacity reservoir for soap reaches to highest window and walls. Set has tough scrub brush for cleaning rough surfaces, hi-pressure spray tip, squeegee attachment to give you streak-free windows, 2 non-slip rubber grips and shut-off valve.
5781 Washer $49.98

5-72

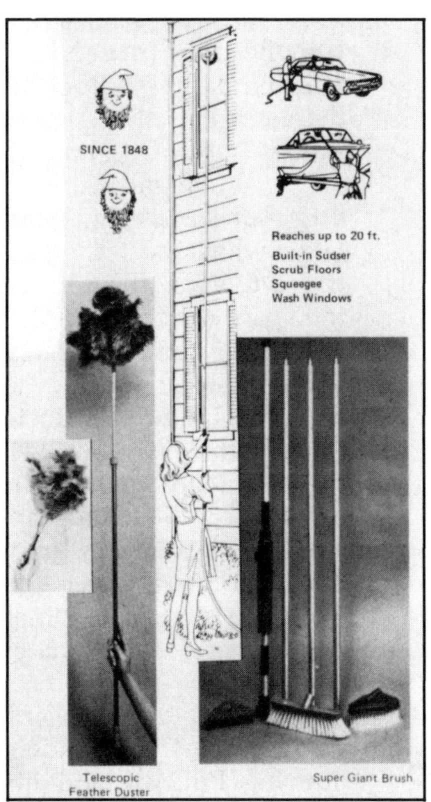

5-73

if an art headline would have been a greater aid toward immediate clarity ("Gutter cleaner available too!").

Figure 5-72 from Taylor Gifts chooses to photograph the item itself, apparently feeling that a visual presentation of all the components is necessary and that the functions are somewhat secondary. The creative staff realized that artwork was the only way to show these functions. But the space which they allowed to accomplish all this is not enough. The upper line drawing shows a car being washed with the item, using only one of the components, which allowed a short-handled usage. The second line drawing is a screen being cleaned. The third is the washing of a boat, and the fourth is the second-story window washing function. Everything is crowded, making the functions hard to isolate. This brings up a point about line drawing in general. This technique is usually used to show a function with the least amount of complication, i.e., a few simple *lines,* rather than the shading and dimension which regular artwork would need. But frequently too much is included in the line drawing, and some of the clarity of the technique is lost. For instance, in the upper line drawing, the male figure could have been eliminated, along with the rear end of the car. This would have allowed the rest of the drawing to be larger, and the function would have been more isolated and consequently clearer for the mind to absorb. So *if you choose to use line drawings, be sure you don't negate their function of simplicity by including too much in the drawing.* The copy headline (not shown) says ''New Deluxe Window Washer,'' which indicates neither the unusual quality of the extra length nor the versatility of the uses. Though it states the name of the item, it does not do so in an illuminating way.

When showing an item visually, *the restrictions you have to work with must always be considered,*, as well as the problems of presentation which the item intrinsically has. There is nothing wrong with trying to show the versatility of this item, for example, but not in the space discipline under which Taylor Gifts had to labor.

Figure 5-73 from Hammacher Schlemmer shows not only the pulsating washer, but also a portion of another piece of artwork, a telescoping feather duster. This is an error in page layout which hurts both items, but particularly the more complicated washer. Although both items are long-handled, their physical juxtaposition confuses each item rather than enhancing any long-handled qualities which each item has. In addition, the layout allowed some air to remain in the upper left section of this presentation, and this air was filled by two little line drawings (presumably Hammacher and Schlemmer?) and a date. This blurb further clutters the item presentation.

Keep drawings simple

Here the washer components have been shown in a photograph. The second-story function is shown in a well-done line drawing. But two more line drawings have lost their effectiveness because of the lack of cohesiveness in the layout. The headlines in the artwork are also barely noticed for the same reasons. The hodgepodge quality of the layout has affected the clarity of the individual presentation. So remember that the *blending of the elements which you determine to be necessary is as important as the decision on which elements to include.*

Remember: no matter how much you gain from the realism of a photo, it does no good if the item is too large to be effectively shown in the camera perspective.

But when a person views artwork instead of a photograph, the mind subconsciously records the fact that it is not looking at ''the real thing,'' and it wonders why. One of the answers which the mind gives us is that the item probably doesn't look very good in "real life." That's a negative, and it is the reason why artwork is avoided unless absolutely necessary. But other situations arise which make photography a poor choice when compared with artwork. When the camera cannot represent the item properly, or positively, go artwork. This often occurs because of:

2. The material of which the item is made. Usually this is a material which is not seen realistically by the camera lens. Sometimes the material obscures the main function of the item. Sometimes the material photographs in such a way as to destroy the shape of the item. (Occasionally these problems can be handled by taking a photograph of the item, making a print of the photograph, and having an artist retouch the print so that the details of the item are clearer to the eye than they were to the camera lens.)

Figure 5-74 from Joan Cook shows a hummingbird feeder which presented several problems from a photographic point of view: window glass is hard to photograph, whatever is behind the glass is a distraction (and if the glass is backed with a sheet of colored paper it doesn't look like glass anymore), clear plastic is hard to photograph, see-through suction cups do not photograph well, and hummingbirds are generally not cooperative subjects, especially when you want them sucking nectar from the feeder. Minus the bird, the item would have had less appeal. The obvious solution was artwork, and it was a happy choice. The plastic of the feeder was controlled in such a way as to not only show the see-through qualities, but to exaggerate the dimensionality as well. The way the feeder attaches to the window is clearly shown, and so is the liquid it holds. These elements would never have stood out so clearly in a photograph.

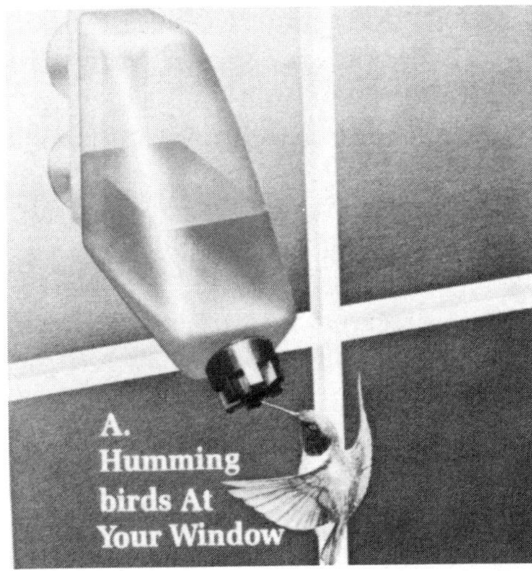

5-74

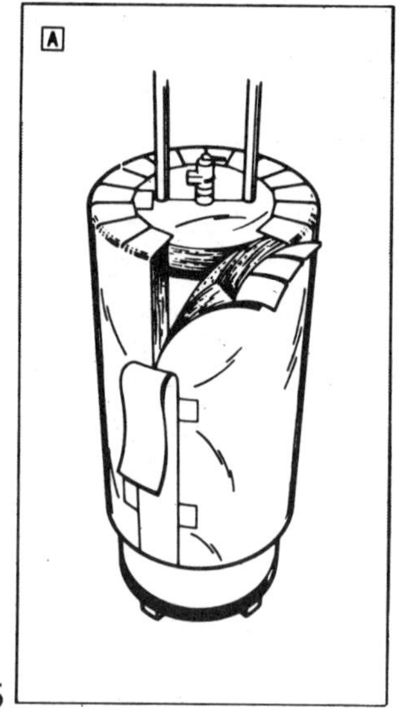

5-75

Figure 5-75 shows a water heater blanket — (a) is from Bruce Bolind, black and white art; (b) is from Old Village Shop, color art. The problem here was to show three essential elements of the blanket: the way the joints wrap around the top of the heater, the method of closing and attaching the blanket, and the insulation. (The color art from Old Village, which loses a bit in our black and white presentation, shows the yellow insulation most effectively against the blue-gray outer covering.) The difficulties presented by photography are that the outer covering of the wrap is shiny vinyl and a light color, creating a hard-to-photograph sheen, plus the problem of showing the light-colored closure tape against the light-colored wrap. Through artwork, the item's elements stand apart from each other, resulting in a far more *interesting* presentation than a blended-into-each-other photograph would have been. In addition, the angle necessary for the optimum presentation would have been a difficult one for the camera, and water heaters are usually crowded into basements (though, of course, a freestanding ''prop'' heater could have been used).

Figure 5-76 from a Harriet Carter catalog (color art) also handles a dull subject with a more interesting visual through the choice of artwork. (Taking a subject which is boring to the camera, and enlivening it with artwork, is also a legitimate reason for choosing art over photography.) The woodpile cover shown here is black — a hard color to photograph and still achieve any detail with, especially when the camera has to back away from the subject to fit it all in. The cover is also vinyl, creating a reflective sheen that discourages detail. It is reinforced with fiberglass — again difficult to see in photography, but relatively easy to show in crisscross artwork. Assembling the logs for the shot is heavy work, the logs perhaps are not already at hand, and the entire project is not easy in a photographer's studio. There is nothing about actual logs that the mind of the viewer will not believe just as well in a drawing. All these reasons add up to the logical choice: art instead of photography.

Figure 5-77, also from Harriet Carter (color art), features a set of 100 luminous glow-in-the-dark Christmas tree icicles, a subject to make any photographer go crazy. Here, the luminous quality has been represented by little ''glow lines'' emanating from each icicle. There are other ways to create a ''glow'' as well — the artists could have represented this with a ''halo'' effect. A choice was made to show a large group of the icicles in the artwork, presumably so that the customer would realize that the set of icicles had many components. In a photograph, the icicles would have blended into each other, creating a mass instead of a group. It also would have been difficult to get the little molded-in hanging hooks to be apparent. Again, art presents the item with far more glamour than a photograph would have achieved.

5-76

5-77

Figure 5-78 from Walter Drake and Sons presents a bookrack which hangs over the top of a door. The rack is made of gold-tone metal, and in actuality it would probably be dwarfed in emphasis by the books it holds. To photograph shiny metal, especially in thin strips, and more especially when the physical qualities of the item are less emphatic than the function it performs, is a difficult chore. Additional problems with this item would be the aspect of the door itself — enough has to show to be recognizable as a door (in order to ''place'' the item), plus the doorway has to be lighted to create dimension in the molding so it looks like a door. (The reason there is so much emphasis on the door appearing as such is that it must immediately register on the mind of the customer that this bookrack is different — it fits over a door.) The lighting needed for this doorway may be entirely different from the lighting needed to best display the product. Consequently, artwork was chosen as the easier path, the path most likely to succeed.

Figure 5-79 from Walter Drake shows a Sensor Night Light. This presents problems similar to the luminous icicles, and here the glow was indeed handled with a "halo." The artwork not only made it easy to create the effect of the light being on at night, but also allowed the details of the plastic faceted cover to show. Attempting to create a "night" shot with photography would have obscured some of the other details, including probably the wall socket. The headline assures that the automatic quality is understood immediately.

Figure 5-80 is again from Walter Drake. The purse and shoe caddies shown here are composed of clear vinyl pockets. Photograph them and chances are you will get glare, wrinkles, and indistinct pocket contents. Choose artwork, and you can control the see-through quality, create an immediate impression of the contents, and let the customer instantly understand the function of the item.

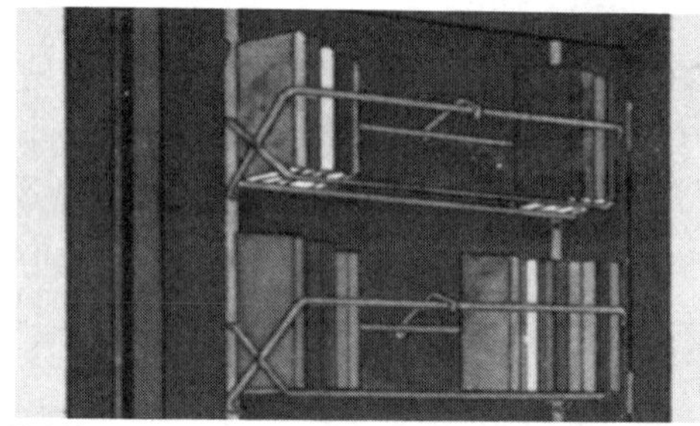

5-78

5-79

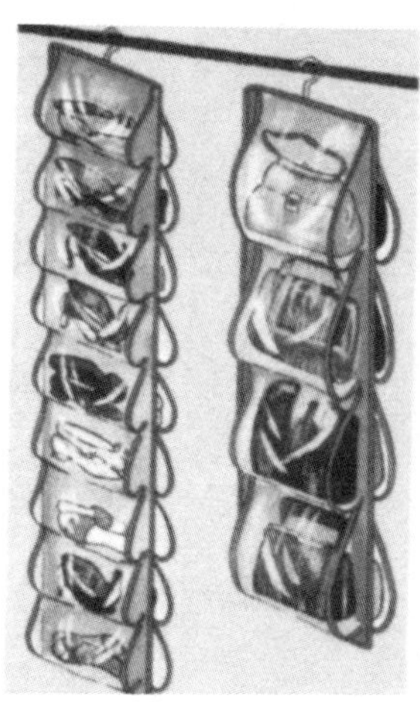

5-80

Artwork. . . A few reasons why, under certain circumstances, it enhances your products. One of the most logical reasons for using artwork instead of photography to present visuals on your items is that *sometimes the artist's brush can show the item better than the camera can.* We've just seen how this will happen when the item is proportioned in such a way that its dimensions do not lend themselves to the camera lens. Another example would be a Christmas tree ornament which is "three dimensional" because three flat planes of silver snowflakes have been assembled at angles to each other. Sometimes artwork is used because the item (or a portion of it) *must* be exaggerated in order to convey the product (an ant "farm', for example, where the tunnels and the ants themselves cannot be easily seen). But these situations are somewhat unusual.

How about a very common item, one which is usually photographed effectively? Why use artwork in a situation like this? One of the more interesting examples is in catalog sales of clothing. The page from a Brooks Brothers catalog shown in Figure 5-88 is a fascinating third example of how artwork has been used to enhance a product.

3. Product enhancement. This becomes necessary when products would look almost boring if photographed in the same manner as the artwork presents them.

The Bermuda-length shorts at the top of the page are shaded by the artist's brush to give them a much less "flat" look than the camera would have shown. Additionally, details of the hem and the pocket stitching are clearly seen. The camera would have been hard put to show these features. The detailing situation is even more apparent in the jacket sketched on the model. Top-stitching on pockets and around lapels would have been diminished by the camera. But drawn by the artist, they add immeasurably to the dimension of the jacket and to the crisp, classy look which otherwise might have seemed merely ordinary. But *most interesting of all in this presentation is the use of photography to the bottom right of the jacket to show the detail of the fabric weave* (as well as the colors in which the jacket is available). *This photograph provides all the realistic reinforcement* needed to show the customer the actual quality of the fabric. And combining this realism with the artwork is a clever way to handle the problem. So here we have a situation where artwork, which can be a negative because customers know they are not looking at the "real thing," has been turned into a positive because it actually shows customers more than the camera could have. And the product is given further credibility by the use of a photograph to show some of the realism of the item.

Art can set mood of catalog

Another highly effective use of artwork rather than photography, again for enhancement, is found throughout the Caswell-Massey catalog. This two-color job is relatively inexpensive when compared with a four-color process. Their product line is composed of a series of bottles, jars, tubes, soaps, shaving brushes, and other bath items. To photograph these products ad infinitum could be boring unless they were elaborately propped with flowers, fruits and ribbons. Tiny photographs of representative products in each listing also would be boring. But the artwork the company used instead is definitely interesting (Figure 5-81), sometimes amusing (Figure 5-82), and there is no intrinsic need dictated by the products to convince the customer of their reality. A photograph of the sponges presented in Figure 5-82 would have been an ordinary treatment, compared to this unusual presentation. However, the drawing of the sponge is unattractive and ineffective. The style of the artwork, like an old-fashioned engraving, suits the products well — but even more importantly, it emphasizes the age of the company, started in 1752 (underlining its reliability, and hence its credibility).

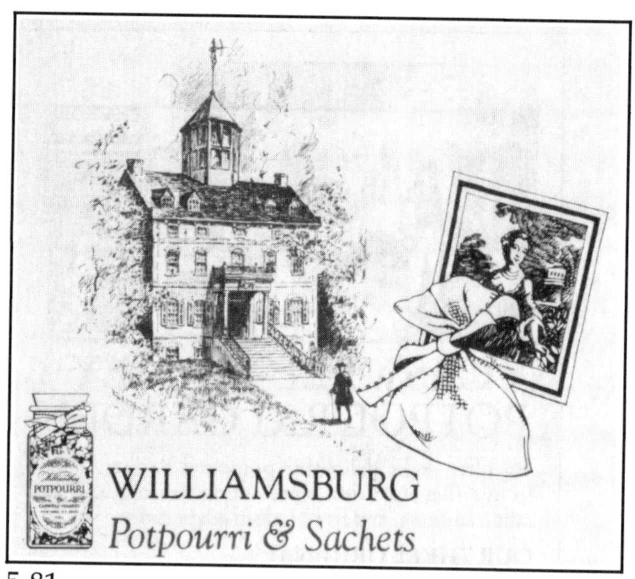

5-81

Oh, the Unfathomable Advantage of a Natural Mediterranean Sponge

The friendly, pleasant feel of the natural sponge has never been surpassed by the most frantic efforts of the plastics industry. That is why we offer a whole range of sizes for all the bathing that we are heir to. Choose from the following sizes:

Natural Sponges:

(26600) Small	*$5.00*
(26601) Hand	*$8.50*
(26602) Medium	*$13.50*
(26603) Large	*$21.50*
(26604) Very Large	*$27.50*

THE BATH 19

5-82

There is plenty to keep in mind here: that art can sometimes be better than photography . . . that photography can be combined with artwork to make an even stronger statement . . . that art can be less expensive (but should not usually be chosen for this reason alone) . . . and that it can sometimes match the mood of your product line, and your company, more effectively than can photography.

Combining Art With Photography . . . An Unusual, But Powerful Technique

Now that we've given you many reasons why artwork can be a more effective device than photography, let's review why catalogers usually object to it. The prevailing feeling is the customer will become suspicious of the item's quality and hesitate to make a purchase. After all, the customer is viewing something that obviously is a drawing and not the real thing. In that viewer's mind, this could mean that the actual item did not look good enough to photograph. Marketers also feel that only occasionally will customers forgive the artwork technique and suspend their disbelief. This occasional lapse might occur if there is an obvious reason for using the art, such as the need to distort perspective to show a long-handled window washing device, previously discussed. *As a general rule, photography is accepted and artwork is not — especially for glamour items* (decorative home accessories) as opposed to nitty-gritty items (the window washer).

Then along comes a catalog which *breaks the rules* — and by doing so, ends up with not merely an acceptable result, but actually an enhancement of the product line. "Coach Leatherware" is an

8½″ × 11″ catalog featuring (among other items) a group of 28 handbags and totes — but *only two of them are photographed*. These two photographs are accomplished in full-page color shots (Figure 5-83). The other 26 handbags are presented via drawings, usually two or three to a page.

What does the customer see in the photograph? The reality of the handbag is observed with its soft sheen, leather grain, lovely tan color, and detailed, even stitching. Now *what does the customer see in the drawings* (Figure 5-84)? An aesthetic "feel" is presented, a sheen is created by the artist's highlighting and shadowing which is much more intense than that which could be achieved by the camera lens, and an "excitement" is developed through the exaggeration of these features. The handbags actually would seem boring if photograph after photograph were viewed. In addition to these marketing advantages made possible by the artwork, *the customer "sees" in each drawing the "memory" of the photograph, with all its reality!* So the photograph has become the realistic support to the aesthetics of the artwork. In fact, the customer actually feels that the artwork is used to give a *better* vision of the products than the camera could possibly do.

Incidentally, there is a great bonus here in the area of catalog economics. Think of the money saved by eliminating color separations and four-color printing — and the fee paid for the artwork probably is much less than a comparably talented photographer would charge. Yet no feeling occurs that catalog quality was compromised or sacrificed. Because these bags are available in ten colors and the drawings cannot show those colors, has a problem been created? On page three of this catalog, all ten color swatches are shown via the "Coach Tag" which hangs from a chain on each bag. The opportunity was taken not only to present the colors for the customer's perusal, but also to feature some information about why the "Coach Tag" stands for a very special product.

What does all this mean to a catalog marketer? It confirms that *in certain cases, the combination of artwork and photography works better than either medium used alone.* In the Coach Leatherware catalog, photographs minus artwork might have become boring, and it might not have been possible to develop certain aesthetics. In addition, photography used exclusively would have created the need to prop some of the bags in order to help prevent the element of boredom.

If artwork had been used without the support of the photographs, a little seed of doubt would have been left in the mind of the viewer: perhaps these handbags are not really as rich and distinctive as the artwork implies.

The technique of combining artwork with photography is *particularly advantageous when a cataloger has a product line with many similar items and certain difficulities in photographing them effectively.* It's worth your consideration the next time this problem arises in your book.

Nº9170 Classic Shoulder Bag..$88
The original Coach® Bag. Simplest of unlined pouches with a minimum of hardware. Inside zipper compartment and an extra compartment under the flap. Adjusting buckles are solid brass.
All ten Coach® Colors shown on page four.
Dimensions: 10" x 9" x 4".
COACH

5-83

Nº9235 Crescent..$88

This body-hugging Coach® Bag is especially contoured for a snug fit. Shoulder strap is 1¼″ wide and adjusts with a pair of matched, solid brass stirrup buckles. The industrial turnlock closure is also made of solid brass. There's an extra compartment inside. *Mocha, British Tan, Black, Navy, Red, Putty, Burgundy, Tabac.* Dimensions: 10″ x 10″ x 3″

Nº8920 Courier Pouch..$104

This Coach® Bag has a large capacity and a distinctive tuck-in flap that adjusts the size of the bag to its contents. Matching solid brass stirrup buckles. Adjustable shoulder strap. Extra zippered compartment inside. *Mocha, British Tan, Black, Navy, Red, Putty, Burgundy, Tabac.* Dimensions: 10″ x 10″ x 5″

5-84

Photography

Advantages	**Disadvantages**
Greater believability due to picture of actual product; heightened credibility because of seeing the "real" thing; greater customer association with product.	Possible misunderstanding of product function; lost product detail; possibility of uninteresting visual.

Art

Advantages	**Disadvantages**
Emphasis on product function for greater customer understanding; easier emphasis on product detail; easy addition of seasonal aspects when preparing catalog in off-season; easy illustration of end-benefit such as bearing fruit trees.	Lost realism, lessened credibility; product distorted.

Photography/Art Combination

Advantages	**Disadvantages**
Emphasis on product detail with art while realism is retained by photography; emphasis on function.	Visual clutter highly possible; more costly production due to double charges (art plus photography) and film stripping in printing pre-stage.

Chapter 6

Copy ... What Role Does It Play?

To Sell Products!

Copy's role is multifaceted — more complicated than that of photography. Copy can attract the customer's attention with a strong benefit or identifying headline. It sells the customer with good, informative body copy and then completes the presentation and sale with the price line. *Copy alone can sell a product — without photography,* whereas a photograph cannot sell without copy. However, once photography has earned the customer's attention through visual command, the primary function of copy in a catalog is to take that attention and *sell* that customer on the product or service offered. The range of this role includes: grabbing the customer's attention, then directing, educating, informing, entertaining, referring, describing — trying the product on for the customer — and finally testing, offering, stroking, befriending, assuring and guaranteeing that customer, too! Company credibility must be built; customer confidence must result. This all needs to be done with an eye for truthfulness that will result in repeat business. How can all of this be accomplished? Where does one start?

Know Your Company and Your Customer

Before thinking about writing any copy for the catalog, the writer needs to study the following:

1. *List Evaluation and Analysis.* You cannot write good selling copy unless you know to whom you are

writing. Who is the catalog being mailed to? What is the buyer like? Does your typical buyer live in town or in the country? Is the list predominantly male or female? What is the average customer's age? What is the average income? Is your customer a value buyer? What is the average dollar order?

2. *Catalog Company Posture*. Knowing what the company is all about and the position it desires is vital for good, convincing copy. Has the company been in the same business for years, or is it just starting out? Is it considered an expert in its product field? Does it specialize in value-priced merchandise, fast delivery, custom service? Is it an authority in its field?

Knowing these two areas will let you choose the tone of the approach which is best for your catalog and product line. A colloquial, conversational style might be just right for a food line from the hill country of Tennessee, whereas a shorter, clipped approach would be better for steaks sold as executive gifts.

Know your company and your customer

Catalog copy has a great deal more to do than describe products. Taken for granted is copy which appears on the front and back covers, and yet these are the two most viable parts of your catalog. Not even the catalog name should be taken for granted. A new company should give a lot of thought to the name. Choice . . . should it be a person's name to denote friendly dependability? Should it be formal? Should it make sense? A full chapter could be written on this choice alone. But for this book, the real questions are — would the catalog name benefit from a descriptive subhead? Should it be prominently displayed?

Front Cover Copy

Copy must share some of the responsibility with art or photography for attracting the customer's attention. Just as a dramatic cover design can grab the customer's attention by sheer beauty, arresting layout, marvelous colors, or subject interest, so too can copy get the customer's attention. It can announce the catalog name, a special sale, a free gift, a value line, company longevity, ordering convenience, or special sweepstakes — it can even sell products directly and indirectly. The artist and copywriter must work carefully together so the final outcome will be desirable and attract the customer.

Catalog Name Subheads

Should a subhead be included to clarify the type of products offered? Adding a subhead is practicing the old adage; never leave a stone unturned. Many companies very successfully use subheads — they tell the prospective customer what products are offered.

General Consumer Figure 6-1 is the cover of the Brookstone catalog, which carries tools for the home hobbyist. The catalog name is visually very prominent in 96 point Perpetua Black style type. Because of the large point size and the fine black outlining of each letter, the reversed color technique is very successful with the white letters popping out on the red background. The subhead, ''Hard-to-Find-Tools and Other Fine Things,'' further clarifies and helps *identify* the category of products to be found inside. Eight different categories of products are referenced by page number (copy area middle right of the cover), further motivating the customer to open the catalog.

6-1

The catalog name and subhead have attracted attention through prominence of position, typestyle, and through verbal explanation.

Business-to-Business The Moore Business Center catalog cover (Figure 6-2) immediately attracts the customer. Just as the front cover illustration tells a story of who the company is and what it does, words also tell the story. The catalog name MOORE bounces right out at the customer because of its size (144 point) and color (blue lettering on a clean white background). This alone immediately draws the attention of the customer already familiar with the catalog. The subhead, "The Most Complete Catalog Selection of Computer Forms and Supplies," announces the type of product inside. Other copy also helps attract the customer's attention, such as the company

6-2

name and the reference to company longevity (lower left) — ''Serving Business For Over 100 Years.'' ''FREE GIFTS'' (lower right) certainly attracts attention, and the announcement of a toll-free number (lower right) attracts attention with thoughts of fast service, courtesy, and a free method of ordering.

Both the Brookstone and Moore catalogs have nicely blended art and copy to the maximum advantage. The artist and copywriter have worked closely to achieve covers which visually and verbally attract the customer.

Inside Reference

The importance of taking advantage of the attention gained through visual and verbal front cover design cannot be stressed enough. In addition, too many catalogs fail to make the most of the opportunity to create a ''contrived hot spot'' (previously discussed in chapter 3) — the opportunity not only to move the customer inside, but to increase sales, too. There are basically three things that can be referenced on the cover: 1) Product category (a grouping of products which have the same function or pertain to a specific area: stationery, garden, cable printers); 2) Special offer (sale, free gift, free trial, sweepstakes); and 3) Specific product (monogrammed label, tweed sports jacket, workstation chair). You may choose to use only one of these points or all three.

General Consumer Figure 6-3 shows the E & B Marine cover, which *references six different products* and *two different product categories, leading the customer to 16 different pages in the catalog.* Reference is also made to six different boat shows where products will be exhibited. This is admittedly an unusual practice, but it's a nice opportunity for regional customers as well as vacationers to take advantage of special offers and to actually see the merchandise. Two other important references are given on this cover. ''Mail Order Hotline'' suggests unusually fast service (even though the number is not toll-free), and this is backed up in the lower right with ''Mail and Phone Orders Shipped Within 48 Hrs.'' While all of this information produces a busy-looking cover, this busyness fits the character of a value-priced catalog.

Photos with inside reference

Figure 6-4 shows that Burpee's garden catalog has a simpler cover, attracting the customer with a dramatic flower shot and then *referencing a special free offer.* The other cover messages are printed in reverse (white) while ''6 *free bulbs*'' is printed in yellow, making it stand out from the rest. Adding page numbers to the five subjects of customer interest mentioned on the cover could easily have turned this area into a quick, easy index besides pulling the customer inside to different sections in the catalog. The toll-free phone reference in the lower right suggests fast service and, because of the inside page reference, helps get the customer to look inside.

One strong attention-getter for inside reference direction is the announcement of a free gift. Figure 6-5 shows The Chelsea Collection picturing a free gift offer on the cover. The words ''Free Gift'' appear in bold red capital letters; ''with any purchase'' qualifies the gift, hopefully encouraging the customer to make a purchase. The product name ''Nail Polish Corrector'' is given, followed by a directive for finding further information: ''See insert.'' Then a negative message almost spoils the whole offer: ''incl. $1.25 gift processing.'' This small fact will turn customers away. Figure 6-6 shows how cleverly The Talbots announces a gift and directs the customer inside. ''Our Gift to You. . .'' is warm and personal, exactly fitting the gift card on which it appears. And instead of naming the gift, the cover directs the customer inside: ''see pages 2 and 3 for details!'' This is wonderful motivational wording. What customer interested in women's apparel wouldn't look inside!

Photos with inside reference

Business-to-Business Garon Products, Inc., a maintenance supply catalog, very neatly references three products which are pictured on the cover *and* identifies a product category for each, thus broadening the subject of interest. Such an approach brings more customers inside. Figure 6-7 illustrates how well this direction was accomplished. A bullet with the product name and page number (''Aluma-Grip, Pg. 29'') appears at the top left of the product photo insert. At the bottom of the photo insert, the product category is identified. In the above left of the cover photo, four benefits are stated, thus building credibility and providing customer information.

6-3

6-4

The Chelsea Collection
Fall 1984
Win a 2-carat diamond ring
50th ANNIVERSARY
$550,000.00 GIVEAWAY!
see the insert
cape coat drama
Special
$99.95
value $138.00
see page 2
FREE GIFT*
with any purchase
Nail Polish Corrector
See insert.
The Chelsea Collection

6-5

SPRING/SUMMER 1984
Our Gift To You...
see pages 2 and 3 for details!
The Talbots

6-6

GARON
PRODUCTS, INC.
Maintenance Power Catalog
• Warehouses and Distribution Centers Coast to Coast for Quick Delivery
• Over 50 New Products in this Issue
• Valuable Premiums - FREE to Qualified Buyers
• All Products 100% Guaranteed
GARON
CRACK-FIL
GARON
GARON
STOP-SLIP
Chuck-Fil Pg. 16
Aluma-Grip Pg. 29
Stop-Slip Pg. 7
Pavement Repair Products
Roof Maintenance Products
Safety Floor Coatings
Spring 1983 • National Edition • $2.00

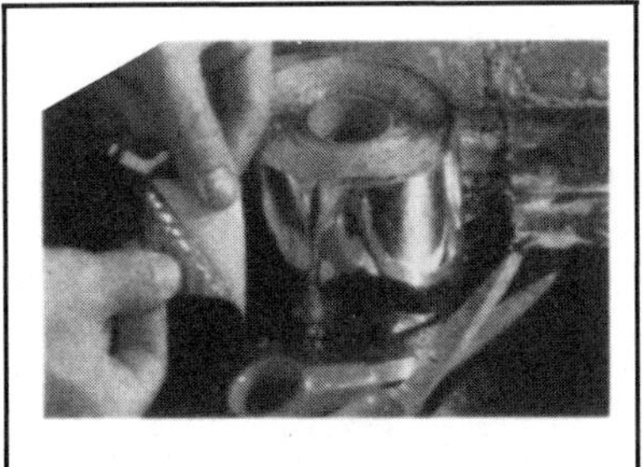

6-7

All of these covers have neatly taken advantage of the customer's attention in the style which best suits each catalog. The customer has been served, and the catalog will realize greater sales.

Direct Selling Copy

The power of the front cover was discussed earlier in Chapter 3. And because the front cover is so powerful, it is logical that it should be utilized to the best, most profitable advantage. Some catalogers strongly feel that only one option is logically available, then — that of selling a product(s) directly off the front cover. If this is the decision made, copy must play a big role because the customer must have enough information to make a buying decision. Generally this means descriptive copy and can require size, color, and style information. How can this be done without destroying the mood of the cover and without clutter? Will an approach such as this misrepresent catalog tone and product line?

General Consumer. The Famous CosmoPedics shoe catalog (Figure 6-8) makes very nice use of a photo of one of their ladies' shoe selections to act as the visual attention-getter. The catalog name, Famous CosmoPedics, is distinct in type design and treatment but not terribly descriptive in meaning. However, the copy headline, "Lovely Cut-out," names the main benefit of the shoe. The descriptive copy block continues with another headline about the cut-out feature and is followed with copy which expands on this product benefit. A little over five of the eight descriptive copy lines are devoted to extolling this benefit: "CUT OUT TO BE A BEAUTY. . . this pretty pump features intricate scalloped detailing and airy openwork for a very feminine look at work or on the town!" The three remaining lines are devoted to product detail such as lining, sole composition, and heel height. The last six lines are devoted to 12 size choices, six widths, and four color choices with their corresponding numbers. Pricing is stated even though it appeared in a 36 point red headline just above. Everything a customer needs to make a buying decision is right on the front cover. It has featured the product benefit (design cut-out), built product credibility (feminine look at work or on the town), and supplied product specifications (lined, material, size, color, price). All of this has been done very simply and in order of selling importance.

Business-to-Business The Frank Eastern Company (Figure 6-9) takes up every inch of the cover to sell three products and inform the customer about many company benefits. Product headlines and descriptive copy are just as they would appear inside. Headlines identify the product; body copy tells of other product benefits and specifications and gives pricing and delivery information. Each of the products is presented the same way. The information/benefit panel builds credibility by stating that Frank Eastern's is "The Original (since 1946) Business and Institutional Discount Catalog," that there are "64 Nationwide Warehouses & Factories to serve you

6-8

from Coast to Coast,'' and that there will be ''Prompt shipments from stock'' out of 15 (named) cities across the nation. Value is indicated with ''Save up to 50%,'' a toll-free number is listed, and an inside page reference is given to help get the customer into the catalog. A lot of information and products for sale are provided here, but distracting clutter is avoided with clean lines and direct, informative copy. The excitement of a bargain is achieved.

6-9

When presenting products on the front cover for direct selling, you can do one of three things:

Three copy techniques

1. Include full-length product copy just as it would appear inside if the item were for sale.
2. Shorten regular copy to include only bare-bone facts but still maintain copy block style.
3. Use facts in short-statement form and list them in bullet fashion.

All approaches perform better with a strong benefit headline pertaining to an outstanding product feature or a special offer or pricing.

Credibility

Nothing builds confidence and encourages ordering quite like credibility. Customers need to feel that a company is trustworthy, reliable, and dependable. How can copy get all of this across on the front cover? Isn't there a possibility of clutter? How do you tell the customer you are *trustworthy* in two words (try: ''Satisfaction Guaranteed''), *reliable* in one (''since'' plus a year, ''1935''), and *dependable* in a few words (''our 62-year commitment''). There are three very strong ways to establish credibility on the front cover.

1. Longevity. Nothing makes a customer more secure than dealing with a company known or perceived to have been in business for a long time. Psychologically, in the mind of the customer, a company that has served the public for more than a few years has to be: (a) smart (b) dependable, and (c) reliable. These abc's equal credibility. The longer a company has been in business, the stronger these features and the more secure the customer is in ordering. Credibility is established!

Here are two approaches which can turn longevity into credibility:

(a) True mail order longevity. This is achieved by a company which has been in the mail order business for a period of time. An established company such as Burpee Gardens may have been in business 109 years, or a relatively new company will have been in business five years. Figure 6-10 from the Spencer Gifts catalog illustrates how a catalog company can incorporate its longevity into a logo design while establishing credibility at the same time. Figure 6-11 shows how Papillon announces a 15th Anniversary Celebration and also establishes credibility!

6-10

6-11

(b) Cumulative age longevity. Many companies have been in the retail or wholesale business for years, selling a product which they now offer by mail. The cumulative number of years in business for retail, wholesale, and mail order are used as a credibility tool. Early's Honey Stand, a food catalog, in Figure 6-12 illustrates use of this information in an attractive "storefront" sign. Wright Line office supply catalog (Figure 6-13) builds in company longevity while indicating service. Longevity of business years can be a powerful credibility builder.

6-12

A 50 year commitment to solving your problems—over 2000 products to satisfy both large and small needs—leading the industry in product innovation and quality.

6-13

2. Guarantee. A guarantee can be presented in a few short words, such as Satisfaction Guaranteed, or it can be fully stated. Companies which most often use this technique on the front cover are new companies that need to project a strong and convincing image in order to compete with existing companies. (Restricting this approach to new companies may be rather ill-conceived, however, since *all* companies must always try as hard as they can in order to maintain their position in the marketplace and be profitable.) The front cover guarantee is also used by companies whose product lines are difficult to sell by mail, such as shoes and wigs where fit is so critical. A good example is the Wright Arch Preserver Shoes catalog. Because this company carries a product line, shoes, where proper fit for comfort is critical, the full guarantee is reproduced prominently right on the front cover (Figure 6-14). This action immediately creates credibility and confidence. Deluxe Computer forms lists the following on the cover: ". . .Unconditional Money-Back Guarantee" and "Guaranteed Software Compatibility," exuding stability and reliability. Again, this builds customer confidence which is vitally important in this highly competitive product area.

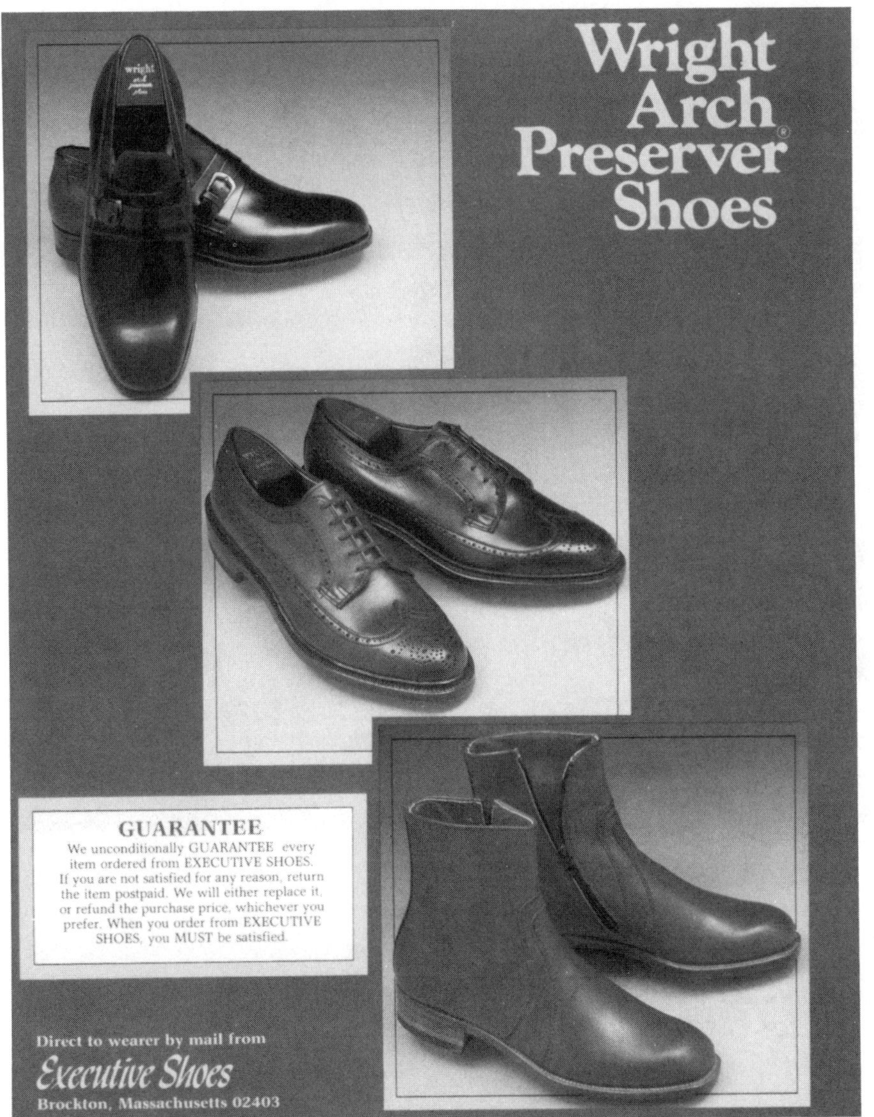

6-14

> **Testimony**
>
> *Testimonials are great credibility-builders. Anyone can brag about how great his product is, but it's much more believable coming from a customer who has bought and used it. And don't neglect using testimonials about your* service, *too — not just your products.*
>
> **Scott Ashley**
> *Annie's Attic*
> *Big Sandy, TX*

3. Testimonials. Hardly anything is more persuasive for making a purchase than a recommendation from a friend or the realization that people who have previously dealt with a company are satisfied. The use of customer testimonials directly on the cover is rare but perhaps so only because it has not traditionally been done. However, there are variations on this theme which are not always recognized as testimonials. Following are some examples:

Lands' End (Figure 6-15) uses a company pricing policy right on the front cover as a testimonial: ''We are able to sell at lower prices because we support no fancy emporiums with their high overhead.'' Inmac (Figure 6-16) gives five reasons for choosing this company, claiming millions of customers have purchased because of these reasons.

The full usage of the traditional testimonial is seen in Figure 6-17, where NEBS, New England Business Services, has pictured

LANDS' END
DIRECT MERCHANTS
"We are able to sell at lower prices because we support no fancy emporiums with their high overhead. Our main location is in the middle of a 10-acre cornfield in rural Wisconsin."

6-15

40th Edition—October '84. Complete Cross-Reference Catalog of Computer Supplies, Accessories, Furniture, Cables and Data Communications Devices.
inmac
Here's the easy way to make short work of a long list!
Find out how one call does it all. Full story next page.
Why millions of computer users have ordered from Inmac.
Highest quality products.
Easy mail or phone ordering.
Super-fast, SAME-DAY shipment.
45-day trial assures your satisfaction.
A friendly, knowledgeable staff.
NEW INMAC LOCATIONS IN SEATTLE, ORLANDO, COLUMBUS & PHOENIX!
INSIDE!

6-16

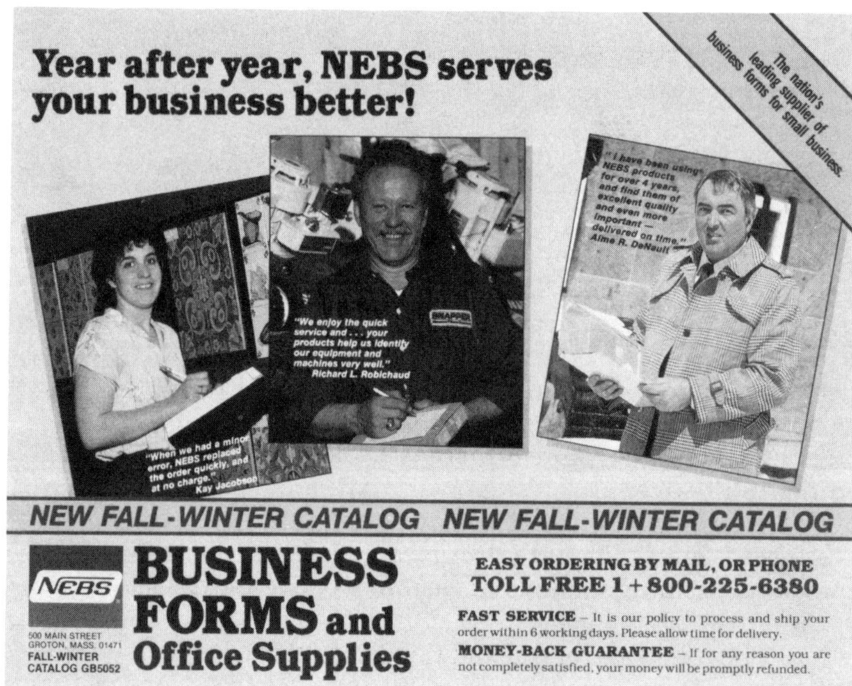
Year after year, NEBS serves your business better!
The nation's leading supplier of business forms for small business.
"When we had a minor error, NEBS replaced the order quickly, and at no charge." Kay Jacobson
"We enjoy the quick service and . . . your products help us identify our equipment and machines very well." Richard L. Robichaud
"I have been using NEBS products for over 4 years, and find them of excellent quality and even more important — delivered on time." Aime R. DeNault
NEW FALL-WINTER CATALOG NEW FALL-WINTER CATALOG
NEBS
BUSINESS FORMS and Office Supplies
500 MAIN STREET GROTON, MASS. 01471
FALL-WINTER CATALOG GB5052
EASY ORDERING BY MAIL, OR PHONE
TOLL FREE 1 + 800-225-6380
FAST SERVICE – It is our policy to process and ship your order within 6 working days. Please allow time for delivery.
MONEY-BACK GUARANTEE – If for any reason you are not completely satisfied, your money will be promptly refunded.

6-17

three customers along with their personal testimonials. All of the testimonials reinforce the guarantee and company dependability. ''When we had a minor error, NEBS replaced the order quickly, and at no charge''; ''We enjoy the quick service. . .''; and ''I have been using NEBS products for over 4 years, and find them of excellent quality and even more important - delivered on time.'' This is excellent reinforcement to credibility! It shouts, ''We are a real company that can be depended on, one which you want to deal with.''

Building credibility must be worked on in every part of your catalog. It is what gives strength and depth to your company — what makes a customer want to purchase again and again.

Convenience

One of the simplest things a cataloger can do for the company as well as its customers is make it easy to shop from the catalog. Two major conveniences that should and can be promoted easily are charge cards and telephone (a toll-free ''800'' number or your regular number). Many general consumer catalogs enjoy 35 percent or more phone orders while business-to-business catalog phone orders may be as high as 90 percent. The high percentages tell us that many people prefer to do their shopping over the phone, that it is a convenience they like using. Charge cards have become a major method of payment and an instantly recognizable ordering convenience wanted by many customers.

Two elements to add for customer ease

1. Telephone Number. The main objective of showing a phone number on the front cover is to let customers know they can order immediately or at their convenience. If you offer a toll-free service nationwide and in your headquarters state, you will need two different numbers. Some catalogs offer a toll-free nationwide number and a regular instate number. Others offer two toll-free numbers (nationwide and in-state). Also, the hours and days the numbers are available can vary. Commonly available is 24-hour service seven days a week, but other options exist, such as restricted hours (8:00 am to 8:00 pm) five, six, or seven days a week. Figure 6-18 shows how three general consumer catalogs have stated their toll-free number availability and how copy helped present and sell the service.

(a) Rick's Automotive Parts strongly encourages the customer to ''use our toll free 'hotline'.'' The word ''hotline'' compounds the convenience by implying that a faster-than-usual method is available. Hours and days of phone order availability are given, too. However, no in-state order number is given, not even on inside pages or the order form.

(b) The Very Thing neatly includes ''Call toll free 1-800-336-4051'' along the border of the front cover photo. Inside pages and the order form give a regular number for in-state residents.

(c) Faith Mountain Country Fare says ''Order toll free'' and gives both a toll-free and a regular number for in-state, Alaska, and Hawaii residents. In Figure 6-17, viewed previously, NEBS plainly states ''Easy ordering by mail, or phone toll free. . .'' only on inside catalog pages two and three; on the order form flap an alternate number is given.

a.

b.

ORDER TOLL FREE
800-822-7238
In VA, AK and HI call: 703-987-8521

c.

6-18

Whenever a phone number is presented, the message to customers is, ''This catalog is easy and convenient to deal with.''

2. Charge Cards. Today the acceptance of charge cards is almost universal among catalogs. Not to use them seems to be self-defeating. Because of this widespread acceptance, catalogers generally choose not to bother with a front cover reference. But with the fierce competition, is this wise? It's so easy to state ''Charge cards happily accepted'' or ''Charge cards welcome.'' Figure 6-19 shows how Walter Drake, a low-end general merchandise catalog, gets the message across. No copy is used; just the two card symbols (Visa and MasterCard) are shown. This gesture does not interrupt or destroy the cover design, but it does say it's convenient to order.

Open every door you can

Other convenience messages or aids besides telephone or charge card references which can appear on the front cover are: quick or mini indexes, a routing list, seasonal identification, new product announcements, or retail store locations.

The front cover can easily become cluttered and out-of-character if not given careful consideration. But remember, when deciding what messages should go on the front cover, that consumers are a fickle lot. If you don't tell them or remind them about convenience pluses, they will quickly go to someone who does.

6-19

Front Cover Checklist:

- ☐ Review the Character of the Mailing List.
- ☐ Understand the Catalog Company's Positioning.
- ☐ Identify Company's Strongest Point.
- ☐ Review Special Offers.

Always

1. Make catalog name prominent.
2. Direct the customer inside.

Strongly Consider

1. Using a subhead to catalog name for product clarification.
2. Stating company longevity.
3. Selling products directly.
4. Announcing special offers.
5. Listing toll-free or regular telephone numbers.
6. Telling of charge card acceptance.
7. Using customer or company testimonials.
8. Offering benefits such as fast service, custom design.

Back Cover Copy

This powerful catalog position must be given every consideration. The products and messages placed on the back cover will have a great deal of impact on the total catalog. Understand that it is the most volatile hot spot you have (next to the front cover), so take every opportunity to use it well. It also is the carrier of your customer's name and address. The post office uses it as a directional vehicle for delivery to the desired individual, and your customer uses it to order or to be directed inside to special pages.

Too often catalogers don't fully analyze what should go on the back cover. There are some questions you should answer when deciding what to tell the customer. Is the company name and address prominently displayed? Is the customer more likely to make a purchase if all information, including price, is given for the products pictured or described? Will the customer look inside if he's told to? Will he order a specific product if it is referenced? Can orders be increased by telephone, credit, and service reference?

Address Panel

The postal department has specific requirements they wish you to follow so they may easily identify and sort according to the customer's address and zip code. For complete specifications, you should refer to the U.S. Government publication, Domestic Mail Manual and Postal Bulletin. This can be obtained by contacting the Superintendent of Documents, U.S. Government Printing Office, Washington, D.C. 20036. The shape (rectangle, square) of the address panel is up to the cataloger, although the address panel is generally no smaller than 2½″ × 4″. You must have the postal permit indicia with specific wording, "Bulk Rate, U.S. Postage Paid," and then the company name or permit number, and you must allow enough room for the address label to be positioned without visual interference with the address. Place in the same area any request for address correction or other delivery message.

Figure 6-20 illustrates how Avon Fashions Inc. dropped out a 4″ × 3″ white square address information area at the lower right of their back cover. The bulk rate permit, company name and address, and address correction are clearly stated in the top of the panel, leaving the major portion for customer name and address label application. Also included is a special message instructing the customer in using the label: "*IMPORTANT*: Please be sure to use the label when ordering. It contains information to help speed the handling of your order." This is rather a lengthy message for the customer

Color yourself luscious with pure cotton in sherbet shades...at just 26.99
THE RIB-STITCH SWEATER shapes up in soft 100% cotton . . . for toss-on chic and unbeatable comfort whatever the season. Styled with boat neck, slouchy shoulders and sleeves to roll or not. In such beautiful colors—and at such an irresistible price—you may not be able to pick just one! Machine washes and dries.
Please state S, M or L when ordering.
Sizes S(5/6-7/8), M(9/10-11/12), L(13/14-15/16)
LV5590 Winter White
LV5608 Dark Peach
LV5574 Pink
LV5582 Green
LV5616 Gray 26.99
AVON FASHIONS MONEY BACK GUARANTEE
You must be completely satisfied with every item purchased from us. If any item fails in any way to meet your expectations, simply return it for prompt exchange or refund, whichever you prefer.
Robert Fry, President
For the most convenient shopping... Charge your order to your Visa, MasterCard or American Express
VISA
MasterCard
CATALOG PRICES VALID UNTIL DECEMBER 31, 1984
AVON FASHIONS INC
AVON LANE, NEWPORT NEWS, VA 23630
IMPORTANT: Please be sure to use this label when ordering. It contains information to help speed the handling of your order.
Address correction requested.
BULK RATE
U.S. Postage
PAID
by Avon
Fashions, Inc.
FF-0013-1

6-20

to read. A more commonly used message is: "Please peel off this label and attach to order form." However, the idea of fast service is good. More successful wording is seen on the back cover of the Leichtung tool catalog: "For fastest possible service" (in red) "Please peel off this label and place it on order form on page 50" (in black).

The customer is promised a reward of faster service for placing the company's coded label on the order form. Leichtung even tells the customer where to find the order form! This is one of many approaches directing the customer to use the self-stick label. Figure 6-21 is an unusual and effective way of getting the customer to utilize the address label. The label has a special discount offer printed directly on it which allows customers to take 10 percent off their orders up until a certain date. While this approach is attractive and unique, careful consideration must be paid to the extra cost incurred with the special design and messages. To further encourage the customer, Rick's Automotive Parts has printed the offer directly on the catalog, as seen to the left, and informs the customer: "This coupon must accompany your order, or give discount coupon number to toll free phone operator on phone orders. Only one coupon per purchase. Discount is not automatic." Here the cataloger is tangibly rewarding the customer for placing the label on the order form or identifying it on the phone. Rick's has found a clever way to help its order entry department receive the correct information, as well as speeding the entry process.

The New England Business Service catalog also drops out a white rectangle area (5½" × 4"). The wording of the bulk rate permit is standard, as is the company name and address. However, NEBS has used a portion of the area for the toll-free number and a personal directive; the whole effort suggests fast service, customer concern, and convenience:

Back Cover Importance

As important as the front. Don't forget, lots of people start their browsing at the back of the book – so save that space for important, great-looking merchandise.

John C. Schenek
Director, Sales Promotion
Avon Fashions

6-21

ORDER NOW!
Call Toll Free 1-800-225-6380

Receipts, Calendar

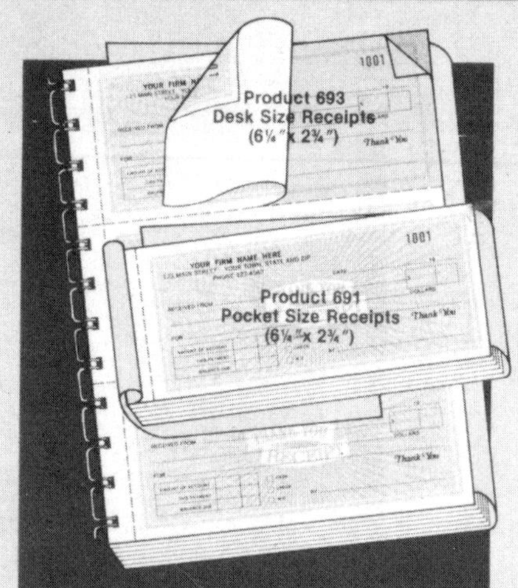

In desk and pocket sizes
RECEIPT BOOKS

For accurate records of payments and original receipts for customers.

- **Available in two sizes.** Order desk size Product 693 or pocket size Product 691.
- **"Carbonless".** Makes clear copies instantly.
- **Handy account section printed on Receipt.** Helps speed collection, reminds customer of amount due.

Product 691 and 693 — Size of Receipt 6¼"x 2¾" detached. Available in two or three-part "carbonless" sets. Prices include printing your heading and consecutive numbering.

QUANTITY	DESK SIZE		POCKET SIZE	
	2-PART Product 693-2	3-PART Product 693-3	2-PART Product 691-2	3-PART Product 691-3
4,000 sets	$114.00	$148.00	$114.00	$148.00
2,000 sets	64.95	86.50	64.95	86.50
1,000 sets	42.50	52.95	42.50	52.95
500 sets	27.50	34.95	27.50	34.95

"NEBS products help make my work go faster and easier. They're indispensable." — David Reed

Product 1515-1
Stick-on Calendar
(3"x 5")

Effective, year 'round advertising
1985 STIK-ON CALENDAR

Promote your name and phone number year 'round for as little as 6¢ per customer! Give your customers this attractively designed calendar!

- **Builds goodwill.** Your customers will appreciate having a readily accessible calendar with all the major holidays highlighted.
- **Easy-to-use.** Just peel and stick. Special adhesive on back permits easy removal from virtually any surface without marking.

Products 1515-1 — Size 3"x 5". Litho stock printed with your name, address and phone number — 5 lines maximum. Counter top dispenser included.

2,000	1,000	500	250
$121.00	$72.95	$44.95	$31.95

FAST SERVICE — Order by mail or phone
TOLL FREE 1+800-225-6380

Questions about previous orders? Call Customer Service TOLL FREE 1+800-225-9540
Please do not use Customer Service phone number for ordering.
PLEASE ROUTE TO person responsible for ordering Business Forms Products.

NEW ENGLAND BUSINESS SERVICE, INC.
500 MAIN STREET, GROTON, MASS. 01471

BULK RATE
U. S. POSTAGE
PAID
NEBS, INC.

6-22 84

"Questions about previous orders? Call Customer Service Toll Free 1+800-225-9540."

"Please do not use Customer Service phone number for ordering."

"Please route to person responsible for ordering Business Forms Products."

Catalog Name

The back cover must not only show the company name prominently enough for identification, but must also bear the address of the company. This identification allows easy reference for both the post office and the customer. Because of the amount of information needed on the back cover, the name should be presented in such a manner that it is easily identifiable. Avon Fashions (Figure 6-20) and New England Business Service (Figure 6-22) both execute this task well. Avon's typestyle and colorful red brush stroke below the name creates a company logo. NEBS relies on a colorful red, white, and blue logo. Always ask yourself, ''Can the customer see my company name easily?'' If the answer is ''No,'' maybe you'd better go back to the drawing board — because this is important.

Inside Reference

The back cover is one of the two most looked-at places in your catalog. What better chance to direct the customer inside to a specific product or product category! Again, many catalogers miss a critical opportunity upon which it is easy to capitalize. Do you want increased sales? Then direct your customer inside your catalog!

Figure 6-23 is the back cover of the Brookstone tool catalog and shows one of the best examples of back cover utilization. A little under one-third of the page is used for the address panel and phone ordering information. All except an eighth of the remaining back cover is used for direct selling. The small lower middle space advises customers of specific products inside. Getting across the idea that the products being referenced are those seen on the front cover is a little complicated, but the actual referencing of the five products and pages is great. The products chosen match the needs of the season for a winter catalog — wind shields, flame-starter crank blower, energy teller, silent electric humidifier, gas water-heater timer. They might have been even more effective if set in bold type to stand out and demand the customer's attention, but the choices are excellent and give the customer even more impetus to take action. Wording backs up the timely selection, too: ''Here are some great ideas for your winter comfort. . .See these and more great weather-tamers in this catalog.'' Copy has helped reinforce the season's needs as well as direct the customer inside. Not all back covers are done as well as Brookstone's.

Figure 6-24 is the Bill Tosetti's catalog. A full three-quarter-page photo pictures five clothing products, but the copy is poorly worded (''Complete description on pg. 31''). The cataloger assumes the customer knows that the clothing is for sale. The five garments could easily have been named, and plenty of room is available for additional page numbers such as, ''See pages 22-29 for quality wool blankets.'' Still, the idea of showing products in a compatible setting is a good choice when trying to maintain a theme or mood.

Inmac, a business-to-business catalog, uses a mini-index on the back cover for referencing new data communications products. Unfortunately, three out of the seven pages are the same, and so much space has been used describing the index that the index type must be in 6 point. Just as effective would have been ''New Product Index'' or ''Mini-Index'' or ''Convenient Index''—all allowing two more lines of extra space for the next index itself.

One innovation that will have a great impact not only on back cover selling but on catalog marketing in general is jet ink printing. Fine-tuned, selective marketing is now available. The process allows on-line personalized messages to be selected for different segments

UNCONDITIONAL GUARANTEE! IF YOU'RE NOT DELIGHTED, RETURN YOUR PURCHASE FOR A PROMPT REFUND.

Order By Phone 24 hours

If you have a Visa, MasterCard or American Express, call our **Credit Card Order Department** any time, 24 hours a day, 7 days a week. During the hours of 9:00 AM to 5:00 PM (Mon.-Fri.) an operator will take your order; other hours, just give your order to our automatic ordering service. In most cases, we'll process and ship that same day.

Remember, this number connects to the order desk only. For other business, including inquiries for our **Customer Service Department**, please call weekdays, 9:00 AM to 5:00 PM; **603-924-7181.**

603.924.9541

Brookstone Company
127 VOSE FARM ROAD
PETERBOROUGH, NEW HAMPSHIRE 03458

BULK RATE
U.S. POSTAGE
PAID
BROOKSTONE
COMPANY

CAR-RT PRESORT **CR02

ADDRESS CORRECTION REQUESTED

BKX 80829SIT50119VA1 1TJ301SA1
MRS. BOBBY SMITH
119 VIA VALLECITO
MANITOU SPRINGS CO 80829

Ultra Light C-Clamp Is Ultra Strong

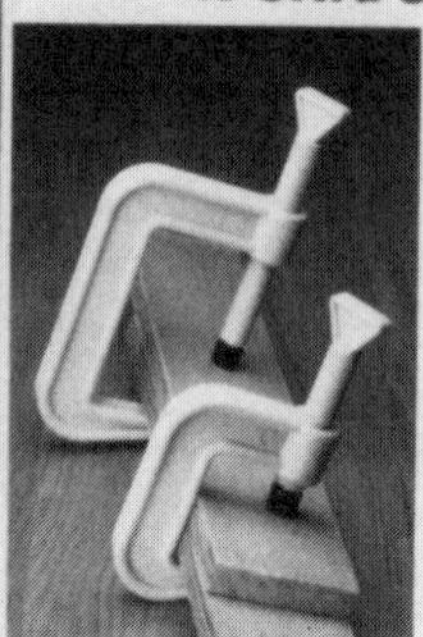

Made entirely of fiber glass-reinforced Capron nylon, this unique new C-clamp is strong and rust-free and weighs far less than conventional steel clamps. Originally developed for the aerospace industry, it's useful in both wood- and metal-working. Really great for delicate woodworking, since it won't damage work if dropped. A self-centering screw makes precise adjustments easy. Comes in 2" (6.5 oz.) or 4" (9oz.) sizes. Gray.

J-10536 Ultra light C-clamp, 2" **$7.95**
J-10537 Ultra light C-clamp, 4" **$9.95**

These Screwdrivers Feel As If They Were Custom-Made For Your Hands

Feature for feature, these German-made screwdrivers are the best we've ever seen. Their octagonal handles fit the hand perfectly for comfort and control. The straight blades are cross-hatched for a better bite, preventing screw damage. Hexagonal shoulders below the handles let you apply a wrench for help on super-high-torque jobs. Set includes 3 straight slots and 2 Phillips (#1 and #2). Vanadium steel alloy shafts, bright red handles. 7" to 10" long.

J-10528 Pro-grip screwdrivers **$18.95**

An Ultrasonic Electric Humidifier That Doesn't Hiss

Silence is just one of the many virtues of this amazing electric humidifier. It ultrasonically vaporizes water into a super-fine mist. There's a variable mist control, and you can direct the flow of moisture where you wish. The humidistat lets you set the level of humidity you desire and maintains that setting automatically. Weighs less than 15 lbs. when full. And it's safe—UL listed. It's so quiet you can use it in the bedroom, or while watching TV.

High impact off-white plastic case, see-through tinted removable reservoir. 11½" x 16½" x 6".

J-07088 Silent electric humidifier **$149.95**

Put Out A Chimney Fire Before The Fire Department Can Arrive

Many fire departments now rely on this extinguisher to put out chimney fires quickly, safely, without water damage to the house or danger of cracking chimney tiles. Works by cutting off the fire's oxygen supply. Just tear the tape, twist the top and snap it off, strike the exposed mixture with the scratcher cap and drop the extinguisher into your stove or fireplace. The combination of gasses released smothers the fire in moments. Easy, safe, and quick to use. For safety's sake, please familiarize yourself and your family with the operation of this product before it's necessary, and always call the fire department when a chimney fire occurs. 13½" long x 1⅛" dia. Weighs 1 lb. Decorative steel container available, finished in matte black, with a brass-toned finial, for storing extinguisher or long fireplace matches.

J-07094 Chimney fire extinguisher **$10.95**
J-10641 Storage container **$12.95**
J-10642 Set, storage container and chimney fire extinguisher **$19.95**

OUR COVER

Winter can be a breeze instead of a blast if you're properly prepared for it. Here are some great ideas for your winter comfort—our draft-stopping wind shields (page 11), flame-starter crank blower (page 3), energy- and money-saving energy teller (page 6), silent electric humidifier (page 76), and gas water-heater timer (page 10). See these and more great weather-tamers in this catalog.

Easy-Set Pantograph Re-Sizes Drawings, Plans And Pictures

The famous old pantograph is back! This timesaving tool reduces or enlarges a drawing, picture, map, plan or diagram from 1/10th to 10 times its size.

All you do is trace the original, and the pantograph retraces simultaneously to the size you want. Ideal for furniture makers working from a small sketch; transfers patterns to wood for cutting; changes shop jigs and patterns to new desired sizes.

Nicely made of aluminum bars, 20" and 21" long; calibrated for 26 ratios of enlargement and reduction. Easy to set. Complete instructions.

J-05488 Easy-set pantograph **$24.50**

6-23

The Pendleton Specialist

17632 CHATSWORTH STREET
GRANADA HILLS, CALIFORNIA 91344

2339 HUNTINGTON DRIVE
SAN MARINO, CALIFORNIA 91108

2801 PACIFIC COAST HWY.
TORRANCE, CALIFORNIA 90505
(New Location)

Prices in this Catalog
effective until July 1, 1985

POSTMAN: DATED MATERIAL
If addressee is no longer living at
residence, leave with occupant

Bulk Rate
U.S. Postage
PAID
Permit No. 1171
PORTLAND, OR

C. JONES
119 VIA VALLECITO
MANITOU SPGS CO 80829

(Complete Description on Pg. 31)

Store hours will vary throughout the year depending on location and time of year, so please contact the store nearest you for their hours.

Granada Hills	818-363-2192
San Marino	818-795-4633
Torrance	213-539-2725

6-24

Lake City, Minnesota 55041
(612) 345-5355

BULK RATE
U.S. POSTAGE
PAID
WILD WINGS

WELCOME TO OUR 1984-85 WILDLIFE SPORTING COLLECTION. WE OFFER YOU THE FINEST SELECTION AVAILABLE OF WILDLIFE LIMITED EDITION PRINTS (PAGES 2-7, 39-64), CONSERVATION PRINTS (PAGES 1, 35-38), HOME AND OFFICE DECORATIONS, GIFTWARE AND BOOKS (PAGES 8-31).

DUPLICATE MAILINGS?
If you receive more than one copy of our catalog, please share this with a friend. Also send us the duplicate addresses and indicate the proper one. We will correct the situation as soon as possible.

If addressee has moved, please deliver this catalog to new resident at address shown.

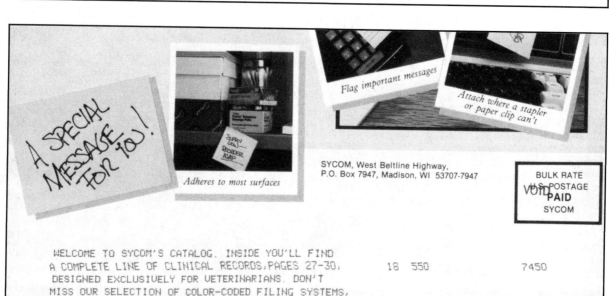

6-25

A SPECIAL MESSAGE FOR YOU!
Adheres to most surfaces

Flag important messages
Attach where a stapler or paper clip can't

SYCOM, West Beltline Highway,
P.O. Box 7947, Madison, WI 53707-7947

BULK RATE
U.S. POSTAGE
PAID
SYCOM
VOID

WELCOME TO SYCOM'S CATALOG. INSIDE YOU'LL FIND A COMPLETE LINE OF CLINICAL RECORDS,PAGES 27-30, DESIGNED EXCLUSIVELY FOR VETERINARIANS. DON'T MISS OUR SELECTION OF COLOR-CODED FILING SYSTEMS, PAGES 2-6. OUR APPOINTMENT AIDS,PAGES 12-27, ARE DESIGNED TO HELP YOU MANAGE YOUR PATIENT FLOW.

18 550 7450

6-26

of your list. Wild Wings, a wildlife gift merchandise catalog (Figure 6-25), directs customers to specific pages in the catalog.

Figure 6-26 shows one of six individual category references sent to the matching customer counterpart. Sycom directs the customer to specific pages bearing products for Chiropractors, Dentists, Optometric Professionals, Veterinarians, Physicians, and Podiatrists, and also to other pages and products. One catalog is turned into seven specialized catalogs just by changing the wording and page references. This fine tuning immediately directs the customers to the areas in which they are interested. Catalogs can be customized according to the customer's buying preference. Also note how a yellow memo with a message makes the customized approach even more special. Handwritten is: "A Special Message For You!"

Exciting promotional opportunity

The opportunities jet ink printing offers are breathtaking: individual personalization, regional product referencing, category highlighting, customer personalization of products offered. Ideas and possibilities are limited only by one's imagination. The possibility of increasing sales through individualized catalogs is here now — take advantage of it!

Direct Selling

Picturing a product along with product copy which includes factual information and the retail price is the most common and successful treatment of a catalog back cover. Products chosen for the back cover should be your best sellers for that season. Full product information must be given in order for the customer to make a buying decision without referencing anywhere else. You may present only one product or a number of products. Your decision on the number of products may be somewhat controlled by the aesthetic feeling desired. But don't let design and aesthetics dominate. Selling products is the job of the catalog.

The Lands' End sportswear catalog (Figure 6-27) takes the full back cover to present one product. A product headline identifier is in the upper right-hand corner. The words "*A Lands' End classic*" attempt to tell customers that this is a popular product which they will want, too. However, the message is almost lost due to the diminished effect of reversed out type on a light blue background. The product name, "The Navy Pea Coat," is a little more legible because of the size of type. The caption headline at the beginning of the descriptive copy block again talks of classic appeal, plus telling the main product benefit. Full-length product copy is provided with complete product information so the customer can immediately decide to purchase. Further encouragement to order, a toll-free number, is right below the product information, providing instant access to ordering. Figure 6-28 shows how another general consumer catalog, Downs' Collectors Showcase, directly sells nine products. Again, the length and style of product copy are typical of that inside. And easy ordering is provided with the presentation of a toll-free number.

Following are two business-to-business catalogs that approach back cover selling in much the same way. Figure 6-29 shows how Inmac directly sells only one product, an adjustable keyboard shelf. The copy is typical of what would be found inside — a benefit headline with medium-length descriptive copy. Added and calling even more attention is a blurb in the upper right corner. Boxed is "An Inmac Exclusive," telling the customer that the product is special and will not be found elsewhere (a good sales motivator).

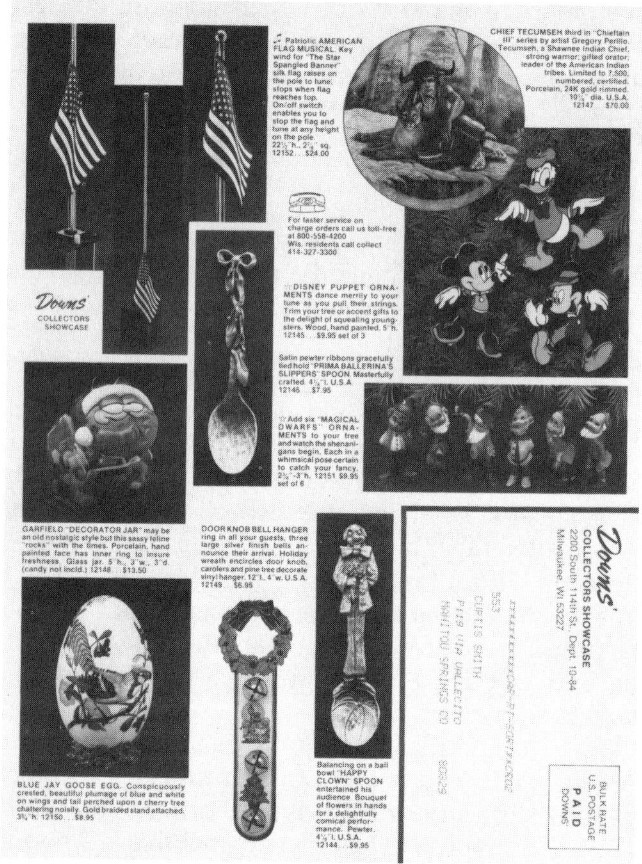

6-28

6-27

Seven product benefits are called out in conjunction with an art presentation. "Low-profile base". . ."Steel extension arm". . . "Attractive oak veneer". . ."Base glides forward". . ."Easy-grip knob". . ."No more strain". . .and "When not in use, it takes no more space than your computer" are explained and act as art headlines. Each solves a problem or provides a benefit which will be appreciated. This type of copy treatment allows easy product benefit selling and shortens the length of the main copy block.

Colorifics, a drill team clothing supplies catalog (Figure 6-30), sells four products directly on the back cover. Again, the copy is the exact style and length it would be if the product were presented inside — a product identifying headline with descriptive copy providing all the information to produce an order. Interestingly enough, neither of the business-to-business catalogs gives a phone number to be used for ordering, and yet business has the largest percentage of phone orders. Something else missed by three out of four catalogs was the opportunity to reference other products or pages inside. Adding a few words with an inside page number takes little space and adds to dollar sales.

6-29

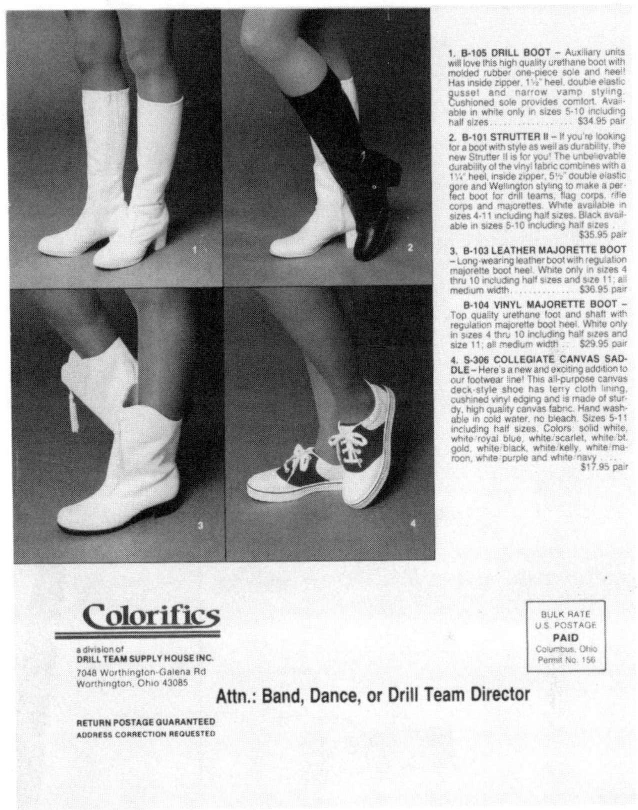

6-30

Back Cover Checklist:

- ☐ Review Character of Front Cover.
- ☐ Choose Back Cover Approach.
- ☐ Check Postal Requirements.
- ☐ Review Special Offers.

Always

1. Include company name and address.
2. Include telephone number.
3. Direct the customer inside.

Strongly Consider

1. Selling product(s) directly.
2. Indicating charge cards accepted.
3. Stating your guarantee.
4. Utilizing jet ink printing for personalized messages.
5. Using customer testimonial(s).
6. Using a routing directive.
7. Using a mini-index.
8. Stating special company benefits.
9. Directing customer to order form.
10. Requesting customer to place label on order form.
11. Rewarding customer for an action taken.

Inside the Catalog

The inside of the catalog is where the real selling begins. It houses the products for which a catalog exists. Copy must now communicate each product's benefits in such a way that the customer will want to purchase the products presented. Copy must welcome the customer to your catalog just as retail stores' proprietors or hosts would welcome a person coming to their place of business or home. Copy must build company credibility, reflect company style, educate customers, and spur them into the action of buying. Let us first explore the basics of writing product copy.

Product Copy

All catalog copy needs to give the customer enough information about a product to make a purchase. The manner in which you impart information varies considerably, depending on the style and image of your company. There is long copy, short copy, medium copy. Copy can be friendly, authoritative, involved, straightforward. But all good copy has basics to which you should be attuned. Copywriters must become familiar with many examples of successful copy structure.

In the beginning of this chapter, it was recommended that a thorough evaluation and analysis of your customer list be made in order for you to know to whom you are writing. Are you appealing to the corporate executive, proprietors of small businesses, retired people, a group of collectors, home chefs, or college attendees? You need to know so you can determine the tone and approach of your copy. You also need to know the catalog company well. What image does it wish to portray? Was the business built on the fact that the owners are experts in a specific area? Do they see their company as a friendly next-door neighbor, or do they pride themselves on fast service and customer attention? Knowing the image will allow the copywriter to determine the approach which should be taken.

In the Product Work Session chapter, we emphasized the need to look at competitors' catalog and advertising copy to see what has worked for others. We also mentioned the manufacturer's material, testing results, and thoroughly reviewing the merchandiser's reasons for selecting the product. Once all this is reviewed, the product is in-hand and hopefully has even been tried by the copywriter. At this point, ask questions. What will be the major benefit, the secondary benefits; what are all the jobs for which the product can be used; is it an exclusive; does it have a warranty; has it been used by professionals or by business prior to public release; does it solve a specific problem? Gain as much knowledge as you can in the time permitted.

Basics of Catalog Copy

A primary fact to realize about catalog copywriting and its major difference from other types of advertising copy is that you get only one chance to contact the customer. Retail stores, when advertising, have several chances at contacting customers: when customers see a newspaper ad, when they hear or see an advertisement on radio or TV, and when they come in the store one, two, or three times. There is no need to give all the information on first contact; the retail store wants only to motivate customers to come into the store. *The cataloger must give complete information about the product. There is only one chance to make the sale.* Failing to give complete information or confusing the customer or inciting someone to write you for more information only delays or discourages the order. Therefore, *the job of the copywriter is to give complete and correct information in such a way that it induces the customer to make a purchase.*

Product Body Copy

Product body copy is the copy which immediately follows the copy headline. It is often referred to as descriptive copy, selling copy, the copy block, or product copy. The primary job of the body copy is to sell the product by describing benefits, attributes, specifications, materials, and price. *Copy has the awesome job of selling the product.* It is by far the most powerful selling tool available to the cataloger. Copy is the secret weapon mail order has over retail stores, providing information which educates, informs, and sells the customer. Retail stores are unable to equal this feat because all clerks cannot know everything about each product in the store; they are often unavailable and are at times less friendly and accommodating than would be desired. Well written copy is always informative, and equally so to all customers.

How To Prepare To Write Product Body Copy

Often catalog marketers and sometimes even writers don't know how to go about researching, writing, or editing a catalog. Chapter 4, Product Work Sessions, should be carefully reviewed and suggested steps followed when you are preparing catalog copy. Here is a five-step summary procedure for getting ready to have your catalog copy written.

Step #1: Consult the merchandiser or buyer who selected the product. This is by far the most important step because the person who selected the product knows why the target customer will purchase the product. The merchandiser is the one who ultimately answers for its success or failure and so has very definite reasons why the product will appeal to the customer.

The merchandiser should be able to tell the writer why the product was selected: that it has been successfully run by competitors in their catalogs or in space advertising, what the main benefit is, what problem the product will solve, what service it will render, or how it is like past or current successful products.

The writer should ask a lot of questions and expect to get answers from the merchandiser which will become the informational backbone of the copy. Information derived from the merchandiser should be given every consideration when the writer is structuring the copy because the merchandiser, not the writer, best knows the appeal of the product.

Step #2: Collect background information. Writing catalog copy seldom requires original research. Usually, the products to be included in the catalog have already been described in previous brochures, flyers, ads, and data sheets. Collecting and organizing this printed material is a crucial step in getting ready to write the catalog copy. The writer should get all pertinent product literature received from the manufacturer. (And if the catalog house doesn't have this literature, it must be solicited.) For an existing product, this information can include ad tear sheets, brochures, old catalogs, article reprints, technical papers, press kits, audio-visual scripts, direct mail promotions, and spec sheets.

If the product is new or manufactured by the catalog company itself, these publications may not exist. But the birth of any new product is accompanied by mounds of paperwork which can be given the writer, including internal memos, letters of technical information, product specifications, engineering drawings, photos of prototypes, business and marketing plans, reports, and sales proposals.

If the catalog house is supplying the copywriter with information on many products, file folders should be used to separate source material by product. Include a brief with each folder indicating whether the enclosed background material is complete and up-to-date and, if not, names of persons the writer can call to fill the gaps.

Be sure to mark the source material to indicate what information should be included in the catalog and what should not. Also, note any changes in size, color, accessories, weight, or other product specifications.

Step #3: Study the previous catalogs, previous ads, and promotional pieces. The writer will have to study all promotional information disseminated over the past few years to decide which ideas, formats, and techniques work and to discard those that don't.

The writer should know about any *mandatory* format or stylistic requirements. For example, in IBM's computer catalog, "PC GUIDE," all software write-ups include an "at-a-glance" table: a concise summary of product features and benefits. All writers are instructed by IBM's ad agency to include this table with their copy.

Step #4: Set a direction. The writer must be aware of any instructions or suggestions the catalog house wants followed. (These should be written down.) The catalogers might have definite ideas on how they want their catalogs arranged and organized. Or they may prefer one style of copy to another. But copywriters can't read anyone's mind; they must know the catalogers' preferences.

Some writers might object, ''But isn't it up to the writer to set the tone, style, content and organization? Isn't that what the writer gets paid for?'' Experience shows that catalogers have their preferred ways of doing things. And rarely does a staff writer (let alone a freelancer or agency) make revolutionary changes from one year's catalog to the next.

Step #5: The catalog merchandiser must be available. Once the background material is ready and the merchandiser's information is supplied, the writer is ready to write the copy. At this point, the merchandiser must be available to answer questions, gather additional information, and review rough drafts, outlines or concepts. If the merchandiser is *not* available, the project will be held up until the writer gets the information, feedback, or approval that is needed.

All merchandisers should make sure their people support the copywriter's efforts. A good bet, if an outside agency or individual is used, is to appoint one employee to act as liaison between catalog company and writer. It's inefficient for a writer to have to track down the many people in a company who are involved with the catalog and its creation.

How To Write Product Copy

Now the writer is ready to sit down and start writing product copy. But before looking at the different copy approaches, let's look at the process of writing itself and specifically *how to write product copy and avoid ''Writer's Block.''* Copywriters who have no trouble dishing up a sales letter or ad may suddenly ''freeze'' when faced with the task of producing 180 lines of 44 characters each for a catalog. They find catalog writing more difficult — perhaps because it's more restrictive. In an ad or sales letter, writers are pretty free to ''let loose.'' But in a catalog they are limited in space and confined to following the catalog's set tone, format, and style.

Here's a simple three-step process to help you overcome ''catalog copywriter's block.''

Start writing

1. In the first stage, *you simply IGNORE the constraints of space, format and style — and just WRITE.* Let the words flow. Write whatever comes naturally. Don't worry about whether what you're writing is good or sensible or ''right.'' You'll have a chance to go back and fix it later. For now, just let the words pour out.

Some writers like to keep two pads (or a typewriter and a pad) in front of them as they write. The first pad is used for composing the copy. Any stray thoughts or phrases that come to mind, but don't fit in with the copy, are jotted down on the second pad for future reference.

2. In the second phase, *you edit your rough first draft to make it better.* Editing consists of:

Edit

☐ Deleting unnecessary words and phrases,

☐ Adjusting the copy to the exact word length the specs call for,

☐ Rewriting awkward phrases,

☐ Making sure all necessary facts are included,

☐ Reordering copy points to make the organization more logical,

☐ Making copy conform to catalog format and style (adding tables, call-outs, charts, or special sections, as needed),

☐ Rewriting to fit the overall "tone" of the catalog.

Polish

3. *The third step is polishing*. Polishing means proofreading, checking for errors in spelling, punctuation, grammar, capitalization, or abbreviation. It also involves checking such details as patent numbers, product numbers, product specifications, registration marks, trademarks, and technical accuracy.

Every writer has a "creative" side and an "analytical" or "editing" side. The creative side comes up with the ideas; the editing side holds the ideas up to the cold light of day and judges their effectiveness. Both sides are needed in copywriting, but should be used in separate and distinct phases of the writing process, as outlined above. When you try to be creative and analytical at the same time, your editing facilities inhibit your creative facilities, and writer's block results. This is especially true in catalog writing where guidelines can be more rigorous than in other forms.

The Long and Short of copy. The old saying, "Copy should be just as long as necessary," often is misrepresented. Some people believe copy should be stripped to the bare bones — just a few exciting words to make the customer's mouth water and that's it. But generally copy needs a lot more. In order to inform the customer about benefits, attributes, basic specifications, and materials — plus make the customer want to buy — most copy will take more than three lines of type. Some products — especially complex products — may require a great deal of explaining and the copy will need to be long. However, let's take a look at how nine lines of copy can say it better than 12. Below are two pieces of copy on the same product. The short copy "B" says everything necessary and says it better. Copy "A" is packed with unnecessary words that only discourage the customer from reading. Notice how headline "B" immediately draws attention by announcing the product benefit.

Copy "A": BRIGHT, CLOSE-UP VIEWS WITH THE ILLUMINATING 30X MAGNIFIER. This convenient pocket magnifier is designed to be a valued companion for work, hobby or recreation. Its diminutive size (5½ × 1¾ × ¾″) allows it to slip easily into pocket or purse; its 30X makes it ideal for detailed examination of plants, gems, stamps, photos. It features a center focus wheel for precise one-hand operation; retractable condenser lens pinpoints light so you can zero in on your subject. Light source is built in; batteries not included. A really handy tool. 30X MAGNIFIER NO. 31,291 $12.95

Copy "B": ILLUMINATING 30X MAGNIFIER IS POCKET-SIZED. Ideal for a detailed inspection of plants, gems, stamps or photos. It features a center focus wheel for precise one-hand operation, a retractable condenser lens to pinpoint light and a built-in light source. Batteries not included. 5½ × 1¾ × ¾″. 30X MAGNIFIER NO. 31,291 $12.95

A good guideline for writing strong, solid, tight copy is to first write as much as you like. Imagine you have twice the space the artist has given you. Then edit. Take a pencil and remove all the "that's." Next, remove any nonselling statements. Next, double check your "check list" to see if you included (or the photography makes clear) all necessary facts: color, size, weight, function, use, etc. And last but not least — *AVOID WORDS BEYOND THE READER'S READING LEVEL.* Now, rewrite. Finally, repeat the above steps. Look at what you have left. You'll have reduced the copy by half and ended up saying everything necessary. So don't worry about the length of your copy. Instead, worry about *what it says and how well it sells.*

Another good way to approach writing catalog copy is to *write copy to solve reader problems*. Your customer doesn't realize it, but actually he thinks: "If the catalog copy identifies my major personal or on-the-job problems, it has a better chance of convincing me to buy."

Before writing, review target mailing lists so you can *identify clusters of names for similar life or job problems*. Then make a *Problem Check List*, and next to each situation note how the particular product or service you're promoting will solve the problems.

You might accumulate the following list in an attempt to sell a special watch to a target group of entrepreneurial managers:

Product Copy

One key thing to keep in mind is making the catalog enjoyable for the reader. *Make it logical, visually appealing, and make the* copy interesting. *The longer you keep them in the "store" the more likely they are to buy.*

Patrick D. Smith, Jr.
Production Manager
California Polytechnic University

PROBLEMS:

- Managers work late, have difficulty waking each day.
- They must budget their time for each job they tackle.
- They must know how long each job took.

SOLUTIONS:

- *You can set multiple wake-up alarms with this watch.*
- *You get an hourly chime to keep you on schedule.*
- *Because this watch functions as a stopwatch, you can time your productivity.*

Notice that the "solution" copy did not state the problem. Rather, when you identify the problem, you should be able to create copy that implies the solution. Allow the readers to "read in" what their problem may be. You state the solution.

Also notice that in each "solution" example, the copy is presented with *clear reader benefits*. "Hourly chime" is insufficient. "Hourly chime to keep you on schedule" tells prospective purchasers why the chime is important and what it can do for them. *The concept is: identify a problem; then write copy that lets the reader see how your product or service solves that problem*. This concept works for every audience, product, or service. By examining your lists before writing, you can find the readers' problems. But in doing this, you'll be flustered when you discover different clusters of readers who have different problems. Then your problem will be how to include all salient points for each cluster.

Solve problems

Your solution is easy: *write more than one benefit* for each product or service feature. Now your copy might read:

> "Soft hourly chime, which only you can hear, keeps you on schedule, and you can switch it to alert you at half-hour intervals, quarter-hour periods, or any minute in any hour."

Give solutions

Now you can see how long problem-solving benefit copy appeals to more segments of your list audience.

Selecting a copy style is important because the tone of the copy should fit the character of your catalog and the market to which you are appealing. If your customer reacts favorably to a bare facts approach, then that is what you will want to use. However, most customers appreciate copy that is friendlier, more informative. Some customer groups want and need to know in detail about the product or product category being offered.

Five very successful copy styles are:

1. **Conversational**, the friendly approach which suggests familiarity — even to the point of the vernacular — to fit the products being offered.
2. **General Category**, where one copy presentation explains and provides information pertaining to a group of related products, allowing shorter copy for individual products.
3. **Involved**, in which copy will go into the aspects of the product more deeply than normal. Benefits and attributes are fully explained.
4. **Bare Facts**, where copy is short and crisp, relating the minimal amount of information. This approach relies heavily on the knowledge or familiarity of the customer.
5. **Benefit Highlighting**, when a single product has several benefits that need to be highlighted.

Now we will go into how these five product copy styles have been used in both general consumer and business-to-business catalogs.

Conversational Copy

General Consumer Eddie Bauer is a master at conversational copy which exudes authority, builds credibility, and informs the customer in a friendly way. And it is done in a convincing manner, selling with every word. Figure 6-31 shows how well the copy is done. After the product identifying headline, the following sentence states the main product benefit (attractive wearability), which is further explained in the second sentence. The next three sentences artfully explain the many product attributes such as epaulets, pockets, cuffs. However, what makes these attributes special is the manner in which they are described: *functional* shoulder epaulets, *expandable* cargo pockets with *security* flaps and *buttoned* cuffs. This is wonderful descriptive writing which is *selling copy*! The copy block ends with a terrific credibility builder: ''We have sold these fine jackets to big-name sportsmen, television correspondents, diplomats and many others who, like you, require comfortable sportswear with definitive style.'' That is almost a celebrity testimonial. It is convincing, informative first-person copy that sells! Specific product specifications are given in brief but complete form, handily above the identifying number and pricing. The conversational style in first person reads so well, encouraging the customer to order.

Catalog Copy

Write as though you are talking *to a customer, because you* are. *Speak a relaxed language, and add your own personal experience whenever possible.*

A. Lee Maynard
Lee Maynard
Santa Fe, NM

Business-to-Business Moore Business Center sells modular furniture in much the same conversational way. An easy, businesslike conversational copy style tells you about the product being offered. Figure 6-32 shows how the headline immediately identifies the product and the product benefits. The second paragraph tells product attributes, ending with a credibility-building sentence reinforced with a problem-solving statement. The conversational tone is achieved by letting the customer know that "The Modular Concept isn't new, but Marvel has executed the concept with flair. . ." and that "Those advantages wouldn't matter very much, however, without durability." This approach has promoted believability in a friendly manner, yet on a business level.

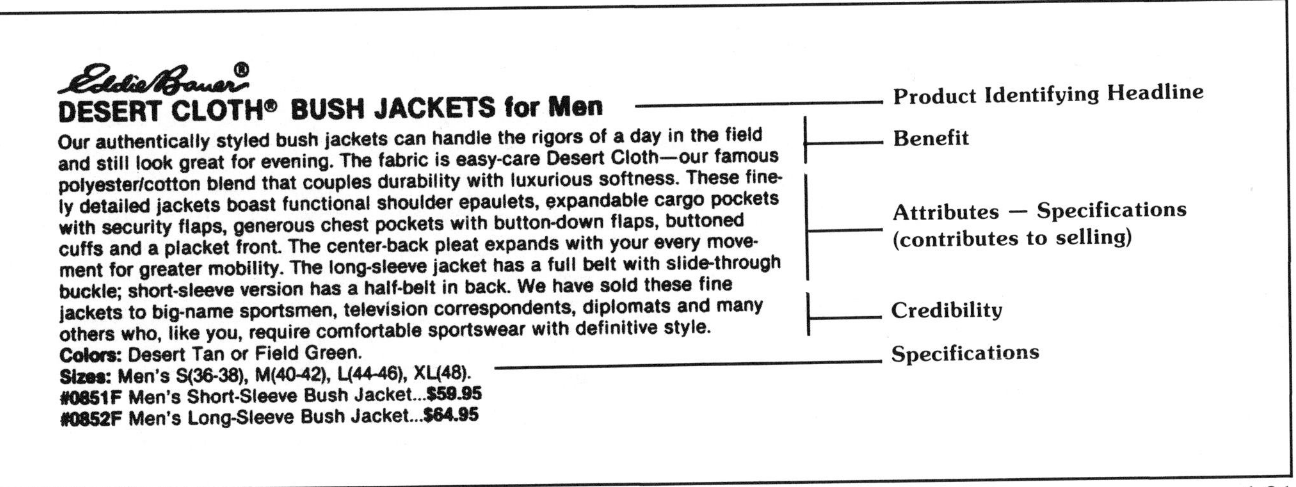

Eddie Bauer®
DESERT CLOTH® BUSH JACKETS for Men
Our authentically styled bush jackets can handle the rigors of a day in the field and still look great for evening. The fabric is easy-care Desert Cloth—our famous polyester/cotton blend that couples durability with luxurious softness. These finely detailed jackets boast functional shoulder epaulets, expandable cargo pockets with security flaps, generous chest pockets with button-down flaps, buttoned cuffs and a placket front. The center-back pleat expands with your every movement for greater mobility. The long-sleeve jacket has a full belt with slide-through buckle; short-sleeve version has a half-belt in back. We have sold these fine jackets to big-name sportsmen, television correspondents, diplomats and many others who, like you, require comfortable sportswear with definitive style.
Colors: Desert Tan or Field Green.
Sizes: Men's S(36-38), M(40-42), L(44-46), XL(48).
#0851F Men's Short-Sleeve Bush Jacket...$59.95
#0852F Men's Long-Sleeve Bush Jacket...$64.95
Product Identifying Headline
Benefit
Attributes — Specifications (contributes to selling)
Credibility
Specifications

6-31

Marvel Modular Furniture Combines Strength and Versatility — Product Identifying Headline

This complete line of high-quality furniture is specifically-designed to provide two very important benefits. 1) It allows you to design your own system to fit the space limitations you have now and add to your system as you grow. And 2) it gives you durable performance for years to come. — Benefits

The modular concept isn't new, but Marvel has executed the concept with flair and precise engineering for total flexibility and adaptability. Those advantages wouldn't matter very much, however, without durability. Each base is solid, 21-gauge steel. Every top is 1½" industrial-grade particle board that's laminated under high pressure to protect against burning, scratching or static. The rounded-corner design and vinyl edging protects operators from scrapes and bruises. — Attributes

And an exclusive feature from Marvel, called Cable Management System, insures you'll never have to fool with tangled cords and cables again. — Credibility

6-32

General Category

General Consumer. L.H. Selman Ltd. produces a Collectors' Paperweights catalog which is also a price guide for collectors and dealers. The products, collectors' paperweights, are classified into two categories (Contemporary and Antique) and then broken down within these categories by individual artisans and studio artists. It is very important that the market to which Selman appeals be informed of many aspects not normally utilized in more common product lines. Figure 6-33 is one of the two introductory pages for the Contemporary paperweights being offered in this catalog. An explanation of Contemporary paperweight production is given, plus the note of excitement in the recreation of nearly lost techniques and the ''renaissance'' of new designers whose fancy has been taken by this 200-year-old art form. Note the interest created by providing a photograph showing a stage of actual production, telling us that these are genuine techniques and skills recovered and newly dedicated to this art form. Elements such as these are very important to collectors — the more they know and understand about production, artists, and the history of skills, the more avid collectors they become, the more legitimate the offer appears. Allotting space to this subject is making use of a subtle selling tool. And the ease with which the art and copy can be referenced is a customer plus.

Figure 6-34 is an example of the pages preceding the presentation of actual paperweights by father and son artist contributors, Ray and Bob Banford. The introduction tells when they started making paperweights, the style they produce, where their work has been displayed, and how their work is signed (so that authenticity can be established). Background information as to how each became interested in this type of work is given, too. The writing style throughout the catalog is casual and personal, and yet it also seems disciplined and reliable — just the right combination to make customers feel at ease, inform them, and let them know this is information that can be trusted. The style and manner in which this education is approached is that of a friendly professor holding class on the lawn at a college campus. The introduction on the Banford artist team says, ''Ray's interest in glass began. . .''; with others there is information such as ''surrounded by Debbie's rose garden and Del's vegetable garden. . .,'' and a gentle suggestion of service: ''We look forward to helping you, too, build an outstanding collection.'' This copy informs and introduces 12 different products.

Create interest

The actual product copy is always short, briefly stating attributes of design and color. The headline consists of the catalog number and the artist's name. A typical product copy block is: ''25. BOB BANFORD. A brilliant, well-designed lampwork bouquet centers around a traditional purple and yellow pansy in this stunning weight set on a clear waffle-cut base. Signed with a 'B' cane at the base of stems. $1440.'' This softly informative copy is all that is needed because of the prior copy concerning the classification and artist.

Copy Content

If space permits, a brief description of product background and suggested use make for interesting reading and may increase sales.

Frank Merritt
Colonial Williamsburg Foundation
Williamsburg, VA

CONTEMPORARY FACTORIES AND STUDIO ARTISTS

Arranging lampwork petals on a template.

In the 1950s, Paul Jokelson, an importer and avid paperweight enthusiast, approached the glass factories of Baccarat and Saint Louis and urged them to revive the classic art of paperweight production.

Paperweights had not been produced in significant numbers for more than 80 years, and glass artisans at the two factories were faced with the difficult and challenging task of rediscovering the almost lost techniques of paperweight making. Once they succeeded, interest in the contemporary weights led to further production and experimentation.

Since then, a number of glass factories have joined Baccarat and Saint Louis in producing modern paperweights. Cristal D'Albret of France, "J" Glass, Perthshire and Caithness of Scotland, and others utilize traditional techniques and classical motifs while exploring exciting new possibilities in design and technology.

With the renewed interest in paperweights, a number of individual glass workers have also been encouraged to experiment with designs and techniques and produce paperweights on their own.

RAY AND BOB BANFORD

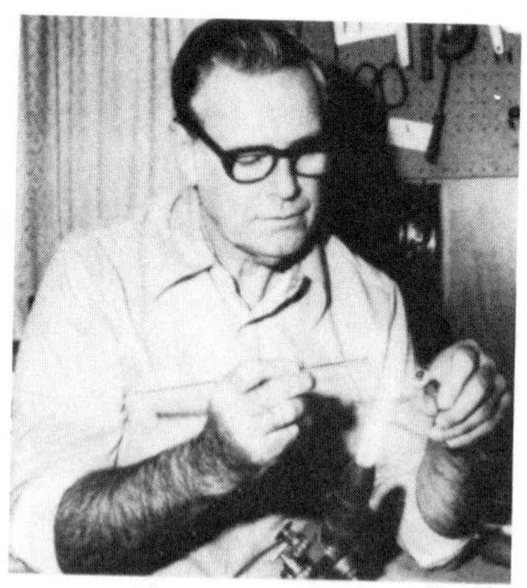

Glass artists Ray and Bob Banford, father and son, have been making French-style paperweights since 1971. The two, who share a workshop behind their home in Hammonton, New Jersey, draw upon each other's expertise but work independently, creating their own designs and functioning as individual craftsmen.

Ray's interest in glass began when he and his wife visited the Corning Museum of Glass and the workshop of an elderly Czechoslovakian glassmaker, Adolph Macho. Ray became fascinated with glass and the glassmaking process, and when Adolph Macho retired, he bought the glassmaker's equipment and began a new career. In addition to paperweights, Ray creates glass buttons and pendants and tends to the business of his and Bob's production.

Bob's glass career began when he received a torch from his parents as a high school graduation gift. With it he began experimenting, first by making ships and carousels of spun glass, then with the challenge of lampwork and paperweight production. Bob's complex lampwork motifs, which include flowers, insects, and reptiles, are realistic and consistently well-designed. His work is displayed at Wheaton Village, the Corning Museum of Glass, and the Smithsonian Institution.

Bob signs his weights with a red, white, and blue "B" initial cane. Ray uses the same initial cane, but in black and white.

6-34

Business-to-Business Day-Timer Executive Gift Catalog (Figure 6-35) takes one full page to illustrate and inform in general about their category of Desk Day-Timer planners appearing on the following nine pages. Day-Timer has utilized this space to talk about their selection of planners. They also cleverly refer the customer to various pages within the category. Following is one paragraph from the page:

> ''All Desk Day-Timer loose-leaf editions, offered on pages 27 thru 31, are designed to fit in a Day Timer 7-ring binder. You can even add your own special pages to custom tailor the Day-Timer to suit your needs exactly. Supplemental Desk Day Timer pages and other accessories, including even a 7-hole paper punch for adding your own special pages, are available on page 34.''

Copy generally references pages 27 through 31 and more specifically references the ''7-hole paper punch'' on page 34. The bulk of the copy extols the benefits in general of using a Day-Timer planner. The following pages, which contain specific variations of the planner, hone in on individual product benefits, information, and specifications.

Involved Copy

General Consumer Early Winters is one of the most outstanding catalogs utilizing an involved copy approach. The type of customer and the type of product that Early Winters handles both demand long product copy — copy that is involved and educates the customer about the product and at the same time sells! Figure 6-36 is a fine example of ''tight'' product copy that leaves nothing to the customer's imagination except the joy of ownership. The headline identifies the product, ''FannySack,'' and the product benefit, ''neat, light convertible,'' and gives a promise: ''does it all.'' The body copy starts right out by suggesting product use in the first paragraph. These suggestions let the customer know the vast versatility this Fanny Pack has over regular packs. The next four paragraphs tell in detail the product makeup, benefits, and attributes — not a detail is missed. Why? Because this type of information is vital to the prospective buyer, every bit of cubic inch storage capability, material, and closure information is important to the product's function and the customer's agility when using it. With the accompanying copy (''Buckle on our Expedition Fanny Pack. . .Two zippers transform. . . a pair of wing pockets keep your snacks and map at hand''), you are practically trying on the pack before you've even left the catalog! The last paragraph invites you to test the product, gives comparisons with similar products, and at the same time suggests that you too are discerning enough to participate in the great outdoor adventure. (''Test it and see if this 18-oz. 'convertible' doesn't admirably fill the gap. . .'') So much information is given and so much selling is done — every pocket and cranny fills a need that would be an-

Inform your customer

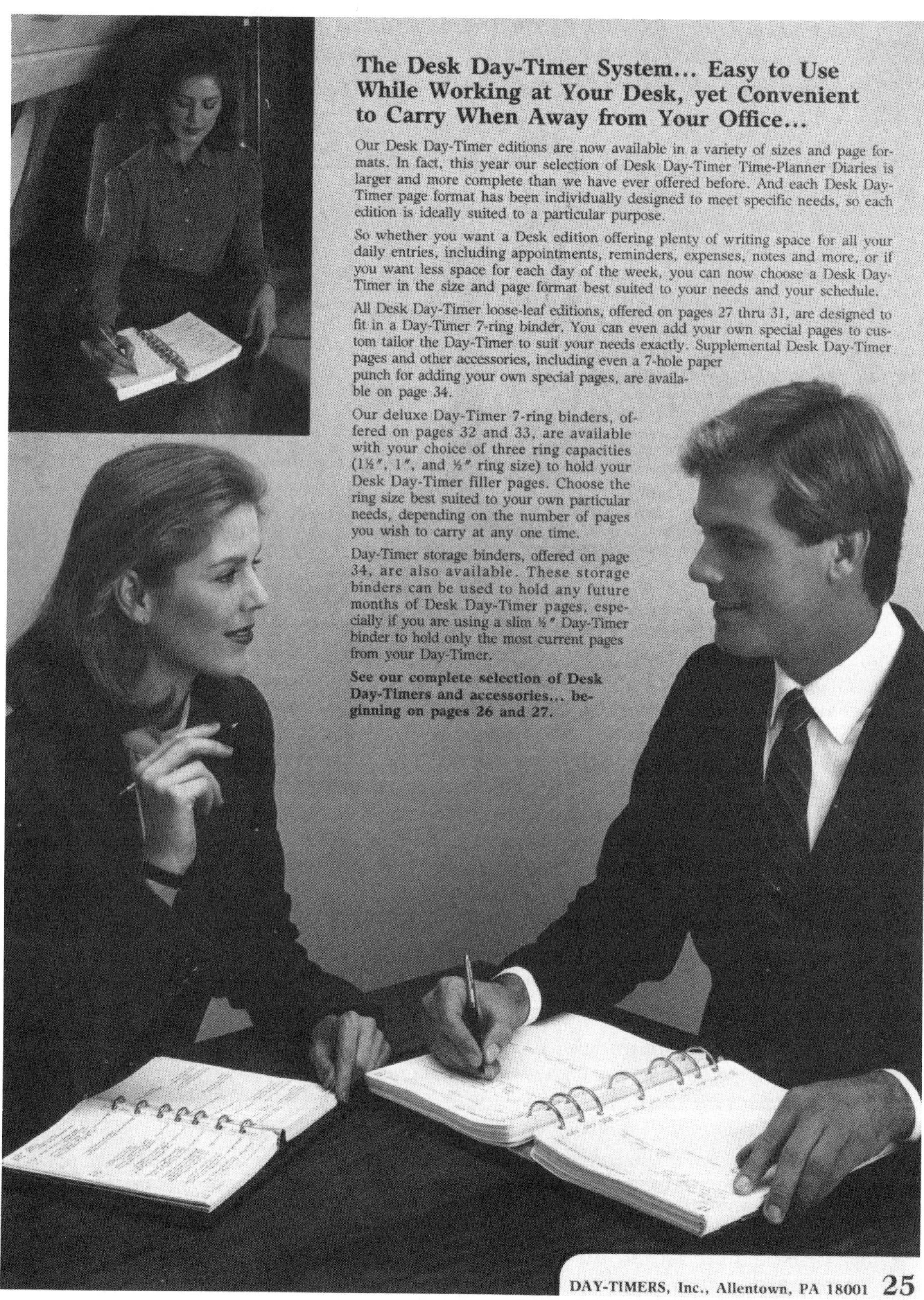

The Desk Day-Timer System... Easy to Use While Working at Your Desk, yet Convenient to Carry When Away from Your Office...
Our Desk Day-Timer editions are now available in a variety of sizes and page formats. In fact, this year our selection of Desk Day-Timer Time-Planner Diaries is larger and more complete than we have ever offered before. And each Desk Day-Timer page format has been individually designed to meet specific needs, so each edition is ideally suited to a particular purpose.
So whether you want a Desk edition offering plenty of writing space for all your daily entries, including appointments, reminders, expenses, notes and more, or if you want less space for each day of the week, you can now choose a Desk Day-Timer in the size and page format best suited to your needs and your schedule.
All Desk Day-Timer loose-leaf editions, offered on pages 27 thru 31, are designed to fit in a Day-Timer 7-ring binder. You can even add your own special pages to custom tailor the Day-Timer to suit your needs exactly. Supplemental Desk Day-Timer pages and other accessories, including even a 7-hole paper punch for adding your own special pages, are available on page 34.
Our deluxe Day-Timer 7-ring binders, offered on pages 32 and 33, are available with your choice of three ring capacities (1½", 1", and ½" ring size) to hold your Desk Day-Timer filler pages. Choose the ring size best suited to your own particular needs, depending on the number of pages you wish to carry at any one time.
Day-Timer storage binders, offered on page 34, are also available. These storage binders can be used to hold any future months of Desk Day-Timer pages, especially if you are using a slim ½" Day-Timer binder to hold only the most current pages from your Day-Timer.
See our complete selection of Desk Day-Timers and accessories... beginning on pages 26 and 27.
DAY-TIMERS, Inc., Allentown, PA 18001 25

6-35

ticipated by the expert hiker — while at the same time copy retains the wonderful, invitingly casual writing approach which is so characteristic of the Early Winters style. Throughout the catalog, headlines about the product benefit and body copy maintain momentum, skillfully educating and selling the customer.

Fanny sack to daypack, our neat, light convertible does it all.

Buckle on our Expedition Fanny Pack and you're ready for ski tour, day hike, or summit assault.

Two zippers transform this 650-cu.-in. fanny pack into a *2050-cu.-in.* hip-suspension pack, with adjustable shoulder straps and a pouch roomy enough to hold a sleeping bag!

Made of Weatherlite,™ a strong, waterproof nylon ripstop, the Fanny Pack has a main pouch & deck pocket that hold a day's supplies.

A pair of wing pockets keep your snacks and map at hand. Two bottle pockets detach for quick refreshment. Pull up the zippered top pack to store layers as you shed them.

A Technolite™ urethane/foam internal frame molds to your back and keeps the load solidly and comfortably on your hips.

Abrasion-resistant nylon ballistics cloth against your back takes the rub with less wear. Seams are bound and reinforced at stress points for years of use.

Order your Expedition Fanny Pack. Test it and see if this 18-oz. "convertible" doesn't admirably fill the gap between mere fanny pack and full-bore backpack.

Fits waists 28-43"

Expedition Fanny Pack, No. 2131 . . . $74.95

6-36

Business-to-Business Following up on the Day-Timer category approach to copy is Figure 6-37, illustrating how the involved copy approach is utilized for this company's most popular planner. Two full pages are devoted to illustration and copy, and they work hand-in-hand. The product-identifying headline spans two pages at the top of the presentation. The major benefit ("The 2-Page-Per-Day Regular Edition offers the Day-Timer 5-in-1 System with Maximum Space for Keeping a Detailed Record of Your Day. . .") lets the busy individual know that there is plenty of room to keep any information needed for one's fullest days. The copy then expands on what five functions make up this benefit. Each is explained and identified by number corresponding to art identification

Art and copy work together

Product Identifying Headline

Desk Day-Timer® System

Major Benefit

The 2-Page-Per-Day Regular Edition Offers the Day-Timer 5-in-1 System with Maximum Space for Keeping a Detailed Record of Your Day...

With this edition, each day of the week is covered on two full pages, so you have plenty of space for scheduling your appointments and planning your day for maximum effectiveness... then recording your results as your day progresses.

This edition offers Day-Timers' five functions in one as described below, with the location of each of these functions numbered 1 thru 5 on the Day-Timer sample page shown here.

Benefit Components

These Five Functions Include...

① **APPOINTMENTS** Hours range from 8 am to 6 pm with four lines per hour, so there's plenty of space for entering all your daily appointments.

② **TO BE DONE TODAY** Use this section to keep a running list of items to be done. Check off items as completed. Reassign unfinished tasks to future dates.

③ **TICKLER REMINDER** Use this same section to enter any items that may require some review or follow-up in the future. List the items on the day action will be taken.

④ **DIARY RECORD** Hours range from 8 am to 6 pm with four lines per hour. This becomes your permanent record of work accomplished during the day. It's a great progress checker.

⑤ **EXPENSE RECORD** This section is combined with the Diary Record, so your expenses are tied-in directly with your daily activities. Can also be used for time-billing.

This edition is available in two sizes:
Sr. Size with 8½" x 11" pages, or
Jr. Size with 5½" x 8½" pages.

Twelve tabbed monthly calendar sheets help you quickly find the current date.

This full-year loose-leaf edition will fit in a Day-Timer 7-ring binder with 1½" ring size, however other ring sizes are available to suit individual needs. See our complete binder selection on pages 32 and 33.

25 MONDAY MARCH, 1985 — MARCH 1985 — 281 Days Left

TO BE DONE TODAY

APPOINTMENTS & SCHEDULED EVENTS

NOTES & MEMOS MADE TODAY

Quantity Discounts: 2-6 units, 5%; 7-12, 7%; 13-25, 10%; 26-50, 12%; 51 or more, 15%.
Orders for all Day-Timer Fillers that are identified by a closed star (★) may be combined f

28 DAY-TIMERS, Inc., Allentown, PA 18001

6-37

-Page-Per-Day Regular Edition

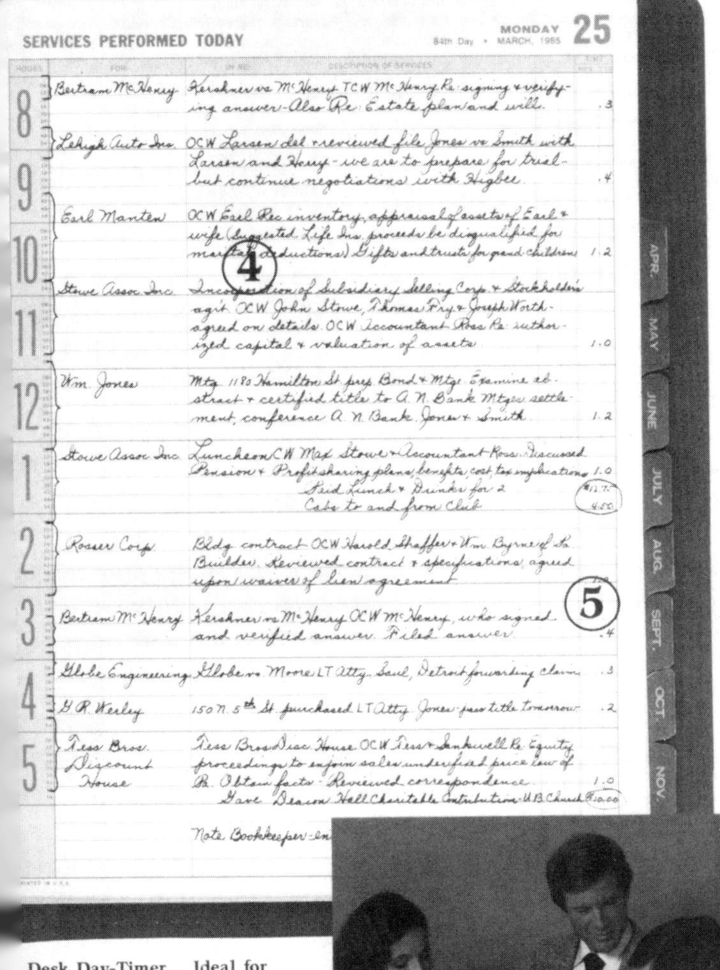

The 2-Page-Per-Day Regular Edition Desk Day-Timer... Our Most Popular Desk Diary!

This is the original Desk Day-Timer... preferred by most busy desk-oriented executives who normally work regular business hours and need maximum space for detailed records. In this 2-Page-Per-Day edition, the left page tells what you must do, while the right page becomes a permanent record of all your activities and work accomplished.

Regular daily coverage is from 8 am until 6 pm, with reduced space for evening hours. Hours for Saturdays are from 8 am until noon, plus ten additional line spaces. Sundays have open hours only, with 16 line spaces. There are four line spaces per hour, with the hourly column notched every tenth of an hour for keeping a decimal time record.

This 2-Page-Per-Day loose-leaf edition is available in two page sizes. Choose Sr. Size with 8½" x 11" pages, or Jr. Size with 5½" x 8½" pages. The full-year edition is designed to fit in a Day-Timer 7-ring binder with 1½" ring size. However, depending on your personal needs, you may prefer to carry only a partial year's supply of pages in either a 1" or ½" 7-ring binder.

As with all Day-Timer loose-leaf editions, you also receive...

- 12 Monthly Calendar/Divider Pages
- Address and Phone Directory
- 6-Year Planning Pages
- 12 Monthly Expense Record Pages
- Extra Pages for Notes and Memos

This edition can start with any month, and includes a full-year set of pages. Specify starting month and year when ordering. Filler pages thru Dec. 31, 1986 are currently available. Prices shown below are for Desk Day-Timer filler pages only. See pages 32 and 33 to order a Day-Timer binder to hold your filler pages.

Sr. Desk 2-Pg-Day Fillers - Regular
#G94010★ $14.95
Jr. Desk 2-Pg-Day Fillers - Regular
#G92010★ $11.95

Functional Information

Desk Day-Timer... Ideal for king at Your Desk, yet Easy arry When on the Road...

Desk Day-Timer makes a beautiful accessory, indispensable for planning busy day, yet easy to carry to meet- and on business trips.

n presented in one of our deluxe 7- leather binders, it makes an elegant t of Success"... one that can help ne to become more effective in iging all their daily activities.

when personalized with name or ini- on the front cover, it becomes a very al gift for your friends and business ciates.

ity discounts. All accesso items, identified with an open star (☆), that are ordered at the time will receive this s ne quantity discount.

DAY-TIMERS, Inc., Allentown, PA 18001 29

End Use Benefits and Attributes

for easy visual reference. Needed specifications are given about size, extra sheets, and a seven-ring holding binder sold on other pages. End-use benefits such as "Ideal for Working at Your Desk. . .indispensable for planning. . .easy to carry" are all what a busy person needs and wants. Then 46 lines of copy are devoted to functional information which is beneficial for the customer to know. In fact, the information given is essential to the education of the customer and the ultimate making of the sale. The product being sold is vitally important to the daily functioning of the person who owns and uses it. That person needs to know what each page is designed to record, the amount of space allowed for recording, the page size, the extra pages included, and how the planner will work. The customer needs to be assured the busiest day will be organized and facts can be easily recorded — Day-Timer offers it all.

Bare Facts

General Consumer Bachrach's is an upscale menswear catalog which became a reality because of a long-established (since 1877) retail store chain. Most products carried are name brand products and the Bachrach customer is a name brand buyer. Figure 6-38 shows how the product copy gives only the bare facts. The "Spanish Mahogany Blazer" headline announces a major benefit (the currently popular color "Mahogany") and identifies the product ("Blazer"). The design is then announced, followed by a few attributes (glove lambskin leather. . .open patch pockets), product specifications, and price. This is good bare-bones copy which gives the customer all the information needed with which to make a decision. Other products not carrying a brand name are as shortly described because Bachrach's feels the quality of their product is a given to those purchasing from the catalog.

F. SPANISH MAHOGANY
BLAZER. By Virany. Rich
glove lambskin leather blazer
features open patch pockets.
Even sizes 36-46 regular, 40-46
long. G2103 $360 (3.45)

6-38

Business-to-Business Harneds' catalog specializes in the butcher supply market. Because their audience is so narrow and the application of their products so specific within that market, the catalog copy can be especially short, containing only the minimal facts.

> Example — product identity headline: "Chicken Dolly"; body copy: "Heavy duty, chrome plated, tubular steel construction. Poly drip pan slides out for easy cleaning. Four swivel casters 22½"W×28½"L"13"H. 849-1015. Chicken dolly complete, ship wgt. 34 lbs. - $101.51."

Benefit Highlighting

General Consumer The Sharper Image utilizes benefit highlighting only occasionally throughout the catalog. But when used, it is very successful in acclaiming the various benefits offered by a single product. Figure 6-39 illustrates how the desired benefit (''Ride in the lap of luxury'') becomes the headline. The following paragraph explains why this is a luxury product by telling where sheep thrive (''steepest alpine crags. . .ice never melts'' and ''hot, arid outback of Australia'') and thus why sheepskin is ''the one material that can keep you cool. . .and. . .warm.'' It is ''the ultimate material for high-quality car and airplane seat covers.'' This method of word usage is the ultimate in building credibility. Benefit highlighting is called to the customer's attention three times for three different benefits throughout the copy in bold typeface. 1) ''The finest pelts for the softest covers.'' 2) ''Custom made to order for years of perfect fit.'' 3) ''Colors to match any interior.'' Each benefit is fully explained. And the three benefits are the most important aspects of a product such as this to the type of customer to whom it appeals.

Ride in the lap of luxury.

From the steepest alpine crags where the ice never melts, to the hot, arid outback of Australia, sheep thrive in some of the most brutal climates in the world. Sheepskin wool is nature's own perfect temperature regulator—the one material that can keep you cool through a long, hot summer and warm in the middle of winter. Which is why sheepskin wool has become the *ultimate* material for high-quality car and airplane seat covers.

The finest pelts for the softest covers.

One company—RamsHead—is known for seat covers of unparalleled softness, fit and construction. Run your fingers through one of these covers, and enjoy the plush feeling of pure, silken wool against your skin. RamsHead works with only the prime, 2–3" thick Australian pelts—the softest, finest wool in the world. Each pelt is combed and sheared numerous times, to an even 1" depth of fleece—a luxurious cushioning between you and your car seat.

On humid summer days, RamsHead seat covers absorb *up to 30%* of their own weight in moisture—without feeling wet. You're protected from scorching seats and your clothes stay fresher, less wrinkled. In winter, snuggle into the warmth of 1" deep pile, instead of icy cold vinyl or leather.

Custom made to order for years of perfect fit.

RamsHead earned its reputation custom-fitting covers for cars like Rolls Royce, Jaguar, and Lamborghini. Now, with a repertoire of over *1500 different seat patterns*, RamsHead can fit virtually any make or model of automobile, truck, RV—even airplane (see chart).

Every RamsHead cover is designed and fashioned with the same precision and workmanship as a fine sheepskin coat. Pelts are matched, then sewn with industrial nylon thread which won't fray or break like cotton thread. Every edge is then finished with the heaviest stretch binding available, so your seat covers stay firmly in place with no wrinkles or bunching. The snug, full fit looks as good from the back as from the front. And because RamsHead uses only the largest, prime pelts available there are fewer stress points than other covers—for improved strength and durability.

RamsHead even replaces the naturally soil-repellant lan-

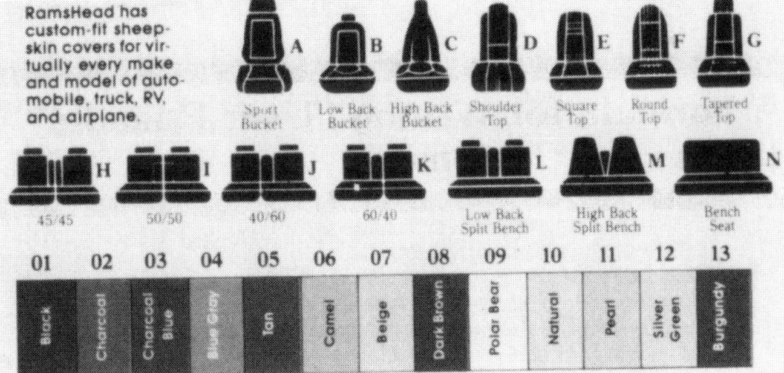

Choose from 13 colorfast colors—each a RamsHead exclusive designed to blend with and complement your vehicle's interior.

stains are easily removed, and your sheepskin only gets softer after each cleaning.

Colors to match any interior.

Select the cover designed and hand-made especially for your car, then choose from 13 rich colors (see chart). RamsHead uses an advanced chrome tanning process, so every color stays fast—as vivid after years of use as on the day you first sink down into it. And every cover is backed up by a *3 year warranty.*

You spend countless hours in your car. Experience what a difference 1" of soft, silken RamsHead sheepskin can make to your driving comfort. Originally created for sports and luxury cars—the finest sheepskin seat covers you can buy are also surprisingly affordable. Order your own custom seat covers now, and turn your next commute into a pleasurable excursion. *How to order:* Please specify seat style and color (from charts, above) and the make, model and year of your vehicle. Custom fitting requires 4–6 weeks for delivery.

- Pair of Seatcovers #URS493 $370 (12.50)
- Pair of Headrest Covers #URS700 $95 (4.50)
- Car Wash Mitt #URS600 $15 (3.50)

With every order receive a Rams Head sheepskin wool wash mitt ($15 value) for a no-scratch professional car washing and polishing.

6-39

Business-to-Business Automatic Business Products highlights main product benefits in red printing. Figure 6-40 shows how three product features give three product benefits to the customer. The "Purchase Orders" headline boldly identifies the product. The body copy both visually (all-caps and red ink) and verbally ("EASY TO USE," "FINANCIAL CONTROL," and "SAVE ADDRESSING TIME") announces the main product benefits. This approach leaves no guesswork as to what the product does and why the customer should buy it. Only brief explanatory copy is needed to make the sale with this type of copy approach.

PURCHASE ORDERS

Document your purchase requirements in writing!

EASY TO USE • Carbonless 3-part set includes original vendor copy, office copy to verify vendor's invoice and receiving copy to check in order.
FINANCIAL CONTROL • Alerts all departments of commitments made, payables due, and shipments expected.
SAVE ADDRESSING TIME • Designed for use with No. 10W Window envelope for convenient and accurate addressing.

Prices inc
Purchase O
Purchase O
No. 10W W

PURCHASE

6-40

A Formula for Writing "User Friendly" Copy: *Inform the Customer!*

An outline that works!

Informing the customer is the basic golden rule which makes it easy for customers to order (because they have enough information to do so) and which should make it easy for the cataloger to sell the product.

Some of the most successful examples of product copy in the mail order business are found in The Sharper Image. Each piece of copy in this company's catalog is like a finely tuned machine operating specifically to inform and sell the customer. Each is an authoritative dissertation that easily engages customers' attention and supplies them with information. The following illustration (Figure 6-41) shows an outstanding example. It *informs* the customer about the product, *validates* the product and its *benefits*, and *builds strong credibility*. This particular example even calls attention to product dangers and legal ordering requirements, and does so in such a way as to strengthen product credibility. This formula can be applied to almost any catalog copy:

1. The product is *identified* and a *benefit announced* immediately with a few short, well-chosen words. Attention is captured!

2. *Credibility is established* immediately by performance test results.

3. How the product is made and *exacting specifications are given.*

4. *An optional listing is introduced* which enhances the product. Vital caution information is given! Mentioning the product warranty makes *product validity* even stronger and eases the customer's mind about placing an order.

Inform!

5. Credibility is highlighted by association: "world's largest cross-bow maker (featured in the James Bond film)." A confidence-building *guarantee,* "30-day home trial," subtly *commands the customer to buy.* And a legal declaration furthers product validity as well.

This outline shows the general style used for every single piece of copy in the entire catalog. It is a successful format causing customers to want to read and thoroughly informing them while doing so. This copy sells products for The Sharper Image.

Space age crossbow fits in your hand.

The most powerful crossbow pistol ever made, Magnum Force Trident sends its arrows (called bolts) at speeds up to 45 miles per hour. It's accurate up to 60 feet and penetration at close range is amazing. At 25 feet, our bolts went through the Yellow Pages to page 339.

Frame is heavy gauge die-cast aluminum. Contoured hard plastic grips. The laminated fiberglass bow is strung with 45 lbs. of tension. Aluminum bolts are perfectly balanced for pistol shooting. Weighs 24 oz. 18″ long with a 16″ bow span. Safety mechanism locks with a flick of a thumb.

Use the precision micro-adjustable sights or the 1.5 × 15 power scope (optional). Comes with two target bolts. Package of 5 more bolts available below. *Target bolts should under no circumstances be used for hunting.* (Game arrows are available directly from Barnett.) One year warranty.

Trident is the newest design from Barnett, the world's largest crossbow-maker (featured in the James Bond film "For Your Eyes Only"). Trident is easy, accurate, and completely free of "kick." Test-fire yours with the security of our 30 day home trial. *Must be 18 or older to purchase.*

- Trident Crossbow #ZBN544 $99 (5.50)
- 1.5 × 15 Scope #ZBN546 $69 (2.50)
- Set of 5 Arrows #ZBN545 $9.75 (1.00)

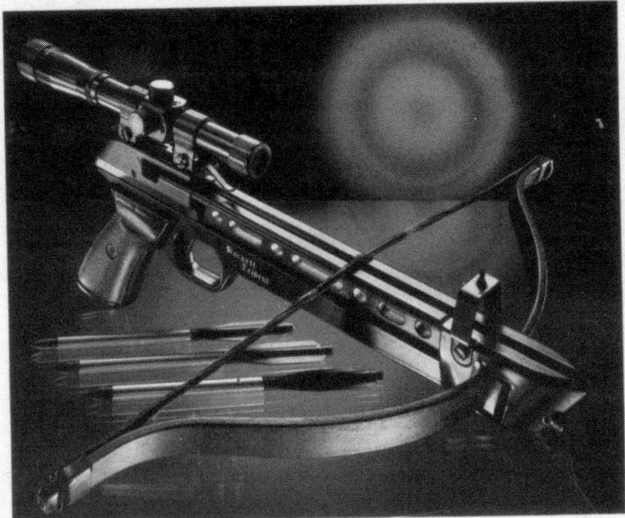

A15

6-41

A catalog which is almost completely opposite in appeal would seem to need a completely different copy approach (Figure 6-42). This copy illustration is from Annie's Attic, a friendly catalog appealing mostly to women from middle America interested in needlework. But, really, how different is their basic copy approach? Not very:

Entertain!

1. The headline *identifies* the product, announcing a *benefit* ("Luscious").

2. *Credibility is established* through a friendly, colloquial description which unveils the true product use.

3. Specific *method of using* the product is given, along with the *material of which it's made*.

4. The ending features a friendly *command to buy*.

Both of these catalog companies inform their customers through a copy approach that fits their individual customer profile. With The Sharper Image this is a macho, fairly affluent 30- to 45-year-old male. With Annie's Attic the profile is a salt-of-the-earth but young-at-heart female, 35 to 50 years old, from the "heartland" of America.

LUSCIOUS FRUIT POTHOLDERS™

IT'S A BUMPER CROP! What an appealing batch of colorful fruit! And, believe it or not, they're really potholders that make a beautiful decorative table centerpiece. Or hang them as singles anywhere. Each luscious fruit is designed to open in back for gripping handles, lids, etc. Each is realistic in size and detail and made from washable acrylic yarn. Simple to crochet from detailed instructions and diagrams. Harvest this collection—they're ripe for the pickin'! Strawberries, Watermelon, Banana, Grapes, Pineapple, Lemon/Lime, Orange and Apple, only **$1.50** each or **all 8 for only $6.60.** Kits only **$3.89** each or **all 8 for only $21.95.**

6-42

The "User Friendly" Formula:

1. *Identify the product* by name and/or *benefit*.
2. Establish product *credibility*.
3. Give product *specifications* concerning the material of which it's made, its components, size, etc.
4. Build in *authority* if you can.
5. *Encourage the customer to buy.*

Above all — inform the customer!

Eight questions you should ask and answer about your copy before you print it.

1. **Is your copy in the right order?** Is there a logical order to the presentation of copy points about your merchandise? And have you been faithful to this organizational principle throughout? Is this the best way to organize the items in your catalog? Or would another method make more sense?

2. **Is it persuasive?** Does your copy begin with a strong selling message? Do individual headlines promise solutions to reader problems and draw readers into the product descriptions? Does the body copy stress user benefits as well as technical features?

3. **Is it complete?** Does your copy include all the information the reader needs to make a buying decision? Does it anticipate and answer all the customer's questions in advance? Have you fully described products and their features? Have you included all important details such as size, color, dimensions, or material of which the products are constructed? Does the copy make it easy for the customer to find the price line, to specify and order the product?

Know your product before you write

4. **Is it clear?** Is the copy understandable and easy to read? Are all terms defined? Don't assume all readers know slang or regional expressions. Is the copy written at the reader's level of understanding?

5. **Is it consistent?** Have you been consistent in your use of logos, trademarks, spellings, abbreviations, punctuation, grammar, capitalization, units of measure, layouts, copy style, visuals?

6. **Is it accurate?** Is the copy technically accurate? Has the copywriter made sure the item functions exactly as described? Has the merchandiser carefully proofread all copy and "fine print" for accuracy (no one knows details about the product better than the merchandiser)? Do the photos show the current models or versions of your product? Have you matched the right photo to each item description?

7. **Is it interesting?** Is the copy lively and informative to read? Or is it boring? Do both the

typeface you have chosen for your copy and the style of layout encourage the viewer to read the copy?

8. **Is it believable?** Is the copy sincere or is it full of ballyhoo? Have you used photos, test results, testimonials, and statistics to back up your product claims, especially those which seem "incredible"?

Fine Tuning Your Copy

How To Find Better Words. A major catalog copy problem is finding and using exciting words for products which may strike the copywriter as boring. But there are some simple solutions:

1. Put yourself in the reader's shoes. You're selling pipe-fitting tools to plumbers. You don't find anything exciting about such tools. But plumbers do. So ask yourself these questions about each tool, pretending you are a plumber:

(a) Which problems will the tool solve?

(b) How will it cut my work load?

(c) Does it fit in my tool kit?

(d) Can I make more money with it?

(e) Can it be used in combination with my other tools?

(f) What accessories does it have?

(g) How will the product make my life easier?

(h) What can I do with the extra time I'll have due to the new tool's performance?

Your answers to these questions form a check list of benefits the plumber will find exciting. Just write your copy to address those benefits and you'll automatically be using more exciting words. Always put yourself in the position of the product user in order to write exciting copy.

Another stimulation method is to spend a day with the plumber on typical jobs. Learn a bit about this field so your copy can address — and solve — the plumber's problems.

2. Use colorful, descriptive language. Product specs and tech-talk don't move buyers to action. Persuasive language does. If it's colorful and descriptive, it paints a picture in the mind of what the product can do for each customer. For example:

Tech-talk:	**Persuasive language**:
"The XYZ mixer is devoid of pinch-points or dead spots where viscous material might accumulate."	"Our mixer is free of sharp edges, nooks and crannies where gunk might get stuck and clog up your pipeline."

3. Use precise language. Beware of language that is either *overly* colloquial or general. You want your writing to be conversational enough to win the reader over without becoming so vague that it doesn't communicate your meaning.

Make Room for Customer Education

Educating the customer is a never-ending job which can pay off in added catalog profits. The more difficult the product is to sell, the greater the payoff for educating the customer! How can you educate the customer? What can you educate the customer about? Talk about the manufacturing of your product when use or fit is especially important with such products as shoes or backpacks. Mention the material from which a product is made if it performs a special function or is the main benefit of the product, the identification and use of a specialized product such as fasteners and wood screws, or the proper way to care for areas with special problems such as septic tanks. The more difficult the product is to sell, the greater the payoff for educating the customer. Two basic ways to approach product education are: (1) Education *within the product body copy,* and (2) Education separately highlighted within the catalog.

1. Education Within the Product Body Copy. Too much product copy contains just specifications, a collection of words that says next to nothing. And there is a whole lot of just plain dull copy. One way to get around these problems is to educate customers while informing and selling them. How can you do this? Won't it take up too much room? Will it interfere with selling? Isn't it hard to do? What will it do for sales? Most of these questions can be answered with one truism: educating the customer will *increase* sales. People are naturally inquisitive and respond when information is provided. And, yes — good educational copy takes skill, so find a writer who is up to the job. Enough area should always be allowed for good selling copy, and educating the customer is often the element which makes the copy good. Following are general consumer examples showing how two catalog companies educate the customer within the body copy.

General Consumer Eddie Bauer is one of the most skilled in the craft of educational copy in the catalog business. Figure 6-43 is a portion of product copy about Fleece Seat Covers. Over half of the copy is devoted to education about the performance of the product material, sheepskin. Eddie Bauer customers expect to order items of the best, most efficient material. The education about what the material is and what the material does is the prime selling point and therefore justifies the area taken.

In Lee Maynard's catalog, the subject of the education is once again the material from which the product is made, but an added element becomes important, the history of "flint-knapping." Three-quarters of the copy is devoted to the history and the technique of

Personal Experience

If the product allows, use personal experience to build a sharp lead; once the customer starts reading, keep him reading.

A. Lee Maynard
Lee Maynard
Santa Fe, NM

Educational highlights of product material and performance

Eddie Bauer®

SHEARLING FLEECE SEAT COVERS

The unparalleled luxury of prime Australian Merino sheepskins—these premium quality seat covers will add a level of comfort to your driving that you'll feel with every mile. Shearling fleece is one of nature's most efficient natural cushions and insulators. These densely piled skins, fully 1" thick, reduce the pinch of pressure points on your legs, seat and back so blood flows more easily and muscles stay relaxed. The thick plush also provides a cushion of air that will keep you cool and dry in summer heat and warm in winter without clinging clothes and static shocks. These skins are specially selected for the length and denseness of the fleece, and are superior to almost all skins on the market. They are tanned by the best methods to give years of strong, supple comfort. The backs are fully lined with durable nylon tricot that won't damage your car's fabric, vinyl or leather seats. The covers secure to seats quickly and easily with elastic straps and hooks, and can be removed for transfer to a new car. The seat covers below fit regular squareback or highback seats, with or without an arm rest or divider. Can be dry cleaned or machine washed. Folks who own these fine seatcovers know they're virtually a driving necessity.
Colors: Champagne or Gray.

6-43

making The Obsidian Dagger as it applies to the product offered. Customers could buy useful and quality knives elsewhere, but because the product is being sold as an art display, the history and crafting technique become the main benefit. (Figure 6-44)

Both of these examples give obvious reasons for utilizing educational copy. The main product benefit depends on the customer's understanding the reason for being so thorough with the catalog copy.

2. Education Separately Highlighted Within The Catalog. Short educational facts in the form of one liners or borderd comments throughout the catalog are very effective. They add interest as well as help sell products.

General Consumer Two difficult-to-sell product categories in the general consumer area are shoes and seeds — shoes because of size variation among manufacturers and the importance of a good fit, and seeds because they are readily available in retail stores at competitive prices.

Executive Shoes' catalog, Wright Arch Preserver Shoes, devotes one full catalog page to educating the customer about its shoe manufacturing process. Figure 6-45 shows a portion of this page, which tells about foot structure and functions and relates how Wright Arch Preserver Shoes accommodate the foot's structure and

Product Description and Presentation

Charge your copy and graphics people to dig for exciting, dramatic and truthful facts about your products and, hopefully, your company's innovative solutions to times that try men's souls

James J. Casey
President-Direct Marketing
Redmond, WA

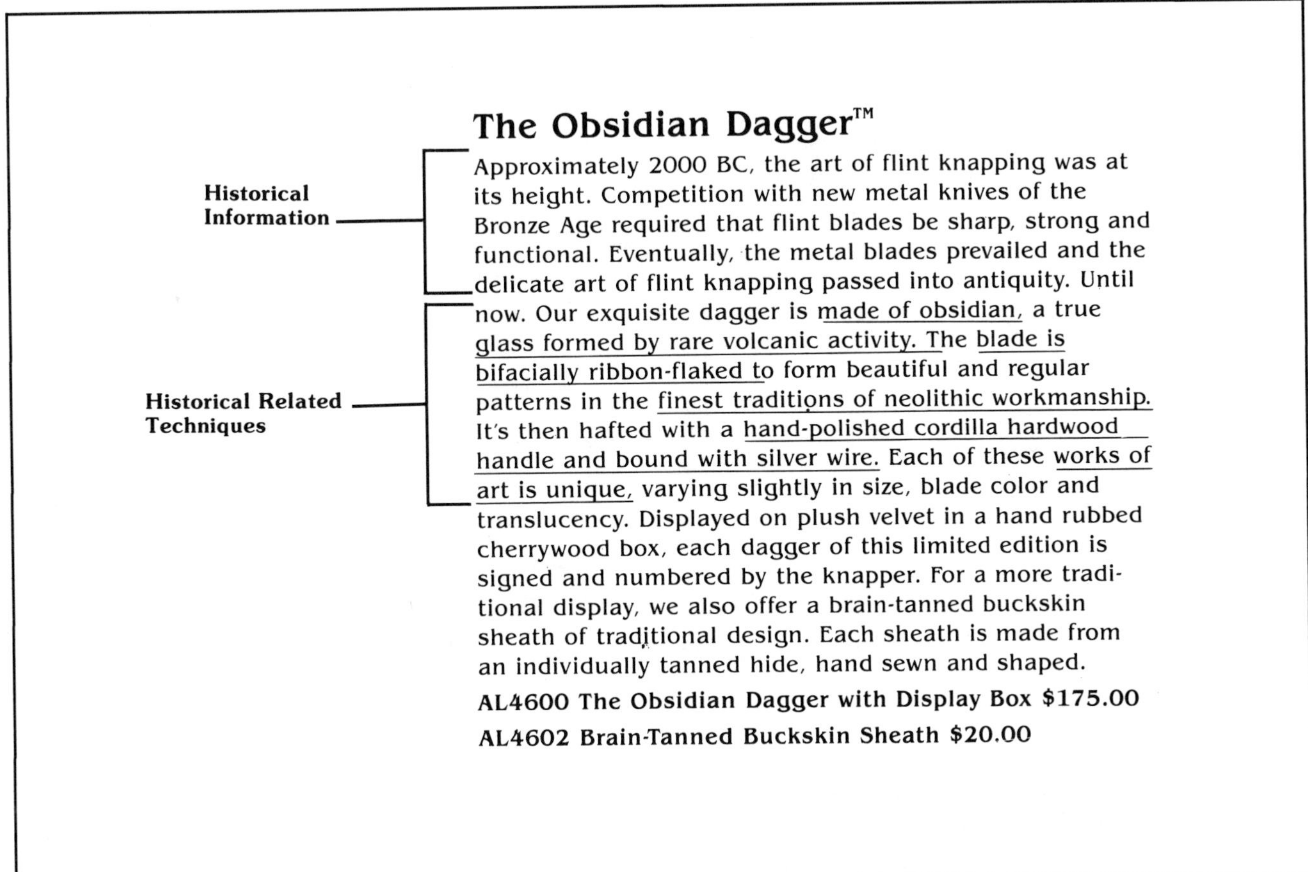

The Obsidian Dagger™
Historical Information
Historical Related Techniques
Approximately 2000 BC, the art of flint knapping was at its height. Competition with new metal knives of the Bronze Age required that flint blades be sharp, strong and functional. Eventually, the metal blades prevailed and the delicate art of flint knapping passed into antiquity. Until now. Our exquisite dagger is made of obsidian, a true glass formed by rare volcanic activity. The blade is bifacially ribbon-flaked to form beautiful and regular patterns in the finest traditions of neolithic workmanship. It's then hafted with a hand-polished cordilla hardwood handle and bound with silver wire. Each of these works of art is unique, varying slightly in size, blade color and translucency. Displayed on plush velvet in a hand rubbed cherrywood box, each dagger of this limited edition is signed and numbered by the knapper. For a more traditional display, we also offer a brain-tanned buckskin sheath of traditional design. Each sheath is made from an individually tanned hide, hand sewn and shaped.
AL4600 The Obsidian Dagger with Display Box $175.00
AL4602 Brain-Tanned Buckskin Sheath $20.00

6-44

functions. This copy is supported by photographs of people involved in the shoe-manufacturing process.

Burpee's seed catalog educates the customer throughout the book with small art and copy blocks. Figure 6-46 is an example of one of the shorter approaches used in the catalog. Look at the areas we've underlined; these few words educate the customer about seed planting while selling a product line and referring the customer to another part of the catalog. This marvelous little education blurb is used on four different pages of the catalog. In addition, Burpee uses a two-page chart to guide the customer regarding heights of various plants for short borders, tall backgrounds, or rock gardens, plus the time of year to sow and whether the plants need sun or shade. The customer cannot help but feel that Burpee offers the easiest way possible to plant a garden. And this has been accomplished through product education, something not available with "rack" seeds.

Business-to-Business Separate highlighting is nicely done in Hewlett Packard's Computer User's Catalog. Hewlett Packard educates the customer on the "cause and effect" of static and gives "Hewlett Packard's answer to static" as a preamble to selling Anti-static Computer Accessories. In Figure 6-47, under "Cause and Effect," the customer is told how electricity is generated and com-

Your Feet Deserve the Best

Yes. . . Wright shoes are well made. But more important is how well they take care of your feet! As you walk, each foot bears the full weight of your body. Each foot has three main arches, placed to hold the body weight. . . to brace your foot. . . to give support and strength to what would otherwise be a weak and delicate arrangement of bones and muscles.

WRIGHT ARCH PRESERVER SHOES protect and support these arches with an insole that is molded under heat and high pressure. The result is not only strength, but a degree of comfort that is simply not experienced in ordinary shoes.

6-45

Use **Burpee's Easy-Sow Straight-Row Seed Tapes.** Easier to plant, precisely spaced seeds reduce thinning, encourage uniform growth. (See page 76.)

6-46

Anti-static accessories

Facts about static protection

If your work area contains electronic circuitry, such as computers and measurement devices, protection against damaging static electricity is a must. HP's static-control products come in a variety of shapes and sizes. To help you make the right choice, we have collected some important facts about static.

Cause and effect

Static electricity is generated when two different materials come into contact and then are separated. Common actions such as walking (shoes leaving floor), sitting (clothes rubbing against upholstery), and standing (clothes rubbing against the body), cause static energy buildup.

When you consider that modern electronic circuitry can operate using levels of 5 volts or less, you can easily see how static discharge through the circuitry can be extremely damaging. (For typical static buildup levels see box on right.)

Nature tends to balance itself. Just as hot and cold water blend to become lukewarm, static charges must become equalized. Therefore, built-up energy continuously seeks a path to ground (neutral charge).

This is one of many reasons HP designs its computers with a ground connection from the chassis to the wall socket. The charge will then have an easy path to balance itself. We suggest you check the building wiring, especially in older buildings, to ascertain that the ground path really exists.

However, even if the discharge path bypasses all the sensitive circuitry, electromagnetic waves (similar to radio or TV waves) will still be generated by the discharge. Because these waves travel through the air, they are able to reach the circuitry with a very high charge.

HP's answer to static

The solution is simple: prevent the damaging charge from reaching the equipment. Hewlett-Packard offers a complete line of products to do just that. The static control mats drain the charge via a ground cord within fractions of a second after you step on the mat; the anti-static carpet mats distribute the charge over a large area, reducing built-up static in any one area (use only where conditions for static buildup are unfavorable); the tabletop mat affords the same protection as the static control mats, but is more convenient and aesthetically pleasing (operator *must* touch the mat before touching the equipment); the Staticide spray and wipes are for use on areas not protected by anti-static carpets and mats.

Static facts

Static damage is described in two ways:

- Catastrophic—when the component is dead; the board/unit will not work.
- Degrading—when a discharge weakens a component, possibly causing premature failures within days, weeks or months after the incident, or characteristic changes such as intermittent failures (usually with temperature shifts, vibrations, or load variations).

	Most common static reading	Highest static reading
Walking across carpet	12,000 volts	39,000 volts
Walking across vinyl tile floor	4,000 volts	13,000 volts
Working at desk	500 volts	3,000 volts

©Institute of Electrical and Electronics Engineers Inc. (IEEE) from 12th Annual Proceedings of IEEE Reliability Physics.

The static charge level is:	When you:
3,500 volts	feel
15,000 volts	see

6-47

mon actions which will cause it. Facts about commonly designed static-preventing features on the Hewlett Packard computers are mentioned, but the customer is also told that electromagnetic waves can still be generated, and can still cause a possible circuitry problem. To substantiate this problem, "Static Facts" are featured in a bordered box. The solution to these problems is then given: "prevent the damaging charge from reaching the equipment." All of this customer education is given as a preamble to a page and one-half of static-preventing products. This "cause and effect" story is well-founded copy designed to educate the customer into making a purchase.

Charts encourage orders

Brown Deer Co., Inc., puts out a concentrated chemical catalog that devotes an entire page to septic tank care, combining art diagrams and copy to educate its customers. Figure 6-48 is a portion of a diagram showing how liquid passes through a septic tank system. Extensive copy explains this flow and identifies some typical problems and how they can be avoided. The opposite page is devoted to a product sold in the catalog which solves septic tank problems. Customer education continues to the next page where related products are illustrated and sold.

DRI Industries carries a half-page "GUIDE TO SELECTION AND USE OF FASTENERS." It tells what to consider before starting a project involving fasteners and educates the customer with illustrations showing the six basic fasteners. Figure 6-49 shows how various styles are identified via line drawings matched to copy describing individual usage. Two following catalog pages sell a large variety of fasteners. Each of these examples skillfully *"educates" the customer into buying*. If you have a difficult or overly common product line, consider educating your customer. Even the easier-to-sell, glamour products also benefit from product education.

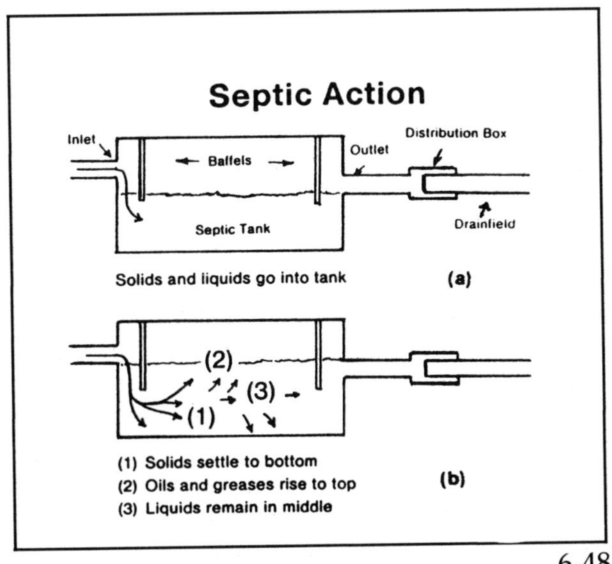

6-48

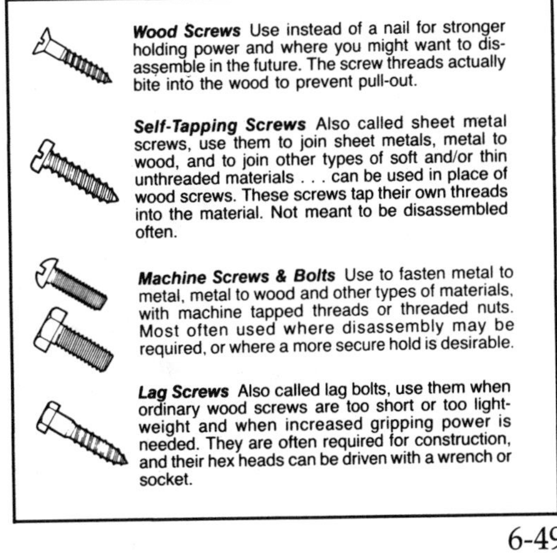

6-49

Combating the Return Factor, While Encouraging the Customer To Order. . .a tough job for the copywriter. The returned-goods factor must be kept at a minimum in the repeat mail order business. Steps must be taken *prior* to the customer's decision to order. But what can be done to keep the return factor low, without discouraging order placement? The *solution* is to gear your catalog toward explaining and describing your merchandise so that *what the customer receives meets his expectations*. The *problem* is to do this in such a way as *not to discourage the placement of the order*.

Let's look at a category where complaints and returns run high and where the customer naturally hesitates to place an order for fear of dissatisfaction — the apparel business.

An apparel catalog which meets the challenge of keeping a *low return factor while encouraging an order* is Lands' End. Throughout the catalog, the writers have done an exceptional job of explaining what materials are used and what features make their products superior — and they've supported this with illustrative diagrams. The most important selling device is a measurement and conversion chart which occupies two-thirds of the back of the order form (Figure 6-50). At the top of the chart, the customer is reassured by being told that Lands' End clothing is traditional in sizing standards. The illustration shows how to measure for various types of clothing; a conversion chart relieves the customer's mind even more. All these features act as insurance against returned goods.

> **Promoting Retail Price**
>
> *Use copy to create a low price image on a high proced product, i.e. "imagine paying so little for the caress of genuine mink surrounding you."*
>
> **Larry Lefavor**
> *Catalog Director*
> *DRI Industries*
> *Boolmington, MN*

The simplicity with which the chart is presented allows ease of interpretation — made even simpler with a conversion table telling what size to order for each article. The problem of size, which once was complex and produced a high return factor, now is solved! Choosing one's size, which once was a deterrent to ordering, becomes simple; now ordering becomes almost automatic.

Such a chart is not new or revolutionary, but two major factors are accomplished:

1. The customer's mind is put at ease about what size to order — therefore *encouraging the placement of an order*.

2. The company is assured of more accurate ordering, thereby *decreasing the percentage of returns* due to improper size.

The merchandiser must put plenty of thought into what can be done to lower returns before order placement.

Write "Seasonal" Copy . . . Your Reward Will Be Higher Response. The writer who fine tunes copy for seasonal impact is a savvy direct marketer. Seasonal catalogs — Easter, Winter, Christmas — must be prepared several months in advance in order to be issued at least six weeks before the holiday or season arrives, with eight weeks being preferable. It's not unusual for a first drop to occur even 12 or more weeks prior to a major holiday, like Christmas.

But when should you write such catalog copy? The most appropriate time is during the season itself. Thus, if you are creating

How To Measure *for* Correct Size

Concerned about fit? Don't be. Our clothing is traditional and fully-cut. Just order your usual size.

SHIRTS:
Neck: Take a shirt with a collar that fits you well. Lay the collar flat, and measure from center of collar button to far end of button hole. Number of inches = size.
Sleeve: Bend elbow, measure from center of neck (backside) to elbow and down to wrist. Number of inches = your size.

BELTS
Measure around waist over pants on which belt will be worn. Number of "even" inches measured is size to order. If between "even" sizes, order next larger size.

GLOVES:
Measure around hand at fullest part (exclude thumb). If right-handed, use right hand, and vice versa. Number of inches = size.

SHOES & SANDALS:
Use your street shoe size.

HATS:
Measure around head with tape above brow ridges. Convert inches to hat size using the chart below.

CHEST:
Measure around fullest part of chest, keeping tape up under arms and around shoulder blades. Number of inches = size.

WAIST:
Measure around waist, over shirt (not over slacks) at the height you normally wear your slacks. Keep one finger between tape and body. Number of inches = size.

SEAT/HIPS:
Stand with heels together, and measure around fullest part.

INSEAM:
Take a pair of pants that fits you well. Measure from the crotch seam to the bottom of the pants. Number of inches (to the nearest ½") = inseam length.
Most dress pants are available unfinished.

How To Convert Measurements *to* Order Size

WOMEN'S SKIRTS & TROUSERS:

	6	8	10	12	14	16
WAIST	25	26	27	28	29½	31
HIP	36	37	38	39	40½	42

MEN'S & WOMEN'S EQUIVALENTS:

Men's Suit Size	Unisex Size	Ladies Dress Size
34-36	XS	8
36-38	S	10-12
38-40	M	14-16
42-44	L	18
46-48	XL	-

HATS:

	21-1/2"	21-7/8"	22-1/4"	22-5/8"	23"	23-1/2"	23-7/8"	24-1/4"
Head size:	6-7/8	7	7-1/8	7-1/4	7-3/8	7-1/2	7-5/8	7-3/4
Order size:	Small		Medium		Large		X-Large	

Our clothing corresponds to these equivalents, unless the catalog description indicates otherwise.

6-50

a Christmas catalog, write it during the prior Christmas season; that's when you are in a festive holiday mood. That joyous attitude will be evidenced in your copy, enabling you to relate much better in the following year.

However, many marketers are forced to prepare Christmas catalog copy in June and July in order to meet production deadlines. Then their mental attitude is oriented toward outdoor activities and sunshine — precisely the wrong atmosphere for preparing Christmas copy.

The same ideal holds true with quarterly catalogs. Try to do your spring catalog during the prior spring when forsythia is in bloom. Don't do it in the fall when the weather is turning chilly. Some writers are able to practice this ideal. Others create a setting most nearly matching the season about which they are writing by traveling to an appropriate locale along with their portable typewriters. *But the key is to get a seasonal flavor. . .not only in your main headlines, not only in theme photography, but also in your product descriptions*. You'll sell more down jackets if you can include a seasonal impression of winter hiking in the description of your item.

Above all, *be enthusiastic* about your product and *remember the customer* by giving complete and accurate information! If you think the words ''easy'' and ''clear'' have been overused in this guideline, you're wrong. Everything you can do to make your message clearer will be reflected in your bottom line.

Product Copy Checklist:

- ☐ Review Customer List.
- ☐ Review Company Image.
- ☐ Attend Product Work Session.
- ☐ Determine Copy Style.

Always

1. Review competitors' copy.
2. Consult merchandiser or buyer.
3. Review manufacturer's material.
4. Clarify product's main benefit.
5. Have the product tested.
6. Identify the product.
7. Inform — include the product specifications needed to make a buying decision.
8. Make every word count.
9. Remember the customer does not have the product in hand.
10. Be truthful.

Strongly consider

1. Testing the product yourself (writer).
2. Hiring a professional writer.

Other Important Catalog Copy

Product copy is certainly the most important form of copy in your catalog, but there are other types of copy which compliment your catalog and can contribute mightily to sales. The most important are headlines and price lines, of course. But there is also copy which warms up your catalog by welcoming the customer. . . copy directing the customer to specific products within the catalog. . . copy establishing credibility. . .copy educating the customer. . . copy encouraging the customer to purchase. . . copy telling the customer how to place an order. These copy extras can be the mortar that pulls the catalog together and makes it complete.

Headlines

Headlines call attention, and are an essential part of copy. They call attention with two strategies:

1. Product benefit
2. Product name/identity.

There are a number of headline applications. Headlines are not all at the beginning of the copy description block. They occur in product photos, at top, bottom, and middle of pages, and alongside copy.

Headlines for Product Photos

First let's look at how to write headlines for product photos. Using copy within photos makes specific demands on the copywriter. Technically, the copy sits within the photo in one of two ways:

1. Overprint copy is printed directly on the photo.
2. Reverse copy is reversed out of the photo, so that the type appears white.

In both cases, writers face one of the toughest copy jobs imaginable, because they must think of typography as they write. It is a good idea to work closely with the artist before starting overprint and reverse copy in order to:

1. Establish type standards
2. Establish character counts
3. Set standard style policy
4. Decide on ornamentation.

The first three goals exist because they determine copy length. The fourth is where the artist rules, deciding on bursts, flags, and other eye-catching devices to spotlight the copy. After establishing these standards, it often is necessary and desirable to create copy to specific character counts per line to aid the reader with a uniform presentation. The writer must trim all phraseology to the bone, so each word communicates, but in the shortest fashion. A typical example of a selling point you might want to communicate in an art or photo headline would be a legend like this: "You get a second beautiful tote bag FREE each time you buy one at our low price!"

That's fine for body copy but *too long* for an art or photo headline. Remember, an art headline is beneficial only when it calls attention to a feature or offer in a short way. Ask yourself the following questions when trying to shorten the wording:

1. Which words are better communicated by the photo? (The reader can see you are selling tote bags.)

2. Which words are duplicated, and in fact are the reader's perception? (The reader can see they are beautiful.)

3. How can it have greater power? (The reader doesn't need so many words.)

Make headline simple

Now the copy becomes: "Buy one, get one FREE" or "TWO for the price of ONE."

This is much stronger copy, communicating the thought more rapidly and clearly. It lends itself much more readily to the disciplines needed for overprint and reverse headlines.

What benefits have occurred through rewriting the original version? And what specific benefits lend themselves directly to the situation of overprint and reverse headlines? The rewritten versions:

Talk about benefit

1. Lend themselves to *larger, bolder type*
2. Are *easier to understand*
3. Imply *urgency*
4. *Stress the bargain aspect*
5. Employ a *command,* letting readers know they *should* do what you suggest.

Those are the Five Commandments of writing overprint or reverse copy for use with photos. Always use them to create greater pull and try these additional techniques when appropriate:

6. *Begin with all caps,* for a word or two
7. Use all caps for the entire legend of overprinted and reversed copy *only when you have very short copy*
8. Present just a *single thought or benefit* in each reverse or overprint . . . though you can use more than one of these graphic insets, or one of each, with a single photo
9. Start and end with *commands,* as in: "Buy one, get one FREE now"
10. Use the *shortest possible words.* John Caples says he once increased response by 20 percent when he changed "repair" to "fix"

11. *Use primary selling points,* never secondary
12. *Reinforce copy statements* from your descriptive copy block
13. Imagine each photo overprint or reverse as a headline. It is! The reader looks at the photo before reading your body copy
14. *Target for the reader's perception,* rather than for fact. "Two for the price of one" really means 50 percent off. But "50 percent off" isn't perceived as quickly. And "50 percent off" forces the reader to do math
15. *Eliminate most adjectives and adverbs.* They belong in copy blocks where you can support them; they're less believable in headlines.

You want your photo to *create great desire.* View your photo inset copy, overprints, and reverses as supportive, punchy phrasing. Complete sentences aren't needed here. Motivation is! But remember, do not utilize a headline in a product photo unless it is beneficial to product sales! Too often, catalogers add headlines that result only in photo and page clutter. If every photo had a headline, *all* would become ineffectual. Generally, low-end or sale catalogs utilize this type of headline.

Figure 6-51 shows how two low-end catalogs use a headline to explain product function. Example (a), from Harriet Carter, simply states "KEEPS PAINT FRESH!" to let the customer know that this

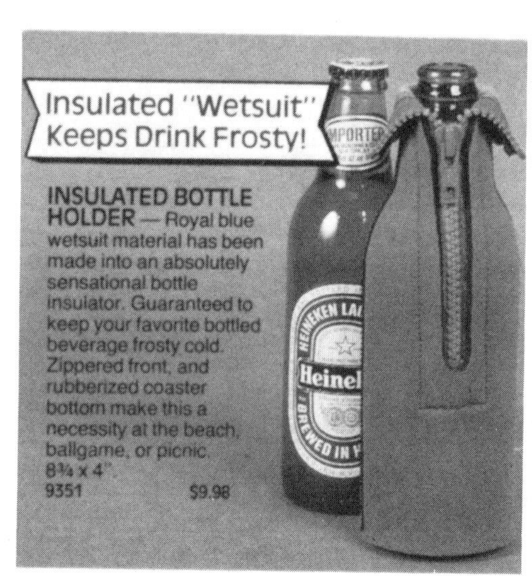

6-51

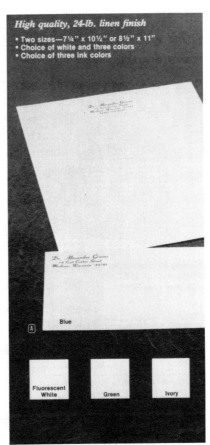

6-52

6-53

is no ordinary artist's palette. The typestyle gives the effect of hand lettering and is reversed out of the blue background. The white type shows more prominently than black would. Example (b) from the Taylor Gifts catalog identifies the product, "INSULATED WET SUIT," as well as stating the product benefit, "Keeps Drink Frosty!" The art treatment, a flag design to hold the headline, makes a clearer, crisper presentation as well as calling attention to the message.

Figure 6-52 is from Grand Finale, a sale catalog. The headline, "Pure Cashmere," identifies that attribute which is the product's strongest selling point, and it prints the sale and regular price. The question that should be asked is, "Did the photograph need the headlines to help attract the customer's attention?" It is doubtful, *but* having a headline in the product photos fits the style of all three catalogs.

Sycom, a forms and supplies catalog, headlines the main product benefit. Figure 6-53 illustrates how the material the product is made of can deserve a photo headline. "High quality, 24-lb. linen finish" is a benefit which would greatly appeal to the professional customer. Three subheads tell of three secondary benefits which are important to the overall quality benefit. Fortunately, the deep blue shade of the background allows the reversed-out type to be easily read.

Product Cluster Headlines

Headlines which are not for one specific product on the page but refer instead to (1) the offer being made, (2) the category of products being offered, or (3) the function the products perform are called Product Cluster Headlines. This headline approach can be used for a page containing an average number of products (generally five) or for pages loaded with second-level (sale or smaller volume) items.

The pages involved should be designed so products with an affinity to each other are adjacent. This aids the customer's search when scanning for a category of interest, and it increases sales by encouraging more desire or need for products in a particular category.

But be sure not to make the common error of simply displaying a photo, some tight copy, and pricing data on each item. Instead, create an enticing headline for each product cluster to lead the customer into the individual products in that cluster.

The first rule for a cluster heading is that it should:

> **1. Clearly identify the nature of the cluster.** Is it a specific area of interest? Do the products perform a special function? Are the products a special value?

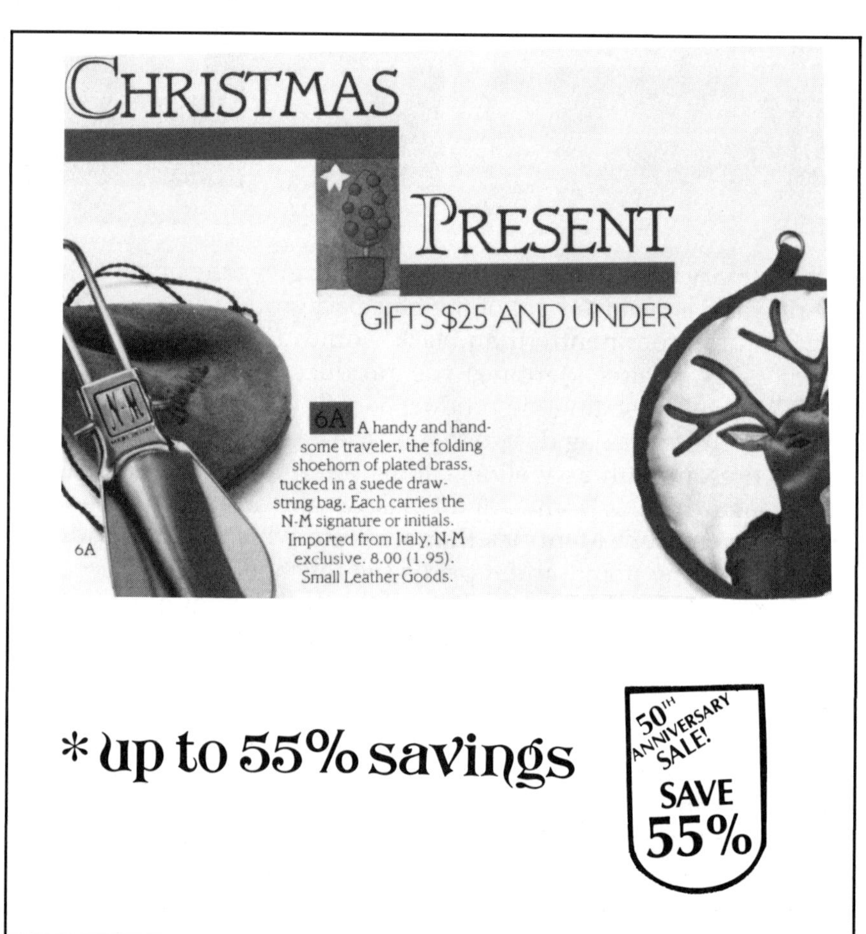

6-54

Three general consumer catalogs grouping products which represent a special offer are seen in Figure 6-54 and Figure 6-55.

Example (a) is from the Neiman-Marcus catalog. The major headline, "Christmas Present," declares the subject matter of the pages. A smaller subhead, "Gifts $25 and Under," tells the customer that products within a certain price range can be found. This is a tremendous headline identifier for a seasonal offer. Example (b) is from The Chelsea Collection catalog. "Up to 55% savings" lets the customer know of the savings which can be found. To let the customer know that the offer stands for the products on the facing page, a blurb with "50th Anniversary Sale! Save 55%" is inset in a product photo. Both headlines are printed in red to add force and excitement to the offer. Figure 6-55 is a double-page spread from the Spencer Gifts catalog. A colorful banner crosses the two pages to let the customer know of special pricing when a specific number of the products is purchased. The left page states, "MIX OR MATCH SALE!" — telling customers they can choose any products they wish at a special price. "Any 6 items on pages 8 thru 33" immediately follows to qualify what the customer must do to take part in the sale. The right-hand page again clarifies how many products must be purchased ("Choose any 6 or more items . . .") in order to qualify for the offer, and "SALE! ONLY 88¢ EACH" states the bargain sale price. Spencer then makes sure the customer understands with: "1 to 5 items priced as marked." This is a common example of a second-level product offer with an abundant number of products on a page.

Informational headline

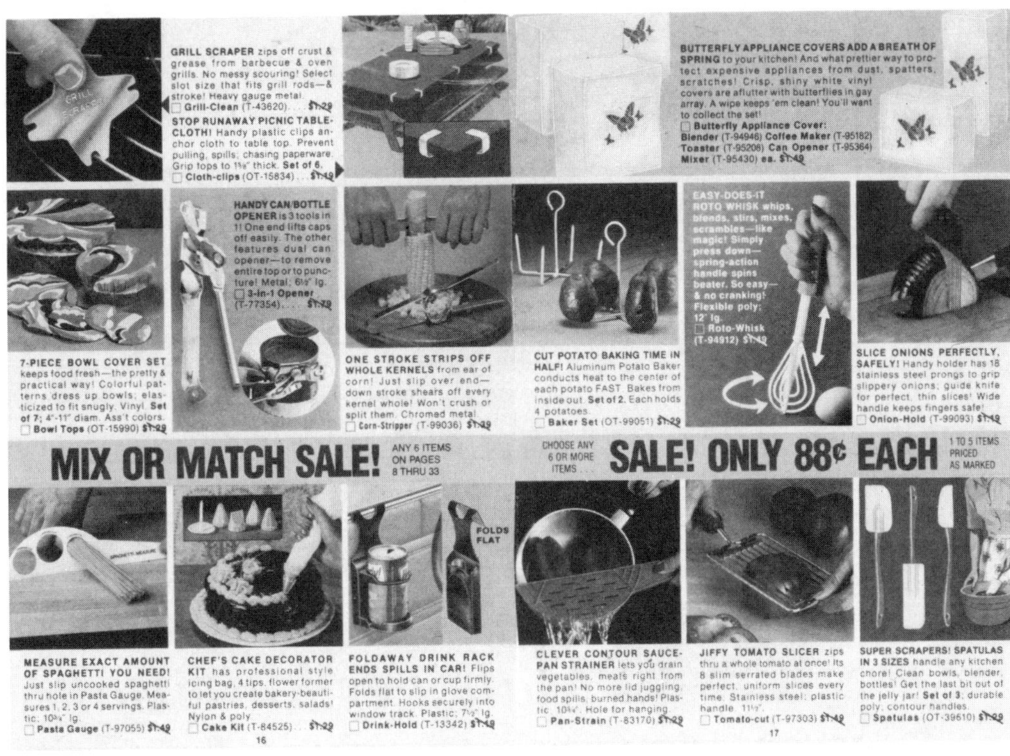

6-55

Figure 6-56 is an interesting use of the product cluster headline. Moore Business Center has used a headline to identify the product category, "Continuous Forms," as a big, bold headline on three different pages. The main category headline is followed by segmented product categories. The main headline defines the product category, while the secondary headline defines the product type within that category. Blanchard Training and Development, Inc., combines a convenient table of contents with individual page

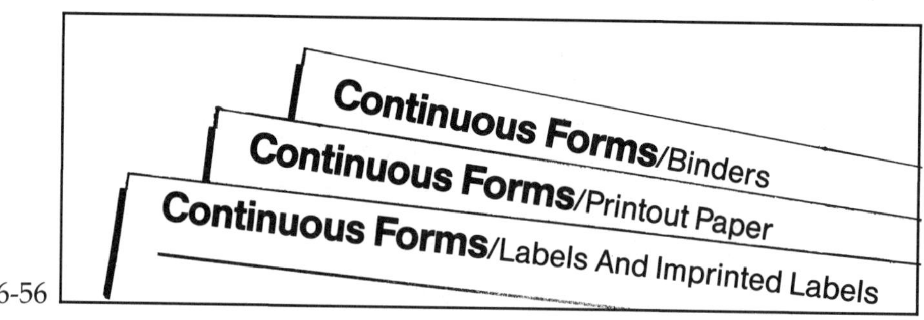

6-56

Contents

3-5 *Situational Leadership Materials* Includes instruments for evaluating leadership style and determining the competence and confidence of subordinates, learning tools for becoming a more effective leader, and case studies

6-9 *One Minute Manager Materials* Includes materials to reinforce and support the three secrets in *The One Minute Manager,* (Goal Setting, Praisings and Reprimands)

10-12 *Putting the One Minute Manager to Work* Like its companion book, *Putting the One Minute Manager To Work* is a runaway best-seller. Materials include a new computer software program and support materials for improving productivity

13 *Video—General* Well-known management specialists and authors show you how to understand human behavior, become a top negotiator, and give excellent presentations

14-15 *Organizational Development* How do your employees perceive organizational practices such as performance appraisal, decision-making and career development? You'll find out that and more with these outstanding tools—"Profile of Organizational Practices,"—"Performax" and "Using Good Management Practices by the Minute"

16 *Books—General* Choose from a variety of best-selling books that help you be a more effective manager, more effective parent and more responsive person

17 *Audio—General* For the first time, hear the thoughts of best-selling authors and practitioners from a wide variety of disciplines

18-19 *Health Promotion* Promote employee health and experience improved performance and an increase in productivity

19 *Newsletters* Promote health and excellence with two quality newsletters

6-57

One Minute Manager Materials

6-58

headlines. Figure 6-57 is the table of contents as seen on page two of the catalog. Note the square blocks immediately preceding each subject. Each block is a different color which visually identifies the subject on the catalog pages. Figure 6-58 is how the color block appears with the headline to identify the products on the inside page. This approach brings continuity to the catalog. Some headlines state the subject of the training being offered, while others identify a general product category.

The second rule for a product cluster headline is that it should:

> **2. Present an "umbrella" user benefit for all items in your cluster**, like increased productivity, reduced costs, greater enjoyment of an avocation. Again, this suggests the need to purchase more than one or two items from the cluster.

Benefits are what the customer buys and so are the logical subjects of any headline. Beautiful flowers, larger tomatoes, twice the closet space, high performance, fast service — these are what we buy. Grouping products which have a general common benefit can help a presentation and allow a headline to be stated in such a way that it is sure to attract customers. Lillian Vernon makes plentiful use of the general benefit method throughout its catalogs with headlines such as "for *neat storage*," "original Italian *space-savers*," "*comforts* for the bath." Just a descriptive word or two (see italicized words) denoting the benefit derived are ideal promoters when declaring a subject category or expressing an attractive benefit alone.

Figure 6-59 is from the First Software catalog. "Hardware and Accessories" identifies the product category while "you get exceptional dealer support from First Software" declares a benefit so important to the customer making a purchase in this category.

The third rule for product cluster headlines is to:

> **3. Use action typography**, such as italics and ellipses, to guide the reader into the cluster.

The use of ellipses gives the effect of pointing or directing the customer to something more, promising there is more to come. Orvis Clothing and Gifts Catalog headlines as follows: "Orvis Country Clothes for Men . . . " The effect is that of anticipation.

Hardware and Accessories —
You get exceptional dealer support
from First Software.

6-59

Here are a couple of tips to consider when preparing a cluster page or headline:

1. Include the total number of all items in the cluster to encourage the reader to review all of them. This also sug-

gests to the customer that a large choice is available or that great value can be had once the choice is made.

2. Hint at urgency to get the customer to review the cluster *NOW*.

Be sure the artist and copywriter get together before the page is designed so ample space is allowed for the cluster headline.

Product Copy Headlines

The importance of headlines cannot be overemphasized! The potential customer looks at the picture — reads the headline — then the price line — then the copy. If the artwork catches his eye, the headline should start the juices flowing by *identifying* the item and *assuring* customers they're reading the copy which matches it. The headline can also pull the customer into the first main advantage (selling point) of the item. If the price then is acceptable and the copy says all the right things, you've got a customer. Picture a newspaper without headlines — how would you determine the items of interest, the ones you want to read? How would you find a particular item for which you may be looking?

It's the same in your catalog. A headline that pops out of the page *calls attention to the item and customers know instantly what the item is* and if it's what they want or need or have been looking for all their lives. The headline saves time for your customers and makes it *easy* for them to respond with a purchase.

Earlier we recommended two main copy headline approaches: (a) product benefit and (b) product name/identity.

Product Benefit

Unless product copy headlines clearly identify the benefit or the product, the customer will not be attracted to read the copy or will not be able to easily match the copy to the product photo. If attention cannot be caught or interest retained, orders will be lost. Some points to consider when writing a headline are: What will make customers feel they need the product? What is the product's greatest asset? Why was the product chosen for the catalog? Answering this type of question will identify the product's greatest benefit. Put the strongest benefit selling point of the product in your headline!

Sometimes identifying the product by name is more satisfactory. This does not necessarily mean the name the manufacturer has given the product. Adding a descriptive word or two to the name of the product to suggest its benefit can be very successful. Ask yourself what would further clarify the product use. What word(s) would help tell of the product's primary attribute? What would give the product strong appeal? Finding these answers will create the maximum amount of interest and demand the most attention of the customer.

The product name/identity headline is widely used by general consumer catalogs. It appeals to all customers because it tells them what they are looking for. Slightly heavy and out-of-shape people don't want a regular home exerciser but one which will help them be trim quickly. People who use canes want one which is fashionable. Hikers don't want ordinary socks but ones which prevent blisters.

Here's how two different general consumer catalogs headline products that answer these needs and desires.

The Sharper Image headlines its Nautilus Abdominal Machine this way: ''Nautilus brings home the fastest way to a trim, tight stomach.'' Immediately the overweight, slightly out-of-shape individual, as well as the physical fitness-conscious person is attracted. A person needing or wanting a firm, flat tummy is going to stop and read more because of the hoped-for benefit — ''a trim, tight stomach'' which can become a realization in the privacy of one's home (''brings home'') and the promise of a speedy result (''fastest way''). If The Sharper Image had used just the product name, ''Nautilus Abdominal Machine,'' not as many customers would have been attracted. Comfortably Yours headlines a group listing, a cane and two cane covers, this way: ''Today, people use canes out of need rather than fashion.'' Right away the real benefit, fashionableness, is communicated to those who use a cane. Fashionableness is also subliminally suggested with the first word, ''Today.'' Understanding is also expressed by the phrase, ''people use canes out of need.'' Imagine how few people would have been attracted if ''Lucite cane and cane covers'' had been the headline. The ultimate benefit of being up-to-date and fashionable even when using a cane would have been lost.

Business-to-business catalogs reap enormous value from the benefit approach. The Sycom Forms and Supplies Catalog, whose market is the health professional, first relates to the customer's problem and then solves it, which is the best of all benefits. Problem: ''Patients forget appointments?'' Benefit Solution: ''Reminder cards can help you.'' The beginning copy head then identifies the product, ''Appointment and Professional Cards.'' Moore Business Center headlines a word processor workstation like this: ''Data-Leggett Work Station Increases Productivity.'' The benefit, ''Increases Productivity,'' is but one of the benefits the product has, but it is the main benefit and therefore the *one* benefit to headline so the customer is attracted but not confused.

Writing Copy

Know your audience. *Who they are, what they like and dislike, what they're interested in. Only then can you write copy that will sell.*

Scott Ashley
Annie's Attic
Big Sandy, TX

Product Name/Identity

This type of headline can be used successfully by every kind of catalog. Still, more can be done than simply stating the name of a product. A Pulse Meter designed especially to be worn while exercising can become a ''Freestyle Pulse Meter'' to indicate freedom of motion and activity, thereby attracting the jogger and exercise buff. A ladies' "Flannel Shirt" becomes a "New/Mini Block Flannel Shirt" because of the newest design look in flannel shirts. Unfortunately, many business-to-business catalogs still use only the product name such as "Bookkeeping Machine Forms," "Statement and Ledger Card."

These are the two most solid headline approaches, but there are other approaches, too. Just remember, the copy headline must gain the customer's interest and work as hard as it can. It should be written as if the art were not there.

Nine headline techniques to consider:

Headlines grab the customers attention

1. **Type Size**. Avoid eye-straining, tiny type. *Your headline is a bridge from photo to copy block* and thus should not be in type that's smaller than the copy block. (The copywriter needs to communicate with the artist.)
2. **Lead-Ins**. When layouts restrict space, it often is intriguing to start a headline in the photo display area and have it wind up as the opening for the copy block. This *draws the reader from headline to selling points.*
3. **Numbers**. When using several headlines for a single photo, *consider numbering them so your reader tackles them in the sequence you prefer* to move that customer into the copy block. Readers subconsciously follow direction, and wind up getting your most potent copy points.
4. **Price**. Price can be presented in the headline if you offer a compelling bargain, an exclusive item, or items priced way under competitive products.
5. **Value**. You can also mention price in your headline if you simultaneously refer to the immense value the product gives. Example: "Just under $25 brings you a full wardrobe."
6. **Color**. Headlines should be printed in the same color as the body copy and that usually means black. *Headlines are not decorative items.* They are part of copy and are meant to draw the reader into the copy. Do not allow a well-meaning artist to display captions in alternate colors.
7. **Sameness**. Headlines begin to train readers how to read body copy. Resist temptations to use alternate italic and roman captions or to use varying typefaces. *Use the same typefaces as used in body copy.*
8. **Anticipation**. Try to make your readers anticipate the great joys, conveniences, and status they will gain with your product or service.

9. **Quiet Excitement.** Usually, when reading headlines, readers are curiously examining your presentation, not making buying decisions. Try to weave the product's excitement into your headlines so your readers will quietly make a decision on their own. Eliminate the exclamation points, which frequently block continued readership anyway. Use extremely strong copy that lets readers provide their own mental exclamations — exclamations of joy, discovery, and desire.

But remember, let your headline *tell the story*. Let your headline *jump out* at the customer. Let it scream with excitement. Use large, bold, black type so it's easy for the customer to read. Use a headline that *stands alone*: "KEEP FLIES OFF YOUR PICNIC." Or use one that *leads into your copy*: "WATER RESISTANT FASHION WATCH to wear at the beach." Make good use of your headlines. They make the customer sit up and take notice. *They Sell Merchandise.*

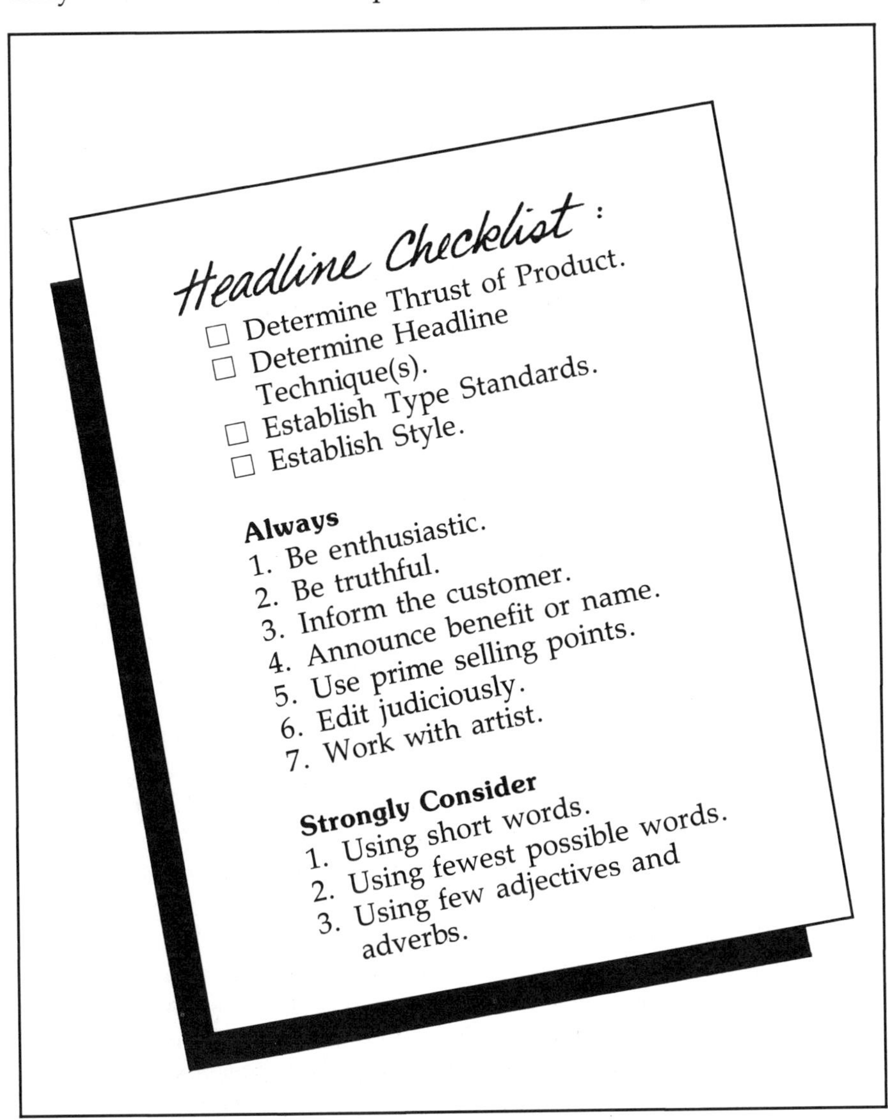

Headline Checklist:
□ Determine Thrust of Product.
□ Determine Headline Technique(s).
□ Establish Type Standards.
□ Establish Style.
Always
1. Be enthusiastic.
2. Be truthful.
3. Inform the customer.
4. Announce benefit or name.
5. Use prime selling points.
6. Edit judiciously.
7. Work with artist.
Strongly Consider
1. Using short words.
2. Using fewest possible words.
3. Using few adjectives and adverbs.

Price Lines

Price lines are part of the body copy but should not be treated as a stepchild or just a product number and pricing identifier. Too often this offhand treatment occurs when a more beneficial solution could be used. The wording used in your price lines can have many psychological effects upon the customer. Changing a word or two can add emphasis, punch, and pizazz to a normally straightforward merchandise action — that of telling your customers what the merchandise is going to cost them. Here are five different pricing strategies (Figure 6-60), each of which has its own special wording and function.

1. **Regular** pricing is the normal retail which reflects the cataloger's required or desired profit. Example 1(a) shows a price line from the Brookstone catalog using the traditional method of product number identification, product name, and retail price — no extras added. Example 1(b) from Annie's Attic identifies the product by reference to "pattern" and "complete kit" and states the retails. The addition of the word "only" by Annie's Attic indicates a value, even though pricing is actually full retail. This is good merchandising.
2. **Sale pricing of original merchandise** shows a markdown from the regular price, usually due to overstock or desire to move seasonal merchandise. Example 2(a) from the Lands' End catalog uses the very effective method of "X"ing out the regular price and printing the sale price in a bright color. The word "OVERSTOCK" tells the customer the merchandise is of normal high quality and "cut to" emphasizes the bargain being passed on. Bergdorf Goodman, 2(b), tells the customer what the regular price is, "Orig.," and what the sale price is "Now." The message to buyers: "This is original, fine-quality merchandise being offered at a special price."
3. **Special purchase** pricing results from a special quantity purchase, close-out merchandise, discontinued production, or some other type of purchasing at lesser cost to the cataloger. Example 3(a) from the Williams-Sonoma catalog states the price "regularly," followed by the "Special Price." "Regularly" represents the recommended or normal price these goods might sell at, with the actual price being lower. To have used "Sale" or "Now" instead of "Special" would imply previously-carried merchandise, which would be inaccurate. The use of "Special" lets the customer feel that the item, as well as the price, is an unusual value. Austad's in 3(b) goes one step further. Not only is their regular price ("your cost") below the manufacturer's recommended retail because of quantity buying, but they also offer a sale price. This indicates a really exceptional bargain.

Price Line Importance

Make your price line a benefit. Substantiate a low price with actual price comparisons.

Larry Lefavor
Catalog Director
DRI Industries
Bloomington, MN

Regular

a. aluminum blower tube. 10" long, weighs only 4¾ ozs.
J-10613 Flame starter **$9.95**

b. finishing touch. **Pattern**
$2.25 or complete **kit**
only **$5.95.**

Membership

a. Mother: 6829 $33.00 (Members $29.70)
(s/h 2.20).
Baby: 6834 $15.00 (Members $13.50)
(s/h 1.60).

b. *Publisher's Edition $14.95*
Members' Edition $11.29 ②

Sale

a. Men's 819474 Women's 814654 ~~$15.00~~
OVERSTOCK Price Cut to $9.00

b. A. **ORIG. $90 NOW $64** (3.25) L18-2A
B. **ORIG. $37.50 NOW $24** (2.65) L18-2B
C. **ORIG. $75 NOW $59** (3.25) L18-2C

Value

210-Piece, Oil Coated Steel $57.60 Value
Half-Moon Key Shop,
Catalog Number 80000029
Your Price Only **$19.99**

Special Purchase

a. SMALL FOLDING TOWEL RACK is 27½" wide and has 5 rods. **#17-13516,** Regularly $32.00 **Special Price $27.00**

b.

MEN'S RIGHT HAND REG. LENGTH REGULAR FLEX	MEN'S RIGHT HAND REG. LENGTH STIFF FLEX	MEN'S LEFT HAND REG. LENGTH REGULAR FLEX	DESCRIPTION	YOUR COST	SALE
SC0813	**SC1813**	**SC2813**	Set 8 Irons (3-9, PW), Set 3 Woods (1,3,5) $579.00	~~$353.40~~	**$279.95**

6-60

4. **Membership** pricing is a special retail offered to customers who become members by paying a fee or who participate in a membership offer which obligates them to a specific amount of purchases. Example 4(a) from the Smithsonian catalog states regular pricing, immediately followed by the "member price." A reader soon realizes that a subscription to the Smithsonian magazine (qualifying one as a member) is paid for by the savings received with just a purchase or two. Literary Guild's pricing, 4(b), reflects the reward that a membership commitment brings. The word "member" associated with a lower price is an obvious benefit and merchandising point.

5. **Value** pricing often results from custom packaging of several same or coordinated products. Example 5 from the DRI catalog refers to the regular price as "Value" because of the savings reaped by purchasing the package instead of the individual components. "Your Price Only" reflects the price resulting from the cataloger's custom packaging efforts. The words imply that the product is priced especially for you, and with DRI's method of merchandising, indeed it is.

Other words and ways of utilizing the price line for subtle merchandising are yours to create. Don't neglect this small but potentially profitable selling opportunity.

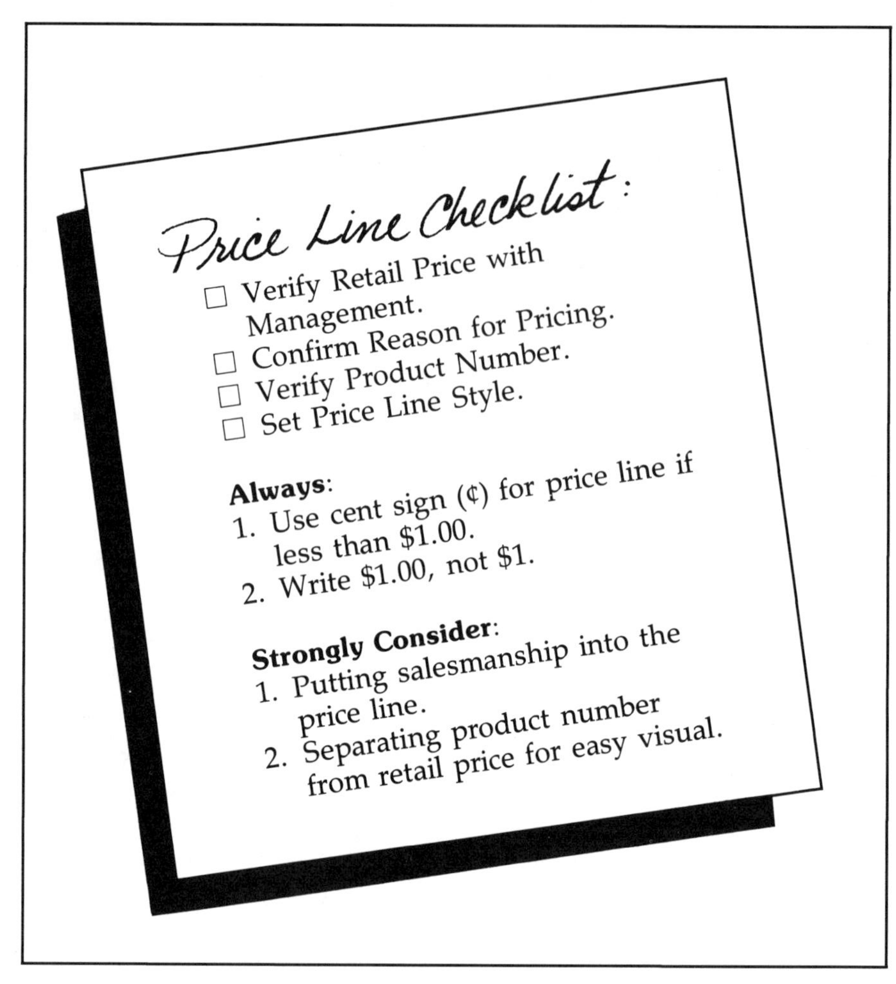

Price Line Checklist:
☐ Verify Retail Price with Management.
☐ Confirm Reason for Pricing.
☐ Verify Product Number.
☐ Set Price Line Style.
Always:
1. Use cent sign (¢) for price line if less than $1.00.
2. Write $1.00, not $1.
Strongly Consider:
1. Putting salesmanship into the price line.
2. Separating product number from retail price for easy visual.

Catalog Credibility

Never before has it been so important to establish and build credibility. The rapid rate of new company start-ups has made competition fierce, and the battle for the customer's catalog dollar is on. One way to get your fair share is to establish your credibility so customers feel confident in placing orders. These four elements will help you build credibility.

1. Company history. What year was your business started? This means your *business*, not the first publication of your catalog. If you published your catalog two years ago, but you have been in business for 25 years, tell your customer about your 25-year-old business. Even if you've started a new division of your company, it still is perfectly valid to say "in business since 1959" or "serving the public for 25 years." Letting the customer know that yours is an established company is one of the best ways to merchandise your credibility. Are you taking advantage of how many years your catalog or company has been in business, or are you ignoring this built-in credibility factor?

2. The Catalog Letter. A mail order catalog must convey to the customer a "feeling" which breaks down resistance to ordering. This "feeling" is credibility. Not being able to examine or touch a product creates in the customer a natural tendency to disbelieve. One avenue to combat this resistance is the Catalog Letter. This is a letter which appears on a page in the catalog or on the order form, not on a separate sheet of paper. Unfortunately, most letters of this type are ineffective because they are very general. They tell what wonderful products the company has to offer (without giving examples); they sometimes mention the guarantee or the fast service (more effective if it were placed elsewhere) and wish the customer the best. They have nothing to say, nothing is accomplished, and space is wasted — a perfect opportunity to build familiarity and credibility is lost.

To make this letter really useful, ask yourself: Do you welcome your customer? Does your catalog introduce itself? Do you worry about first impressions? What about an actual greeting? Just what kind of welcoming posture do you take, and how important is it to your catalog?

Are introductions and greetings necessary to the business of selling merchandise by mail? They're certainly designed to put customers at ease, to make them feel comfortable about your catalog, merchandise, and services. They're designed to create the impression that someone cares; they add a "personal" element and remove the institutional feel. They imply that customers are welcome to browse and, of course, to buy.

Catalog Credibility

To build Credibility and Authority, your key ingredient is Truth in Advertising. Neither your catalog copy nor your illustrations should invent, guess or approximate.

James J. Casey
Eddie Bauer
Redmond, WA

Welcome your customer

Sign your name

Where should introductions be positioned? By their very nature, they should be up front. If you use a wrap-around, it becomes an excellent location for a greeting. Greetings often are located on pages two or three, just inside the front cover. Many companies welcome their customers in the middle of the book, or sometimes on the order form. But this diminishes the effect — somewhat like saying ''hello'' to one's guests as they are leaving the party, rather than upon their arrival. In cases where the greeting is positioned on the order form, it alters its impression by underlining the company's appreciation toward its customers, rather than by welcoming potential buyers.

What format should be used — an unsigned message or a signed letter? And from whom? Your decision here depends greatly on the impression you wish your catalog to make. One favorable format is the ''letter from the president.'' Such letters tell potential customers that bosses are around, involved. . .and available, should customers ever want them. A less formal, more homey approach is to use a ''home economist'' or a ''personal shopper'' — usually a fictitious person created to make the customer feel that a specially chosen individual is available to serve the customer's specific needs. Some catalogs combine the two feelings of these separate approaches by issuing welcomes from the entire staff or the whole family. These letters promote the feeling that ''we are real friends, personally interested in YOU.'' And often you'll find this technique used by family-owned catalog businesses.

Should the signer's photograph be included? This certainly enhances the ''real person'' approach, and when used in every edition of your catalog, it establishes easy recognition. The face becomes familiar, like an ''old friend,'' and creates an atmosphere of trust. It's not unusual for the individual who appears in these photos and signs these ''letters'' to receive fan mail from new and old customers. If you use a photograph, you'll probably want to change it once in a while. Especially with a photograph of a woman, hair styles and clothing change, and can easily give a dated appearance. Mary Ann Spencer, a fictitious personality of Spencer Gifts, has changed considerably over the years; she is not the ''same person'' she was 20 years ago. In fact, she's a lot younger now. (And Spencer Gifts' long-time customers must wonder how she does it!) Alberta Kimball (not fictitious), of the Miles Kimball catalog, hasn't changed a bit in as many years.

What should you say? You can use opening salutations such as "Dear Friend," or "Dear Customer," or just "Hi!" Or you can use a headline such as "President's Message." But a lot of what you say and how you say it depends on the philosophy behind your company image — the impression you want your company to make. Mentioning your guarantee and how long you've been in business is a fine credibility builder, and adding something about your toll-free phone service is an ordering incentive. If you are publishing your first catalog, you may wish to relate your special, unique merchandising and service philosophies. . .and assure the customer of your intent to be around forever. *It's important to develop your greeting in a believable, sincere manner — and to keep it coordinated with the perceptions you wish your customer to have about your business.*

Sell your company

How much space should be devoted to this greeting? The more prominence and the more space given to this effort, the more effective it should be (for example, a full-page letter on page two, as opposed to 10 lines of copy at the bottom of the order form). BUT space is expensive; prime space is usually reserved for selling your best merchandise. Compromises are usually made (10 lines on page two). The most important reason for taking customer greetings seriously is a realization that the end result of this greeting is to aid in a sale, establish company credibility, and encourage customers to remain with you forever.

General Consumer A perfect example of what a credibility letter should and can do is that of Burpee Seed. Read the letter carefully (Figure 6-61) and see how each paragraph builds credibility. Paragraph one speaks of the longevity of the company (credibility); paragraph two, the scope of Burpee's market (credibility); paragraph three, the nationwide testing program of impressive groups, such as county agents, universities. Even the map which interrupts the letter serves its purpose in adding to credibility — it is an attention-getter and shows where Burpee seeds are sold (credibility). Paragraph four calls attention to product weakness which it then cleverly turns into a benefit — customized order fulfillment (more credibility). The last paragraph and single sentence are left to wishing the customer well. This is hard-sell credibility at its best. This letter was not put together haphazardly. A copywriter spent much time building the credibility elements and capitalizing on the well known Burpee name.

Mary of Puddin Hill combines two elements, a letter and photograph, to make a powerful presentation. Figure 6-62 illustrates how the warmth and *familiarity* of mother's kitchen are achieved by this photo and letter from Mary herself. Mary's photo presents the familiar image that everyone longs for and which we *associate* with

Dear Friends and Fellow Gardeners:

My grandfather, W. Atlee Burpee, first trumpeted the famous slogan "Burpee's Seeds Grow" more than 80 years ago. Since then the phrase has been recognized and trusted by four generations of gardeners all over America.

From Maine to Texas, from New York to California, Burpee's seeds grow!

To be sure our flowers and vegetables do well under varied soil conditions and climates, we conduct extensive annual field trials on the East and West Coasts, and in several locations in between. We send advance samples of new Burpee varieties to thousands

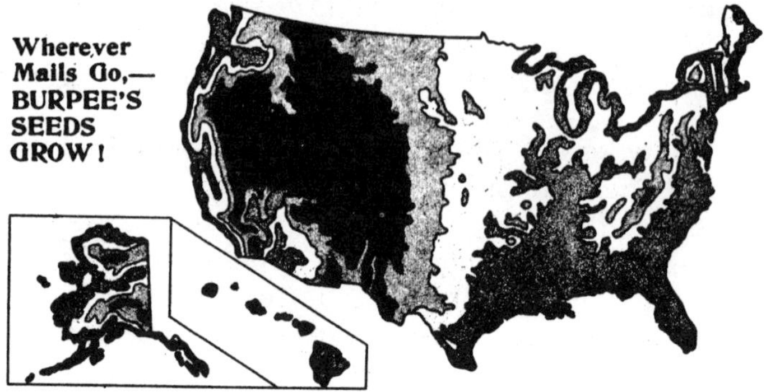
Wherever Mails Go,—
BURPEE'S
SEEDS
GROW!

of county agents, horticulturists and garden writers in every state of the union. We work closely with agricultural departments of universities throughout the U.S. We keep up-to-date with world-wide developments of new varieties useful to American home gardeners. In addition, thousands of Burpee customers help our research team by writing us about their experiences with our products.

Of course, not every Burpee variety grows equally well all over. In fact, all plants have specific needs and preferences. For example, marigolds and most other annuals bloom better in sun than shade...carrots grow best in porous or sandy soil...Tropic tomato feels most at home in the South. The information we get from our trials, our customers and our country-wide associates helps us recommend the best varieties for <u>your</u> area, with <u>your</u> climate and soil. Our catalogs are filled with many hints for the home gardener.

By choosing varieties carefully and giving them the care they need -- and by using only Burpee's "seeds that grow" -- you'll have a garden to be proud of.

Best wishes for your most satisfying, productive and joyful year of gardening ever!

Jonathan Burpee

Jonathan Burpee

6-61

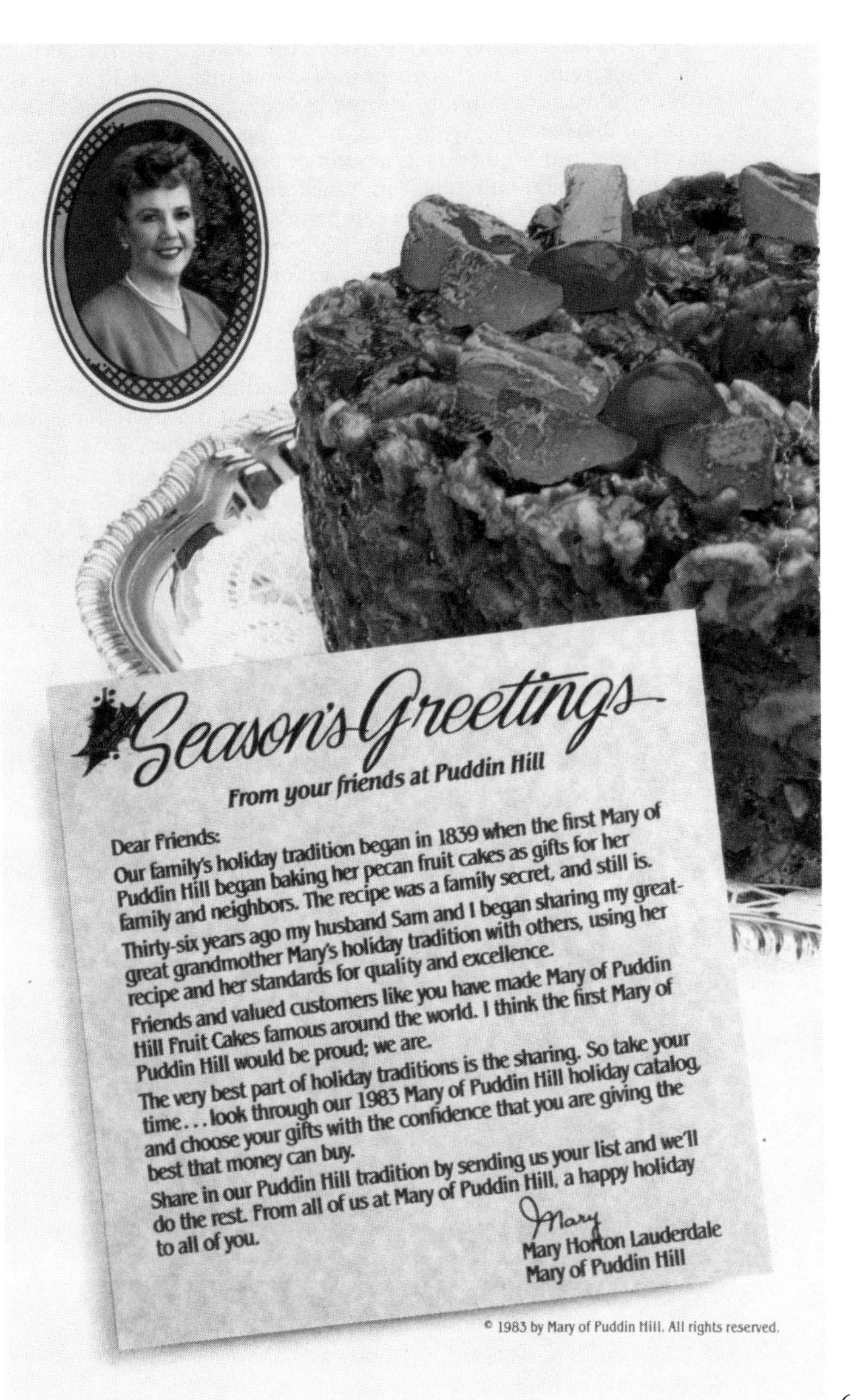
Season's Greetings
From your friends at Puddin Hill
Dear Friends:
Our family's holiday tradition began in 1839 when the first Mary of Puddin Hill began baking her pecan fruit cakes as gifts for her family and neighbors. The recipe was a family secret, and still is.
Thirty-six years ago my husband Sam and I began sharing my great-great grandmother Mary's holiday tradition with others, using her recipe and her standards for quality and excellence.
Friends and valued customers like you have made Mary of Puddin Hill Fruit Cakes famous around the world. I think the first Mary of Puddin Hill would be proud; we are.
The very best part of holiday traditions is the sharing. So take your time... look through our 1983 Mary of Puddin Hill holiday catalog, and choose your gifts with the confidence that you are giving the best that money can buy.
Share in our Puddin Hill tradition by sending us your list and we'll do the rest. From all of us at Mary of Puddin Hill, a happy holiday to all of you.
Mary
Mary Horton Lauderdale
Mary of Puddin Hill
© 1983 by Mary of Puddin Hill. All rights reserved.

6-62

the perfect Mom. Mary is a "perfect" picture of a "perfect" Mom. The letter reinforces this feeling of familiarity by telling of the wonderful family tradition, started in 1839, of baking fruitcakes at home to use for gifts. Even though the company was only started in 1947, one hundred and eight additional years have been used for reference by mentioning the earlier historical moment when the idea was born. The copy shares the company's history with the customer and ties it to the present; to say "Share in our Puddin Hill tradition" gives the customer a real sense of knowing and belonging. All elements have been brought together expertly to produce an encompassing warmth that melts away sales resistance. The customer is now primed to purchase!

In Austad's sports equipment and clothing catalog (Figure 6-63), a bond of familiarity and association is produced by the image of father and sons — every American father's dream of a perfect business situation. And it's a perfect approach to the sales resistance problem. Austad's brings both visual and verbal reinforcement of this dream in the photo of the father and his two sons working together in the family business. Copy builds on this ideal by confirming

OSCAR SEZ:

This is our 21st summer in business!

When I started Austad's back in 1963, one of my goals was to provide golfers throughout the country with a good, reliable source for quality equipment at affordable prices. I think we've done just that—but then only you can be the true judge.

Over the past 20 years I've really enjoyed the challenge of offering you better selections, service and quality each year. Last year we were fortunate enough to have almost 200,000 golfers buy their golf supplies from us. Dave thinks we'll have even more this year (he works in our Marketing Department, so he'd better be right).

As in previous years, my sons, Randy and Dave, helped make our 1983 selections. We've literally "shopped the world" for the best values we can find. We've used the expertise we've developed over the years, customers' comments, plus the ideas of leading manufacturers in the golf industry to come up with some excellent items at prices we think you'll like. To make sure we offer you only the best quality products at the best possible price, we've had many of our products made exclusively for us and we stand behind them with a strong guarantee.

Take a few minutes to look through your catalog and join the thousands of fellow golfers who do their shopping for quality equipment the easy Austad's way. It can all be done from the comfort of your home or office. If you see something you'd like to order, simply give us a call or fill out the handy order form and drop it in the mail. Your order will be delivered right to your door, usually in a matter of days.

Let us help you get in on the fun this summer and enjoy your leisure to the fullest!

Best personal regards,

Dave Randy Oscar

DAVE, RANDY AND OSCAR AUSTAD

6-63

in the customer's mind that this type of business partnership results in the same virtues this country was built on: trust, faith, dependability. When the President says, ". . .one of my goals was to provide golfers throughout the country with a good, reliable source for quality equipment at affordable prices," this partial sentence coupled with the family photo tends to break any customer's resistance to ordering. The letter goes on to increase this feeling of credibility with phrases such as: ". . .better selections, service and quality each year. . .200,000 golfers buy. . .my sons, Randy and Dave, helped make our selections. . .prices we think you'll like." This presentation gives a powerful wallop to customer sales resistance. And yes, Dave, you'll "have even more (orders) this year" because the feeling of *familiarity* and *association* has been built so strongly!

Copy Tip

Consider Question & Answer formats to control and direct reader to the issues and facts you want him *to know about* your *product. Use it for complex technical products; it makes it easy to read, interpret and reference.*

Richard Halpern
Data General
Milford, MA

Business-to-Business AMT (American Machine and Tool Company) has been a tool manufacturer for 56 years. The cover of their catalog (Figure 6-64) uses an attention-getting fold-out panel in a business letter format to promote AMT's "special reason for being." At right you see the visual impression created by this businesslike approach to promoting the reliability and longevity of the company, along with the savings for the customer. The copy informs the customer in a proud, yet understated (and consequently believable) manner of these various facts:

- ☐ 23rd Annual Sale (longevity, implying reliability)
- ☐ Company continues as THE world leader (more reliability, world status!)
- ☐ Prices from 25% to 50% below competition
- ☐ Competitors don't come close
- ☐ Discounts below price levels of two years ago (this comment and the signature are underlined with blue ink, making the comment stand out and creating the impression that it was personally emphasized by the individual "signing" the letter)
- ☐ 10-day money-back guarantee
- ☐ 10-year parts and repair guarantee.

The businesslike letterhead approach to this promotion, combined with the statements of reliability and savings, constitutes a highly credible presentation. Mentioning the unusual guarantee in the letter format gives it added support in the believability department, as though a real person stood behind it, and assures the customer that the guarantee were not merely a printed promotional blurb. Because all this information is printed on the fold-over flap, it is hard to resist opening the flap to see what's hidden underneath it. And what is found? "The AMT Story" and a panel of customer testimonials (Figure 6-65). The subhead on this page says "A highly respected 56-year-old firm stands behind this tool line" and gives reasons why ''no one else has a quality power tool line at such sensational prices.'' The comments from customers are printed in a typewriter style, just as though reproduced from actual letters. Now prospective customers can identify with other businesses who are ordering from AMT, businesses just like their own. The customer letters are used to reassure any doubting prospects that AMT is indeed exactly what it says it is: ''It is certainly gratifying to know that at least one company in the United States fully honors their warranty. I thought your 10-year warranty was just an advertising gimmick, but now I know it's true. . .(thanks) for standing behind it without hassling your customers for their receipt or invoice — I can just see me trying to locate my original invoice that I received with the drill press 9 years ago.'' This style of promotion has now established a partnership between company and customer. The letter is a fine credibility builder and booster in a first-rate promotional effort.

Figure 6-66 is from the inside front cover of the Harneds catalog. This company is targeted to butchers and the meat-packing industry. The catalog uses a letter along with photos of the staff. The customer is told that Harneds is a family business, now being manned by the fourth generation. The company's goals are expressed (''a better job of serving you'') and directed toward motivating the customer to place an order (''If you haven't used Harneds before — try us! I promise we will all do everything we can to earn your orders''). Photos of the family and staff are shown next to the letter, punctuated by the headline, ''OUR FAMILY. . .WE CARE!'' Now, if *you* needed a new wall thermometer for your meat freezer, wouldn't *you* try Harneds? If a company like this can take the policies and goals stated in the catalog copy and follow through with service, there's no reason for a customer to shop anywhere else.

If you have an individual or group in your company upon whom you can base this approach, *merchandise this plus*! If not, consider creating a personality. When you can merchandise attitudes of *familiarity* and *association*, you help *break customer ordering resistance*!

In these days of greater-than-ever competition for the catalog sales dollar, it's important to establish a bond between you and your customer. Letting your customers know that you care, and that you take a personal interest in their satisfaction via a catalog letter, may be your first step toward holding those customers for a long time to come.

3. Guarantee. Make your guarantee as strong as possible. Almost without exception you can make your guarantee unconditional (a 100 percent guarantee to return customers' money if they are not satisfied). Don't be afraid that every product you sell will come back. The fact is that a strong guarantee coupled with fast service encourages a minimal return rate. Naturally, this assumes that your product is of average-to-good quality. Are you offering the strongest guarantee possible, or are you letting fear of high refunds water it down with too many qualifiers? Qualifiers that can hurt your

AMERICAN MACHINE & TOOL COMPANY, INC. OF PENNSYLVANIA

FOURTH AVE. AND SPRING ST., P. O. BOX 70, ROYERSFORD, PENNSYLVANIA 19468 • 215-948-0400

January 2, 1984

23rd ANNUAL

MAXIMUM DISCOUNT POWER TOOL SALE

COMPETITORS DON'T COME CLOSE!

Our company continues as THE world leader in small bench power tools at prices from 25% to 50% lower than competition.

Even though we've had some cost increases this past year, we decided not to increase prices last fall. Business levels have been good and we've been running our factory at full tilt. Now we find that in order to maintain these low price levels, we have to keep our factory at 100% production. To insure this we are repeating last year's special extra discounts. These are discounts below price levels of two years ago.

This special printing of our catalog shows these low discounted prices in red. These special prices will expire March 12, 1984.

If you're near Royersford, visit our Factory Showroom. Bring this letter with you and we will honor these discounted prices. We're open 9:00 AM to 4:30 PM on weekdays, and 9:00 AM to Noon on Saturdays.

Remember, our 10-day money-back guarantee and our 10-year parts and repair guarantee still apply.

Very truly yours,

AMERICAN MACHINE & TOOL CO.

Dan Bechtel

Dan Bechtel
Sales Department

P.S. Note that a $5.00 deposit is required for each item ordered C.O.D.

REMEMBER, THIS OFFER EXPIRES MARCH 12, 1984!

6-64

THE AMT STORY

A HIGHLY RESPECTED 56-YEAR OLD FIRM STANDS BEHIND THIS TOOL LINE

No one else has a quality power tool line at such sensational prices and stands behind their products the way AMT does. What makes AMT so special?

MANUFACTURERS—We sell quality tools, and make most of them, and have been doing so since 1928. There are literally millions of satisfied customers who own tools made in our Royersford, PA factory. You are invited to visit our factory showroom and see for yourself.*

ENGINEERING—Our staff includes some of the most highly qualified designers in the field. They know what woodworkers want and how to deliver it to them. The products we sell have got to be the best because we put our guarantees on everything.

5 REASONS WHY AMT POWER TOOLS COST LESS:

1. **NO FRILLS**—no gimmicks, no fancy chrome. Just good, solid tools that do the job right!
2. **FASTER MACHINING**—our special equipment machines all parts automatically, in far less time.
3. **STANDARD PARTS**—they're easy to find, so they cost us less to begin with, and will still be readily available if they need replacing years from now.
4. **LARGE VOLUME**—we make bench power tools by the thousands—so we buy materials in quantity and pass the savings on to you!
5. **DIRECT-FROM-FACTORY SAVINGS**—means you save a bundle.

WE BACK WHAT WE SELL—We stand behind everything we sell one hundred percent. No other power tool manufacturer, no other power tool catalog sales firm offers such all-encompassing guarantees and warranties...a ten day money-back guarantee (no questions asked) and a ten year limited warranty (motors one year). And when you need a part, when you need service, we are here to help you. See the back cover for the guarantee and limited warranty.

**Royersford is three miles south of Route 422 on Township Line Road, which becomes Walnut Street. Turn left off Walnut Street onto Fourth Avenue to our location at Fourth and Spring Street. (20 miles west of Philadelphia.) Our hours are from 9 to 4:30 on weekdays and 9 to noon on Saturdays.*

American Machine and Tool Company • Fourth and Spring Streets, Royersford, PA 19468
Phone 215-948-0400

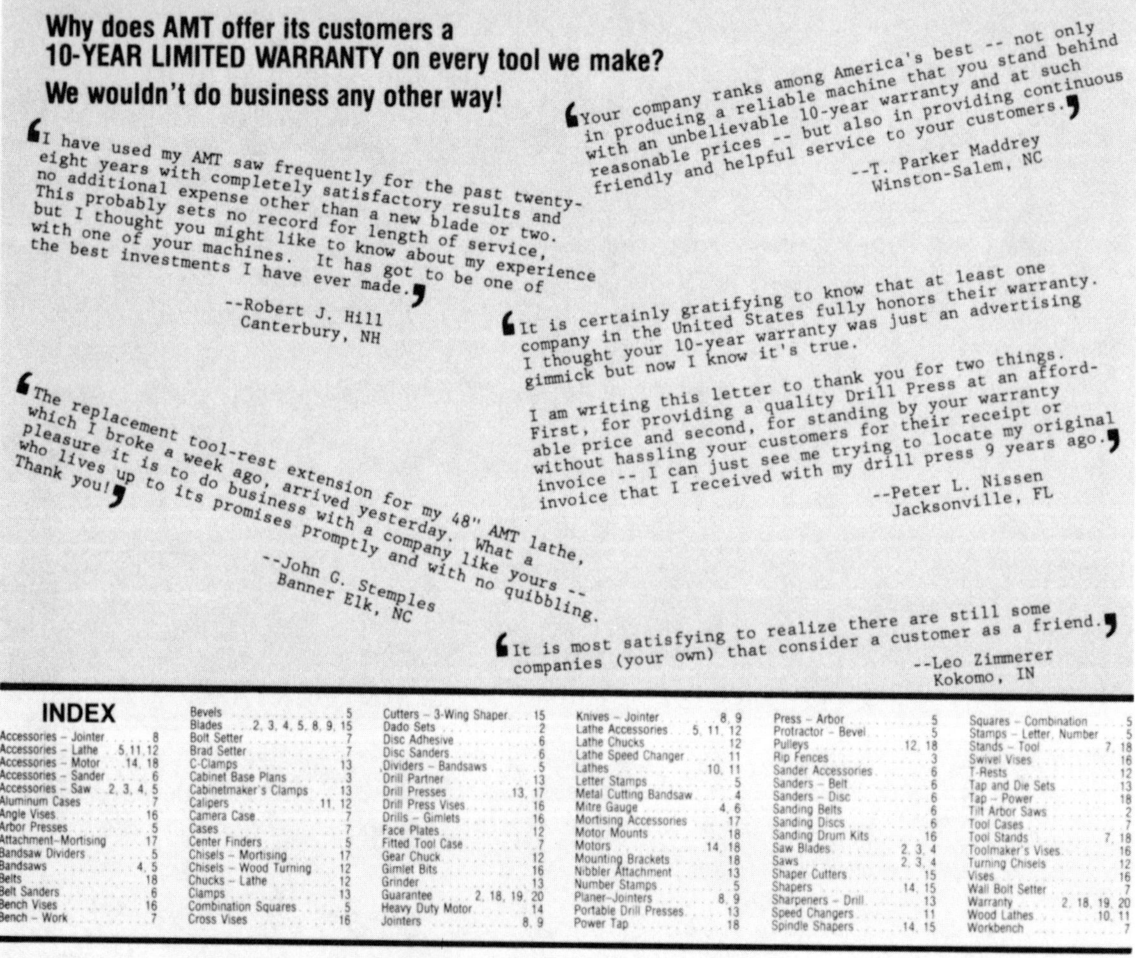

Why does AMT offer its customers a
10-YEAR LIMITED WARRANTY on every tool we make?
We wouldn't do business any other way!
"Your company ranks among America's best -- not only in producing a reliable machine that you stand behind with an unbelievable 10-year warranty and at such reasonable prices -- but also in providing continuous friendly and helpful service to your customers."
--T. Parker Maddrey
Winston-Salem, NC
"I have used my AMT saw frequently for the past twenty-eight years with completely satisfactory results and no additional expense other than a new blade or two. This probably sets no record for length of service, but I thought you might like to know about my experience with one of your machines. It has got to be one of the best investments I have ever made."
--Robert J. Hill
Canterbury, NH
"It is certainly gratifying to know that at least one company in the United States fully honors their warranty. I thought your 10-year warranty was just an advertising gimmick but now I know it's true.
I am writing this letter to thank you for two things. First, for providing a quality Drill Press at an affordable price and second, for standing by your warranty without hassling your customers for their receipt or invoice -- I can just see me trying to locate my original invoice that I received with my drill press 9 years ago."
--Peter L. Nissen
Jacksonville, FL
"The replacement tool-rest extension for my 48" AMT lathe, which I broke a week ago, arrived yesterday. What a pleasure it is to do business with a company like yours -- who lives up to its promises promptly and with no quibbling. Thank you!"
--John G. Stemples
Banner Elk, NC
"It is most satisfying to realize there are still some companies (your own) that consider a customer as a friend."
--Leo Zimmerer
Kokomo, IN

INDEX

6-65

September 1, 1983

WELCOME . . . to Harneds 1983-84 catalog!

It's our 60th anniversary! Thank you for your support and loyalty. We are proud to have been a part of your operations and the meat industry for over half a century.

Harneds is a family business. My grandfather, Walter Harned, started selling out of his Model T in 1923. Today I am third generation and proud that the fourth generation, my son Bruce, is also working hard to serve your needs.

My goal is to make Harneds your best supplier. In that effort many of you received a questionnaire with your catalog last year. Your responses have been very helpful and most appreciated. In view of your comments and suggestions we have made major changes in our catalog format this year. I hope these changes will meet with your approval.

Please continue to make comments and suggestions. It helps us do a better job of serving you. Call us, toll free, any time you need help! If we don't have what you need we will try to help you find it.

If you haven't used Harneds before — try us! I promise we will all do everything we can to earn your orders. With your support Harneds future generations will be working to serve you 60 years from now.

Thank you,

Jake Hartmetz

Jake Hartmetz

616 PENNSYLVANIA · BOX 2333 · WICHITA, KS. 67201 · 316-262-0651
MEMBER: AMERICAN ASSOCIATION OF MEAT PROCESSORS

OUR FAMILY . . .

JAKE HARTMETZ

BRUCE HARTMETZ

BARBARA BROOKS

BETTY MARTINEZ

ANNE TRIMMELL

DEBBIE STICKNEY

H.M. BEARD

BOB MORRISON

. . . WE CARE!

6-66

business would be time limits for returning merchandise, or issuance of credit for future orders rather than refunding cash.

4. Testimonials. They come from your own customers in your daily mail or through phone conversations. Nothing is more believable or reassuring to a prospective customer than knowing that prior customers have been satisfied with your products and service. Testimonials skillfully placed throughout your catalog and order form are strong ways to merchandise your credibility. Are you utilizing favorable customer comments, or are you throwing into the wastebasket this golden opportunity to merchandise your credibility?

If you are not taking advantage of at least two of these four elements of credibility merchandising, you are losing sales.

Blurbs and Insets

Not to utilize one or both of these techniques is to miss an opportunity to catch the customer's attention, instill customer confidence, build credibility, or direct the customer to place an order. A blurb can be just a word or two, a copy line, or a visual and verbal message combined. An inset, for example, is most often a combination of a visual and verbal message clarifying product components or use.

Service and ordering information is the most simply relayed. It can generally be conveyed in short messages and so can be used prolifically throughout the catalog due to the small space required. A telephone number or charge card information can signal the customer that your catalog is a convenient place to shop and that ordering is easy. Such blurbs can also relate to your customer that service is fast. Many expert catalogers feel that a constant reminder throughout the catalog can subliminally act as a directive to order.

The following illustrations show how three general consumer catalogs promote telephone ordering and charge cards. In Figure 6-67 The Sharper Image promotes toll-free ordering. Included in a small space is a directive (''Order Toll-free''), qualifying information (''24-hours every day. . .Toll-free ordering by credit card only''), and the toll-free number plus a regular number for Canadian and overseas orders. This blurb is reproduced throughout the catalog in various sizes depending on the space available.

ORDER TOLL-FREE. 24 HRS. EVERY DAY.

800 344-4444

Canadian/overseas orders 415-344-4444

Toll free ordering by credit card only.

6-67

Lillian Vernon (Figure 6-68) combines a visual design (telephone silhouette) with a verbal command (''CHARGE IT!'') along with a regular phone number. This small message appears in a red and white design 27 times in one of her 60-page catalogs.

6-68

Norm Thompson (Figure 6-69) takes the opportunity to tell the customer what is available ''For fastest service.'' Hewlett Packard Computer User's Catalog places two separate blurbs (see Figure 6-70) throughout the company's catalog — one for ordering (a) and one for charge card acceptance (b). All of these blurbs can be used anywhere throughout the catalog because of their general subject matter and referencing.

For fastest service, order TOLL FREE anytime by calling 1-800-547-1160. Oregon call 1-800-772-7226. Alaska & Hawaii call (503) 644-2666, Mon.-Fri., 8-5 PST.

6-69

6-70

Credibility can be built in little ways such as one-sentence statements used throughout a catalog or fully quoted testimonials and company policy guarantees.

The use of short testimonial blurbs is a fine way to build customer confidence in your company and products! Every company has the opportunity to utilize testimonials. All catalog companies get letters from customers who are pleased. Sometimes an entire letter can be used effectively, but more often highlighting a comment or two is the way to go.

An efficient way to utilize these customer comments is in combination with a design, sprinkled judiciously throughout the catalog. This method not only *calls attention to supportive remarks* about your company and products as your customer browses through your pages, but it also *makes efficient use of catalog space*. A small blurb can almost always fit in an area that otherwise would be wasted. Figure 6-71 from REI (Recreational Equipment Inc.), grabs the customer's attention with graphics that look like notepaper and with a salutation headline (''Dear REI. . .''). This particular testimonial comment pertains to a product being sold on the same page. Figure 6-72 is from the Walter Drake and Sons catalog. The headline (''Our Customers Say:'') calls attention to the comments wherever they are placed throughout the catalog. Because this comment is general in nature, it could be used on any page in the book.

Save the favorable customer comments you receive and use them in your catalog. It's a great way to *merchandise your credibility!*

Use of Key Benefits

Intersperse 'how to order' information, ordering telephone numbers and key benefits of the entire catalog (new low prices, discounts, free freight, 100's of new products, etc.) throughout the catalog – *including Terms & Conditions page. Remember how readers read a catalog. It's not a novel; it's to be browsed.*

Richard Halpern
Data General
Milford, MA

Inmac uses two very effective methods of testimonial blurbs. Figure 6-73 shows two customer testimonials that are a little lengthier, extolling the benefits of the product being sold on the same page, Inmac computer ribbons. The testimonials are letter-length and are effectively presented in a crisp one-point rule border. They were carefully chosen to emphasize quality, price, and print quality comparison with a competing brand. In another approach (Figure 6-74), Inmac uses a four-color photograph of the customer along with her testimonial regarding fast service. This brings even more credibility and believability to the company, thereby building a bond for future business.

Guarantees are very effective because they say, ''Don't worry, it's okay to order from us''; they should be stated often. Simply stating, in one-line blurbs, ''Satisfaction Guaranteed'' throughout the catalog is beneficial. However, Inmac utilizes the guarantee blurb to the fullest. Even though their ''Double Guarantee'' has been stated on page two of the catalog, they have also placed throughout the catalog blurb guarantees which pertain to specific products. Figure 6-75 shows how art and copy make up a guarantee blurb about the computer pens carried. The copy headline (''We guarantee freshness!'') pertains only to the computer pens being sold on the two facing pages. The following copy guarantee stating the freshness is strong: ''We unconditionally guarantee the absolute freshness and color brilliancy of each Inmac plotter pen as long as the package seal remains intact. If any pen ever fails to perform flawlessly upon breaking the seal, return it to Inmac and receive a full refund.'' This art/copy inset has added credibility to the product as well as to the company. It has become a full-fledged promotional tool.

Customer education is another primary use for short blurb-type copy, often in conjunction with art or graphic highlighting. All companies can use small space available throughout the catalog for customer education about either the product or the catalog company.

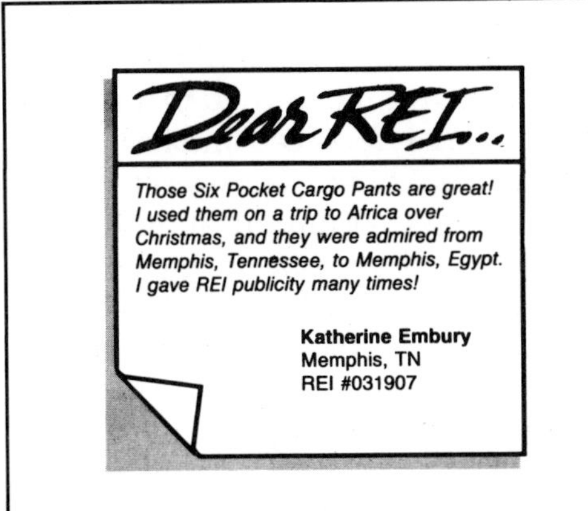

Dear REI...
Those Six Pocket Cargo Pants are great! I used them on a trip to Africa over Christmas, and they were admired from Memphis, Tennessee, to Memphis, Egypt. I gave REI publicity many times!
Katherine Embury
Memphis, TN
REI #031907

6-71

Our Customers Say:
"Your catalogs are so neat and I have been very pleased with all my orders from you."
T. J. R., Hawaii

6-72

What our customers say about Inmac ribbons:

"Just wanted to let you know how pleased I am with your ribbons.

"I've checked around and you've by far got the cheapest prices on ribbons for my Xerox 1720!

"Besides the price, I appreciate the quality. My Inmac ribbons don't break like others I've used.

"Thanks again."

—Jakki Carey,
Word-Processing Secretary,
Core Labs Int., Dallas, Texas

"We've got an LP2 printer that we really put through the paces. We wanted to improve our printer quality so we switched to your 'Good Impressions' ribbons.

"Right from the start they printed much darker—they're easily 100% better than the Data General ribbons we were getting before! Keep up the good work."

—Kevin Reed, Data Processing Manager
Thomas Systems, Fort Worth, Texas

6-73

"Everything I've ordered from Inmac has been great. We're especially happy with your customer service people. Sometimes I don't realize I'm low on a supply until the last minute, but they always get it here before I run out—even though we're in Wyoming."

—Laurie Pankey
Secretary
Crayton Smith Agency
Jackson, Wyoming

6-74

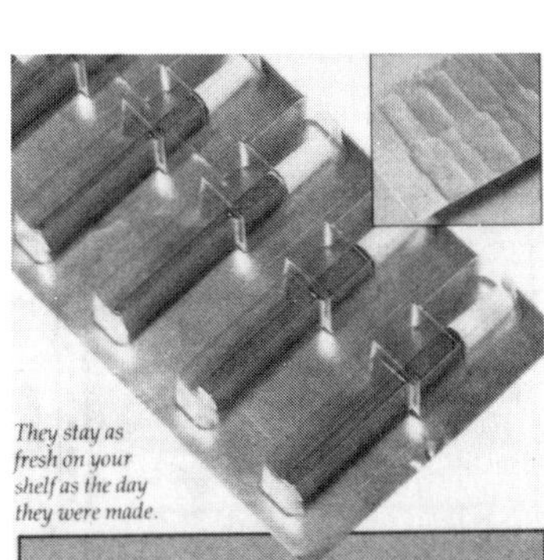

They stay as fresh on your shelf as the day they were made.

We guarantee freshness!

With our unique perforated blister-pak, you tear off only the pens you need. The rest stay factory fresh in airtight compartments. We unconditionally guarantee the absolute freshness and color brilliancy of each Inmac plotter pen as long as the package seal remains intact. If any pen ever fails to perform flawlessly upon breaking the seal, return it to Inmac and receive a full refund.

6-75

Inmac puts its educational material in the form of "Hints." Figure 6-76 shows how very valuable Inmac considers this technique. This little "Helpful Hints" index is on page two, highlighted in an "index card" design. Twelve different pages are referenced and bear educational hints. Figure 6-77 from the Inmac catalog shows seven hints in the care and use of floppy discs. This bit of education helps in cementing the loyalty of the customer. Educational insets which inform the customer in the use of a product will encourage orders because the customer can more clearly understand the product and associate it with his own needs.

Product facts interest customers

DRI's use of a line drawing inset carefully defines the products more clearly for the customer and visually explains their use (Figure 6-78). Part (a) illustrates a Disc-Lock Washer. The line drawing conveys the makeup of one component of the set being sold and is clearly identified with copy; the remainder of the illustration shows where and how the product is used. Every product sold within the first 24 pages of DRI's Complete Shops has line drawing insets such as these. DRI says it is a "hardware store in your mailbox," and this is the point where a customer at a retail hardware store would "pick up" the item and examine it.

The Dickson Company, which markets recording and testing instruments, uses an inset to educate the customer on the vitally important construction of the capillary tube found in sensing bulbs for distant-reading temperature recorders. Figure 6-79 illustrates how art and copy, as a team, educate the customer concerning the construction and quality of the tube.

Helpful Hints

Caring for floppy disks 11
How to select a floppy disk 19
Ordering the right printer ribbon 31,34
A guide to ordering data communications equipment for your system 49,52,54,56
Selecting EIA cables 62
How to choose the right testing device 71
The truth about 120 volt power & your computer 76
How to control cable clutter 78

6-76

Carelessness with your floppies could cost you weeks of work.

Prevent data disasters! Avoid these common floppy disk dangers.

Good habits pay-off! Simply taking basic precautions in caring for disks could save you megabytes of unexpected, frustrating and costly data loss.

- **Don't bend or fold:** creases can cause permanent disfiguration. Vertical storage is recommended.
- **Don't expose to strong sunlight** or any heat source.
- **Don't expose to magnetic fields.** Telephones, radios, and even paperclip holders can cause minor or major data erasures.
- **Don't contaminate.** Smoke particles, dust, dirt, face powder, graphite dust or erasure crumbs from pencils can cause very expensive data loss.
- **Don't put pressure on the disk.** Writing on a label with a ballpoint pen, or even the weight of an empty soda can, might cripple disk performance.
- **Always return your disk to its envelope** for maximum support and continual protection.
- **Always protect your disks by storing them properly** in vinyl envelopes, binders, library cases, or specially designed cabinets.

6-77

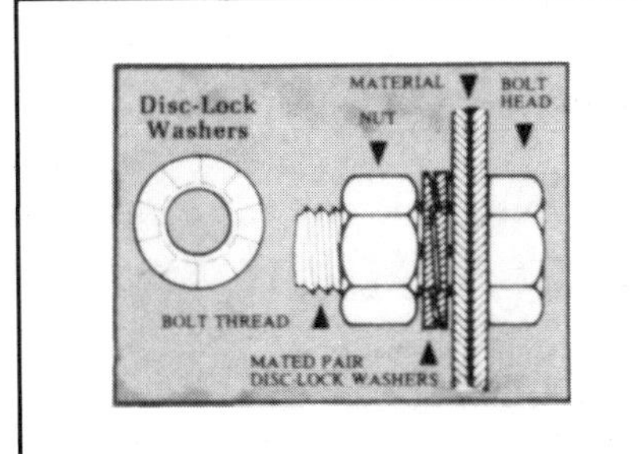

6-78(a)

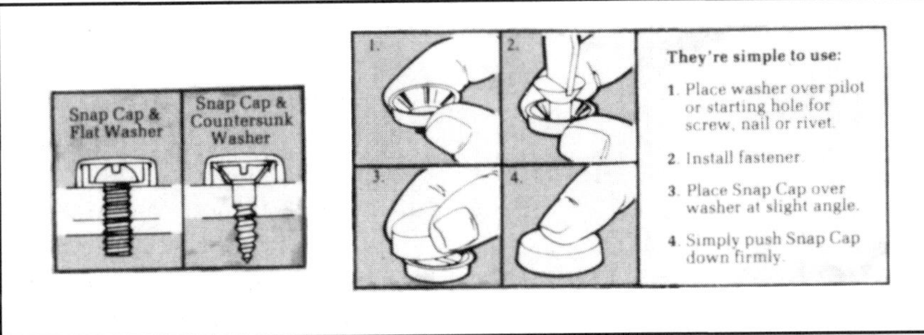

6-78(b)

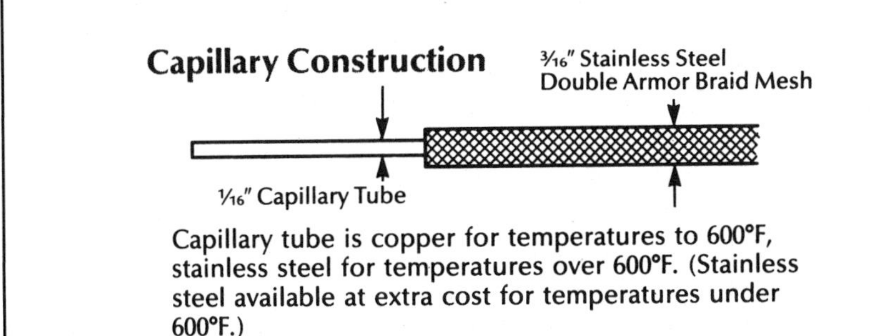

Capillary Construction
3/16" Stainless Steel Double Armor Braid Mesh
1/16" Capillary Tube
Capillary tube is copper for temperatures to 600°F, stainless steel for temperatures over 600°F. (Stainless steel available at extra cost for temperatures under 600°F.)

6-79

Information is another prime use for blurbs and insets. Telling the customer about different product features, company practices, and related product material can help add to sales. Specific product information can be worked in nicely on the same page with a product to which it pertains; general information can be placed anywhere in the catalog. When a standard product is changed, it is a good idea to let the customer know before ordering.

For example, L.L. Bean (Figure 6-80) utilizes an informational blurb to let the customer know about a color and design change in a standard product the company expects to continue to carry. This allows the customer currently ordering to match merchandise previously ordered: ''If you purchased a piece prior to 1984 and would like to match an 'old' color, we will continue to offer the luggage in the 'old' colors, and designs. Please direct orders. . .'' This information keeps customer service work down, refunds down, and customers happy. DRI (Figure 6-81) uses a blurb informing the customer where to find component parts of workshops offered in bulk form in another part of the catalog. This is a sharp technique as it also gets the customer through the catalog.

The Sportsman's Luggage underwent changes in color and design in 1984. If you purchased a piece prior to 1984 and would like to match an "old" color, we will continue to offer the luggage in the "old" colors, and designs. Please direct orders to attention of the Special Order Department. Specify "old" Green, "old" Navy, "old" Tan, or "old" Gray.

6-80

For bulk Stainless Steel Threaded Fasteners, see Pages, 32-35.

6-81

Williams-Sonoma, a kitchen and housewares catalog, cleverly uses blurbs for informing the customer about pricing and about policies referred to in the product copy, as well as giving the customer full recipes which match a product on the same page. Figure 6-82 (a) explains that favorable foreign exchange rates mean better prices for the customer. On the same page, two products have reduced special prices. Figure 6-82 (b) clarifies a point made in the copy throughout the catalog: ''NOTE: When we say 'recipe included' we will enclose with your order a complimentary 3″ × 5″ printed recipe card. . .'' Figure 6-83 illustrates how Williams-Sonoma includes recipes in the catalog to match products carried. This particular recipe, ''Terrine of France,'' is for a pate which can, of course, be made in the product being sold, an Oval Terrine from France. Note how the recipe is enclosed in a fine line border exactly the same height as the product photo. All informational blurbs originated by Williams-Sonoma are ''signed'' with a special company logo.

Other beneficial aspects of product quality or company policies can be highlighted in blurbs and insets. Using them not only serves customers with information and attracts their attention, but it also adds a finishing touch which makes a catalog a polished presentation.

Many of the reduced special prices in this book reflect the favorable foreign exchange rates experienced by us on recent purchases in Europe. We are pleased to pass them on to you.

NOTE: When we say "recipe included" we will enclose with your order a complimentary 3" x 5" printed recipe card, tested by — and in fact often originated by Chuck Williams. We have started publishing our recipes in this form in response to requests from customers.

6-82

TERRINE OF FRANCE
Mix together 1 lb. each ground fresh pork and ground lean beef, ½ lb. ground pork or calves' liver, 2 Tbs. brandy, 1 egg, 1-2 cloves of minced garlic, 6 minced juniper berries, ¼ tsp. ground mace, ground pepper, 2 tsp. salt and 3 slices of bacon, diced. Let stand for 2-3 hours. Pack into terrine (or terrines). Cover and place in a baking pan filled with 1-2" of boiling water. Bake in a 350° oven for 1-1¼ hrs. or until internal temperature of meat registers 165°. Remove from oven and let cool to a warm temperature. Drain off fat and juices. Make an aspic with well-flavored beef stock or Haco aspic jelly powder and fill space around pâté. Chill before serving. Yield: 4-4½ cups.

6-83

A Few Words about Truth. Catalog copywriters must recognize one essential fact before writing anything: they are not in a one-shot business. Because catalog marketers achieve their greatest profits by acquiring and *retaining* customers, the writer must review all copy with an eye for truthfulness.

School yourself with this credo: you really are creating copy to get long-term customers who will try you once, like you, and then have faith that they can continue to deal with you.

In your eagerness to create copy that sells, it is natural to want to describe every product in the most glowing terms you can devise. *Be careful*. Readers search your copy to find points with which they can disagree, unbelievable points, or obviously false claims. When they find those stretched truths, they don't buy. If your claims are so extravagant that an unsuspecting reader is convinced, buys, and then is disappointed because the product didn't live up to your claims, refund requests go up.

Victoria's Secret very skillfully combines both the essential facts (which a customer needs to make a buying decision) and the beautiful benefits (enthusiastically expressed) received by purchasing the product — and disciplines itself into never overwhelming or overstating. Its copy might tell the reader to "slip into another world where nights are glamorous and romance is in the air." It might say the gown is "bias-cut to flatter your figure" or that the fashions are "sensuous." But it does not say that your figure will look magnificent in the gown or that you will be sensuous. It merely implies — and does so in a gentle and genteel manner — and consequently remains credible in the mind of the customer.

You can make your copy more believable, and thus create longer-term customers, by following these 10 editing techniques:

1. Do not use the word "best" for every item
2. Avoid superlatives when possible
3. Avoid strings of adjectives
4. Do not exaggerate. . .eliminate puffery
5. Avoid imprecise copy
6. Do not mislead to get a sale
7. Do not use subtleties or nuances that may not be understood quickly by fast readers
8. Avoid disorganized copy which confuses the reader
9. Do not overly stress the legitimacy of your company
10. Avoid excessive enthusiasm

Another frequent problem is that your copy may be 100 percent truthful, but the reader's perception of your wording may lead to an impression of falsity or exaggeration. This problem is licked by switching to short words and phrases, often in a staccato presentation minus complete sentences.

Example:
"From the very first moment that you start using this handsome executive calendar, you'll discover how marvelous it is to have the ultimate convenience of highlighted, easily-accessed, color-coded separate sections for important appointments, personal notations, expense memorandums, things-to-do listings, and staff schedules. And it's all yours in a modern, spring-loaded loose-leaf binder so you can insert special company memos at key reminder dates."

Editing:
"Instant ring-binder convenience is yours. Add memos at key dates. Use color-coded separate sections for appointments, personal notes, expenses, reminders, schedules. Modern. Handsome, executive styling.

The edited version contains every sales point from the longer version but is less argumentative, and the staccato copy implies enthusiasm — a much more convincing approach than using enthusiastic wording.

Typography

Deciding which typestyles or sizes to use in your catalog is a decision as important as how to best present a product or how best to describe it.

The use of type is as critical to total visual image as the style, approach, or props are to a photograph. At the most basic level, type makes the product description readable. Its legibility helps move the customer from sentence to sentence — page to page. How do you know what type style to choose? What do you look for when judging a layout? Can type be attractive (not just the plain old accounting form type) and readable, too? *Selecting the right typestyle for your catalog, plus the right size and weight, and then executing it well in the presentation call for skills approaching art.*

Selecting Typestyles. The Right Way, The Wrong Way . . . and Some Helpful Hints. Of the hundreds of typestyles, most typesetters will carry from fifteen to twenty. Nobody, of course, carries everything that is available.

So, how do you choose the styles needed for your particular catalog or promotion? Here are two basic rules to keep in mind:

1. Keep it simple
2. Make it easy to read

Yes, it can be easy to read and attractive, too — in fact, it should be! Type is used to create a ''look'' and to convey a mood: excitement, masculinity, femininity, quality, strength, and so on. But no matter what look or mood you wish to create, the type must be *easy to read*. Following are three recommendations for choosing type:

1. Use fancy typestyles only for your logo or occasionally to create an accent
2. Keep the rest of your copy in a style that is easy to read
3. Most typestyles come in light, medium, bold, and italic. Use light for body copy, medium for subheads, bold for heads, and italic for accents

In Figure 6-84 we see just a few typestyles which are both common and readable.

There are two basic typestyles: serif and sans-serif. Serif type has small shoulders or crosslines at the ends (tops and bottoms of letter strokes) of each letter. The line strokes of serif letters are generally thick-thin in design, providing interest to the eye. Serif type has a ''feel'' that is old-fashioned and warmer than sans-serif. *Sans-serif* type is plainer, with line strokes that are generally even in design and weight (no thick-thin). This is a popular style of type because of its simplicity, but it must be used with care to avoid a cold, rigid appearance.

Line spacing or leading (the amount of space between lines) is also important to the readability of your catalog. Lines should be set so the type is easy to read and so the eye travels over the page with little effort. Lines set too close together or too far apart produce both poor readability and eye strain, discouraging the customer from reading the product description or other catalog copy.

SERIF	SANS-SERIF
Korinna	Avant Garde
Souvenir	Helvetica
Palatino	Optima
Times Roman	Serif Gothic

6-84

Choosing the right size of type for headlines, body copy, and the order form is crucial to both the readability (ease of reading the page) as well as the legibility (ease of letter recognition) of your catalog. A six point type, for example (see Figure 6-85 from the Inmac catalog) should never be used for the main selling copy of a product because it is neither that readable (the eye fights to distinguish each line and travel easily along the page) nor that legible (the letters are not easily recognized for an extended period of time without strain). Nine point type (see Figure 6-86, also from the Inmac catalog) is much more desirable because the eye easily travels over each line. Each letter is instantly recognizable — the eye can and wants to sustain the visual path through which the type is leading it. Readable-sized type is generally in eight or nine point.

Here are some suggestions to help you select the right style of type for your catalog:

1. **Value catalogs** should select no-nonsense type to correspond with their approach to value pricing.
2. **High-ticket** catalogs need a softer, friendlier approach. Fancier, scrolled type can be used for accents — but still only sparingly. Body copy should be neat, clean, and crisp.
3. **Electronic and high-tech** catalogs can use modern, plain type for a high-tech effect. But do not use electronic computer typestyles for body copy: they are hard to read. Again, stick to clean, crisp type.

Description	Color	Line Width	Inmac Order #	Price-Pkg. of 5 1–4	5–9	10–19
Paper/Water Base Compatible with HP plotter numbers: 7220A/B, 7221A/B, 7225A/B, 7470A, 7475A, 7580A, 7585A & 9872A/B; Sweet•P and other similar plotters.	Red	.3mm*	6001-1	$6.95	$6.25	$5.85
	Blue	.3mm*	6001-2	$6.95	$6.25	$5.85
	Green	.3mm*	6001-3	$6.95	$6.25	$5.85
	Black	.3mm*	6001-4	$6.95	$6.25	$5.85
	Brown	.3mm*	6001-5	$6.95	$6.25	$5.85
	Violet	.3mm*	6001-6	$6.95	$6.25	$5.85
	Yellow	.3mm*	6001-7	$6.95	$6.25	$5.85
Film/Transparency-Permanent Compatible with HP Plotter numbers: 7220A/B, 7221A/B, 7225A/B, 7470A & 9872A/B; and other similar plotters.	Red	.3mm**	6002-1	$6.95	$6.25	$5.85
	Blue	.3mm**	6002-2	$6.95	$6.25	$5.85
	Green	.3mm**	6002-3	$6.95	$6.25	$5.85
	Black	.3mm**	6002-4	$6.95	$6.25	$5.85
	Brown	.3mm**	6002-5	$6.95	$6.25	$5.85
	Violet	.3mm**	6002-6	$6.95	$6.25	$5.85
	Yellow	.3mm**	6002-7	$6.95	$$6.25	$5.85
Ballpoint/Paper Compatible with HP 7470A, 7475A, 7580A, 7585A, 9872A/B and other similar plotters.	Red	Standard Line	6003-1	$16.95	$15.25	$13.95
	Blue	Standard Line	6003-2	$16.95	$15.25	$13.95
	Green	Standard Line	6003-3	$16.95	$15.25	$13.95
	Black	Standard Line	6003-4	$16.95	$15.25	$13.95

6-85

Imagine yourself in the conference room. Your colleagues and supervisor just sat through two visual presentations. Now it's your turn. You hope their response is favorable.

You introduce your topic, wondering if you'll lose them with the dry statistics you're about to present. Your palms start to sweat.

You turn on the overhead projector. Your first 4 transparencies are typed summaries of what you intend to cover.

Two people twist in their seats. Someone puts down a cup of coffee. Someone else coughs.

You put your next transparency in the projector. A simple bar chart created on your plotter with Inmac plotter pens. The color is incredibly brilliant.

You sense a subtle mood change and steal a quick glance across the room.

To your relief, the fidgeting has stopped. All eyes are on the screen.

You begin to address the chart, and now the room comes alive. Questions fly, a colleague takes notes, your supervisor makes a point based on your graph.

You move to the next transparency...a color curve showing sales growth by product group. The colors are richer, more vibrant than any graph they've ever seen. Their attention is 100% yours.

6-86

Proofreader's Marks and Meanings

Symbol	Meaning	Example	Corrected
e	Take out	This is easy(?) e	This is easy
(e)	Delete and close up	This is(not)easy. (e)	This is easy.
#	Insert space (air)	This is^easy. #	This is easy.
eq#	Equal space	This^is^easy eq#	This is easy.
⁐	Close up	This ⁐ is easy	This is easy.
‿	Less space between words	This‿is‿easy.	This is easy.
tr	Transpose letters	This (si) easy	This is easy.
tr	Transpose words	is easy (This)	This is easy.
wf	Wrong style of type	This (**is easy.**)	This is easy.
lc	Set in lower case	T(HIS) is easy. lc	This is easy.
ls	Letter space	This is e a s y.	This is easy.
caps	Set in caps	this is easy. caps	THIS is easy.
sc	Set in small caps	THIS is easy. sc	THIS IS EASY.
ital	Set in italic type	*This* is easy. ital	*This is easy.*
rom	Set in roman type	(*This is easy.*) rom	This is easy.
bf	Set in bold face	This is easy. bf	This **is easy.**
stet	Let it stand	This is (easy.) e stet	This is easy.
sp	Spell out	This is (e-z.) sp	This is easy.
¶	Start paragraph	¶ This is easy.	This is easy.
no ¶	No paragraph	This is easy.	This is easy.
|←	Flush left	|←This is easy.	This is easy.
⊓	Raise	This is easy.	This is easy.

Symbol	Meaning	Example	Corrected
⊔	Lower	This⌊is⌋easy.	This is easy.
⊏	Move left	⊏ This is easy.	This is easy.
⊐	Move right	This is easy. ⊐	This is easy.
‖	Align type	This is easy. ‖	This is easy.
═	Straighten line	This is easy. ═	This is easy.
⊙	Insert period	This is easy; ⊙	This is easy.
(,)	Insert comma	This is easy. (,)	This is easy,
(:)	Insert colon	This is easy. (:)	This is easy:
(;)	Insert semicolon	This is easy. (;)	This is easy;
∨'	Insert apostrophe	Thiss easy.	This's easy.
∨" ∨"	Insert quotation marks	∨"This is easy.∨"	"This is easy."
=/	Insert hyphen	This is easy. =/	This is easy-
!∨	Insert exclamation mark	This is easy!	This is easy!
?∨	Insert question mark	This is easy?	This is easy?
(?)	Query for author	This is easy.(?)	Oh yeh!
[/]	Insert brackets	[This is easy.]	[This is easy.]
(/)	Insert parenthesis	(/) This is easy.(/)	(This is easy.)
□	Indent 1 em	□ This is easy.	This is easy.
□□	Indent 2 ems	□□ This is easy.	This is easy.
X	Broken type	X This is easy.	This is easy.
ok w/c	OK "with corrections"		
ok a/c	OK "as corrected"		

Three areas of concern when reviewing a layout:

1. How *will the type reproduce* against the background design?
2. What color will the type be printed in — and *is this color suitable for easy reading*?
3. Is the type legible?

1. Backgrounds. When striving for creativity, designers sometimes prepare layouts with bold colors and designs against which type can be lost. Because of the number of products that must be printed per catalog page, most type is set in six point or eight point or nine point size — which is small. Deep-colored backgrounds, such as navy blue, burgundy, or dark grey, can create havoc when this small type is reproduced against them. When a layout is submitted for approval, the type is indicated as thin lines drawn against the background (either in black, indicating overprinting, or in white, indicating drop-out). But when type is set, the thin lines turn into blocks which create a completely different (and sometimes unattractive) appearance. Thus a layout which seemed attractive, no longer is.

Blocks of type placed against dark backgrounds must be reproduced in drop-out white type. Picture six small blocks of small type reproduced on a page, dropped out of a four-color separation. When running on high-speed equipment, this size type will ''fill in'' and reproduce out of register. This type will contain hues of the different processing colors, which means the color plates are out of exact alignment and the copy will be difficult to read. If the designer has called for horizontal or diagonal patterns as background for the type, the color goes from dark to light to pure white, also making type reproduction difficult. The leading (pronounced leding, and indicating spacing between lines of type) can ease this problem to some extent.

2. Type Color. When designers tire of black type on every page they get creative by specifying colored type such as light grey (30 per cent of black), mustard or yellow. Now a problem of readability must be faced. Small type not only carries less weight and impact in these colors, but also reproduces badly because the colors diminish the type's quality. In a small size type, it is wise to use Gothic typefaces. Gothic (or sans serif types) have no contrasting heavy or light strokes or crosslines at the ends of the strokes. Gothic typefaces have an overall even weight with little contrast between the thick and thin strokes. Helvetica, Futura, and New Gothic fall in this family. If serif faces are used, a designer must consider appropriate leading and even spacing between letters to enhance readability.

3. Legibility is affected greatly by leading and lettering spaces. To establish a mood, a designer may choose a serif typeface with large ascenders or descenders (vertical strokes). If the face is delicate and the type must reproduce in small sizes, the serifs can fill in or break off, giving the type an unfinished appearance. In certain types, ascenders and descenders touch, giving the type an artistic but untidy appearance. Additional leading can clean up the look. It's sometimes necessary to add space between words or letters for better readability.

Proofing Your Copy

Besides choosing a typestyle that ensures legibility, you must ensure that your set copy is correct. The typesetter will send you a galley proof or ''proofs'' (a copy of the type before it is printed for reproduction). This is the time to proofread your copy carefully, making all changes, deletions, and additions. In fact, you may need to have more than one proof pulled to make sure all the corrections are made and the type will fit the designated area. Figures 6-81 and 6-82 are proofreaders' marks. They are common to the art, copy, and typesetting worlds, so their use is important when correcting your proofs.

Seven Hints To Keep You AND The Typesetter Happy

To get error-free typesetting for yourself and goodwill from your typesetter, here are a few hints to follow.

1. Submit typewritten, double-spaced copy. Handwritten copy usually costs more because it's harder to read and consequently takes more time to typeset.
2. Proofread your copy carefully. Check for uniform style of punctuation, spelling, capitalization, indentation, and so on. Changes you make to your copy after it is typeset are ''author's alterations'' (known as AA's) for which you will be charged extra.
3. Give the typesetter a layout. It will help as a guideline to what you want to accomplish.
4. If space is at a premium, remember that copy flushed left or right usually takes up more lines than justified copy (when both left and right margins are flush).
5. Do not let anyone — not typesetters, not layout artists, not anyone — talk you into a typestyle that is hard to read. It will hurt sales.
6. Do not be talked into hard-to-find type. Usually the person selling it to you is making an extra profit.

7. Do not be misled that big point type (thirty point, seventy-two point) is more expensive than smaller type (eight point, ten point). It isn't.

Typography should be the concern of both the art and copy people, but also the merchandiser. Attractive, readable type helps sell products, too.

Chapter 7

The Guarantee . . . What Is Its Role?

To Build Company Credibility and Customer Confidence!

The guarantee is important because it symbolizes trustworthiness, builds confidence, and reflects the company's attitude toward its customers and its own products. When customers read the guarantee, they feel they can order with confidence — that what they have seen and read about a product in the catalog can be believed because the cataloger has a real stake in every customer's satisfaction. It breaks down the customer's resistance to ordering because of concerns over fit, quality, workability, color matching, or just plain change of mind. A strong guarantee also tells the customer that the quality expected is what the customer is going to receive, and — if there are any problems — that money will be refunded, credit will be given, and products can be exchanged.

In convincing the customer that there is no risk in the purchase of a product previously untried, unseen, and untouched, ''GUARANTEED'' is one terrific, magical word. Your guarantee policies and how they are presented can mean the difference between the customer's writing an order or throwing the catalog away. When your buyer-beware-educated audience sees the word ''guaranteed,'' it can feel more secure. When your customers read your particular guarantee, they will decide whether it covers their particular needs.

Are you leery of giving a strong, full money-back guarantee? Do you feel you'll receive too many returns? Will customers take advantage of you? Don't be afraid of giving the strongest guarantee your product line will allow. The stronger the guarantee, the greater the number of orders you'll receive because the customer will trust you and feel confident in your products and company. Returns won't mount up because of a strong guarantee; in fact, they won't be any higher than with a weak guarantee. As long as you are truthful, not overly zealous in your claims, and represent the product well, you have very little to worry about. Most customers will not take advantage of your goodwill. For one thing, it is too much trouble to return goods or write about problems. But, again, if you represent the product fairly, the customer will treat you fairly, too — that's just human nature.

What Do You Guarantee?

The answer may seem obvious — the product, of course! And the product is the typical reason for and subject of a guarantee. The product is the major concern of both the customer and the cataloger; it is what is being sold and bought. The product isn't in the customer's hand for inspection when it is being purchased, so it is possible for some dissatisfaction to occur upon receipt. On the other hand, the product may be perfectly satisfactory upon receipt but not after it has been tried. Or maybe it does not function properly — a computer pen could leak, a kitchen slicer not adjust, a tomato seed not come up, a piece of clothing not fit — or steak could be tough. Do you want to cover all of the above possibilities, or limit the possibilities?

And is there anything else you want to include in your guarantee? What about service — delivery — packaging — price?

Guarantee for specific time period

Service to your customer starts right in your catalog with honest and complete product presentation and representation. An "800" number and the option of charge cards or in-house credit are other important service factors. Other considerations of service are: being polite, communicative, and informative on the phone when a customer calls to place an order or make a complaint; giving the customer a reasonable option of product substitution or refund when the product ordered is no longer available; offering a gift-wrapping service or method of return packaging for difficult-to-handle products when making a return. What do you offer in service . . . can you guarantee it?

Delivery is a terribly important mail order factor and the biggest challenge for the cataloger today. Catalogs have become very successful in visual presentation and relating product information. In many instances they do a better job than a retail store. But the time it takes for the customer to receive the product after placing an order is a deterrent to sales. If the product is ordered through regular mail, it will generally be fifteen days or more before receipt.

If ordered by phone, general consumer catalog products will take up to ten days or more to arrive. Some business-to-business catalogs can deliver within five days or less because of strategically placed distribution centers. Turnaround time within your plant becomes critical to timely product delivery. Special delivery services, may be added to "buy" time, too.

Packaging of the product is intrinsic to its safe arrival. Mail order demands are different from retail demands. With some exceptions for the image you desire and the type of products you carry, packaging for beauty's sake can be kept to a minimum. In retail stores the packaging is sometimes what must attract the customer. In mail order, catalogs sell the product. Many times a plain box or poly bag is all that is needed for an individual product. The important factor is that the shipping box be substantial enough to sustain the rigors of the U.S. mail or other shipping means. Nothing is more disappointing or more irritating to the customer than receiving a damaged product due to inadequate packaging. Can you guarantee your packaging?

Price is of vital importance and interest to the customer. It can also be a major concern to the cataloger when suppliers raise their prices. Guaranteeing the price for a specific period of time assures customers. But it can also act as an incentive for them to place their orders, as well as providing protection to you.

All of these elements can be included in a guarantee, if you want. Including them will make a stronger, more complete guarantee and will build customer confidence. And remember, a guarantee is one of the most important factors within a catalog because it reflects your company's attitude toward your customers and your products! It should tell the customer in a credible way that the company offers good products and that your service is dependable. *A strong guarantee, worded well and positioned properly, is a major persuasive element in giving the customer enough confidence to place an order.*

The Basic Guarantee . . . Two Approaches

There are a lot of different guarantees, but there are only two basic structures to build upon — *unconditional* and *conditional*. The base you build upon depends on how confident you are of your product and the other elements you choose to include: service, delivery, packaging, price. Or the limitations which you choose to impose: time, exchange, product use, or exceptions. The type of product carried can influence your guarantee policy in several different ways. If you sell animal vaccine, for example, federal law prohibits its return, so requesting that the customer return it before receiving a refund would be useless. Personalized products, as well as fresh or frozen food products, have little benefit if returned. Large pieces of furniture or valuable pieces of art may have to be packaged a certain way to insure their safe return, so you may wish to provide help in packaging or instructions for sending. Or perhaps your products are low-end retail and therefore not worth the cost of returning or rehandling in your own plant. Or maybe you simply wish to know why the customer is returning the product so you can help prevent future returns.

Unconditional Guarantee means exactly what it says: no conditions are placed on the customer's satisfaction with what is being guaranteed. The customer may return the product for any reason. The product may be defective, or not the right color or size, or — the customer may simply no longer want the product. A truly unconditional guarantee will also offer the choice of a cash refund, charge card credit, or an exchange for the same or a different product. No limitations are placed.

The Unconditional, Unlimited Time Guarantee.

Eddie Bauer (Figure 7-1) states a strong, simple, unconditional guarantee. Note particularly the one word which has been used with effective psychology: *will*. ''Every item we sell *will* give you complete satisfaction . . .'' Most companies would say ''*must* give you complete satisfaction,'' which implies that there might be some doubt. ''Will'' leaves no doubt; it says, ''Our products are tops!'' The company places this guarantee on page two and on the back of the ordering envelope. *Eddie Bauer promotes the guarantee with deceptively simple, subtle wording and with positioning . . . creating an extremely strong impression.*

Keep it simple!

OUR GUARANTEE

Every item we sell will give complete satisfaction or you may return it for a full refund.

7-1

Bird 'n Hand (Figure 7-2), a catalog dealing primarily in bird seed, also gives an unconditional guarantee, highlighted on an order form panel under ''Extra Customer Benefits.'' It would seem that bird seed might be a difficult product to guarantee, but Bird 'n Hand guarantees that ''If, *for any reason*, our Pure Seed Bird Feeds do not live up to your expectation, we will refund your purchase price in full.'' And in the letter from owner Len Short, another guarantee is given: ''. . .almost 100% edible, and *guaranteed to attract a wonderful variety of birds*.'' Mr. Short has to have a lot of confidence in his product to make that kind of guarantee. With a product of this nature, which is competing with other varieties that can easily be found in supermarkets, discount stores and garden shops, you must give a powerful guarantee in order to convince the customer to purchase from your catalog instead.

- **100% Guarantee**
  If, *for any reason,* our Pure Seed Bird Feeds do not live up to your expectation, we will refund your purchase price in full.

7-2

Three other highly competitive and difficult products to sell by mail are wigs, crafts, and shoes. Figures 7-3 and 7-4 are guarantees from catalogs representing these product categories. Figure 7-3 is from Eva Gabor Wigs by Paula. This guarantee is no doubt the company's strongest motivational sales tool. The guarantee is completely unconditional — no strings attached, no time limit. There is NO RISK . . . the product must satisfy the customer completely . . . you can get your money back at any time, just ask. And Paula's tells you this is not only their guarantee; it is also the philosophy of the company. YOU are the most important consideration. All doubts about ordering are overcome.

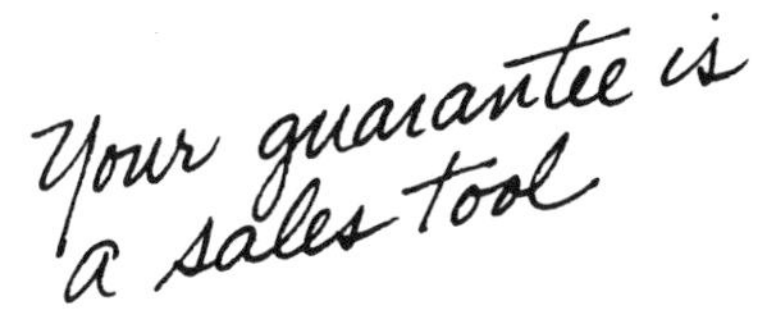
Your guarantee is a sales tool

Our Unconditional Guarantee

You take NO risk. Everything you order MUST live up to YOUR expectations. If you are not satisfied with ANY item for ANY reason, return it for prompt refund or exchange, whichever you prefer. You MUST be satisfied when you shop with WIGS BY PAULA!

7-3

Figure 7-4 is the guarantee from Herrschner's Quality Needlecrafts, a company which has been in business since 1899. Note the underlined areas. Not only is your satisfaction guaranteed — no matter what; they will also refund your money in full, plus "any transportation charges you have paid," and you can "return to us at OUR expense." Competition has been displaced, customer confidence built, company credibility established.

GUARANTEE OF SATISFACTION

Herrschners guarantees you must be satisfied! If for any reason you are not, return merchandise and we will exchange it or refund your money in full including shipping and handling charges.

7-4

Executive Shoes publishes the Wright Arch Preserver Shoes catalog. "Shoes of quality . . . that provide superb COMFORT for the normal foot." These are wonderful-sounding words. The catalog devotes two pages to a special letter from the sales manager and to details about company history and caring craftsmanship, making a very readily available product like shoes sound special indeed. But because shoes are so difficult to sell by mail (the customer worries about fit and the ultimate comfort), an exceptionally strong guarantee is given. Here is the company's guarantee as stated in the sales manager's letter:

> "Your satisfaction is GUARANTEED UNCONDITIONALLY! Any shoes may be returned for *ANY REASON . . . AT ANY TIME* . . . for exchange or refund!"

Any hesitation which may have arisen is quickly dispelled — customers need only make their selections and place their orders.

Include it in a letter

A business-to-business catalog company that has a powerful guarantee is American Computer Supply. Figure 7-5 shows how prominently their guarantee is displayed at the top of page three. If any of their computer supplies do not "perform to your satisfaction," just call and tell them — they will replace or exchange the product, or refund your money. The crowded computer supply catalog field has been tamed. Orders will be placed because of this unconditional guarantee.

The Oxford Company, a personalized stationery catalog serving the law profession, makes a strong, simple guarantee the main attraction for their discerning audience in a personal letter from Bill Oxford. Figure 7-6 illustrates how bold type and a half-point rule within the letter make the guarantee special. This strong guarantee, an order re-run or money fully refunded, backs the company's "Customer satisfaction is important to us" statement. Attorneys are hard to please and the first to take advantage of a guarantee such as this. The Oxfords believe in their product — it must be quality-produced with no personalizing errors, or profit goes out the window. This is a good, simply stated guarantee brilliantly presented to stand out and reassure the customer.

The Unconditional Limited Time Guarantee

A majority of catalogers stipulate a time period within which a customer must express dissatisfaction with a product in order to receive a refund or other desired action. The time requirements can be anything the cataloger wishes as long as they are stated clearly and in a reasonably conspicuous place for the customer to see. The most commonly applied time periods are: 10 days, two weeks, 30 days, one year. All product types can be successfully guaranteed within a specific time limit — even categories such as seeds and plants

Read What Our Customers Say:

"Very glad to deal with someone who understands my job and the equipment I use." **S.B., Roseville, MI.** "I especially like the fact that you offer name-brand products at discount prices, and give premiums, too! It's a great deal. .**J.E. Eugene, OR.** "Thanks for making the delivery date I needed. My personal sales rep. handled everything well, and really was nice." **G.K., Albany, GA.** "Placed my order yesterday and got it today. Thanks American, I was down to my last ribbon!" **J. G., Orlando, FL.** "Talk about coming through — my job needed 10 cartons of paper and **same day** delivery. Your same-day courier service saved the day!" **M.M., Tulsa, OK.**

FROM AMERICAN COMPUTER SUPPLY

Gifts For Home Or Office . . .
Earn Yours Free From American Computer Supply

Earn your choice of the great items shown here, absolutely FREE! Just place your order for the dollar value shown below and tell us which item you would like. Take your pick, from a handy office pencil sharpener to any size RCA color TV you'd like. They're all FREE with the appropriate dollar amount puchase. Place your order today — call TOLL-FREE 1-800-527-0832. In Texas, call (214) 243-3232.

A. **FREE when you "Bank" Your Premium Credits:** Any size G.E. or RCA solid-state color TVs, from 10" portables to wall-size projection video. Call for details.
B. **FREE With $2000 Purchase:** AM/FM Stereo Cassette Player. Gives rich sound, saves space. Records direct off radio, too!
C. **FREE With $1000 Purchase:** La Machine Food Processor. Full function, 2.5 qt. gourmet helper; slices, shreds, chops & blends.
D. **FREE With $700 Purchase:** Digital AM/FM Clock Radio/Telephone. Music alarm, snooze, AFC, battery back-up. Auto redial phone.
E. **FREE With $500 Purchase:** Digital AM/FM Clock Radio. Wake to music, snooze, AFC. 100% solid state. Large LED read-out.
F. **FREE With $400 Purchase:** 10-Cup Drip Coffeemaker. Makes 1-10 cups of tea or coffee. Mini-miser basket. Rugged, easy to clean.
G. **FREE With $250 Purchase:** Electric Pencil Sharpener. Solid steel cutters last long.
H. **FREE With $250 Purchase:** Titleist Golf Balls. One dozen of America's finest.
J. **FREE With $200 Purchase:** Poly Pop Popcorn Popper. Makes up to 4 qts. See-thru cover is dishwasher safe.
K. **FREE With $100 Purchase:** Pocket Calculator. Multi-function, memory too!

Here's How To Earn Your FREE Vacation Travel With American Computer Supply

1. When you purchase your computer supplies from American Computer Supply, just ask your personal sales representative to "bank" your Premium Credit Bonus Points* towards vacation travel.
2. Once you decide where you'd like to travel and when, just ask your personal sales representative to obtain a Trip Quote for your exact plans.
3. We'll give you all of the travel details you need, and tell you how many Premium Credit Bonus Points* you'll need to earn your FREE vacation travel.

That's all it takes! You'll be on your way to great vacation travel, FREE from American Computer Supply. All prices and offers subject to change or may be discontinued without prior notice.

IN 1903 JOHN DEWBERRY, THE great grandfather of Bill Oxford, opened a stationery engraving company in Birmingham, Alabama. His goal was to produce the finest quality engraved stationery available. With hard work and a dedication to quality and service, John felt his business venture could survive.

It did survive. For more than 80 years the art of producing quality stationery has been handed down from father to son. John Dewberry had no way of knowing that a family tradition would emerge from his humble enterprise.

The Oxford Company is the culmination of this proud tradition. But we don't rest on our history; we acknowledge it with harder work, better service, newer products and higher quality.

Seals Oxford, President
Bill Oxford, Vice President

Presented in this catalog are the products we supply to the legal community. Each is backed by a simple guarantee which states;

If for any reason you are dissatisfied with your order we will either re-run it or return your money. Customer satisfaction is important to us.

So please, consider our company the next time you place an order for stationery items. Our experienced sales department will gladly send you samples and assist you with placing your orders. And if you have any questions regarding our company, feel free to contact me or my father. We are never too busy to talk to you, because the backbone of our family tradition is our customers — and we never forget that.

I look forward to receiving your order.

Very truly yours,

Bill Oxford

7-6

that need an extended time period to allow the customer to test the product.

Figure 7-7 is Clothkit's guarantee. This catalog sells mainly kits for clothing. Clothing kits raise the difficulty of customers not knowing what the end result (or end benefit) will be until they have completed the kit. Clothkit goes all the way — without question they will refund or exchange even after the product has been used; you need only to return it. The wording qualifying this policy is simple: "The kit may even be sewn or partially sewn! Our wish is that you be completely satisfied with your Clothkit." The two negatives, they don't pay postage, and the 30-day limitation are softened because of the genuine and considerate tone of the guarantee. The headline, "Money Back Guarantee," builds company credibility and customer confidence immediately. Note the underlined portions in the guarantee. The words and phrasing are thoughtful, not demanding or dry. People respond to this type of communication. Clothkit will be rewarded for this thoughtfulness with orders.

Considerate tone

MONEY BACK GUARANTEE. We will credit or refund (without question or delay) the full amount (less postage) of any kit or knitwear you wish to return. The kit may even be sewn or partially sewn! Our wish is that you be completely satisfied with your Clothkit. We ask only that the return be made within 30 days from the receipt of merchandise. (We are also happy to exchange styles, colours or sizes when possible.)

7-7

Golden Moments (Figure 7-8) has a good guarantee but takes a slightly different approach which adds a completely different tone. They start off with a bang: "YOUR SATISFACTION IS GUARANTEED. Order with assurance." This is strong wording that quickly builds customer confidence. But the next sentence ("Our items are chosen for quality and accurately represented") — even though it is meant to give reassurance to the lead headline and sentence — does just the opposite. The clipped wording and inconclusiveness of the statement result in an unbelievable and cold communication. Much more appropriate phrasing might be: "We strive to select only high-quality merchandise and to represent each clearly and realistically." Despite the time period of only 14 days, the coverage is so complete that it results in a fine guarantee.

YOUR SATISFACTION IS GUARANTEED.
Order with assurance. Our items are chosen for quality and accurately represented. If, for any reason, you are not delighted with your selection, simply return it within 14 days for a full, prompt refund of purchase price (except shipping & handling), no questions asked.
Our Policy is to process all orders promptly. All credit card orders are processed upon credit approval. If we are out of stock on an item, we shall notify you promptly and we guarantee shipment within 60 days.
We Reserve the right to substitute merchandise of equal or better quality.
Warranties: Where applicable tne manufacturer's written warranty is enclosed with the product. A free copy is available on request prior to purchase. Write to Warranty Requests, at address above.

7-8

READ THIS FANTASTIC GUARANTEE
It applies to everything in This Catalog
Try it, use it. Do anything you like except break it. Keep it for up to 30 days. If you decide not to keep it, return it undamaged for a 100% refund

7-9

New Horizons puts a little zip into their wording and it comes off well. (See Figure 7-9.) They sell their guarantee by the wording they use. They direct you to "Read this" and tell you it is "Fantastic" and "applies to everything." They encourage you to "Try it, use it." Even the one negative about product use is stated so it is not a negative: "Do anything you like except break it." Most important is the positioning of the two most critical elements of the guarantee: (1) identifying what it is in a bold headline, "Fantastic Guarantee," and (2) telling the coverage at the end, "100% refund." The beginning and end of any copy presentation are the natural areas the customer's eye automatically goes to first. If what is seen in those two areas is attractive, then further action is taken, whether it is reading the full copy presentation, looking at the products carried, or placing an order. The important fact is — the customer continues to look at *your* catalog!

Customer reads beginning and end first

Moore Computer Forms and Supplies catalog has a good, 30-day guarantee to cover the products they carry. The headline wording lets the customers know that it's a clean, 100 percent guarantee and that they can order with full confidence. The words "No-Nonsense" immediately clear the air, telling customers no red tape is involved in getting their money back if they are not satisfied. The copy following states the stipulations of the guarantee. It asks that the customer call an "800" number for a "Return Authorization Number" before returning the merchandise. This request is a plus, too — only the customer doesn't know it. Getting a Return Authorization Number allows the company to process the credit or refund more quickly because: (1) when the number is assigned, it has been registered in the company's computer system and is ready for acceptance; (2) when the returned merchandise arrives at the company's warehouse, it can be acted upon much more expeditiously because the number tells what action needs to be taken; and (3) it assures the customer of receiving the proper credit amount, cash refund, or other desired action. This is a fine service!

Advantages: Builds strong customer confidence; builds company credibility; presents no negatives; establishes product credibility; promotes ordering.	**Disadvantages**: Company and products carried subjected to high quality expectations.

Conditional Guarantee

The conditional guarantee promises to completely satisfy the customer by refunding, crediting, or exchanging *if* the personalizing mistake was the catalog company's error; *if* you have not used the product; and so on. The most commonly seen conditional guarantee is the one excluding personalized products.

Neiman-Marcus (Figure 7-10) says: "YOUR COMPLETE SATISFACTION IS OUR AIM" . . . but "THE EXCEPTIONS TO THIS are personalized items, which cannot be returned unless incorrectly personalized." What a negative! And a glance through this beautiful catalog, with hundreds of products retailing up to $250,000.00, reveals that only two products offered were personalized, one a $21.00 engraved pocket knife! There is another negative in this guarantee which is not so obvious: "You may return, *for full credit,* merchandise . . ." Neiman-Marcus evidently doesn't even give a cash refund. That's what this guarantee is saying.

YOUR COMPLETE SATISFACTION IS OUR AIM

It is Neiman-Marcus policy that you may return, for full credit, merchandise with which you are not satisfied. THE EXCEPTIONS TO THIS are personalized items, which cannot be returned unless incorrectly personalized.

7-10

Another negative limited guarantee is that of Olympic Sales Company, which puts out a wholesale catalog of calculators, personal computers, software, accessories, copiers, etc. This guarantee presents a subhead, "Warranty Service," under which the customer is advised that "We take pleasure and pride in selling well known and established major brands of equipment. These firms each guarantee and/or warranty their respective equipment." Below, and in bold type, the customer is notified (forewarned?) that "OLYMPIC SALES COMPANY DOES NOT GUARANTEE OR WARRANTY

ANY OF THE PRODUCTS SOLD OR OFFERED BY THEM. DO NOT RETURN DEFECTIVE MERCHANDISE TO OLYMPIC SALES, IT WILL BE REFUSED.'' This is an unbelievable turnoff! But limited guarantees do not need to be so negative. Rewording could help a lot: ''One way Olympic Sales keeps its prices so low is by reducing the product handling. Should you have a problem or need to return a product, please deal directly with the manufacturers.'' This is a little longer, but it has ceased to be a turnoff. It lets customers know that Olympic Sales has low prices and cares about their satisfaction by telling them how to take care of their problems.

The limited guarantee of the Wine Enthusiast catalog simply states the restrictions (Figure 7-11): ''. . .return merchandise in new condition, complete with all packing materials and your receipt. Sorry, no returns on food items.'' Even though there are some negative connotations simply because of the limitations, attention

A GUARANTEE OF SATISFACTION: You must be completely satisfied with your purchase or simply return the item within 10 days for a quick refund, exchange or charge card credit. We only ask that you return merchandise in new condition, complete with all packing materials and your receipt. Sorry, no returns on food items. Not responsible for typographical errors.

7-11

Satisfaction Guaranteed

At Montgomery Ward, we believe a loyal customer is more important than an individual sale . . . we want to keep you satisfied so you'll keep coming back!

If, when you receive your purchase, you find that it is not completely satisfactory, return it. We will gladly exchange it, or if you prefer, refund the price and transportation and handling charges (within Continental United States) you paid.

If, after you have used your purchase, you find that it is not completely satisfactory, simply let us know what is wrong. We will strive to assure your satisfaction by means of our special warranties or make an adjustment in cash, credit exchange or repair.

MONTGOMERY WARD & COMPANY

7-12

is not called to them with bold or capital letters and they are not worded in an offensive manner.

Montgomery Ward gives an unconditional guarantee on one condition — that the product not be used. Figure 7-12 shows how positively this guarantee is presented with a bold headline of "Satisfaction Guaranteed." The first paragraph strokes the customer: "we believe a loyal customer is more important than an individual sale . . . we want to keep you satisfied so you'll keep coming back!" The second paragraph heartily reinforces this positive tone by promising to refund the money or exchange the merchandise. The company goes one step further by refunding the "transportation and handling charges (within Continental United States) you paid." Then the third paragraph lowers the boom with the condition: "If, after you have used your purchase . . . we will strive to assure your satisfaction by means of our special warranties or make an adjustment in cash, credit, exchange or repair." All this is meant to be for the customer's benefit, but it sounds as if major negotiations will be entered into and that product usage can be somewhat hazardous to your health! How much better to have declared warranty coverage and to have said something like this: "Even once the product has been used, we strive to assure your satisfaction. Just contact our customer service department so we can make an adjustment in cash, credit, exchange or repair."

Advantages:
Allows cataloger to select desired products or services to be limited in guarantee; time period pricing allows cataloger to plan more efficiently.

Disadvantages:
Can be negative; produces customer hesitation to order; deters sales of products which are restricted in any way.

Three Different Approaches Where Personalization Is a Factor.

Joan Cook has a gift and novelty catalog that is 112 pages long and carries somewhere around 450 products. Under two percent of the products are personalized. Here is the company's guarantee as seen in Figure 7-13. The headline says it all. "No Risk Guarantee . . . Full Satisfaction or Full Refund." It is straightforward, easily seen, builds credibility instantly, and gives complete confidence to the customer. The copy goes on to back up this feeling even more: "You may return any item for full refund of the purchase price, for any reason. This includes personalized items." What fine credibility for the company and assurance to the customer! The reference to personalized items is not lost on mail order buyers.

No Risk Guarantee...
Full Satisfaction or
Full Refund

You may return any item for full refund of the purchase price, for any reason. This includes personalized items. All we ask is that you return products unused and undamaged, along with your receipt, within 60 days of delivery. We are bound by the U.S. Post Office and the magazines in which we advertise to live up to this guarantee.

MEMBER: New England Mail Order Association, U.S. Post Office Mail User's Council, Chamber of Commerce, Parcel Post Association.

REFERENCE: American National Bank of Fort Lauderdale, Dun & Bradstreet.

7-13

OUR GUARANTEE: If, for any reason, you are not totally satisfied with our merchandise, return it within 30 days and we will replace it or refund the purchase price, whichever you prefer. Bathing suits or items which have been altered, laundered, or personalized are, regretfully, unreturnable.

7-14

OUR GUARANTEE

You must be fully satisfied with every item you buy from Walter Drake. If you are not pleased with your purchase for any reason, you may return it for a full cash refund.

7-15

Knight's Ltd. Catalogue sells basically casual apparel. Their guarantee is boldly stated on the back of the ordering envelope. Of the over 200 products offered in their 72-page catalog, about 30 are personalized. Their guarantee is shown in Figure 7-14. Again, they guarantee the customer's satisfaction with this exception: "Bathing suits or items which have been altered, laundered, or personalized are, regretfully, unreturnable." This is a big negative to end up with for such a small portion of the products carried. Ordering is immediately discouraged.

The totally unconditional guarantee that is also the simplest comes from the catalog which carries the greatest number of personalized products, Walter Drake and Sons. Their catalog is 104 pages with over 600 products; approximately 25 percent, or around 145, are personalized. Here is their guarantee (Figure 7-15). The words are simple and few — no guesswork is left for the customer about any product Walter Drake carries.

The chance of a delivered product being incorrect is much greater with Walter Drake and Sons because of the number of personalized products. Joan Cook has the least chance for error because of the lowest number of personalized products and the limited amount of apparel carried. And yet Walter Drake has the strongest and most worry-free headline message, and even bothers to assure the customer that all products, including personalized, are covered by the guarantee.

Price is Guaranteed, Too.

More and more catalogs are stating a time period during which the prices quoted in the catalog are valid. This approach does a number of things. It protects the cataloger from supplier cost increases, allowing a legitimate period of time in which prices can be raised. And it subtly reminds customers that they can keep the catalog a while before ordering. Also, if they order after the stated date, perhaps they will have to pay more — this kind of message urges the customer to place an order.

Lands' End simply states on the order form: ''Prices in this catalog are guaranteed through (date).'' Trifles (a gift catalog) states its price guarantee on the back of the catalog along with other ordering information. An interesting element is added in the Trifles guarantee:

> ''All prices in this book are guaranteed through (date), except gold and silver items, which due to fluctuation of the world metals market, are subject to change without notice.''

The mention of ''without notice'' is commonly used for jewelry and flatware, and by gift catalogs carrying such products. This type of protection is needed because of the movement in price of these precious metals. Some catalogs will even give a lower price to customers if a metal's price is down considerably from when the catalog was printed.

Another kind of pricing guarantee is given by some catalogs — a comparison pricing guarantee. Customers are challenged to find a better price if they can. This may sound risky, but it's really not. Catalogers promise to refund the difference between their own

Contents of Guarantee

Keep your guarantee of satisfaction direct and to the point. Avoid legalese . . . let your lawyer read it if you must, but never let him write it.

Estin Kiger
Corporate Creative Director
Inmac
Santa Clara, CA

Price comparison guarantee

advertised price and the found lower price, with proof of discovery generally being a copy of the ad. This approach allows customers, in fact encourages customers, to place their order right now! Don't worry about looking anywhere else (including retail stores) for a lower price! This is a very clever approach. At first, the cataloger might worry that there will be an inundation of requests. But this does not happen. The increase in orders easily makes up for the few "takers" of the offer. This happens, of course, only if the products are competitively priced.

An example of a price comparison guarantee executed well within a regular 30-day guarantee is that of The Sharper Image. Figure 7-16 shows one of the three guarantees made and stated on an order form panel in The Sharper Image catalog. The guarantee headline is stated very positively: *"You get the best value. We match any advertised price."* This is so strong, the customer may not even read on for the particulars, but just place an order. If the customer does read on, what is found will be painless: ". . .just

Four reasons why you enjoy shopping more with The Sharper Image.

1. You have 30 days to make up your mind.
If not satisified, simply return the item (in new condition, please) within 30 days for a prompt, courteous refund, whatever the reason. Your satisfaction is the only judge.

2. You get the best value. We match any advertised price.
You won't see the same item advertised for less elsewhere. If you do, just send us the advertisement within 30 days of receiving the item. We'll refund or credit the difference to you.

3. You own a durable, well-made product, with a one-year quality guarantee.
We make sure every product is backed by a reputable manufacturer's service center. If you don't get prompt satisfactory service, in or out of warranty, call our Customer Relations representatives. Use the toll free Customer Relations number—800-344-5555. We'll make sure your item is fixed or replaced in a reasonable time, or your money will be refunded—up to a full year after purchase.

4. You receive the Frequent Buyers™ Reward.
By purchasing regularly, you can earn gift certificates worth $50, $150, and $300. It's easy to qualify—just save your receipts. (Full details are on the front page of this order form.)

7-16

send us the advertisement within 30 days of receiving the item. We'll refund . . . the difference to you.'' Except for a few items, the products The Sharper Image carries are not that common.

And, of course, since this is Beauty Buy Book, your satisfaction is 100% guaranteed. If you're not completely satisfied with any item you order from Beauty Buy Book, or if you find lower prices advertised anywhere, just let us know and we'll refund the difference in full.

Lowest prices and Satisfaction Guaranteed
Your complete satisfaction is guaranteed (or your money back) and so are BEAUTY BUY BOOK cosmetic prices. They're the lowest advertised prices in the marketplace. See Guarantee for full details.

THE BEAUTY BUY BOOK GUARANTEE
We guarantee that BEAUTY BUY BOOK cosmetic prices are the lowest prices advertised anywhere in the marketplace. If you find any cosmetic product advertised for less that is identical to one you purchased from BEAUTY BUY BOOK, just send us a copy of the ad, together with your BEAUTY BUY BOOK proof of purchase, on or before December 31, 1984, and we'll gladly refund the difference in purchase price.
We also guarantee your complete satisfaction with your purchase or you may return them at any time you want and we'll refund the selling price of the item or items returned.

7-17

A more commonly found category of product is cosmetics, such as carried by the catalog, Beauty Buy Book. Name brand perfume, lipstick, nail polish, powders and creams are offered. Figure 7-17 shows how the guarantee, which includes the price comparison policy, is stated in three different locations on the order form flaps and envelope. The first (a) is a letter from a company personality, Joanna King. The second paragraph of this letter is devoted to the 100 percent guarantee which includes the price comparison guarantee. Joanna states that ''if you find lower prices advertised anywhere, just let us know and we'll refund the difference in full.'' This is a nice personal message carrying reassurance to the customer. On the back of the order form (b) is another presentation of the guarantee. A great headline attracts and reassures the customer: *Lowest prices and satisfaction guaranteed.* The copy following refers the customer to the guarantee for details. On the order form flap we find (c), the full ''Beauty Buy Book Guarantee.'' A stronger and more persuasive headline could have been used. The price comparison guarantee takes precedence over the full unconditional guarantee — and rightfully so, as cosmetics are easily found in supermarkets, drugstores, department stores and beauty shops. Competition is tough. The Beauty Buy Book meets it head on.

Delivery

This subject is the most worrisome of all for catalogers. Even at its best, when the order is placed by mail, customer receipt can hardly be faster than 10 days. Some general consumer companies pride themselves in getting an order turned around in their own plants within twenty-four hours. And that is fast! Business-to-business companies strive for even faster order processing, shipping the same day the order is received. The faster you can ship, the happier your customers are going to be and the more orders you will receive. The fall and holiday seasons are especially difficult times, and customers become concerned about delivery.

Miles Kimball, a low-end gift catalog dealing in a large number of personalized products, unconditionally guarantees delivery to the customer by Christmas if the order is placed by a certain time. Figure 7-18 is the letter from Alberta Kimball appearing in the front of the catalog. Two full paragraphs, three and four, are devoted to the company's guarantees. The fourth paragraph deals solely with delivery. Orders that are *postmarked* before December 15th are unconditionally guaranteed to reach the customer before Christmas! This is strong and will bring in orders. Another long-time catalog company, L.L. Bean (privately owned since 1912), guarantees four-day delivery. Figure 7-19 shows their delivery guarantee. ''If you place your order before 5:00 p.m., Monday through Friday, it will be shipped the next business day.'' A good visual of Santa and sleigh with a Federal Express sign on the back acts as a positive credibility builder for fast delivery.

Service-oriented Inmac, a computer supplies catalog, has a special six-point presentation in its catalog. Figure 7-20 headlines, ''How to get your products fast!'' Points one through five are hints on how to fill out the order form, the importance of including your I.D. number, how credit can be received quickly, how you can save money, and how fast Inmac's order turnaround service is. This is all good company P.R., but point number six gets down to the most important aspect for the customer — delivery. ''Need it faster?'' (Almost every business person will relate immediately as it seems everything always should have been done yesterday.) Inmac comes to the rescue with: ''We'll use guaranteed overnight package service.'' The guarantee that is offered by most fast freight services now becomes Inmac's guarantee. This is clever usage of another company's service to make customers happy and build credibility for Inmac.

Business Guarantee

Guarantee of satisfaction in business-to-business catalogs is even more important than with consumer goods. It's the final clincher that assures the prospect he's making a sound business decision. It's his proof that your product and service claims are true.

Estin Kiger
Corporate Creative Director
Inmac
Santa Clara, CA

Miles Kimball Company

41 West Eighth Avenue Oshkosh, Wisconsin 54901

Fall, 1984

Dear Customer,

The coming of Christmas and the New Year to Oshkosh gives all of us at Kimball's pause to reflect on the many friends we've made during the past 50 years. We are pleased to count you among them, and to share with you the joy of the season.

To help with your gift-giving plans we are sending you this catalog collection of gifts, housewares and toys. Among these pages you'll find many new and unusual items as well as some familiar old-time favorites.

Just as we take pride in offering fast, personalized service, we feel it's important to picture and describe each item realistically and honestly. However, should you find anything to be other than you expected, you'll receive a full, prompt refund (the famous Kimball guarantee).

Because most orders are shipped within 48 hours after we receive them in Oshkosh, we unconditionally guarantee delivery to you before Christmas if your order is postmarked before Saturday, December 15th.

As you page through this catalog you will find tucked in, here and there, some recipes for Christmas fare that are nostalgic to the season. We hope you will enjoy trying some of them.

May your Christmas and New Year be full of many good things.

Sincerely,

Alberta Kimball

P.S. The October, 1983, CONSUMER REPORTS article on mail-order buying mentions Miles Kimball. You will find this report at your local public library.

P.P.S. Please keep this catalog until August, 1985. We'll try to keep all items in stock until then.

7-18

We Offer Guaranteed 4 Day Delivery

This Christmas, phone toll free for Federal Express Delivery. It is available for just $7.50 per order per address. If you place your order before 5:00 PM, Monday through Friday, it will be shipped the next business day. L. L. Bean guarantees your order to reach its destination in just four days. See order form for details. For more information and faster service, call our operators 24 hours a day, 7 days a week.

7-19

How to get your products fast!

1. **Fill out the order form completely.** Even if you're phoning or TWXing your order, having all the information in front of you will save time and prevent errors.

2. **Always include your customer I.D. code.** You'll find it on the back cover, above your name on the mailing label.

MR JOHN SAMPLE 999033
ABC COMPANY
000 FIRST STREET
ANYTOWN, ST 00000

3. **Credit is available on approval.** Speed your credit order by providing the name and address of your bank and 2 major trade references. Installment Terms: Half of invoice amount due NET 15 days; remainder due NET 30 days from invoice date.

4. **Send a check—save freight charges!** When you include a check with your order, *we* pay surface freight, within the continental U.S., on most items. IMPORTANT: See product pages for exclusions.

5. **Your order is normally shipped within hours.** Most orders under 100 lbs. are sent via UPS or USPS, FOB our distribution centers, with freight and handling added to your invoice. Orders 100 lbs. and over are shipped via our choice of common carrier.

6. **Need it faster? We'll use guaranted overnight package service.** The overnight carriers are the fastest delivery services available. Call us by noon to place your order and to confirm your location in an overnight service area.

Prices in this catalog are effective with orders received on Apr. 16, 1984 and supersede all prices in previous catalogs. Prices subject to change without notice. We reserve the right to correct typographical pricing errors.

7-20

Positioning

Positioning of the guarantee is more important than most catalogers realize. Just as a company should choose the strongest guarantee possible in order to build company credibility and customer confidence, so should it choose a strong placement of the guarantee and for the very same reason. If the customer cannot see the guarantee, it becomes ineffectual. Reassurance of a strong guarantee is a persuasive element for placing orders. What are the strategic areas? Does the type of merchandise offered make a difference as to where guarantees are placed?

Two of the most powerful places to put a guarantee are the front and back cover. Products which are especially hard to sell by mail benefit enormously from this placement. Executive Shoes, which sells Wright Arch Preserver Shoes exclusively by mail, puts its unconditional guarantee on both the front and back cover (Figure 7-21). So important is the fit of shoes to people for their everyday comfort that Executive Shoes feels it is necessary for the customer to be immediately reassured of satisfaction. This strong placement acts not only as reassurance but also as a sales tool. The guarantee is saying to the customer, "These shoes are superior in every way and are just right for you."

Yield House is less obvious with its front cover reference but nevertheless takes the opportunity to let the customer know of its guarantee. Figure 7-22 just states "Satisfaction Guaranteed" and then refers the customer to an inside page. This is good. The type of product carried, furniture and furniture kits, is readily available in retail stores. Yield House wants to get across the general message of low prices via sales and factory-direct furniture and at the same time reassure customers that quality and satisfaction are theirs.

The back cover of the Day-Timers catalog is laden with stationery products which can be found many other places. Day-Timers'

7-21

Our Annual

Winter/Spring 1985 • $1.00
Prices good through April 30, 1985
Dept. 9700, North Conway, N.H. 03860

SHOP-AT-HOME SALE!

Save even more on our low, factory-direct furniture prices!

Sale! $50 off our pine Country Entertainment Center
Page 7

Sale! Up to 20% off our pine Country Plate Rails
Page 17

Special savings on our pine Barrister Bookshelves Up to $450 off when you buy sets!
Pages 38 and 39

Sale! 50% off the Tole Pin-Up Lamp
Page 66

More than 130 sale items • More than 100 new furnishings and accessories
Order toll-free: 1-800-258-4720 • Satisfaction guaranteed. See page 26B

Your factory-direct furniture catalog.
Home of affordable pine and oak furniture and furniture kits. Since 1947.

7-22

guarantee is there, too, to meet the competition. Attention is called by a certificate border and a large, powerful headline: "100% Satisfaction Guarantee." The wording is especially good for a business-to-business catalog offering office supplies, personalized certificates, plaques, and stationery. (See Figure 7-23.)

> "You have our unconditional guarantee of satisfaction on every item you order from Day-Timers. Merchandise not acceptable for any reason (and you are the sole judge) may be returned within 30 days for prompt exchange, refund or credit, at your option. This guarantee includes even imprinted or personalized items."
>
> Robert C. Dorney, President

This is businesslike yet warm in feeling and expression. It is believable — and even more so as the president of the company signed it.

The two most common areas for guarantee placement are company/personal letter and the order form/envelope. The catalog letter is one obvious choice because it relates to the customer and the building of company credibility: hence the importance of including the guarantee. Earlier in this chapter we saw how the Miles Kimball Company devoted two paragraphs to the guarantee in Alberta Kimball's personal letter to catalog customers. Executive Shoes (Figure 7-24) devotes a full catalog page to a letter from the Sales Manager. It is packed full of credibility builders like company longevity, quality product construction, the number of satisfied customers, ordering convenience, and the company guarantee. It is an ideal place to reassure the customer. Sycom Forms and Supplies includes its guarantee as one of the five company commitments to the customer in a letter from the General Manager. Figure 7-25 shows the effectiveness of this presentation. Each commitment is underlined and within the indented area for ultimate attraction.

Typical order form/envelope positioning is seen in Figures 7-26 and 7-27. The back of the order form (Figure 7-26) becomes the envelope back when folded and it boldly carries the Orvis guarantee. On the order form (Figure 7-27), the guarantee is again stated. These are good positions as they reassure the customer when placing an order and may even be a deciding element in either placing an order or increasing the size of an order. Some catalogers feel that many potential customers get as far as the order form and yet do not place an order, from lack of confidence either in ordering by mail or in the company itself. A strong guarantee is a positive element and therefore should be beneficially placed in strategic areas such as these.

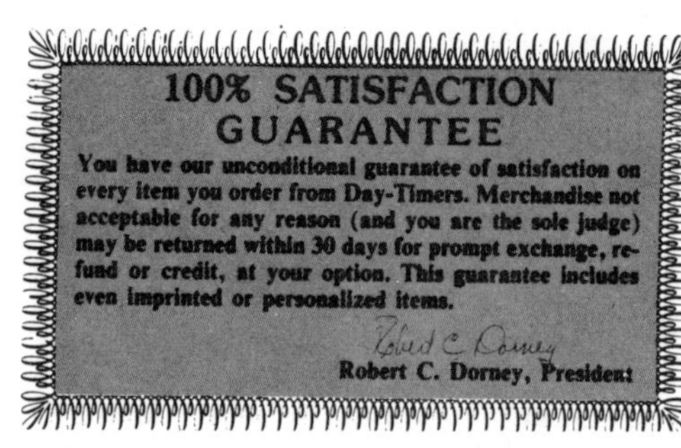

100% SATISFACTION GUARANTEE

You have our unconditional guarantee of satisfaction on every item you order from Day-Timers. Merchandise not acceptable for any reason (and you are the sole judge) may be returned within 30 days for prompt exchange, refund or credit, at your option. This guarantee includes even imprinted or personalized items.

Robert C. Dorney, President

7-23

Executive Shoes

Box 488, Brockton, Mass. 02403
Toll Free Order Line: 1-800-343-1022
Mass. Residents Call: 617-584-7360

I'm happy to know you are interested in America's finest shoes.

For 107 years, the E.T. Wright Co. has made shoes of quality in every detail. PLUS...exclusive features that provide superb COMFORT for the normal foot.

This catalog shows a wide selection of WRIGHT ARCH PRESERVER SHOES...the ONLY shoe uniquely constructed inside to fit the contours of your foot perfectly. The result is natural support and complete comfort, unlike that found in any other shoes.

On the outside, you will find WRIGHT ARCH PRESERVER quality... luxurious leathers meticulous workmanship - - born of experienced Yankee craftsmanship since 1876.

EXECUTIVE SHOES sells by mail only - - nothing but famous WRIGHT ARCH PRESERVER SHOES.

In three years, over 50,000 men have enjoyed ordering these shoes by mail because...

All orders are shipped from the Wright factory, from their stock of over 30,000 pairs.
We offer sizes from 6 to 16, widths from AAA to EEE...thousands of men who wear sizes hard to find, welcome this service.
Men like the convenience of ordering in the comfort of their homes or offices...simply by picking up the phone and calling our TOLL FREE number 1-800-343-1022.
Your satisfaction is GUARANTEED UNCONDITIONALLY! Any shoes may be returned for ANY REASON...AT ANY TIME...for exchange or refund!

We know of no shoe with the comfort...quality...satisfaction ...value - of WRIGHT ARCH PRESERVER SHOES. Try the comfort over a million men swear by. Mail or phone your order TODAY!

Cordially yours,

Jim Crispin

Jim Crispin, Sales Manager

P.S. We save on orders for 2 or more pairs, and we pass the savings on to you! Get 2 pair of Cedar Shoe Trees for $1.00 when you order ANY 2 pair of shoes.

The only company selling Wright Arch Preserver Shoes exclusively by mail.

7-24

Dear Doctor:

At SYCOM, we have tradition to uphold. We were founded almost 50 years ago dedicated to the idea of serving the business side of the nation's health care practices.

We know you are committed to giving your patients the best possible service, and we have the same commitment to you. Therefore, we:

-- Ship orders for standard forms and supplies within 24 hours after we receive the order.

-- Ship most specially imprinted forms within five working days after your order is received.

-- Make it very convenient to order. Why not pick up the telephone and call us toll-free and we'll prove it to you.

-- Provide technical assistance for you any time. Just call Joe Fass in our Customer Services Department. Joe has been consulting the business end of health care practices for 25 years.

-- Guarantee every product we sell. If you ever have any problem with a product we sell, we have two specially trained Customer Services Representatives, Mona and Sue, to help you.

Why not order today? More than 75,000 health care practices already rely on SYCOM for their professional forms and supplies. We look forward to making you part of our tradition.

Cordially,

R. E. Rehberg
General Manager

P.S. We have a new product on our back cover, Post-it Notes, we know you'll need. Once you've tried them, you'll wonder how your office did without them.

7-25

Wording

Wording can be tricky — warm, short, long, colloquial, simple, or complex. While many catalogers use very brief and simple wording, others employ a more personal approach by adopting a colloquial flavor. Can a guarantee be too long? Yes! — and therefore, not read. Can a guarantee be confusing? Yes! — especially when a company is trying to get around a condition they themselves have chosen. Can a guarantee be worded to sell? Yes! And always should be.

Food is especially hard to sell by mail to a first-time customer. Why? Because food is very personal. People tend to be especially particular about what they eat and what they serve their guests. And oftentimes food-by-mail seems quite expensive. Strong customer confidence must be built. Let's see how two food catalogs meet four very important confidence-building criteria through the guarantees they choose and the *wording* of their guarantees.

Four requirements of a customer confidence-building guarantee are met by:

1. Choosing the strongest guarantee possible.
2. Wording the guarantee appropriately for products sold.
3. Strategically placing the guarantee for customer viewing.
4. Selling confidence through the wording of the guarantee.

DETACH HERE

Bottoms-Up Glasses

NEW . . . A wonderful way to toast an enjoyable hunt. Designed by and made exclusively for Orvis. The black hand-screened duck design is a new angle on decorative waterfowl designs. Glasses are 14 oz. double old-fashion, available in sets of six so everyone at dinner can enjoy the whimsical design.
E1308-00-14 - Bottoms-Up Old-Fashion Glasses - Set of Six . . . $21.50

Micro-Lith Lite

Even after 10 years of storage, **this 4", 1.5 oz. palm-sized flashlight will run for over 3 hours.** It uses a 3v. Lithium battery, similar to an AA cell but 4 times the energy storage capacity. Micro-Lith's unique Krypton bulb is 100% brighter than normal bulbs. Waterproof, unbreakable, the lens even doubles as a magnifier-fire starter. With its 1400 candlepower rating, this excellent product is a real innovation and possibly a lifesaver.
E2555-00-00 – Micro-Lith Lite (includes power cell). $19.95
E2554-00-00 – Replacement Power Cell $6.95

FIRST FOLD

FIRST FOLD

Please do not tape.

PLACE STAMP HERE

FOLD FOR FLAP HERE

Please do not staple.

THIRD FOLD

Orvis Guarantee

Our products are guaranteed to be 100% satisfactory. Return anything that proves otherwise. We will replace it or refund your money, as you wish.

Order by Phone

CALL 1 - 802 - 362-1300
AND USE YOUR CREDIT CARD

VISA, MASTERCARD OR AMERICAN EXPRESS

SECOND FOLD

SECOND FOLD

DETACH HERE

Vermont Maple Syrup

Probably you have never tasted Grade Fancy Syrup. While the snow is still in the sugarbush, the first sunny days of early spring start a tender tentative brief flow of sap. These first brief runs produce a maple syrup of very pale straw color and exquisitely delicate flavor which lingers on the tongue. Our syrup is still packed in old fashioned metal tins which will not affect the flavor.
E8300-00-00 – 1/2 Gallon Grade Fancy Syrup. $22.50
E8301-00-00 – 1 Quart Grade Fancy Syrup. $11.75

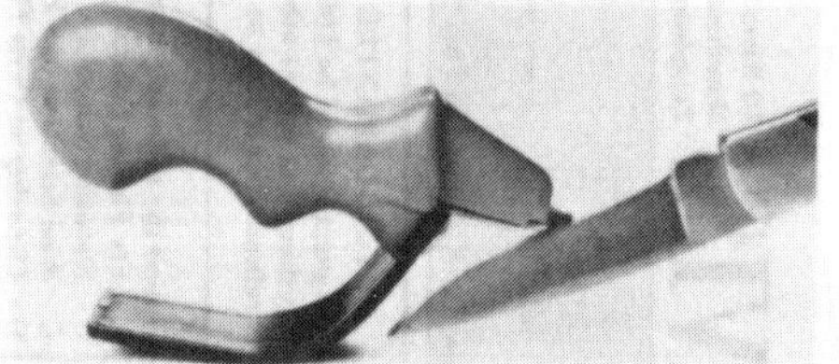

Foolproof Knife Sharpener

Sharpener holds your knife blade and sharpens both edges simultaneously. Just rest your knife, blade up, against a table top and draw the sharpener over your knife blade. Three or four firm strokes will sharpen knives and tools to a keen edge. Sharpener features a comfortable handle, safety hand guard and fast-cutting carbide teeth.
E1034-00-00 – Foolproof Knife Sharpener . . . . each $9.95

7-26

ORVIS®

10 River Road
Manchester, Vermont 05254
Telephone 1 - 802 - 362-1300

Please Do Not Write In This Space

ORVIS GUARANTEE
Our products are guaranteed to be 100% satisfactory. Please return anything that proves otherwise. We will replace or refund your money as you wish.

Please send the following booklets:
[ ] A - Fly Fishing School
[ ] B - Shooting School
[ ] C - Wise Selection of a Fly Rod
[ ] D - Choosing an Orvis Fly Line
[ ] E - Custom Built Shotguns

PLEASE FILL IN ALL INFORMATION BELOW

ORDERED BY:
444003

____

____

____

______________________ Zip __________

DAYTIME
TELEPHONE NUMBER: ______________

I enclose [ ] Check [ ] Money Order [ ] Visa [ ] MasterCard
[ ] American Express (No C.O.D.'s, Stamps or Currency)

Expiration Date for
Visa, MasterCard, American Express [| | |]

Account All Digits
[| | | | | | | | | | | | | | | |]

SIGNATURE
Must Be Signed ______________________

DETACH HERE

The Orvis Company, Inc. A Sporting Tradition Since 1856

Quantity	Item Number	Size or Pattern #	Description	Other: (inseam, sleeve monogram, etc.)	Price Each	Total Price

SHIP TO: (Use only if different from ORDERED BY:)

____

____

____

______________________ Zip __________

For additional Ship To Orders, use separate sheet of paper.

Ship To Greeting: ______________________

Merchandise Total	
Add applicable Vermont or California Tax of Merchandise Total for Orders Delivered in Vermont or California	
Packing, Shipping and Guaranteed Delivery - $3.50 per shipment	3 50
Additional Shipping Address — $3.50 each	
Additional Shipping Charges as Noted on Special Items	
Add $5.00 for Air Service and/or $3.00 for Special Delivery	
TOTAL AMOUNT ENCLOSED OR CHARGED	

MOISTEN FLAP TO SEAL

DETACH HERE

7-27

Harry and David has sold fruit by mail for decades, with the same guarantee from the start:

> "Our *guarantee since 1936,* Harry and I have *promised to* always please you — *no matter what. Our lawyer,* who used to be *a good pear-picker, says farmers can't guarantee anything* because of hailstorms, wind, drought crop failures, freezes, mistakes, hazards of farming, birds and bees and everything else. You'll find his fine print on our order blank—but *remember — we guarantee your complete satisfaction or your money back.*"

This is a 100 percent guarantee. The wording is warm and intimate; hard, solid confidence is instilled with a soft, personal touch. The cozy, social approach which relates to the whole psychology of food is used. The guarantees appear on page two and on the back of the order form. Every word sells! Those underlined caress the customer into ordering.

Mary of Puddin' Hill offers a guarantee which psychologically encompasses the feelings Americans have toward food:

> "MARY'S *PROOF OF THE PUDDIN' GUARANTEE.* We're *proud* of our *products* and also proud of our *customer's confidence*. We will *not knowingly permit a dissatisfied customer.* If you aren't *100% satisfied* with any item from Mary of Puddin' Hill, we will *send your money back immediately!* This *includes products, packaging, delivery and service.*"

Again we have a 100 percent guarantee. Friendliness, honesty, and warmth glow throughout the wording. Guarantees appear prominently in Mary's letter to the customer, on a page in the catalog, and on the upper left corner of the order form. Mary comes right out and says that her customers are confident of her products, packaging, delivery, and service; there is no need for customers to interpret confidence. Words underlined are selling hard.

Prism Optical, Inc. Eyeglasses must be one of the hardest products to sell by mail. People's lives — their enjoyment and livelihood — depend on eye care. Convincing people of a company's credibility and dependability, plus product quality, is an enormous job. Prism Optical's catalog has a wonderfully full, complete guarantee!

Prism Optical, Inc. hereby guarantees that your eyeglasses will: 1) look right on your face 2) fit right over your ears, eyes and nose bridge 3) have the right prescription, just as your doctor ordered it for you. You have 30 days from the time you receive your glasses to examine them. If you are not fully satisfied, you can return them to us for a full, prompt refund.

The three major points guaranteed are: (1) *appearance* — relieving the customer of obligation if a wrong style choice is made; (2) *fit* — assuring proper fit and comfort; (3) *accuracy* — guaranteeing a perfect match to the doctor's instructions. In addition to these reassuring, confidence-building points, the customer gets to wear the glasses on a trial basis for up to 30 days. This guarantee is placed on page nine (the back of the lens-choosing guide); it is shortened and printed in red within the "owner's letter," and it is again shortened and critically placed at the bottom of the order form. *Prism Optical does an exceptional job of forming an extra strong guarantee in simple words that inspire customer confidence.*

Acknowledge customer doubts

Master Vaccine. Vaccine, plus health and grooming supplies for animals, is serious business and is approached exactly that way. Master Vaccine has a money-back satisfaction guarantee and must deal with more issues than the normal cataloger does because of the product carried. Figure 7-28 shows how a formal point-by-point approach is successfully executed. The first sentence acknowledges many people's negative thoughts and proposes to alleviate these thoughts. "To buy sight unseen, by mail or phone, is an act of confidence. We understand that and we want to be worthy of it. Our guarantee is simple . . . it has no 'fine print'." That's a pretty good way to counteract a customer's negative thoughts — by being straightforward and using simple language that cannot be

SATISFACTION GUARANTEED
OR YOUR MONEY BACK

To buy sight unseen, by mail or by phone, is an act of confidence. We understand that, and we want to be worthy of it. Our GUARANTEE is simple . . . it has no "fine print".

1. You must be satisfied -- you are the only judge.
2. Federal law prohibits the return of vaccine.
3. If anything else you order is not to your liking, for any reason or for no reason at all, or if anything arrives in less than perfect condition, you may return it within one month of receipt.
4. You may request exchange, replacement or refund for the full amount of purchase, except shipping charges.
5. Please include your Order Number with any product returned

So, browse through the following pages and order with the complete confidence that every single product will perform to YOUR expectations...OR WE TAKE IT BACK.

Wayne W Nurmi

Wayne W Nurmi
President, Master Vaccine

7-28

misunderstood. Point number one declares an unqualified requirement of satisfaction: ". . .you are the only judge." Point number two meets and states a federal requirement by stating, "Federal law prohibits the return of Vaccine." Points three, four, and five state other stipulations: return of merchandise, amount refunded or credited, and order number included with the return. These are all worded simply and softly — not in a dictatorial way. The genuine concern of the owner and president, Wayne W. Nurmi, shows through.

Careful wording can make a regular time-limit guarantee sound like a free-trial period. True free-trial guarantees, generally employed by book companies, give the customer a stated period of time in which to examine the product. During this time, no monies need be paid — only after the declared period of time must the customer pay, if the product is satisfactory. If it is not satisfactory, the product may be returned without any monies being paid toward the product. An example of how simply a regular 30-day guarantee is turned into a free-trial period is seen in Figure 7-29 from The Sharper Image: "You have 30 days to make up your mind." This can be very easily interpreted as a period of trying out at no charge. The fact is, the customer has already paid . . . even though money will be refunded if the product is not satisfactory.

1. You have 30 days to make up your mind.
If not satisified, simply return the item (in new condition, please) within 30 days for a prompt, courteous refund, whatever the reason. Your satisfaction is the only judge.

7-29

Another example of this treatment is seen in an excerpt from the Bedford Fair catalog guarantee. (See Figure 7-30.) The underlined portion shows how a 15-day time-limited unconditional guarantee sounds like a free trial. Bedford Fair comes much closer to this interpretation by just eliminating the word "free" and using "15-day trial." This is clever wording and ambitious selling of a guarantee.

YOUR GUARANTEE OF SATISFACTION
Shopping "direct" with Bedford Fair not only entitles you to extraordinary savings, but also enables you to order our fine products on a 15-day trial. Unless fully satisfied, you may return any items for an immediate refund of the purchase price (except shipping & handling), no questions asked.

7-30

Extra-effort guarantee promoting

Extra-effort guarantee promoting is a specialty of Inmac. This company makes a 45-day regular guarantee and a one-year performance guarantee into a ''happening.'' And they do not simply place a guarantee only where it is convenient or just in the traditional places such as a company letter and on the order form/envelope. They fully promote it starting right on page two with a letter from the president (Figure 7-31). The headline is a simple statement, ''How we guarantee your satisfaction,'' but it entices the customer to read on and find out how. Again, the simplicity of the first sentence shows through by establishing a quiet credibility. ''Every product you buy from our catalog must meet your expectations . . . not ours.'' The further offer, ''So we let you try them out in your own facility for 45 days,'' builds the company credibility even more. To keep it simple and natural, an ending sentence is power packed: ''We also back each item with the industry's strongest quality guarantees. (See inside back cover).'' What strength and how natural! The president, Ken Eldred, signs the letter, and a president never goes into nitty-gritty details. The simplicity of effort and wording is laden with credibility. On page two is the company's double guarantee. Note number five in the six reasons for ordering from Inmac. (See Figure 7-32). A short, crisp sentence names both guarantees. ''We give you a 45-day trial period and a minimum 1-year performance guarantee.'' And simplicity again declares strength of service: ''No one else offers this kind of protection.'' The merely simple presentation of the guarantee stops here. Now, through the entire catalog, Inmac initiates an intense guarantee selling program. Following are five basic approaches Inmac takes throughout the catalog.

How we guarantee your satisfaction.

Every product you buy from our catalog must meet your expectations... not ours.

So we let you try them out in your own facility for 45 days. If you're not satisfied, return them for a refund, credit or exchange. We also back each item with the industry's strongest quality guarantees. (See inside back cover).

So, browse through these pages now and order with complete confidence.

Kenneth A. Eldred

Ken Eldred
President, Inmac

7-31

6 reasons to order from Inmac.

1. Assured Quality.
We put each product through relentless tests for performance and durability. If they don't pass, you won't find them in our catalog!

2. Fast Shipment.
Other companies often make you wait 4 to 6 weeks for shipment. Not Inmac. We ship the day you order!

3. Easy Ordering.
Order from any of our sales and distribution centers by mail or phone. Verbal P.O.'s are welcomed.

4. A Helpful Staff.
For answers to technical questions or product compatibility information, our friendly, knowledgeable staff is glad to help.

5. Double Guarantee
We give you a 45-day trial period and a minimum 1-year performance guarantee. No one else offers this kind of protection.

6. One-stop Shopping
Your time is too valuable to spend hours searching through source books. Rely on Inmac for all the computer-related products you need!

**Subject to inventory availability.*

7-32

How to choose the Inmac floppy that's right for you. When you need the very best: Inmac Plus™ Disks ...absolute read/write accuracy, lifetime guarantee.

If you believe that the least expensive disks to own are the ones that always work, then Inmac Plus Flexible Disks are right for you.

Guaranteed to work the first time, every time–for life!

Inmac Plus Diskettes surpass every applicable performance standard in the industry. They're guaranteed to work flawlessly for as long as you own them.

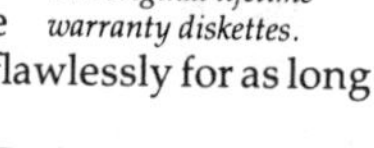

The original lifetime warranty diskettes.

Trust Inmac Plus Diskettes with your most critical work – for programs and data you can't afford to lose. Use them confidently on "finicky" drives that demand state-of-the-art diskette performance.

For the ultimate in quality and a lifetime guarantee, choose Inmac Plus.

Recommended Use: Applications where flawless performance is paramount. Best choice for your critical programs data.
Performance Specifications: Certified 100% error-free at 60% clipping level. (Surpasses ANSI, ECMA, ISO standards).
Special Features: Manufactured with hub-rings. Individual serial numbers.
Guarantee: Lifetime 100% error-free for as long as you own your disks.
See full details on pages 24-25.

7-33

1. Main headline declaration. The company often makes a version of one of its guarantees work as headline-quality selling copy. Inmac considers its strong guarantees a benefit and treats them as such. Figures 7-33 and 7-34 illustrate how the company applies its own and the manufacturer's guarantee to enhance headline quality. Figure 7-33 is Inmac's own brand name floppy disk. The product is named in the first two lines; the third line is devoted to the benefit, a lifetime guarantee. Figure 7-34 is the headline for a brand name product, Porta-Files. The manufacturer's guarantee becomes one of the two benefits in the headline.

2. Copy highlight headlines. Benefits and selling points are emphasized in bold type within the product copy. Inmac uses its own 45-day trial guarantee to challenge the customer into making a purchase of a product (Figure 7-35). The challenge headline, "Give it a 45-day trial," is followed by customer application of the offer: "If after 45 days you think you can bear to part with the added flexibility and comfort it gives, you can return it for a prompt refund." This exudes product confidence. Inmac also utilizes a product performance element to highlight a guarantee within their Fast Talk Modem copy. "Auto-answer guarantees you'll never miss a call" is highlighted in bold in the middle of the copy. The commonly shared problem of missing telephone calls is solved. Customer confidence and desire are built.

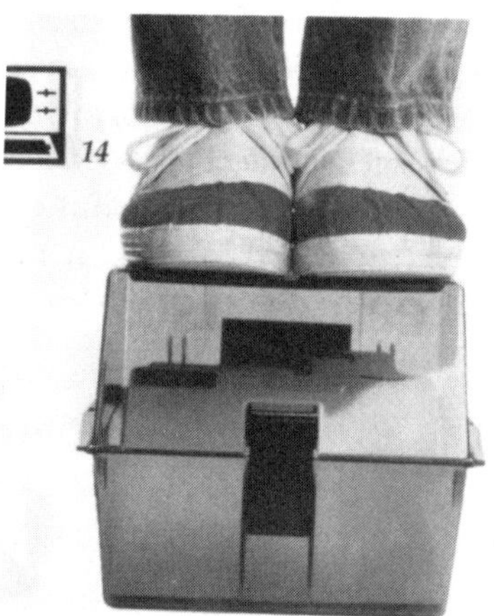

Porta-Files are made of Lexan®, a material so tough, we have the confidence to guarantee these cases for life!

Store 50 disks in a case so rugged, it's guaranteed for life!

Porta-File protects, organizes and transports up to fifty of your 5¼" floppies in a case so strong, we guarantee it won't crack, break or warp for as long as you own it.

If you take your disks home at night you'll find a Porta-File is the safest, easiest way to carry them.

Doubles as a desktop file.

At your desk or workstation, a Porta-File will keep fifty of your disks organized and

7-34

3. Punch line selling is accomplished by using the guarantee as a selling point, or punch line, at the end of the copy: ''We guarantee Micro Master for life against defects in materials and workmanship.'' This is a strong selling point for an IBM workstation. Another time, a command (''Order yours!'') is followed by a superb confidence statement from the double guarantee: ''Try it risk-free for 45 days.''

4. Benefit call-outs bulleted in a listing format include guarantees, too. Figure 7-36 shows that two out of nine ''Inmac Plus Specifications'' are guarantee features.

Give it a 45-day trial.

Order your monitor pedestal today. It matches the color of your IBM exactly and will quickly become an integral part of your system.

If after 45 days, you think you can bear to part with the added flexibility and comfort it gives, you can return it for a prompt refund.

PC Monitor Pedestal. Dim: 4"h. x 11"w. x

7-35

Hard-sell guarantee

5. Boxed super-blurbs highlight many different guarantees throughout the catalog. Here are four different guarantees used for individual product reinforcement.

(a) 5-year guarantee on Inmac Data Cartridges (Figure 7-37).

(b) One-year freshness guarantee. (Figure 7-38).

Inmac Plus Specifications

- Guaranteed 100% read/write accuracy at 60% clipping level.
- Performance exceeds all applicable industry standards: ANSI (U.S.A.), ECMA (Europe), ISO (Japan).
- Coating thickness:
  48 TPI disks: 2.5 µm ± 0.2µm.
  96 TPI disks: 2.5 µm ± 0.2µm.
- Biaxially oriented polyester substrate and special annealing process assure dimensional stability. Disks are punched from non-tensioned web for maximum dimensional accuracy.
- Quality control procedures: 32 separate quality tests throughout the manufacturing process . . . for each diskette. Final visual inspection. Each individual disk tested in a drop-through gauge for jacket flatness.
- Registration: each disk individually serialized and tracked throughout the manufacturing process.
- Protective envelopes: tear-resistant Tyvec®.
- Liner material: non-woven cloth chosen after tests on 400 different materials. Offers minimal fiber-extrusion with excellent cleaning effect.
- Guaranteed to read/write with 100% accuracy for as long as you own the diskettes.

7-36

(c) The Data Master lifetime guarantee (Figure 7-39).

(d) Your guarantee of complete satisfaction (Figure 7-40).

And, finally, there is Inmac's double-protection guarantee of your satisfaction on the inside back cover (Figure 7-41).

There are many more promotions throughout the Inmac 130-page catalog for strong and frequent selling. This approach has certainly proven to be successful, as the company went to $70,000,000 in only nine years.

5-Year Guarantee on Inmac Data Cartridges

All Inmac data cartridges are guaranteed to read and write for five years from the date of purchase. Should you discover a defect in a cartridge, simply return it to us postage paid and we'll replace it at no charge.

7-37

One-Year Freshness Guarantee.

The quality control is so tight on these ribbons that every single Good Impressions ribbon you order is guaranteed to be "factory fresh" for one full year from your date of purchase.

Who makes the freshness determination? You do! If for any reason you're not completely satisfied, simply return them for a prompt refund, exchange or credit.

7-38

The DataMaster™ Lifetime Guarantee.

With furniture this flexible, you'll want it to last a long time. That's exactly why we've gone to such great lengths to insure that only the finest materials and construction techniques are used.

This furniture is so well made that if anything should ever go wrong with it, we'll replace the defective item free. Simply return it to us for a prompt exchange.

7-39

Your Guarantee of Complete Satisfaction

You can buy any of these CRT and printer stands and use them in your own facility for 45 days, risk-free.

If you aren't completely satisfied, for any reason whatsoever, simply return them for a prompt refund, exchange or credit.

7-40

Inmac's Double-Protection Guarantee of Your Satisfaction

Every product you buy from this catalog must live up to your expectations, not ours. That's why we offer this unique, "DOUBLE-PROTECTION" Plan.

1. 45-Day No-Nonsense Trial Period. *Any product in this catalog may be returned within 45 days if you're not completely satisfied. No hassles, no phone calls. Just send it back with proof of purchase to the nearest Inmac branch, freight prepaid, for prompt exchange, refund or credit. We would appreciate a note explaining why you are returning the product.*

2. One-Year Replacement Guarantee. *Except for consumable items (paper, ribbons, printwheels, plotter pens and filters), all catalog products are guaranteed for extended periods against defects in material and workmanship. Guarantee period is one year unless otherwise stated on product pages. If a product fails during this period, we'll promptly replace it. Just call you Inmac distribution center for an accelerated return number and return the product, freight prepaid.*

Understandably, we cannot warranty damage resulting from misuse. Nor can we assume responsibility for consequential damage.

7-41

Guarantee Checklist:

- ☐ Choose Strongest Guarantee Possible.
- ☐ Investigate Manufacturer's Guarantees.

Always:

1. Display guarantee prominently.
2. Be careful in the wording and claims — be prepared to follow through with them.
3. Use guarantee as selling element.

Strongly Consider:

1. Placing your guarantee on front and/or back cover.
2. Utilizing your guarantee in headlines, copy, punch lines, blurbs.
3. Placing your guarantee on the order form.
4. Using manufacturer's guarantee as yours.

Chapter 8

The Order Form . . . What is its Role?

To Close the Sale — With Ease!

Closing the sale. The order form must wind up the sale — get the customer to take the final step in ordering — by filling out the order form. And, that is often hard to do. A lot of complications can get in the way, including complication itself. What does that mean? If an order form is so complicated that it is hard to understand what needs to be included, or if too much information is requested, the customer becomes discouraged and decides against placing an order. Having a complicated and confusing design, or not allowing enough room for the requested information, will also discourage the customer. In fact, one of the easiest ways to unknowingly reduce order response is to unnecessarily complicate and confuse your order form. People do not like wrestling with details, and when they must, they want a simple way of doing it. Internal company battles have raged over what the order form should do, not for the customer, but for the data entry department. Just keep one thing in mind: if there are few or no orders coming in, the data entry department won't have anything to do. Customers are the important factor, so design the order form for their needs. The layout for information needed by all company departments is vitally important. But always keep in mind that *the easier it is for the customer to understand and fill out the order form, the better response you will have.*

Information To Include. . . Your first consideration.

No planning or designing can take place until you know the information you need to work with. There are two basic areas to consider: (1) the customer, and (2) your order entry and record keeping departments. Since number one is by far the more important of the two, the information needed by order entry and record keeping should be designed around the needs and ease of the customer. Simplicity can be realized, even in large-volume, multi-million-dollar companies.

Four Basic Areas

You can use the order form (or ''bind-in'') for a lot more than than just an ordering device. Because of design, panels and the envelope provide areas which can be utilized.

There are four basic categories of use:

1. Order form panel.
2. Information panel.
3. Product panel.
4. Ordering envelope.

Order Form Panel

Your order form must make it easy for the customer to place that order. *This form is the final step in closing the sale.* Too many times, order forms present roadblocks, even visual and mechanical turnoffs. These can confuse the customer, or make the form look difficult, or make it seem overwhelming to read and fill in. The end result is that a poorly designed form stops the customer from making a purchase. But *if you create an order form which is easy to use, you will actually increase sales!*

Knowing what information you need is of prime importance. The catalog product line influences needs, but there is some basic information which is required for all types of product lines, as well as the information customers need so they may order easily. What are the essential needs?

Bare-fact information

1. Customer full name and address.
2. Product identity number.
3. Quantity desired.
4. Name of product.
5. Size, color and personalization requirements.
6. Retail price.
7. Shipping, handling, insurance charges.
8. State tax requirements.
9. Method of payment.
10. Company name and address.
11. Company telephone number (regular and toll-free).
12. Catalog code number.
13. Total dollar column.

Other beneficial information

1. "Ship to" name and address.
2. Customer's telephone number.
3. Page number product appears on.
4. Request for change of address.
5. Minimum order information.
6. Company guarantee.
7. Special shipping information.
8. Mr., Mrs., Miss or Ms. designation.
9. Quantity discount or free gift information.
10. Thank you.

Simple Demands, Simple Order Forms

One of the simplest order forms is that of Walter Drake and Sons (Figure 8-1). Eleven out of the twelve needed basics have been included. Number 11, the company telephone number, is missing and could easily be added. Only two of the other beneficial information points are included, however: Number 2, the customer's telephone number, and Number 4, the request for change of address. This example shows how a company doing a large volume of business is able to keep the order form demands to a minimum and the design simple for the customer. Not including a "thank you" is unforgivable, however. Now let's see how another catalog, Leichtung, Inc., manages to get even more information on approximately the same size order form and not look any more crowded. Figure 8-2 shows that twelve of the thirteen basics are included. (The one omitted is Number 5, but size, color and personalization requirements do not apply to the line of products carried — tools.) On the beneficial information list, only three points are excluded: the page number, guarantee, and "thank you." The page number is most likely inconsequential to internal company workings anyway. The full guarantee is placed opposite the order form on the back of the envelope, so not a great deal is lost. But a "thank you" could so easily have been added and would let customers know how much they are appreciated. One aspect handled especially well here, and which adds to customer interest and visual appeal, is the "Free" gift information filled in with handwriting. This is a clever way to draw attention to an order incentive, as well as showing the customer how easy it is to fill out the order form. An added push for placing the order *now* is the offer expiration date under the total line, also in handwriting.

Attention called with handwriting

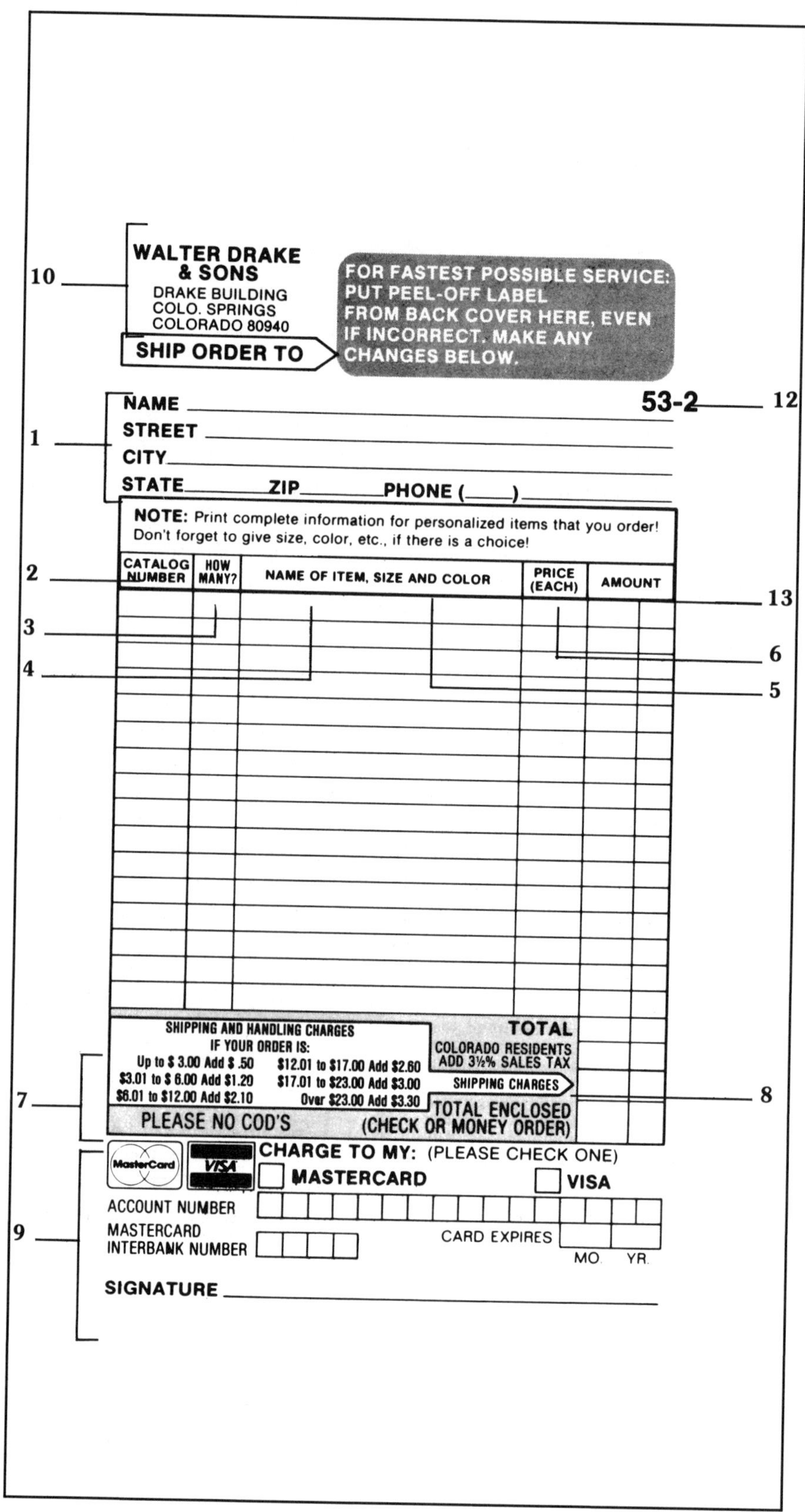

WALTER DRAKE
& SONS
DRAKE BUILDING
COLO. SPRINGS
COLORADO 80940

FOR FASTEST POSSIBLE SERVICE: PUT PEEL-OFF LABEL FROM BACK COVER HERE, EVEN IF INCORRECT. MAKE ANY CHANGES BELOW.

SHIP ORDER TO

53-2

NAME ______
STREET ______
CITY ______
STATE ______ ZIP ______ PHONE (____) ______

NOTE: Print complete information for personalized items that you order! Don't forget to give size, color, etc., if there is a choice!

CATALOG NUMBER	HOW MANY?	NAME OF ITEM, SIZE AND COLOR	PRICE (EACH)	AMOUNT

SHIPPING AND HANDLING CHARGES
IF YOUR ORDER IS:

Up to $ 3.00 Add $ .50	$12.01 to $17.00 Add $2.60
$3.01 to $ 6.00 Add $1.20	$17.01 to $23.00 Add $3.00
$6.01 to $12.00 Add $2.10	Over $23.00 Add $3.30

PLEASE NO COD'S

TOTAL
COLORADO RESIDENTS ADD 3½% SALES TAX
SHIPPING CHARGES
TOTAL ENCLOSED (CHECK OR MONEY ORDER)

CHARGE TO MY: (PLEASE CHECK ONE)
☐ MASTERCARD ☐ VISA

ACCOUNT NUMBER
MASTERCARD INTERBANK NUMBER
CARD EXPIRES MO. YR.

SIGNATURE ______

8-1

10 LEICHTUNG inc.
"THE Workbench People"
4944 Commerce Parkway Cleveland, Ohio 44128-5985
Phone 216-831-6191

May we have your daytime phone number? It will help if we need to call you about your order.

Area Code ___ Phone Number ___

SOLD TO:
(Please correct name and address label if necessary)

SHIP TO: (If different from SOLD TO or if "SOLD TO" is a P.O. Box.)

1
Name ___
Address ___
City ___ State ___ Zip ___

PLEASE USE PEEL-OFF ADDRESS LABEL FROM BACK COVER

6
13
3

How Many?	Item Number	Name of Item	Price Each Dollars	Price Each Cents	Total Price Dollars	Total Price Cents
1	G33	WOOD DRILL SAW	FREE WITH ANY ORDER*			

2
4

MINIMUM NET ORDER: Due to sharply rising processing and handling costs, we must establish a minimum NET order of $10.00. It helps keep prices down.) Thanks for your understanding.

Net Amount of Order
If Layaway: Down Payment

7
SHIPPING, HANDLING AND INSURANCE

IF YOUR ORDER IS:
Under $25.00 .... $3.50
From $25.01 to $50.00 ..... $4.95
From $50.01 to $120.00 .... $6.95

FREE SHIPPING FOR ORDERS OVER $120.00

Note: Workbench and Miter Saw orders are shipped FREIGHT COLLECT

Shipping, Handling and Insurance
Ohio Residents Add 6½% Tax 8
TOTAL PAYMENT

* OFFER EXPIRES FEB. 28, 1983

METHOD OF PAYMENT:

9
☐ Check or Money Order Enclosed
☐ Layaway Plan (See page 47)
Charge Full Payment to:
☐ MasterCard ☐ VISA

My Bank Credit Card Number is ___

Credit Card Good Thru ___ Signature ___

MasterCard VISA

You Can Order By Phone:
CALL TOLL FREE
800-321-6840 11
Ohio Residents Call: (216) 831-6191

H942 12

50

8-2

Information Panel

This is where the cataloger should go into detail about services offered, such as toll-free ordering, fast delivery service, mail preference notification, special instructions for returning merchandise, and full guarantee declarations. Often a full panel of the order form plus the back of the ordering envelope is used for this information. How much room is needed depends on your product line. Do you sell clothing where fit is important? A sizing chart, diagram, or other explanation might not only be appropriate but also help keep the refund rate down. (This kind of information also instills customer confidence and encourages an order.) Business-to-business catalogs may need to state their terms and conditions of sale, including product patent and copyright policies. Or, if your needs don't require use of a full panel for ordering information, you might include explanations of special offers, free gifts, or even a product for sale to utilize the space judiciously.

Basic facts to tell your customer

1. Toll-free service. Explain your toll-free service. What hours is it available? If you offer 24-hour service, tell your customers! If the service is limited, tell them what hours to call and what days are available. If certain hours are better times to call for quicker service, mention this, too. Do you have more than one toll-free number? Maybe you have a national ''800'' number and a different toll-free number for your home state — tell them this. Do you offer a separate toll-free or regular number for customer service and inquiries? Be sure to say so.

2. Shipping information. This is where you should tell the customer about the different shipping methods your company offers. It's even a good idea to explain turnaround time if you ship regular parcel post or United Parcel Service. Do you ship all of your orders the same day or the next day? This is a bonus — tell the customer. Do you offer any special methods of shipping? State what they are: air delivery, special delivery, COD, air express — or even trucking for large items. Tell the charges for each, too. Are conditions for delivery outside the continental United States and for foreign delivery different? Be sure to say so. *Promote fast delivery strongly*.

3. Return policies. Should customers be dissatisfied or need to return the merchandise, it is beneficial to them to know how to return the goods. Do you have a preferred way you want the merchandise returned? Tell them how — insured and prepaid, original order included, special packaging for product protection. Letting the customer know merchandise can be returned (plus how to do it) strengthens customer confidence in the company.

4. Customer inquiries. You may have a special person or department assigned to this function, depending on your order volume and product line. If you do, tell the customer — this may be a big plus and something to promote heavily. For added friendliness, some companies even give the name of a particular person to call.

5. Guarantee. State your guarantee in full, whether it is only one sentence or several. Have you stated it elsewhere in the catalog? That's good — but be sure to state it again on the information panel. This is a very influential place, one referred to by most customers. The opportunity to build company credibility and instill customer confidence should be promoted here via your guarantee.

6. How-to-order basics. Telling customers how to order step-by-step, so they can easily check off the steps and place the order correctly, ensures proper order fulfillment and fast service — a big bonus for the customer. Number these steps to correspond with the steps needed on the order form, or give customers a check list to mark off for accuracy. Separate the requirements for ordering by mail and by phone — the phone customer needs additional information, such as telephone number and hours to place the order. Some companies encourage customers to fill in the order form before placing their phone order to ensure accuracy and speed of handling.

7. Mailing preference policy and service. Most catalog companies rent their lists to other catalog companies. By letting your customers know this and giving them the option of not receiving mailings from other companies, you help the mail order industry be its own watchdog. The more companies that comply, the less likely the federal government will become the watchdog.

Additional information pluses

1. Free catalog for a friend request and form. Personal referrals are considered wonderfully responsive names to add to your mailing list. Some catalogs take a lot of room for this type of promotion, providing two or three areas for friends' names and addresses. In turn, the company sends each referral a free catalog.

Eva Gabor Wigs by Paula (Figure 8-3) has a friendly message on the back of the ordering envelope asking, "Would you like us to send a catalog to a friend?" This position makes it easy for the mail opening department to separate this information from order entry processing.

2. Gift service. Announcing this service is important, especially if your product line is conducive to gift-giving. A gift service can take many different forms. (1) You may want to offer a full gift-wrapping and card enclosure service. A general gift-wrap may be provided at a minimal charge. Often an illustration is not needed because no choice is involved. However, when special selection of wrap choices with different dollar charges is offered, it is better to have an illustration picturing the choices. (2) A card enclosure provided by the catalog company can be combined with the gift-wrap service or can be offered separately. Some catalogs ask that customers provide their own cards with their own messages.

Would you like us to send a catalog to a friend?

If you have friends who might enjoy receiving our catalog, write their names below, and we will see that they receive their own catalog of EVA GABOR wigs.

Thank you.

Paula

Name ______

Address ______

City ______

State ______ Zip ______

Name ______

Address ______

City ______

State ______ Zip ______

Fold and seal gummed flap.

THANK YOU FOR YOUR ORDER

Have you enclosed check, money order, or credit-card information?

We can not be responsible for cash sent through the mail.

Do Not Detach

Hair Sample Envelope

If you wish personal color-matching, place a small sample of your hair or hair from another wig in this envelope. If we cannot match your color exactly would you prefer a color that is slightly lighter or darker?

☐ slightly lighter ☐ slightly darker

If you are sending a hair sample, please insert here. ←

8-3

An unusually large area of the Neiman-Marcus Christmas catalog order form is devoted to a gift-wrapping service and a "gift bond" service. Figure 8-4 shows two panels of four-color illustrations with eight gift-wrap choices, each for a nominal fee. It's an attractive presentation that dominates the information area. The high percent of gift ordering from the Neiman-Marcus Christmas catalog justifies the unusually large area. The gift bond presentation is also attractive and visually clear. Most catalogs choose to make a much more modest presentation, such as the gift selection service from The Siri Vail Collection, noted under point number four on a following page.

3. Gift certificate opportunity. More and more companies are telling customers how they may acquire a gift certificate, by mail or phone or both. If a special design, engraving, or folder is used, be sure to specify this, too. If the dollar value of the gift certificate is limited, customers need to know. If you will send the gift certificate directly to the recipient, along with a catalog to aid in selection, you have a special service your customers will want to know about. (A good visual presentation was seen in Figure 8-5 from the Neiman-Marcus catalog.)

Specify all services

4. Gift selection service. Helping the customer select gifts can be a big drawing card. General suggestions, such as "gifts for men," vacation wardrobe, gifts under $25, $50, or $100, can be presented right on the order form panel. A more sophisticated service may ask the customer to provide the dollar amount wanted and the recipient's likes, sizes, and so on — maybe even specifying a particular order department person or having the customer call a special phone number. A high-ticket catalog, The Siri Vail Collection, does a nice job of encouraging gift orders by suggesting gift ideas for men and women from the products in its catalog; customers are directed to the specific catalog page (see Figure 8-6). Siri Vail even offers a customized service: "Still Stumped? Call us and tell us a little about your friend. We'll put a package together specially suited to him or her. We're ready to serve your gift giving needs, from 9-5, Monday thru Friday at (312) 774-2023 Central Time."

126A

126B

126C

126D

126E

126F

S H O P P I N G A

CALL TOLL FREE TO ORDER

For Neiman-Marcus credit card purchases, the fastest and most personal service is via our TOLL FREE phone service. In Continental U.S. dial 1-800-NEIMANS. (1-800-634-6267). Place calls from 8:00 a.m. to 8:00 p.m. Central time, Monday through Saturday.

QUESTIONS ABOUT ORDERS

Our expanded service allows you to follow up on orders already placed, or to inquire about shipments. CALL TOLL FREE. In Continental U.S., dial 1-800-322-INFO. Place calls from 8:00 a.m. to 8:00 p.m. Central time, Monday through Saturday.

YOUR COMPLETE SATISFACTION IS OUR AIM

It is Neiman-Marcus policy that you may return, for full credit, merchandise with which you are not satisfied. THE EXCEPTIONS TO THIS are personalized items, which cannot be returned unless incorrectly personalized.

PRICES AND AVAILABILITY

Order by Jan. 15, 1984, to assure that all merchandise depicted in this book will be available at prices stated. We will notify you within 7 days of our receipt of your order of any shipping delays or discontinued items. All orders delivered to an alternate address, and all personalized orders will be confirmed to you by letter.

Please note that items ordered on the same
may not be shipped on the same day.

IT MAY NOT BE IN THE STORES

Merchandise in this book may not always b
your local Neiman-Marcus store. However,
dise may be obtained with the Mail Order f

OUR CATALOGS ARE TO SHARE

If you already have a subscription, perhaps
give us the name of a friend who might like
Neiman-Marcus by mail. Send the name a

8-4

N-M GIFT WRAPS

126G

126H

126J

THE FINISHING TOUCH

Neiman-Marcus gift wraps are the only things that can make a Neiman-Marcus gift more exciting. To order, add the price of each wrap to the price of the item it will enclose. Any item priced over 300.00 will be wrapped gratis. Substitutions may occasionally be necessary, and wraps are not available on items marked with an asterisk (*) after the price. Please note that the Mini-wraps (items 12G,H), are for small scale merchandise only. Regretfully, we cannot accept orders for the wrapping materials alone.

126A. The Christmas Cat, 4.00.
126B. Rockaway Reindeer, 4.00.
126C. Santa the Decorator, 4.00.
126D. Broomstraw Wreath, 4.00.
126E. Happy Hannukah, 4.00
126F. Victorian Wreath, 4.00.
126G. Mini-Straw Angel, 3.00.
126H. Mini-Silver Wreath, 3.00.

126J. A shopping trip at Neiman-Marcus, via the choice of an N-M Gift Bond. Available in any denomination from 25.00 up, the Gift Bond is automatically sent in a Christmas red envelope. If you'd like the Bond gift wrapped, add price of wrap (see above) plus 1.95 for delivery fees to the amount of the bond ordered. Bonds over 300.00 are wrapped gratis. Be sure to include the recipient's name and address when ordering.

D D E N D U M

Neiman-Marcus Mail Order Division, Subscription Manager, P.O. Box 2968, Dallas, Texas 75221.

MAILING LISTS PREFERENCE

We occasionally make our Mail Order customers' names and addresses available to carefully screened companies and organizations whose products might be of interest to you. If you prefer not to receive such mailings, please copy your mailing label exactly and mail it with your request to Neiman-Marcus Mail Order Division, Marketing Management, P.O. Box 2968, Dallas, Texas 75221.

TO ASSURE CHRISTMAS DELIVERY

PERSONALIZED ITEMS: order by Nov. 1 for surface delivery, by Nov. 7 for Air Mail. FRESH FOODS: order by Dec. 1 for surface delivery, by Dec. 7 for Air Mail. OTHER ITEMS: order by Dec. 3 for surface delivery, by Dec. 9 for Air Mail. FOREIGN DELIVERY: orders must be received by Nov. 7th. After Nov. 7th, these orders will automatically be shipped and billed Air Mail unless otherwise requested. NOTE: all your orders to be sent outside the United States will be consolidated for shipment whenever possible. The additional charges for foreign shipments will be billed separately.

SIRI'S GIFT SUGGESTIONS

To the Men: Wondering what to get her for the holidays? What would your loved one simply die for? (Well, hopefully everything here, but I'll be more specific!)

- The lace camisole—in black or cream (for the different moods you share!). Page 8.
- The necklace that does everything—because **she** does. Page 10.
- The cashmere plaid muffler—pure luxury. Page 17.
- A 14K gold ring in her favorite color(s). She especially loves fine jewelry when it's a surprise from you! Page: back cover.

For the Working Woman: Essentials for Business Travel

- The multi-currency wallet. A Siri Vail exclusive and a time-saving necessity for quick jaunts on the Continent. Page 19.
- A colorful shawl for keeping warm as temperatures drop between destinations. Also, to glamourize that ever-so-basic black dress. Page 3.
- The oversize tote on page 18, with all or any of the following in it (all in black, that best ever neutral): The weekly agenda, page 19; black kidskin clutch, page 19; Rain poncho that folds into a pouch. Page: order blank.

For Those Spending Their Holidays in the Sun:

- A pair of black sunglasses. Page 6.
- Bright lacquered jewelry adds color to white cottons. Page 7.
- A silk tie for your hair in a pretty color for those moonlit, tropical evenings. Page 5.

Still Stumped? Call us and tell us a little about your friend. We'll put a package together specially suited to him or her. We're ready to serve your gift giving needs, from 9–5, Monday thru Friday at (312) 774-2023 Central Time.

All of the products in The Siri Vail Collection have been selected because of their fine quality. Some products have been exclusively designed to offer you originality.

Your satisfaction means everything to us! If you are not satisfied, simply return the product within 30 days for a prompt refund or credit. It will help us if you give us the reason for your return so we can serve you better in the future.

8-5

5. Delayed delivery service. This allows the customer to order now for delivery at a later specified time. It's an especially nice service for Christmas or Thanksgiving time. It allows the customer to place one order early for different people and different delivery times. The categories utilizing delayed delivery most often are garden and food. Plants, bulbs, trees, and shrubs must be shipped at specific times of the year; most orders are shipped to the customer placing the order. However, the percentage of gift orders for food products is very high. Figure 8-6 is from Breck's Advance Sale catalog for bulbs. It is mailed early in the year for fall delivery. Early ordering is promoted heavily on page two of the catalog, while the order form takes care of the particulars of method of payment. Because the order is being placed so early, with shipment

If Necessary

FOUR WAYS TO ORDER

☐ Payment enclosed. Amount $________

☐ Charge my VISA Account when my bulbs are delivered this fall.

☐ Charge my MasterCard Account when my bulbs are delivered this fall.

☐ I authorize you to establish an account for me and bill this account when my bulbs are delivered. Orders subject to approval.

No need to fill in this area unless you are sending cash with your order. We will do necessary calculations for credit orders.

TOTAL AMOUNT ME[R]

SHIPPING AND INSURA[NCE] SEE CHART

SALES TAX ILLINO[IS] RESID[ENTS]

TOTAL AMOU[NT]

MY CARD EXPIRES ______ MO/YR

Credit Card Number

SIGNATURE ______

Phone: Area Code______

Please include your only if there is a q

8-6

to be made much later (over 30 days) and at the catalog company's discretion, an explanation of deferred payment is made clear, too. (This deferral complies with Federal Trade Commission rulings.) Note that customers using VISA or MasterCard are explicitly notified of the delay in charging their accounts: ''Charge my MasterCard account, when my bulbs are delivered this fall.'' If the customer chooses to use an in-house Breck account, then the following is stated: ''I authorize you to establish an account for me and bill this account when my bulbs are delivered.''

Don't forget delayed shipping notice

Figure 8-7, a portion of the Omaha Steaks order form, shows how easy it is for the customer to indicate the desired week of ar-

Please ship the following gifts to the names below:

Shipment No. 2

Name ______

Address ______ Apt.# ______

City ______ State ______ Zip ______

Telephone ( )

Ship to Arrive* ☐ Now ☐ Week of ______

Gift Greeting to Read:

8-7

rival with one simple line: ''Ship to arrive ______now ______ week of ______.'' The notice of delayed billing is taken care of on the information panel: ''Delayed shipping service — order now for any future shipping date. You will not be billed until your order is ready to ship.''

6. Telephone specials. It is smart telephone marketing to offer customers catalog specials when they call to place an order. Merchandise offers may be overstock or a special purchase. In either case, this type of offer is a big plus and deserves special promotion. Trifles, a gift catalog, highlights its ''DAILY PHONE SPECIAL'' on

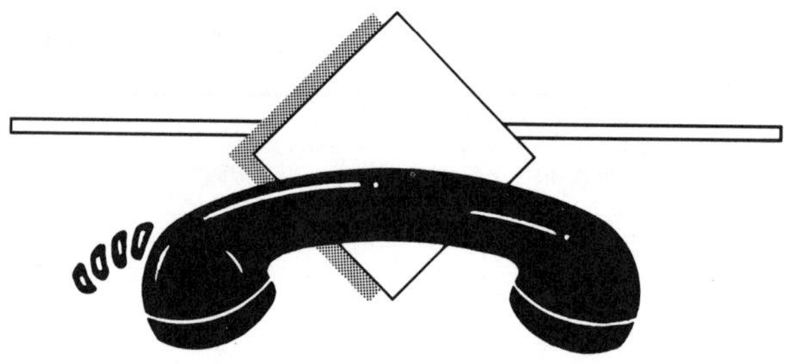

TO ORDER BY PHONE
7 A.M.-11 P.M. CENTRAL TIME
7 DAYS A WEEK

FIRST FOLD

From anywhere IN ALL
FIFTY UNITED STATES,
order toll-free
800-527-0277
EXCEPT IN TEXAS,
order toll-free
800-442-5801
IN DALLAS,
call 233-0643

Please have your catalogue and credit card readily available. Only credit card orders can be accepted by phone.

For faster answers to inquiries about an order, delivery dates or availability of items from past catalogues, CALL 214-385-2792, Monday-Friday, 8 a.m.-5 p.m. C. T. Our Customer Service operators have the information at their finger tips. (Sorry, we cannot accept collect calls.)

DAILY PHONE SPECIAL

When you order by toll-free telephone, you will be offered a favorite Trifles item at a special unadvertised reduced price. Not available with mail-in orders and you must place an order to take advantage of the phone special of the day.

8-8

the back of the order form, which also becomes the back of the ordering envelope when folded for mailing. The offer is especially well positioned, right under the toll-free ordering information. (See Figure 8-8.) The customer is enticed with the following: "Not available with mail-in orders and you must place an order to take advantage of the phone special of the day." This qualifies the offer, as well as encouraging customers to place their orders *now*.

7. Product line aids. Some categories of merchandise benefit a great deal from extra attention. For product lines where personalization is a big factor, or if you have clothing, stationery, or metal products, you might want to include special instructions on how to order. Clothing is one obvious candidate for special attention since complaints run high and the customer naturally hesitates to place an order for fear of dissatisfaction. Charts telling how to determine one's correct size not only build customer confidence in placing an order, but also benefit the catalog company by cutting down on the number of refunds and exchanges. Size conversion tables can be helpful, as are simple instructions.

Charts are good customer aids

An apparel catalog which meets the challenge of keeping a *low return factor while encouraging an order* is Lands' End. Throughout the catalog, Lands' End people have done an exceptional job of explaining what materials are used and what features make their products superior — and they've supported all this with illustrative diagrams. The most important feature is a measurement and conversion chart which occupies two-thirds of the back of the order form (Figure 8-9). At the top of the chart, the customer is reassured by being told that Lands' End clothing is traditional in size. The illustration shows how to measure for various types of clothing; a conversion chart relieves the customer's mind even more. All these features act as insurance against returned goods.

The simplicity with which the chart is presented allows ease of interpretation, especially since the conversion table tells what size to order for each article. The problem of size, which once was complex, deterred ordering, and produced a high return factor, now is solved so ordering becomes almost automatic.

The chart is not new or revolutionary, but it does accomplish two major goals: (1) The customer's mind is put at ease about what size to order — therefore *encouraging the placement of an order*. (2) The company is assured of more accurate ordering, therefore *decreasing the percentage of returns* due to improper size. This is excellent use of an order form panel by an apparel company.

8-9 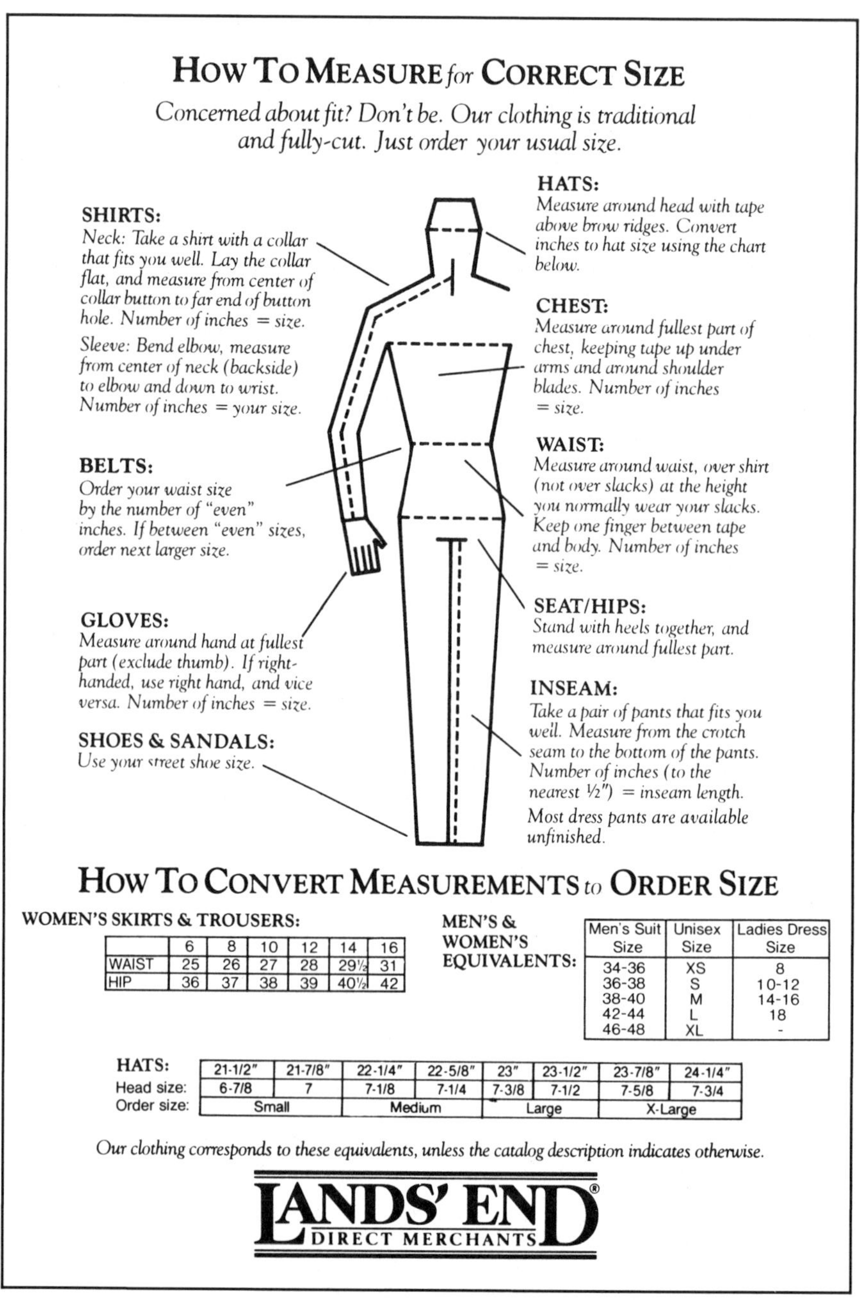

How To Measure *for* Correct Size

Concerned about fit? Don't be. Our clothing is traditional and fully-cut. Just order your usual size.

SHIRTS:
Neck: Take a shirt with a collar that fits you well. Lay the collar flat, and measure from center of collar button to far end of button hole. Number of inches = size.
Sleeve: Bend elbow, measure from center of neck (backside) to elbow and down to wrist. Number of inches = your size.

BELTS:
Order your waist size by the number of "even" inches. If between "even" sizes, order next larger size.

GLOVES:
Measure around hand at fullest part (exclude thumb). If right-handed, use right hand, and vice versa. Number of inches = size.

SHOES & SANDALS:
Use your street shoe size.

HATS:
Measure around head with tape above brow ridges. Convert inches to hat size using the chart below.

CHEST:
Measure around fullest part of chest, keeping tape up under arms and around shoulder blades. Number of inches = size.

WAIST:
Measure around waist, over shirt (not over slacks) at the height you normally wear your slacks. Keep one finger between tape and body. Number of inches = size.

SEAT/HIPS:
Stand with heels together, and measure around fullest part.

INSEAM:
Take a pair of pants that fits you well. Measure from the crotch seam to the bottom of the pants. Number of inches (to the nearest ½") = inseam length.
Most dress pants are available unfinished.

How To Convert Measurements *to* Order Size

WOMEN'S SKIRTS & TROUSERS:

	6	8	10	12	14	16
WAIST	25	26	27	28	29½	31
HIP	36	37	38	39	40½	42

MEN'S & WOMEN'S EQUIVALENTS:

Men's Suit Size	Unisex Size	Ladies Dress Size
34-36	XS	8
36-38	S	10-12
38-40	M	14-16
42-44	L	18
46-48	XL	-

HATS:

	21-1/2"	21-7/8"	22-1/4"	22-5/8"	23"	23-1/2"	23-7/8"	24-1/4"
Head size:	6-7/8	7	7-1/8	7-1/4	7-3/8	7-1/2	7-5/8	7-3/4
Order size:	Small		Medium		Large		X-Large	

Our clothing corresponds to these equivalents, unless the catalog description indicates otherwise.

LANDS' END®
DIRECT MERCHANTS

8. Credibility builders. The order form area is where the customer is going to place an order or consider placing an order. And building company credibility will certainly help make this decision a positive one. Hence the order form is an ideal place for you to present customer testimonials, have a letter from the president, or tell about your retail store locations.

Early Winters uses more than one panel for a letter from the founder, Bill Nicolai, plus fourteen customer testimonial letters. Figure 8-10 shows how Early Winters has created interest amidst a mass of very tight type by means of a line drawing of a typewriter and a strong horizontal line focus bearing solicitation versions: ''Dear Early Winters, Dear Mr. Nicolai, Hello Everyone, Greetings, Dear Sir or Madam, Hi Folks.'' This mass of credibility is all visually directed to a special information block on Gore-Tex (Figure 8-11), a material used in many Early Winters products. The material itself further aids company credibility.

The business-to-business catalog, Rio Grande (tools and equipment), uses part of a panel for a letter from Vice President Alan Bell (Figure 8-12). The letter is visually attractive and is realistically presented in typewriter type. Information on ordering is briefly reviewed with reference to page two for ''more detailed information on ordering, pricing, and shipping.'' While making customers search elsewhere for ordering information at the time they are about to place the order may not be the wisest thing to do (a deterrent and postponement), it does take them through the catalog. The time zone ''call'' map used to tell customers when the company is open in different time zones is a good idea but a bit confusing; it is not clear which time is for which area.

Personal letter is informative

The L.L. Bean catalog has a very tightly designed information panel loaded with elements to help the customer. Figure 8-13 shows the importance placed on *toll-free ordering* and even a *toll-free customer service* number. *Shipping information* goes into the different types (even foreign) and includes a breakdown of the charges. A brief statement is made about L.L. Bean's special *four-day delivery* (also highlighted on page two of the catalog). The company reaches out to the customer by encouraging *correspondence*. *Size guidelines* plus conversion charts are given for clothing and accessories. *Mail preference* policy is stated. By turning the panel sideways, the designers have made available space for two friends' addresses. This jam-packed panel (the back of the order form) manages to look appealing and easy to use because of the style and size of type. Headlines declaring the subject of the information are in Cheltenham bold, 16 point, while the body copy is 11 point Cheltenham light face. The type size in the information blocks of the size guidelines drops to an 8 point, which is still very readable.

A business-to-business catalog which also packs its information panel full of elements to benefit and educate the customer is Modern Farm (Figure 8-14). An attractive line design of a barn acts as an attention-getter for the different subject areas. All-cap headlines in 12 point Helvetica condensed complete the subject call-out. How to order, guarantee, ten reasons to shop with confidence, customer service, returns, correspondence, and mailing lists all become special — each declaring its own informational importance. Nine point Times Roman type provides easy reading. The three-column format separated by one point rules clearly defines and holds together the information. Modern Farm does an especially fine job of building company credibility and customer confidence with the ''Ten Reasons to Shop With Confidence through Modern Farm'' column. Some

Dear Customer,

Welcome once again to the pages of Early Winters' newest catalog.

Last year we celebrated our tenth anniversary with a special section of outdoor writing. You liked it so much, we decided to do it again. Turn to page 51, and enjoy the reading.

If *you* have an outdoor story or article you think Early Winters customers might like, send it in. See page 50 for details.

See pages 16 and 17 for a selection of new items that keep the beer cold, the wine chilled, and the palate perked. Our new Picnic Kit makes it easy to act on the "picnic impulse." Just add good food and friends.

Another item you'll find useful is the Pop-Up Lens Cap. If you're like me, you lose—or come close to losing—your lens cap whenever you take a picture. Our pop-up cap (p. 94) does away with the searching and reduces

Dear Early Winters, Dear Mr. Nicolai, Hello everyone,

Let me begin by complimenting you on your 10th anniversary catalog. I received it last spring and was truly impressed that you devoted so many pages to non-advertising—an enjoyable "gift," so to speak, for your customers.

. . . it helped me to decide to upgrade some of my basic backpacking gear by mail order—and I'm very well pleased.

All of the items I purchased from you have been trail-tested this season and have lived up to, or exceeded, all of my expectations.

During a 25-day trek of the John Muir Trail in August, from Yosemite to Whitney Portal, my son and I experienced nine days of rain, and although the abnormal weather caused many ill-prepared hikers to depart the High Country, we continued on in comfort.

We were most thankful to Early Winters for our Gore-Tex Summerfall parkas, but also appreciated our Norwegian-style Body Warmers, Silver Lining vests, and Silver Lining Sleeping Bags (despite their light weight and compressibility, they performed with rugged durability).

Thanks, also, for your fast, dependable, no-hassle service . . . Although I've never written a letter like this before, I believe that your reasonable prices for real quality merchandise, together with outstanding service, deserve recognition. Thanks, Early Winters! Thank you, Bill!

—William Marshall, Little Rock, AR

The Alpinist's Lantern I bought last year kept two of us very comfortable in the Catskills in -15° weather. It is simple and well-designed, and those candles burn forever! It's a grand product. —L. Strom, New York

. . . there I was, alone, at 3,100 ft. on the upper floor of the King Ravine. Black fly season should have been two months past, but this summer's weather conditions had hatched an August crop . . . They were so thick that they fell upon me.

I had already put up my yellow and orange Pocket Hotel because it was quick and easy, and I desired its cheery presence in this lonely and magnificent place . . . I got into the tent, fastened the fly screen and squashed the seven or eight other living creatures that sat on my bright yellow ceiling, then read some Thomas Jefferson, then put down the book and laughed aloud.

An image from your catalog flashed into my mind; the pretty girl reading in the Pocket Hotel wasting broad daylight. I'd thought it catalog "hype," and here I was luxuriating in much the same way.

By and by, a firm breeze rolled down from Thunderstorm junction (or Mt. Adams?) grounding the flies. I got out of my cocoon, finished preparations, and supped in the remaining evening light. I rate all of my nights of sleep in the bush on a scale of 0-10, and once again, I scored an 8 that night in the Pocket Hotel. And that's about as good as I do anywhere.

—Edmund H. Geschickter, Framingham, MA

During a car camping & day-hike weekend in the Cairngorms (Scottish highlands), I noticed a cluster of tents and decided camping with some others would be a pleasant change. Shouldering my trusty Lowe Triolet, I crunched on over.

The first indication that I was going to provide food for British humor was when I pulled out my Light Dimension.

"What's that?"

"My tent."

"You mean your bivouac sack."

"Just hold the sack while I pull it out, okay?"

Unroll tent, pick up the poles, snickety-snick of poles assuming proper shape.

"What? Well, you Yanks have some good ideas there." Grudgingly.

Unfold the tent. It's camouflage. Nothing said, but they thought it pretty amusing. I'm used to that.

So the tent's up. Discussion, explanation of Gore-Tex. The general concensus among my British neighbors was summed up in one sentence:

"Nice idea, but I doubt it's really waterproof, and you best hope it doesn't storm tonight. That'll never stand up to a storm around here."

As usual in these mountains, it drizzled that evening. Nobody laughed as I cooked supper warm and dry in my Lost World and Rainpants. *Everybody* enjoyed my Sigg bottle full of Glenmorangie whiskey!

As luck would have it, there was a hell of a storm that night. Lying in my Light Dimension, warm and dry, my initial chuckles soon turned to gleeful chortling, listening to the usual mayhem where rainfly tents are concerned.

Hark! What sound from yonder darkness breaks? Tis a rainfly, seeking an end to drab, earth-bound existence, to fly like a bird in the Tempest.

Nope, somebody got to it. Maybe next time.

Like any good hiker, I came to the assistance of my fellows, by opening the door a bit and shining my flashlight for them. Very delighted to holler advice. I received some, too, although it had nothing to do with camping.

Needless to say, I'm delighted with my Light Dimension. The careful craftsmanship, excellent design, and ruggedness is more than I would have expected. We've been through some gales together . . . —C.F. Dwyer, Stavanger, Norway

I've been meaning to write for some time to tell you how much I enjoy my Silver Lining Jupiter Jacket. The design and attention to detail make it not only the lightest, warmest jacket I've owned, but also the finest fitting and quality functional unit. So much for all the superlatives. I love it! It works well and looks great!! Keep up the innovative thought.

—M.B., Austin, TX

I probably bought one of your first Gore-Tex Anoraks, in first-generation Gore-Tex!

Since then I have bought your Sprint jacket for myself, and three other rain parkas for gifts. My one *major complaint* is that you no longer make this anorak.

I have crossed the Allagash twice, crossed the Algonquin twice, backpacked the Northville Lake Placid trail in winter and summer, and skied down Mt. Marcy—all in torrential downpours, and all in my Early Winters first-generation Gore-Tex anorak. And I have yet to get one drop of water on my clothing.

Nobody makes rain gear like you do! But please start making an anorak like your last one, because mine may just wear out in the next few years . . . —R.R., Auburn, NY

. . . Since I received it some 5 weeks ago, my Terrashell parka has been subjected to wind-whipped rain and sleet while bicycling in New York; salt-spray, wind, and water while scuba diving in St. Kitts, and, as if the foregoing were not enough, a 4000 ft. climb through a tropical rain forest up the appropriately named Mt. Misery. I loaned my parka to friends for the latter adventure, and they too had nothing but praise for your product. I must say that it was worth every penny . . .

—Bill Halligan, Yonkers, NY

the danger of harming your lens.

See page 8 for a new and good-looking jacket that combines bunting with a wind- and water-repellent shell.

If you own a Light Dimension or Winterlight tent, you may want to add a detachable front door "lobby." See our new Weatherlid, page 38.

You'll find lots more new and exciting items throughout these pages. They await your test.

Browse through now and let Early Winters help with your equipment needs. Take advantage of our 30-day money-back guarantee to test our products in actual conditions.

We wish you a summer filled with good times in the outdoors.

Sincerely,

Bill Nicolai

Bill Nicolai

Greetings, Dear Sir or Madam, Hi folks

I ordered the John Muir Trail Case because it sounded good. When it arrived I wasn't impressed until I tried it for a month. Now I take it everywhere I go. It's become my gym bag, day pack, first aid/survival kit, and even an extra pocket on my backpack. It's handier than an American Express card.

—Susan Shinkai, San Francisco, CA

I've often thought that if the government were run as well as Early Winters, we'd have a darn fine country again. In a time of notoriously bad service from too many places, E.W.'s service amazes and delights me. Keep it up!

—Richard Thurman, Salt Lake City, UT

We are retired, in our mid-fifties, and travel mostly by bicycle with full camping gear. We are always looking for well-made, compact, and light gear to use while travelling.

Many items we take must serve two or more purposes to insure we keep the weight to a minimum. All hills that we climb while bicycling provide this constant reminder: Keep weight and bulk to a minimum.

I thought you would appreciate our comments on items we have purchased from Early Winters over the years:

Camper's Valet—We use these in all of our travels. Everyone wants to know from where and how much. They replace the old ditty bag—thank God!

Lightning Bug—The best and smallest item you can carry at night in your pocket, bags, tent, or even auto.

Silk T-Shirt—Real comfortable and good looking but don't stand near a fry pan, the grease stains will stay in the shirt. Easy to maintain while travelling and great for layering in cold weather.

Norwegian Turtleneck—Excellent as an outer layer for winter in Florida. Good in layering over the silk t-shirt for lower temps. Easy to maintain while travelling. (One time I goofed—threw it in the dryer by mistake and out came a melted blob.)

Silver Lining Insulators—Especially appreciated here in Florida during April to October. We use them continuously on our daily trips around town and on the open road.

Complete Sprint Suit—Again, the best design on the market and it works well. It is my favorite wet weather gear, even off the bike.

Winterlight tent—Our pride and joy on the road. Extra, extra dry, bug free, warm, and easy to set up . . . We feel at home when using it.

Netting Sacks—We found a new use on the bike. We place damp clothes in a netting sack and attach to our rear bike packs while touring. The clothes dry quick and our bikes don't look like a travelling clothesline going down the road.

Last but not least, I believe your service is excellent. Thank you for providing good products.

—Bill Quinn, St. Petersburg, FL

Living on an island in Southeast Alaska, we sure appreciate your interesting catalog (anything new to read), your high standards of quality, and your money-back guarantee. We've always been very pleased with the service we've gotten from you. Thanks so much. We look forward very much to our new Early Winters catalog.

—Roger & Marcia Kringen, Wrangell, AK

. . I'd like to thank you all for the excellent service and products you offer.

For some time you have led the equipment industry in offering worthwhile products incorporating advanced materials and construction: Gore-Tex tents and shell parkas, nylon fiberpile, polypropylene underwear, lithium-cell flashlights. Naturally, one cannot afford to try them all, but I look to you first to keep abreast of changes.

. . . I look forward to doing business with you again.

—Will Brown, Corpus Christi, TX

I want to tell you how much I enjoy wearing my Bunting Jacket. I put it to work last week, backpacking in the wind and rain at Mt. Hood. The jacket kept me warm and dry, even though it was pretty wet. That night I put it in my sleeping bag and the next morning it was almost dry. Thanks again for making such a wonderful jacket.

—Katie O'Shea, Corvallis, OR

Even though I live on the opposite side of the country, I can always expect to receive my Early Winters order within a week. Few other places can match E.W. service.

—David Saville, Covington, VA

What to look for in a Gore-Tex garment.

In a secret process patented by W.L. Gore and Associates of Elkton, Maryland, fabric of nylon (or Taslan, or Tricot, etc.) is laminated to a thin membrane of expanded PTFE (the resin from which Teflon® is made) to form Gore-Tex fabric.

The millions of pores in PTFE are so small that liquid water cannot get through them, but large enough to let water vapor—like your body's moisture—pass out.

In other words, it's waterproof *and* it breathes.

Material	Water Entry Pressure (lbs. per sq. inch*)	Moisture Vapor Transmission (grams per sq. meter per day)
Gore-Tex®	85-110	12,980 gm.
Storm Shed	2.5	2,971 gm.
Klimate	37-45	11,676 gm.
60/40 cloth	failed test	18,626 gm.
Super K Kote	105	925 gm.

*U.S. Military waterproofness specifications require a fabric to withstand water entry pressure of 25 pounds per square inch.

Early Winters pioneered the outdoor use of Gore-Tex and carries the widest selection available.

Every inch of our Gore-Tex fabric is inspected before it goes into your Early Winters parka.

The seams are stitched *twice* and major seams are sealed for waterproofness here at the factory, by heat bonding waterproof tape to the finished seam for a lifetime weld.

Our products are made with good looks *and* function in mind. That's why Early Winters parkas include such features as: • Underarm zippers to vent excess heat. • Double drawstring hoods that protect without reducing vision. • Water-resistant zippers that won't freeze up in cold weather. • Cordura lace zipper pulls for easier operation when you're wearing gloves. • Underarm "action ease" cut for a comfortable, non-binding fit. • Universal® snaps that won't swivel, pull out, or break. • The nicest, sturdiest toggles you've ever seen. • Adjustable wrists for venting, or sealing arms from the wind.

Only if the garment meets Early Winters' standards at final inspection will it be sent to you. If you don't like it, send it back.

Gore-Tex® galore! The charts below help you compare features of some of our Gore-Tex® wear.

GARMENT		Trainer Jacket	Terra-shell	Lost World	Ultralight Parka	Sprint
Weight (oz.)		8.4	22	25	12.5	9.5
Sleeve Length (inches) Nape to wrist	XS	30	30	30	30	30
	S	32	32	32	32	32
	M	34	34	34	34	34
	L	36	36	36	36	36
	XL	38	38	38	38	38
Neck-to-Hem length (inches)	XS	22	27	27	27	28
	S	24	29	29	29	30
	M	26	31	31	31	32
	L	28	33	33	33	34
	XL	30	35	35	35	36
Taslan						
Nylon ripstop						
Water resistant zippers						
Heat vents						
Storm skirt						Butt flap
Factory-sealed seams						

Dear Customer,

Our latest catalog continues efforts to offer you more products and better quality merchandise. In order to bring you the hundreds of new products included, we traveled the world over.

As I write this, my brother, Eddie, is returning from yet another buying trip in Europe. In addition, our purchasing department scours this country for new items which would be helpful to you.

We hope you enjoy our new presentation and the many new products we've added. We are, of course, as committed as ever to the fast, friendly service and fair prices you have come to expect from us.

Sincerely,

Alan Bell - VP
Rio Grande Albuquerque

P.S. See page 2 for new shipping and handling information. FREE shipping on orders over $250.00.

EASY ORDERING INFORMATION

For fast, personal service just pick up the phone and charge it to your MasterCard or Visa.

We accept MasterCard and Visa, your personal check, certified checks, money orders or bank wire transfers. We will also accept C.O.D. if requested.

Order TOLL FREE 1-800-545-6566 and use your Visa or MasterCard for fast service. If you send us a check, certified check or money order, it is wise to send a little more than the amount of your order to cover fluctuations in the market. We will credit or refund, whichever you prefer.

OPEN ACCOUNTS: If you don't already have an open account with us and are listed with Jewelers Board of Trade, we can open an account for you with this order. If you are not currently rated with JBT and you would still like to open an account, just ask and we'll be happy to forward our credit policy information.

For more detailed information on Ordering, Pricing and Shipping, see page 2 of this catalog.

When To Call

We are open Monday-Friday from 8:30-5:30 Mountain Time.
This easy reference shows when we are open in your time zone.

FROM 5:30 TO 2:30 — FROM 6:30 TO 3:30 — FROM 7:30 TO 4:30 — FROM 7:30 TO 4:30 — FROM 8:30 TO 5:30 — FROM 9:30 TO 6:30 — FROM 10:30 TO 7:30

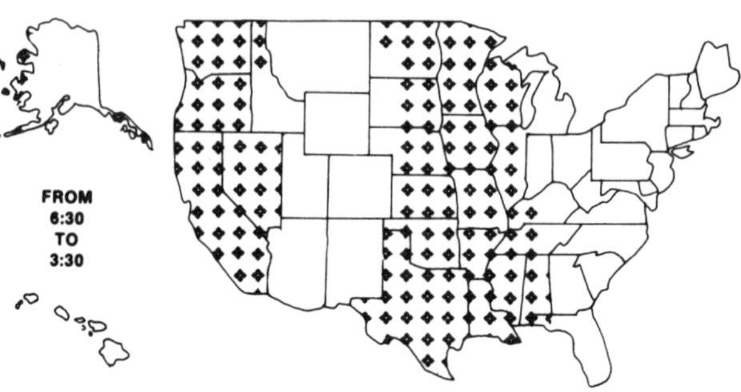

8-12

Toll Free Telephone Orders

Our telephone order number is **800-221-4221.** Our operators are available 24 hours each day, 7 days a week. For best service call between 4PM and 11PM EST. You may use your MasterCard®, VISA or American Express Cards for convenience when ordering.

Toll Free Customer Service

Our Customer Service number is **800-341-4341.** Open 24 hours each day, 7 days a week. When writing, please address to Customer Service Department.

Shipping Information

We ship primarily UPS. If you prefer United States Postal Service (USPS), be sure to specify this.

POSTPAID (PPD.) We pay regular shipping and handling charges on all orders delivered in the U.S. and its possessions, unless otherwise stated in this catalog.

SPECIAL SHIPMENT may be requested. The special shipment charge per delivery address in the **United States** is:

REGULAR	USPS AIR DELIVERY		SPECIAL DELIVERY
Paid by L. L. Bean	Item Total:	Charge:	Add $3.50 onto REGULAR or AIR DELIVERY Charge.
	Under $50.00	$3.00	
	$50.01-$100.00	$4.50	
	$100.01-200.00	$6.00	
	Over $200.00	$7.50	

FOREIGN SHIPMENT postage is paid by the customer. Please check your Customs and Postal Departments for regulations, rates and restrictions.

Four Day Delivery.

Orders received by 5PM can be shipped **Federal Express Standard Air** next business day for $7.50 per delivery address within the continental U.S. Sorry, no P.O. Box or Rural Rte. addresses. To assist us in delivery, please enter your telephone number on the order.

Returns and Exchanges

Should you wish to return your purchase for Exchange, please do this:

1. Wrap return securely in a good box using strong tape.
2. Include inside the package the packing slip we sent with your purchase telling us why you are returning your purchase and what you desire in exchange. If the packing slip is not available, please include a letter with the exchange information.
3. Be sure your package is insured and prepaid.

We will make every effort to speed delivery of your exchange. Please remember that it takes time for us to receive your merchandise, carefully process your request and ship your package back to you.

Correspondence

We appreciate any suggestions, comments or questions. We consider our customers a part of our organization and want you to feel free to make any criticism you see fit in regard to our merchandise or service.

Please use separate sheet of paper for faster handling and address to Customer Service Department.

SIZE GUIDELINES

Chest

Measure just under the arms and across shoulder blades holding tape firm and level. Women measure at the fullest point of the bust and across shoulder blades holding tape firm and level.

Gloves and Mitts

Measurement in inches around the knuckles with hand flat. (Exclude thumb.) Number of inches equals glove size.

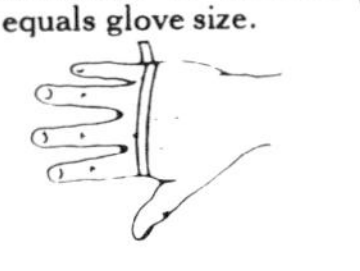

Footwear

Give size and width of dress shoe and/or enclose outline of bare foot. Hold pencil straight up when tracing foot. Also advise type of stockings you plan to wear (light, heavy, etc.)

Hat and Caps

Measurement in inches around the largest part of the head with tape above brow ridges. Convert to hat size using the chart below.

Shirts

Measurement in inches of a shirt collar that fits you well. Lay collar flat. Measure from center of collar button to far end of button hole.

Belts

Measurement in inches around the outside of the waistband of trousers that fit you well.

Inseam

Measure pants from the crotch seam to the bottom of the pants along inside pant leg seam.

Trousers, Slacks, Skirts

Measurement in inches over shirt around your waist, where you normally wear trousers or slacks. Hold tape firmly but not tight.

Hat Sizes: Unless otherwise stated the following conversions apply:

Head Measurement:	20½	20¾	21⅛	21½	21⅞	22¼	22⅝	23	23½
Hat Size:	6½	6⅝	6¾	6⅞	7	7⅛	7¼	7⅜	7½

Women's Shirts and Jackets:

Size:	Sm.	Med.	Lg.	XLg.
	6-8	10-12	14-16	18-20

Women's Skirts and Slacks (Actual Body Measurements)

Waist:	25	26	27	28	30	31	33	35
Size:	6	8	10	12	14	16	18	20

Stockings:

Shoe Size:	4-5½	6-8	8½-10	10½-11	11½-12½	13-14
Sock Size:	9(S)	10(M)	11(M)	12(L)	13(L)	14(XL)

Mailing Lists

We occasionally make our customer list of names and addresses available to carefully screened companies and organizations whose products and activities might be of interest to you. If you prefer not to receive such mailings, please copy your mailing label exactly and mail it to:

L. L. Bean, Inc., Mail Preference Service
Freeport, ME 04033

Please let us know if you have a friend who would like our catalog.

☐ Mr. ☐ Mrs. ☐ Ms. First Name — Middle Initial — Last Name
Street or Box No. — Route
City — State — Zip

☐ Mr. ☐ Mrs. ☐ Ms. First Name — Middle Initial — Last Name
Street of Box No. — Route
City — State — Zip

8-13

Close-Outs...While Supplies Last!

Portable Kerosene Heaters.

Save 70%!

Model #6090
Toyokuni 9,800 BTU/hour for 360 square feet one-sided radiant heater. 1 gallon fuel capacity at 0.3 quart use per hour. Size: 18'' high x 25'' deep. Weight 23 lbs. Glass burner. Grille guards. Glass wool wick. Auto-ignition. Auto-extinquishing if flame is bumped or jarred. Manual fuel siphon. U.L. listed.

#6090 Toyokuni 9,800 BTU/hour, ~~$189.00~~ NOW $57.50

Model #6091
Toyokuni 15,000 BTU/hour for 550 square feet full circle convection heater. 1.3 gallon fuel capacity at 0.45 quarts use per hour. Size: 23'' high x 18'' wide x 18'' deep. Weight 13 lbs. Glass burner. Grille guards. Glass wool wick. Auto ignition. Auto-extinguishing if flame is bumped or jarred. Manual fuel siphon. U.L. listed.

#6091 Toyokuni 15,000 BTU/hour, ~~$229.00~~ NOW $64.50

Acreage Counter

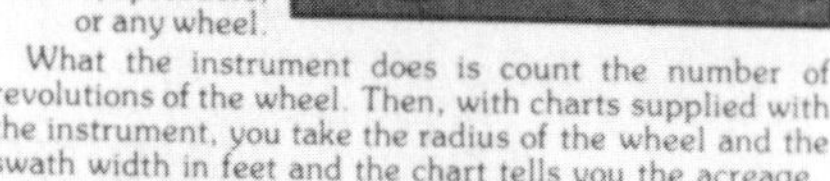

Put this on your tractor wheel, or your machinery wheel, and know how much acreage you've covered. Tested and proven in the trucking industry for over 25 years. Use it on tractors, planters, combines, spreaders, or any wheel.

What the instrument does is count the number of revolutions of the wheel. Then, with charts supplied with the instrument, you take the radius of the wheel and the swath width in feet and the chart tells you the acreage.

No maintenance required. Easy to install. Tamper-proof. Mounting brackets are included.

#6403 Acreage Counter, $67.00

HOW TO ORDER FROM MODERN FARM

Order by mail

Use the order blank enclosed. Or write a letter giving product name, item number, and size or color. Send to Modern Farm, 1825 Big Horn Avenue, Cody, Wyoming 82414.

Order by telephone

Phone toll-free 800-443-4934. Operators are on duty from 7:30—4:30 Mountain Time Monday—Friday. 7:30—Noon Saturday. Closed Sundays. Dial direct and order with a charge to your VISA, Mastercard, American Express, or Diners Club credit card. In Wyoming call 587-5946 collect.

Terms

Terms are payment-with-order. Please include your check, bank draft, money order or use your MasterCard, VISA, Diners Club or American Express card. Sales tax at the rate of 3% is required only on orders shipped to a State of Wyoming address. Merchandise shipped outside Wyoming is not taxable.

Shipping

We ship UPS wherever possible. If you prefer Parcel Post, be sure to specify this. On request we will ship your order by Air UPS Blue Label and bill you for the added cost, about $1 per pound. We process your order immediately upon request and often the shipment leaves our building within 48 hours.

OUR GUARANTEE
Modern Farm Ear Tags carry a no-questions-asked Lifetime Guarantee. All other products carry an **iron-clad** satisfaction guarantee. If you're unhappy with your purchase for **any** reason, send it back within 30 days for a replacement or a **full refund.** You **must** be satisfied.

TEN REASONS TO SHOP WITH CONFIDENCE THROUGH MODERN FARM

1. **Over 200,000 satisfied customers**
   Modern Farm has over 200,000 customers who come to us year after year for all their ear tag and other ranch supply needs. They keep coming back because they know they'll get fair prices, great merchandise and excellent service!
2. **A unit of an established family-owned business.**
   Modern Farm is a unit of a 23-year old business which has been family-owned in Cody, Wyoming, for all of its years.
3. **Nation-wide merchandise selection.**
   With contacts around the entire country, we offer a unique selection of merchandise, hard-to-find farm and ranch tools, often not found in stores.
4. **Only good quality offers.**
   With Modern Farm's guarantee, we only offer good quality merchandise. We want you to be satisfied.
5. **Lowest possible prices consistent with quality.**
   No seconds, or inferior quality items are offered, so the value offered for the money is outstanding. You eliminate the middle-man when buying "farm direct."
6. **Reliable product descriptions.**
   All of the products are described in this catalog in an honest, straightforward manner without exaggeration. We deal with many people. We know if an item is complicated and try to answer all of your questions in advance. Often you get much more information in the catalog than you could from a store clerk.
7. **Prompt shipments.**
   Items ordered from Modern Farm are shipped promptly from our building, often within 48 hours of receipt of your order. You will be notified of any unforeseen delay. Some items are shipped from warehouses where fast service is their specialty.
8. **Satisfaction guaranteed.**
   You must be completely satisfied with anything ordered or you may return it immediately for a cheerful refund, or replacement.
9. **Performance underwritten by reputation.**
   As part of a 23-year old family business operating in the small town of Cody, Wyoming, we must provide excellent service or we wouldn't be permitted to continue.
10. **Toll-free number to answer any questions.**
   If you have any questions regarding merchandise or your order, please call our customer service department (toll-free 800-443-4934).

CUSTOMER SERVICE

Our toll-free phone number is 800-443-4934. When phoning about an order already placed, please call between 7:30 a.m. and 4:30 p.m. Mountain Time Monday through Friday. Ask for Customer Service. If you call or write about your order, be sure to include: our order number (if available); date of order; your name, address, and telephone number; amount of payment; charge card number; catalog name of item, including quantity, size, color and price. Write to Customer Service.

RETURNS AND EXCHANGES

How to return: Should your order be damaged or if you wish a different size or color, please do this: (1) Use a good carton. Wrap, using good tape. (2) Inside the package, include the papers that we sent you, plus a note saying why you are returning your purchase and what you desire. (3) Address your package to: Modern Farm, Big Horn Avenue, Cody, Wyoming 82414. (4) Ship insured and prepaid. We will make every effort to speed delivery of your exchange. Please remember that it takes time for us to receive your merchandise, carefully process your request, and ship your package back to you.

CORRESPONDENCE

We appreciate any suggestions, comments or questions. Our customers are a vital part of our organization. We want you to feel free to make any criticism you see fit in regard to our merchandise or service. Please use separate sheet of paper for faster handling and address to Customer Service Department.

MAILING LISTS

We occasionally make our customer list of names and addresses available to carefully screened companies and organizations whose products and activities might be of interest to you. If you prefer not to receive such mailings, please copy your mailing label exactly and mail it to:
Modern Farm Mail Preference Service
Cody, Wyoming 82414

good points can be gleaned by reviewing these ten reasons:

1. Over 200,000 satisfied customers. The headline alone tells customers and prospects that a lot of people believe in the company enough to purchase.

2. Family-owned business is a wonderful fact to tell customers because it builds camaraderie and suggests the dependability and tradition of a solid American family.

3. Nationwide merchandise selection lets the customer know that Modern Farm searches for the best, most up-to-date merchandise.

4. Only good quality is reinforced by the guarantee and tells the customer the company is proud of its products.

5. Lowest possible prices reminds customers that Modern Farm considers their pocketbooks, too.

6. Reliable product descriptions reinforces company credibility and belief in the company's products by truth in advertising. This also brings up a point which is very valid and influential in mail order shopping: *''Often you get much more information in the catalog than you could from a store clerk.''*

7. Prompt shipments tells customers the company cares about serving them quickly . . . ''often within 48 hours of receipt of your order.''

Info panel can sell company

8. Satisfaction guaranteed emphasizes the desire to please the customer.

9. Performance is emphasized by again pointing out the dependability of the ''23-year old family business . . .''

10. Toll-free number to answer any questions is yet another way of letting customers know the company backs up its products and truly cares about and welcomes customer interest.

Most of these ten ''reasons'' have already been explained elsewhere on the page, but *this is promoting them — selling the product, service, delivery, dependability, and credibility*. It's space well used. And at the top of the page, three close-out products are offered at sale prices — the proceeds will no doubt pay for the order form.

In summary, the details given on the information panel will build customer confidence. In some cases this information allows the customer to try out vicariously the service or ''try on'' a product, thus eliminating fear of ordering. Clarifying the process of ordering will benefit the company, too, by allowing smoother order processing. And carefully worded information will help keep down refunds due to misunderstandings or to incorrect sizing or personalization.

Product Panel

The order form is a popular area for sale merchandise and impulse products. The product panel has often been compared to a checkout line in a grocery or discount store where impulse items are sold. Regular merchandise can be presented, too. But often the choice of product is determined by the number of ink colors used. Some products simply will not present well in black-and-white. If the order form is black-and-white or two-color, then a lemon jelly roll, navy jacket, or an intricately designed motif cannot easily be presented in a manner which will attract attention or sell the product.

Lillian Vernon uses a three-panel foldout to picture eight products for sale. Figure 8-15 illustrates how four-color printing allows freedom of product choice. The page layout follows that of the catalog for tight coordination and strong purchasing appeal.

The same effect is achieved by the Fidelity Products Company envelope flap (Figure 8-16). Product presentation is four-color and the layout is similar to a catalog page. Note the "In stock," "Quick shipment," and UPS symbols; these are used throughout the catalog for products that are in stock and can be shipped instantly . . . all good order incentives.

8-15

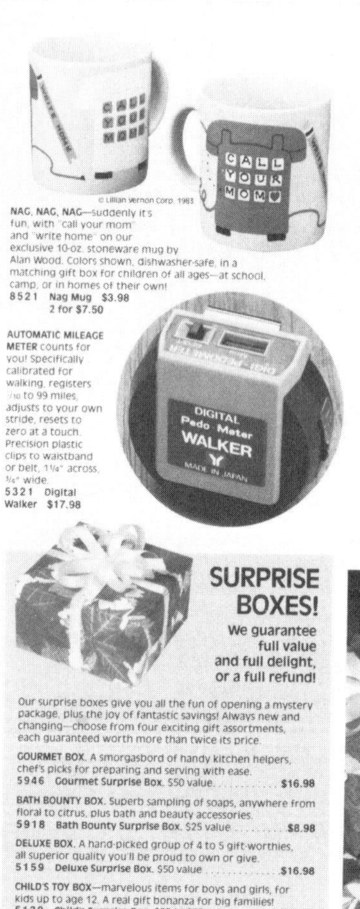

In many cases, both the front or address side and the back of the envelope are used for customer education, imparting information, and selling products — and sometimes for special promotions such as free gift, bonus offer, and value boxes. Should this area really be used for promotion and selling? Absolutely! The ordering envelope, like any other part of the catalog, should be expected to pay its way. Even though it's normally the carrier which brings the catalog customer orders, it can do more (as you can see in the following illustrations).

Front, address side. The most commonly practiced function for the address side of the envelope is just what it says — the catalog company's name and address plus bar coding to be used by the post office for automatic sorting. Lines for the customer to fill in a return address are usually provided, too. Figure 8-17 from the Williams-Sonoma catalog shows the typical approach. General consumer

8-16

2-Year Parts and 3-Year CRT Warranty

Compatible with most computers

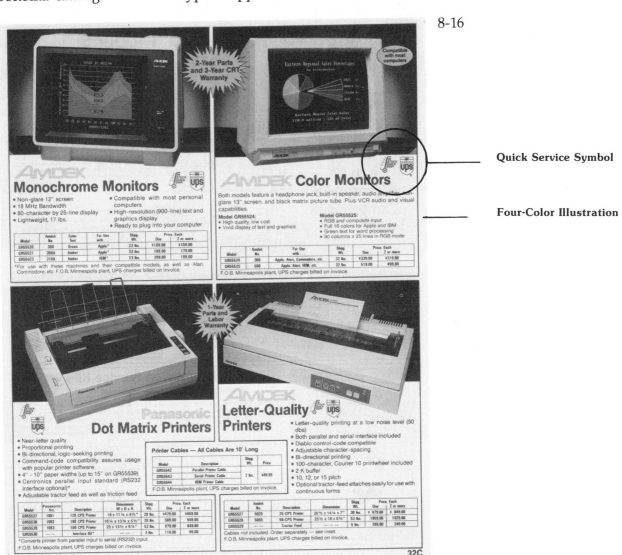

Quick Service Symbol

Four-Color Illustration

AMDEK

Monochrome Monitors

- Non-glare 12" screen
- 18 MHz Bandwidth
- 80-character by 25-line display
- Lightweight, 17 lbs.
- Compatible with most personal computers
- High-resolution (900-line) text and graphics display
- Ready to plug into your computer

Model	Amdek No.	Color Text	For Use with . . .	Shpg. Wt.	Price, Each One	Price, Each 2 or more
GR55520	300	Green	Apple*	23 lbs.	$189.00	$159.00
GR55521	300A	Amber	Apple*	23 lbs.	189.00	179.00
GR55523	310A	Amber	IBM*	23 lbs.	209.00	199.00

*For use with these machines and their compatible models, as well as Atari, Commodore, etc. F.O.B. Minneapolis plant, UPS charges billed on invoice.

AMDEK **Color Monitors**

Both models feature a headphone jack, built-in speaker, audio amplifier, non-glare 13" screen, and black matrix picture tube. Plus VCR audio and visual capabilities.

Model GR55524:
- High quality, low cost
- Vivid display of text and graphics

Model GR55525:
- RGB and composite input
- Full 16 colors for Apple and IBM
- Green text for word processing
- 80 columns x 25 lines in RGB mode

Model	Amdek No.	For Use with . . .	Shpg. Wt.	Price, Each One	Price, Each 2 or more
GR55524	300	Apple, Atari, Commodore, etc.	32 lbs.	$339.00	$319.00
GR55525	500	Apple, Atari, IBM, etc.	32 lbs.	519.00	499.00

F.O.B. Minneapolis plant, UPS charges billed on invoice.

1-Year Parts and Labor Warranty

Panasonic **Dot Matrix Printers**

- Near-letter quality
- Proportional printing
- Bi-directional, logic-seeking printing
- Command-code compatibility assures usage with popular printer software
- 4" - 10" paper widths (up to 15" on GR55539)
- Centronics parallel input standard (RS232 interface optional)*
- Adjustable tractor feed as well as friction feed

Model	Panasonic No.	Description	Dimensions W x D x H	Shpg. Wt.	Price, Each One	Price, Each 2 or more
GR55537	1091	120 CPS Printer	16 x 11¼ x 4½"	20 lbs.	$479.00	$459.00
GR55538	1092	180 CPS Printer	16¼ x 13¾ x 5½"	20 lbs.	569.00	549.00
GR55539	1093	160 CPS Printer	25 x 13½ x 6¼"	53 lbs.	879.00	849.00
GR55530	— —	Interface Kit*	— —	3 lbs.	110.00	99.00

*Converts printer from parallel input to serial (RS232) input.
F.O.B. Minneapolis plant, UPS charges billed on invoice.

Printer Cables — All Cables Are 10' Long

Model	Description	Shpg. Wt.	Price
GR55542	Parallel Printer Cable	2 lbs.	$49.95
GR55543	Serial Printer Cable		
GR55544	IBM Printer Cable		

F.O.B. Minneapolis plant, UPS charges billed on invoice.

AMDEK **Letter-Quality Printers**

- Letter-quality printing at a low noise level (50 dba)
- Both parallel and serial interface included
- Diablo control-code compatible
- Adjustable character-spacing
- Bi-directional printing
- 100-character, Courier 10 printwheel included
- 2 K buffer
- 10, 12, or 15 pitch
- Optional tractor-feed attaches easily for use with continuous forms

Model	Amdek No.	Description	Dimensions	Shpg. Wt.	Price, Each One	Price, Each 2 or more
GR55527	5025	25-CPS Printer	20½ x 14¼ x 7"	30 lbs.	$ 879.00	$ 849.00
GR55528	5055	55-CPS Printer	25½ x 18 x 8¾"	53 lbs.	1959.00	1929.00
GR55529	— —	Tractor Feed	— — —	5 lbs.	289.00	249.00

Cables not included. Order separately — see inset.
F.O.B. Minneapolis plant, UPS charges billed on invoice.

32C

catalogs indicate an area for customers to place their own stamp, while the majority of the business-to-business catalogs provide a prepaid business reply envelope as seen in Figure 8-18 from Omaha Steaks. Specific design requirements are requested by the United States Post Office. These specifications can be obtained from your local post office.

A more attractive and internally efficient approach — and certainly a more profitable one — is to utilize the left area of the envelope for a design, message, function, or even for selling a product. Figure 8-19, again from Omaha Steaks, shows how effectively this area can be used for a "Rush this order!" message. The printing, in red ink, simulates a rubber stamp. This message indicates no expectation that the post office will deliver any faster; it's just an indicator to the customer that the company cares about receiving the order. An important addition is the message right below the return address area: "Check here if yours is a new address." If only twenty percent of the customers who really do have a new address check the box, it will save hours of time in data processing over a year's time. Eddie Bauer chooses to add a wildlife motif to add appeal to its outdoor clothing and camping catalog (Figure 8-20). This costs no more and makes the envelope more distinctive. Just below is the message "Order-Rush," again indicating to the customer that this company cares about receiving an order and a catalog code number, too. This code number allows both fast mail sorting and proper credit assignment.

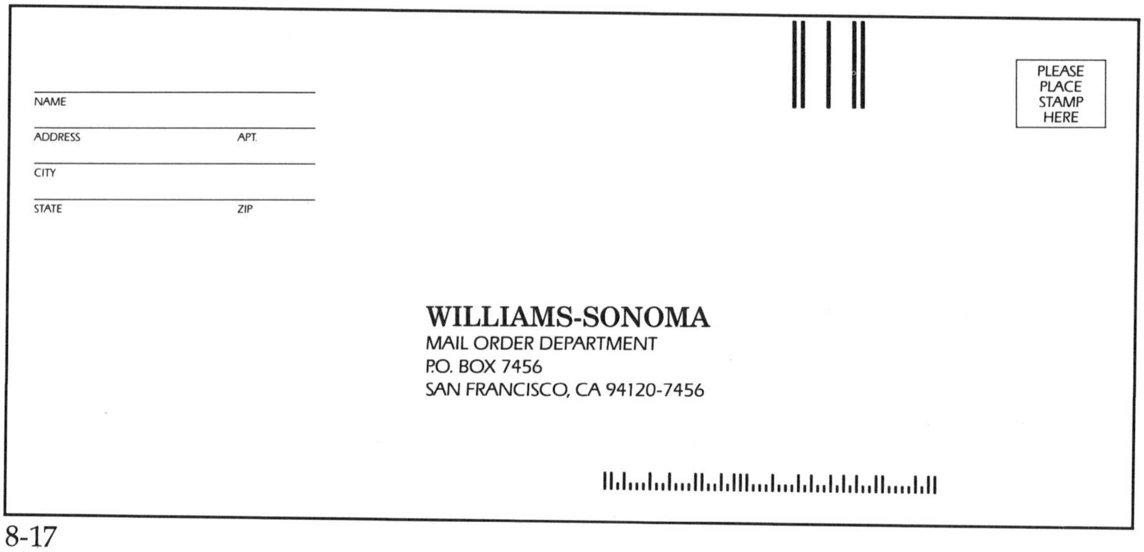

NAME
ADDRESS APT.
CITY
STATE ZIP

PLEASE PLACE STAMP HERE

WILLIAMS-SONOMA
MAIL ORDER DEPARTMENT
P.O. BOX 7456
SAN FRANCISCO, CA 94120-7456

8-17

Back of the envelope. The back of the envelope can and does bear more serious selling and promotion. There are no postal requirements for this space, so not to use it in some way is foolish. Williams-Sonoma, the sample seen in Figure 8-17, goes all out on the back of the envelope (Figure 8-21). Two products are pictured

RUSH ORDER ENCLOSED FROM:

NO POSTAGE NECESSARY IF MAILED IN THE UNITED STATES

BUSINESS REPLY MAIL

FIRST CLASS PERMIT NO. 263 OMAHA, NEBRASKA

POSTAGE WILL BE PAID BY ADDRESSEE

Omaha Steaks International®

FREDERICK J. SIMON
4400 SOUTH 96TH STREET
P.O. BOX 3300
OMAHA, NEBRASKA 68172

8-18

RUSH ORDER ENCLOSED FROM:

☐ CHECK HERE IF YOURS IS A NEW ADDRESS

NO POSTAGE NECESSARY IF MAILED IN THE UNITED STATES

BUSINESS REPLY MAIL

FIRST CLASS PERMIT NO. 263 OMAHA, NEBRASKA

POSTAGE WILL BE PAID BY ADDRESSEE

PRIORITY HANDLING: Rush This Order!

Omaha Steaks International®

4400 SOUTH 96TH STREET
P.O. BOX 3300
OMAHA, NEBRASKA 68172

8-19

for sale, along with complete selling copy. The illustrations are even in four-color. And ample area is provided for the customer to fill in a friend's name to receive a Williams-Sonoma catalog. Figure 8-22 from the Country Curtains catalog *promotes phone ordering even though a regular number is given where the customer pays the tab.* Three spaces are provided for friends' names! And reinforcement is given to the customer by stating the company's unconditional guarantee. L.L. Bean uses the back of the envelope for reinforcing customer confidence with its *100 Percent Guarantee,* promoting its *toll-free telephone ordering* service, providing the customer with a final *ordering check list,* and reminding the customer to include any *address change.* Also in Figure 8-23, we see how L.L. Bean promotes its *Gift Certificate* service. Omaha Steaks promotes its superior packaging to assure customers that the food they order will arrive safely. A diagram shows the packaging components (Figure 8-24) very effectively.

Smart use of space

NAME
ADDRESS
CITY STATE ZIP

PLACE STAMP HERE

Eddie Bauer®
FIFTH & UNION
P.O. BOX 3700
SEATTLE, WASHINGTON
98130

ORDER–RUSH

8-20 U9

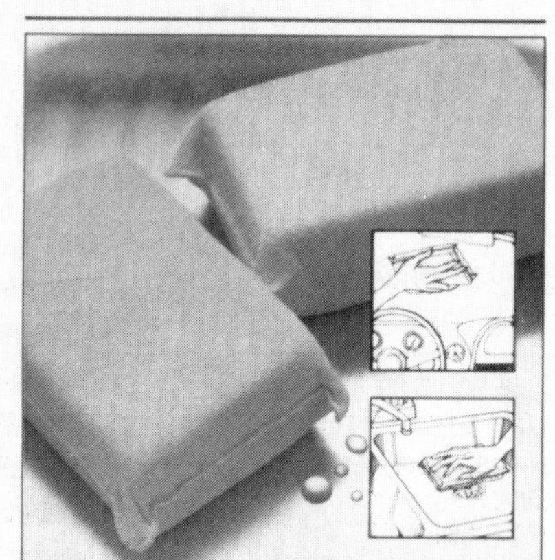

This **Chamois Covered Sponge** does a super job of keeping stainless steel sinks and countertops or windows sparkling and free of water stains. (The sponge absorbs water from the natural chamois skin.) Keep one in the car to defog windows in wet weather. 3" x 4¼" x 1½", made in Holland. Set of two #36-13334 $6.50

Old fashioned, no nonsense **Flour Sack Towels** are snowy white, lintless 100% cotton, and measure an extra-large 38" x 32". Made in USA. Set of eight #36-08391 $14.00

May we send a catalog to a friend?
Please **print** the name and address below:

NAME
(36215)
ADDRESS APT.
CITY
STATE ZIP

8-21

Country Curtains... ...
Old-Fashioned Quality and Conscientious Service

PHONE ORDERS
(Please have your MasterCard or Visa information and your catalog at hand when you place your order.)

Please call: (413) 243-1805.
Monday-Friday, 8 AM - Midnight
Saturday, 9 AM - 5 PM (Eastern)

CUSTOMER SERVICE
Please call (413) 243-9910
Monday-Friday, 8:30 AM - 4 PM (Eastern)

Dear Jane Fitzpatrick,
Please send your free Country Curtains catalog to these friends:

NAME
ADDRESS
CITY
STATE ZIP

NAME
ADDRESS
CITY
STATE ZIP

NAME
ADDRESS
CITY
STATE ZIP

SATISFACTION GUARANTEED . . . If you are not totally pleased, just let us know. We will be happy to make an exchange or refund. Please do so promptly and let us know the reason so we may serve you better in the future.
Please allow additional time for package to arrive here and be processed.

8-22

8-23

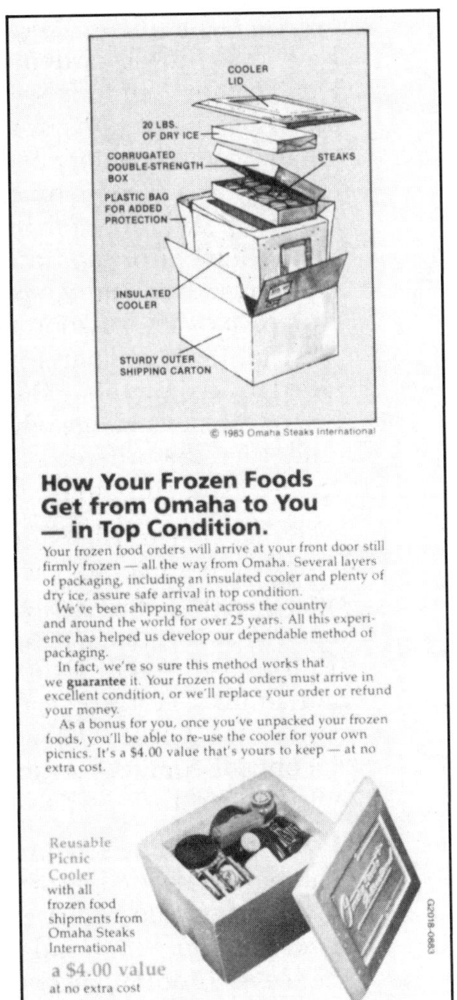

8-24

The copy strongly promotes such facts as, "We've been shipping meat across the country and around the world for over 25 years," and states the company's emphatic guarantee. Because the insulated cooler box holding the frozen food is so sturdy, it is promoted as a picnic cooler and as a $4.00 value which is the customer's at no extra cost. This is smart promotion — something the customer can appreciate.

Order Form Design

It is no small trick to design an order form that looks appealing, is logical for the customer to use, includes everything required by the type of products carried, and meets the internal needs of the catalog company. A lot of planning must be done in the beginning and an expert designer sought. When working with your designer, keep the following three words in mind and let them guide your planning, your discussion with the designer, and the final assessment of the ordering area itself. The three words are: *(1) simplicity*, (2) *space*, and (3) *logic*.

1. Simplicity. Above all, keep your design clean and simple. Keep the requests or demands you make upon your customer few. Don't clutter your form with seemingly clever design elements which are visual distractions from the process of ordering. Keep the color scheme complimentary and don't highlight or screen too many areas for emphasis. Too many elements will only distract the customer's attention. Ask only for information which is directly pertinent to the fulfillment of the order, such as product code, name of item, price, quantity desired, and shipping charges. Special products may require such information as size and personalization. If you do not preprint the customer's name and address, an area must be provided to accommodate this, too. Method of payment must be clearly requested. Catalogs which accommodate shipping to an address other than the orderer's (such as a gift service) must have an area for the extra shipping address and name.

2. Space. Allow enough room on the ordering lines for the customer to comfortably write or print the needed information. Many catalogs don't leave enough width and yet leave an extraordinary amount of height, which makes this area unsightly as well as difficult to use. Also be sure there is enough room to write a name and address, if needed, for personalization. Make sure the boxes or lines for charge card numbers are large enough. Cramped space not only discourages action, but also makes it difficult for your order entry department to decipher the numbers.

3. Logic. Use common sense about the sequence in which you request needed information, not only for the customer's sake, but also for your order entry department. Their needs can work hand-in-hand with a satisfactory solution for the customer. (*But* if there ever is doubt, *make it easy for your customer*.) If the customer's name and address is different from the ship-to address, put the space for the shipping address in the same area — generally at the top. Ordering information comes next, with the total, tax, and shipping and handling data right below. Method of payment should be near the total for easy referral. Your telephone number should be placed either at the top of the order form so your customer can find it without searching, or at the bottom near the charge and totaling information to encourage quick and accurate phone orders.

In Figure 8-25 we see the Early Winters catalog, which concentrates on sports gear for the general consumer, doing an exceptional job of making its order form ''user friendly'' for its customers.

This catalog separates the needed information into three easy segments:

(a) Shipping information
(b) Ordering information
(c) Payment method information

In addition, the designer has numbered each step in the natural sequence a customer would take when filling out the order form, making it exceptionally easy to place an order. The resulting visual appeal also encourages order placement. The easy use of this form closes the sale!

Figure 8-26 shows how a business-to-business computer forms and business supplies catalog, Moore, applies the same principles. Cleanly defined shipping information is asked for in steps one, two, and three. Ordering information is requested in five, six, and seven. Payment method information is also kept in one area, the lower one-fourth (numbers four and eight) of the order form. What is hard to see here is the skilled use of a second color (blue) to accent the steps needed. A screening of the color is used to separate each area of the form, making the ordering process seem even simpler.

Closer examination of both examples reveals three very important features that make the order form appealing and easy to use: numbering the steps, allowing generous room to fill in information, and providing sectioned areas for charge card numbers.

Early Winters takes the customer through eleven steps of order fulfillment. Again refer to Figure 8-25.

1. The name and address area provides space for customer number, telephone number, and birthdate (account number recorded in company's records). Customers are encouraged to ''Place peel-off label here'' — a great aid to the order entry and record keeping departments. The unusual request for birthdate not only allows the company a prime opportunity for individual promotion via special mailings and highly personalized letters, but it also provides the company with exacting information about the customer which will benefit overall customer profile analysis and product selection.

2. The address of the person the merchandise is to be shipped to assures the customer and the company of minimal error.

3. The address correction area allows the company to keep its record file current. The house list will remain credible and costs for postal handling and catalogs are kept down.

4. Product ordering information has been kept very simple, asking only for quantity, product code, product size and color choices, product name with desired personalizing information, price each, and total price. This is the minimum amount of information needed for a catalog carrying a large proportion of apparel. No extras such as page number or weight are asked for — the computer can be programmed to give the catalog company that information.

Step-by-step guidance

Steps 5, 6, 7, 8, 9, and 10 tally the business details. Two of the steps seem questionable for either the company's or the customer's benefit. Six, for example (credit, gift cer-

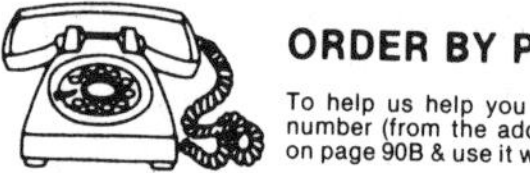

ORDER BY PHONE (206) 624-5599

To help us help you better, please copy your customer number (from the address label) into the space provided on page 90B & use it with future orders or correspondence.

Shipping Information

1 Ordered by: If peel-off label is incorrect, print your name, address, and customer number here. **DEX**

Customer Number

Mr. / Mrs. / Ms. / Miss

Street

City — State — Zipcode

PLACE PEEL-OFF LABEL HERE

Your daytime phone number (Speeds order should we have a question)

Month Day Year — May we have your birthdate?

2 Ship to: (If different from name & address at left)

Mr. / Mrs. / Ms. / Miss

Street

City — State — Zipcode

3 If you've moved since last ordering, print OLD address here:

Street — City — State — Zipcode

Ordering Information

4

Qty.	Product code	Size	Color 1st choice	Color 2nd choice	Product Name (or words/name for engraving or embroidery)	Monogram Initials First name	Monogram Initials Middle name	Monogram Initials Last name	Price Each	Total price

Need more room? Attach a separate sheet.

Payment Method

11 MY METHOD OF PAYMENT IS:

☐ Check or Money Order—U.S. funds.
☐ Traveler's Checks—made out in the higher amount than your order. We'll refund the difference.
☐ MasterCard ☐ Diner's Club
☐ Carte Blanche ☐ Visa
☐ American Express

Card Number

Expiration date

X
Cardholder's signature

DO NOT WRITE IN THIS BOX
CK
MO
CA

8 Handling, packing, insurance

Order Amt.	$0 to $15	$15.01 to $50	$50.01 to $100	$100.01 to $200	$200.01 & over
Surface	$2.55	$3.45	$4.40	$5.85	1% of total
Air	$5.95	$6.95	$7.90	$9.35	1% of total + $3.50

5	Total of items above	
6	Credit, gift cert, or discount. Enclose appropriate document	
7	Item total $500-$900, deduct 5%; $900 or more, deduct 8%	
8	Handling, packing, insurance (See chart at left)	
9	Sales tax. Add 7.8% for WA deliveries only.	
10	TOTAL	

Check over your order, use the envelope provided, and mail today!

8-25

tificate, or discount), is a bookkeeping chore and constitutes a minimal number of total orders. Would this be better off on the information panel? The same is true for line seven. The percentage of orders totaling more than $500 is no doubt small compared with the total number of orders. Do these functions really act as incentives to increase orders, or are they just another line adding confusion to the process? Handling, packing and insurance, line eight, is nicely conveyed with a fee chart.

11. Method of payment is handled well — especially the area for the customer to fill in the numbers. A slight line indication is given each number box, acting as a guide for

the customer to neatly fill in and making sure no numbers have been omitted.

Moore Business Forms (Figure 8-26) also numbers the steps to be taken. Billing and shipping information is clearly designed for customer ease. Ample space is given for information to be filled in through a progressive vertical format, steps 1, 2, 3, 4.

The 5, 6, and 7 areas are exceptional in design. Requested product information consists of five simple sections: catalog number, quantity, item description, unit price, and total amount. Two separate areas are devoted to personalization information for the stationery items offered. The request for typestyle selection, logo, and numbering requirements demands careful company handling and adequate space for the desired personalization (7). Again, the area allowed is roomy to encourage ordering and accuracy. What might look like excessive allowance for space only seems so because of exceptional design elements. The payment area (8) is good, with individual boxes for charge card numbers — again assuring accuracy and also acting as a simple guide.

1 BILL TO

☐ Check here if name and/or address are incorrect, and enter corrections.

Name_____
Title_____
Company_____
Address_____
City_____ State_____ Zip_____

AFFIX PEEL-OFF ADDRESS LABEL HERE

2 SHIP TO (if different from address above)

Name_____
Title_____
Company_____
Address_____
City_____ State_____ Zip_____
Person Ordering_____
Title_____ Date_____ (   ) Business Phone
Signature_____

3 SHIPPING (CHECK ONE PLEASE)

☐ Regular Delivery (usually UPS, Except for heavy, bulky items) ☐ Emergency Delivery (Air Courier)

EMERGENCY NEXT-DAY DELIVERY requires the slightly higher charge for air courier service. Phone order by 2 P.M. CST. Delivered by 5 P.M. next business day to most U.S. locations. Also, UPS "2nd Day Air Service" is available to selected cities at approximately half the cost of overnight air courier cost. Please call to see if your city is qualified. ☐ UPS 2nd Day Air Service

4 NEW ACCOUNT INFORMATION

To help us expedite your order, please provide your DUN & BRADSTREET numbcr (if you have one):_____
if you've bought from the Moore Catalog before, enter your Moore Customer No._____
Bank Name:_____
Account Number (if known):_____
City_____ State_____ Zip_____
(Bank reference not required if you are listed and acceptably rated with D&B or have bought from Moore before.)

MOORE

COMPUTER FORMS AND SUPPLIES CATALOG ORDER FORM

P.O. BOX 20, WHEELING, IL 60090

ALL PRICES GUARANTEED THROUGH DECEMBER 31, 1983

Shipping information: Imprinted items usually ship within 6 working days, Non-Imprinted items will be processed and shipped within 48 hours. Therefore, imprinted forms and other stock items may be shipped separately. **For Imprinted Orders:** Please fill out all pertinent information in Sections 6 and 7. If ordering by phone, give complete imprinting information to our sales representative. If no type preference is stated, we will print your order in typestyle B, Alphatura Book. For all check orders a "voided" bank check or a magnetic ink encoding form filled in by your bank must accompany your order. See pages 55 and 57 for ordering instructions. If ordering by phone, use the attached envelope to return your check material.

5 CATALOG NUMBER	QUANTITY	ITEM DESCRIPTION	UNIT PRICE (each, doz., etc.)	TOTAL AMOUNT

ORDER NON-IMPRINTED ITEMS HERE

ORDER IMPRINTED ITEMS BELOW

6 CATALOG NUMBER	QUANTITY	ITEM DESCRIPTION	UNIT PRICE (each, doz., etc.)	TOTAL AMOUNT

Type Style ☐ Garamond ☐ Alphatura Book ☐ Alphatura Medium ☐ Kaufman Bold — Logo Code ☐ ☐ — No Logo ☐ — Starting No. (Sequentially Numbered forms only)_____

Type Style ☐ Garamond ☐ Alphatura Book ☐ Alphatura Medium ☐ Kaufman Bold — Logo Code ☐ ☐ — No Logo ☐ — Starting No. (Sequentially Numbered forms only)_____

Type Style ☐ Garamond ☐ Alphatura Book ☐ Alphatura Medium ☐ Kaufman Bold — Logo Code ☐ ☐ — No Logo ☐ — Starting No. (Sequentially Numbered forms only)_____

7 IMPRINT INFORMATION: See page 55 for complete details and specifications regarding the ordering of imprinted forms and checks.

PLEASE PRINT CLEARLY

Your Firm Name_____ (Maximum 40 characters, including blanks & punctuation)
Street or Mailing Address_____ (Maximum 25 characters, including blanks & punctuation)
City, State, Zip Code_____ (Maximum 49 characters, including blanks & punctuation)
Phone Number_____ (Maximum 20 characters, including blanks & punctuation)

MINIMUM ORDER $15.00

Applicable sales tax must be added unless your tax-exempt number is shown here ☐ Sales Tax_____

Shipping charges will be added to your invoice. Total $_____

8 PAYMENT (check one) PLEASE: NO C.O.D.'s
TERMS: NET 30 DAYS FROM DATE OF INVOICE
(CHECK ONE)
☐ Check or Money Order enclosed
☐ Open Account—new customers, see left
☐ Company Purchase Order (required on orders over $1,000)

Purchase Order No._____

Authorized Signature:_____ Title_____
☐ Visa ☐ MasterCard ☐ American Express
Account Number ☐☐☐☐☐☐☐☐☐☐☐☐☐☐☐☐
American Express account number ends here
Signature_____
Expiration Date_____

8-26

Both companies have been considerate by providing *simplification of design* and the progressive numbering system that guides the customer through the ordering steps. The most glaring omission from the Moore Business Forms illustration is their own telephone number for ordering! Telephone orders constitute up to 90 percent of total business-to-business orders; not to have the number on the order form seems a major oversight. Both companies have neglected to say ''thank you'' to the customer, even though it's a nice and easy thing to do.

Following is a brief review of three very good order forms, highlighting their good points and calling attention to what is missing.

Simplicity is most important

1. Figure 8-27, Omaha Steaks. An immediate positive reaction registers because of design and obvious *ease of ordering*. A *bonus* enticing the customer to order is prominently displayed at the top of the order form. Ample space is given to *fill-in* areas; many food companies unnecessarily complicate this procedure. At the bottom, the order summary is prominent. A good visual emphasizes the toll-free number. *What is missing? A guarantee.*

2. Figure 8-28, Ambassador. A plethora of information is assembled on this form — and yet with an overall effect of *simplicity*. Ambassador shows right away an easy-to-use three-step formula for *filling in* needed information. Steps 1 and 2 are the application of the peel-off address label, plus an area to manually fill in the needed information if the label is missing or incorrect. Step 3 leads the customer through *method of payment*. The *bonus* area is kept simple, even though chock-full of information, and is well placed for encouraging larger orders. *Postage and Handling* is clear. The *guarantee* is well placed and highlighted. *What's missing? A telephone number . . .* toll-free or regular.

3. Figure 8-29, Eva Gabor Wigs by Paula. Here we have clean lines, discretionary use of color, and *simplicity* of presentation. The customer is set at ease right away by the prominent placement of the *guarantee* which is so vital with this type of product. *Order information* is kept simple with adequate fill-in room. *Shipping and Handling* is easily taken care of by one charge, $3.00, preprinted on the form. A *toll-free number* is displayed prominently with added graphics. *Method of payment* is so simply presented it looks easy, and an extra *bonus* is offered at just the right time — when the customer is ready to finalize the order. *What's missing? Nothing vital.*

But what do all three order forms lack? A *''Thank you for your order''* message to the customer.

Omaha Steaks International®
4400 South 96th Street
P.O. Box 3300 • Omaha, Nebraska 68103

ORDER FORM

CHICKEN BREAST BONUS!

Order No. 806 - two 6 oz. Chicken Kiev, two 6 oz. Chicken Cordon Bleu, two 6 oz. Chicken Alfredo, and two 7 oz. Chicken Venezzia. Regularly $47.00, *it's yours for just $33.00* - but only when ordered with another selection from this catalog. You'll save $14.00. Order now!

Make checks out to "Omaha Steaks International."
Please specify:

☐ Check or Money Order enclosed $__________.
☐ VISA ☐ Diners Club
☐ Master Card ☐ Carte Blanche
☐ American Express ☐ Omaha Steaks — if you have an approved account **

SHOW CREDIT CARD NUMBER BELOW:

Card Expires Month Year

In case we have a question about your order, may we have your phone number? ☐Home: ( ) ☐Office: ( )

Please print
Name
Address Apt.#
City State Zip

Peel label from back of catalog and attach here.

Please be sure we have your correct mailing address in the space above.

Please ship these selections to my address:

Shipment No. 1	Description	Selection Number	How Many of this Selection	Unit Price	Total Price
Name					
Address Apt.#					
City State Zip					
Telephone ( )					
Ship to Arrive * ☐ Now ☐ Week of					

Please ship the following gifts to the names below:

Shipment No. 2	Description	Selection Number	How Many of this Selection	Unit Price	Total Price
Name					
Address Apt.#					
City State Zip					
Telephone ( )					
Ship to Arrive * ☐ Now ☐ Week of					
Gift Greeting to Read:					

Shipment No. 3	Description	Selection Number	How Many of this Selection	Unit Price	Total Price
Name					
Address Apt.#					
City State Zip					
Telephone ( )					
Ship to Arrive * ☐ Now ☐ Week of					
Gift Greeting to Read:					

This Order Summary area is for your use only. ➡

To guarantee delivery to R.R. or P.O. Box, we need receiver's telephone number.
*Please allow two to three weeks for delivery.
**☐ Check here if you would like an application for an Omaha Steaks charge account.
☐ Check here if you need more order forms.

Order Summary		
	Subtotal	$
		$
	Postage and Handling Charge = No. of Shipments x $3.00	$
	Nebraska resident sales tax	$
	TOTAL DUE	$

To Order by phone, call **FREE 1-800-228-9055**
Nebraska residents, phone (0-402-391-3660) collect

G2019A-0883 8-27

Placement of the Order Form

Where to put the order form within your catalog is an important decision; don't shortchange yourself by letting the creative staff determine the placement. What difference does it make? Sales - Sales - Sales! The pages of the catalog adjacent to the order form benefit from added sales. Why? Because the catalog naturally "opens up" to the bound-in order form, affording higher visibility to the pages next to be form. And, when placing an order, customers are exposed to more products. These pages become one of the "contrived hot spots" discussed in Chapter 3. Very few catalogs use a catalog page for their order form, since it is felt that customers

8-28

JOY HALL'S EASY-TO-USE ORDER FORM
(Just 3 simple steps to follow)

AMBASSADOR® 7822 S. 46th Street Phoenix, Arizona 85044

1. Your order can be shipped more quickly if you will peel off the **WHITE LABEL** from the back of this catalog, and stick it onto this space by pressing firmly (no glue needed).

If your address on the white label is NOT correct, stick the label here anyhow, and make corrections in the spaces at right.

2. If **WHITE LABEL** is missing from back cover or address on white label is not correct, please print your correct mailing address below:

Please Print
☐ Mr. ☐ Mrs. ☐ Miss ______ First Name ______ Last Name
Address ______ Apt. No ______
City ______ State ______ ZIP ______

415ZB8

3. Please check (✓) method of payment:

☐ I am enclosing a check made payable to Ambassador.

CHARGE TO MY:
☐ MASTER CARD
☐ VISA
☐ AMERICAN EXPRESS
☐ DINERS CLUB

Account Card No. (Print ALL digits, please)

Card expires: Mo. Yr. Signature X ______

Item numbers ending with the letter "A" are custom made to your order and shipped directly from the factory. Please allow up to 8 weeks for processing and delivery.

ITEM NO.	HOW MANY	CATALOG NUMBER	NAME OF ITEM	PAGE NUMBER	SIZE (if needed)	COLOR NAME	COLOR NUMBER	PRINT INITIALS in normal order First Middle Last	AMOUNT
1									
2									
3									
4									
5									
6									
7									
8									
9									
10									
11									
12									

Ambassador Guarantees Your Satisfaction

If for any reason (or no reason at all) you are not completely satisfied with the design, color, workmanship, size or material of any product you buy from Ambassador, simply return it to us **within 30 days of receiving it,** and we will **refund** the purchase price promptly — or, if you desire, **replace** the product you bought free of charge.

CHECK (✓) YOUR FREE GIFT!

☐ FREE GIFT—A BEAUTIFUL CHRISTMAS TREE ORNAMENT!

The fourth in our exclusive collection...and it's yours FREE with every catalog order over $10.00.

POSTAGE AND HANDLING CHARGES

If your order is:
Under $15 .... add $2.45
$15 to $30 .... add $3.45
$30 to $45 .... add $4.45
Over $45 .... add $5.45

TOTAL AMOUNT OF ORDER	
SEND MY TREE ORNAMENT	FREE
Your Package Fully Insured if Lost or Damaged	.90
Postage and Handling Charges	
Total Payment Enclosed or Charged to Credit Card*	$

MINIMUM ORDER: $10.00
Arizona Residents add Sales Tax. Sorry, no C.O.D.'s or stamps, please!

Ambassador's Mail Preference Service

Ambassador occasionally makes it customer list available to other reputable companies who also offer products and services by mail. If you DO NOT WANT to receive such offers, please do the following: (1) Tear out this Request Form. (2) Mail it with your mailing label (or the name and address printed **exactly** as shown on label) to: Mail Preference Service Dept., Ambassador International, 7822 S. 46th St., Phoenix, Arizona 85044.

LET US MAIL YOUR GIFTS FOR YOU!

Item No.	Qty.	Style No.	Color	Free Initials	Item No.	Qty.	Style No.	Color	Free Initials

Name ______ Address ______ City ______ State ______ ZIP ______

Name ______ Address ______ City ______ State ______ ZIP ______

hesitate to tear the catalog apart. Also, a catalog page provides no return envelope.

Three placements for the order form:

1. Catalog page
2. Middle of catalog
3. Between catalog signatures

1. Catalog Page. The catalog page, as mentioned above, has some drawbacks. But first look at Figure 8-30 from Vocational Educa-

ORDER FORM

PLACE PEEL-OFF LABEL FROM BACK COVER HERE.
Please print address corrections if necessary.

Name __________

Address __________

City _____ State _____ Zip _____

Telephone number (Area Code) __________

SHIP TO: (if different from above name and address)

Address __________

City __________

State _____ Zip Code _____

EVA GABOR
WIGS
BY PAULA
Brockton, MA 02403

Our Unconditional Guarantee
You take NO risk. Everything you order MUST live up to YOUR expectations. If you are not satisfied with ANY item for ANY reason, return it for prompt refund or exchange, whichever you prefer. You MUST be satisfied when you shop with WIGS BY PAULA!

Please check to be sure your color is available in the style you want.

FOR OFFICE USE ONLY	How Many	Name or Stock Number	COLOR 1st Choice	COLOR 2nd Choice	Price	Office Use Only
AMT. PD.						
METHOD						
SPECIALS						
COMMENTS						

TOTAL AMOUNT		
Mass. residents add 5% sales tax		
Shipping, Handling, & Insurance	$3.00	
TOTAL AMOUNT DUE		

CHARGE CARD CUSTOMERS For easier, faster and more personal shopping please use our toll free number

1-800-343-9695
in Massachusetts Call Collect 617-584-7360

We will NOT be undersold! If you find one of our EVA GABOR styles offered for less than our price, send us the advertisement or catalog page, and we will honor the lower price.

☐ Payment in full is enclosed
☐ Charge to MASTERCARD ☐ VISA
(give ALL numbers on your card)

Expiration Date

Charge Card Customers must sign here:

Signature

*EXTRA BONUS: Order 2 or more wigs, and receive a FREE wig-care accessory for EACH wig ordered!
Example: Order 2 wigs, get 2 FREE Accessories
Order 3 wigs, get 3 FREE Accessories
Remember, you must order MORE than one wig to get FREE Accessories. See Page 25 for list of accessories. Write your choices on this order form.

8-29

tion Production. The order form takes up only two-thirds of a page. It is simple in design and easy for the customer to use with a steps-one-through-seven procedure for placing an order. And, just like a regular bind-in, this order form (Figure 8-31) asks the customer to use the peel-off label from the back cover. The back of the order form not only serves as a prepaid business reply vehicle, but it sells a product, too.

Advantages	**Disadvantges**
Lower costs for printing and bindery; more than one order form easily included.	Loss of contrived hot spot and, therefore, loss of sales; customer must destroy catalog when using; writing surface ''slick'' because of coated stock used for catalog pages, so writing is more difficult; hard for customers to find.

2. Middle of catalog. The catalog parts naturally in the middle when collated and bound because of the staples or gluing used in binding. This has traditionally been the place to locate the order form because of ease in bindery and the natural space available. And, depending on the number of pages in the catalog, this can be the only space available to bind-in the envelope. Figure 8-32 illustrates the placement of the ''middle'' bind-in.

Advantages	**Disadvantages**
Easy bindery function; order form easily found by customer; envelope and order form always together.	Loss of contrived hot spot (hot pages created when order form is bound between signatures) and, therefore, loss of sales.

3. Between catalog signatures. This is probably the most advantageous positioning for an order form. And it is as easy as the middle binding position. A signature is the number of pages a press will print at one time. (See Chapter 9 for full explanation.) If a press printed only 16 pages at one time and you had an 80-page catalog, there would be five signatures in the catalog and you would have four opportunities to bind-in an order form. Eliminating the middle binding spot, you would have three possibilities — between pages 8-9 and 72-73, 16-17 and 64-65, 24-25 and 56-57. The greatest problem is that the envelope might become separated from the order

Vocational Education Productions
California Polytechnic State University
San Luis Obispo, California 93407

ORDER FORM

PLEASE APPLY PEEL-OFF LABEL FROM BACK COVER HERE.
FILL IN ALL BILLING AND SHIPPING INFORMATION BELOW.

1 **BILL TO:** Purchase Order No. ____

Name

Organization

Address

City/State/ZIP Code**

Purchaser's Phone Ext.

2 **SHIP TO** (If different than BILL TO):

Name

Organization

Street Address

City/State/ZIP Code**

Business Office Phone Ext.

**Your ZIP CODE insures prompt delivery.

3 VEP Order No.	Title or Description	Qty.	Price Each	Total Price

IMPORTANT! Insert seven-digit VEP Order Number. Please PRINT clearly or type.

CALL TOLL-FREE TO ORDER
1-800-235-4146
CALIFORNIA: (805)546-2295

Unconditional Guarantee

Vocational Education Productions unconditionally guarantees that all VEP materials will satisfy your instructional needs, or you may return them for a full refund. Simply return any item that you are unable to use within 30 days of receipt and your account will be properly credited. (Please include a copy of your invoice with any materials you return.)

4 Sub-Total	
5 Sales Tax*	
6 Shipping*	
7 TOTAL	

Thank You, VEP appreciates your order.

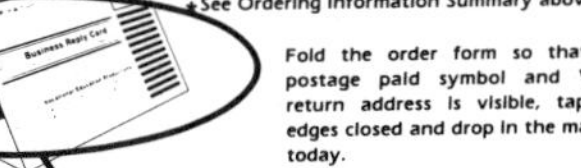

*See Ordering Information Summary above/left.

Fold the order form so that the postage paid symbol and VEP's return address is visible, tape all edges closed and drop in the mailbox today.

11

8-30

ORDER FORM

If You Teach OH, You've Got To Have It!

Nursery Teacher's Survival Guide

Make sure you're getting the most out of your OH classes with the popular new Nursery Teachers' Survival Guide.

This essential teaching resource covers occupations in the nursery industry, nursery practice topics, greenhouses and greenhouse selection, as well as the equipment and supplies needed for teaching a class of 25 students.

You get thorough guidance in selecting and purchasing suitable plants for cuttings, groundcovers, bedding plants, vegetable and ornamental seeds, novelty plants and much more. There's even sound advice on marketing your cash crops.

The Nursery Teacher's Survival Guide really puts it all together for you. Order this one-of-a kind book today and make sure you get the most out of your OH classes.

(1-200-820) **$10.95**

NO POSTAGE NECESSARY IF MAILED IN THE UNITED STATES

Business Reply Mail

FIRST CLASS Permit No. 4337 Long Beach, CA

POSTAGE WILL BE PAID BY ADDRESSEE:

Vocational Education Productions
California Polytechnic State University
San Luis Obispo, California 93407

8-31

*See Ordering Information Summary above/left.

Fold the order form so that the postage paid symbol and VEP's return address is visible, tape all edges closed and drop in the mailbox today.

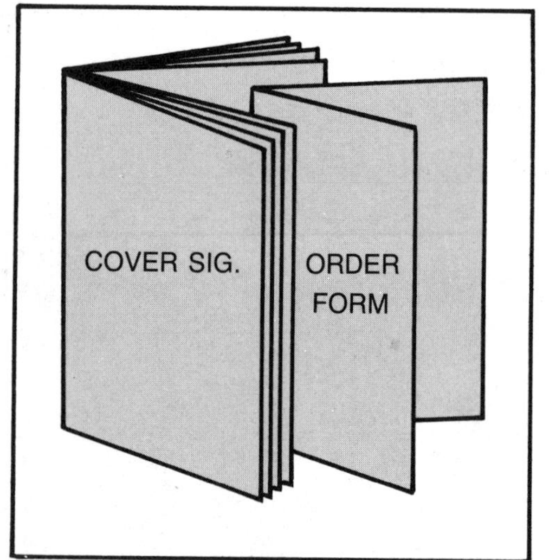

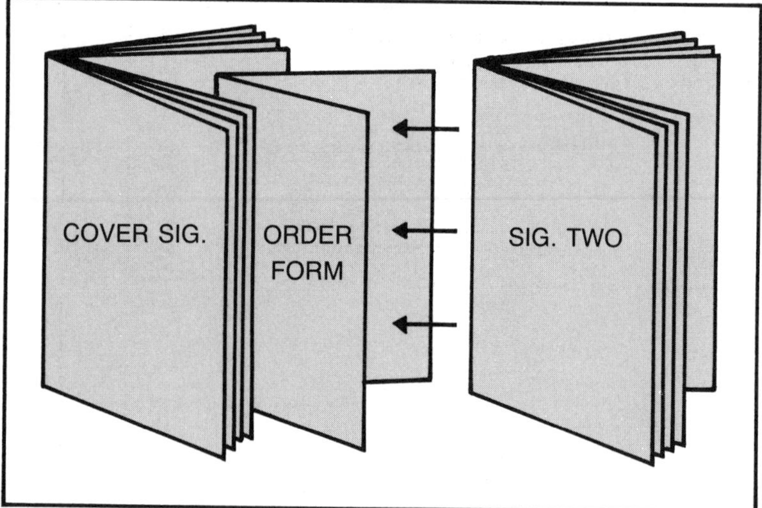

8-32

Advantages	**Disadvantages**
Creates two extra hot spots, meaning four pages of boosted sales; easy to bind; feasibility of two order forms and two envelopes.	Possible separation of envelope and order form.

form, whereupon the irritated customer fails to place an order. However, a good designer and flexible envelope printer can get around this. In Figure 8-33 we see how. Frederick's of Hollywood has cleverly designed a 28½-inch sheet of paper so that it provides two order forms and two envelopes. Part (a) shows one-half of the completely printed order form as it appears between pages 16 and 17. The front or address side of the envelope is to the left, with a "How to order" information panel to the right. When the gateflap (b) is folded out, the back of the envelope and the middle panel together become the order form. The envelope pocket is still available for checks or notes, and the ordering information becomes private when the envelope is sealed (c).

a. Folded as bound in catalog

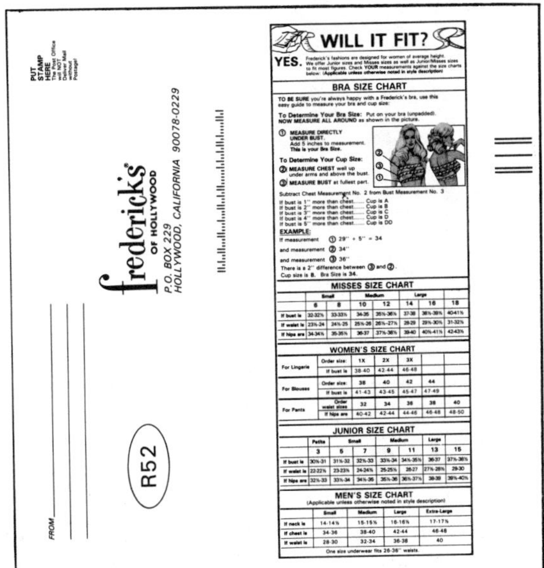

b. Envelope

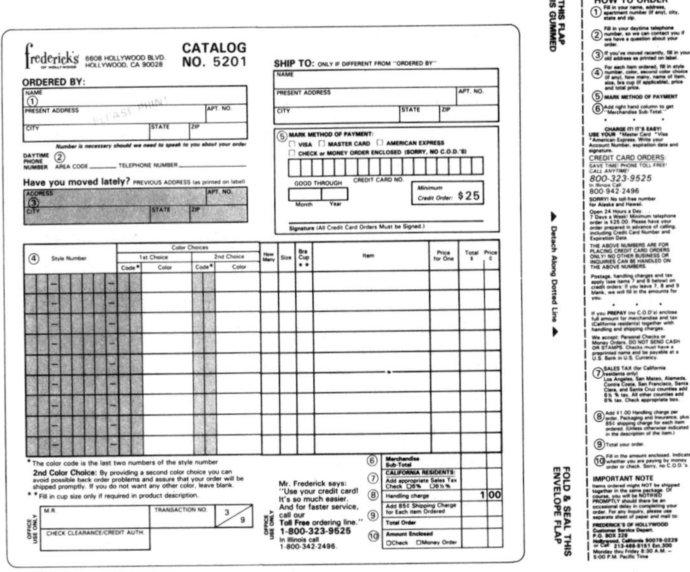

c. Sealed Envelope

8-33

Order Form Design Tips:

1. Keep it clean. Use lots of white space. Keep your form open and attractive. An order form that looks complicated IS complicated. This can result in missing or wrong information . . . or no order at all.

2. Leave room to write. Make your form easy to fill out. If necessary, increase the form's size to assure the order's legibility.

3. Remember your order entry system. The form should be compatible with your order entry system, especially if your system is computerized. A form with the same design as your computer format will speed order entry and fulfillment, while reducing input errors.

4. Keep it simple. Use of color can be confusing and distracting. Use basic black or some other dark color for important information. Colors should be used to highlight and enhance.

5. Attract attention. Use screens of black or second colors where you want to draw attention or create sections. Shade the areas you don't want filled in. Use screens sparingly.

6. Color stripe your envelope. If you get many kinds of mail, color stripe the edges of your return envelopes so rapid sorting can cut down your processing time.

7. Don't confuse your customer. Be consistent in layout and design. If you need to improve your order form, make changes that will present minimal confusion to customers.

8. One step at a time. Lead your customer step-by-step in filling out the order form. Doing so makes your form seem simple, even if you require lots of information. Consider numbering the steps.

Give Information:

1. Explain your exchange policy. Provide specifics on returns and exchanges, including postage. The Federal Trade Commission is becoming increasingly strict about this requirement.

2. Reinforce your guarantee. The order form is an ideal place to restate your guarantee, instilling confidence when the customer is about to place an order.

3. Put postage charges on the order form. Psychologically, including them in the price of the item or placing them next to the price raises the perceived cost. Put postage charges on the order form in a spot where they're seen after the customers have committed themselves to placing an order.

4. Give your customer a mail preference option. Offer not to extend use of the customer's name to other mailers.

5. Tell customers how to pay. If your company name is different from your catalog name, tell the customer so that checks can be made out properly. An alternative is to set up a system with your bank to accept checks made out both ways.

6. Explain the minimum order on charge cards. To assure that you cover costs, put a minimum on your charge orders.

7. State delivery time. This increases credibility by telling customers what you will do for them . . . and it reminds customers that you are concerned about fulfillment of the order.

8. Date your prices and your catalog. State when your catalog prices expire. "guaranteed until . . ." is better than "expire on . . . ." After that date, refer inquiries to your customer service department to ascertain the current price.

Ask for Information:

1. Ask customers to use the label. Remind people to affix mailing labels in the proper place on the order form; this is important for tracking codes. Try to reduce your costs by asking recipients of multiple catalogs to return the labels so you can eliminate duplicates from your lists.

2. Ask for names for your mailing list. Solicit the names of your customers' friends (they're likely to have similar interests). This is an excellent way to build your list of prospects at virtually no cost.

3. Ask for a phone number. Always ask for a way to contact the customer just in case there's a question about the order. Specify both a work and home number so you'll be able to reach the customer without delay.

4. Ask for change of address information. Also ask the customer to correct his address if necessary. Provide a separate box to write in a new address. Put old information in a nixy file to use for merge/purge purposes.

5. Ask for a street address for UPS. UPS will not deliver to a post office box. Without proper information, delivery is impossible.

6. Always find out where to ship the order. **Ask for "ship to" information or a gift address.**

And always thank customers for their orders!

Order Form Checklist:

- ☐ Gather Information To Include.
- ☐ Decide On Position Within The Catalog.

Always:

1. Design with simplicity.
2. Keep customer uppermost in mind.
3. State information clearly and simply.
4. Include your company name and address.
5. Provide a phone number.
6. Allow ample room for customer to fill in information.
7. Thank the customer.

Strongly Consider:

1. Including guarantee on order form panel.
2. Taking the customer through the order steps via a numbering system.

Chapter 9

Production Planning

. . . Getting Ready To Publish Your Catalog.

Production planning consists of establishing the deadline dates upon which copy, art, and photography operate. It also includes the process of acquiring printers, selecting paper and color separators, and choosing a lettershop. Production planning is the non-creative part of preparing a catalog. (Not that printing and lettershop can't be creative in their own way.) You can easily establish the time periods for printing the catalog and the mechanics of the lettershop because printing presses go only so fast. Labeling, bagging, and sorting have their recognized pace, too. The deadlines which they establish are based on the *mailing date of the catalog . . . and that's one date that cannot be missed.* So the often-used saying, "The buck stops here," applies to the printing and lettershop deadlines because there is no more time left. Printing presses and the people running them are costly; presses must be tightly scheduled in order to operate profitably. What all of this means is that the creative production schedule must be realistic enough so that it can be met and the printer's deadline can be made. Chapter 2 discusses the creative scheduling. Here we will look at finding printers, choosing paper stock, selecting color separators, finding a lettershop, and communicating instructions — plus understanding the function of all these steps and avoiding errors. Production planning and good printing go together.

Step Number 1: The Printer

First, you'll need to select a printer. One of the first things you will want to check is the financial strength of a new printer. The condition of the economy goes up and down, and so does the condition of a company. Avoid the trauma of having a printer falter while committed to producing your catalog: weed out the undesirables in the beginning.

How To Get Proper Bids On Your Printing Job.

Whether you get bids on a per-catalog publishing basis or on a year's contract, you will want to have several printers in mind to bid on the requested material. But what do you ask them to bid on?

Prepare a bid sheet containing the following points. This is the only way you can be sure that all bids will be based on the same set of specifications. Many of these points will be discussed in detail later in this chapter.

Check off each step

1. **Title** — allows you to identify the job so that you and your printer will be able to call the job by a common name.
2. **Unit** — identifies the type of job: a folder, booklet, letter, envelope, catalog.
3. **Quantity** — is the amount you wish to purchase. It's a good idea to investigate quantity cost breaks as well.
4. **Size** — is 8½ × 11 inches or 5½ × 8½ inches, or whatever size you choose.
5. **Number Of Lots** — identifies more than one version, for testing different copy, using different codes, etc.
6. **Fold To** — is whether the catalog or brochure folds to fit a #10 envelope, a 6 × 9 inch, or a fancy fold.
7. **Number Of Pages** — is 8, 16, 24, 32 or more pages. A letter could be two, four or more pages.
8. **Colors** — should indicate two, three, four or however many colors. Does it print one or two sides of the sheet?
9. **Bleed** — is whether the ink should run off the page (without margins) making it bleed — or not? Bleeds usually cost more.

10. Ink Coverage — is something a purchaser may forget to establish when bidding a job. But it is very important when you consider that the press sheet could have very light ink coverage (20 percent) and a great deal of white space, or heavy ink coverage (75 to 85 percent), which can influence reproduction of the job.

11. Stock — is the kind of paper (coated, uncoated) you will be using. Always specify the name of the sheet or grade, e.g., number one, two, three grade. Often purchasing agents will think they're getting a great buy, only to discover that the printer has substituted an inferior grade of paper to lower the price. When recommending an alternate stock, the printer should specify the name and grade. (Be sure to examine a printed sample.)

12. Art and Preparation — is your specification of how your art will be prepared. For example, in the case of four-color, mechanicals with dyes, or chromes . . . will the chromes be 35mm or 5 × 7? How many of each? If your four-color art is assembled in position, how many assemblies? If your mechanicals are two-color, will the second color be an acetate overlay? Is all color type indicated properly?

13. Finishing and Binding—is establishing whether your catalog will have a saddle stitch; does it perfect-bind or side-wire stitch? (See Figure 9-1.) In the *saddle stitch,* staples are bound in the spine of the catalog. This is the simplest and least expensive method. In the *side-wire stitch,* staples are inserted along the left front side of the catalog through to the back side. This method is generally used when the bulk is too great for saddle stitching — for the most part, covers are glued in place. In *perfect binding,* the catalog pages are collated, the left side ground off, and adhesive applied. Covers are glued on. Catalogers who expect their books to be kept over a period of time generally prefer this type of binding — especially for business-to-business catalogs.

Must decide on proof quality

14. Proofs — require several specifications. If the printer is doing your color separations, how many blues (proofs) do you need? Will you accept color keys of some type, or do you want full-color press proofs? How many sets do you need? Do you expect a second press proof, adding to the cost, or are chromalins acceptable? Chromalins are a less expensive way of seeing color. Due to the advent of scanners, color separators now can supply excellent chromalins for approval.

15. Packing — specifies whether the printed material should be delivered bulk, in cartons, or on skids. Again,

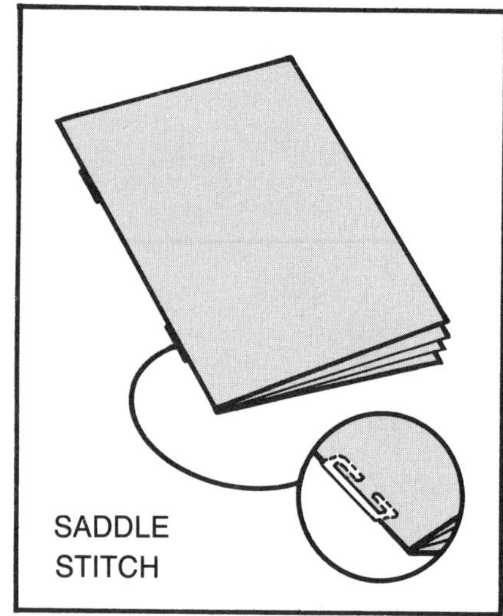

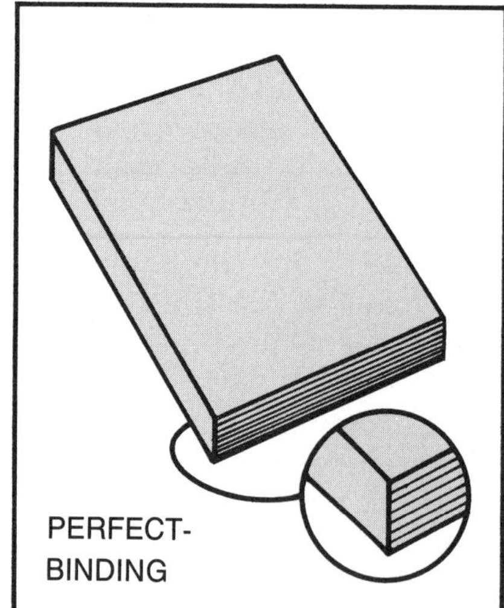

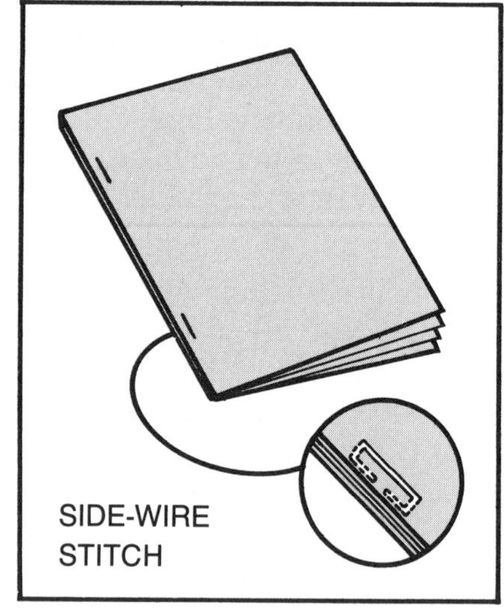

9-1

packing material in cartons is more costly.

16. Destination — specifies whether the printer will deliver the material to your mailing house or to a distributor.

17. Delivery Date — is the date by which all material must arrive at its destination.

In addition, ask suppliers to give you a *breakdown* when submitting bids, to separate costs into four categories: printing, paper, separations, and freight.

You will soon discover the printers who have a tendency to low-bid a job, figuring they can make up the differences in author's alterations. Asking for a breakdown will force them to be up-front with each item. Also, the use of a lesser grade of paper would be highlighted in the individual cost breakdown. This is also true of color separations.

If you prepare a proper bid sheet, *all your printers will bid on the same specifications*, and you will be able to make an valid comparison.

Know the types of printing available

Basically there are three printing processes — letterpress, offset lithography, and gravure — which are used in catalog printing.

1. **Letterpress**: the image is transferred by means of raised areas on a plate. When the pressure of the press is exerted, the raised areas apply ink to the paper, making a printing impression. *This process is especially conducive to short runs, under 50,000 catalogs.*
2. **Offset Lithography**: the image is transferred to the printed page via a blanket wrapped around a cylinder, not directly from the original plate — hence the term "offset." *Web offset is by far the most popular method of catalog printing.*

The main advantage of web printing is its speed. Some web presses can print up to 1,800 feet per minute (five to six times faster than a sheet-fed press). Commonly, a speed of 1,000 feet per minute can be achieved while at the same time signatures (eight, sixteen, thirty-two pages) are being folded. Some web presses include operations such as paste binding (gluing the spine), perforating, and slitting. The main disadvantage of web offset is that all catalog sheets must be cut the same length.

3. **Gravure**: in this cylinder printing process, ink is transferred to paper via ''wells'' which are etched in the cylinder. Although cylinders are expensive, the process starts to become economical for press runs of one million or more — which is also the life of the cylinder. Most large mail order companies print their catalogs by this process.

Presses are either sheet-fed or roll-fed (web). Catalogs with small runs of 50,000 or less are generally run by a sheet-fed process because it is more cost effective. The speed of the web press is so great that bringing the color and registration to a point of acceptability might not be achieved before hundreds of catalogs have been run, thus creating an unallowable amount of waste for small catalog runs. The web process allows *double ending* or printing on both sides of the paper simultaneously.

Price, Quality, Service

Price, Quality, Service — Should You Expect All Three? All three objectives are attainable. But if price is your main goal, will you have to give up quality or service — or vice versa? In most instances, you'll receive the job at the price, quality, and service you expect. *But you must give your printer the material according to the printer's specifications, and allow the time required to produce the job.* If, for some reason, you are not able to meet agreed-upon specifications, then you must expect a change in what you are going to receive. In some circumstances, you may get only two of your three objectives. When you select a printer, consider the alternatives:

Price: If your main concern is to buy the job at a set price, you may preclude your supplier's ability to maintain quality. Or perhaps your quality standards can be met for the quoted price, but the printer may not be able to deliver the job on time. Say, on the other hand, that you've selected a supplier who has quoted your job at a higher figure, but who meets your quality and service requirements; such a printer may take longer to okay a sheet, or might pull a job because of a bad plate, and so on. So you risk maintaining price and quality, but losing service.

Quality: Say that you have a source that offers the quality you demand and the service you require . . . but some surprise comes up and the job is not running right. Now you may be faced with a decision to change your price and delivery. For example, when the printer receives the film and goes to press, there's a photo of a sweater that looks pink, and your copy describes it as "tomato red." If the color can't be corrected on press, you face the decision of going with what you have, or pulling the job — which will affect the price and possibly delivery.

Service: Say that you're locked into a mailing date, you've selected a supplier who can produce the job on time, the price is right, and you are confident that the quality will meet your standards. Knowing that the mailing date is the reason you have selected this print shop, your supplier may handle an emergency by having the material ready but at a higher price . . . or by sacrificing quality in an effort to make the mailing.

Don't miss these two basic steps:

Visit printing plants

1. When considering the abilities of a new printer, ask to see as many job samples as possible. Most salespeople will not display poorly printed samples; still, *any* samples can tell you a lot about the company. Ask how current the samples are. If many of them are a year or so old, it may mean there's a severe turnover in customers — and for a good reason.

Examine samples printed on the grade of paper you normally use. If you're low-ticket, don't be swayed by a portfolio of high-fashion catalogs printed on quality sheets. You need to know if this printer can print well on commodity-grade paper. And if the wares displayed were all produced on commodity grades and you're looking for a "Rembrandt" . . . beware. If you are impressed with a particular sample relating to your standards, ask to see the proof. See how well the proof was matched on press. Perhaps talented press people were able to improve the quality.

2. Ask for a list of catalogers that the salesperson personally deals with. It is important for the printer's liaison to understand the catalog business, as well as the printing business. You'll often hear radically different critiques of the same print shop. The difference frequently rests with the representative and how much dedication is shown to understanding and satisfying your needs.

There is one more thing you should do if time and budget allow: *visit the printing plant*. Talk to the people who make it happen. Walk through the press area; examine what's running at the time if you can. Is the plant clean? Are the people busy but not hurried (panicked)? Is the atmosphere businesslike? Do people seem alert and enthusiastic about their jobs? Are you received with a degree of excitement?

Step Number 2: The Paper.

The material that will show your product is paper, and it should be selected with the same care used in choosing your photographer, separator, and printer. If your company is large and your paper usage volume is large, you may have a paper and purchasing expert as part of your staff. In that case, you'll want to purchase paper directly from the paper mill and save the commission that would be realized if your catalog printer made the purchase. But few companies are large enough to take advantage of this situation. The average catalog company will want the catalog printer to negotiate and make long-term commitments protecting paper supply and cost. But as an end-user whose product means so much, you need to consider features such as finish, grain, weight, and bulk; these areas will affect print quality and price.

Finish: This term refers to the feel and smoothness of the sheet. You can use paper as it comes from the driers of a paper machine, or you can buy machine-calendered paper for a smoother finish or supercalendered paper for an even smoother finish. ("Calendered" is a term indicating the smoothing of the paper by passing it through rollers.) For even smoother finishes and paper with better ink holdout, you will want to buy coated paper. ("Holdout" is the ability of the ink to sit on the paper, rather than being absorbed into it.) Coated papers can reproduce finer halftone screens, and have greater ink holdout and higher opacity than uncoated sheets. Application of a coating, from a dull finish to a very glossy finish, can control the weight and bulk of a sheet to give you the look and feel you require for your catalog.

Weight and Bulk: With few exceptions, paper is identified by basis weight in pounds of a ream (500 sheets) in its grade size. **Grades** are given below:

Grade	Standard Sheet Size
Book	25″ × 38″
Bond	17″ × 22″
Cover	20″ × 26″
Bristol	22½″ × 28½″
Index	25½″ × 30½″

For example, 500 sheets (one ream) of 100 pound book (25″ × 38″) weighs 100 pounds. Five hundred sheets of 50 pound cover (20″ × 26″) weighs 50 pounds.

When selecting the stock you're going to use, keep in mind that in addition to the weight of the sheet, you will want to know how much that sheet bulks. Bulk for book paper is expressed as the number of pages per inch for a given basis weight. For example, the bulking range for a 50 pound book stock can vary from 310 to 800 pages per inch.

Grain: When ordering paper, keep in mind these three facts about grain direction:

1. Paper folds smoothly with the grain direction and roughens or cracks when folded across the grain.
2. Paper is stiffer in the grain direction.
3. Paper expands or contracts more in the cross-grain direction when exposed to moisture changes. Figure 9-2 shows a few simple tests that will illustrate how paper tears and folds.

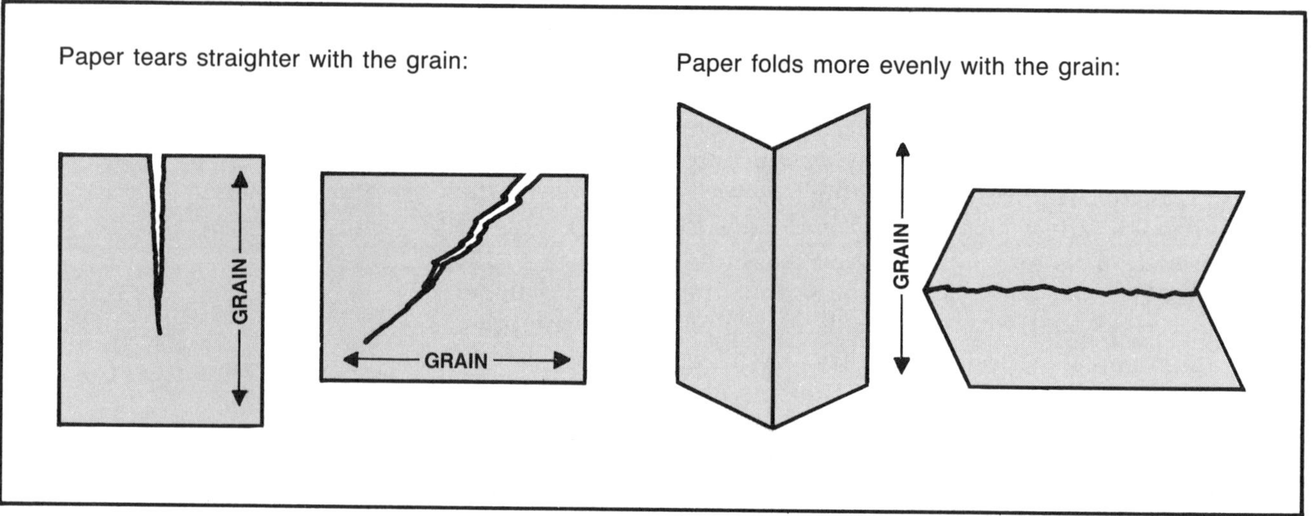
Paper tears straighter with the grain:
GRAIN
GRAIN
Paper folds more evenly with the grain:
GRAIN

9-2

Print Quality: The factors listed below affect print quality.

Color of paper plays a large role in how your piece will look after it's been printed. Type, for instance, is more easily read on a soft white, while process colors are most accurately reproduced on a neutral white.

Brightness of paper affects the contrast, brilliance, and snap of the printed subject. Artificial brighteners added to paper can affect reproduction because most are not neutral in color, but have excess blue reflectance.

Opacity refers to the show-through of the printed image from the opposite side of the sheet or the adjoining sheet. Opacity is affected by the thickness of the sheet and the use of fillers, such as titanium dioxide.

Gloss affects the appearance of the ink film on the paper.

Refractiveness is light absorption in the surface of the paper, causing halftones to appear darker than they should.

Paper chosen for web presses (presses which operate on a continous feeding of roll-paper through cylinders of the press) should be rolled with the grain direction paralleling the web. When accepting orders for large runs, your printer and the mill should work closely to determine the exact specifications for your job. Because web shutdowns can be costly in both time and money, rolls must be properly wound, protected, stored on end, and have good tensile strength to minimize tearing or breaking on the web. Your paper should be uniform in thickness, and free from scum, holes, spots, slitter dust, fiber picking, and lint. Your paper should have a minimum of contraction and expansion, contain a minimum number of splices, and have sound cores for winding and delivery.

Keep current on paper technology

Paper Selection . . . What it can mean in dollars and cents.

Paper buyers must search constantly for anything new that will *reduce cost while maintaining quality*. Keeping on top of correspondence and comparisons from different paper manufacturers can be highly informative about important new developments in the industry. The field is complicated, and constantly changing.

The characteristics of coated paper finishes:

Matte Coated is fully coated paper with a nonglare finish. There is no off-the-paper-machines supercalendering. (Again, calendering is a process of pressing paper between revolving cylinders to smooth the finish.) This means that the mattes, as a group, are the *bulkiest of the coated papers* and have a somewhat grainy surface, though they are still far superior to uncoated sheets in print quality.

Gloss Coated is double coated on both sides. The sheet is supercalendered off the paper machine. Supercalendering brings up a gloss through heat and friction, but also reduces sheet bulk, brightness, and opacity. The *gloss coated surface is smooth and sealed and, thus, most suitable for true dot reproduction*. Basically, five quality categories exist in gloss paper, with gloss, brightness, shade, and surface smoothness being the major differentials which affect pricing.

Dull Coated is also coated on both sides. The sheet is supercalendered off the machine, but with composition rollers rather than the steel rollers used in gloss calendering. Steam is injected into the dull coating process to retard gloss. The *bulk loss is not as great as in a gloss paper, but the dull coated surface is not as smooth as a gloss sheet*. Dull coated papers are smoother than matte grades.

> **Selecting Paper**
>
> *The highest quality paper is not always the best choice. Some number-one grades will blister when run on heat set web equipment. Number two or three grades perform well and are not prone to this problem.*
>
> **Frank Merritt**
> *Colonial Williamsburg Foundation*
> *Williamsburg, VA*

Warrenflo is coated on both sides, but the gloss surface is attained without supercalendering. The combination of a *gloss surface and lack of supercalendering results in a sheet approximately 20 percent bulkier than conventional gloss coated paper*. The following example shows that the weight of 70 pound Warrenflo bulks out higher than a conventional 80 pound gloss paper. What does that mean to you as a buyer? Take these comparisons using four-sheet thickness as the bulk comparison:

	70#	**80#**	**100#**
Regular coated gloss	13.0	15.0	19.0
Warrenflo	15.5	18.0	24.0

Why is bulk important? For small catalogs, 8- or 16- or 24-page, where a more bulky paper would give the feel of a larger catalog, Warrenflo would give you the greater thickness you desire for less weight. This would mean a savings to you of approximately 12½ percent to 20 percent, depending on the kind of paper you had used previously. On cover weight of 8 point, the savings could range from 5 percent to 15 percent, again depending on your prior paper choice.

What does all this mean to you in dollars and cents? If paper for your catalog costs $10,000 and the cover an additional $2,500, the use of Warrenflo would save from $1,200 to $2,000. Cover savings would run from $125 to $375 . . . giving you a total savings of anywhere from $1,325 to $2,375.

Besides different paper finishes, there are different grades of paper, too. The better grade stocks are brighter, whiter, and cost more; the lesser grades are cheaper and grayer in tone.

Groundwood Paper. All papers start as wood pulp, and come in various grades. Groundwood is usually a lesser grade of coated or offset stock. Many of these feel coated, and because of their gloss or shiny finish, they are the preferred stock. In speaking of coated finishes, *the better grade is called free sheet, the lesser grade groundwood.*

In its initial stage, paper is brown; brighteners are added to make it white. The more brighteners, the whiter the sheet. Here, we will use this oversimplification merely to distinguish a free sheet from groundwood.

The better grade free sheet is very white and has a high-gloss look. The top grade free sheet stocks are Mead's Black and White enamel, Warren's Lustro enamel, and Northwest Vintage, to name just three. If you are producing a top-of-the-line catalog for fashions or valued art, these, and others like them, are the papers you would consider. At the other end of the spectrum are the groundwood sheets. In this area you would find Crown's Monterey or Sufa Web, and Champion's Panaprint. These are classified as number-four sheets; while they do not have the brightness of the top-of-the-line number-one sheets, they can be used very successfully for merchandise catalogs.

The finished product of number-four sheets is less refined, less bright, and has a grayish appearance. It is very serviceable for two-color and four-color catalogs which have maximum coverage. *The use of groundwood gives you an initial savings of approximately 22 percent over a coated free sheet.*

One sheet, Monterey Web, is used by many companies for their monthly catalogs. While this sheet doesn't pretend to have the look of the number-one gloss-coated sheet, the savings you would realize by using it make it worth investigation.

Another cost-saving consideration is the weight of the stock you presently use. Many companies prefer 60 pound, 70 pound, or perhaps 80 pound because of the bulk it provides. You should consider reducing the weight from, for example, your present 60 pound to 50 — or from 50 to 45 pound.

Considering the increased postal costs, *the lighter weight stock would also afford you an advantage in mailing rates.* A 24-page self-cover catalog in 60 pound stock would weigh 106 pounds per 1,000 catalogs. A 24-page self-cover catalog in 45 pound would weigh 80 pounds per 1,000 catalogs . . . *a savings of 25 percent.* The reduced weight would then allow additional inserts as part of your mailing, or an increase in the number of catalog pages, which in turn would increase profit.

Get cost breakdowns

Test a 45 pound groundwood for opacity and appearance against your present stock; groundwood may be an excellent cost-saving solution for your catalog. Most paper merchants would gladly supply a few rolls as a test for your run.

Think about ink when designing your catalog and ordering paper! Ink can play a very important part in the reproduction of your artwork and photography. *Ink is either transparent or opaque,* but the bulk of your print job is done by process printing and requires transparent inks. Such reproduction uses three subtractive secondary colors: magenta (red), yellow, and cyan (blue), plus black.

Transparent ink modifies light by subtracting some colors from the light source and transmitting other colors. For example, look at something that appears to be green. That item subtracts red and some blue and shows you yellow and some blue to give your vision a shade of green. If your printer were to use *an opaque ink, it would reflect light and not allow you to see the underlying colors,* thus eliminating the intermediate colors that create the effect and versatility of process printing.

Your paper stock becomes the reflecting light source for the ink which is placed on it. The paper is the immediate source of illumination for a transparent ink, and this is called reflected illumination. Because of the limitations of process inks, you may want to select a paper stock that is very white in order to show the colors in their purest form.

Paper has the property of absorbing some colors and reflecting others. A sheet that both absorbs and reflects colors equally is known as a *balanced sheet*. One that absorbs some colors and reflects others will have a tint and is known as an *unbalanced sheet*. For example, if a sheet absorbs more red and green, it will have a blue tint. If a sheet absorbs all white light, you have a paper that is black.

When viewing a sheet of paper, consider that the area which will be unprinted is going to be the brightest portion of the overall page. The areas where ink has been applied will be less bright because the sheet has absorbed light (color). *The most accurate color reproduction is obtained on papers that reflect the light that strikes them without changing its quality*. In addition, the most brilliant color reproductions are obtained on papers with high, balanced reflectance.

Some cost-saving alternatives, in addition to paper choice

1. Think about printing a two-color catalog. No one will say that two-color catalogs duplicate the brightness or attractiveness of four-color pieces or that sales for most product lines will be as great as when presented in four-color. But, some product lines (wire, cement repair material, nuts and bolts) can do very well with two-color printing. Here are some cost-saving factors you should consider:

(a) **Separations**. For a two-color catalog, the cost of separations is usually included in the printing price. To separate a 24-page catalog in four colors would currently cost approximately $12,000 to $15,000 — exclusive of photography. The cost of two-color 3M proofs (matchprint) would be approximately $2,000. In addition, you would have to allow another eight to twelve working days for proofing four colors.

Consider using lighter paper stock

(b) **Use of two-color**. When running a 24-page 8½″ × 11″ catalog, you will probably use a web and a half. This means that your catalog will run with one 16-page signature and one 8-page signature. This can be to your advantage. On a 16-page signature, you can use a black and a PMS color you choose; on the 8-page signature, you can use black and a different PMS color. (PMS stands for Pantone Matching System — a standardized color designation system.) For instance, you can use black and PMS 485 (a certain red) on the 16 pages, and then black and PMS 124 (a mustard gold) on the 8 pages. When the 8 and 16 pages are combined, the illusion of a multi-color catalog is created. Also, rather than black, you might choose another color, like dark blue.

Combining colors. Through the use of different percentages of tints of blue and red, the combining of blue and red tints, plus percentages of other combined colors, you can create a multi-colored effect on each page.

With two-color, the use of tints can work to your advantage. Tints of color, ranging anywhere from a pin-point to a heavier 40 percent, can be inserted underneath your black-printed copy. But when using tints, you must be careful which size of type you use. (See Figure 9-3.) For example, 6 point italic type with thin serifs is not suitable, because it is not strong enough to stand out clearly against a tinted background. But a gothic sans serif typeface or an 8 point sans serif can be used with deeper tints, because of the weight of the type.

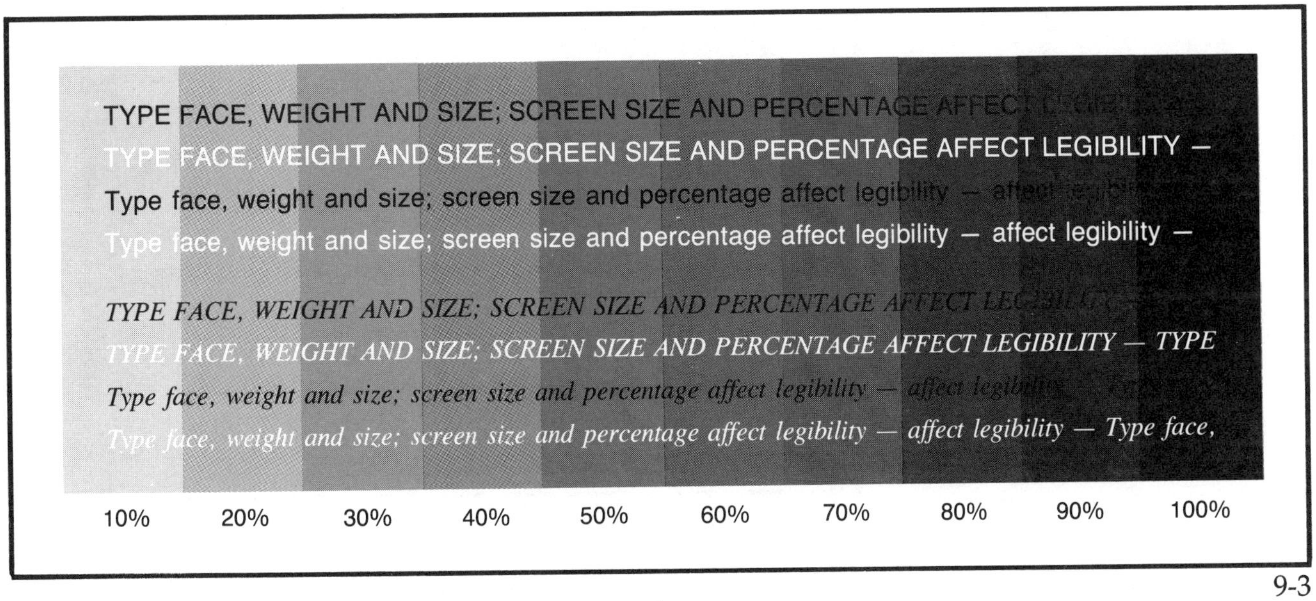

TYPE FACE, WEIGHT AND SIZE; SCREEN SIZE AND PERCENTAGE AFFECT

TYPE FACE, WEIGHT AND SIZE; SCREEN SIZE AND PERCENTAGE AFFECT LEGIBILITY —

Type face, weight and size; screen size and percentage affect legibility — affect

Type face, weight and size; screen size and percentage affect legibility — affect legibility —

TYPE FACE, WEIGHT AND SIZE; SCREEN SIZE AND PERCENTAGE AFFECT

TYPE FACE, WEIGHT AND SIZE; SCREEN SIZE AND PERCENTAGE AFFECT LEGIBILITY — TYPE

Type face, weight and size; screen size and percentage affect legibility — affect legibility

Type face, weight and size; screen size and percentage affect legibility — affect legibility — Type face,

10% 20% 30% 40% 50% 60% 70% 80% 90% 100%

9-3

How to design a catalog or brochure that creates the illusion of more than two colors.

Let's look at how a two-color print job can be aesthectically accomplished with a colorful look. In reality this is relatively simple to accomplish. Suppose you have an eight-page catalog you'd like to design on a low budget, but with a colorful effect. When you lay out the piece, side one will contain four pages: one, four, five and eight. Side two will hold pages two, three, six and seven.

Print side one in two-color. This means your front and back cover (pages one and eight) and centerspread (pages four and five) will print in single color. The layout form in Figure 9-4 shows how this works to create a multicolor appearance.

When the catalog is assembled, you will create a *look* of more than two colors. Creativity plays a part in

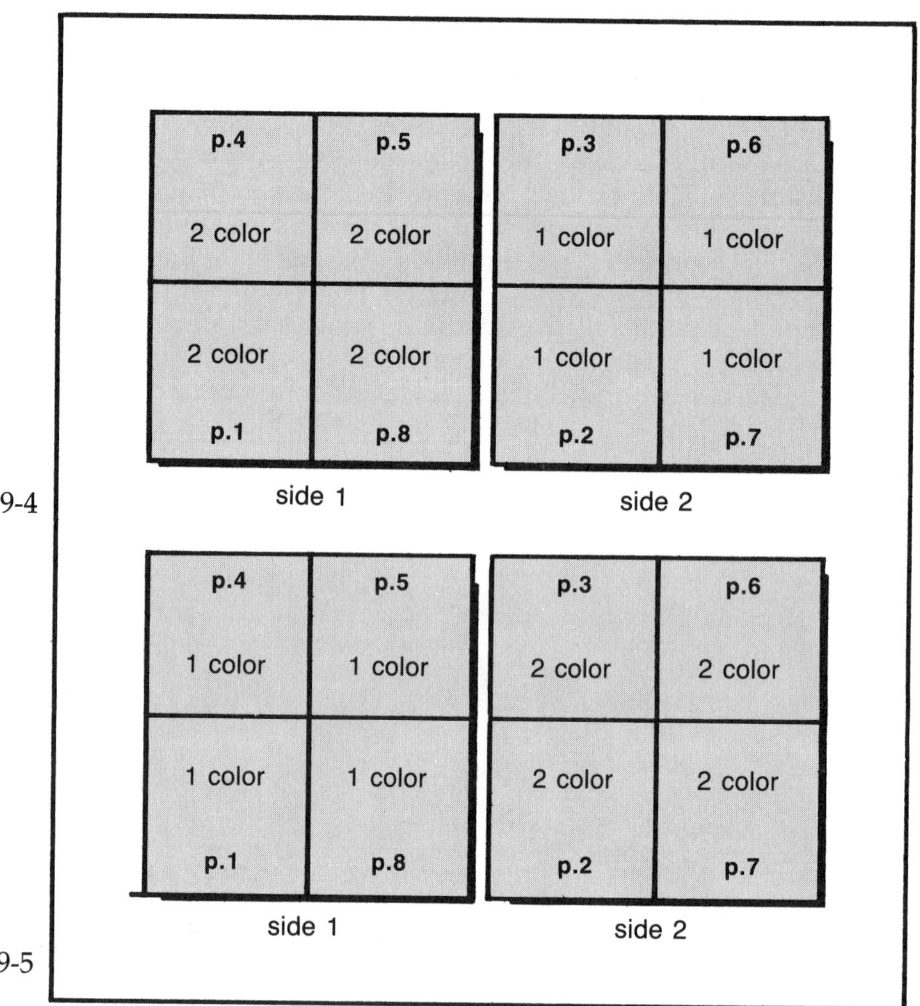

9-4

9-5

p.4
1 color
1 color
p.1
p.5
2nd
1 color
2nd
1 color
p.8
side 1
p.3
2 color
2 color
p.2
p.6
2 color
2 color
p.7
side 2

9-6

similar illusions. In addition to the layout just proposed, let us take another example.

Using the same format, the page layout now looks like the one shown in Figure 9-5. We have reversed the color format, using the single color on side one. What does this accomplish? Page one, your front cover, now can be designed with bold type or an illustration using the mezzotint technique advantageously in a single color.

Remember that black does not necessarily have to be used. Dark blues or grays work well. This technique allows you to print the first two inside facing pages (two and three) in two colors, further enhancing the illusion of more color in your book. Pages six and seven now are your two-color pages, which creates a problem: your centerspread (pages four and five) must appear in a single color.

One solution is a technique called a split fountain. This is a method by which you can add an additional color across the sheet by separating and dividing the ink fountain approximately in half, using two different colors across the page. The example in Figure 9-6 explains what happens to pages one, four, five, and eight when they are kept in a single color, but with a split fountain.

As the ink fountain prints and moves over the side one form, the two different colors on the single color side are printed at the same time. In addition, if the proper colors are chosen on side two, you can blend the two colors to form a range of colors, such as blue, yellow, and a blend of the two which is green.

You can imagine what a catalog using this technique will look like. Also, note that your back cover, page eight, prints in a different color from your front cover, page one.

2. A second area of savings involves planning in the design stage, prior to the actual printing process.

Stay with black

Type. Stick to the norm — black on white — for the greatest economy. Deviations from this norm will affect price. For example, type can be printed in *many colors*, but special matches will affect costs. Type can be made *white on a colored background* (knockout type), but this will again add to costs. *Outlined type* (bordered letters) requires delicate work, and this added time translates into dollars.

Original copy. (''Copy'' in a printing sense is the term used for artwork.) What is your original piece of art? Is it a transparency (through which light must pass in order for the art to be seen or reproduced — like a slide or a negative), or is it reflective art (which reflects light from its surface — a photograph or drawing)? Working from reflective art costs more.

But even more important from the standpoint of added expense is the quality of the original art you're giving to your separator. Is it underexposed or overexposed; does it have high contrast or low contrast? Contrast is the tonal gradation among the highlights, middle tones, and shadows in the artwork. Any work which requires adjusting the exposure or contrast will increase your costs. Be sure you give the separator the best possible art or photography you can supply.

Quality of result. It's your choice. Do you want your color separator to provide you with separations that are of pleasing quality, high quality, or something in the middle? The time required to reach each plateau affects price. Here's what to expect at each quality level.

Highest: Good copy normally exposed can be printed or proofed to the client's satisfaction. This may require three or four on-press proofings and special retouching to achieve complete satisfaction.

Medium: Normal copy is printed or proofed for one overall change. For instance, you might want to lighten or darken the final result overall, as opposed to subtle changes in highlight areas. At this level, you can expect two on-press proofs.

Normal: The trade term for this is ''pleasing'' quality. You won't get a press proof. Instead, you'll get a prepress proof — a color key, matchprint or chromalin — each of which is less accurate than a press proof. Basically, what you see separated is what you'll get. No changes will be offered.

Time. It's always money. To produce work on short notice or within a short time frame will cost more. Most color separators specify a normal turnaround of eight working days. Anything less will require overtime and affect price. In addition, customer approval at press side will require additonal press time and also increase costs.

Essentially, price is affected by the needs of the client and the amount of service required. Only you can be the judge of what you want and how much help you'll need in obtaining your desired results.

3. A third cost-saver is deciding not to change plates for address or coding changes. Suppose you face the problem of adding a number of different branch addresses to your catalog. (Though in this example we've used branch addresses, the identical situation would exist if you needed to change codes, for instance.) *You can change these addresses as part of your press run; this is the most expensive way*. It's necessary to stop the presses when you reach the desired amount for a certain address, change to another address, and so on. Of course, one way to save money by this method is

Two-color Catalogs

We've had very good luck with two-color catalogs. A good artist can do a LOT with two colors, so you can print an attractive catalog that is quite cost effective . . . the savings allow you to mail more frequently.

Patrick D. Smith, Jr.
Production Manager
California Polytechnic University

to "gang" addresses which need the same quantity of brochures. You can do this when your press sheet is large enough to accommodate producing, for example, six brochures on the same plate (Figure 9-7). Address A, B, and C are printed concurrently (if you need equal quantities of each address). For instance, if these three addresses need 10,000 pieces each, you will get two each of the three addresses every time a sheet goes through the press. If you have twenty or thirty branches, you can see the number of times you must stop the press, replace plates, and continue.

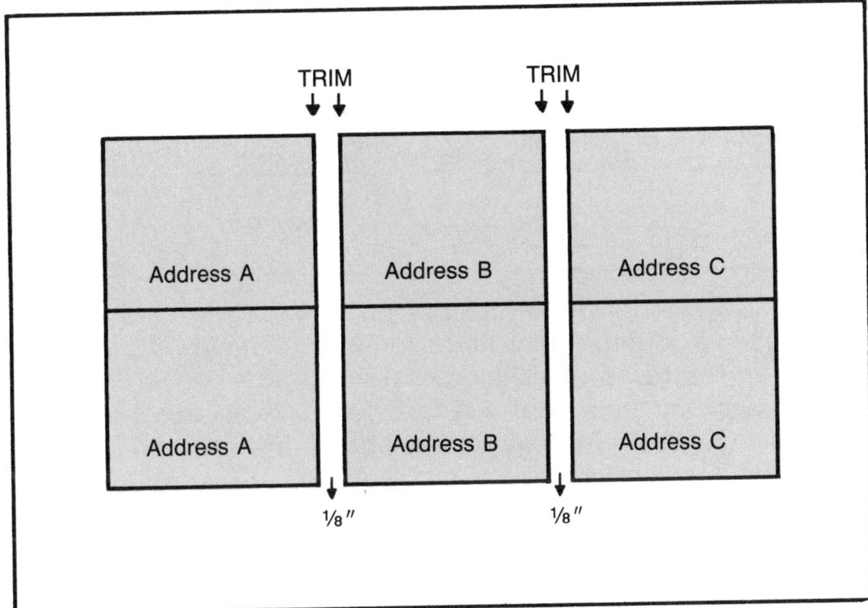

9-7

Quality ÷ cost

A less expensive alternative is imprinting off press. All your brochures or catalogs would be printed at one time and the necessary addresses would then be imprinted as a separate operation. The danger in this method is "roller marks." Your printed piece must pass under wheels to hold it in place when it is traveling along the belt before and after it is imprinted. If these wheels are too tight, they'll leave marks (resembling black streaks) running the length of your piece. This will happen on both coated and dull stocks. It may not always happen, but in many instances it does. *If quality is important, changing address plates on press is the better answer, although it is more costly.*

4. Another cost-saver is using a "common chop" to trim your printed piece. If you want to do this, you should allow at least one-eighth of an inch on either side of an illustration for trimming or cutting away. Let us suppose you have a press sheet with six pieces laid on the sheet, as was shown in Figure 9-8. But when preparing the brochure, some printers butt two pieces together (Figure 9-8). The illustrations are placed beside each other with a thin white hairline between them. This saves cost and (sometimes) gets more pieces on a press sheet. When the pieces are cut, it is necessary to come as close to the white hairline as possible. This

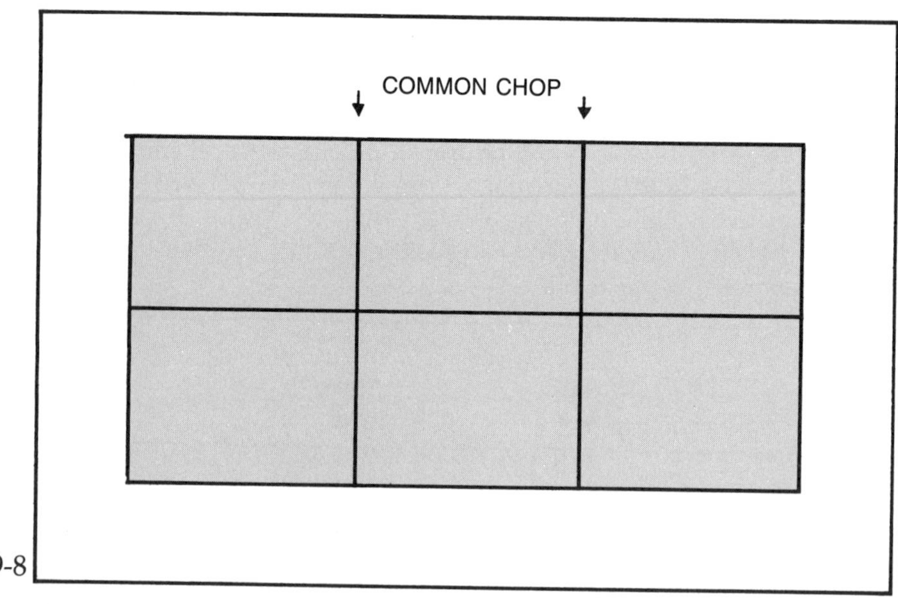

9-8

doesn't always work. Thus you can trim between two hairlines and find you have portions of the illustrations from the first piece sliced off and appearing on the piece next to it. It's wise, if you want to obtain a clean-cut piece, to allow that one-eighth-inch bleed between each piece to get the proper cut (as shown in Figure 9-7). **If you don't, and if your trim is not exact, your effort to save money will have proved costly — you won't have received the printed piece you wanted.**

Keep problems like this in mind when some supplier suggests money-saving shortcuts. Be sure you know the liabilities which can threaten the quality you wish to maintain (or ask your printer to explain the risks involved in any suggested cost-saving methods).

How To Choose The Most Economical Size For Your Order Form and Envelope.

Just as there are standard, economical sizes for catalogs (such as 8½″ × 11″, 5½″ × 8½″ and 6″ × 9″), there are also standard sizes for bindable order forms and envelopes. What these standard sizes are depends upon the size of the printing press on which they are produced. Standard-size formats are shown in Figures 9-9 and 9-10.

One of the most common sizes is 8¾″ (or 8⅞″) by 13″. This size is a cost-effective format for mini-web presses (smaller than average paper size acceptance, 26″ × 31″ versus 38″), allowing four pieces out of each printing impression. Using the same press, other sizes would also be economical, but would yield only two pieces per impression. Some examples are 8¾″ × 19″ or 8¾″ × 26″. *The 8¾″ size is suitable for binding into all of the most common catalog sizes.*

Other order form sizes might be just as economical, depending upon the printing press and your order quantity. A 7½″ × 17″ order form might seem irregular, but in large quantities could be printed with even greater efficiency than the 3¾″ × 13″. Some sizes you might consider are:

5⅝″ × 13″	5⅝″ × 19″	7½″ × 12⅔″
9⅝″ × 15″	11⅜″ × 18″	

Many other configurations can use these same dimensions in other combinations (e.g., 11⅜″ × 17″, 11⅜″ × 12⅔″, etc.). There are even larger presses where 11¾″, 12¾″, and other head-to-foot dimensions can be printed, but these sizes are often difficult to fit inside your catalog. *Ideally the order form/envelope should be two inches shorter than your full catalog size, so the order form becomes a natural page break.* This will make your order form easy to find, especially when it is not bound into the middle of the catalog.

You might wish to consider using a double order form format — that is, two order forms and one or two reply envelopes. This allows pass-along readers to order using an actual form. Economical sizes for a double order form and envelope are 8¾″ × 26″ or 7½″ × 30″. Two reply envelopes and order forms can be created by perforating the standard 11⅜″ × 17″ size, forming two envelopes which are 5$\frac{3}{16}$″. *Always be careful that you stay within the postal regulations for legal reply envelope sizes.*

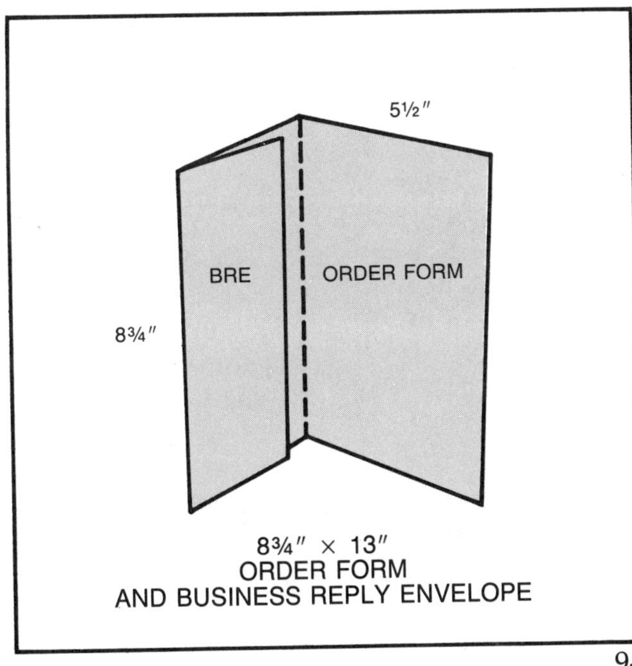

9-9

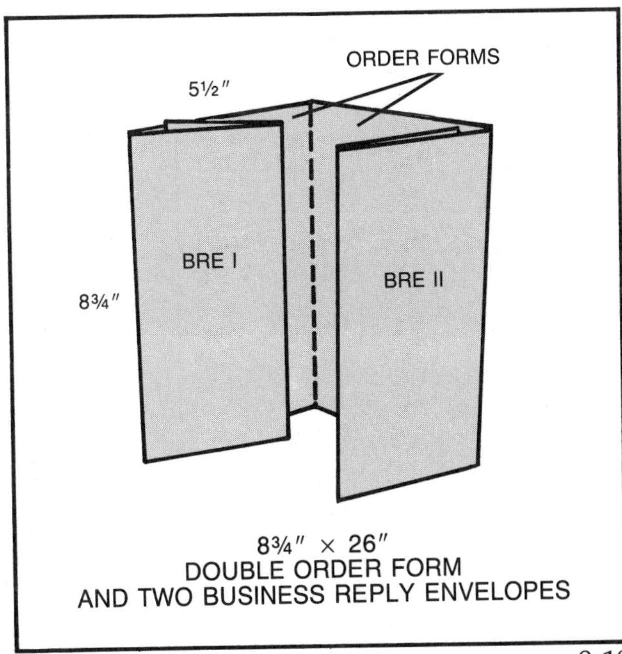

9-10

Catalog Printing Checklist

- ☐ Prepare a Bid Sheet.
- ☐ Define Your Printing Needs for Quality, Price, and Service.
- ☐ Identify Early Your Method of Addressing.

Always:

1. Ask for printing samples on same kind of paper you intend to use.
2. Be uniform and thorough about job specifications with all printers.
3. Select paper to match your products and image.
4. Consider weight of paper.
5. Project your printing volume needs.

Strongly Consider:

1. Visiting the printing plant prior to a final decision.
2. A slightly lighter or lesser grade paper than prime.
3. A two-color catalog, if only for an off season or sale version.
4. Being on site as the catalog is printed.

Step Number 3: The Color Separator.

Your photographer took superb shots for your new catalog, but will your printed piece convey the full impact of those photographs and sell your products? Make sure you get the right supplier to provide color separations and film to your printer. But who is right for you? Many times, catalog printers have separators with whom they work well so the printer will do the coordinating for you. Or, some printers have their own color separating facilities. But if you need to find a separator yourself, visit the shops you're considering. Here's what to look for and ask about:

The Facility. Be certain your prospective separator has a modern plant layout. Many separators have let their facilities grow sporadically through the years without anticipating their growth or planning for it. A stripper has been put here, a photographer there, a dot etcher anywhere. Look for the separator who places crafts-people in positions to coordinate efforts with an economical flow from one work station to the next. This guarantees efficiency of operation, reduces error, and helps assure that you'll receive your materials on time.

The White Glove Test. A clean, environmentally sound plant will help guarantee a better product. Be certain there's a modern, efficient air conditioning system, with filters changed regularly to ensure dust and static control. If a stray speck of dust gets on your film, it will be on every catalog you print. Ask how your separator controls this problem; giving the plant the ''white glove test'' will help you determine the cleanliness of the plant environment.

The Equipment. Does your separator have state-of-the-art equipment? Let's divide this subject into four areas: (1) computerized imaging; (2) prepress proofing; (3) computer proof evaluation and quality control devices; and (4) press proofing.

1. Computerized Imaging. This is the better mousetrap — tomorrow's world today, the best in high-tech for the graphic arts industry. A computerized imaging system (some manufacturers are Scitex, HELL, or Crossfield) can do in a fraction of the time and with better quality what used to take a highly skilled craftsperson hours to do. Some functions of particular interest to the catalog producer include retouching, color correcting, silhouetting, resizing, color matching, and page makeup. Computerized imaging will not reduce the price of your color separation, but costs for items such as dye transfers and retouching will be drastically slashed.

2. Prepress Proofing. What will your separator show you prior to ink on paper? Ideally your separator should be prepared to show you a matchprint (3M product) or chromalin (DuPont) prepress proof to give you a visual check of film. This pretty much duplicates press condition; you save time and money by making needed corrections before the presses are running.

3. Computer Proof Evaluation and Quality Control Devices. Certain computer systems inspect and measure film quality to help guarantee "the perfect job."

(a) **Hazeltine Previewer** is an electro-optical system which simulates accurately the color printing process from film separation through press production. It gives your separator a color video display including the effects of all photographic and photomechanical processes, enabling the separator to evaluate separations individually and as progressives (all four colors — black, cyan, magenta, yellow) in both offset and gravure.

(b) **Spectronics** is a sophisticated little system which inspects your final proof against the film. The two should match, and then your printed piece will match your proof.

(c) **Densitometers** measure ink and film densities to guarantee more uniform printing across the entire page. The Tobias densitometer goes a step beyond by scanning four colors in repetitive sequence, giving a visual display of those areas in or out of spec, and providing a printout of all color values at the same time. The Tobias is faster, more precise, and provides more data than conventional densitometers.

4. Press Proofing. Make sure your color separator has clean, modern presses so your proof will reflect what ultimately comes off your production press. Nobody wants to approve a press proof only to see a different job once the press is off and running. The art of color proofing is addressed in greater detail later in this chapter.

A Written Estimate is needed to detail all aspects of the job and the estimated price for completion. Your final bill should exactly coincide, the only exception being author's alterations and changes you made after the job was initiated. Make sure it's the separator's policy to give you a written estimate — it's the only way to stick within your budget.

If you keep the above points in mind when you're searching for your color separator, you should have no problem finding a qualified, efficient plant to handle your specific needs.

How To Communicate With Your Color Separator

There is a fine line between a good and a superb catalog. What you send to your separator and how you communicate can help you cross that line. Accurate communication, the correct preparation of your materials, and attention to how designs and type will reproduce make all the difference.

Communications. The burden is yours to tell your separator what you want. The separator will ask you to fill out a purchase order including obvious information such as your company's name, due dates, key contacts, and the project title, as well as:

The **size of each page** . . . and whether or not the page should bleed (in a "bleed," color or a printed image is applied past the edges of the trimmed sheet or page).

The **materials you are supplying to your separator** . . . and in what quantities. Chapter 5 discussed different types of photography, but are you providing reflective art such as photographs, drawings or other illustrative copy that is viewed and photographed by light reflected from its surface? Or are you providing transparencies, slides or illustrative copy through which light must pass in order for the art to be seen or reproduced?

The **kind of type reproduction** . . . freestanding (black type), color, or knockout ("white" type "reversed out" of a color background).

The more accurate you are in the details of your specifications, the less chance of error.

The mechanical. "Mechanical" is a term for the camera-ready pasteup of artwork. It includes type, photos, line art — all on one piece of art board. It is the road map your separator will follow in preparing each page of your catalog. Your art department should:

Make certain the stats you furnish of your four-color and halftone art are of actual size and in position. Artwork on your mechanical is for position only. The separations will be made from the actual artwork (transparencies or reflective) that you supply.

Figure 9-11 shows the assembly of a mechanical. A mixture of artwork is used for the purpose of this illustration. Generally, a catalog page will be made up of one major type of art, such as transparencies, and type. The art board, in the center, has all type and line art (headline and product copy) to-size and in the exact position in which it will appear in the catalog. The position of original art, color prints, and color transparencies is indicated directly on the art board by outline drawings which are in the exact shape, position, and size they will occupy on the catalog page. This finished art board is photographed for use in the photomechanical reproduction process.

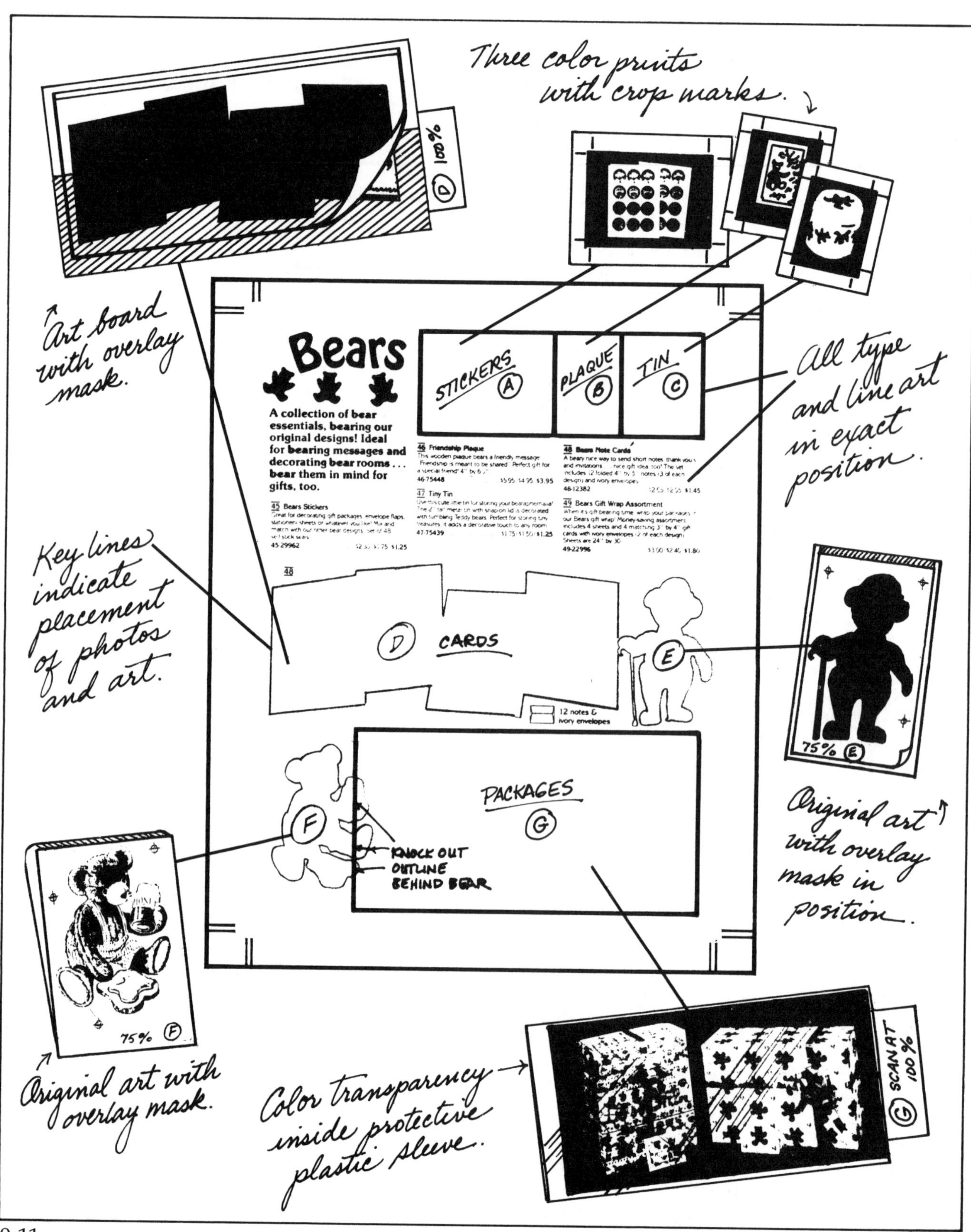
100%
D
Three color prints with crop marks.
Art board with overlay mask.
Bears
A collection of bear essentials, bearing our original designs! Ideal for bearing messages and decorating bear rooms . . . bear them in mind for gifts, too.
STICKERS A
PLAQUE B
TIN C
All type and line art in exact position.
45 Bears Stickers
45-29962
46 Friendship Plaque
46-75448
47 Tiny Tin
47-75439
48 Bears Note Cards
48-12382
49 Bears Gift Wrap Assortment
49-22996
Key lines indicate placement of photos and art.
48
D CARDS
E
12 notes & ivory envelopes
75% E
Original art with overlay mask in position.
PACKAGES G
F
KNOCK OUT OUTLINE BEHIND BEAR
75% F
Original art with overlay mask.
Color transparency inside protective plastic sleeve.
SCAN AT 100%
G

9-11

Specify whether borders around the page or around specific pieces of art are black, knockout, or a specific color. Tracing paper is overlaid on your boards to show specific color breaks and to list other pertinent information. This is called a "color key." (See Figure 9-12.) Note how the artist has traced the forms and positions of the art and copy on the tissue overlay to indicate the color of type, borders, and artwork. Background color tint is also specified (lower left of page) as well as a tint bleed: "Background tint bleeds off this page 10% yellow." The instructions on a tissue overlay must be specific, indicating all color breaks and corrections. Figure 9-13 is the final printed catalog page as it appears in the Current, Inc. catalog.

Hazards to watch out for when preparing material to be color separated.

1. **Photo retouching** can be dangerous and fraught with problems during the stage of color separation. Bloodshot eyes, red finger knuckles, blotching or discolored areas may seem very acceptable to the naked eye but look disastrous when the camera's turn comes around.

You face two choices when the decision to retouch has been made:

(a) Produce a *dye transfer* (*a color print* made from your own chrome), or

(b) Color correct (retouch) *the chrome directly*.

Because correcting directly on the chrome is so limited, retouching is almost always accomplished on a color print. To make the print from the chrome, each color is laid down (one color at a time) until the color chrome is physically reproduced. When the color print is reviewed, it must match the quality of the original chrome. If not, further retouching will be necessary in addition to the retouching needed to correct your original problem.

About 35 chemical dyes and bleaches are used for the retouching process. Sometimes, retouchers (people who correct prints and chromes) must airbrush to improve or remove color. Air brushing adds color to the print or chrome by spraying it on — much like spray painting a wall in your home. But the artist has a more delicate hand. Often, the retoucher is forced to use fluorescent paints for the corrections. These paints, when placed on the scanner or in front of the bright lights of the camera, create a "bloom" in the engraver's proof (showing a shine or hot spot on the retouched area). *Retouched material often looks excellent to the naked eye, but the camera/scanner picks up the fluorescent imperfection*. Your retoucher should warn you about "blooms."

2. **When preparing color prints** for separation (whether they are retouched or not), keep in mind the *size and thickness of boards used to back the print*. Since material is usually placed on a scanner, and since the scanner operates with a cylinder around which the material must wrap, all art should be no larger than 8″ × 10″ and no thicker than .006″. (There is no way to wrap hardboard around

Cost Savings

Some products just don't need four-color. A good two-color catalog can effectively merchandise the product, highlight benefits and features, and save you money that's better spent somewhere else.

Patrick D. Smith, Jr.
Production Manager
California Polytechnic University

10% CYAN
50% MAGENTA
50% YELLOW
OUTLINES 100% MAGENTA, 10% YELLOW
KNOCK OUT TYPE TO WHITE
Bears
A
4 CL
B
4 CL
C
4 CL
100% YELLOW
50% MAGENTA
SOLID BLACK
D
4 COLOR
E
BLACK
BACKGROUND TINT BLEEDS OFF THIS PAGE
10% YELLOW
OUTLINE 100% MAGENTA
F
G
KNOCK OUT TO WHITE
+ PRINT BACK
100% YELLOW, 10% RED
BLACK
KNOCK OUT TYPE TO WHITE

9-12

A collection of bear essentials, bearing our original designs! Ideal for bearing messages and decorating bear rooms . . . bear them in mind for gifts, too.

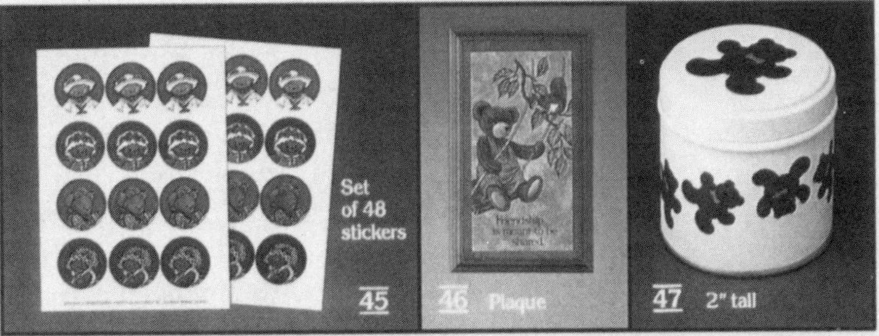

45 Bears Stickers
Great for decorating gift packages, envelope flaps, stationery sheets or whatever you like! Mix and match with our other bear designs. Set of 48 self-stick seals.
45-29962 . . . . $2.30/$1.75/**$1.25**

46 Friendship Plaque
This wooden plaque bears a friendly message: "Friendship is meant to be shared." Perfect gift for a special friend! 4" by 6½".
46-75448 . . . . $5.95/$4.95/**$3.95**

47 Tiny Tin
Use this cute little tin for storing your bearaphernalia! The 2" tall metal tin with snap-on lid is decorated with tumbling Teddy bears. Perfect for storing tiny treasures, it adds a decorative touch to any room.
47-75439 . . . . $1.75/$1.50/**$1.25**

48 Bears Note Cards
A beary nice way to send short notes, thank-you's and invitations . . . nice gift idea, too! The set includes 12 folded 4" by 5" notes (3 of each design) and ivory envelopes.
48-12382 . . . . $2.65/$2.05/**$1.45**

49 Bears Gift Wrap Assortment
When it's gift-bearing time, wrap your packages in our Bears gift wrap! Money-saving assortment includes 4 sheets and 4 matching 3" by 4" gift cards with ivory envelopes (2 of each design). Sheets are 24" by 30".
49-22996 . . . . $3.00/$2.40/**$1.80**

a cylinder without completely cracking the board.) If your art arrives mounted on a board which is too thick, the separator will strip the print from the mounted board, reducing the print to its thinnest layer.

Another way to overcome this problem is for the engraver to shoot a transparency of the art, instead of stripping it from the board, but this added step can cause a loss of clarity. As a last resort, a print mounted on a too-thick board can be color separated by shooting it with a special camera. This old-fashioned method shoots the print four times, once for each of the four colors of the separation.

Three-Way Communication. It is imperative that your color separator know all the details of how your printer is ultimately going to print the catalog. Your separator must know the type of press to be used, paper stock, type of printing plates, type of ink, and ink layout rotation. Here are some specifics:

> **Ink rotation** refers to the fact that different printers print colors in different sequences, e.g., yellow, red, blue, black. The order chosen will affect the final color appearance, so your press proof from the separator should be run in the same rotation. In addition, ink is a chemical and *all inks differ,* creating subtle differences in the same color.
>
> The **type of paper** your job will be printed on will affect the final color appearance. You should have your printer supply the color separator with samples of paper stock and ink in order to proof identically to the way the job ultimately will be run.

Some hints about color. All color transparencies have a *color cast* (for instance, in Kodachrome it's red and in Ecktachrome it's blue). It is imperative that you let your color separator know whether you want this cast left there or whether you want it removed.

Do you want **more or less contrast**? Remember, in the actual printing, you automatically get less.

What part of the art do you want to **highlight?** It's your choice. There are two different types of highlight: ''Specular'' gives the brightest effect (i.e., the whitest white, which means there are no dots of color appearing in the white at all, and the white you get is the white of your paper). ''Diffue'' is a ''neutral'' white; it has a minimum of dots in it. The decision should be made by your art department. Also, inform your color separator if you want to *darken or lighten your art,* enhance or subdue details.

There are many questions you have to answer so your color separator can do the job correctly. The more thoroughly you answer these questions, the better chance you have of receiving a catalog which can best sell your product. Remember, your catalog communicates to your customers — you must communicate with your color separator.

Another approach to communication is to have your engraver (color separator) work with your printer directly. This allows you to communicate with both suppliers while assuring vital communication between the two of them.

A brief explanation about how color separations are made may improve your communication abilities as well as help you to proof and to understand correction possibilities.

How color separations are made . . . and how to take your artwork (either illustrations or photography) and transform it into a rich color plate that will print as a faithful reproduction.

To the separator's eye, all color is made up of just four basic process colors: magenta (process red), cyan (process blue), process yellow, and process black. Combinations of these four produce almost any color imaginable. The photoplatemaker begins by separating the four basic colors from your artwork using one of two methods: *indirect separation* or *electronic color scanning*. The indirect method separates by camera and is a two-step process (continuous tone and then a halftone negative). This is a complex and time-consuming process. The second method, electronic color scanning, is restricted to flexible materials that can be wrapped around the scanner's cylinder, producing four halftone negatives, ready for stripping. *Both methods do the same thing: they separate your raw materials into the four basic colors.*

Halftone photography converts your print or transparency into the four basic colors, each being a series of dots of different diameters. This is done by photographing the artwork through a grid pattern, much like a window screen in your home. Each color is separated at a different angle of the screen to produce a rosette pattern of dots (see Figure 9-14). If the screen angles weren't varied, each dot would print on top of another, and the result would look like a black and white halftone.

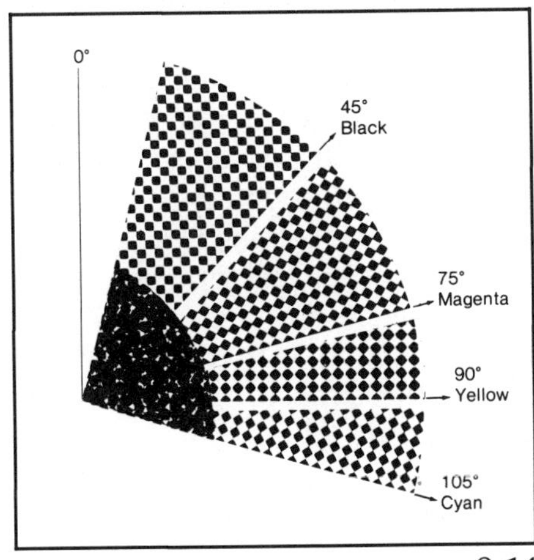

9-14

Undercover Removal. Getting a deep, rich black can be a problem. As mentioned earlier, black results from printing the four separate colors on top of each other. But this gives you a printed piece appearing flat and muddy. The answer is undercolor removal. By reducing magenta, cyan and yellow, and increasing black through photographic means or dot etching, you create the rich black required for color with definition.

Screen Selection. Separators produce the finest quality from your artwork only if they are aware of the paper and inks your printer will use. If the paper is coarse and uncoated, a coarse screen (55 to 65 lines per inch) is required. As the paper choice becomes smoother with a harder finish, a finer screen (150 and upwards) is possible. Your separator should learn the capabilities of your printer's press. The ability of your printer is important, too — some printers are more capable of handling finer screen, even using the same equipment as their competition, because of their skill. Figure 9-15 shows the gradation range of tones, each with an inset showing the corresponding size of the dot pattern.

The Densitometer enables your printer to more closely match the proof you have supplied. This instrument reads and measures the optical density of your separations and the evenness of the color bars. Color bars are as important as the color proof itself. Without the bars, your printer will be in the dark as to how the film and proofs read across the sheet. If the readings vary during the press run, the color bars help your printer adjust the equipment to match the supplied proof.

Though the densitometer is valuable, it must be used with other available materials. For example, let's say the printer can't match your press proofs. The densitometer readings are very close to the separator's . . . but they just can't come up to color. The answer is simple, but not obvious. The separator had used a warmer red than specified in order to make the color more vibrant.

Dot Etching is the final, manual process before preparing the type of proof you have requested. The dot etcher goes into the particular area where the size of the dot is off and alters the dots by hand, thickening or thinning them (strengthening or weakening the color perceived in that area) so the color matches your artwork. The hand process is being gradually replaced by photographic and electronic methods.

Contact Correction is another technique that thins or fattens the dots. By means of photographic exposure, the dots are reduced or thickened throughout the entire film.

After your separator has shown you proofs and you've approved them, the film is ready to go to the printer for platemaking and printing.

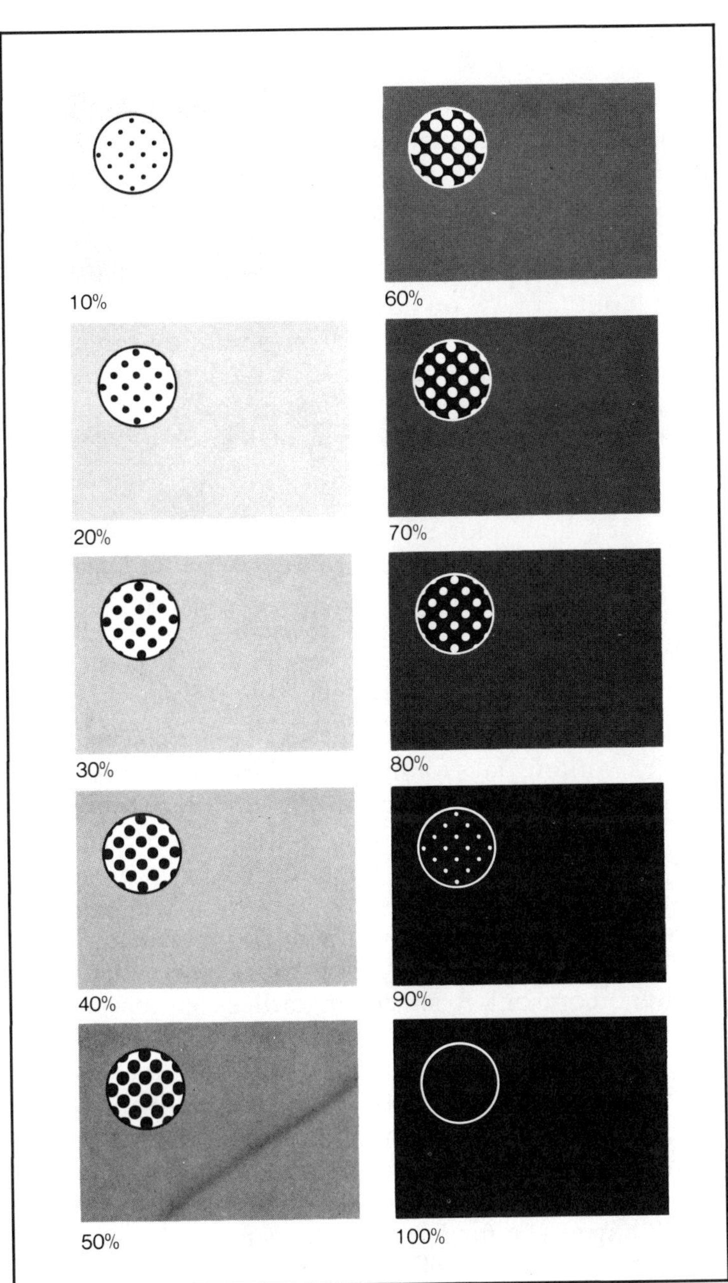

9-15

How To Proof Your Four-Color Work

A few simple techniques in this mysterious area of color proofing can help you get the results you expect in the printing of your catalog. Always *start by making sure you deliver to the engraver (color separator) film which meets your printer's needs,* as discussed above.

Be sure you deliver your film and your mechanicals (paste-ups) on time. Production people too often hear, ''I know I'm late, but you can get it out!'' or, ''You have to make the scheduled mail date anyway.'' Sometimes the job still does get out on time — but more often than not some quality has had to be sacrificed in so doing.

From the production point of view, here are areas you must take seriously when preparing to print a catalog:

(a) Allow enough *time* for each step of the job.

(b) Prove your four-color subjects *in position,* as they will run.

(c) Insist proofs be on the *stock* you will use for the job.

(d) *Develop an eye* for translating the look of chromes (transparencies) to the look they will have on paper.

1. After final mechanical approval, you must allow a minimum of eight working days for first four-color proofs. Ten working days to two weeks would be normal. The engraver must have ample time to shoot and assemble chromes in position for proper proofing — proofs which reflect how the job will run on press with type and chromes in position.

2. There is an alternate method called ''loose proving.'' This term applies to a situation where all the four-color subjects are gathered together on one or two sheets, regardless of their position in a catalog, and run at one time. Obviously, there is a cost-saving factor in using this method, but it does not guarantee quality reproduction. When the engraver pulls a four-color proof at random, and not in the sequence in which individual illustrations will appear on the press (and in your catalog), you will have subjects of different intensities juxtaposed when actually running the job. Then adjustments will have to be made to compensate for this variation in color, and these adjustments will in turn affect all the other colors for the other products.

Must decide on proof quality

3. Often you will receive engraver's proofs on an 80 pound Mead enamel, which is fine if you are producing your catalog on that stock. But if you are using a lesser grade, say 60 pound Escanba, you will find your four-color will differ — sometimes dramatically. For your proofs, insist the engraver use the stock on which you are actually printing. Figure 9-16 shows what a typical press proof sheet might look like once the artist has reviewed it and marked corrections. Let's take a look at what color corrections the artist has requested, starting at the top and going clockwise. (1) ''Y in flesh tones.'' The flesh tones in the model's hands are off-color and would

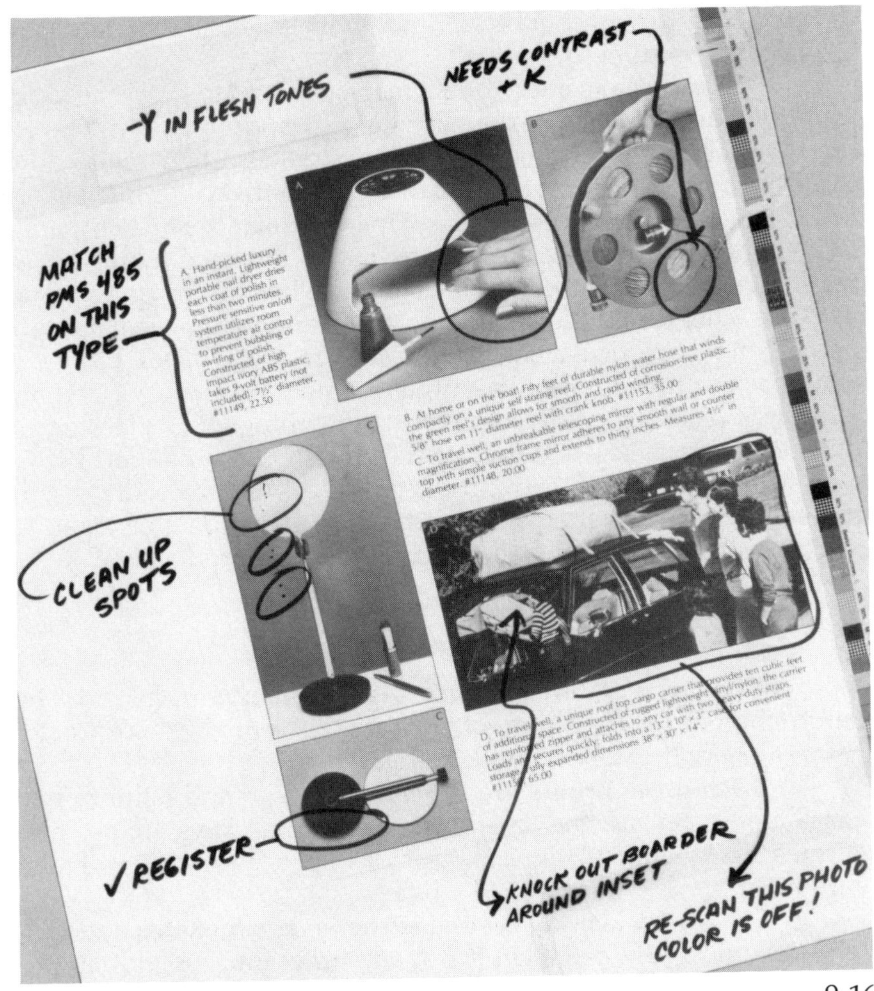

9-16

benefit from removing a little yellow. (2) ''Needs contrast + K.'' The product is appearing flat and blending too much with the background — needs more black. (3) ''Re-scan this photo, color is off!'' The artist is asking that the photograph be scanned again for modification so the colors become correct. (4) ''Knock out border around inset.'' The artist is asking that the inset be cleaned up by removing a partial border which was meant for size guidance only. (5) ''Check register.'' The printing images seem to be out of alignment and need to be corrected. (6) ''Clean up spots.'' Spots can be as harmless as pieces of dust the printer has overlooked (these are easily removed). Spots on the transparency could also have been overlooked and these, unfortunately, are on the plates and therefore much harder to correct. (7) ''Match PMS 485 on this type.'' The artist is calling for a specific ink color in which the designated type is to appear. If a second proof is required, allow at least three working days for that proof. Again, this will allow your engraver ample time to check and correct. And don't forget that when the second proof comes in, you need ample time for review. In some instances, one day will be sufficient; but other times your in-house schedule may require two to three days.

4. Art directors and product managers tend to expect an exact reproduction on paper of the chrome as it appears when viewed on a light box. But chromes are transparent, so light must flow through them to show color brilliance. When that color is transferred to paper, some concession in color and brilliance must be made. One of the top art directors in direct marketing used to use an interesting technique. He viewed the chrome when the first proof came in to see what the engravers had obtained and to know what to expect when that particular chrome was transferred to paper. He never went back to the chrome. From that moment on, he corrected for what was pleasing to the eye. When something looks pleasing, it may not be necessary to duplicate the chrome that was shot. Those who insist the chrome be reproduced exactly will be sadly disappointed over and over again. Liberties can and should be taken to insure proper, though not necessarily exact, reproduction.

An Overview of Proofing Systems

When you're buying color separations, your cost will be determined by the type of proof you want. Essentially there are *two types of proofs:* 1. Prepress and 2. Press.

1. Prepress proofs are the *least expensive* and fall into two basic types: (a) *overlay systems* such as color keys, naps, and chromacheck, and (b) *dry proof systems* such as matchprint and chromalin.

(a) **An overlay system is the least expensive** and the quickest to produce. It is made up of four individual films which lie on top of one another (Figure 9-17), each bearing one of the four colors in the printing process: magenta (red), cyan (blue), yellow, and black. The material you are going to print is separated into each of these four colors in a dot pattern. The dots are thinner and there are fewer of them in the areas which look lighter, and vice versa. When all four sheets are overlaid, you see the four-color look. As you lift up each sheet of film, you see your material in each of the four colors. This method requires some interpretation because the overlay film itself has a slight "cast" and colors may be distorted when you look through four sheets of it. An overlay system is *not the best way to judge how your separations will actually print.*

(b) **Dry proof systems are an extremely accurate way to judge how your separations will actually print.** The dry proof system puts simulated ink on paper much the same way the actual press does, and the result looks similar to a color print. The dry proof system can also incorporate press characteristics such as dot gain (when the dots take ink on press, getting "fatter" and making the color appear darker), which will make your separations look darker than you expected. This is the *second best method of proofing*.

2. Press proofs are undeniably the best way to evaluate your color separations. They are also the *most expensive*. A press proof will show all of the actual printing characteristics and press problems that can be avoided, such as ink trap (when colors or screens of colors overlap and one color is "trapped" under another), dot gain, and sharpness. A press proof (which looks like the actual printed product) will show your separations with basically the same ingredients (same paper and ink) that will print the job.

All three systems — *overlay, dry proof, and press proof — can get the job done for you*. Depending on your needs and budget, discuss with your printer which is best for you.

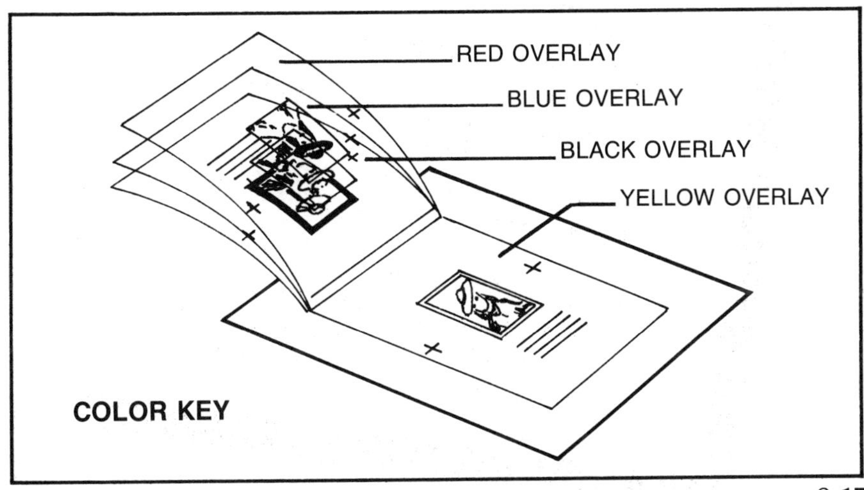

9-17

Color Separation Checklist:

- ☐ Identify Method of Color Separation Needed.
- ☐ Establish Type of Proof Required.

Always:

1. Request a written estimate per job.
2. Furnish separator with a list of specifications.
3. Furnish a clean and complete mechanical to follow.
4. Furnish to-size artwork.
5. Identify desired special effects.

Strongly Consider:

1. Having the printer and color separator communicate directly to clarify the printer's needs.

The Major Labeling Methods

The major leading methods . . . Their assets and liabilities. Thoughts Before Taking the Next Step. Labeling your catalog serves two purposes. First, it bears the name and address of your customer for the purpose of delivery. Second, it often contains information needed internally to establish what list the order came from and, of course, who placed the order. The importance of choosing the right type of labeling may not seem obvious to you at first, so you might put off the decision. However, choosing which labeling method to use should be done early in the planning schedule so that different internal needs and promotional opportunities can be fulfilled. The lettershop you choose will be able to give you a choice of different kinds, but maybe not all you want. The services you'll find in a lettershop can be divided roughly into two areas: production and backup. Production services are those such as labeling, inserting, metering, mailing, etc. Backup services include materials handling, inventory control, etc. So labeling is a production service.

One word you'll run into frequently to identify label type is "Cheshire." But it's really the name of a company which manufactures a line of labeling machines and is the brand name of those machines. Cheshire labelers, as well as those produced by other manufacturers, are designed to take labels produced on a continuous form (by computer or otherwise), cut them into individual labels, and affix the labels to a mailing piece. A lettershop may have more than one type of labeler, as each make and model has its special attributes: ease of setup, flexibility, speed, and so on.

The various types of labels which you can use are categorized according to the type of affixing adhesive:

Plain paper labels are the most common. They are sometimes referred to as "Cheshire" labels because they are designed to be affixed by a Cheshire (or similar) labeler. They are affixed by cutting the labels apart, applying glue to the back, and placing them on the mailing piece. Plain paper labels are the least expensive of all label stock. *Caution:* Some plain paper stock is very thin to permit reduction in bulk of computer-generated data files. This is distinctly not an advantage in labeling. Do not use stock under 18 pound basis without consulting your lettershop. There should be no perforation, except at the fanfold. Stock too thin and with perforations will not run well on standard lettershop equipment.

Gummed labels are backed with glue like that used on postage stamps or envelope flaps. These labels usually come on sheets or continuous forms that are perforated and are primarily intended to be hand-separated and affixed. They usually can be affixed by machine, but then the gumming and perforation are of no advantage and most lettershops will play it safe and apply glue anyway. Gummed label stock costs about four times as much as plain paper label stock.

Heat-activated adhesive labels are normally affixed by machine and can be made to adhere to just about any surface. (Their other advantage, particularly for short, in-house office runs, is that they do not require the use and subsequent wash-up of a glue pot.) *Problems*: They require a heating element for the labeling machine; they cost about as much as gummed labels; the lettershop will usually charge more to run them. They should be used only when demanded by a specific situation.

Pressure-sensitive labels are also referred to as ''Kleen-Stik'' (a trade name for a brand of pressure-sensitive material), sticky-back, and piggyback labels. In their simplest form, they are die-cut with a latex adhesive backing (similar to the back of cellophane tape) and then placed on a waxy paper which allows their relatively easy removal. They can be affixed by removing the backing and applying them directly to the mailing piece. (See Figure 9-18.) They also may be left on the backing and applied similarly to plain paper labels (with the pressure-sensitive label still riding on the backing paper) — hence the name ''piggyback.'' These labels cost about three times more than gummed or heat-activated labels, and the lettershop may charge slightly more to machine-affix them (and considerably more to affix them by hand). Advantages may be improved response — particularly with catalogs. The elimination of record error (because of the company-provided information such as name, address, catalog key identifier appearing on the label) could more than offset their additional cost.

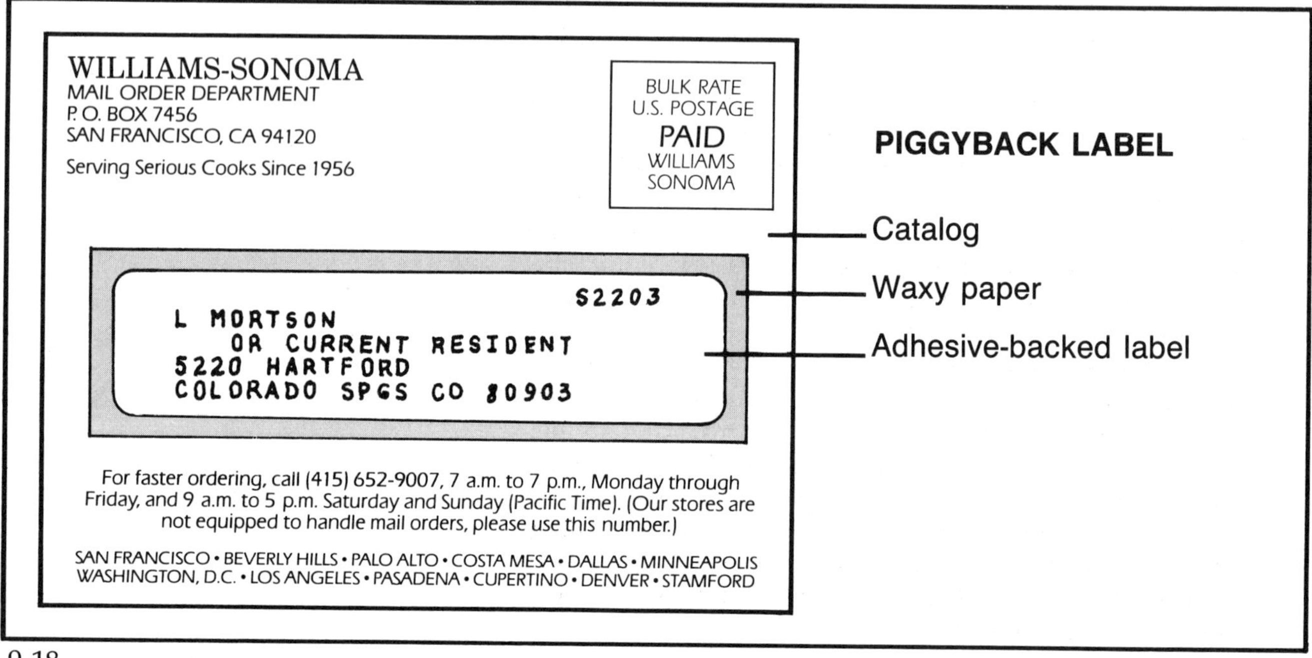

9-18

Ink jet addressing lacks one ingredient — a label — but puts all information usually found on a label directly on the mailing piece. (This process should not be confused with ink jet letters, which are like to computer letters and an entirely different category.) The ink jet addresser uses a magnetic tape as its input (furnished by the cataloger), with a format similar to that used to run a computer label printer. Besides the fact that label stock cost is zero, the absence of a paper label allows fuller use of the labeling area: it allows caps and lower case characters or mixed type styles (if programmed on the mag tape), and it affords aesthetic advantages, especially when addressing on colored or textured stock. Depending on specifics, costs can be higher or lower than with a paper label. Ask to see samples of actual ink jet addressing done by the lettershop, as the quality varies widely.

The Ink Jet "Revolution"

The Ink Jet "Revolution" . . . a technology that has been part of the direct marketing industry for over a decade. Ink jet printing capabilities have opened up a whole new world for catalogs and have solved many problems. What is ink jet printing? As we have just said in our discussion of this technology, ink jet is a non-impact printing process which places droplets of ink on paper using information supplied in magnetic tape form. Originally used as an addressing medium, ink jet later was adapted to duplicate the name and address on the inside order form. This order form placement has the *potential* (along with the use of coding data which we will discuss below) *to revolutionize the catalog industry.*

Consider the experiences of several catalog firms which tested the concept of coding order forms along with address information. The *inability to trace orders has been a continuing problem* for many of these mail order companies; it was not unusual for them to experience an average of thirty-five percent untraceable orders — even with the use of pressure-sensitive labels. But *the problem was virtually eliminated, with a remaining average of only two percent untraceable orders, after ink jet coding the order form.* The implications are encouraging for assessing the viability of outside lists, as well as increasing the statistical certainty that response results can be duplicated — especially in an area where response rates have been declining.

Here's why ink jet addressing allows better order processing. Using peel-off labels may be the least expensive way to address your catalog, but it's probably not the most *cost-effective.* By using ink jet addressing instead, you can enjoy a number of profit-building benefits:

1. More control over the quality of names/addresses you mail.
2. Dramatic increase of data captured on orders received.
3. Simplified order processing.

4. Improved response by personalizing each catalog.

Converting to ink jet addressing won't be a snap. Your address file may need reformatting. If your printer doesn't have ink jet capability, it will even mean changing printers — unless your current vendor can be persuaded to invest in the equipment. But let's look at the long-term advantages of ink jet addressing and how you might determine if the switch is worth the trouble.

Source Codes. Tracking orders by source is valuable to your overall marketing effort. Using peel-off labels that must be transferred to your catalog's order form may result in as many as *one-third* of your orders received *without* the label affixed. It may be possible to reconstruct the key code on orders placed by customers already on the house file. But it will be quite costly, if not impossible, to source the orders from rented names. With most ink jet addressing systems, on the other hand, the order form is personalized along with the address block or the wrap as the catalog passes through the bindery line. *All source codes (and any other coded or noncoded information you desire) will appear automatically on the order form in the catalog.* If you use more than one order form (business-to-business catalogs issued quarterly, for example, should have at least two order forms), even the most conscientious customer can't stick the one peel-off label on the additional forms. But some ink jet systems can personalize multiple order forms, increasing subsequent built-in order sourcing from zero percent to 100 percent. Even without multiple personalized forms, the original codes remain on the address block for transcription from cooperative buyers.

Ink jet codes can also be used to identify the catalog in which the order form appears or to distinguish special sale catalog mailings, allowing you to print a large quantity of order forms in advance to save on printing costs. How you use the flexibility of the ink jet system is up to you . . . but you certainly should take advantage of opportunities to *streamline your own production, in addition to the tracking and marketing benefits of ink jet systems.*

Tracking of source codes is invaluable in improving every catalog marketer's profit picture. It's *essential in building the kind of data base that can guide list rental selection, determine optimum frequency of mailings by market segment, and target customer needs.* If you have only a vague idea of who your customers are, you're missing the full potential of catalog marketing.

Clean Lists. With on-line ink jet addressing, you can incorporate changes of address and other data updates virtually up to the day you mail. Labels have to be printed much earlier and limit your flexibility in mailing to a clean (or updated and error-free) list. Factor in the number of labels that are lost in the mail and you'll see that permanent *ink jet addressing will increase the number of catalogs actually received, perhaps by as much as five percent.*

Individualized Mailings. Many ink jet addressing systems allow you to print up to six additional lines of copy on the address block or the order form, using a variety of type fonts. These can be used to alert specific types of customers to special discounts or to make special offers on the order form. Such options can *boost dollar volume* of orders dramatically. One successful utilization of the ink jet procedure is in "personalization," or the use of *special targeted messages.* Applying an ink jet message on the back cover of your catalog, requesting the nonbuyer to order from the current catalog or have the name eliminated from the mailing list, has shown a thirty percent increase in some cases, with an average order size comparable to the house list average.

The use of special messages in association with targeted market segmentation and particular buying patterns is just one approach the ink jet printing technique has made possible. While ink jet is not a panacea, its utilization can benefit the analysis of results, and can impact the bottom line directly, particularly in the case of targeted special messages. Ink jet addressing can eliminate guesswork, improve deliverability, increase response rates and average order values, and add new flexibility to your catalog mailing. It costs more in initial programming and slightly more for production, but the return on investment is substantial.

Ink jetting requires precise planning with your printer. It is essential that scheduling requirements be covered as far in advance as possible.

Physical characteristics of labels can affect their compatibility with lettershop capability. It's wise to furnish your lettershop with a list of these characteristics. That way you can be sure the lettershop can accept any deviations from the norm.

	4-Up	**5-Up**
Width of printout paper:	14⅞″	14⅞″
Vertical distance between fanfolds:	11″	11″
Label width:	3.4″	2.6″
Number of labels across:	4	5
Maximum number of characters per line:	33	23
Minimum distance from labels to pinfeed holes:	0.3″	0.3″
Centering of labels on printout paper:	Yes	Yes
Label height:	1″	1″
Number of lines per inch:	6 or 8	6 or 8
Maximum number of lines per label:	5 or 7	5 or 7
Whether labels print across fanfold "perf":	No	No
Sequence of labels in printout (NS or EW):	EW	EW

Information needed by list processor. If your list processing house will provide the lettershop with bag tags — usually required if your list is to be carrier route or five-digit presorted — it is important to provide the list processor with the following information:

(a) **Name, city and state** of your lettershop;
(b) **Complete weight** of your mailing piece;
(c) **Size** of your mailing piece;
(d) **Maximum weight per mailing bag**
(e) **Minimum number** of pieces per bag.

Size and weight of the mailing piece must come from you. The other information usually is worked out between you, your lettershop, and the list processing house. Establish size and weight from an actual sample of the mailing piece . . . or if that is unavailable, from an accurate dummy made of the same materials you'll print on. Lacking that, a fairly accurate estimate of weight can be made using the flat trim size and basis weight of each item in the mailing. In the case of a bound book or catalog, the estimate can be made from the number of pages, page size, and basis weight. Take note if some pages are on a different weight stock.

All this is routine for most list processing houses. But if you get a list which your lettershop can't handle easily, you may find yourself facing unexpected costs and delays.

Step Number 4: The Lettershop.

How To Get Lettershop Estimates and Quotes . . . And When To Get Them! Before you get a quotation (firm costing information), before you start printing, before your artwork is drawn up — while you're still in the layout stage — *you should have an estimate* (approximate costing information). An early discussion with your lettershop can save grief later on. You will receive not only estimates of the costs to prepare your alternate packages, but also suggestions to help reduce lettershop costs in each case.

It's important to *differentiate between a quotation and an estimate,* two words often used synonymously, though they are different. When you are planning a mailing and specifications can still be changed, be sure the lettershop knows you are looking for an *estimate based on those specifications.* That way, the lettershop will put pencil to paper knowing that specs may be adjusted if there is sufficient justification. Estimating can lead to cost-cutting suggestions or to a mention of available techniques which, although they may not save on lettershop costs, may save in label production, postage, fulfillment, or other costs. (Of course, a reputable lettershop will treat the estimate as a legitimate quotation, if the actual job comes through conforming to the original specs.)

What does a lettershop need to know in order to give you a quote? Not everything, but some things you may not consider significant may be exceedingly important. For example, though it makes no difference to the lettershop whether or not a catalog is printed in black or four-color, it matters greatly whether the catalog is to be inserted into an outer envelope.

Your lettershop will assume you know what you are buying . . . that you know the types of equipment used in the industry and their capabilities and limitations. It's your responsibility to alert the lettershop to any specifications which may affect the ultimate cost figures. The *safest way to get a quote is to have you and the lettershop rep sit down with as accurate a dummy of the proposed job as you can muster.*

There are still other areas to be covered. Will postage be paid by meter, stamps, or permit imprint (as discussed in Chapter 3)? Will the mailing be first, second, or third class mail? (Most catalogs go third class.) Will any portion qualify for carrier route or five-digit presort? How much time will there be to produce the job? (And how many machines must be set up and manned?) What time of year will the job run? (And will the lettershop have sufficient capacity available then?)

Many lettershops are capable of handling printing, list maintenance, addressing, list procurement, list processing, bursting, folding, imprinting, coding, collating, nesting, packing, shipping — as well as a host of other related services. Be prepared to answer additional questions if you want your lettershop to quote in these areas. And be sure to establish some kind of identification for each quote. The best is a combination of a project or job number, and a title for the mailing. Then, when revised quotes are needed later on — or when the job is ultimately produced — you and the lettershop are assured you're referring to the same quote.

There are lots of questions, but they divide into just two categories: *catalog configuration* and *list configuration*. Both affect lettershop cost. List configuration can have the greatest effect on lettershop costs. A list of 50,000 names consisting of a single ZIP sequence may cost less per thousand to mail than a list of 100,000 names consisting of four segments of 25,000 each. A single list of 25,000 in a local area may cost less per thousand to mail than a list of 100,000 with national distribution.

The most obvious questions have to do with the package — size, weight, thickness. For jobs which must be labeled, questions include the size of the piece to be labeled, the position of the label, the size of the label and the space into which it must be placed, and the type of paper and ink coverage where the label will be placed, as well as the type of label paper.

Getting The Catalog From Bindery To Lettershop

You envision your brilliantly conceived and executed catalog easily transported from the folder-trimmer to the feed station of the labeling or inserting machine. But this magic won't occur — not without one essential: *Packing*.

If material is to run smoothly and quickly, it must be in good condition when it's put on the machine (whether the catalog will be labeled as a self-mailer or enclosed in a plastic or paper envelope). Otherwise, you may suffer lowered production rates, not only delaying the mailing, but also increasing the lettershop's costs, which legitimately may be charged back to you. Make sure your printer (or separate bindery) knows the catalog will be machine processed on a mass production basis. *It must arrive at the lettershop flat, undamaged, with a minimum number of "turns"* . . . and packed so that when it's opened, it won't slither down the aisle in a river of brightly printed coated paper.

Remember, your material moves many times before it ever reaches the final machine. After the final bindery operation, it's packed, moved first to a storage area and then to the loading dock, loaded onto a truck, driven to the lettershop, unloaded, inspected on the dock, moved into storage, removed to the production floor, and finally moved to the labeling machine. Intercity shipments may require additional trucking and handling in the originating and destination cities. That's a lot of handling. But there are ways to trim the possibilities of damage.

First, find out how your lettershop wants the material packed. This is the basis upon which they quoted the job: size, weight, and paper stock of the catalog; total quantity to be mailed; number and sizes of different codes and versions; whether all material will be mailed at once or over a series of drops. In some cases, banded lifts in cartons will be the only acceptable preparation. In others, it would be a wretched nuisance.

Second, tell the printer these needs. The print shop people must understand the handling the material will get and the *reasons* the material must arrive at the lettershop in good condition. If they have any problems with particular requests, what alternatives can they offer? Their alternatives may be perfectly acceptable to the lettershop. Don't be afraid to arrange a three-way conversation among the printer, the lettershop, and yourself. A brief conference call can save a series of two-party conversations.

Third, make sure the material is properly marked and identified. Proper marking of direct mail material is not automatic for all printers. It's surprising how many lettershops receive shipments consisting of three unmarked skids, a waybill reading only "3 skds advg printed matter," and the name of the printer. If the shipment contains your name, you're lucky — you can be called to identify your material. But suppose the shipment has two catalog versions which bear the same cover — is your name clearly identified? Will the lettershop know it's for you? Will they know there are two versions which need to go to two different lists? Suppose it looks extremely similar to another, different catalog you have designed? Take the precaution of giving explicit instructions for the marking of your well-designed, effective, and very expensive catalogs. And take the time to spot-check to make sure these instructions are being religiously followed.

> **1. Identify the contents of every container**, be it carton or skid. Remember what you are trying to do, and give enough information!
>
> **2. Distinguish those contents from every other item in the mailing**. Include codes, flights, packages.
>
> **3. Distinguish it from your other material which may be at the lettershop already**, or which may subsequently arrive. And identify it as *your* material to avoid confusion with similar material from other mailers.
>
> **4. Indicate the quantity in each carton**. If it's very thin material, also indicate the amount in each band. If skid loaded, mention total skid contents *and* the number of pieces per turn or brick, *and* the number of bricks per layer. This is easy to do when the material is being packed,

and it saves time and the cost of a physical inventory, as well as increasing inventory accuracy.

5. Make sure every shipment includes a detailed packing slip indicating the items, packing, and quantity of *everything delivered*. This is the only way the lettershop can be sure it has received all items shipped . . . and has all it needs to produce the job.

Examples of marking which would usually be adequate:

SMITH & CO.	THE JONES COMPANY
Knife Bonus Offer	Spring White Sale Catalog
Code K-23	Western version
Contents: 12,000	Code GLR-37
Banded: 500	Contents: 475

Figure 9-19 shows what a simple outside identification label might look like. Labels could be printed in different colored stock or ink colors so a single color could be identified as a particular code. Imagine the printing on the label printed in red, the details filled in with handwriting. All fifty boxes of code 84 going to the lettershop would be visually color coded as well as identified with filled-in information. With just a little extra effort, a sample piece could be attached to each individual carton, too, for even more insurance against error. Specifics concerning mail date, type of labeling, and class of mail will be sent along separately with any other needed information.

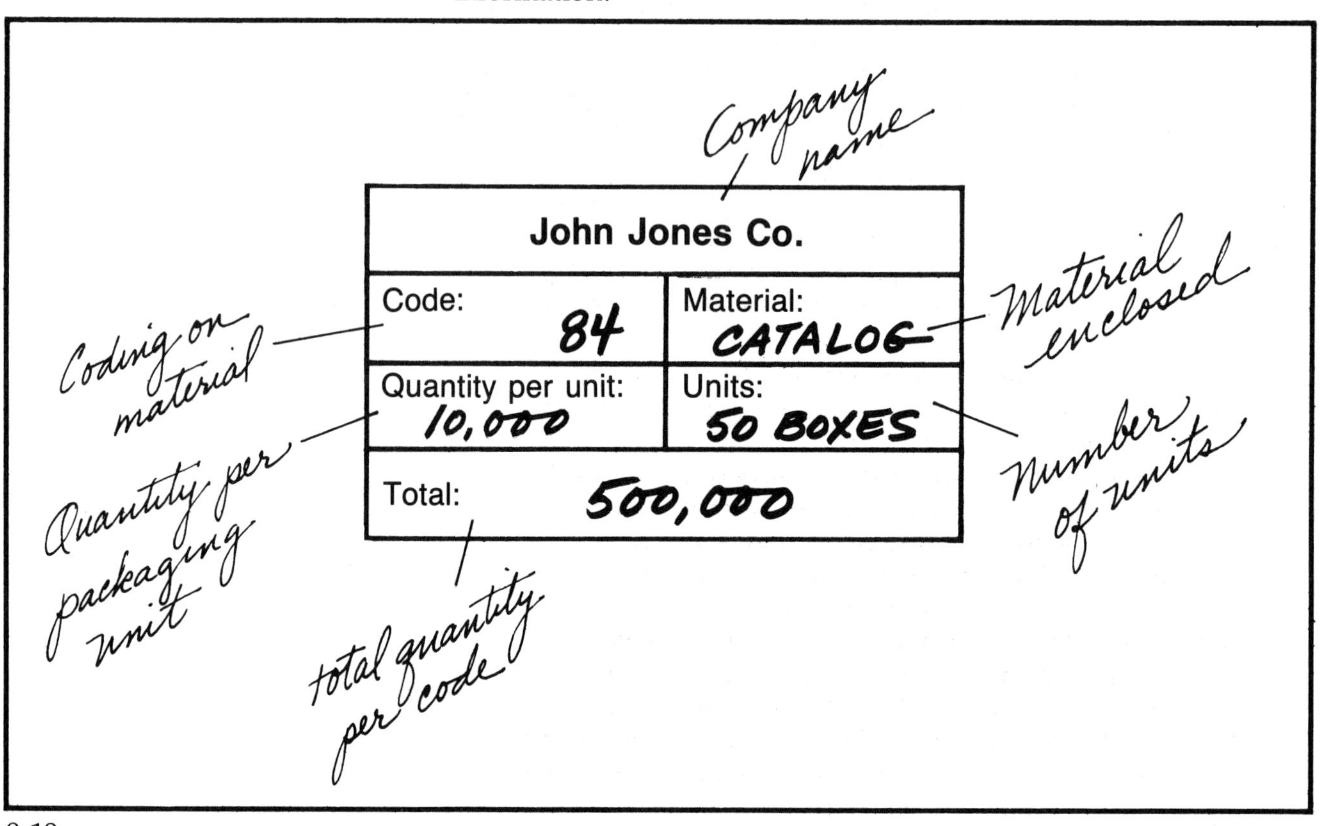

9-19

Things to avoid: Never put more than one item in a carton. If this must be done, all enclosed items must be identified on the outside, including quantity. The items must be wrapped separately and each package marked. The same principle applies to skid loading.

Long, complex codes are difficult to differentiate. Unless there is a compelling reason for lengthy codes, keep them as short and simple as possible.

Things to do: Code all pieces, if possible, especially in a place where the code can be seen without opening or unfolding the piece. Doing this will make it far easier to describe a specific item, as well as greatly reducing the chances of error in production.

You'll get far better service with less chance of error, and your lettershop people will be grateful if they don't have to spend much of their time playing detective! And, if you are a regular customer, the lettershop may charge less because your material is always in good shape and well identified — it costs them less time and hassle!

The next step in making certain your material gets where it's supposed to (and when) is to tell your lettershop what you want them to do with it through order writing.

How To Write Instructions To Your Lettershop

You have taken great pains to see that your lettershop will receive your material well identified and with correct information. Your next responsibility is to *make sure the lettershop knows precisely what to do with it.*

Instructions must be in writing. There are many reasons for this and almost all are for your benefit. Putting instructions in writing will:

1. Help you to state your plans in precise language.
2. Help you to define in your own mind all aspects of the mailing.
3. Make sure your lettershop acts on instructions exactly as you understand them.
4. Allow your lettershop to question any part of the entire mailing procedure which they may not understand clearly.
5. Provide a reference point if a question arises later as to what was to be done.

For simple mailings, writing instructions won't require much work. More complicated mailings will require more effort, but the effort is absolutely essential. *No professional lettershop buyer should even consider accepting a complex mailing without detailed instructions in writing.*

For a simple mailing, the following information should be provided:

1. Title of mailing.
2. Drop dates. (Drop all material on one date, on a scheduled series of dates, within a time span, or as completed?)
3. Total pieces of mail to be dropped.
4. How to mail. (First class, presorted first class, bulk third class, five-digit presorted bulk third class, carrier route presorted first or third class?)
5. How to affix postage. (Permit imprint/indicia, meter, or postage stamps?)
6. Description and expected arrival date of printed materials. (The source of these materials, while not essential, can be helpful.)
7. Description and expected arrival date of lists. (Sources of lists and any coding will be helpful in identifying lists.)

If your mailing will be going out in an envelope, also include:

8. Number of enclosures and description of each.
9. Sequence of pieces in the envelope and whether this sequence is preferred, or required, or of no importance. (A sample envelope, with the pieces inserted as desired, is helpful.)
10. The correct piece to label and the position in which the address label is to be placed.

For a complex mailing, a matrix is a handy way to describe in simple terms what would otherwise be a tedious and cumbersome set of instructions. This substitutes for the list of enclosures and coding information of a simple mailing (but includes that information in a different format). A matrix for a small mailing might look like the sample in Figure 9-20. This tells the lettershop what it needs to know to put the correct pieces in the correct envelope and to label with the correct list. Other matrix formats are used by many mailers. Just convey your intentions clearly!

Finally, some clean-up items should be included. A new supplier should receive billing instructions, if these are not included on

9-20

Piece / Panel	Outer Envelope	Letter	Catalog	Order Form	BRE	List
1-25,000	OA - 1	LA - 1	CA - 1	OFA - 1	RA - 1	A - 1
2- 5,000	OA - 1	LA - 2	CA - 1	OFA - 2	RA - 1	A - 2
3- 5,000	OA - 1	LA - 1	CA - 2	OFA - 3	RA - 1	A - 3
4- 5,000	OA - 2	LA - 1	CA - 1	OFA - 4	RA - 1	A - 4
4- 5,000	OA - 1	----	CA - 1	OFA - 5	RA - 1	A - 5
5- 5,000	OA - 1	LA - 1	CA - 1	OFA - 6	----	A - 6

a formal purchase order. State the price which you understand applies to the mailing, or refer to an applicable quotation.

Overstock instructions should be provided at the beginning of the job. This will save a lot of urgent conversations at the end of the run and prevent extra handling. The choices are few: place back in stock, destroy, or ship (to whom, and how).

This list is but a minimum requirement: each job is different and therefore needs different information. And remember, common sense helps! Use a little forethought on all the areas where errors could occur because of cloudy instructions, and you'll be on your way to accurate mailings!

Lettershop Errors . . . How to avoid them.

Though a good start is to put everything in writing . . . there's more. One of the best ways to prevent lettershop errors is to *call in the lettershop representative during the planning stages* to discuss what you intend to accomplish with the mailing. This doesn't mean you have to give away your marketing secrets — just reveal enough so that the rep can make informed suggestions to help you install the controls essential to preventing errors.

What are these controls? Here are some suggestions. Not all will be appropriate in every situation, but give each some thought before using or rejecting it.

1. Assign a **code number** to all pieces in the mailing.
2. Prepare a matrix showing **which pieces go with which packages.**
3. Make sure your printer and/or binder **marks all containers** properly.
4. Make sure your list source **marks all lists** properly. If the list source is to provide sack labels for presorting (or for any reason), you'll need to provide information as to the weight of the mailing piece, its dimensions, and the minimum and maximum bag loading limits. If this information is not carefully determined, you could end up paying a premium for your mail preparation.
5. **Show your mailer a dummy** of the outside cover of your catalog or of the outer envelope for inserted mail. Covers and outers which are improperly designed and fail to meet postal regulations are among the errors most frequently encountered by lettershops. Even if you have great confidence in yourself, your agency, art studio, and printer, it can't hurt to check with your lettershop.
6. Be sure you have a clear and early understanding with your lettershop about **mailing dates, material, and list delivery dates**. This not only will ensure that the lettershop will be expecting your mailing, but also will make certain that sufficient manpower and equipment to produce the mailing will be provided at the required time.

Remember, common sense is a major ingredient in any error-prevention program. One final suggestion: admit to your mailer that you do not know all there is to know about mailing. (This should be easy, since nobody does.) Then your mailer will feel more comfortable about making suggestions which will have the net effect of protecting *you*.

How To Detect Lettershop Errors

Despite your best efforts to avoid lettershop errors, they do occur. It's important for you to know about them, but how will you detect their occurrence? You won't — unless you take precautions, some of which require planning well in advance of the mailing.

Most errors fall in one of three categories: lists, materials, dates. Though other things can go wrong, these are the most frequent problem areas.

The first and easiest tracking device is to *salt your name in every mailing list you use.* This will show you what happened with each list: when you receive the piece in your mailbox, you'll know that the list, material, and mailing date were (or were not) as desired. You may want to use the names of others in your marketing organization, as well as friends, relatives, and business associates who'll add to this group and help provide a broader base. (As both a courtesy and a precaution, let everyone know what to expect, when to expect it, and what you want them to do.)

> Caution: unless the names on each list are highly distinctive, you may not know which list was used if the labels are not coded. But you still can make deductions as to the mailing dates. And you will know whether the mailing piece was put together exactly as you specified and sent to the right people.

Another way to get samples of mailed pieces is to *use the address correction service* of the U.S. Postal Service. Since undeliverable pieces will be representative of the entire mailing, they'll provide useful information as to the material mailed and the approximate date it arrived at the destination post office. The greatest effectiveness will be realized for your own lists.

You can get documentation of mailing dates by *requiring postal receipts for all mailings.* If the postage was paid by permit imprint (indicia), you should request form 3602. This form is filled out by the mailer on the front and by the Postal Service on the reverse. The date filled in by the Postal Service is the date of acceptance, not necessarily the date the mail was delivered to the post office. If the postage was paid by stamps or meter, the form to request is 3606. This is filled in on one side only, with charges based on the number of pieces in the mailing. Copies of 3602 can be obtained after the mailing, but doing so requires a written request to the Postal Service and can take some time. Copies of 3606 cannot be requested after the mailing. These forms can also be used to *check on quantities mailed* and are especially useful if a separate form is used for each cell of a mailing, with a notation as to which cell each represents. Comparison with expected cell counts is useful.

Reconcile materials on hand at the start of a mailing with materials used and inventory remaining at the end. Significant differences require explanation.

Remember, these are suggestions on how to determine *after the fact* if there may have been an error. It's best to take, as well, the steps listed earlier to prevent error *before the mailing*. And don't feel that taking any of these steps indicates lack of confidence in your lettershop. It's just prudent management.

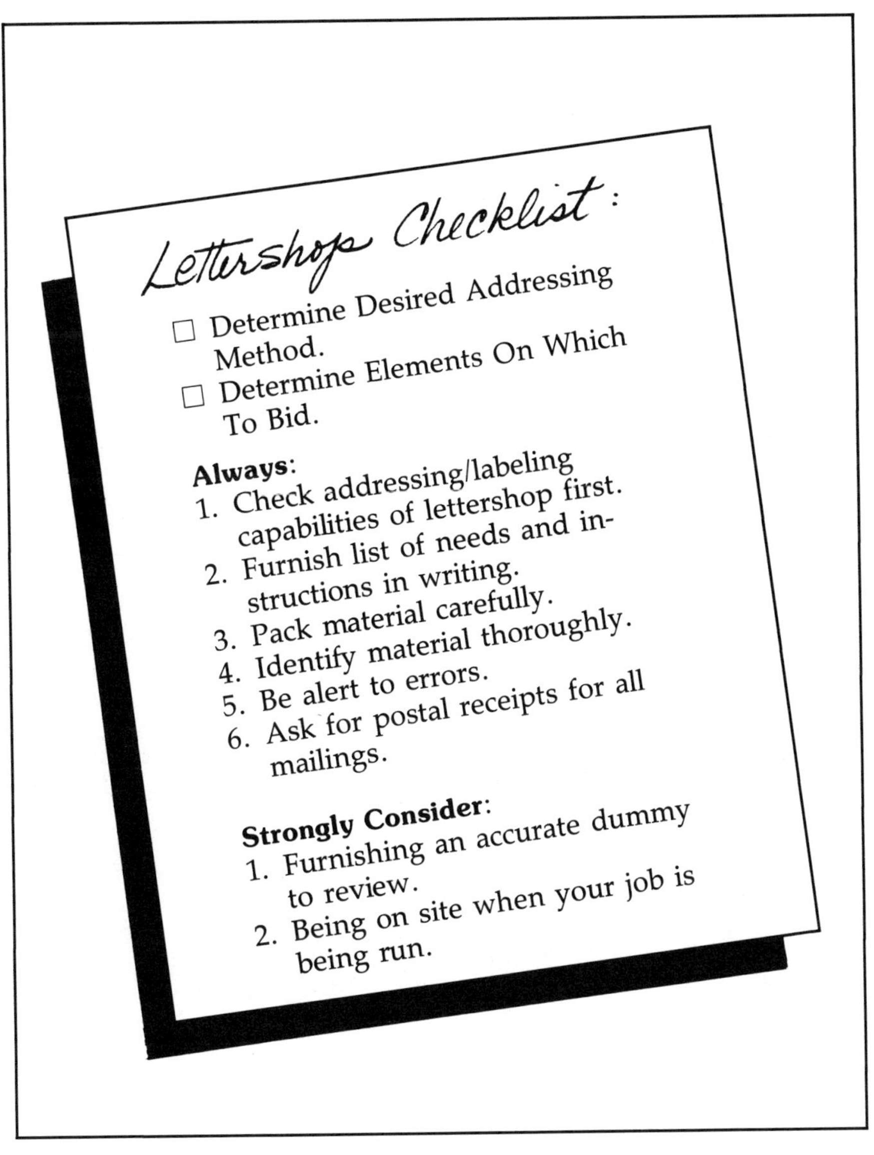

Lettershop Checklist:
☐ Determine Desired Addressing Method.
☐ Determine Elements On Which To Bid.
Always:
1. Check addressing/labeling capabilities of lettershop first.
2. Furnish list of needs and instructions in writing.
3. Pack material carefully.
4. Identify material thoroughly.
5. Be alert to errors.
6. Ask for postal receipts for all mailings.
Strongly Consider:
1. Furnishing an accurate dummy to review.
2. Being on site when your job is being run.

Chapter 10

Legal Matters

Your responsibility to your catalog

The thought of laws, regulations, and restrictions may at first suggest limitation of activities. But, indeed, the effect is just the opposite. Catalog companies practicing good ethics and not trying to stretch the limit of state and federal regulations build customer confidence and strengthen the mail order industry. A good example of self-regulation benefiting the mail order industry is the Mail Preference Service, where individual catalogs voluntarily reveal list rental practices and offer to remove customers' names from their mailing lists. Direct Marketing Association records show that for every one person asking to be dropped, almost two people have asked to be added. Other less tangible or publicized factors heavily influence the public's favorable attitude toward mail order companies. Fast delivery, truthful copy and illustrations, strong guarantees fully stated and backed-up — all these factors influence the positioning of mail order in the customer's view and mold the character of the industry. How can you help make the character positive? What areas influence your catalog? Where can you get help?

People like to get catalogs

How To Create Successful Catalogs does not pretend to act as a legal advisor. The next few pages will call your attention to just a few of the more obvious areas to be aware of, areas that influence the stability of the mail order industry.

Four prominent laws and regulations affecting the catalog marketer. During the past several years many laws and regulations were designed to protect the consumer, and at the same time also targeted the mail order industry.

Truth in Lending: Regulation Z (passed 1969 and amended). Deals with all companies engaged in selling on credit to the consumer, including property, money, or a service primarily for personal, household, or family use. The act runs more than 100 pages and even sets forth definitions of the goods and services and intended users. The Equal Credit Provisions prohibiting discrimination were passed in 1975 and 1977. Familiarity with this act is essential in any sale on credit.

Fair Credit Billing Act: (passed in 1975 and amended). This Act provides for a procedure to settle disputed billing.

Where to get copies of laws

Fair Credit Reporting Agency: (passed in 1971 and amended). Covers the consumer obligations of a user of credit information from credit agencies including the right and procedures for the consumer to examine those reports.

Fair Debt Collections Practices Act: (passed in 1978). Applies only to collection agencies and not to creditors, but the direct mailer should be aware of the prohibited abuses. Some states, and at least one major city (New York) are considering making the law apply to creditors.

Numerous Federal Trade Commission Regulations directly affect the direct mail industry, including regulations such as:

a. Magnuson-Moss Warranty Act dealing with the disclosure and use of a warranty.

b. The Mail Order Rule.

c. Negative option mode of selling.

d. Guarantees and deceptive advertising.

There are many other areas which are covered by the Federal Trade Commission, such as a ruling that computer-grams, which are used for many other purposes in the direct mail field, may not be used as a collection device. At the same time the ruling exempts mailgrams from the restriction. Copies of these regulations are available from the Federal Trade Commission, Office of Public Information, 6th and Pennsylvania Avenue NW, Washington, DC, 20580. In addition, the FTC issues free of charge a weekly FTC News Summary, which we recommend — especially since the price is affordable. Copies of the above acts are also available free of charge. The summary can be ordered by mailing a request to the above address.

The Mail Order Rule was issued by the Federal Trade Commission as a result of consumer complaints about mail order problems. The major complaints were: failure to deliver merchandise, late delivery of merchandise, failure to make prompt refunds, and failure to answer customer inquiries about delayed or lost orders. Under this rule, the cataloger must ship merchandise on time, or follow procedures that the rule requires when the ordered merchandise cannot be shipped on time. When there is a shipping delay, notices of the delay must be sent and the customer must be given the option of accepting the delay or receiving a prompt refund. For each additional delay, the catalog company must receive a signed consent from the customer or it must refund the customer's money. In short, merchandise must be shipped within a reasonable amount of time (30 days) after receipt of the order unless otherwise stated in an advertisement. If merchandise cannot be shipped within the 30 days, or the stated period, a notice must be sent stating the expected shipping date. The notice must be sent before the 30-day expiration and by first class mail, a postage-paid reply must be furnished, an expected shipping date given, and an option of refund provided. One question frequently asked by new catalogers is:

Regarding the 30-day FTC ruling . . . are those 30 days counted from when the order is placed or from when it is received by the mail order house?

The 30 days are counted from the time the order is received. The FTC mail order merchandise 30-day rule provides that sellers may not solicit any order for the sale of merchandise through the mail unless, at the time of solicitation, the sellers expect that they will be able to ship any ordered merchandise to the buyer:

1. Within that time clearly and conspicuously stated in any such solicitation, or
2. If no time is clearly and conspicuously stated, within 30 days *after receipt of a properly completed order* from the buyer (emphasis supplied).

"Receipt of a properly completed order" is defined as follows:

(a) where there is a credit sale and the buyer has not previously tendered partial payment, *the time at which the seller charges the buyer's account;*

(b) where the buyer tenders full or partial payment in the proper amount in the form of cash, check, or money order, the time at which the seller has received both said payment and an order from the buyer, containing all the information needed by the seller to process and ship the order.

Another question which should always be considered by the cataloger when trying to salvage the order for the company as well as for the customer is:

Is it legal to substitute a "like" product for the one originally ordered without the customer's permission?

The FTC rules provide that selling, shipping, or invoicing goods different from those ordered is an unfair and deceptive practice. The FTC has held that in connection with bicycles, for example, substituting merchandise not identical in all respects to the order, except with the consent of the customer, is a deceptive practice. The conclusion is, a seller cannot substitute a like product for the original without the customer's permission.

How To Avoid Sending A "Delayed Merchandise" Shipment Notice. Rather than being concerned with what to do if you violate this ruling, *you should first be concerned with how to keep from making the violation.* Six distinctly different classifications of merchandise require six distinctively different approaches. Let's see what the classifications are and what approach is needed for each.

1. **Merchandise warehoused by the catalog company.** You should have a system to take care of problem products *before they are listed in your catalog.* Develop systems to assure that merchandise will be in your warehouse before you mail your catalog. The main steps to incorporate are:
   (a) Notify suppliers of your intention to list the product and the approximate volume you expect to use.
   (b) Ask suppliers to verify (preferably in writing) the availability of the product . . . and the supplier's ability to ship your quantity estimates when needed.
   (c) Delete from the catalog any product which does not have availability and shipping dates that comply with your needs.

Monitor your drop shipping

2. **Merchandise drop shipped.** If you must rely on others to ship products for you (because of limitations or product completion needs such as personalization), you still should verify the supply . . . just as you do for the products you warehouse yourself. You should have a fulfillment contract with the drop-ship supplier stating a required shipping time. (You also should have a monitoring system to place decoy orders to make sure the drop shipper is complying.) State in your catalog the

the amount of time these products will take to ship . . . an additional two to four weeks is not unusual, depending on your order relay system to the drop shipper: for example, "Please allow six weeks for personalization." And smooth out your system of relaying orders, so that no time is wasted at *your* end.

3. **Seasonal merchandise.** Most plants, trees, bulbs or shrubs need to be planted at different times of the year in different areas of the country. These items do not fall prey to the 30-day rule. Chocolate candy would melt if sent during the hot summer months. Many pastries and cakes would spoil. For products such as these, a catalog notice of availability is provided: for example, "Available for delivery until May 15 to all 50 states."
4. **Delayed shipment by customer request.** Many people order gifts and wish the recipient to receive them at a specific time. Catalog companies set up a system internally to accommodate these wishes. Food catalogs thrive on this business and provide a special area on the order form for the customer to fill in the desired arrival date.
5. **Made-to-order merchandise.** Products such as furniture and limited-edition pieces of art fall under this classification. A special piece of furniture may take as long as six months to be completed and shipped to the customer. The catalog must state this. A limited-edition bronze sculpture may not be in a casting production for several months after ordering. Copy should read something like this: "Shipment about the first of January 1986."
6. **Search-and-send merchandise.** Replacement services, such as sterling silver flatware, and china and glass companies will often accept an order based on fulfillment when they locate the product. The advantage to the customer of placing a firm order for a hard-to-find product and paying for it when the order is placed is the privilege of ownership and receipt when the product is found. The catalog company must clearly state this procedure and provide for a signed document by the customer in order to operate safely in this manner.

Delay notices

These general guidelines will help you avoid sending costly delay notices. Knowing the FTC rules and having your lawyer inform you as to actions which may be exceptions are the best steps to take. Then you'll know how to comply with the law . . . and still avoid the expense of sending delay notices!

Following are yet more areas of concern and tips on dealing with them:

"Bait Advertising" . . . A Trap To Avoid

The violation of FTC guidelines regarding ''bait advertising'' subjects the violator to federal fines and injunctive relief, as well as to possible fraud actions by victimized purchasers. Never jeopardize a good mail order business with overtones of the old ''bait and switch'' scheme. In the long run, you will not only subject yourself to litigation and legal ramifications, but you will also find your business activities short-lived.

''Bait Advertising'' is defined in Federal Trade Commission guidelines as an alluring, but insincere, offer to sell a product or service which the advertiser, in truth, does not intend or want to sell. The primary goal is to switch consumers from buying the advertised merchandise in order to sell something else, usually at a higher price or on a basis more advantageous to the advertiser. Sometimes the real aim of a bait advertisement is to obtain leads on persons interested in buying merchandise similar to what was featured in a particular ad. The merchandiser may not send the same product as originally featured in the ad. The guideline on ''Bait Advertising'' clearly states that no advertisement should create a false impression of grade, quality, make, value, currency of a model, size, color, usability, or origin of the product offered, or which may otherwise misrepresent the product so that later, on disclosure of the true facts, the purchaser may be switched from the advertised product to another. Note that, even if the mail order merchandiser makes known the true facts to the buyer at a subsequent time, the law is still violated if the first contact or interview is secured by deception.

The same regulation also covers the practice of trying to discourage the purchase of advertised merchandise in order to sell other merchandise. Practices which are considered by the FTC in determining whether or not the advertisement is a bona fide offer are:

1. Refusal to show, demonstrate, or sell the product offered in accordance with the terms of the offer, as well as failure to ship the product advertised (instead shipping a different product).
2. Disparagement of the advertised product by acts or words.
3. Failure to have available at all advertised outlets a sufficient quantity of the product to meet reasonable anticipated demands . . . unless it is clearly disclosed in the advertising that the supply is limited or available only at a designated location.
4. Refusal to take order for the advertised merchandise to be delivered within a reasonable period of time.
5. Showing or demonstrating a product which is defective, unusable, or impracticable for the purpose represented.
6. Use of compensation or penalization of salesmen,

designed to prevent or discourage them from selling the advertised product.

In essence, the merchandiser should not pursue a practice of ''unselling'' with the intention of selling other merchandise in its place. The following practices constitute evidence of whether or not the initial sale was in good faith:

1. Accepting a deposit for the advertised product; then switching the purchaser to a higher-priced product.
2. Failure to either deliver the advertised product within a reasonable time or make refund.
3. Disparagement by acts or words of the advertised product, the guarantee, credit terms, service availability, repairs, or any other aspect of the product.
4. The delivery of an advertised product which is defective, unusable, or impracticable for the purpose represented or implied in the advertisement.

The guideline for ''Bait Advertising'' as adopted by the FTC is contained in 16 CFR 238 and was adopted on November 24, 1959.

Avoid Deceptive Advertising of Guarantees

One of the most popular methods of selling mail order merchandise is to guarantee the product. The Federal Trade Commission, on April 26, 1960, adopted a rule regarding ''Deceptive Advertising of Guarantees'' (which can be found in 16 CFR 239). This federal regulation sets forth *what should be contained in a guarantee.*

In general, any advertisement of a guarantee must clearly and conspicuously *disclose the nature and extent of the guarantee.* This means that the disclosure should contain:

1. What product or part of the product is guaranteed.
2. What characteristics or properties of the product or designated part thereof are covered by, or excluded from, the guarantee.
3. What is the duration of the guarantee.
4. What, it anything, anyone claiming under the guarantee must do before the guarantor will furnish his obligation under the guarantee (such as returning the product or paying for the services or labor charges).

What to state in a guarantee

In addition, the mail order advertiser must clearly and conspicuously disclose the identity and manner in which the guarantor will perform, i.e., whether he will repair, replace, or refund. If the guarantee is on a pro rata basis (such as tires), the advertising should clearly disclose this fact, particularly the basis on which the article will be prorated (e.g., the time for which the guaranteed product has been used and any deductions made based on that issue). In addition, if the guarantees are to be adjusted on the basis of a price other than the price actually paid by the purchaser, this price should be clearly and conspicuously disclosed.

Such advertising comments as "satisfaction or your money back," "10-day free trial" or similar representations will be *construed as a guarantee* that the full purchase price will be refunded at the option of the purchaser. If this type of guarantee is subject to any conditions or limitations whatsoever, these conditions or limitations must be set forth. If the words "life," "lifetime" or the like are used in advertising to show the duration of the guarantee, and they relate to any life other than that of the purchaser or original user, the life referred to also must be clearly and conspicuously disclosed.

Some mail order advertisers like to state in their ads "guaranteed to save you 50 percent," "guaranteed never to be undersold," or "guaranteed lowest prices in town." When these advertisements are made, they should include a clear and conspicuous disclosure of what the guarantor will do if the savings are not realized, together with any time or other limitations that the advertiser/guarantor may impose. Thus, if you use "guaranteed lowest price in town," you should accompany that ad with a disclosure such as, "If within 30 days from the date you buy a Widge from me, you are not satisfied I will refund your money." Also note that guaranteeing under a situation where the guarantor does not or cannot perform is also a violation of the FTC rules. Therefore, a mail order seller may not advertise or represent that a product is guaranteed when said seller cannot or does not promptly and scrupulously fulfill all guarantee obligations. Don't advertise "satisfaction or your money back" when you cannot or do not intend promptly to make full refund upon request.

Realize that a guarantee can also be a *misrepresentation*, subjecting the representor to a possible fraud action. Therefore, if a mail order merchandiser runs an ad stating "guaranteed for 36 months," the merchandiser is representing that the product normally can be expected to last for 36 months. Such a guarantee should never be used on a product that cannot last for the period stated in the guarantee wording. A vivid example of this type of guarantee would be an ad stating "Guaranteed to grow hair or money back." This can be a *fraudulent* misrepresentation in and of itself, *even if money is returned*. The unhappy bald person could have an action for fraud to recover any actual damages suffered by the inability to grow hair, as well as for punitive damages which are permissible for recovery by the plaintiff in such fraud actions.

Shipment guaranteed

Does stating a shipping time, i.e., "guaranteed shipment within 24 hours after receipt of order," legally bind a cataloger in any way?

The FTC has found that the failure to fill orders, or failure to fill them in the time promised, or within a reasonable time after acceptance of the order constitutes an unfair and deceptive practice.

Additionally, the FTC mail order merchandise 30-day rule provides that it is an unfair or deceptive act for sellers to solicit any order for the sale of merchandise to be ordered by the buyer through the mail, unless the sellers have a reasonable expectation of being able to ship any order or merchandise to the buyer *within the time clearly and conspicuously stated in any such solicitation.* In other words, if shipment is guaranteed within 24 hours after receipt of order and shipment is not so made, the FTC may find that the seller has engaged in an unfair or deceptive practice.

Be careful! Don't suggest that a product is made of something it's not. To regulate unfair and misleading practices, the Federal Trade Commission has developed certain rules which are intended to have the force of law. Such rules are set out and referred to as ''Federal Trade Commission Guides and Policies.'' A violation can subject offenders to fines and injunctive remedies by the FTC, as well as to civil actions by purchasers who have been victims of wrongful advertising or a breach of these federal rules.

These misleading practices are covered by general acts, as well as very specific ones. Usually the specific situations have arisen because the FTC wishes to direct attention to a particular product area (such as shoes and slippers) . . . or because of requests from specific businesses that wish to have something from the general acts clarified in their special area. One can gain insight regarding not only the letter of the law, but also its intention, by perusing the specific situations. Such is the case with advertising shoes, for example. Say that a shoe or slipper is visually depicted in advertising with sufficient clarity to create the impression that the pictorially visible non-leather parts (exclusive of heels) are composed of leather or split leather (or that pictorially visible leather parts are composed of a different kind or type of leather than is the case). The *advertising must contain a statement* clearly and conspicuously disclosing that the visible part or parts are simulated or imitation leather, or the general nature of the visible part or parts must be depicted to show they are not leather or not the type of leather they seem.

It should also be noted by the mail order merchandiser that the term ''leather'' or other terms suggestive of leather may be unqualifiedly used only when the shoes or slippers are composed in all *substantial* parts of top grain leather, exclusive of heels, stiffening, and ornamentation. If the shoe or slipper is substantially leather, such terms may be used, if immediately *qualified to show clearly* what parts are leather, provided no leather content shall be emphasized to exaggerate or otherwise deceptively represent the quantity, quality, or extent of leather present.

State true components

The federal rule prohibits the unqualified use of the term ''leather'' and any other terms suggestive of leather to describe shoes and slippers or parts thereof made from split leather or from ground, pulverized, or shredded leather. The term may be used only if qualified so as to provide an *accurate, non-deceptive description.*

Terms suggestive of leather to describe the appearance of a non-leather material must be immediately accompanied by a disclosure that the terms refer only to the appearance and that the material is not leather. An example of this would be ''imitation alligator.'' Furthermore, no trade name, coin name, trademark, depiction symbol, or other words or terms may be used which would *convey the impression* that the shoes or slippers advertised are made with a certain kind or type of material when they are not. An example of such an identification would be the use of ''Duraleather'' or ''Bark Hyde.''

"Free" . . . How To Use This Powerful Word Legally. The words ''free'' merchandise or service are promotional devices frequently used by mail order merchandisers to attract customers. Because of the effect on the purchaser, *all such advertising must be pursued with extreme caution to avoid any possibility that the buyer will be misled or deceived.* The most common advertising language includes ''free,'' ''buy one — get one free,'' ''two-for-one sale,'' ''50% off with purchase of two,'' or ''1 cent sale.'' Some related advertising gimmicks, including ''Cents Off,'' ''Half-Price Sale,'' ''One-Half Off,'' may raise many of the same questions.

Be careful about "free"

One of the FTC guidelines is entitled *''Use of the Word 'Free' and Similar Representations,''* contained in 16 CFR 251; 36 Federal Register 21517. Under this guideline, the word ''free'' indicates that the purchaser is paying nothing for the article, or no more than the regular price for another article, where this is a condition of getting the free merchandise. The FTC feels a purchaser has a right to believe that a merchant will not directly and immediately recover, in whole or in part, the cost of the free merchandise or service by marking up the price of the article which must be purchased or by the substitution of inferior merchandise or service. The article to be purchased must be sold at its regular price, i.e., the price at which the seller has openly and actively sold the product, in the geographic market in which he is now making the ''free'' offer, in the most recent and regular course of his business, and for a reasonably substantial period of time. The FTC generally considers this period to be 30 days or more. Where consumer products or services fluctuate in price, the regular price is the lowest price of any substantial sales during the 30 days. Note that, except in the case of an introductory offer, if no substantial sales actually are made at the regular price, a ''free'' or similar offer would not be proper.

The merchandiser of a ''free'' offer should clearly state all terms, conditions, and obligations at the outset, leaving no reasonable probability that the terms of the offer might be misunderstood (subjecting the merchandiser to liability). A disclosure of terms in a footnote of an ad to which reference is made by an asterisk or other symbol, *is not* regarded as making disclosure at the outset. The FTC even carries the obligation for wrongful advertising of ''free'' to the supplier: if a supplier knows that a retailer is improperly advertising the word ''free,'' it is improper for the supplier to continue offering the product to this retailer. The supplier should take appropriate action to bring an end to the description, including the withdrawal of the word "free" from the offer. The supplier is also required to offer the product as promoted to all competing retailers or resalers, under the same terms and conditions. If suppliers advertise the promotion, they should identify areas where the offer *is not available,* if the ad is likely to be seen in such areas. They should clearly state that it is available through participating resalers, indicating the extent of participation by using terms such as "some," "all," "a majority," or "a few," as the situation may dictate.

Introductory offers are covered by another rule. In essence, no "free" offer should occur when introducing a new product or service at a specified price unless the offerer expects, in good faith, to discontinue the offer after a limited time. The merchandiser must intend to then sell the product minus the "free" offer, but at the same price at which it was promoted with the "free" offer.

A single size of product or single kind of service should not be advertised with a "free" offer in a trade area for more than six months in any twelve-month period . . . and at least 30 days should elapse before another such offer is promoted in the same trade area. No more than three such offers should be made in the same area in any twelve-month period. Furthermore, during this period, the merchandiser's sale of the product in the size promoted with a "free" offer (in that trade area) should not exceed 50 percent of the total volume of the merchandiser's sale of the product, in the same size, in that trade area.

Don't think you can skirt the law by substituting different words such as "gift," "Given without charge," "bonus," or other words or terms which tend to convey the impression to the consumer public that an article of merchandise or service is "free." By following these FTC guidelines, you can not only help avoid governmental intervention and civil lawsuits, but you can also successfully conduct your sale.

Trademarks . . . What They Mean To Your Business. Frequently overlooked is the possibility of acquiring *one of the most valuable business assets* available under U.S. and international law — the exclusive protection of your right to business goodwill as reflected in a registered trademark or service mark . . . names and designs that describe products or services to form mental concepts or identification in purchasers' minds.

The primary function of any trademark or service mark is to identify the particular product or service of one business from that of another. This identification is called a Trademark to identify a particular physical product, and a Service Mark to identify *intangible actions or services.* Unlike patents and copyrights, a *trademark can remain exclusive property in perpetuity* . . . if the businessman does not abandon it by ceasing to use the mark — or through such conduct, including acts of omission or commission, which causes the mark to lose its significance as an indication of its origin. Substantial monies are spent in promoting the name of a product or service. So trademarks can develop into valuable business assets . . . even a major factor in the continued success of a particular marketing program.

The Name. The cardinal rule when choosing a trademark is that *registrable trademark or service mark words must be adjectives* and, therefore, must modify a noun that is a generic name of a product or service. For example, ''Universal'' is a registered trademark to identify the exercise equipment of a particular manufacturer. ''Universal,'' the adjective, modifies ''exercise equipment,'' the noun, and designates to the buying public that they should not just buy *any* exercise equipment, but should buy ''*Universal* exercise equipment.''

If the consuming public comes to treat the trademark as a noun or the name of a type of product or service, rather than as an adjective and a designation for one particular brand of product or service, the mark will no longer identify and distinguish the business' goods or services but may become a generic term. The Otis Elevator Company, after 50 years of use, lost a trademark on the word ''escalator'' by using it as a noun rather than referring to an ''Escalator moving staircase.''

Proper use of a trademark is such that if you eliminated the trademark from the advertising copy it would still give you a completed sentence. Example: ''Build your body with Universal exercise equipment.'' Note the difference if you eliminate ''Universal'' from copy that reads ''Build your body with Universal.''

Mail Preference Service

In 1971 the Direct Marketing Association (DMA) initiated this service as a self-regulating protection for the mail order consumer and industry. This service offers consumers the chance to be added to or removed from lists before a rental occurs or at the time of the consumer's request. As mentioned in the beginning of this chapter, more people have asked to be put on lists than to be taken off. The DMA also urges catalogers to disclose their list rental practices (in general) to the consumer.

The Talbots catalog uses a fairly standard mail preference message (Figure 10-1). They disclose their rental practices in general: ''Occasionally we make customer names available to firms offering merchandise that may be of interest to you.'' They then give customers the option of not having their names rented: ''If you would prefer not to receive these mailings, please copy your label exactly as it appears on this catalog and send it to . . .'' The message is friendly and not offensive to the customer or to the company's rental practices.

Delmart, a business-to-business office supplies catalog, takes a shorter and different tack. Figure 10-3 shows a bordered panel on the back of the order form. The information included in the panel, The Delmart Pledge, 30-day money-back guarantee, and free catalogs for your friends, is positive. The heading ''Your Name'' is attention-getting, though the message is a little blunt: ''If you would like your name removed from our mailing list, please send us the mailing label from this catalog or drop us a note.'' There are some nice words — ''please,'' ''drop us a note,'' but the message translates poorly. ''Removed'' is a harsh word as used. If the company rents its list, does not rent its list, or does not wish to state so, maybe the following wording would be better: ''Should you, for any reason, wish not to receive our catalog, please send us your mailing label from this catalog or drop us a note.''

Clymer's of Bucks County, a gift catalog, changes the wording slightly to fit their company's friendly image (see Figure 10-2). They start out with, ''We believe that a benefit of being a Clymer's customer is the availability of merchandise and services which we feel may be of interest to you.'' The option of not receiving catalogs and how to accomplish it is nicely done, too: ''If you do not wish to receive solicitations from other fine companies, please write our MAIL PREFERENCE DEPARTMENT and enclose your catalog label.'' The action is made to sound easy and nonoffensive, maintaining the company's friendly tone.

What's the worst that could happen by putting this type of message in your catalog? A customer (yours) could ask not to be sent any future catalogs of yours. All this would do is save you money — the printing of the catalog and postage — since this customer most likely would not purchase anyway. But, chances are, your customers will stay with you and recommend you to their friends. By complying with this service, you are lessening the possibility of mandatory federal legislation.

MAIL PREFERENCE SERVICE: Occasionally we make customer names available to firms offering merchandise that may be of interest to you. If you would prefer not to receive these mailings, please copy your label exactly as it appears on this catalog and send it to: The Talbots Mail Preference Service, 164 North Street, Hingham, MA 02043.

10-1

MAIL PREFERENCE SERVICE
We believe that a benefit of being a Clymer's customer is the availability of merchandise and services which we feel may be of interest to you. If you do not wish to receive solicitations from other fine companies, please write our MAIL PREFERENCE DEPARTMENT and enclose your catalog label.

10-2

The Delmart Pledge

We want to save you time and money ...and make shopping and buying as easy as possible from the comfort of your office or home...by offering quality products, unique special values and items that can make your business and personal life more enjoyable. We pledge to serve your needs with promptness, courtesy, and guaranteed satisfaction. Thank you.

30-Day, Money-Back Guarantee

Your 100% satisfaction is our goal, therefore, we offer you the opportunity to see and/or try a product and return it within 30 days (for a full refund) if you're not completely satisfied.

Warranties: For a copy of a manufacturer's warranty, just write Delmart.

Free Catalogs for Your Friends

We would be happy to send a copy of this catalog to anyone you think would be interested. Just send us name and address.

Name ____________

Firm ____________

Street ____________

City ____________

State ____________ Zip ________

Your Name

If you would like your name removed from our mailing list, please send us the mailing label from this catalog or drop us a note.

Thank you

FOR FASTEST SERVICE, ORDER TOLL-FREE: 1-800-328-9697

Mon.-Fri., Central Time, 8 a.m.-4:30 p.m. (Minnesotans call 612-483-7888.)

10-3

Depends on state laws

Here are just a few questions of concern:

Sales tax: Is it legal to charge sales tax *after* the handling, shipping, and insurance are added up? What should you charge? (The answer depends on the state laws in which the transaction occurred.)

Plants and pesticides: Can plants be shipped from and to all states . . . do pesticides need clearance other than federal? (Again, it depends on individual state laws.)

Duty charges: What duty (if any) is levied on goods being shipped to Canada or abroad? (The amount of duty levied varies according to the nature of the article — the duty is fixed by the importing country's customs officials.)

As you can see, there are many variables which concern the catalog marketer. You need to be aware of individual state requirements and federal laws and requirements. The advice of highly competent legal counsel is to your benefit. Also, contacts with state district attorneys' offices and foreign customs offices are helpful. Above all, venture forth with truthfulness . . . treat each customer with consideration and fairness. You'll be rewarded with satisfied customers and repeat orders and, after all, that's what the catalog business is all about.

Glossary

Additive primaries: In color reproduction, red, green, and blue.

Address correction requested (ACR): When printed in the upper left-hand corner of the address portion of the mailing piece (just below the return address), an ACR endorsement authorizes the U.S. Postal Service, for a fee, to furnish the known new address of a person no longer at the address on the mailing piece. Also, undeliverable and unforwardable mail is returned to the sender.

Advertising: Any paid communication through various media by business firms, nonprofit organizations, or individuals who are generally identified in the message and who hope to inform or persuade members of a specific audience.

Against the grain: Folding or feeding paper at right angles to (against) the grain of the paper.

Agate line: A standard of measurement for depth of columns of advertising space. One column inch equals fourteen agate lines.

Airbrush: In artwork, a small pressure gun shaped like a pencil that sprays watercolor pigment by means of compressed air. Used to correct and obtain tone or graduated tonal effects, especially on reflective art.

Antique finish: Surface of the sheet which features a natural rough finish; usually used for cover papers.

Art: Illustrations used in catalogs and advertising for the purpose of visually selling a product.

Basis size: Wide variety of papers, each having specific dimensions — e.g., cover paper is 20 inches × 26 inches, bond paper is 17 inches × 22 inches.

Basis weight: Weight in pounds of 500 sheets (a ream) of paper cut to certain standard sizes; which are 25 × 38, 20 × 26. This may be referred to as, "80 lb." stock, "60 lb." stock, and so on.

Bible paper: Very lightweight, bright, strong, opaque paper, commonly made from rag pulp and mineral filler.

Bindery: Where books, magazines, or pamphlets are bound. A trade bindery generally serves printers. An edition bindery handles publishers' work in quantities. A job bindery does miscellaneous work; a pamphlet bindery devotes itself to paper-covered publications, magazines, and self-covered catalogs. Here, printed signatures of catalog and order forms are assembled, stapled, and trimmed.

Black-and-white: Originals or reproductions (photographs, printing) in single color, as distinguished from multicolor.

Bleed: When the printed image extends to the trim edge of the sheet or page, hence "bleeding off the page."

Blister: Blemish or bubble caused by too-sudden drying.

Blueprint: A photoprint made from stripped-up negatives or positives, used as a proof to check position of all image elements (copy, photos, art).

Body copy: The main wording of a selling message, not including the headlines.

Body type: A type used for the main text of a catalog, as distinguished from the headings and headlines.

Boldface: Type having thick, heavy face, used for emphasis.

Boldface type: Type that is bold in line and heavier than the text type, which is light in line.

Bond paper: A grade of writing or printing paper with the essentials of durability and strength; used on letterheads and business forms.

Book paper: A general term for a group of papers made for the printing trade, excluding newsprint.

Book papers — premium: High-cost papers. Their most important qualities are high opacity with low caliper.

Break for color: To separate parts which are to be printed in different colors.

Brightness: The degree of perceived whiteness of a pulp.

Bringing color up: The task of improving the color once the job is on press, to meet the standards of an acceptable job.

Broadside: A single sheet of paper which can be printed on one or both sides. Folded for mailing in an envelope, as a self-mailer, or for direct distribution, it opens into a single, large advertisement.

Brochure: In the strict sense of the word, a brochure is a high-quality pamphlet, with carefully planned layout, typography and illustrations. The term may also be used for any promotional pamphlet or booklet.

Bulk: The degree of thickness of paper.

Bulk mail: A category of third-class mail specially processed for mailing before delivery to the post office. It consists of a large quantity of identical pieces, each addressed to a different name. The Postal Department's definition of bulk: nonpreferential second, third, and fourth-class mail. Includes parcel post, ordinary papers, and circulars.

Buyer: One who orders merchandise or a service.

C/A: Change of Address.

Calendering: The smoothing of paper by cast-iron rollers which are attached at the end of the paper-making machines.

Calender rolls: A set or stack of horizontal cast-iron rolls at the end of a paper machine. Paper is passed between the rolls to increase the smoothness and gloss of the paper's surface.

Caliper: The thickness of paper, usually expressed in thousandths of an inch (mils).

Caps and small caps: Two sizes of capital letters, made within one size and family of type.

Catalog: A book or booklet displaying merchandise, with descriptive details and prices, usually for the purpose of placing an order.

Catalog buyer: One who purchases merchandise or a service from a catalog.

Chemical pulp: The treatment of groundwood chips with chemicals to remove impurities such as lignin, resins, and gums. The two primary chemicals are sulfite and sulfate.

Cheshire label: Specially prepared paper to be mechanically affixed to a mailing piece. In rolls, fanfold, or accordion fold, the paper contains names and addresses printed by a computer in a special format — usually 4 across and 11 down, or 44 to a page — for processing on a Cheshire labeling machine.

Chrome: An abbreviation of Ektachrome, Kodachrome, or any other transparency film. The trade name, ''Chromalin,'' is a color proofing system by DuPont.

Chromalin: A way of producing a color proof (less expensive than press proofs). It is color applied to a Khromkote stock (looks like clear plastic sheets) in 4 separate ''sheets'' one color at a time, which when overlaid, show what your 4-color will look like when run.

Coated book paper: A paper which is coated on both sides, most often used for letterpress printing. Available in glossy and dull finish.

Coated offset: A paper which is coated on both sides; used in offset printing. It has a high resistance to picking. Available in glossy and dull finish.

Coated paper: Paper with a surface coating which produces a smooth finish.

Coding: A group of letters and numbers used to identify certain characteristics of an address on a list. Also, a code used on reply devices to identify the source from which the address was obtained, such as a mailing list, magazaine, or newspaper.

Cold type: Type which is set by a direct impression method such as linotype or typewriter composing machines.

Collate: To assemble the various elements of a mailing in sequence for insertion in a mailing envelope. Also, the combining of two or more ordered files to produce a single ordered file. The same as merge, as in Merge-Purge.

Color bars: Bars of the three primary colors plus black located at the edge of a printed sheet so that they can be read with a densitometer to determine ink density.

Color correction: Any method, such as masking, dot-etching, re-etching, and scanning, used to improve color image.

Color print: A inexpensive version of a Dye Transfer. It is shot photographically, and provides less quality.

Color separation: The process of separating full-color originals into the primary printing colors in negative or positive form by photographic process. An artist can also make separations by manually making separate overlays for each color.

Composition: Either the setting of type or the material set in type.

Comprehensive layout: A detailed artist's rendition of an advertisement or brochure indicating positioning of all elements.

Computer personalization: The printing of a letter or other promotional communication by computer, using the recipient's name, address, and information based on data from one or more computer records in order to tailor the promotional message to that specific individual.

Condensed type: A narrow or slender width type face.

Contact print: A photographic print made from a negative or positive in contact with sensitized paper, film, or printing plate.

Contact screen: A photographically-made halftone screen on film having a dot structure of graded density.

Continuous tone: An unscreened photographic image containing variable tones from black to white.

Contrast: Tonal gradation among the highlights, middle tones, and shadows.

Contrived hot spots: Pages of the catalog to which the customer is specifically referred and which therefore tend to produce extra sales.

Copy: Text, headlines, or manuscript used to explain a product or service.

Cover paper: A term applied to a variety of papers used for the covers of catalogs; usually heavier than the inside pages.

Crop: The removal of portions of a photograph or illustration as indicated by lines ("cropmarks") around the subject.

Cross direction: The direction across the grain of paper.

Curl: The distortion of a sheet due to differences in structure or coating from one side to the other. Also, the waving of paper due to the absorption of moisture.

Cyan: One of the subtractive primaries used for one of the four-color process inks. It reflects blue and green light and absorbs red light.

Dandy roll: A wire cylinder on a paper-making machine that adds wove or laid effects to the texture.

Deckle: The width of the wet sheet as it comes off the wire of a paper machine.

Deckle edge: The untrimmed, feathery edge of paper formed where the pulp flows agains the deckle.

Densitometer: A sensitive photoelectric instrument which measures the density of photographic images and colors.

Density: A measure of the relative darkening or blackening of photographic images.

Digest-sized catalog: Catalog measuring 5½ × 8½ inches.

Direct Marketing Association (DMA): International trade association representing direct marketing. Founded in 1917.

Display Type: Type that is larger and generally fancier than text. Generally used for main headlines.

Dot: The individual element of a halftone.

Dot etching: Chemical etching used to increase or reduce the amount of color to be printed. Dot etching negatives increases color; dot etching positives reduces color.

Drop-out: Portions of originals that do not reproduce, especially colored lines or background areas (often on purpose).

Dull finish: Low-gloss finish.

Dummy: A preliminary layout showing the position of illustrations and text as they are to appear in the final catalog reproduction.

Duplex paper: Paper with a different color or finish on each side.

Dye transfer: A print of art (which looks like a color print) in which the four colors have been produced one color at a time to closely approximate the original art. Used as a vehicle for retouching, when retouching is necessary.

Em: The square (area) of a type body.

Embossed finish: Paper with a raised or depressed surface resembling wood, cloth, or other patterns.

En: One-half the width of an em.

Enamel: A term applied to a coated paper or to a coating material on a paper.

Enamel paper: High-gloss polish paper, coated on one side.

English finish: A grade of book paper with a smooth, uniform finish.

Engraver's proofs: Proofs pulled on stock to show you what the chromes look like on paper.

Etch: The production of an image on a photographic plate by chemical or electrolytic action.

Face: The printing surface of a piece of type.

Federal Trade Commission (FTC): Government regulatory bureau overseeing advertising claims and practices.

Felt side: The smoother side of the paper.

Filter: In color separation photography, a colored piece of gelatin used over the lens or between lenses.

Fine paper: Includes printing, writing, and cover papers.

Flush left (or right): In composition, type set to be aligned along the left (or right) edge.

Focus: Defines the sharpness of a photograph. To the separator and printer, focus delineates the percentage scale of the original to the final image reproduced in print; i.e., focus at 50 percent (half size).

Foil: Paper coated with either aluminum or bronze powder finish or leaf finish.

Folio: The page number.

Font: The complete assortment of type of one size and face.

Format: The size, style, type, margins, printing requirements, etc. of a printed piece.

Four-color process: Use of four printing plates — magenta, yellow, cyan, plus black — to reproduce a full-color printed piece.

Free sheet: Paper free of mechanical wood pulp.

Friend-of-a-friend (friend recommendation): The name of an prospective customer sent to a catalog company by an established customer so the ''friend'' will receive a catalog. Generally derived by specific request or a specific program. A third-party inquiry; a referral name.

Fuzz: Fibers projecting from the surface of paper.

Galley proof: A proof taken of metal type standing in a galley, before being made up into pages.

Gate fold, gate flap: An extension of a page in an order form or in any printed piece that is folded so it swings out gatewise when unfolded for reading.

Generation: Each succeeding stage in reproduction from the original copy.

Gloss: Surface quality that reflects light.

Grade: A means of ranking various kinds of paper by quality.

Grain: In papermaking, the direction in which most fibers lie (corresponds with the direction the paper is made on paper machine).

Grain long: When paper grain (fibers) runs parallel to the long direction of the sheet.

Grain short: When paper grain (fibers) runs parallel to the short direction of the sheet.

Grammage: A metric term for expressing the basis width of paper.

Groundwood pulp: A mechanically-prepared wood pulp used in the manufacture of newsprint and publication papers.

Guarantee: The pledge of satisfaction made by seller to buyer which specifies the terms by which the seller will honor his pledge.

Gutter: The blank space, after printing area, or inner (center) margin of catalog.

Hard copy: Typewritten copy reproduced simultaneously from magnetic, paper, or perforated tape.

High contrast: A reproduction in which the difference in darkness (density) between neighboring areas is greater than in the original.

High finish: A smooth finish.

Highlight: The lightest or whitest parts in a photograph represented in a halftone reproduction by the finest dots or the absence of all dots in a specific portion of a photograph.

Hot spot: An area of a catalog which naturally produces added sales such as: front cover, back cover, pages two and three, middle pages.

Imposition: Laying out pages in a press form so that they will be in the correct order after the printed sheet is folded.

Impression: The pressure of type, plate or blanket or the effect of that pressure as it comes in contact with the paper.

Impression cylinder: The cylinder on a printing press against which the paper picks up the impression.

Ink density: The ability of ink to absorb light. Can be measured by densitometer.

Ink fountain: The device which stores ink and supplies it to the inking rollers of a press.

Insert: A printed piece placed (inserted) into a catalog or another printed piece.

Italic: The style of letters that slope forward as opposed to the upright or roman; often used when indicating a quote or for words requiring emphasis.

Justify: To align both right and left margins or to indicate the exact number of characters to fit a given space.

Key: To code copy to a dummy by means of symbols or letters. Also, a number or group of numbers which identifies a specific item.

Keyline: A mechanical outline used to indicate the exact shape, position, and size of artwork elements such as halftones, line sketches, copy.

Kodachromes: A specific brand name of the Eastman Kodak Company; their transparencies and/or reproduction of same. Often used in reference to color transparencies.

Kraft: A paper or board containing unbleached wood pulp (brown in color).

Kromekote: Coated paper rolled under pressure against a polished, heated cylinder to produce a highly glossed enamel finish. A brand name.

Kromolite: Method of producing drop-out halftones photographically through use of filters and combination of line and halftone negatives.

Label: A piece of paper with the name and address of the recipient to be affixed to a mailing.

Lacquer: A clear coating, usually glossy, applied to a printed sheet for protection or effect.

Laid paper: Paper with parallel lines on the surface, giving a ribbed effect.

Laser: An intense light beam with very narrow band width that can produce images by electronic impulses. It makes possible imaging by remote control from computers or facsimile transmission.

Laser platemaking: The use of lasers for scanning pasteups and/or exposing plates in the same or remote locations.

Leaders: Rows of dashes or dots used to guide the eye across the page.

Letterpress: Any printing which is done direct from type. The term is used in contrast to printing done by the offset process.

Letterset (dry offset): The printing process which uses a blanket (like conventional offset) for transferring the image from plate to paper.

Lettershop: A company that handles the mechanical details of mailing: addressing, imprinting, collating, inserting.

Letterspacing: The placing of additional space between each letter of a word.

Lifestyle: An individual's behavior pattern as manifested by activities, possessions, attitudes and beliefs.

Lightface: A description given to type having a face with thin lines which prints a light tone, as opposed to bold or black-face type.

Line copy: Any copy suitable for reproduction without using a halftone screen.

Line drawings: Artwork with solid black lines which can be reproduced without using halftone screens.

Linotype: A typesetting machine in which the letters are set in lead slugs from a keyboard similar to that of a typewriter.

Lithography: A printing process which prints from plates made from photographs. Offset lithography is usually called simply "offset."

Machine coated: Paper which is coated on one or two sides on the paper machine.

Machine finish (M.F.): Any finish produced on papermaking machines.

Machine glazed (M.G.): High-gloss finish produced mechanically on papermaking machines.

Mail date(s): Date(s) on which a company mails a specific promotion. If rented lists are used, the date(s) on which a list user, by prior arrangement with list owner, is obligated to mail a specific list. No other date is acceptable without express approval of the list owner.

Mailer: An advertiser who uses the mail to promote a product or service. A direct mail advertising piece. A wrapper, tube, or a folding carton used to protect materials in the mail.

Mailing machine: A machine that attaches labels to mailing pieces and otherwise prepares them for deposit in the postal system.

Mail key: An identifier usually four to six characters in length assigned to the record and appearing on the printed label. Usually based on the list code, it enables the client to track the performance of lists and packages when responses come back. Refers also to the set of records identified by the mail key.

Mail order: A method of conducting business wherein merchandise is offered by mail; orders are received by mail, by telephone, or electronically; and/or merchandise is shipped by mail.

Mail order action line (MOAL): A service of the Direct Marketing Association, MOAL assists consumers in resolving problems with their mail order purchases.

Mail order buyer: One who orders and pays for a product or service through the mail. While those who telephone or telegraph to order from direct response advertising may be included in this category, technically they are not mail order buyers.

Mail oriented: The characteristic of responding to mail order offers.

Mail Preference Service (MPS): A service of the Direct Marketing Association by which consumers can request to have their names removed from or added to mailing lists. The names are made available to both association members and nonmembers.

Make ready: Material used on a printing press to bring all type matter and illustrations to the point of reproductive quality. Also the process of preparing material on the press.

Make ready sheets: Sheets used in getting reproductive quality when starting a production press run. These sheets are generally waste.

Makeup: The arrangement of lines of type and illustrations into pages.

Market: A group of people having both purchasing power and the willingness to spend to meet either needs or desires.

Marketing: Those business activities that direct the flow of goods and services from the producer to the consumer.

Marketing concept: Combines consumer orientation with the organization of a firm in the service of the consumer for profit.

Marketing mix: The manipulation of marketing variables into a suitable marketing program for a particular firm. Includes product, package, price, distribution, channels, personal selling, advertising, and sales promotions.

Marketing plan: A formal, written ''blueprint'' for an organization's entire marketing program.

Marketing research: The systematic gathering, recording, and analyzing of data about problems concerning the marketing of goods and services. Includes the study of size, structure, composition, disposable income, and other factors of a particular segment of the broader market.

Market profile: Description of the demographics and psychographics of a target market. Notes the sex, age, income, and other characteristics of persons making up a specific market.

Market segmentation: The division of the total market into homogeneous subsets. This marketing strategy makes it possible for each subset to be addressed most appropriately.

Market share: That percentage of a market controlled by a particular company or product line.

Market test: The controlled testing of a limited but carefully chosen sector of a market in order to predict sales or profits of one or several marketing actions, either in absolute or relative terms.

Matrix: A mold in which type is cast in linecasting machines. The paper mold or mat made from a type form.

Matte finish: Dull paper finish without gloss or luster.

Matte print: Photoprint having a dull finish.

Measure (type): The length, usually expressed in picas or ems, of a single line of type.

Mechanical: A term for a camera-ready pasteup of artwork. It includes type, photos, and line art, all on one artboard.

Mechanical pulp: Groundwood pulp produced by mechanically grinding wood chips.

Mechanical screen: The dot or line pattern used by a photoengraver for reproducing an illustration.

Mechanical separations: Art prepared with separate overlays for each color to be used in printing.

Middle tones: The tonal range between highlights and shadows of a photograph or reproduction.

Moire: Undesirable pattern which results when a cut is made from the print of a halftone or certain other types of printed illustrations; i.e., by photographing a printed illustration.

Mylar: In offset preparation, a polyester film made by Du Pont and, because of its mechanical strength and dimensional stability, specially suited for shipping positives.

Name-removal service: Part of the Mail Preference Service of the Direct Marketing Association providing a form which a consumer can fill out and return, requesting that his name be removed from all mailing lists used by participating members of the Association and other direct mail users.

Negative: Film containing an image in which the values of the original are reversed so that the dark areas appear light and vice versa.

Newsprint: Paper made mostly from groundwood pulp and small amounts of chemical pulp.

North/south labels: Reading from top to bottom, these mailing labels are designed to be affixed with Cheshire equipment.

Odd page: Right-hand pages, which carry odd folios (3, 5, 7, etc.).

Off color: Paper or ink which does not match a specified sample.

Offset: Printing process using an intermediate blanket cylinder to transfer an image from the image carrier to the substrate. Short for offset lithography.

Offset printing: A term used in contrast to letterpress. Offset printing is a kind of lithography in which the impression is made from the surface of a roll (usually rubber) to which an image has been transferred from a photographic plate.

O.K. A/C: Proofreader's mark to indicate a proof is without error.

O.K'd sheet: A sheet signed to indicate the job is okayed and can be printed.

O.K. W/C: Proof is okay except for indicated corrections.

Opacity: That property of paper which minimizes the "show-through" of printing from the back side or the next sheet.

Opaque: In photoengraving and offset lithography, to paint out areas on a negative not wanted on the plate. In paper, the property which makes it less transparent.

Opaque ink: An ink that conceals all color beneath it.

Optical character recognition (OCR): The use of light-sensitive devices for the machine identification of printed characters.

Optical scanner: A device that optically scans printed data and converts each character into an electronic equivalent for processing.

Order blank envelopes: Business reply envelopes with an order form printed on one side of a sheet and the address reply form on the other. Recipient fills in order, folds and seals envelope for mailing.

Order card: A reply card — often a self-mailer — to be filled out, checked or initialed by prospect or customer, and mailed back to the advertiser for the purpose of initiating a reply or order.

Out of register: When color plates are out of alignment or are not printed in perfect relationship for accurate reproduction.

Overlay: A transparent covering over artwork where color break, instructions, or corrections are marked.

Overrun: That printing which is in excess of the amount specified — up to 10 percent usually acceptable.

Page makeup: Assembly of all elements to make up a page. Phototypesetting electronically assembles page elements to compose a complete page with all elements in place on a video display terminal and on the phototypesetter.

Page proof: A proof of type matter which has been made up from galleys into pages.

Pagination: Arranging type so it will print pages in proper sequence.

Paper grain: Grain of paper runs parallel with length of paper as it is received from the mill.

Pasteup: Placing elements such as type and art into position for platemaking.

Peel-off-label: A self-adhesive label on a backing sheet which is attached to a mailing piece. Designed to be removed and placed on order blank or card.

Perfect binding: Machine binding method wherein the back folds are cut off, leaf edges roughed, glue applied, and a cover then attached without the use of binding wire or sewing.

Perfecting press: Rotary printing two sides of paper during one operation.

Personalizing: Individualizing direct mail pieces by adding the name of the recipient.

Photo-composing: The assembly of separate elements into an integrated page layout.

Photolettering: Display type lines created by photographically printing individual characters on photosensitive paper or film.

Photomechanical: Any platemaking process using photographic negatives or positives exposed onto plates or cylinders covered with photosensitive coatings.

Photostat: A positive reproduction of a piece of art on paper. A trade name.

Phototypesetting: The method of setting type photographically.

Pick: The small particles of paper that loosen from the surface during printing.

Picking: The lifting of the paper surface during printing. It occurs when pulling force (tack) of ink is greater than surface strength of paper.

Piggy-back: An offer riding along with another offer at no charge.

Pigment: In printing inks, the fine solid particles used to give color, body or opacity.

Pinpoint dot: The finest halftone dot used in photoengravings.

Pin register: The use of accurately positioned holes and special pins on copy, film, plates and presses to insure proper register or fit of colors.

Platen: Flat surface upon which paper rests when it comes in contact with printing surfaces. Also short for platen press.

Platen press: Any press that gives a printed impression by bringing together two flat surfaces, one of which is called a bed and the other a platen.

Plates: Flat, smooth pieces of metal which have been treated to create a printing surface.

Plough/fold: A special piece of equipment attached to web presses which allows a printed piece to be folded while a job is running, thus reducing costs.

Plugging: A condition in which the nonprint area between dots fills in with ink so that it is solid black.

PMS colors: Refers to *P*antone *M*atching *S*ystem, an established color system which gives the percentage of (red) Cyan, Blue, Black, and Yellow needed to match a color sample. Colors are designated as PMS 265, for example.

Point size: Standardized measurement system for type. There are twelve points (approximately 1/72 inch) to a pica and six picas to an inch.

Positive: In photography, film containing an image in which the dark and light values are the same as in the original.

Pre-press proofs: Proofs made by photographic techniques to eliminate the expense of making press proofs.

Press proofs: In color reproduction, a proof of color from a proof press, in advance of the production run.

Press sheet: The printed sheet.

Pressure-sensitive paper: Material with an adhesive coating, protected by a backing sheet until used, and which will stick without moistening.

Primary letters: Lower-case characters which have no ascenders or descenders.

Print quality: The properties of paper that affect its appearance and the quality of printing reproduction.

Process colors: In printing, the subtractive primaries: yellow, magenta, and cyan, plus black in four-color process printing.

Process four-color printing: The use of yellow, red, blue, and black positives for reproducing almost any color.

Process plates: Color plates, two or more, used in combination with each other to produce other colors and shades.

Process printing: Use of primary colors printed over each other with nonopaque inks to produce a variety of tints and hues.

Product life cycle: The concept that the life of a product has definite stages: introductory, growth, maturity, and decline. A different marketing approach is required by each stage.

Product positioning: Communication techniques to develop a marketing strategy insuring that a product or service is viewed and understood by potential customers as what the seller wants it to represent.

Progressive proofs: A set of proofs separated into color sequence starting with black, blue, red, and ending with yellow. Each set will show what the single color looks like when separated out of a four-color chrome. As each color is overlayed on top of another, the printer finally arrives at the four-color appearance. Progressives are extremely helpful in determining any color corrections.

Proofing: Denotes the operation of pulling proofs of plates for proofreading, revising, trial, approval of illustration, and other purposes prior to printing.

Proof press: A small printing press, usually hand-operated, for pulling proofs.

Prove: To pull a proof.

Psychographics: Statistical description of a group of consumers based on characteristics of interests, lifestyles, or attitudes.

Pull sheets: Sheets removed from the run after every press stop. They are considered good sheets.

Pulling a proof: Printer's term for making a copy of a cut or type matter on a proof press.

Pulp: Papermaking material existing in a disintegrated fibrous wet or dry state.

Qualified leads: Truly interested prospects as distinguished from the merely curious. Individuals who have taken some type of positive action in their inquiries about a given product or service, such as sending a small fee for a catalog.

Rag book: High-quality book with longevity, made from rag content paper.

Rag content paper: Bond and ledger papers containing from 25 per cent to 100 percent rag fibers.

Ream: Five hundred sheets of paper.

Ream weight: The weight of one ream of paper (also called basis weight).

Reduction: Decreasing the density or opacity of a negative by removing some of the metallic silver forming the image.

Reflection copy (reflective art): An illustration that is viewed and must be photographed by light reflected from its surface, such as photographs, drawings.

Register: In printing, fitting of two or more printing images on the same paper in exact alignment with each other.

Register marks: Crosses, lines, or other devices applied to original copy prior to photography; used for positioning negatives in register, or for register of two or more colors in process printing.

Reproduction proof: A reproducible copy of an illustration or type pulled on a special proof press; used for camera ready art to be photographed for offset reproduction or engraving. Commonly called ''Repro''; (also called ''Hacker Proof'').

Retouching: A process that adds or takes away color to improve the printing reproduction of artwork.

Return postage guaranteed: Legend which should be imprinted on the address face of envelopes or other mailing pieces if the mailer wishes the Postal Service to return undeliverable third class bulk mail. There is a charge equivalent to the single piece third class rate for each such piece returned.

Rotary press: Letterpress in which paper fed from a continuous roll is printed as it passes between an impression cylinder and a curved printing plate.

Rotogravure paper: A specially finished paper used for rotogravure printing.

Rough: A loose layout in sketchy form generally used in the planning stages of product presentation or catalog page layout.

Run-around: In composition, the term describing a type area set in line lengths that are adjusted to fit around a picture or another element of the design.

Saddle stitching: A method of binding, with wire staples fastened through the back fold, enabling a catalog to open out flat.

Saddle wire: The fastening of a booklet by wire through the middle fold of the sheets (saddle stitch).

Sans serif: Letters without serifs (or shoulders).

Satin finish: A special smooth paper finish suggesting satin.

Scaling: Determining the proper size of a printed image by reducing or enlarging the original.

Scanner: An electronic device used to correct and separate color.

Score: To impress a mark with a string or rule in the paper to make folding easier.

Scratchboard: An art technique which involves scratching away portions of a black coating on white board so that the illustration is formed by the scratched lines.

Screen: A pattern consisting of the number of dots per square inch in a halftone. Ben Day (inventor's name) are sheets of screens, dots, or lines used to save artist time.

Secondary color: Violet, orange, green produced by mixing two primary colors.

Self-mailer: A direct mail piece that needs no outer envelope or special wrapper.

Separation negative: A negative made from any single color of a multicolor illustration.

Serif: The short cross-lines (also called shoulders) at the ends of the main strokes of many letters in some type faces.

Shadow: The darkest parts in a photograph, represented in a halftone by the largest dots.

Sheet fed: Gravure printing produced on separate sheets of paper (in contrast to rotogravure, which is done on a continuous web or roll of paper).

Short grain paper: Paper made with the machine direction in the shortest sheet dimension.

Show-through: The printing of text or illustrations which can be seen through the sheet on the reverse side under normal lighting conditions.

Side-stitching: A binding method with wire staples driven through the far left side of a catalog, entering from the cover and fastening on the back cover. Also Side Wire.

Side-wire: In binding, to wire the pages or signatures of a catalog on the left side front near the backbone.

Signature: A section of printed sheets in 8, 12, 16, or 32 pages made by folding a single printed sheet.

Silhouette: An illustration from which the background of the image has been cut or etched away (dropped out).

Silverprint: A photocopy used as a proof.

Skid: A platform support for a pile of cut sheets, boxes, or catalogs.

Slitting: Cutting printed paper into two or more sections by means of cutting wheels on a press or folder.

Slug: In composition, a one-piece line of type. Also, a strip of metal, usually 6 points, used for spacing between lines.

Small caps: An alphabet of smaller capital letters approximately the size of the lower case letters.

Soft dot: In photography, a dot whose halation or fringe is excessive. Conversely, when the fringe is so slight as to be barely noticeable and the dot is very sharp, it is called 'hard.'

Solid (type): Type matter set with no added leading.

Solids: One hundred percent tones or colors which have no dots in them when printed.

Spacing: Separation between characters or groups of characters in type. Letterspacing between individual characters. Wordspacing between words. Linespacing between lines.

Spectrum: The complete range of colors in the rainbow, from short wavelengths (blue) to long wavelengths (red).

Spine: Backbone of a catalog or book.

Splice: The joining of two webs of paper.

Spot glue: Glue added to a printed piece or envelope in a ''spot'' which allows another piece to be attached to it, or which allows a position to be maintained.

Square halftone: A finishing style in which the halftone screen runs to the edge of the printing plate, which is trimmed straight both vertically and horizontally.

Step-and-repeat: The procedure of reproducing the same image from one negative or positive any number of times on a printing plate.

Stet: A proofreader's mark, written in the margin, signifying that the original copy, marked for corrections, should remain unchanged.

Stitch: The number of staples used in the spine of a catalog — usually two.

Stock: Paper or other material to be printed.

Stock photo: Photographs by professional photographers on a variety of subjects available for reproduction commercially for a determined fee. Users choose an appropriate photograph for a fee rather than commissioning a specific shot.

Strip-in: To insert additional material into a photographic negative or positive used for platemaking.

Stripping: In offset-lithography, the positioning of negatives (or positives) on a flat (goldenrod) prior to platemaking.

Studio: A commercial organization which prepares artwork or photography for advertising.

Supercalender stock: A paper stock with a high glossy finish, produced by calendering.

Tack: The pulling power of separation force of ink. A tacky ink has high separation forces and can cause surface picking or splitting of weak papers.

Tensile strength: Resistance to force parallel to the plane of a specific size sheet of paper.

Text: The body matter (editorial) of a page or book, as distinguished from the headings.

Third class mail: Non-personalized mail with delayed handling. Most direct mail advertising is sent third class.

Three-color process: The reproduction of a full-color original by using three colors, usually red, yellow, and blue.

Tints: Various even tone areas (strenghs) of a solid color.

Tissue overlay: A thin, translucent paper placed over artwork (mostly mechanicals) for protection; used to indicate color break and corrections.

Tone: The shade or degree of a color. A quality or value of a color.

Tone value: Intensity of a color or a mass of type, as compared to black, white, and gray.

Translucency: Ability to transmit light without being transparent.

Transparency: A photographic image on film which allows images to be seen through a sheet. Black and white and four-color.

Transpose: To exchange the position of a letter, word, or line with that of another letter, word, or line.

Trim: The maximum width of finished paper that can be made by a particular machine.

Type gauge: A printer's tool calibrated in picas and used for type measurement.

Type metal: Usually an alloy of lead, antimony, tin, and brass used in typemaking.

Typographic error: Mistake made when type is set.

Typography: The process of setting material in type for printing.

Typro: Machine for setting display type by cold type composition.

U.C.: Upper-case or capital letters.

U&LC: Upper and Lower case. Capital and small letters.

Unbleached: Paper not treated by bleaching; has a light brown hue.

Undercoat: A clear coating sometimes applied to foil during printing, but before laying on ink. Frequently used under white ink to emphasize white ink color.

Underlay: Pieces of paper pasted under type or cut to bring it to the proper level for printing.

Unit: In multicolor presses, refers to the combination of inking, plate and impression operations to print each color. A four-color press has four printing units, each with its own inking, plate, and impression functions.

-up: In printing, two-up, three-up, etc., refers to imposition of material to be printed on a larger size sheet to take advantage of full press capacity.

UPS: United Parcel Service.

USPS: United States Postal Service.

Vellum finish: In papermaking, a toothy finish which is relatively absorbent for fast ink penetration.

Velox: An engraver's halftone print of a photograph. Used for placement or reproduction, and also for retouching.

Vignette: An illustration in which the background gradually fades away, in contrast to a silhouette or an illustration with a full background. Also, a halftone in which the tone of the engraving blends into the white of the paper.

Warm color: In printing, a color which has a yellowish or reddish cast.

Wash: A drawing done in a wet medium as opposed to a line drawing.

Wash drawing: Drawing in which a water-soluble color is applied as a wash.

Whiteness: The extent to which a paper approaches ideal white.

White envelope: Envelope having a die-cut window on the front, exposing address printed on enclosure. Window may be open or covered with transparent material. See also window envelope, die-cut envelope.

White mail: An order or reply that is not on coded order form sent out by advertiser, making it difficult or impossible to trace which promotional piece prompted response. Refers also to all mail other than orders and payments.

Wire stitching: The fastening together (binding) of pages with wire staples.

With the grain: Folding or feeding paper into a press parallel to the grain of the paper.

Woodcut: Printing plate made by carving nonprinting areas out of a type-high block of wood.

Wove paper: Paper having a uniform, unlined surface and a soft, smooth finish.

Yellow: One of the subtractive primaries, the hue of which is used for one of the four-color process inks. It reflects red and green light and absorbs blue light.

Index

ADDITIONAL SERVICES FROM MAXWELL SROGE PUBLISHING

THE CATALOG MARKETER newsletter. Catalog industry experts share their ideas and experiences with you on every phase of the catalog business — "how-to" advice on design, lists, economics, printing, merchandise, telephone, cost controls, analysis . . . every two weeks.

THE BUSINESS-TO-BUSINESS CATALOG MARKETER newsletter. How to do it advice written especially for producers of business-to-business and industrial catalogs. Eight pages every two weeks.

NON-STORE MARKETING REPORT. The leading source of non-store marketing trends, forecasts, analysis, company profiles, facts, and figures. For industry leaders and industry watchers! Published every two weeks.

DIRECTECH REPORT. How you can use electronic marketing today! Cuts through all the hype and jargon and gives you straightforward advice and ideas for selling via electronic marketing.

BEST IN CATALOGS, Volumes I & II. A goldmine of information on what makes a catalog a winner. Illustrates, analyzes, shows you why renowned experts in the catalog mail order business selected 25 winners, 50 finalists in each volume of "Best in Catalogs." Page after page offers insight, valuable information to anyone involved in the production of any type catalog.

INSIDE THE LEADING MAIL ORDER HOUSES, Second Edition. A behind-the-scenes look at 250 of America's largest mail order houses. Reveals sales, profits, who own thems, who runs them, prices, brand names, list size, company history, and more. Includes commentary and analysis by Maxwell Sroge Publishing editors.

INDUSTRY STUDY REPORTS. In-depth research on major segments of the mail order industry. Comprehensive overviews with valuable statistics, charts for each of these industries: Ready-To-Wear-By-Mail (1985 update), Food-By-Mail (1985 update), Books-By-Mail, Crafts-By-Mail, and Sporting Goods-By-Mail.

CATALOG ANALYSIS/REVIEW/EVALUATION. Have your catalog evaluated by the experts from Maxwell Sroge Publishing. Creative aspects of your catalog are reviewed with you via telephone. Your questions are answered instantaneously by someone who has consulted, instructed, and written about the catalog industry.

CATALOG MARKETING SEMINARS. Personally led by Maxwell Sroge, these seminars show you how to produce more profitable catalogs, whether you're planning a catalog start-up, or searching for fresh ideas for your current catalog.

COMPANY VALUATIONS, MERGERS AND ACQUISITIONS. Maxwell Sroge Consultants specializes in valuations, acquisitions and mergers, with emphasis on tax and estate planning and public offerings. Our range of professional services is designed to assist owners and potential owners in the acquisition, development, structuring, management and divestiture of mail order businesses.

For more information on our services, contact us at our office in Colorado Springs.

Maxwell Sroge Publishing

Maxwell Sroge Publishing
731 North Cascade Avenue
Colorado Springs, CO 80903-3205
(303) 633-5556